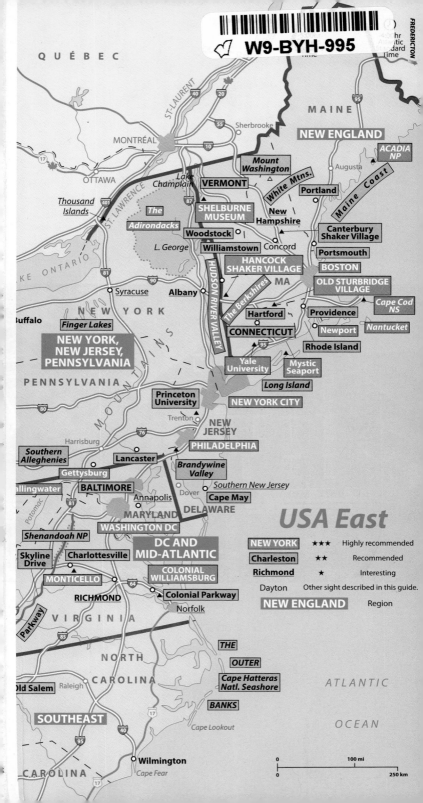

Hancock Shaker Village, Pittsfield, Massachusetts
Courtesy of Hancock Shaker Village, Pittsfield, MA

THEGREENGUIDE
USA East

How to...

Plan Your Trip

Understand USA East

Discover USA East

Green Guides - Discover the Destination

Main sections

PLANNING YOUR TRIP
The blue-tabbed section gives you **ideas for your trip** and **practical information.**

INTRODUCTION
The orange-tabbed section explores **Nature, History, Art and Culture** and the **Region Today.**

DISCOVERING
The green-tabbed section features Principal Sights by region, **Sights, Walking Tours, Excursions,** and **Driving Tours.**

Region intros

At the start of each region in the Discovering section is a brief introduction. Accompanied by the regional map, the intro provides an overview of the main tourism areas and their background.

City maps

Star ratings

Michelin has given star ratings for more than 100 years. If you're pressed for time, we recommend you visit the three or two star sights first:

★★★ Highly Recommended

★★ Recommended

★ Interesting

Tours

We've selected driving and walking tours that show you the best of each town or region. Step by step directions are accompanied by detailed maps with marked routes. If you are short on time, you can follow the star ratings to decide where to stop. Selected addresses give you options for accommodation and dining en route.

Addresses

We've selected the best hotels, restaurants, cafés, shops, nightlife and entertainment to fit all budgets. See the Legend on the cover flap for an explanation of the price categories. See the back of the guide for an index of where to find hotels and restaurants.

Other reading

+ Green Guide New England
+ Green Guide New York City
+ Green Guide Florida
+ Must Sees Chicago
+ Must Sees Washington,DC
+ North America Road Atlas

Welcome to USA East

Thirty-one states make up the eastern portion of the United States presented in this guide—it's an immense and enormously diverse landscape that handsomely rewards the visitor. Let the regions below guide your approach to this land's wealth of cosmopolitan cities, natural wonders, cultural institutions and recreational adventures. Then relax, and enjoy the USA East in all its wonderful variety.

New York, New Jersey, Pennsylvania ◆ New England ◆
DC and Mid-Atlantic ◆ Great Lakes ◆ Minneapolis, Iowa, Missouri ◆
Mid-South ◆ Southeast ◆ Florida

Old lobster buoys © PhotoDisc, Inc.

Planning Your Trip

Introducing USA East

Discovering USA East

New York New Jersey Pennsylvania

Regions of USA East

New York, New Jersey, Pennsylvania (pp120-191)

The varied landscape of Pennsylvania encompasses modern industrial centers like Pittsburgh; placid Amish communities where time seems to stand still; forests and mountains looming rural and isolated; and the great historical city of Philadelphia, the Cradle of Independence. New Jersey's casinos and shorelines beckon risk-takers and sunbathers, while winter snows draw skiers to New York's Adirondacks and Catskill resorts. If you're ready for your bite of the Big Apple, make tracks for the world-class museums, Broadway shows, culinary adventures and endless fascinations of New York City, tourism mecca of the eastern US.

Pemaquid Point Lighthouse, Maine
© Jon Hicks/Corbis

New England (pp192-231)

Compactly located in the country's northeastern corner, New England is one of the loveliest regions in the US. Cosmopolitan Boston and the towns of Massachusetts around it proudly preserve sights related to the Revolutionary War and the region's whaling industry. The winter sports resorts in Vermont and New Hampshire are world-renowned, while tiny hamlets dot the rocky Maine coast, perfect for summer getaways. The smallest state in the nation, Rhode Island looms large in fame for its extravagant Gilded Age mansions of Newport. The state of Connecticut draws visitors to its Mystic Seaport and t University. But New England is best known for its fall foliage, when changing leaves swath hills and mountains in breathtaking displays of oranges, reds, golds and yellows.

DC and Mid-Atlantic (pp232-267)

The nation's capital of Washington, D.C., boasts awe-inspiring monuments and memorials to the country's heroes and an incredible number of museums, many of them free of charge. To the east lies Annapolis, Maryland, home to the US Naval Academy. North of DC sits modern Baltimore with its shiny Inner Harbor. Just south in Virginia, the Colonial Parkway links historic Jamestown, site of the first English colonies, with Yorktown, where independence from England was won. Tour the James River plantations, the estates of Virginia's colonial gentry, and visit popular Colonial Williamsburg, which preserves its 17C period as Virginia's capital.

Great Lakes (pp268-319)

Rising at the edge of Lake Michigan, dynamic Chicago bustles as the cultural capital of the Midwest. Come here for historic and contemporary architecture, noteworthy museums and great shopping. Then venture forth into the cities of America's heartland. Industrial Detroit is renewing itself and its cultural

Henry Ford Museum and Greenfield Village, Dearborn, Michigan
© Craig Lovell / age fotostock

institutions; Milwaukee offers charming ethnic neighborhoods and lakefront parks, while Cleveland has fine museums and historic ships. Ohio's other river cities, Cincinnati, Dayton and Columbus, have varied attractions of their own.

Minneapolis, Iowa, Missouri (pp320-347)

The Twin Cities sport different characters: Minneapolis is the more progressive, with modern architecture, a vibrant theater scene and cutting-edge music. Quieter St. Paul, capital of Minnesota, has a traditional feel. Embodying American capitalism, Bloomington's Mall of America is the largest shopping and entertainment complex in the US. Farther south spreads the agrarian state of Iowa, epitomizing America's heartland with its famous Iowa State Fair, while Des Moines shows off its regal state capitol building. Missouri, known as the gateway to the American West, boasts the tallest man-made monument in the US, St. Louis' stunning Gateway Arch.

Mid-South (pp348-418)

In this region, savor BBQ with a side of slaw, soak in an Arkansas hot spring, honor America's Civil Rights leaders in Birmingham and Montgomery, tour the home of the Kentucky Derby, gawk at rockets in Huntsville, and listen to American roots music (country in Nashville, blues in Memphis, bluegrass in Tennessee and Kentucky, and Cajun and zydeco in Louisiana). To the west rise the lovely Ozark highlands. Farther south Vicksburg preserves a key Civil War battlefield, while Natchez showcases its antebellum homes. Famous New Orleans fascinates visitors with its heady cuisine, wild Mardi Gras celebration and bawdy French Quarter.

Southeast (pp419-463)

Atlanta's throbbing thoroughfares testify to the Georgia capital's large size and population, which shares space with the Carter Library, Coca-Cola, CNN and M.L. King, Jr.'s birth home. In contrast are the genteel streets of Charleston

Everglades National Park
©VISIT FLORIDA

and Savannah, grande dames of the southeast coast. Resort islands Jekyll, St. Simon's, Hilton Head and Kiawah invite visitors to rounds of golf, beachwalking and afternoons lazing in the sun. To the north, the wild dunes of North Carolina's Outer Banks are studded with historic lighthouses and memorials. The majestic Great Smoky Mountains rise in the western part of the region, traced by Skyline Drive and the Blue Ridge Parkway, two of the nation's most scenic byways.

Florida (pp464-503)

This state has been a holiday playground since the late 19C when wealthy northern families targeted historic St. Augustine for their winter getaways. Today popular Walt Disney World, Universal Studios and SeaWorld bring visitors in droves, as does the city of Miami, with its enticing tropical flair. Mile upon mile of white-sand beaches ring the state right down to the pristine swamps of the Everglades in the southwest. The Florida Keys archipelago extends into the gulf, offering adventure in the form of snorkeling, scuba-diving and other watersports.

Planning
Your Trip

Ancient Spanish Monastery, North Miami
© Zain Deane/Michelin

Planning Your Trip

Virginia International Tattoo, Virginia Arts Festival
© Todd Owyoung, Virginia Arts Festival

Inspiration

WHAT'S HOT

– **Walt Disney World** debuted two new themed areas in 2013: the Enchanted Forest, inspired by Beauty and the Beast, and Storybook Circus (p489).

– In **Atlanta** the new National Center for Civil and Human Rights is slated to open in spring 2014. (p423)

– **St. Petersburg**'s Dalí Museum occupies a striking new building (2011) with a massive geodesic bubble on the exterior (p501).

– **Miami**'s new 40-acre Museum Park will host the new home of the Pérez Art Museum Miami in late 2013 (p469).

– **New York City** will open the doors of its 911 Museum in 2014. (p126).

– **Washington, DC**'s reinstated streetcar service begins in late 2013 (p235).

– The Barnes Foundation's Galleries and Arboretum opened in 2012 in a stunning new building in **Philadelphia** (p166).

Fall Colors in West Virginia ©PhotoDisc, Inc

Michelin Driving Tours

Y ou've got your car, you know the rules of the road, now get ready to go. We've outlined below several driving tours that will lead you to the highlights of the East's diverse regions, from the gleaming skyscrapers of New York City to the gracious plantations of the South.

Whiteface Mountain area, Adirondacks

© Victor Kapas/iStockphoto.com

MEET NEW ENGLAND

15 days

Rich in both cultural and natural attractions, New England encompasses the states of Connecticut, Maine, Massachusetts, New Hampshire, Rhode Island and Vermont. Fall, when the leaves turn blazing shades of red, orange and gold, is the most popular time to visit. Begin in **Boston** by exploring the city's Colonial heritage along the **Freedom Trail** and visiting the **Museum of Fine Arts** and the **Isabella Stewart Gardner Museum**. If you're in Boston during baseball season, catch a Red Sox game at Fenway Park. Stroll the campus of venerable Harvard University, with its many museums, leaving time to peruse **Cambridge's** myriad bookstores.

Then it's southeast via Route 3 and US-6 to **Cape Cod**, Massachusetts, where you can walk the beaches of **Cape Cod National Seashore**, poke around quaint villages like **Chatham**,

or do the club circuit at **Provincetown** on the Cape's northern tip. From the Cape, you can take a ferry to the charming islands of **Nantucket** or **Martha's Vineyard**.

Drive southwest from Cape Cod to **Newport**, Rhode Island, via I-195, stopping to visit the **New Bedford Whaling Museum**. Touring Newport's fabulous mansions gives new meaning to "lifestyles of the rich and famous." Spend a day in nearby **Mystic Seaport**, Connecticut and continue west through **New Haven**, home of **Yale University**, then drive north on I-91. From **Hartford**, it's a short jaunt on I-84 northeast to the popular living-history museum **Old Sturbridge Village**, re-creating the 1790s to1840. Back in Massachusetts, head west on I-90 through **Stockbridge** to the undulating foothills of **The Berkshires**. North of Stockbridge on US-7, you'll come to bucolic **Hancock Shaker Village** and farther on, to the pristine Colonial burg of **Williamstown**.

Continue north on US-7 through southern Vermont to historic **Bennington**, and farther north to the stellar **Shelburne Museum**. Then swing east across Vermont and into New Hampshire for a scenic drive through the **White Mountains**; en route, leave time for a tour of **Ben & Jerry's Ice Cream Factory** in Waterbury, Vermont.

Loop south via I-93 to **Canterbury Shaker Village** and cut east on Route 100 and north on I-95 to **Portsmouth**. From New Hampshire's only seaport, you can head back to Boston via I-95 South, or take a leisurely drive up US-1 along the **Maine coast**. If you choose the latter option, stop often to admire the spectacular views of rocky shores and lonely lighthouses, and to dine on lobster, fresh off the boat. End your coastal sojourn at **Acadia National Park** and return to Boston via I-95 South.

FLORIDA SUNSHINE
15 days

Distinguished by its 1,197mi coastline, the Sunshine State's peninsula is edged by beautiful beaches. Warm winter temperatures make Florida a year-round playground, from Orlando's theme parks to the international flavor of Miami and the unique ecosystem of the watery Everglades.

Begin in **Orlando**, where a visit to **Walt Disney World** is *de rigueur*. The city's other theme parks, **Universal Studios** and **SeaWorld**, will easily occupy an additional couple of days with animal shows, thrill rides and family fun.

An hour's drive east of Orlando via the Beachline Expressway (Rte. 528), science fiction comes alive at **Kennedy Space Center**, home to some of the world's most sophisticated technology. Plan a visit here to coincide with a **rocket launch**. History buffs will enjoy a detour north via scenic Route A1A to **St. Augustine**, the oldest continuously occupied European settlement in the US, to see its 18C masonry fort and nearby alligator farm.

For a leisurely coastal drive, head south on US-1 to **Palm Beach** and scout out the elite boutiques along Worth Avenue. Then it's on to **Miami**, to sample the Cuban cuisine in **Little Havana**, soak up some rays on the beach, and admire Art Deco architecture in trendy **Miami Beach**. Be sure to try succulent stone crab claws if they're in season.

South of Miami, the vast "river of grass" protected by **Everglades National Park** harbors some 750 species of animals. To truly experience this rare subtropical wetland, spend time hiking its trails, canoeing its waters and taking park-sponsored wilderness cruises.

Everglades National Park, Florida

For a glimpse of Florida at its most bohemian, drive down to **Key West** along the dramatic Overseas Highway (US-1). A walking tour of Old Town, including bar-hopping along Duval Street and watching the sunset at Mallory Square Dock, will make it clear what has lured artists and writers—such as Ernest Hemingway—to this tiny isle.

Wind up your Florida tour with a drive up the Gulf Coast on Route 41. Along the way, enjoy the elegant city of **Naples** and spend time shelling on the beaches of **Sanibel and Captiva Islands**. Heading north, the cities of **Sarasota, St. Petersburg** and **Tampa** draw culture mavens and sun seekers. From Tampa, return to Orlando via I-4.

SOUTHERN SOJOURN
14 days

A tour through the southern states of **Georgia, Alabama, Tennessee, Mississippi** and **Louisiana** reveals antebellum plantations alongside international cities. As you go, you'll uncover the roots of America's classic music forms: jazz, blues and country. Begin in bustling **Atlanta**, where shopping in the upscale **Buckhead** neighborhood vies with the city's many cultural attractions for visitors' time. For a soupçon of stately 19C architecture, detour east on I-16 to the lovely coastal city of **Savannah**. Re-live the drama of the American civil rights movement in Alabama (via I-20 West) at the famed **Birmingham Civil Rights Institute**. Then it's north on I-65 toward Nashville, with a requisite stop at the **US Space and Rocket Center** in Huntsville, Alabama. Home of the Grand Ole Opry, **Nashville** is the US country-music capital.

From Nashville, take I-40 West to **Memphis**. Here you'll find **Graceland**, former residence of the city's most famous son, Elvis Presley, and the **Beale Street Historic District**, where the Memphis **blues** evolved in smoky backstreet clubs.

Head south on US-61 through Mississippi, leaving time for a stop at **Vicksburg National Military Park** and an overnight stay in one of the antebellum B&Bs a bit farther south in **Natchez**—including a paddlewheeler cruise on the Mississippi River. Continue south through **Baton Rouge** and follow the **River Road**, lined with a mix of stately plantations and Creole cottages, to New Orleans, Louisiana. Lauded for its Cajun and Creole cuisine as well as for its **jazz** clubs, **New Orleans** kicks up its heels before Lent at the annual bacchanalian bash known as **Mardi Gras**.

Head back toward Atlanta on I-10 East, first taking a break on the white-sand beaches of the **Gulf Coast**. At **Mobile**, pick up I-65 North and swing through **Montgomery**, Alabama, to catch a performance at the **Alabama Shakespeare Festival**. From Montgomery, I-85 North will take you back to Atlanta.

EASTERN SEABOARD'S CULTURAL CAPITALS
13 days

Within the I-95 corridor that runs from New York City south to Washington, DC *(roughly 230mi)*, you'll find some of the nation's greatest museums and its most revered monuments. Begin in **New York City**; see a Broadway show, take the ferry out to the **Statue of Liberty**, and visit the **Metropolitan Museum of Art**. Then break from the city's bustle; take US-9 North through the painterly landscapes of the **Hudson River Valley**.

Head south on I-95 to **Philadelphia**, Pennsylvania, where the cradle of US independence is re-created at **Independence National Historical Park**. Feast your eyes on the many works in the **Philadelphia Institute of Art**, then feast yourself on a Philly cheesesteak at the Italian Market in **South Philly**.

South of Philadelphia, you can detour east on the Atlantic City Expressway and try your luck in the casinos of **Atlantic City**, or take the Garden State Parkway south to the beaches of Victorian **Cape May**. Then on to

Washington Monument, Washington, DC

GREAT LAKES ODYSSEY

14 days

Lining Lake Michigan and Lake Erie, the cities of Chicago, Milwaukee, Detroit and Cleveland have reigned as the Midwest's industrial and transportation centers since the early 19C. Try to plan your visit here for warm weather; winter brings snow and bone-chilling winds off the lakes. Begin your tour in **Chicago**, which prides itself as much on its ethnic neighborhoods as on its downtown architecture. America's third-largest city by population, Chicago contains the world-class **Art Institute of Chicago, Field Museum of Natural History**, the **Adler Planetarium** and the **John G. Shedd Aquarium**. Be sure to do some upscale shopping on the **Magnificent Mile** and take in the city views from the top of the **Willis Tower**. Then, head south on I-65 to **Indianapolis**, Indiana, site of the world-famous **Indy 500** car race. From there, take I-74 East to **Cincinnati**, Ohio. Spend time at the **Cincinnati Art Museum**; then drive to Mt. Adams and explore its cozy shops, eateries and Victorian houses. Over the Ohio River, a short jaunt south on I-75 brings you to **Lexington** in the heart of Kentucky's **Bluegrass Country**. Nearby **Louisville** is home to the renowned **Kentucky Derby** horse race.

Interstate 71 North will lead you through Ohio to **Cleveland**, which claims the **Rock and Roll Hall of Fame**. Several hours north of Cleveland via I-90 in New York lies one of the East's most popular attractions, **Niagara Falls**.

From Cleveland, head west on I-90 and north on I-75 to the "Motor City"— **Detroit**, Michigan—where attractions highlight the automobile industry. Don't miss the **Henry Ford Museum and Greenfield Village** in neighboring **Dearborn**.

Return to Chicago via I-94 West. If time permits, continue past Chicago on I-94 to **Milwaukee**, Wisconsin, to experience the city's German heritage and to tour its breweries.

Baltimore, Maryland, where you can tour the **National Aquarium** at the Inner Harbor; don't miss the **Baltimore Museum of Art** and the **Walters Gallery** nearby. Worthwhile excursions include historic **Annapolis** *(south on I-97)* and Maryland's **Eastern Shore** *(east on US-50)*, where you can sample the area's charming inns and enjoy the Chesapeake Bay's bountiful catch of **blue crabs**.

Make your way south on I-95 and end your tour at **Washington, DC**. Home to the **White House** and **The US Capitol**, DC also boasts many fabulous museums—including the **National Gallery of Art, the Museum of Natural History** and the ever-popular **National Air and Space Museum**— most all of them free of charge. The revered monuments on **The Mall** pay tribute to the nation's heroes and to those who lost their lives in wartime. If you happen to wind up with an extra day in DC, head to **Colonial Williamsburg** *(via I-95 South & I-64 East)* in Virginia, where the early days of the nation come to life on a re-created 18C town site.

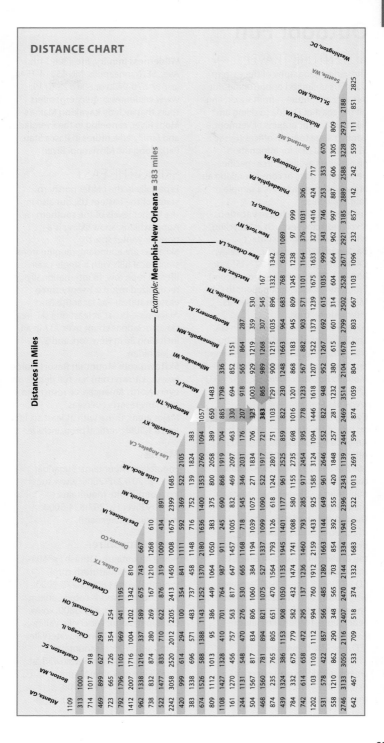

DISTANCE CHART

Distances in Miles

Example: Memphis–New Orleans = 383 miles

Outdoor Fun

ADVENTURE TRAVEL

The varied geography of the eastern US offers unlimited opportunities for outdoor adventure—from snorkeling off the coast of Florida to skiing and hiking in the mountains of Vermont. Contact state tourism offices (☝ see BEFORE YOU GO) for information on activities available in a specific geographic area, or consider taking an organized tour. Below is a sample of tour providers:

For exciting **all–inclusive vacations** involving activities such as bicycling, hiking and kayaking, contact **Backroads** (801 Cedar St., Berkeley, CA 94710-1800; ✆510-527-1555 or 800-462-2848; www.backroads.com). Programs include destinations in GA, MA, ME, MS, SC, and VT, as well as international trips.

For adventures on **horseback** in GA and VT—including riding tours, horse and cattle drives and visits to working ranches—contact **Hidden Trails**, 659A Moberly Rd., Vancouver, B.C. V5Z 4B3, ✆604-323-1141 or 888-987-2457, www.hiddentrails.com.

Cycling enthusiasts can see the US on one of several tours offered by **America by Bicycle** (P.O. Box 805, Atkinson, NH 03811-0805; ✆603-382-1662 or 888-797-7057; www.abbike.com). Excursions range from 5-11 day mini-tours to 52-day coast-to-coast programs.

Guides and Outfitters – A list of accredited **mountaineering organizations** can be obtained from the **American Mountain Guides Association** (P.O. Box 1739, Boulder, CO 80306; ✆303-271-0984; www.amga.com), a nonprofit organization and member of the International Federation of Mountain Guides Association. **America Outdoors** (P.O. Box 10847, Knoxville, TN 37939; ✆800-524-4814 www.americaoutdoors.org) offers an extensive outfitter database on their website.

Wilderness Inquiry, Inc. (808 14th Ave., SE, Minneapolis, MN 55414-1546; ✆612-676-9400 or 800-728-0719; www.wildernessinquiry.org) offers tours that include **kayaking** Maine's Moos River, **canoeing** in the Everglades and family adventures in Itasca State Park along the Mississippi River.

SKIING THE EAST

Especially in the colder northern states of the eastern US, but also in the higher levels of the southern Appalachians, snow skiing is a popular winter sport.

Ski areas are abundant, ranging from small local hills with a single chair lift and rope tow, to internationally recognized resorts. Twenty-three eastern states—as far south as Alabama—boast at least one ski area; ski associations count over 237 in all, including 36 in New York and 37 in Michigan.

SkiTown.com Mountain Resort Guide (www.skitown.com) has full details on every North American ski resort and on many resorts overseas.

Major areas, those with at least six lifts and a 1,500ft vertical drop, include:

Maine

Longfellow Mountains: Sugarloaf USA (✆207-237-2000; www.sugarloaf.com). White Mountains: Sunday River (✆207-824-3000, www.sundayriver.com).

New Hampshire

White Mountains: Attitash (✆603-374-2600, www.attitash.com); Bretton Woods (✆603-278-1000, www.brettonwoods.com); Cannon Mountain (✆603-823-8800, www.cannonmt.com); Waterville Valley (✆603-236-8311, www.waterville.com); and Wildcat Mountain (✆603-466-3326, www.skiwildcat.com). Lebanon area: Mount Sunapee (✆603-763-3500, www.mountsunapee.com).

New York

Adirondacks: Gore Mountain (✆ 518-251-2411, www.goremountain.com) and Whiteface Mountain/Lake Placid (✆ 518-946-2223, www.whiteface.com). Catskills: Hunter Mountain (✆ 518-263-4223, www.huntermtn.com) and Windham Mountain (✆ 518-734-4300, www.windham mountain.com).

Vermont

Green Mountains: Bolton Valley (✆ 802-434-3444, www.boltonvalley.com); Killington (✆ 802-422-6200, www.killington.com); Mount Snow (✆ 802-464-3333, www.mountsnow.com); Okemo (✆ 802-228-1600, www.okemo.com); Smugglers' Notch (✆ 802-644-8851, www.smuggs.com); Stowe Mountain (✆ 802-253-3000, www.stowe.com); Stratton Mountain (✆ 802-297-4000, www.stratton.com); and Sugarbush (✆ 802-583-6300, www.sugarbush.com); Cold Hollow Mountains: Jay Peak (✆ 802-988-2611, www.jaypeakresort.com).

West Virginia

Allegheny Mountains: Snowshoe (✆ 304-572-1000, www.snowshoe mtn.com).

NATURE AND SAFETY

Wildlife

In most parks, tampering with plants or wildlife is prohibited by law. When visiting any natural areas, remember that while the disturbance of a single person may be small, the cumulative impact of a large number of visitors may be disastrous. Avoid direct contact with any wildlife; an animal that does not shy away from humans may be sick. Some wildlife—bears in particular—may approach cars or campsites out of curiosity or if they smell food. **Food storage guidelines:** hang food 12ft off the ground and 10ft away from tree trunk, or store in a locking ice chest, car trunk or in lockers provided at some campgrounds. Improper storage of food is a violation of federal law and subject to fine. If a bear approaches, try to frighten it by yelling and throwing rocks in its direction (not at the bear). Never approach a mother with cubs, as she will attack to protect her young.

Hurricanes

Beginning as tropical depressions, hurricanes can measure upward of 500mi in diameter and contain winds up to 200mph (a tropical depression is classified as a hurricane once its winds reach 74mph). The East Coast of the US and the Gulf Coast region are vulnerable to these low-pressure storms from June to November, but the greatest activity occurs between August and October. The National Hurricane Center in Coral Gables and Miami, Florida, tracks all storms and issues advisories every six hours; a hurricane **watch** is announced if a storm may threaten an area within 36

HURRICANE PRECAUTIONS

- ◆ Check your car battery, fill the gas tank, and be sure you have a good supply of cash.
- ◆ Make sure you have a battery-operated radio and extra batteries.
- ◆ Collect fresh water in containers and bathtubs.
- ◆ When staying in coastal areas, be familiar with evacuation routes.
- ◆ Stay indoors during the hurricane.
- ◆ Don't ride out a storm in mobile homes or RVs; seek sturdier shelter.
- ◆ Avoid low-lying areas that are subject to flooding.
- ◆ Be aware of storm surges in coastal regions.
- ◆ Never take a hurricane lightly; follow instructions issued by local authorities, especially if evacuation is mandated.

hours; a hurricane **warning** is issued if landfall is expected within 24 hours.

Thunderstorms and Tornadoes

Prevalent throughout the Deep South and Midwest during summer months, towering thunderheads can develop quickly. Some thunderstorms can be severe, producing hail and dangerous lightning. These severe storms can spawn **tornadoes**, or twisters, violently rotating columns of air reaching from the storm clouds to the ground. Winds generated by tornadoes can reach 300mph, powerful enough to lift trucks and destroy buildings.

Beach and Water Safety

In the strong sun of coastal areas where white sand and water increase the sun's intensity, visitors risk sunburn, even in winter. Apply sunscreen even on overcast days, since ultraviolet rays penetrate the cloud cover. In summer when temperatures can be extreme, avoid strenuous exercise during midday and drink plenty of liquids.

Along public beaches warning flags are posted every mile: **blue flags** signify calm waters; **yellow flags** indicate choppy waters; **red flags** warn of dangerous swimming conditions such as riptides—strong underlying currents that pull swimmers seaward. Take precautions even when venturing into calm waters: never swim, snorkel or scuba dive alone, and supervise children at all times. Most public beaches employ lifeguards seasonally; swim at your own risk at unguarded beaches. Stinging creatures such as jellyfish, men-of-war and sea urchins can inhabit shallow waters. Although most jellyfish stings produce little more than an itchy skin rash, some can cause painful swelling; treat the affected area with papain-type meat tenderizer. Stingrays and men-of-war can inflict a more serious sting; seek medical treatment immediately.

"FOR THE ENJOYMENT OF FUTURE GENERATIONS"

The seeds of America's national park system were planted in 1832 when the federal government created Hot Springs Reservation in central Arkansas to preserve the beneficial mineral springs there for the use of all. But not until 1872 did fierce lobbying by a dedicated group of citizens bring about the creation of Wyoming's Yellowstone National Park—America's first national park.

Preserving parklands east of the Mississippi River proved complicated by the early 20C, because so much territory was already developed or privately owned. In some cases, state parks were transferred to the care of the US government; in others, property was purchased outright with federal funds. American citizens mounted fundraising drives to buy and donate land for Great Smoky Mountain National Park, while industrialist John D. Rockefeller donated 11,000 acres of his personal property in Maine to help create Acadia National Park.

Established in 1916, the **National Park Service's** mandate is to conserve the scenery and the natural and historic objects therein "for the enjoyment of future generations." Today it oversees 58 national parks and 334 other monuments, historic sites, trails, seashores, military parks, recreation areas and byways. Great Smoky Mountains National Park is the most-visited park in the system, while the former Hot Springs Reservation is today Hot Springs National Park, the smallest, and only, urban park. Even the White House is a national park.

Check with local authorities for information on water and weather conditions. If you rent a canoe or charter a boat, familiarize yourself with the craft, obtain charts of the area and advise someone of your itinerary before setting out. **Life jackets** must be worn when boating. Many equipment-rental facilities also offer instruction; be sure to choose a reputable outfitter.

Mountain and Hiking Safety

When hiking in the backcountry, stay on marked trails; taking shortcuts is dangerous and causes erosion. It's best not to hike alone in the backcountry,but if you do, notify someone of your destination and planned return time. Since mountain roads tend to be narrow, steep and twisting, be cautious when driving. Observe road signs and posted speed limits. Always check weather

HITTING THE LINKS

From multi-course complexes and resorts to municipal and daily-fee courses, US golfing facilities provide challenging play, beautiful natural scenery and gracious amenities for enthusiasts of all skill levels. Following is a list of some top-rated public-access courses in the eastern US:

COURSE	LOCATION	WEBSITE
Bay Hill	Orlando, FL	407-876-2429 www.bayhill.com
Bethpage	Farmingdale, NY	516-249-0707 www.bethpageproshop.com
Cog Hill	Lemont, IL	866-264-4455 www.coghillgolf.com
Doral	Miami, FL	305-592-2030 www.doralresort.com
Grand National	Opelika, AL	334-749-9042 www.rtjgolf.com/grandnational/
Sea Pines Harbour Town	Hilton Head Island, SC	800-723-7463 www.seapines.com/golf/harbour-town-golf-links.aspx
Kiawah Island	Kiawah Island, SC	800-654-2924 or 843-768-2121 www.kiawahresort.com/golf
Pinehurst	Pinehurst, NC	910-235-8507 www.pinehurst.com/north-carolina-golf-course.php
Sugarloaf	Carrabassett Valley, ME	207-237-2000 www.sugarloaf.com/GolfCourse
The Dunes	Myrtle Beach, SC	843-449-5236 www.thedunesclub.net/Golf.aspx
The Greenbrier	White Sulphur Springs, WV	800-453-4858 www.greenbrier.com/Golf.aspx
The Homestead	Hot Springs, VA	800-838-1766 www.thehomestead.com/golf
TPC at Sawgrass	Ponte Vedra Beach, FL	904-273-3430 www.tpc.com/tpc-sawgrass
Treetops Sylvan	Gaylord, MI	989-732-6711 http://treetops.com/courses/

conditions before driving or hiking in mountainous areas. Flooding due to heavy rains can cause roads and bridges to become impassable and make camping and hiking in low terrain hazardous. Be prepared for snowstorms if you are in the mountains in winter.

NATIONAL AND STATE LANDS

The US boasts an extensive network of federal and state lands, including national and state parks that offer year-round recreational opportunities such as camping (see WHERE TO STAY AND EAT), fishing, horseback riding, snowmobiling and boating. US federal land-management agencies support a comprehensive online database (www.recreation. gov) with information on all federal recreation areas.

The National Park Service provides a listing of National Wild and Scenic Rivers on its website (www.nps.gov/ncrc/programs/rtca/nri/index.html).

Both national and state parks offer season passes. The America the Beautiful Annual Pass (see BEFORE YOU GO) is good for one year and includes admission to all national parks, sites and areas. Purchase at any park entrance; by calling 888-275-8747 x1; or online at http://store.usgs.gov/pass. Most parks have information centers equipped with trail maps and literature on park facilities and activities. Contact the following agencies for further information:

◆ National Forests
US Department of Agriculture
Forest Service National Headquarters
1400 Independence Ave., SW
Washington, DC 20250-0003
202-205-8333 or www.fs.fed.us

◆ National Parks
The Department of the Interior
National Park Service
1849 C St. NW
Washington, DC 20240
202-208-3818 or www.nps.gov

◆ State Parks
Alabama State Lands Division
31115 Five Rivers Blvd.
Spanish Fort, AL 36507
334-242-3484
www.outdooralabama.com
Arkansas Department of Parks & Tourism
One Capitol Mall
Little Rock, AR 72201
501-682-7777
www.arkansas.com
Connecticut State Parks Division
79 Elm St.
Hartford, CT 06106
860-424-3200
www.ct.gov/deep
Delaware Division of Parks & Recreation
89 Kings Highway
Dover, DE 19901
302-739-9220
www.destateparks.com
District of Columbia Recreation & Parks Department
1250 U St. NW

Great Falls Park, Maryland

©La Wanda Wilson/Dreamstime.com

Washington, DC 20009
℘(202) 673-7647
http://dpr.dc.gov

**Florida Division of Recreation
and Parks**
3900 Commonwealth Blvd.
Tallahassee, FL 32399
℘850-245-2157
www.floridastateparks.org

Georgia State Parks & Historic Sites
781 Red Top Mountain Rd. SE
Cartersville, GA 30121
℘404-656-2770
www.gastateparks.org

**Illinois Department of
Natural Resources**
One Natural Resources Way
Springfield, IL 62702-1271
℘217-782-6302
www.dnr.Illinois.com

Indiana State Parks and Reservoirs
402 W. Washington St.
Room W298
Indianapolis, IN 46204
℘317-232-4124
www.in.gov/dnr/parklake/

**Iowa Division of Parks,
Recreation & Preserves**
Wallace State Office Building
Des Moines, Iowa 50319-0034
℘515-281-5918
www.parks.iowadnr.gov

Kentucky Department of Parks
Capital Plaza Tower
500 Mero St., Suite 1100
Frankfort, KY 40601-1974
℘502-564-2172 or 800-255-7275
www.parks.ky.gov

Louisiana Office of State Parks
P.O. Box 44426
Baton Rouge, LA 70804-4426
℘225-342-8111
www.crt.state.la.us/parks

Maine Bureau of Parks & Lands
22 State House Station
18 Elkins Lane (AMHI Campus)
Augusta, ME 04333-0022
℘207-287-3821
www.maine.gov/doc/parks

Maryland State Park & Forest Service
580 Taylor Ave.
Annapolis, MD 21401
℘410-260-8186 or 877-620-8367
www.dnr.state.md.us/publiclands

**Massachusetts Department of
Conservation and Recreation**
251 Causeway St., Suite 900
Boston, MA 02114-2104
℘617-626-1250
www.mass.gov/dcr/forparks.htm

Michigan Parks & Recreation Division
P.O. Box 30028
Lansing, MI 48909
℘517-373-9900
www.michigan.gov/dnr

Minnesota State Parks
500 Lafayette Rd.
St. Paul, MN 55155-4040
℘651-296-6157
www.dnr.state.mn.us/state_parks

Mississippi Wildlife, Fisheries & Parks
1505 Eastover Dr.
Jackson, MS 39211
℘601-432-2400
www.mdwfp.com

TIPS FOR VISITING PUBLIC LANDS

- Spray clothes with insect repellent (particularly around cuffs and waistline) and check for ticks every 3-4 hours when participating in outdoor activities.
- Do not feed wild animals.
- Do not litter; pack out everything you pack in.
- Boil (5min) or chemically treat water from streams and lakes.
- Cutting wood for fires is prohibited; only dead or fallen wood should be used. Campfires are limited to fire pits.
- Hunting is prohibited in most parks; contact individual parks for hunting information.
- All pets must be leashed and may be prohibited from certain park areas.
- All plants and animals within parks are protected.
- Taking natural objects (antlers/horns, historical objects, plants, rocks) is prohibited.

Missouri Division of State Parks
P.O. Box 176
Jefferson City, MO 65102
☎800-334-6946 or 573-751-2479
www.mostateparks.com

New Hampshire Division of Parks & Recreation
P.O. Box 1856
Concord, NH 03302
☎603-271-3556
www.nhstateparks.org

New Jersey Division of Parks & Forestry
Mail Code: 501-04, P.O. Box 402
Trenton, NJ 08625
☎609-984-0370
www.state.nj.us/depparksandforests

New York State Office of Parks, Recreation & Historic Preservation
Albany, NY 12238
☎518-474-0456
www.nysparks.com

North Carolina Division of Parks & Recreation
1615 MSC
Raleigh, NC 27699
☎919-707-9300
www.ncparks.gov

Ohio State Parks
2045 Morse Rd.
Columbus, OH 43229
☎614-265-6565
www.ohiodnr.com

Pennsylvania Bureau of State Parks
P.O. Box 8551
Harrisburg, PA 17105
☎888-727-2757
www.dcnr.state.pa.us/stateparks

Rhode Island Division of Parks & Recreation
2321 Hartford Ave.
Johnston, RI 02919
☎401-222-2632
www.riparks.com

South Carolina Department of Parks, Recreation & Tourism
1205 Pendleton St.
Columbia, SC 29201
☎803-734-1700
www.southcarolinaparks.com

Tennessee State Parks
401 Church St.
L&C Tower, 7th Floor
Nashville, TN 37243
☎615-532-0001
www.tn.gov/environment/parks/

Vermont Department of Forests, Parks & Recreation
1 National Life Drive, Davis 2
Montpelier, VT 05620-3801
☎802-522-0841
www.vtfpr.org

Virginia State Parks Division
600 E. Main St., 24th Floor
Richmond, VA 23219
☎804-786-1712
www.dcr.virginia.gov/state_parks

West Virginia State Parks & Forests
324 4th Ave.
South Charleston, WV 25303
☎304-558-2764
www.wvparks.com

Wisconsin State Park System
P.O. Box 7921
Madison, WI 53707-7921
☎608-266-2621
www.wiparks.net

HIKING TRAILS

The National Park Service, USDA Forest Service and Bureau of Land Management administer numerous national scenic and national historic trails throughout the US.

For information on specific trail systems and recreational activities offered, download The *National Trails System Map and Guide* from the Federal Citizen Information Center (Pueblo CO 81009; http://publications.usa.gov/USAPubs.php?PubID=1262; email: Pueblo@gpo.gov).

National Trails System Branch of the National Park Service
1849 C Street NW
Washington, DC 20240
www.nps.gov/nts

Appalachian National Scenic Trail
Appalachian Trail Conservancy,
P.O. Box 807, Harpers Ferry,
WV 25425
☎304-535-6331
www.appalachiantrail.org

National Park Service, Appalachian National Scenic Trail
P.O. Box 50, Harpers Ferry,
WV 25425
☎304-535-6278

Captain John Smith Chesapeake National Historic Trail
NPS–Chesapeake Bay Program Office, 410 Severn Ave., Suite 314, Annapolis, MD 21403
✆410-260-2471

Florida National Scenic Trail
Florida Trail Association, 5415 S.W. 13th St., Gainesville, FL 32608
✆352-378-8823 or 877-445-3352 (US)
www.floridatrail.org

USDA Forest Service
Greenways & Trails, 1400 Independence Ave., SW., Washington, D.C. 20250-0003
✆202-205-8333

Ice Age National Scenic Trail
Ice Age Trail Alliance, 2110 Main St., Cross Plains, WI 53528
✆800-227-0046, www.iceagetrail.org

National Park Service
Ice Age National Scenic Trail, 700 Rayovac Dr., Suite 100, Madison, WI 53711
✆608-441-5610
www.nps.gov/iatr

Natchez Trace National Scenic Trail
National Park Service, 2680 Natchez Trace Parkway, Tupelo, MS 38804
✆601-680-4014

New England National Scenic Trail
National Park Service, 15 State St., Boston, MA 02109
✆617-223-5210

North Country National Scenic Trail
North Country Trail Association, 229 E. Main St., Lowell, MI 49331
✆866-897-5987
National Park Service, North Country National Scenic Trail, PO Box 288, Lowell, MI 49331
✆616-340-2004

Overmountain Victory National Historic Trail
Overmountain Victory Trail Association, 1780 Muster Place, Abingdon, VA 24210
✆276-525-1050

© Natan Blaney/iStockphoto.com

National Park Service, 2635 Park Rd. Blacksburg, SC 29702
✆864-936-3477

Potomac Heritage National Scenic Trail
For a list of partners and volunteer associations, visit www.nps.gov/pohe/
National Park Service, Potomac Heritage National Scenic Trail Office, P.O. Box B, Harpers Ferry, WV, 25425
✆304-535-4014

Selma to Montgomery National Historic Trail
National Park Service Office, 7001 US Hwy. 80 W, Hayneville, AL: 36040
✆334-877-1984

Star-Spangled Banner National Historic Trail
NPS–Chesapeake Bay Program Office, 410 Severn Ave., Suite 314, Annapolis, MD 21403
✆410-260-2470

Trail of Tears National Historic Trail
Trail of Tears Association, 1100 N. University Ave., #143, Little Rock, AR 72207
✆501-666-9032
National Park Service, Intermountain Region, P.O. Box 728, Santa Fe, NM 87504-0728
✆505-988-6098

Spectator Sports

MAJOR LEAGUE BASEBALL (MLB)

APR–OCT

www.majorleaguebaseball.com

Atlanta Braves
Turner Field ☎404-522-7630

Baltimore Orioles
Oriole Park at Camden Yards
☎410-685-9800

Boston Red Sox
Fenway Park ☎617-267-9440

Chicago Cubs
Wrigley Field ☎773-404-2827

Chicago White Sox
US Cellular Field ☎312-674-1000

Cincinnati Reds
Great American Ball Park
☎513-765-7000

Cleveland Indians
Progressive Field ☎216-420-4200

Detroit Tigers
Comerica Park ☎313-471-2000

Kansas City Royals
Kauffman Stadium ☎816-921-8000

Miami Marlins
Marlins Park ☎305-480-1300

Milwaukee Brewers
Miller Park ☎414-902-4400

Minnesota Twins
Target Field, Minneapolis, MN
☎612-659-3400

New York Mets
Citi Field, Flushing, NY
☎718-507-6387

New York Yankees
Yankee Stadium, Bronx, NY
☎718-293-4300

Philadelphia Phillies
Citizens Bank Park ☎215-463-6000

Pittsburgh Pirates
PNC Park ☎412-323-5000

St. Louis Cardinals
Busch Stadium ☎314-345-9600

Tampa Bay Rays
Tropicana Field ☎727-825-3137

Washington Nationals
Nationals Park ☎202-675-6287

NATIONAL BASKETBALL ASSOCIATION (NBA)

OCT–APR

www.nba.com

Atlanta Hawks
Philips Arena
☎(404) 878-3000

Boston Celtics
TD Garden
☎866-423-5849

Brooklyn Nets
Barclays Center, Brooklyn, NY
☎917-618-6700

Charlotte Bobcats
Time Warner Cable Arena
☎704-688-8600

Chicago Bulls
United Center
☎312-455-4000

Cleveland Cavaliers
Quicken Loans Arena
☎216-420-2000

Detroit Pistons
The Palace of Auburn Hills
☎248-377-0100

Indiana Pacers
Bankers Life Fieldhouse
☎317-917-2500

Memphis Grizzlies
FedExForum
☎901-205-2525

Miami Heat
AmericanAirlines Arena
☎786-777-1000

Milwaukee Bucks
BMO Harris Bradley Center
☎414-227-0400

Minnesota Timberwolves
Target Center, Minneapolis, MN
☎612-673-1600

New Orleans Hornets
New Orleans Arena
☎504-587-3663

New York Knicks
Madison Square Garden
☎212-465-6741

Orlando Magic
Amway Center
☎866-239-9666

Philadelphia 76ers
Wells Fargo Center ☎215-336-3600

Washington Wizards
Verizon Center
202-661-5000

NATIONAL FOOTBALL LEAGUE (NFL)
SEPT–DEC
www.nfl.com
Atlanta Falcons
Georgia Dome
404 223-8444
Baltimore Ravens
M&T Bank Stadium
410-261-7283
Buffalo Bills
Ralph Wilson Stadium
716-648-1800
Carolina Panthers
Bank of America Stadium,
Charlotte, NC
704-358-7800
Chicago Bears
Soldier Field
847-615-2327
Cincinnati Bengals
Paul Brown Stadium
513-621-3550
Cleveland Browns
FirstEnergy Stadium
440-891-5001
Detroit Lions
Ford Field
313-262-2031
Green Bay Packers
Lambeau Field
920-569-7500
Indianapolis Colts
Lucas Oil Stadium
317-297-2658
Jacksonville Jaguars
EverBank Field
904-633-2000
Kansas City Chiefs
Arrowhead Stadium
816-920-9400
Miami Dolphins
Sun Life Stadium
305-943-8000
Minnesota Vikings
Mall of America Field at the
Hubert H. Humphrey Metrodome
(the new Vikings Stadium to
open 2016)
612-338-4537

New England Patriots
Gillette Stadium, Foxboro, MA
508-543-1776
New Orleans Saints
Mercedes-Benz Superdome
504-731-1700
New York Giants
MetLife Stadium,
East Rutherford, NJ
201-935-8222
New York Jets
MetLife Stadium,
East Rutherford, NJ
973-549-4800
Philadelphia Eagles
Lincoln Financial Field
215-463-5500
Pittsburgh Steelers
Heinz Field
412-323-1200
Tampa Bay Buccaneers
Raymond James Stadium
813-870-2700
Tennessee Titans
LP Field, Nashville, TN
615-565-4300
Washington Redskins
FedEx Field 301-276-6800

NATIONAL HOCKEY LEAGUE (NHL)
OCT–APR
www.nhl.com
Boston Bruins
TD Garden
617-624-2327
Buffalo Sabres
First Niagara Center
716-855-4100
Carolina Hurricanes
PNC Arena
919-861-2323
Chicago Blackhawks
United Center
312-455-7000
Columbus Blue Jackets
Nationwide Arena
614-246-2000
Detroit Red Wings
Joe Louis Arena
313-396-7444
Florida Panthers
BB&T Center, Sunrise, FL
954-835-7825

Minnesota Wild
Xcel Energy Center
✐651-602-6000
Nashville Predators
Bridgestone Arena
✐615-770-7825
New Jersey Devils
Prudential Center
Newark, NJ
✐973-757-6200
New York Islanders
Nassau Veterans
Memorial Coliseum
✐516-501-6700
New York Rangers
Madison Square Garden
✐212-465-6000

Philadelphia Flyers
Wells Fargo Center
✐215-218-7825
Pittsburgh Penguins
Consol Energy Arena
✐412-642-1842
St. Louis Blues
Scottrade Center
✐314-622-2583
Tampa Bay Lightning
Tampa Bay Times Forum
✐813-301-2500
Washington Capitals
Verizon Center
✐202-397-7328

Activities for Kids

I n this guide, sights of particular interest to children are indicated with a ♟♙ symbol. Many of these attractions offer special children's programs. Some attractions offer discounted (if not free) admission to visitors under 12 years of age. In addition, many hotels and resorts offer family discount packages.

Entertainment

Atlanta Civic Center
✐404-523-6275
www.atlantaciviccenter.com
Aaron's Amphitheatre, Atlanta
✐404-443-5090
www.facebook.com/
aaronsamphitheatreatlakewood
Boston Opera House
✐617-259-3400
www.bostonoperahouseonline.com
Orpheum Theatre, Boston, MA
✐617-482-0106
www.orpheumtheatreboston.com
Civic Opera House, Chicago, IL
✐312-419-0033
www.civicoperahouse.com
Steppenwolf Theater Co., Chicago, IL
✐312-335-1650
www.steppenwolf.org
Riverbend Music Center, Cincinnati, OH
✐513-232-6220
www.riverbend.org

Max M. Fisher Music Center, Detroit, MI
✐313-576-5111
www.dso.org
Clowes Memorial Hall, Indianapolis, IN
✐317- 940-9697
www.cloweshall.org
Byron Carlyle Theater, Miami, FL
✐305-867-4194
Milwaukee Theatre
✐414-908-6000
www.milwaukeetheatre.com
Plymouth Playhouse, Plymouth, MN
✐763-553-1600
www.plymouthplayhouse.com
Radio City Music Hall, New York, NY
✐(212) 247-4777
www.radiocity.com
First Niagara Pavilion, Pittsburgh, PA
✐724-947-7400
www.firstniagarapavilion.net

Sightseeing

National and City Tours – Several national tour companies provide all-inclusive packages for motorcoach tours of the US (below). The scope of tours may vary among tour operators, but most offer packages of varying length, geographic coverage and cost. **TrekAmerica** (✆UK: 0844 576 1400, US: 800-873-5872, Other: +44 (0) 208 682 8920; www.trekamerica.com) caters to travelers who prefer small groups, varied sightseeing/sporting activities and flexible itineraries. For those interested in more educational offerings, **Smithsonian Journeys** (✆855-330-1542 or www.smithsonian journeys.org), sponsored by the Smithsonian Institute in Washington, DC, offers a variety of single- and multi-day thematic programs covering topics such as architecture, performing arts, cuisine and Civil War history. Educators specializing in related fields lead these tours.

Discover the rolling Mississippi River aboard the 4-decker paddlewheeler Celebration Belle operated by **Celebration River Cruises** (2501 River Rd., Moline, IL 61265; ✆800-297-0034 www.celebrationbelle.com). Themed itineraries focus on the river between Illinois and Iowa.

Backroads (✆510-527-1555; www.backroads.com) organizes multisport trips geared toward the active traveler.

Itineraries include biking in Vermont; biking and kayaking in Maine; walking in Massachusetts; and biking and kayaking along the South Carolina/ Georgia coast.

Information on **city tours** can be obtained by contacting the convention and visitors bureaus in large US cities. **Gray Line Tours** provides half- and full-day sightseeing motor-coach tours for more than 70 US cities: For information, contact: **Gray Line Worldwide**, ✆303-394-6920, www.grayline.com.

National Tour Companies

Collette Vacations
✆800-340-5158
www.collettevacations.com

Globus and Cosmos
5301 S. Federal Circle
Littleton, CO 80123
✆877-245-6287
www.globusandcosmos.com

Mayflower Tours
1225 Warren Ave.
Downers Grove, IL 60515
✆630-435-8500 or 800-323-7604
www.mayflowertours.com

Trafalgar Tours
✆866-544-4434.www.trafalgar.com

Tauck Tours
10 Norden Pl., Norwalk, CT 06855
✆203-899-6500 or 800-788-7885
www.tauck.com

What to Buy & Where to Shop

S hopping is a main event in many parts of the east, south and midwest US. In some cities, discount and outlet malls are the main tourist attraction, drawing more visitors each year than local museums and other landmarks.

In general in the US, people do not bargain in stores; they pay the marked price. Exceptions are flea markets and antique malls, where negotiating is expected. Sales tax varies by state, city and county and is added to the purchase price. Occasionally, merchants will offer discounts for cash payments. Different regions of the country have different shopping specialties, just as they have varied regional cuisines. Look for furniture in North Carolina, antiques in New England, handicrafts in the South and clothing (◖see Conversion Tables p63) in major metropolitan areas.

Books

The eastern half of the US is well represented in the country's literary offerings. Read some of these books before you go.

The Adventures of Tom Sawyer
Mark Twain (1876)
This classic tale recounts the childhood exploits of mischief-maker Tom Sawyer, set on the Mississippi River in the town of Petersburg, MO.

Devil in the White City
Erik Larson (2003)
Through the lives of two men during Chicago's landmark World's Fair—a renowned architect and infamous serial killer—this tale sheds light on Chicago's rich architectural history.

Lost Man's River
Peter Matthiessen (1997)
The second novel in this author's trilogy paints a rich landscape of the unconventional characters residing in the Florida Everglades.

A Prayer for the City
Buzz Bissinger (1998)
The factual story of Democratic Philadelphia mayor Ed Rendell's efforts to save this East-coast city from bankruptcy in the early '90s.

A Streetcar Named Desire
Tennessee Williams (1947)
New Orleans' dazzling French Quarter provides the backdrop for this renowned play, which tells the story of a wilting Southern belle who comes to stay with her sister and dominating brother-in-law.

To Kill A Mockingbird
Harper Lee (1960)
This story of a widowed father and his two children provides a personal window into the judicial system and racism in Alabama during the Great Depression.

A Tree Grows in Brooklyn
Betty Smith (1943)
Set in the early 20C, this collection of five books charts the lives of a struggling Irish-American family in the impoverished Williamsburg neighborhood of Brooklyn, NY.

Films

In America, most stories are about to become a movie, or are inspired by one. Catch one of these flicks to get a glimpse of eastern US cities on screen.

Chicago (2002)
This feature-film version of the classic Broadway musical weaves a sultry web of crime, stardom and sensationalism in 1920s Chicago.

Nashville (1975)
An ensemble cast of characters intertwined in Nashville's music business take center stage in this song-laden film directed by Robert Altman.

The Last of the Mohicans (1992)
Historical drama of the French and Indian War, set in Albany, NY, but filmed in the North Carolina mountains.

New York Stories (1989)
Three favorite directors, including Woody Allen, Francis Ford Coppola and Martin Scorsese, tell their own stories about the Big Apple.

Fever Pitch (2005)
Nick Hornby may be a Brit, but this movie, based on his book by the same name, is as American as it gets. Set in Boston, it's about an obsession with the Boston Red Sox, one of the teams involved in America's pastime: baseball.

When The Levees Broke (2006)
Directed by Spike Lee, this documentary provides a close-up of the lives of New Orleans natives

in the tragic aftermath of Hurricane Katrina. The film was originally created for Home Box Office (HBO) cable television.

The Color Purple (1985)
Based on the 1982 novel by Alice Walker, Stephen Spielberg's powerful film chronicles the life of a poor African-American girl growing up in rural Georgia.

Rent (2005)
This movie version of Jonathan Larson's Tony-award winning musical (loosely based on the opera La Bohème) tells the story of eight friends struggling with their relationships, drug addictions and AIDS in the tenement-filled streets of New York City's gritty Alphabet City in the late '80s.

All The President's Men (1975)
This iconic Washington, DC-set film follows investigative journalists Bob Woodward and Carl Bernstein as they break open the Nixon administration Watergate scandal, thanks to the help of an anonymous source named Deep Throat.

Walk The Line (2005)
This Memphis-set film follows the tumultuous path of rising country music star Johnny Cash as he records his chart-topping tunes alongside legends such as Elvis Presley.

The Help (2011)
Rich in history and atmosphere, this fictional film follows a white journalist in 1960s segregated Mississippi as she records the stories of African-American maids working for white families.

Festivals & Events

SPRING

MARCH

EARLY MAR
Philadelphia Flower Show, Philadelphia, PA
Carnaval Miami, Miami, FL
Sanibel Shell Fair, Sanibel Island, FL
Bike Week, Daytona Beach, FL

MAR–EARLY APR
Natchez Spring Pilgrimage, Natchez, MS

MID-MAR
St. Patrick's Day Parades, Atlanta, GA, New Orleans, LA, Savannah, GA, New York City, NY

MID-MAR–MID-APR
Festival of Houses & Gardens, Charleston, SC

LATE MAR
Savannah Tour of Homes & Gardens, Savannah, GA
Spanish Night Watch, St. Augustine, FL

MID-MAR–EARLY APR
Vicksburg Spring Pilgrimage, Vicksburg, MS

International Artexpo New York, New York City, NY

EARLY MAR–MID-APR
Festival of States, St. Petersburg, FL

APRIL

EASTER SUNDAY
Easter Sunday Parade, New York City, NY
Easter Sunrise Service, Arlington National Cemetery, Arlington VA

EASTER MONDAY
Easter Egg Roll and Egg Hunt, White House, Washington, DC
Seven Mile Bridge Run, Marathon, FL
Wildflower Pilgrimage, Great Smoky Mountains NP, TN
National Cherry Blossom Festival, Washington, DC

APR–MAY
Smoky Mountain Music Festival, Gatlinburg, TN

2ND WEEKEND APR
French Quarter Festival, New Orleans, LA

APRIL: National Cherry Blossom Festival, Washington, DC

© Ron Engle for National Cherry Blossom Festival

JAN–MID-MAY
Chicago Park District Spring Flower Show, Chicago, IL

APR–MAY
The 500 Festival, Indianapolis, IN

EARLY APR
Atlanta Dogwood Festival, Atlanta, GA

MID–LATE APR
Tampa Bay Blues Festival, St. Petersburg, FL
Tri-C Jazzfest, Cleveland, OH

MID-APR–MAY
Kentucky Derby Festival, Louisville, KY

3RD WEEK APR
Fayetteville Dogwood Festival, Fayetteville, NC

3RD MON IN APR
Boston Marathon, Boston, MA

LAST WEEK APR
Historic Garden Week, Virginia, statewide

LAST WEEKEND APR
Annual Main Street Festival, Franklin, TN

4TH SUN APR
Blessing of the Fleet and Seafood Festival, Charleston, SC

LATE APR–MAY
Spring Festival, Cape May, NJ
New Orleans Jazz & Heritage Festival, New Orleans, LA

Hudson River White Water Derby, North Creek, NY
Virginia Arts Festival, Norfolk, VA

LATE APR–JUN
Georgia Renaissance Festival, Atlanta, GA

MAY

MAY–JUN
Cape May Music Festival, Cape May, NJ

1ST WEEKEND MAY
TACA Tennessee Craft Fair, Nashville, TN

© Paul Denny/Tulip Time Festival

MAY: Tulip Time Festival, Holland, Michigan

EARLY MAY
Schaeffer Eye Center Crawfish Boil, Birmingham, AL
Tulip Time Festival, Holland, MI

2ND WEEKEND MAY
International BBQ Festival, Owensboro, KY

MID-MAY
Crawdad Days Music Festival, Harrison, AR
Philadelphia Open House, Philadelphia, PA
Annual Hang Gliding Spectacular, Nags Head, NC

LATE MAY
Indianapolis 500, Indianapolis, IN
Old School & Blues Festival, Hunstville, AL

MEMORIAL DAY WEEKEND
Lobster Days, Mystic, CT

LATE MAY–MID-JUN
Spoleto Festival USA, Charleston, SC

SUMMER

JUNE

Sarasota Music Festival, Sarasota, FL

EARLY JUN
Goombay Festival, Coconut Grove, Miami, FL
Yale-Harvard Regatta, New London, CT
Belmont Stakes, Belmont, NY

MID-JUN
Festival of the Bluegrass, Kentucky Horse Park, Lexington, KY
Chicago Gospel Festival, Chicago, IL
CMA Music Festival, Nashville, TN
Festival of Historic Houses, Providence, RI
Chicago Blues Festival, Chicago, IL

MID–LATE JUN
River Days, Detroit, MI

JUN–AUG
'Unto These Hills' Cherokee History drama, Cherokee, NC
Shakespeare in the Park, New York City, NY
The Lost Colony symphonic outdoor drama, Manteo, NC

JUN–LATE AUG
Jacob's Pillow Dance Festival, Becket, MA

MID-JUN–MID AUG:
Grant Park Music Festival, Chicago, IL

MID-JUN–EARLY SEPT
Ravinia Festival, Chicago, IL

LATE JUN- EARLY JUL
Summerfest, Milwaukee, WI

JULY

Minneapolis Aquatennial, Minneapolis, MN
Hemingway Days, Key West, FL
NY Philharmonic Parks Concerts in the Parks, New York City, NY
Taste of Chicago, Chicago, IL

JUL 4
Boston Harborfest, Boston, MA
Macy's 4th of July Fireworks, New York City, NY
National Independence Day Celebrations, Washington, DC

EARLY JUL
Smithsonian Folklife Festival, Washington, DC
Essence Music Festival, New Orleans, LA
M&T Syracuse Jazz Fest, Syracuse, NY
National Tom Sawyer Days, Hannibal, MO

MID-JUL
Grandfather Mountain Highland Games, near Linville, NC

LATE JUL
Chicago Yacht Club Race to Mackinac, Mackinac Island, MI
Pony Penning (Pony Swim) and Carnival, Chincoteague, VA
Ozark Empire Fair, Springfield, MO

JUL-AUG
Mostly Mozart Festival, Lincoln Center, New York City
Metropolitan Opera Parks Concerts, New York City, NY

LATE JUL–AUG
Racing Season, Saratoga Springs, NY

AUGUST

EARLY AUG
Uptown Art Fair, Minneapolis, MN
Craftsmen's Fair, Newbury, NH

Newport Jazz Festival, Newport, RI
Festival of Contemporary Music, Lenox, MA

MID-AUG
Iowa State Fair, Des Moines, IA
Bayfront Blues Festival, Duluth, MN
Chicago Air & Water Show, Chicago, IL

AUG 18
Virginia Dare Birthday Celebration, Fort Raleigh NHS, Manteo, NC

AUG 25
National Park Service Founders Day, all National Parks

LAST WEEKEND AUG:
Viva! Chicago Latin Music Festival, Chicago, IL

LABOR DAY WEEKEND
Chicago Jazz Festival, Chicago, IL
Cleveland National Air Show, Cleveland, OH

FALL

SEPTEMBER
Mountain Life Festival, Great Smoky Mountains NP, TN
Maryland State Fair, Timonium, MD

MID-SEPT
Kentucky Bourbon Festival, Bardstown, KY
Virginia Wine Festival, Centreville, VA
Indy Jazz Fest, Indianapolis, IN

Miss America Pageant, Atlantic City, NJ

LATE SEPT
Adirondack Balloon Festival, Glens Falls, NY

LAST WEEKEND SEPT
Wide Open Bluegrass Festival, Raleigh, NC

LATE SEPT-OCT
Natchez Fall Pilgrimage, Natchez, MS
Northeast Kingdom Fall Foliage Festival, Northeast Kingdom, VT
Penn's Colony Festival, Saxonburg, PA

OCTOBER

Chicago International Film Festival, Chicago, IL

EARLY OCT
Oktoberfest, Amana Colonies, IA
Grand Ole Opry Birthday Bash, Nashville, TN
Williamsburg Scottish Festival, Williamsburg, VA

MID OCT
Victorian Week, Cape May, NJ
National Shrimp Festival, Gulf Shores, AL

3RD WEEKEND OCT
Great Mississippi River Balloon Race, Natchez, MS

LATE OCT
Guavaween, Ybor City, FL

JANUARY-FEBRUARY:
Chinese Paper Dragon at the New Year Parade, New York City

© Steffen Foerster/iStockphoto.com

NOVEMBER: Magnificent Mile Lights Festival, Chicago

© Charles Cherney Photography

NOVEMBER

MID-NOV
Veterans Day Ceremonies, Washington, DC
Magnificent Mile Lights Festival, Chicago, IL
City of Chicago Tree-Lighting Ceremony, Chicago, IL

THANKSGIVING DAY (3RD THURS IN NOV)
Macy's Thanksgiving Day Parade, New York City, NY
Pilgrim Progress Procession, Plymouth, MA

DAY AFTER THANKSGIVING DAY
Rockefeller Center Christmas Tree Lighting, New York City, NY

WINTER

DECEMBER
EARLY DEC
Art Miami, Miami, FL
National Christmas Tree Lighting, Washington, DC
Williamsburg Grand Illumination, Williamsburg, VA

LATE DEC
King Mango Strut, Coconut Grove, FL

DEC 24–25
Christmas Celebration, National Cathedral, Washington, DC

LAST WEEK OF DEC
Indian Arts Festival, Miccosukee Indian Village, Everglades, FL

DEC 31
New Year's Eve Celebration, New York City, NY

JANUARY
JAN 1
Mummers Parade, Philadelphia, PA

MID-JAN–MID-MAR (ASH WEDNESDAY)
Mardi Gras Season, New Orleans, LA

MID-JAN
Art Deco Weekend, Miami Beach, FL
Stowe Winter Carnival, Stowe, VT
Gasparilla Pirate Festival, Tampa, FL

LATE JAN
Lowcountry Oyster Festival, Charleston, SC

LATE JAN–FEB
Chinese New Year Parade, New York City, NY
St. Paul Winter Carnival, St. Paul, MN

FEBRUARY

Daytona 500, Daytona Beach, FL
World Championship Sled Dog Derby, Laconia, NH

FEB–MAR
Chinese New Year Parade & Festival, Washington, DC

Practical Info

TOP TIPS

Best time to go: Early autumn or late spring.
Best way around: Personal vehicle or rental car, for the most freedom.
Best for sightseeing: Avoid Mondays, when restaurants may be closed.
Most authentic accommodation: Bed and breakfasts and country inns.
Need to know: Road regulations and the weather forecast, if driving.
Need to taste: New England clam chowder, BBQ ribs, jambalaya.

CITY	JANUARY			JUNE		
	avg. high °F / °C	avg. low °F / °C	precip. in. / cen.	avg. high °F / °C	avg. low °F / °C	precip. in. / cen.
ATLANTA, GA	33 / 1	17 / −8	2.2 / 5.5	79 / 26	57 / 14	3.2 / 8.1
ATLANTIC CITY, NJ	40 / 4	21 / −6	3.5 / 8.8	80 / 27	59 / 15	2.6 / 6.7
BALTIMORE, MD	40 / 4	23 / −5	3.1 / 7.7	83 / 28	62 / 17	3.7 / 9.3
BATON ROUGE, LA	60 / 16	40 / 4	4.9 / 12.5	91 / 33	70 / 21	4.5 / 11.4
BOSTON, MA	36 / 2	22 / −6	3.6 / 9.1	76 / 24	59 / 15	3.1 / 7.8
BURLINGTON, VT	25 / −4	8 / −13	1.8 / 4.6	76 / 24	55 / 13	3.5 / 8.8
CHARLESTON, SC	58 / 14	38 / 3	3.5 / 8.8	88 / 31	69 / 21	6.4 / 16.3
CHICAGO, IL	29 / −2	13 / −11	1.5 / 3.9	80 / 27	58 / 14	3.8 / 9.6
CINCINNATI, OH	38 / 3	20 / −6.7	3.1 / 7.7	85 / 29	57 / 14	4.9 / 12.4
CLEVELAND, OH	32 / 0	18 / −8	2.0 / 5.2	78 / 26	57 / 14	3.7 / 9.4
DES MOINES, IA	28 / −2	11 / −12	1.0 / 2.4	82 / 28	61 / 16	4.5 / 11.3
DETROIT, MI	30 / −1	16 / −9	1.8 / 4.5	79 / 26	56 / 13	3.6 / 9.2
DULUTH, MN	16 / −9	−2 / −19	1.2 / 3.1	71 / 22	49 / 9	3.8 / 9.6
GREEN BAY, WI	23 / −5	6 / −14	1.2 / 3.1	76 / 24	54 / 12	3.4 / 8.6
INDIANAPOLIS, IN	34 / 1	17 / −8	2.3 / 5.9	83 / 28	61 / 16	3.5 / 8.9
JACKSON, MS	56 / 13	33 / 1	5.2 / 13.3	91 / 33	67 / 19	3.2 / 8.1
KANSAS CITY, MO	35 / 2	17 / −8	1.1 / 2.8	83 / 28	63 / 17	4.7 / 12.0
LEXINGTON, KY	39 / 4	22 / −6	2.9 / 7.3	83 / 28	62 / 17	3.7 / 9.4
LITTLE ROCK, AR	49 / 9	29 / −2	3.9 / 9.9	89 / 32	67 / 19	7.8 / 19.9

CITY	JANUARY			JUNE		
	avg. high °F / °C	avg. low °F / °C	precip. in. / cen.	avg. high °F / °C	avg. low °F / °C	precip. in. / cen.
LOUISVILLE, KY	40 / 4	23 / –5	2.9 / 7.3	84 / 29	63 / 17	3.5 / 8.8
MADISON, WI	25 / –4	7 / –14	1.1 / 2.7	78 / 26	54 / 12	3.7 / 9.4
MEMPHIS, TN	49 / 9	31 / –1	3.7 / 9.5	89 / 32	69 / 21	3.6 / 9.1
MIAMI, FL	75 / 24	59 / 15	2.0 / 5.1	88 / 31	45 / 7	9.3 / 23.7
MILWAUKEE, WI	26 / –3	12 / –11	1.6 / 4.1	75 / 24	55 / 13	3.2 / 8.2
MINNEAPOLIS, MN	21 / –6	7 / –14	1.0 / 2.5	79 / 26	57 / 14	4.5 / 11.2
MOBILE, AL	60 / 16	40 / 4	4.8 / 12.1	90 / 32	71 / 22	5.0 / 12.8
NASHVILLE, TN	46 / 8	27 / –3	3.6 / 9.1	87 / 31	65 / 18	3.6 / 9.1
NEW ORLEANS, LA	61 / 16	42 / 6	5.1 / 12.8	89 / 32	71 / 22	5.8 / 14.8
NEW YORK, NY	38 / 3	25 / –4	3.8 / 9.6	77 / 25	61 / 16	3.4 / 8.4
NORFOLK, VA	47 / 8	31 / –1	3.8 / 9.6	83 / 28	65 / 18	3.8 / 9.6
ORLANDO, FL	71 / 22	49 / 9	2.3 / 5.8	91 / 33	72 / 22	7.3 / 18.6
PHILADELPHIA, PA	38 / 3	23 / –5	3.2 / 8.2	82 / 28	62 / 17	3.7 / 9.4
PITTSBURGH, PA	34 / 1	19 / –7	2.5 / 6.5	79 / 26	57 / 14	3.7 / 9.4
PORTLAND, ME	30 / –1	11 / –12	3.5 / 9.0	73 / 23	52 / 11	3.4 / 8.7
PROVIDENCE, RI	37 / 3	19 / –7	3.9 / 9.9	77 / 25	57 / 14	3.3 8.5
RICHMOND, VA	46 / 8	26 / –3	3.2 / 8.2	85 / 29	63 / 17	3.6 / 9.2
SAVANNAH, GA	60 / 16	38 / 3	3.6 / 9.1	89 / 32	69 / 21	5.7 / 14.4
ST. LOUIS, MO	38 / 3	25 / –4	2.3 / 5.8	85 / 29	66 / 19	4.6 / 11.4
TAMPA, FL	70 / 21	50 / 10	2.0 / 5.1	90 / 32	73 / 23	5.5 / 13.9
WASHINGTON, DC	42 / 6	27 / –3	2.7 / 6.9	85 / 29	67 / 19	3.3 / 8.4
WINSTON–SALEM, NC	47 / 8	27 / –3	3.2 / 8.1	84 / 29	63 / 17	3.8 / 9.6

Before You Go

WHEN TO GO

The eastern states have diverse climates (see INTRODUCTION) and weather patterns that are determined by geography, latitude, elevation, and proximity to the ocean and other bodies of water (chart opposite). Most attractions in major cities are open year-round.

The **Northeast** is a year-round vacation destination with four distinct seasons. Summer months are moderate and daytime temperatures (70-80°F) are comfortable without air conditioning. This region is especially popular in autumn, when hordes of "leaf peepers" come to see the brilliant **fall foliage**. Winter snowfall brings skiers to resorts in New England, New York and Pennsylvania. Moving south, the **Mid-Atlantic** states—Maryland, Delaware, Virginia, Washington, DC, West Virginia—have warmer, humid summers (average temperature 80°F). Though snow is common in winter, warm spells often break up the cold winter weeks. Beginning in April, mild spring temperatures foster the bloom of dogwood and cherry trees, and countless crocuses, tulips and daffodils. The **Southern** states, known for their torpid summer heat and humidity, are most affected by tropical storms and hurricanes (storm season is from June–November). Fortunately, such tempests are generally limited to the coastal areas. Summer temperatures average between 85°F and 90°F, with frequent afternoon thunderstorms. Sunny days are abundant in winter, when temperatures dip down to 50°F. Winter is high tourist season in south Florida, which boasts average temperatures in the 70s.

The **Great Lakes** area experiences one of the most varied climates in the north. The influence of the large masses of water and resulting jet streams lead to variable weather year-round. Summers are warm and humid, with temperatures around 70°F. The duration of the seasons is also affected by the lakes, whose influence extends cool autumn weather and delays the arrival of summer. Winter makes its presence felt by strong winds blowing off the lakes and frequent snows.

Harsh winters, consisting of strong wind chills and hearty snowstorms, usually keep winter temperatures in the **Midwest** around 32°F. Midwest summers don't begin until mid-June, with temperatures between 70°F and 80°F. In summer, fierce thunderstorms can spawn occasional tornadoes (⚓see INSPIRATION, Nature and Safety). *For up-to-the-minute weather conditions, check www.weather.com.*

USEFUL WEBSITES

www.flightstats.com—Flight departure/arrival boards.

FlyerTalk.com—Looking for ways to make the most of your frequent flyer miles? Benefit from the experiences of others.

SeatGuru.com—Tired of getting assigned cramped middle seats? Check out different plane seating charts here.

HotelChatter.com—Before you book the hotel—starred or otherwise—see what others who have slept there have to say.

IgoUgo.com—Need inspiration for your travels? You'll find it here.

Kayak.com—One of the best flight and hotel booking websites around, Kayak also lets you hire a car with ease; all through a simple search-engine style interface.

VRBO.com—If traditional hotels aren't your thing, consider renting a privately-owned home from Vacation Rentals by Owner.

AirBNB.com—Break out of the hotel habit by renting furnished rooms, apartments and homes in a variety of neighborhoods, short- or long-term.

Breezenet.com—Find great deals on US car rentals at this user-friendly website.

Concierge.com—The inside track from Condé Nast Traveler—from hotel recommendations to travel advice—is compiled here.

lastminute.com—Looking for a last-minute getaway? This site compiles leads for trips that don't require months of planning.

TOURISM OFFICES
US Embassies and Consulates

In addition to tourism offices, visitors from outside the US may obtain information from the nearest **US embassy or consulate** in their country of residence (⚓see details below). For a complete list of American consulates and embassies abroad, access the US State Department on the Internet at: www.usembassy.gov.

◆ **Australia**
  Moonah Place, Yarralumla ACT 2600
  ☎02 6214 5600
◆ **Belgium**
  27, boul. du Régent, B-1000 Brussels
  ☎(32-2) 811 4000
◆ **Canada**
  490 Sussex Drive, Ottawa
  Ontario K1N 1G8,
  ☎613-688-5335 (US & Canada)
◆ **China**
  55 An Jia Lou Lu, Beijing 100600
  ☎(86-10) 8531 3000
◆ **France**
  2, av. Gabriel, 75382 Paris
  ☎01 43 12 22 22 / 01 48 60 57 15
  (Tourism information line)

◆ **Germany**
   Clayallee 170, 14191 Berlin
   ✆030 8305-0
◆ **Italy**
   Via Vittorio Veneto 121, 00187 Rome
   ✆06 4674 1
◆ **Japan**
   1-10-5 Akasaka, Minato-ku Tokyo
   107-8420, ✆81-3-3224-5000
◆ **Mexico**
   Paseo de la Reforma 305, Col.
   Cuauhtémoc, 06500 México, D.F.
   ✆55 5080-2000
◆ **Netherlands**
   Lange Voorhout 102, 2514 EJ
   The Hague, The Netherlands
   ✆70 310 2209
◆ **Spain**
   Calle Serrano 75, 28006 Madrid
   ✆91587 2200
◆ **Switzerland**
   Sulgeneckstrasse 19, CH-3007 Bern
   ✆31 357 7011
◆ **United Kingdom**
   24 Grosvenor Square, London W1K
   6AH, ✆0 20 7499-9000

State Tourism Offices

State tourism offices provide information and brochures on points of interest, seasonal events and accommodations, as well as road and city maps. Local tourist offices (⬤ listed below) provide additional information regarding accommodations, shopping, entertainment, festivals and recreation. Many countries maintain consular offices in major cities.

Alabama
   Alabama Tourism Department
   401 Adams Ave., P.O. Box 4927,
   Montgomery, AL 36103-4927
   ✆334-242-4169, 800-252-2262
   www.alabama.travel

Arkansas
   Arkansas Department of
   Parks & Tourism, One Capitol Mall,
   Little Rock, AR 72201.
   ✆501-682-7777
   www.arkansas.com

Connecticut
   Commission on Culture and Tourism,

One Constitution Plaza, 2nd Floor
Hartford, CT 06103
✆860-256-2800, 888-288-4748
www.ctvisit.com

Delaware
   Delaware Tourism Office,
   99 Kings Highway, Dover, DE 19901,
   ✆866-284-7483
   www.visitdelaware.com

District of Columbia
   Destination DC, 901 7th St. N.W., 4th
   Floor Washington, DC 20001-3719
   ✆202-789-7000
   http://washington.org

Florida
   VISIT FLORIDA, P.O. Box 1100,
   Tallahassee, FL 32302-1100,
   ✆850-488-5607
   www.visitflorida.com

Georgia
   Georgia Department of Economic
   Development 75 Fifth St., NW, Suite
   1200, Atlanta, GA 30308
   ✆800-847-4842
   www.exploregeorgia.com

Illinois
   Illinois Bureau of Tourism
   100 Randolph St., Suite 3-400
   Chicago, IL 6060, ✆800-226-6632
   www.enjoyillinois.com

Indiana
   Indiana Office of Tourism
   Development, 1 N. Capitol Ave.,
   Suite 600, Indianapolis,
   IN 46204-2288
   ✆800-677-9800
   www.enjoyindiana.com

Iowa
   Iowa Department of Economic
   Development, 200 E. Grand Ave.,
   Des Moines, IA 50309
   ✆515-725-3084
   www.traveliowa.com

Kentucky
   Kentucky Department of Tourism
   500 Mero St., 22nd Floor
   Frankfort, KY 40601-1968
   ✆502-564-4930
   www.kentuckytourism.com

Louisiana
   Louisiana Office of Tourism
   P.O. Box 94291, Baton Rouge,
   LA 70804-9291

😊 A Bit of Advice 😊

Bad Weather Precautions

Thunderstorm
- If outdoors, take cover and stay away from trees and metal objects.
- If riding in a vehicle, remain inside until the storm has passed.
- Avoid being in or near water.
- If in a boat, head for the nearest shore.
- Do not use electrical appliances, especially the telephone.

Tornado
- If indoors, move to a predesignated shelter (usually a basement or stairwell); otherwise find an interior room without windows (such as a bathroom).
- Stay away from windows.
- Do not attempt to outrun the storm in a car; get out of the automobile and lie flat in a ditch or low-lying area.

☎225-342-8119
www.louisianatravel.com

Maine
Maine Tourism Association, 327 Water St., Hallowell, ME 04347-1341.
☎207-623-0388
www.mainetourism.com

Maryland
Maryland Office of Tourism Development, 401 E. Pratt St., 14th Floor, Baltimore, MD 21202
☎866-639-3526
www.visitmaryland.org

Massachusetts
Massachusetts Office of Travel & Tourism, 10 Park Plaza, Suite 4510, Boston, MA 02116,
☎617-973-8500
www.massvacation.com

Michigan
Travel Michigan, 300 N. Washington Sq. Lansing, MI 48913,

☎888-784-7328
www.michigan.org

Minnesota
Explore Minnesota Tourism 121 7th Pl. E., Metro Square, Ste. 100, St. Paul, MN 55101-2146
☎651-296-5029
www.exploreminnesota.com

Mississippi
Mississippi Development Authority Tourism Division, P.O. Box 849 Jackson, MS 39205
☎601-359-3297
www.visitmississippi.org

Missouri
Missouri Division of Tourism P.O. Box 1055, Jefferson City, MO 65102
☎573-751-4133, 800-519-2100
www.visitmo.com

New Hampshire
State of NH Division of Travel and Tourism Development, P.O. Box 1856, 172 Pembroke Rd., Concord, NH 03302-1856
☎603-271-2665
www.visitnh.gov

New Jersey
New Jersey Division of Travel and Tourism, P.O. Box 460, Trenton, NJ 08625.
☎609-599-6540
www.visitnj.org

New York
New York State Department of Economic Development Division of Tourism, 30 S. Pearl St., Albany, NY 12245
☎518-474-4116, 800-225-5697
iloveny.com

North Carolina
North Carolina Travel and Tourism Division, Department of Commerce, 4324 Mail Service Center, Raleigh, NC 27699-4324
☎919-733-4171, 800-847-4862
www.visitnc.com

Ohio
TourismOhio, P.O. Box 1001 Columbus, OH 43216-1001
☎800-282-5393
www.discoverohio.com

Pennsylvania
Pennsylvania Department of Community & Economic Development, 400 North St., 4th Floor, Harrisburg, PA 17120-0225
℘800-847-4872
www.visitpa.com

Rhode Island
Rhode Island Tourism Division 315 Iron Horse Way, Ste. 101 Providence, RI 02908
℘800-556-2484
www.visitrhodeisland.com

South Carolina
South Carolina Department of Parks, Recreation & Tourism 1205 Pendleton St., Columbia, SC 29201
℘803-734-1700
www.discoversouthcarolina.com

Tennessee
Tennessee's Department of Tourism Development Wm. Snodgrass/Tennessee Tower 312 Rosa L. Parks Ave. Nashville, TN 37243,
℘615-741-2159
www.tnvacation.com

Vermont
Vermont Department of Tourism and Marketing, One National Life Dr., 6th Floor, Montpelier, VT 05620-0501
℘802-828-3237
www.vermontvacation.com

Virginia
Virginia Tourism Corporation 901 E. Byrd St., Richmond, VA 23219
℘800-847-4882
www.virginia.org

West Virginia
West Virginia Division of Tourism 90 MacCorkle Ave., SW South Charleston, WV 25303
℘304-558-2200
www.wvtourism.com

Wisconsin
Wisconsin Department of Tourism 201 W. Washington Ave., P.O. Box 8690, Madison, WI 53708-8690
℘608-266-2161
www.travelwisconsin.com

INTERNATIONAL VISITORS
Entry Requirements
Travelers entering the United States under the **Visa Waiver Program** (VWP) must present a machine-readable passport to enter the US without a visa; otherwise a US visa is required. Visa Waiver Program requirements can be found on http://travel.state.gov. Citizens of countries participating in the VWP are permitted to enter the US for general business or tourism for up to 90 days without a visa provided they have obtained prior electronic authorization (ESTA). For a list of countries participating in the VWP and ESTA procedures, check the US Department of State website at http://travel.state.gov. Citizens of nonparticipating countries must have a visa. Upon entry, nonresident foreign visitors must present a **valid passport** and round-trip ticket. Travelers to and from Canada must present a passport or other secure, accepted document to enter or re-enter the US. Inoculations are generally not required, but check with the US embassy or consulate.

Customs Regulations
All articles brought into the US must be declared at the time of entry. **Exempt** from customs regulations: personal effects; one liter (33.8 fl oz) of alcoholic beverages (providing visitor is at least 21 years old); either 200 cigarettes, 50 cigars or 2 kilograms of smoking tobacco; and gifts (to persons in the US) that do not exceed $100 in value. **Prohibited items** include plant material; firearms and ammunition (if not intended for sporting purposes); meat or poultry products. For other prohibited items, exemptions and information, contact the US embassy or consulate before departing, or the US Customs Service (℘202-325-8000; www.cbp.gov) to download their helpful brochure *Before You Go*, containing updated restrictions and regulations.

Health

The United States does not have a national health program that covers foreign nationals; doctors' visits and hospitalization costs may seem high to international visitors. Check with your insurance company to determine if your medical insurance covers doctors' visits, medication and hospitalization in the US. If not, it is wise to enroll in a travel insurance plan before departing. Prescription drugs should be properly identified and accompanied by a copy of the prescription.

&.ACCESSIBILITY

Many of the sights described in this guide are accessible to people with special needs. Sights marked with the &. symbol offer access for wheelchairs. However, it is advisable to check beforehand by telephone. Federal law requires that existing businesses (including hotels and restaurants) increase accessibility and provide specially designed accommodations for the disabled. It also requires that wheelchair access, devices for the hearing impaired, and designated parking spaces be available at hotels and restaurants. Many public buses are equipped with wheelchair lifts; most hotels have rooms designed for visitors with special needs. All national and most state **parks** have restrooms and other facilities for the disabled (such as wheelchair-accessible nature trails). Permanently disabled US citizens and permanent residents are eligible for a free **America the Beautiful-National Parks and Federal Recreational Lands Pass, Access Pass** (www.nps. gov/fees_passes.htm), which entitles the carrier to free admission to all national parks and often a 50 percent discount on user fees (campsites, boat launches). For everyone else the pass is available at a single annual fee of $80, at any national park entrance. Buy online at http://store.usgs.gov/

pass/index.html, or call ℘888-275-8747 extension 1O.

Many attractions can make special arrangements for disabled visitors. For information about travel for individuals or groups, contact the **Society for Accessible Travel & Hospitality** (347 5th Ave., Suite 605, New York, NY 10016; ℘212-447-7284; www.sath.org).

Travel by Train

Train passengers who will need assistance should give 24hrs advance notice. Amtrak offers discounts for persons with disabilities. You must reserve accessible space by phone or in person and present written documentation of disability to qualify for rail fare discounts. Amtrak's website provides detailed information on Amtrak's services for disabled travelers (www.amtrak.com ℘800-872-7245 and 800-523-6590 TDD).

Travel by Bus

Disabled travelers are strongly encouraged to notify Greyhound 48hrs in advance. For up-to-date information, visit the Customers with Disabilities section of Greyhound's website or call the Travel Assistance Line: ℘800-752-4841 or 800-345-3109 (TDD), www.greyhound.com.

Rental Cars

Reservations for hand-controlled cars should be made well in advance with the individual car rental agency.

Senior Citizens

Many hotels, attractions and restaurants offer discounts to visitors age 62 or older (proof of age may be required). Discounts and additional information are available to members of the AARP (601 E St. N.W. Washington, DC 20049; ℘888-687-2277, www.aarp.org).

GETTING THERE AND GETTING AROUND
BY PLANE
Major Airports

Atlanta, GA
Hartsfield-Jackson Atlanta International Airport (ATL), 10mi south of downtown
✆800-897-1910
www.atlanta-airport.com

Boston, MA
Logan International Airport (BOS), 2mi northeast of downtown
✆800-235-6426
www.massport.com

Chicago, IL
O'Hare International Airport (ORD), 14mi northwest of downtown
✆773-686-2200
Chicago Midway Airport (MDW), 10mi southwest of downtown
✆773-686-2200
www.flychicago.com

Charlotte, NC
Charlotte-Douglas International Airport (CLT), 10mi west of downtown, ✆704-359-4013
www.charlotteairport.com

Cincinnati, OH
Cincinnati/Northern Kentucky International Airport (CVG), 13mi southwest of downtown
✆859-767-3151
www.cvgairport.com

Cleveland, OH
Cleveland Hopkins International Airport (CLE), 11mi southwest of downtown, ✆216-265-6000
www.clevelandairport.com

Detroit, MI
Detroit Metropolitan Wayne County Airport (DTW), 20mi south of downtown, ✆734-247-7678
www.metroairport.com

Memphis, TN
Memphis International Airport (MEM), 11mi southeast of downtown ✆901-922-8000
www.mscaa.com

Miami, FL
Miami International Airport (MIA), 7mi northwest of downtown
✆305-876-7000
www.miami-airport.com

Milwaukee, WI
General Mitchell International Airport (MKE), 11mi south of downtown, ✆414-747-5300
www.mitchellairport.com

Minneapolis-St. Paul, MN
Minneapolis-St. Paul International Airport (MSP), 16mi south of Minneapolis and St. Paul,
✆612-726-5555
www.mspairport.com

Nashville, TN
Nashville International Airport (BNA), 8mi east of downtown
✆615-275-1675
www.nashintl.com

New Orleans, LA
Louis Armstrong New Orleans International Airport (MSY), 15mi west of downtown,
✆504-303-7500
www.flymsy.com

New York City, NY
John F. Kennedy International Airport (JFK), 15mi southeast of Midtown, ✆718-244-4444
www.kennedyairport.com
LaGuardia Airport (LGA), 8mi northeast of Midtown
✆718-533-3400
www.laguardiaairport.com
Newark Liberty International Aiport (EWR), 16mi southeast of Midtown, ✆973-961-6000
www.newarkairport.com

Orlando, FL
Orlando International Airport (MCO), 9mi southeast of downtown, 22mi northeast of Walt Disney World
✆407-825-2001
www.orlandoairports.net

Philadelphia, PA
Philadelphia International Airport (PHL), 8mi southwest of Center City, ✆215-937-6937, www.phl.org

St. Louis, MO
Lambert-St. Louis International Airport (STL), 13mi northwest of downtown, ✆314-890-1333
www.flystl.com

Washington, DC

Ronald Reagan Washington National Airport (DCA), 4.5mi south of downtown, ☎703-417-8000 www.metwashairports.com

Washington Dulles International Airport (DIA), 26mi west of downtown, ☎703-572-2700 www.metwashairports.com

Baltimore/Washington Thurgood Marshall International Airport (BWI), 28mi north of Washington; 8mi south of Baltimore, MD ☎410-859-7111 www.bwiairport.com

BY TRAIN

The Amtrak rail network offers a relaxing alternative for the traveler with time to spare. Advance reservations are recommended to ensure reduced fares and availability of desired accommodations. On some trains, reservations are required; smoking is not allowed on any Amtrak train. Depending on the train and route, passengers can choose from first class, coach and cars with panoramic windows. In the East, service is provided along the following routes:

◆ **Adirondack**
New York City–Montreal
Adirondacks, Lake Placid & Saratoga Springs, Albany, NY

◆ **Auto Train**
Lorton, VA–Sanford, FL
Alternative to driving I-95

◆ **Capitol Limited**
Chicago–Washington, DC
Pittsburgh, PA. Cleveland, OH

◆ **Cardinal/Hoosier State**
Chicago–Washington, DC–New York
Virginia's Blue Ridge
West Virginia
Cincinnati, OH

◆ **Carolinian/ Piedmont**
New York City–Raleigh–Charlotte
New York City, NY
Philadelphia, PA
Washington, DC
Richmond, VA
Raleigh, NC

◆ **City of New Orleans**
Chicago–Memphis–New Orleans
Memphis, TN

◆ **Crescent**
New York City–New Orleans
Washington, DC
Virginia's Blue Ridge
Atlanta, GA
Birmingham, AL

◆ **Empire Service**
New York City–Niagara Falls
Hudson River Valley & Finger Lakes, NY

◆ **Keystone Service**
Harrisburg–Philadelphia–New York
Lancaster County, PA

◆ **Lake Shore Limited**
Chicago–New York/Boston–Albany
Great Lakes
Cleveland, OH
Berkshires, MA

◆ **Silver Services/Palmetto**
New York–Jacksonville–Miami
Richmond, VA. Charleston, SC
Savannah, GA. Orlando, FL

◆ **Vermonter**
Washington–New York–St. Albans
Baltimore, MD
Philadelphia, PA
New York City

USA RailPass offers unlimited travel within Amtrak-designated regions at discounted rates; 15-, 30- and 45-day passes are available. For schedules, prices and route information, call ☎800-872-7245 or www.amtrak.com *(outside North America, contact your travel agent).*

BY BUS/COACH

Greyhound is the largest bus company in the US with lower fares overall than other forms of transportation. Some travelers may find long-distance bus travel uncomfortable due to the lack of sleeping accommodations. Advance reservations are suggested. Greyhound's **North America Discovery Pass** allow unlimited travel for 7, 15, 30 or 60 days, with stops along the way, for all routes in the US and Canada. Schedules, prices and route information: www. greyhound.com, ✆800-231-2222 *(US only)* Greyhound Lines, Inc.; P.O. Box 660362, Dallas, TX 75266-0362 **Peter Pan** (✆800-343-9999; www. peterpanbus.com) offers service throughout the Northeastern US.

BY CAR

North-south **interstate highways** in the US have odd numbers (I-85, I-95) and east-west interstates have even numbers (I-20, I-80). Numbers increase from west to east (I-5 along the West Coast; I-95 along the East Coast) and from south to north (I-10 runs through the Sunbelt from Florida to Los Angeles, California; I-94 runs along the northern US from Milwaukee, Wisconsin to Billings, Montana).

Interstate **beltways** surround cities and have three digits: the first is an even number and the last two name the interstate off which they branch (I-290 around Chicago branches off I-90). There can be exceptions and duplication across states (there are I-495 beltways around Washington, DC, New York City and Boston). Interstate **spurs** entering cities also have three digits: the first is an odd number and the last two represent the originating interstate as for beltways (I-395 into Washington DC and I-195 into Philadelphia). Highways and roads that are not interstates are organized into US Routes, State Routes and County Routes. **US Routes** range from winding two-lane roads to major highways. North-south US Routes have odd numbers (US-23, US-1) and east-west routes have even numbers (US-6, US-50). All US Route numbers can have one, two or three digits. **State Routes** may also range from tiny two-lane roads to large highways; **County Routes** are usually smaller local or connector roads.

Rental Cars

The national rental car companies (✆ see chart) have offices at most airports and in the downtown areas of most major cities.

Aside from these agencies, there are local companies that offer reasonable rental rates. Renters must possess a major credit card (such as Visa/ Carte Bleue, American Express or MasterCard/Eurocard) and a valid driver's license (international driver's license not required). Minimum age for rental is 21 in most states. A variety of service packages offer unlimited mileage and discounted prices, often in conjunction with major airlines or hotel chains. Since prices vary from one company to another, be sure to research different companies before you reserve. All rentals are subject to a local tax not included in quoted prices. (To reserve a car from Europe, it is best to contact your local travel agent before you leave.) Liability **insurance** is not automatically included in the terms of the lease. Be sure to check for proper insurance coverage, offered at an extra charge. Most large rental companies provide assistance in case of breakdown.

RENTAL COMPANY	✆RESERVATIONS
Alamo	800-233-8749 www.alamo.com
Avis	800-633-3469 www.avis.com
Budget	800-218-7992 www.budget.com
Dollar	800-800-4000 www.dollar.com
Hertz	800-654-3131 www.hertz.com
National	800-222-9058 www.nationalcar.com
Thrifty	800-331-4200 www.thrifty.com
Enterprise	800-261-7331 www.enterprise.com

Cars may be rented by the day, week or month, and mileage is usually unlimited. Only the person who signed the contract may drive the rental car; but for an additional fee, and upon presentation of the required papers, additional drivers may be approved.

A drop fee may be charged for one-way rentals. You must either fill the gasoline tank of the car before returning it or pre-pay for a tank of gasoline when you rent the car. Otherwise, the rental company will fill it for you at a higher price per gallon.

Rental car information and reservations across the US may be accessed on the Internet (www. breezenet.com) or by calling one of the companies listed on p 53.

Recreational Vehicle (RV) Rentals

One-way rentals range from a basic camper to full-size motor homes that can accommodate up to seven people and offer a full range of amenities including bathroom,

Alligator Crossing Road Sign in Florida

©PhotoDisc

shower and kitchen with microwave oven. Reservations should be made several months in advance. There may be a minimum number of rental days required. A drop fee will be charged for one-way rentals. Cruise America RV (✆800-671-8042, www. cruiseamerica.com) features rentals with 24-hour customer assistance. The **Recreational Vehicle Rental Association** hosts an online directory of RV rental locations in the US, www. rvra.org or www.gorving.com, or 3930 University Dr., Fairfax, VA 22030, ✆703-591-7130,. **RV America** (www. rvamerica.com) also offers an online database of RV rental companies as well as information on campgrounds and RV associations.

Road Regulations and Insurance

The speed limit on most interstate highways in the contiguous US ranges from 55mph (88km/h) to 70mph (112km/h), depending on the state. On state highways outside of populated areas, the speed limit is 55mph (88km/h) unless otherwise posted. Within cities, speed limits are generally 35mph (56km/h), and average 25-30mph (40-48km/h) in residential areas. You must turn your headlights on when driving in fog and rain. Unless traveling on a divided road, motorists in both directions must bring their vehicle to a full stop when the warning signals on a **school bus** are activated. Parking spaces with are reserved for persons with disabilities; anyone parking in these spaces without proper identification will be ticketed and/or their vehicle will be towed. The use of **seat belts** is mandatory for all persons in the car. Children's safety seats are available at most rental car agencies; be sure to inquire when making reservations. In some states, motorcyclists and their passengers are required to wear helmets. Hitchhiking along interstate highways is prohibited by law.

Unless otherwise posted, it is permissible to **turn right at a red light,** after coming to a complete stop.

If you're visiting the US from abroad, check with your **automobile insurance** provider to be sure that your policy will cover you in case of an accident. It may be necessary to purchase additional coverage for the duration of your trip, particularly if you will be driving a vehicle other than a covered rental car. Keep your driver's license, passport and proof of insurance with you at when driving.

In Case of an Accident

If you are involved in an auto accident resulting in personal or property damage, you must notify the local police and remain at the scene until dismissed. If blocking traffic, vehicles should be moved as soon as possible.

Automobile associations such as the **American Automobile Association (AAA), Mobil Auto Club** (☏800-621-5581) and **Shell Motorist Club** (☏800-355-7263) provide their members with emergency road service. Members of AAA-affiliated automobile clubs overseas benefit from reciprocal services:

Australia
- Australian Automobile Association (AAA),
☏02 6247 7311
www.aaa.asn.au

Belgium
- Royal Automobile Club de Belgique (RACB),
☏02 287 09 11,
www.racb.com
- Touring Club de Belgique (TCB),
☏02 233 22 02, www.touring.be

Canada
- Canadian Automobile Association (CAA),
☏613 820 1890, www.caa.ca

France
- Automobile-Club de France (ACF),
☏01 43 12 43 12
www.automobileclubdefrance.fr

Germany
- Allgemeiner Deutscher Automobil-Club E.V. (ADAC),
☏0 180 2 22 22 22 (landline), 22 22 22 (mobile), www.adac.de
- Automobilclub von Deutschland E.V. (AvD),
☏69 6606 300, www.avd.de

Great Britain
- The Automobile Association (AA),
☏0906 888 4322 (landline), 84322 (mobile), www.theaa.com
- The Camping & Caravanning Club (CCC),
☏024 7647 5448
www.campingandcaravanning club.co.uk
- The Caravan Club (CC),
☏01 342 326 944
www.caravanclub.co.uk

Ireland
- The Automobile Association Ireland Ltd. (AA Ireland),
☏01 617 9104
www.theaa.ie

Italy
- Automobile Club d'Italia (ACI),
☏06 49 11 15, www.aci.it
- Federazione Italiana del Campeggio e del Caravanning (Federcampeggio),
☏55 88 23 91
www.federcampeggio.it
- Touring Club Italiano (TCI),
☏840 88 88 02
www.touringclub.it

Netherlands
- Koninklijke Nederlandsche Automobiel Club (KNAC),
☏70 383 1612
www.knac.nl
- Koninklijke Nederlandse Toeristenbond (ANWB),
☏088 269 22 22, www.anwb.nl

Spain
- Real Automóvil Club de España (RACE),
☏902 40 45 45, www.race.es

Switzerland
- Automobile Club de Suisse (ACS),
☏031 328 31 11, www.acs.ch
- Touring Club Suisse (TCS),
☏0844 888 111, www.tcs.ch

On Arrival

♿ Hotels and Restaurants are described in the Addresses within the Discovering USA East section. For price ranges, see the Legend on this guide's cover flap.

PLACES TO STAY AND EAT

For a listing of recommended accommodations in the areas described in this guide, consult the **Address Book** sections included in each chapter. Luxury **hotels** generally are found in major cities, while **motels** normally are clustered on the outskirts of towns and off the interstates. **Bed-and-breakfast inns** (B&Bs) are found in residential areas of cities and towns, as well as in more secluded natural areas. Many properties offer special packages and weekend rates that may not be extended during peak summer months (late May–late Aug) and during winter holiday seasons, especially near ski resorts. Advance reservations are recommended for peak seasons. Many resort properties include outdoor recreational facilities such as golf courses, tennis courts, swimming pools and fitness centers. Activities—hiking, mountain biking and horseback riding—often can be arranged by contacting the hotel staff. Many cities and communities levy a hotel occupancy tax that is not reflected in hotel rates. Local tourist offices provide free brochures that give details about area accommodations *(telephone numbers and websites are listed under blue entry headings in each chapter)*.

HOTELS AND MOTELS

Rates for hotels and motels vary greatly depending on season and location. Expect to pay higher rates during holiday and peak seasons. For deluxe hotels, plan to pay at least $300/night per room, based on double occupancy. Moderate hotels will charge between $100

and $200/night, while budget motels charge from $50 to $90/night. In most hotels, children under 18 stay free when sharing a room with their parents. When making a reservation, ask about packages including meals, passes to local attractions and weekend specials. Typical amenities at hotels and motels include television, Internet, alarm clock, coffee makers, smoking/non-smoking rooms, restaurants and swimming pools.

An increasing number of chain hotels offer free breakfast and free Wi-Fi. In-room kitchenettes are available at some hotels and motels. Always advise the reservations clerk of late arrival; unless confirmed with a credit card, rooms may not be held after 6pm.

Hotel Reservation Services

Hotel reservation services are plentiful in the US, especially on the Internet. For a complete listing, search the Internet using the keyword "reservation services" or ask your travel agent. Following is a brief selection of reservation services.

- ◆ **Booking.com**
  ✆888-850-3958, 203-320-2609 (outside the US),
  www.booking.com
- ◆ **Central Reservation Service**
  ✆800-894-0680, 407-740-6442 (outside the US),
  www.crshotels.com
- ◆ **Expedia**
  ✆877-787-7186, 404-728-8787 (outside the US), www.expedia.com
- ◆ **Hotels.com**
  ✆800-246-8357, www.hotels.com
- ◆ **Hotwire**
  ✆866-468-9473, 417-520-1680, www.hotwire.com
- ◆ **Orbitz**
  ✆888-656-4546 (there may be a fee for booking by phone), 312-416-0018 (outside the US), www.orbitz.com
- ◆ **Priceline.com**
  ✆877-477-5807,www.priceline.com

- **Quikbook**
  (certain major cities only), ☎800-789-9887, 212-779-7666 (outside the US), www.quikbook.com
- **Kayak**
  Compares hotel prices listed on other websites, www.kayak.com
- **Travelocity**
  ☎888-872-8356, 210.477.1089, www.travelocity.com
- **Trivago**
  Compares hotel prices listed on other websites, www.trivago.com

BED & BREAKFASTS AND COUNTRY INNS

Most B&Bs are privately owned historic residences. Bed-and-breakfast inns are usually cozy homes with fewer than 10 guest rooms; breakfast is generally the only meal provided. Country inns are larger establishments; full-service dining is typically available. B&B amenities usually include complimentary breakfast and use of common areas such as garden spots and sitting rooms with fireplaces. Some guest rooms may not have private bathrooms. Reservations should be made well in advance, especially during holiday and peak tourist seasons. Minimum-stay, cancellation and refund policies may also be more stringent during these times. Most establishments will accept major credit cards. Rates vary seasonally but generally range from $125 to $200 for a double room per night. Rates will be higher for rooms with such amenities as hot tubs, private entrances and scenic views.

Reservation Services

Numerous organizations offer reservation services for B&Bs and country inns. Many services tend to be regional. **Select Registry** (☎269-789-0393; www.selectregistry.com) publishes an annual register listing B&Bs and country inns by state. For a complete listing, search the Internet using the keyword "bed and

breakfast," or check the destination's official website. The following are suggested nationwide services:

- **BedandBreakfast.com**
  ☎512-322-2710, www.bedandbreakfast.com
- **BBOnline**
  ☎800-215-7365, www.bbonline.com

HOSTELS

A simple, no-frills alternative to hotels and inns, hostels are inexpensive, dormitory-style accommodations with separate quarters for males and females. Many have private family/couples rooms that may be reserved in advance. Amenities include fully equipped self-service kitchens, dining areas and common rooms. Rates average $15–$20 a night, but in big cities $25–$45 a night. Hostelling International members receive discounts on room rates and other travel-related expenses (airfare, railway and ferry tickets, car rentals, ski-lifts, passes, etc.). Hostels often organize special programs and activities for guests. When booking, ask for available discounts at area attractions, rental car companies and restaurants.

For information and a free directory, contact **Hostelling International USA** (8401 Colesville Rd., Suite 600, Silver Spring, MD 20910; ☎240-650-2100; www.hiusa.org). For more general information on hostels, try www.hostels.com. From outside the US, contact your local **Hostelling International** center.

- **Australia**
  Australian Youth Hostels Association, ☎2-9261-1111, www.yha.org.au.
- **Belgium**
  Les Auberges de Jeunesse, ☎02-219-56-76, www.laj.be.
- **Canada**
  Hostelling International-Canada, ☎613-237-7884, www.hihostels.ca.
- **France**
  Fédération Unie des Auberges de Jeunesse (FUAJ), ☎01-44-89-8727, www.fuaj.org.

- **Ireland (Northern)**
  Hostelling International Northern Ireland, ✆028 9032 4733, www.hini.org.uk.
- **Italy**
  Associazione Italiana Alberghi per la Gioventù, ✆06-487-1152, www.aighostels.com.
- **Netherlands**
  StayOkay, www.stayokay.com.
- **Spain**
  Red Española de Albergues Juveniles, ✆91-298-7245, www.reaj.com.
- **Switzerland**
  Schweizer Jugendherbergen, ✆01-360-1414, www.youthhostel.ch.
- **United Kingdom**
  YHA (England & Wales) Ltd., ✆01629 592700, www.yha.org.uk.

SPAS

Popular in large resort hotels, modern spas specialize in a variety of programs: fitness, beauty, wellness, stress relief, relaxation, and weight management. Guests may be pampered with mud baths and daily massages and are often given access to state-of-the-art fitness and exercise programs, cooking classes and nutritional counseling. Many spas offer luxurious facilities in settings that can include championship golf courses, equestrian centers and even formal gardens.

Spa packages usually range from 2 to 10 nights; weekly rates *(per person, double occupancy)* vary from $800/week in summer to $3,500/week during the winter season, depending on choice of program *(age restrictions may apply)*. Spa packages generally include all meals, special diets, use of facilities, tax, gratuities and airport transportation. For more information, contact **SpaFinder Wellness,** 257 Park Ave. S., 10th Floor, New York, NY 10010, ✆212-924-6800, www.spafinder.com.

CONDOMINIUMS

For families with children or larger groups, furnished apartments or houses are more cost-effective than hotels since they offer separate living quarters, fully equipped kitchens with dining areas, several bedrooms and bathrooms, and laundry facilities. Most condos provide televisions, basic linens, Internet and maid service. Depending on location, properties can include sports and recreational facilities or beach access. Most require a minimum stay of three nights or one week, especially during peak season. When making reservations, ask about cancellation penalties and refund policies. Chambers of commerce and convention and visitors bureaus keep listings of local property-management agencies that can assist with the selection. Vacation Rental By Owner *(www.vrbo.com)* and AirBNB.com also include condo listings.

CAMPING AND RV PARKS

Campsites are located in national parks, state parks, national forests, along beaches and in private campgrounds. Most offer full utility hookups for recreational vehicles (RVs), lodges or cabins, backcountry sites and recreational facilities. Advance reservations are advised, especially in summer and on holidays. In most parks and forests, campgrounds are available on a first-come, first-served basis.

National park and state park campgrounds are inexpensive, but fill quickly, especially during school holidays. Facilities range from simple tent sites to full RV hookups *(reserve 60 days in advance)* or rustic cabins *(reserve one year in advance)*. Fees vary according to season and available facilities (picnic tables, water/electric hookups, used-water disposal, recreational equipment, showers, restrooms): camping & RV sites $8–$21/day; cabins $20–$110/day. For all US national park reservations, contact the park you are visiting or the **US National Park Reservation Service** (✆877-444-6777, ✆518-885-

MAJOR US HOTEL CHAINS	PHONE NUMBER, WEBSITE
Best Western	800-780-7234, www.bestwestern.com
Clarion, Comfort Inn, Quality Inn, Sleep Inn	877-424-6423, www.choicehotels.com
Days Inn	800-225-3297, www.daysinn.com
Four Seasons	800-819-5053, www.fourseasons.com
Hampton Inn	800-426-7866, www.hamptoninn.com
Hilton	800-445-8667, www.hilton.com
Holiday Inn	800-465-4329, www.holidayinn.com
Howard Johnson	800-221-5801, www.hojo.com
Hyatt	800-591-1234, www.hyatt.com
Marriott	800-236-2427, www.marriott.com
Omni	800-843-6664, www.omnihotels.com
Radisson	800-967-9033, www.radisson.com
Ramada	800-854-9517, www.ramada.com
Ritz-Carlton	800-542-8680, www.ritzcarlton.com
Sheraton, W and Westin	800-328-6242, www.starwoodhotels.com

3639 outside US; www.recreation.gov). For **state parks,** contact the state tourism office (&see BEFORE YOU GO) for information.

Private campgrounds offering facilities from simple tent sites to full RV hookups are plentiful. They are slightly more expensive *($10–$60/day for tent sites, $20–$75/day for RVs)* but offer amenities such as hot showers, laundry facilities, convenience stores, children's playgrounds, pools, air-conditioned cabins and outdoor recreational facilities. Most accept daily, weekly or monthly occupancy. During the winter months *(Nov–Apr)*, campgrounds in northern regions may be closed. Reservations are advised, especially for longer stays and in popular resort areas. Kampgrounds of America (KOA) operates campsites for tents, cabins/cottages and RV hookups throughout the US. For a directory *(include $6 for shipping)*, contact **KOA Kampgrounds,** P.O. Box 30558, Billings, MT 59114, &888-562-0000, www.koakampgrounds.com. Listings of campgrounds throughout the US are easily found on the Internet. Search using keyword "campground directories."

The following is a selection of campground directories.

◆ **Camping USA**
  www.camping-usa.com
◆ **CIS' RV-America Travel & Service Center**
  www.rv-america.com
◆ **Go Camping America Directory**
  www.gocampingamerica.com

WHERE TO EAT

&See Food and Drink p75.

The eastern US serves up a bounty of culinary specialties, which vary from region to region. In America, food portion sizes tend to be large. Most restaurants will accommodate special dietary concerns, such as food allergies and vegetarian diets. Kosher meals can be difficult to find outside of major metropolitan areas. When in doubt, call ahead and ask.

&For a selection of restaurants, see the ADDRESSES within the Discovering USA East section of this guidebook.

Practical A–Z

BUSINESS HOURS

In general, most businesses operate Mon–Fri 9am–5pm. Banks are normally open Mon–Thu 9am–5pm, Fri until 5pm or 6pm. Some banks, especially in larger cities, may open on Saturday morning. Most retail stores are open Mon–Sat 10am–6pm. Malls and shopping centers are usually open Mon–Sat 10am–9pm, Sun 10am–6pm. Some restaurants close Mondays. In the South, especially in smaller towns, some retail stores are closed on Sundays, or open after noon.

ELECTRICITY

Voltage in the US is 120 Volts AC, 60 Hz. Foreign-made appliances may need AC adapters (available at specialty travel and electronics stores) and North American flat-blade plugs.

EMERGENCIES

In the US (and Canada) there is one single phone number (9-1-1) that can be used to call for emergency assistance anywhere in the country. Even inactive cell phones may be programmed to make 9-1-1 calls. However, operators cannot determine a caller's location instantly, as is possible when calling from a land-based telephone line. Like 9-9-9 in the United Kingdom, 9-1-1 is reserved for true emergencies, such as when you need medical attention, are in a threatening situation such as a fire, or are witnessing suspicious behavior. In many cities, dialing 3-1-1 will connect you to police or city operators who can assist in non-emergency situations. If you need more assistance than local authorities can provide, turn to the Travelers Aid *(www.travelersaid. org)* organization. Volunteers staff information and help booths at many airports, and also can provide referrals to appropriate groups. Travelers Aid volunteers are trained to deal with emergency situations.

INTERNET

Smart phones and tablets should be able to access the Internet almost everywhere in the US, though coverage can be weak or intermittent in rural or mountainous areas, depending on the service provider. Wi-Fi service is widely available throughout the US, though often it is password protected. Find free Wi-Fi service at most coffee shops and fast-food restaurants, libraries, and some retail stores. A few towns and cities have free Wi-Fi available in downtown areas. Some hotels offer free Wi-Fi to guests; others bill by the hour or day for Internet access (cost and details are listed on the log-in screen). Airports and airplanes vary in offering free or paid access. If you need an ethernet connection to go online, hotels and airports often—but don't always—offer connections, and fees may apply.

LIQUOR LAWS

The minimum age for purchase and consumption of alcoholic beverages is 21; proof of age may be required. Local municipalities may limit and restrict sales; laws differ among states. In many states, liquor stores sell beer, wine and liquor. Beer and wine may also be purchased in package-goods stores and grocery stores. In some states you can buy beer in gas-station convenience stores. However, in other states, wine and liquor are sold at state-operated shops and beer may be sold only by licensed distributors. Certain states, especially in New England and the Southeast, do not permit alcohol sales on Sundays, even in restaurants (exceptions can apply in metropolitan and tourist areas).

MAIL/POST

First-class postage rates within the US are: 46¢/letter (or one Forever Stamp) (up to 1oz); 29¢/postcard. To Europe: $1.10/letter (under 1oz); $1.10/postcard. Most post offices are open Mon–Fri 9am–5pm; some may open Sat 9am–noon. Companies such as

Mail Boxes Etc. and Pak Mail (consult the Yellow Pages under Mailing Services) also provide mail service for everything from postcards to large packages, at slightly higher prices, and sell packaging materials. For mail service as well as photocopying, fax service, Internet and computer access, FedEx Office has locations throughout the US (℘800-463-3339; www.fedex.com) or consult the Yellow Pages under Copying Services for a listing of local companies.

MAJOR HOLIDAYS
Banks and government offices are closed on the legal holidays shown in the table below.

New Year's Day	January 1
Martin Luther King, Jr.'s Birthday*	3rd Monday in January
President's Day*	3rd Monday in February
Memorial Day*	May 30 or last Monday in May
Independence Day	July 4
Labor Day*	1st Monday in September
Columbus Day*	2nd Monday in October
Veterans Day*	November 11
Thanksgiving Day	4th Thursday in November
Christmas Day	December 25

Many retail stores and restaurants remain open on these days

MONEY
The American **dollar** is divided into 100 **cents**. A **penny** = 1 cent; a **nickel** = 5 cents; a **dime** = 10 cents; a **quarter** = 25 cents. Most national banks and Travelex (locations throughout the US; ℘516-300-1622; www.travelex.com) **exchange foreign currency** in local offices and charge a fee for the service.

SMOKING
The **Americans for Nonsmokers' Rights** (www.no-smoke.org) estimates that 50 percent of Americans live somewhere regulated by some sort of smoking ban. Many major cities, including New York and Chicago, restrict smoking in public places, such as sports arenas, restaurants and bars, as well as workplaces and within 15ft of entrances to such places. Most venues clearly post their smoking rules and regulations, so it should be easy to be sure that you do not violate them. Most hotels offer non-smoking rooms, which you may request when making reservations.

TAXES AND TIPPING
In the US, with the occasional exception of certain food products and gasoline, **sales tax** is not included in the quoted price and is added at the time of payment. Sales taxes vary by state and range from 3 percent to 7 percent (except for Delaware and New Hampshire, which charge no sales tax). Sales tax may often be higher in major cities due to local taxes. In some states, the **restaurant tax** appearing on your bill when you dine out may be higher than the state tax; also, expect additional **hotel taxes** and surcharges. In restaurants, it is customary to leave the server a gratuity, or **tip,** of 15–20 percent of the total bill (unless the menu specifies that gratuity is included). Taxi drivers are generally tipped 15 percent of the fare. In hotels, bellmen are tipped $1 per suitcase and housekeeping $1 per night. Salon professionals may be tipped at the client's discretion.

TELEPHONES
For **long-distance** calls in the US and Canada, dial 1 + area code (3 digits) + number (7 digits). To place a **local call,** dial the 7-digit number without 1 or the area code (unless the local calling area includes several area codes). To place an **international call,** dial 011 + country code + area code + number (country and city codes are listed at the beginning of local phone books). To obtain help from an **operator,** dial 0

for local and 00 for long-distance. For **information** on a number within your area code, dial 411. For long-distance information, dial 1 + area code + 555-1212. To place a **collect call,** dial 0 + area or country code + number; at the operator's prompt, give your name. For all **emergencies,** dial **911.**

Since most **hotels** add a surcharge for local and long-distance calls charged to the room, it is less expensive to use your calling card or cellular telephone. Pre-paid calling cards are available at stores all over the country. These can be the most frugal way to place a call. Many require dialing a toll-free access number; some hotels charge for these calls. **Public telephones** (a rarity as customers increasingly rely on cell phones) cost 50¢ or more for local calls; some accept all coins, others only quarters. You may also use your calling card or credit card. Instructions for using public telephones are listed on or near the phone.

Unless otherwise indicated, telephone numbers that start with the area codes **800, 888, 866** and **877** are toll-free within the US. If visiting the US from another country, check with your cell phone service provider to be sure your phone or tablet will function in the US as GSM phones must be unlocked to use a SIM card for a North American network. Companies such as T-Mobile, Verizon, Sprint and AT&T, as well as many electronics stores, may offer short-term contracts and rental phones.

In some cities and states, talking on a cell phone (even when using a hands-free device) while driving is illegal and punishable by a fine, as is sending text messages while driving.

TIME ZONES

There are four different time zones in the contiguous United States: Eastern Standard Time (EST), Central Standard (CST), Mountain Standard (MST) and Pacific Standard Time (PST). Daylight Saving Time is observed in all states (except Arizona and Hawaii) from the second Sunday in March to the first Sunday in November when clocks are set forward one hour to Eastern Daylight Time (EDT), Central Daylight Time (CDT), Mountain Daylight Time (MDT) and Pacific Daylight Time (PDT). Eastern Standard Time is five hours behind Greenwich Mean Time (GMT), or Universal Time (UT).

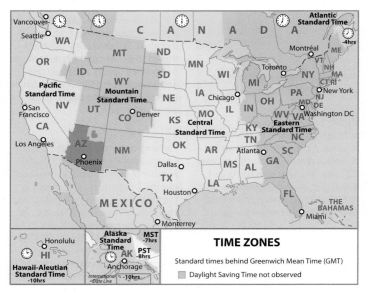

TIME ZONES

Standard times behind Greenwich Mean Time (GMT)

Daylight Saving Time not observed

CONVERSION TABLES

Weights and Measures

EU	US	UK	
1 kilogram (kg)	**2.2 pounds (lb)**	**2.2 pounds**	*To convert*
6.35 kilograms	14 pounds	1 stone (st)	*kilograms*
0.45 kilograms	16 ounces (oz)	16 ounces	*to pounds,*
1 metric ton (tn)	**1.1 tons**	**1.1 tons**	*multiply by 2.2*
1 litre (l)	**2.11 pints (pt)**	**1.76 pints**	*To convert litres*
3.79 litres	1 gallon (gal)	0.83 gallon	*to gallons, multiply*
4.55 litres	1.20 gallon	1 gallon	*by 0.26 (US)*
			or 0.22 (UK)
1 hectare (ha)	**2.47 acres**	**2.47 acres**	*To convert*
1 sq kilometre	**0.38 sq. miles**	**0.38 sq. miles**	*hectares to*
(km²)	**(sq mi)**		*acres, multiply*
			by 2.4
1 centimetre (cm)	**0.39 inches (in)**	**0.39 inches**	*To convert metres*
1 metre (m)	**3.28 feet (ft) or 39.37 inches**		*to feet, multiply*
	or 1.09 yards (yd)		*by 3.28; for*
			kilometres to miles,
1 kilometre (km)	**0.62 miles (mi)**	**0.62 miles**	*multiply by 0.6*

Clothing

Women	EU	US	UK		Men	EU	US	UK
	35	4	2½			40	7½	7
	36	5	3½			41	8½	8
	37	6	4½			42	9½	9
Shoes	38	7	5½		Shoes	43	10½	10
	39	8	6½			44	11½	11
	40	9	7½			45	12½	12
	41	10	8½			46	13½	13
	36	6	8			46	36	36
	38	8	10			48	38	38
Dresses	40	10	12		Suits	50	40	40
& suits	42	12	14			52	42	42
	44	14	16			54	44	44
	46	16	18			56	46	48
	36	6	30			37	14½	14½
	38	8	32			38	15	15
Blouses &	40	10	34		Shirts	39	15½	15½
sweaters	42	12	36			40	15¾	15¾
	44	14	38			41	16	16
	46	16	40			42	16½	16½

Sizes often vary depending on the designer. These equivalents are given for guidance only.

Speed

KPH	10	30	50	70	80	90	100	110	120	130
MPH	6	19	31	43	50	56	62	68	75	81

Temperature

Celsius (°C)	0°	5°	10°	15°	20°	25°	30°	40°	60°	80°	100°
Fahrenheit (°F)	32°	41°	50°	59°	68°	77°	86°	104°	140°	176°	212°

To convert Celsius into Fahrenheit, multiply °C by 9, divide by 5, and add 32.
To convert Fahrenheit into Celsius, subtract 32 from °F, multiply by 5, and divide by 9.
NB: Conversion factors on this page are approximate.

Introducing
USA East

National Museum of African Art, Washington, DC
© Gwen Cannon/Michelin

Features

Blue Ridge Parkway, near Rocky Knob
Recreational Area, Milepost 170, Virginia

USA East Today

Though the 31 states that make up the eastern half of the US are individual in character, there are definitely regions that are defined by terrain, climate, ethnicity, speech (accents) and food.

US Capitol, Washington, DC ©PhotoDisc, Inc

People and Society

From the time the Puritans established their colonies here in the 17C, America has had a reputation as a land of hope, a place to wipe the slate clean and start anew. Its population today is largely made up of immigrants and descendants of immigrants, people who fled economic hardship, religious intolerance or political persecution in their homelands in the hopes of living the "American Dream" of equal opportunity for all. This steady influx has resulted in a heady mix of cultural traditions, influences and customs that is commonly described as a "melting pot." Multiculturalism pervades American society, and diversity is perhaps its chief characteristic—in the 2000 census, just 7 percent of the country's residents claimed to be of "American" ancestry.

New York City, the major port of entry to the New World, nurtures an exceptional number of strong, closely-knit immigrant communities, as do Chicago, Miami, Milwaukee and Washington, DC. The state of New York claims more Polish-Americans and Italian-Americans than any other state, and the Northeast boasts the highest concentrations of immigrants from the Dominican Republic, Puerto Rico, Ecuador, Syria, Jamaica and Haiti. More than half of the nation's persons of Scandinavian and Slavic origin are clustered in the Midwest—Minnesota has more Norwegian-descended residents than any other state. Close to half of Americans claiming Scotch-Irish ancestry live in the South, and large numbers of immigrants from the Caribbean and Central America have settled in Florida, giving that state one of the largest Hispanic populations in the nation.

Most African Americans in the US are descended from slaves who were brought here in the 18C-19C to work on massive plantations south of the Mason-Dixon Line, the boundary between Pennsylvania and Maryland that served as a symbolic border between slave and free states.

After the Civil War, industry boomed in Chicago, Detroit, Cleveland, Philadelphia and other cities in the North and Midwest, attracting newly freed slaves and contributing to a black diaspora that carried the African-American culture to those regions. Today some 3 million African Americans live in New York State, the highest concentration in the nation.

REGIONAL IDENTITY

Descended from hard-working, frugal Puritans, **New Englanders** are characterized by their manner of self-reliance and reserve. The region's academic tinge comes from the presence of many of the nation's top-ranked colleges and universities—some of them referred to as the "Ivy League" in reference to their long histories. With low crime levels and high home-ownership rates, the New England states rank among the nation's top places to raise children.

The **Mid-Atlantic** region is the nation's most populous, and an urban lifestyle prevails in cities such as New York City, Philadelphia, Baltimore and Washington, DC. Seat of the nation's government, Washington is characterized by its political power brokers. Sharing a reputation for brusqueness, residents of the financial and cultural capital of New York City include high-rolling Wall Street types as well as many of the movers and shakers of the performing- and visual-arts scene.

Known for its conservative traditional values and friendly people, the **Midwest** contrasts the brawny industrialized cities of Chicago, Detroit and Minneapolis with pastoral farm communities. Every four years, presidential hopefuls, looking to confirm their viability as candidates, hold a "straw poll" in Iowa—indicating a belief that the pulse of mainstream America beats in the Heartland.

In a country in which everything seems to be on the move, **Southerners** tend to live life at a slower pace. They are known for their open manner toward strangers—hence the term "Southern hospitality." With the rise to prominence of dynamic cities such as Atlanta, New Orleans and Miami, the region has lately shrugged off its undeserved reputation as a cultural backwater, and a new influx of foreign investment in the Carolinas and Georgia makes for a distinctly cosmopolitan atmosphere in some areas.

Regardless of where they live, Americans are known to be ardent defenders of the individual rights and freedoms defined in their Constitution—to exercise free speech, to assemble, to keep and bear arms, and to enjoy privacy and freedom of religion, among others. Such liberties come at a price, however, as recent debates over gun control and abortion attest.

The people of the United States—a country still in the process of defining itself—defy most attempts at classification. Social scientists, demographers and the media are quick to tag segments of society with labels such as "Baby Boomers" (the generation born after World War II) and "Gen-Xers" (persons born in the late 1960s-70s). Yet exceptions contradict every rule, keeping alive the challenge to create a definitive description of mainstream America.

GOVERNMENT AND POLITICS

When the delegates gathered in Philadelphia in 1787 to organize the government of their young country, they held varying ideas as to how it should be set up. Influenced by the theories of 18C philosophers, they believed that government should exist to protect the rights of the people, and that the will of the people—rather than that of a monarch—should prevail. Delegates also distrusted placing too much power in popular hands, worrying that it could lead to mob rule. Similarly, they saw the need for a strong leader, but not one so powerful as to become a tyrant. What they came up with was a federal structure with divided powers and a system of checks and balances whereby no one branch of government could wield total power.

Three levels of government operate in the US: federal, state and local. The structure of most **state governments** closely resembles that of the federal government, with a governor as chief executive, a two-house legislature (except for Nebraska, which has only one house) and a system of trial and appellate courts. Local governments also function along the lines of a three-pronged system, but with more variations. All states in the eastern US have **county government** units, with the exception of Rhode Island and Connecticut. Counties levy and collect taxes, provide services, enact ordinances applicable to county residents and enforce state and local laws under some form of commission/executive government—whereby an elected three-to-five-member commission sets policy and an elected or appointed executive administers those policies.

Farther down the line are the **municipal governments,** which perform many of the same functions as county governments. Traditionally, municipal governments in large cities have operated with an elected mayor as executive and an elected council as the legislative arm.

Federal Government

The US Constitution divides the government into three separate branches with varying responsibilities. Although the Constitution leaves all powers not specifically delegated to the federal government to the states and municipalities, there is overlap in certain areas.

Executive Branch

The executive branch consists of a president and vice president—both elected together to a maximum of two four-year terms of office. In addition, 15 **cabinet departments,** whose heads are appointed by the president, and numerous agencies help carry out executive-branch functions and advise the president frequently on issues of state. The cabinet departments are: State, Treasury, Defense, Justice, Interior, Agriculture, Commerce, Labor, Health and Human Services, Education, Transportation, Homeland Security, Housing and Urban Development, Energy, and Veterans Affairs. The Executive Office also includes a number of independent agencies, such as the Central Intelligence Agency, the National Security Agency, and the National Aeronautics and Space Administration.

The main function of the executive branch is to carry out and enforce laws and regulations. Both the president and vice president must be at least 35 years old, be native US citizens, and have lived in the US for at least 14 years prior to taking office. Although their candidacies are submitted to popular vote, both the president and vice president are actually elected by an elaborate system called the **electoral college.** Under this system, voters casting their ballots for a certain candidate actually vote for a slate of electors committed to that candidate. Electors cast their pro forma votes several weeks after the popular election at the electoral college meeting.

The Constitution designates the president as head of state, chief treaty maker, and commander-in-chief of the armed forces. He has wide-ranging appointive powers, including that of ambassadors, Supreme Court justices and lower court judges, and heads of federal departments "with the advice and consent of the Senate."

As a check on the Congress, the president has the power to veto legislation; but that veto can be overridden by a two-thirds vote of both houses of Congress.

Although not specifically granted him by the Constitution, the president's responsibilities have expanded over the years to include drafting domestic legislation and devising and implementing foreign policy.

The vice president presides over the Senate; otherwise, that office has no specific duties except to step into the presidency if the president dies or becomes so disabled that he is unable to perform his duties.

Most of the administrative work of the executive departments and agencies is performed by nonpartisan civilian employees. This civilian cadre of about 2.6 million works primarily in Washington, DC. A significant majority (70 percent) are employed by just four federal agencies: Defense, Veterans Affairs, Homeland Security, and Justice.

Legislative Branch

The legislative, or lawmaking, branch is made up of two sections—a **House of Representatives** and a smaller **Senate,** collectively known as the Congress. The House, where states are represented according to population, at present numbers 435 members. The Senate, in contrast, contains two members from each of the 50 states no matter how large or small the state.

Senate candidates run for six-year terms in staggered years—thus about one-third of the Senate faces re-election every two years. To run for office, Senate candidates must be at least 30 years old. Representatives, who run for office every two years, must be at least 25 years old. Unlike the presidency or vice presidency, neither senators nor representatives are required to be native-born. Senators must have lived in the US for nine years, representatives for seven.

By far the largest part of contemporary congressional business is taken up with drafting and passing laws. Other powers granted to the Congress include declaring war, levying taxes, regulating interstate commerce, and impeaching and trying other government officials, including presidents and judges.

As a check on the president, the Senate must confirm all presidential appointees and ratify all treaties made with other governments by the executive branch. Responsibility for originating tax and appropriations bills rests with the House of Representatives.

Judicial Branch

Smallest of the three branches of government, the judiciary interprets the law of the land. It consists of the **US Supreme Court** (the country's highest tribunal), some 94 courts of original federal jurisdiction called **district courts,** and 13 **appellate courts.** There are also a number of special courts, among them US Claims Court, US Tax Court and the US Court of Military Appeals.

The Supreme Court considers constitutional questions arising from both the lower federal courts and the state court system. This power gives it a check on the Congress by allowing review of laws passed by that body.

Its nine justices—one chief justice and eight associates—are appointed by the president, confirmed by the Senate, and have lifetime tenure. The last provision gives judges a large measure of independence, helping to ensure that political pressures do not unduly influence judicial opinions. District and appeals-court judges are likewise appointed to lifetime terms. Beginning its term the first Monday in October and lasting through June, the court usually hears about 80 cases per year.

Revenue

Approximately $2 trillion is collected each year to operate the US government, the lion's share from personal income taxes. Other revenue sources include corporate income taxes; excise taxes on items such as gasoline, cigarettes and liquor; energy and timber sales; Social Security taxes; customs duties; and estate taxes.

Armed Forces

The US maintains military bases around the world and forces numbering some 1.5 million in the form of a full-time army, navy, marine corps and air force. Additional forces are available from reserves, which may be called upon in times of war. Military service has been voluntary since 1973, when conscription ended.

State Governments

As in the federal system, the chief executive and legislators in each state are elected. While most state judges previously were elected, that practice has begun to change, with many now being appointed by the governor.

The US Constitution stipulates that each state operates under its own constitution. Thus, state governments have a number of responsibilities, including maintaining state roads and facilities, regulating businesses and professions, regulating driver and motor-vehicle licensing, setting standards for educational institutions, regulating the sale of liquor and tobacco products, and passing and enforcing laws.

State laws and regulations can vary widely. Some allow civilians to carry a concealed firearm as long as they have a valid permit; in other states, this practice is strictly forbidden. Liquor laws and motor-vehicle speed limits also vary considerably from state to state.

Frequently, state and local responsibilities overlap with federal regulations. The operation of public schools, for example, is the responsibility of local school boards, even though public schools must also meet various federal requirements.

Political Parties

Since the presidency of Abraham Lincoln (1861-65), two major political parties—the generally liberal **Democrats** and the relatively conservative **Republicans**—have dominated US politics. While third parties, such as the Libertarian and Green parties, often field candidates, it's difficult for them to gain enough followers to win an election because most voters choose to remain within the mainstream rather than vote for a candidate who has little chance of winning.

Although most Americans over the age of 18 are eligible to vote, only about 50 percent of registered voters participate in national elections.

ECONOMY

The democratic and economic mythology of the United States remains hugely appealing. According to the American ideal, any enterprising person, regardless of race, creed or social class, should have equal opportunity to work hard, earn money by any legal means, and improve his or her lot. As the rags-to-riches lives of countless immigrants, celebrities and CEOs attest, the "American Dream" has come true for millions. On average, US citizens enjoy a higher per capita income and a higher standard of living than any other people on earth.

The US economy thrives on its unique historical system of free enterprise—a laissez-faire capitalism whereby individuals can create, own and control the production of virtually any marketable good or commodity they can conceive, without undue government interference, except in matters of consumer protection.

A **federal income tax** on earnings helps support state and federal government activities, including national defense, space exploration, the public school system, and major public works projects such as airports and interstate highways.

In addition, most Americans contribute a I percentage of their annual income to the federal Social Security system, which provides retirement benefits and medical care for older citizens.

Like other industrialized nations, the US has transformed itself over the last few generations from an agriculturally based economy to one based on service industries and manufacturing.

Today the nation's $15.6 trillion (2012) **gross domestic product (GDP)**—the combined value of all goods and services—is the largest in the world. Rich farming areas, manufacturing and trade centers, and large metropolitan areas of the eastern US account for almost 70 percent of this output. However, the economies of individual states vary widely according to their natural resources, labor pools, transportation networks and geography.

For example, many residents in the urban Northeast (Connecticut, Massachusetts, New York, Pennsylvania) work in high-end professional services such as banking, finance and law, earning per capita personal incomes among the highest in the nation. In the New York City financial district, dubbed "Wall Street," investors buy and sell millions of shares of corporate stock through the three major US stock exchanges—the **New York Stock Exchange** (NYSE), the **American Stock Exchange** (AMEX) and **NASDAQ** (an electronic network regulated by the National Association of Securities Dealers).

To the west, by contrast, the five **Great Lakes** anchor a region characterized by its fertile farmland, abundant natural resources and navigable inland waterways, which support prosperous agribusinesses, heavy industry and the shipping trade.

Natural Resources

Few economies are as abundantly supplied with natural resources as the eastern US. In addition to fertile soils, a favorable climate and adequate water supplies for agriculture and hydroelectric power, this varied terrain contains a wealth of fossil fuels, minerals, stone, timber and freshwater and ocean fish. Throughout the East, extractive industries harvest coal, natural gas, kaolin, crushed stone and sand, marble and granite, iron ore, gems and even gold. Altogether, mining accounts for some $225 billion of the US GDP.

In general, the most flagrant and careless examples of environmental damage from strip mining and agricultural practices have been regulated out of existence in the eastern US in recent decades. However, as the nation burns an ever-growing tonnage of fossil fuels (oil, coal and natural gas) for electricity, manufacturing and transportation, air and water quality have suffered. Many eastern cities from Atlanta to Boston suffer visibly high levels of air pollution (haze and smog).

Agriculture

In the 21C, US agriculture coexists uneasily with global markets and expanding urbanization. Today California, Iowa and Texas lead the nation in overall agricultural production. The picturesque scenes of American farm life still dominate large swaths of the Midwest and the South, though farmland is giving way to development in many places. Iowa is a cornerstone of the **Corn Belt,** a broad warm-summer region nestled between the Ohio and the lower Missouri rivers. To the north, cooler summers yield crops of clover, hay and small grains, supporting an elongated **Dairy Belt** from Wisconsin (famous for its cheeses) eastward along the Great Lakes into New England. With its upstate agricultural areas, New York ranks second to Vermont in the production of maple syrup.

Among the southern states, North Carolina, the top tobacco-grower, ranks highest—seventh nationally—in cash receipts from total agricultural production. Florida, the nation's leading grower of oranges and other citrus fruits, ranks ninth agriculturally; and Georgia, the largest state east of the Mississippi, ranks tenth in total agricultural output and leads the nation in the production of peanuts.

But the decline of family farms in America remains a concern; the number of farms in the country has declined from more than 5.3 million in 1950 to 2.2 million by the 2007 farm census (though that number was up slightly from a census taken earlier in the decade).

Service Industries

Even in states where agriculture and manufacturing are major parts of local economies, service industries are a prominent and fast-growing segment—23 percent of earnings in Alabama, 33 percent in Florida, 28 percent in Illinois, 27 percent in New Hampshire. A broad collective category, service industries vary from low-paying retail or food-service businesses to high-level executive consulting. The largest non-government, private-sector service industry in the US is **health services**, which accounted for 17 percent of the total US GDP in 2011.

Tourism and travel-related services (lodging, transportation, meals, entertainment) also account for an increasing proportion of US employment, goods and services, and tax revenues—as much as $1.9 trillion in 2012. With 9.7 million international visitors in 2010, New York City ranks as the top US city. But Florida, home to sunny beaches, Walt Disney World and multicultural Miami, is also a popular destination, attracting 8 million overseas visitors in 2010 of the total 60 million international visitors to the US that year.

Manufacturing

While many US businesses desire a national or global focus for their marketing and product lines, production for specific industries continues to decentralize. Leading telecommunications or pharmaceutical companies may have signature buildings in New York and other cities, while production and research facilities are scattered from West Virginia to Florida. The high-tech industry, birthed in upstate New York in the 1950s by International Business Machines (IBM), now occupies a prominent role not only in California's Silicon Valley, but also in the Washington, DC area; the Research Triangle in Raleigh-Durham, North Carolina; Atlanta, Georgia, and many points in between.

The US space industry, officially based in Washington, DC (home to the National Aeronautics and Space Administration), also concentrates thousands of high-tech employees in Virginia, Ohio, Alabama, and Florida. Similarly, the big three US automobile manufacturers (General Motors, Ford and Chrysler) are headquartered in Michigan but have large plants in other states.

The US continues to lead world production in many categories of manufacturing, including the making of aluminum, numerous chemicals and plastics, forest products, and paper and paperboard.

Food and Drink

B lessed with an impressive variety of locally produced ingredients and myriad foods imported by immigrant populations, the eastern US serves up a bounty of culinary specialties, which differ from region to region.

NORTHEASTERN TRADITIONS

Casual clam shacks and rural supper halls invite seafood lovers to sample the abundance of fish and shellfish drawn from the cold Atlantic waters off New England. Crab, clams, blue mussels, oysters and bay scallops are served steamed, boiled, fried or simmered in thick, milk-based chowders such as the popular New England clam chowder. **Maine lobster** wins the day here—whether you order it boiled whole with butter in an elegant restaurant presentation, or eat the succulent meat lightly tossed with mayonnaise and stuffed into bread on a **lobster roll** at a waterside fish joint. Regional menus also feature striped bass, Atlantic salmon, bluefish, tuna, cod and haddock. Held on the beach, a traditional **New England clambake** includes lobsters, shellfish, onions, new potatoes and ears of corn packed in wet seaweed and steamed atop charcoal-heated stones in a pit dug into the sand. Orchards and bogs yield ingredients

for apple cider, Concord grape jam, and cranberry juice. In Vermont, sap from sugar-maple trees is boiled down into thick **maple syrup** and eaten on pancakes, drizzled over ice cream and baked into pies, cookies and puddings. Don't miss an opportunity to try tart Maine **blueberries** (in pies, pancakes or muffins), **Vermont Cheddar** cheese, or **Boston baked beans** and **brown bread**.

MID-ATLANTIC MELTING POT

A mustard-laced hotdog from a street vendor; lox and bagels or a slice of creamy cheesecake in a Jewish deli; dim sum in a family-owned Chinatown eatery; trendsetting cuisine in a world-class restaurant—all qualify as a typical culinary experience in New York City. New York's wine-growing region around the upstate Finger Lakes produces fine vintages from European varietals.
Crab (see BALTIMORE) is king along the eastern shore of Maryland and Virginia, where mouth-watering crabcakes are a signature dish. Salty slices of

Collecting sap from maple trees, Vermont

Vermont Department of Tourism & Marketing/Stephen Goodhue

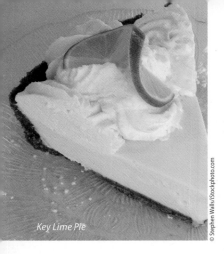

Key Lime Pie

© Stephen Walls/iStockphoto.com

Cincinnati chili (served over spaghetti and topped with cheese) was created in Greek-owned chili parlors, and many of Milwaukee's famed **breweries** were founded by German immigrant families. The first Europeans called North America "Vinland' owing to the grape varieties they found; French-American hybrid grapes are the staples of East Coast **wine** production.

DOWN-HOME COOKIN'

Barbecue is a high art in the South: experts rub pork with a mix of dry spices, smoke the meat slowly over a hickory fire, and dress it with tangy vinegar and red pepper or a tomato-based sauce (sauce preferences vary regionally). Traditional barbecue is served with a side of "slaw"—a creamy salad of shredded cabbage, carrots, mayonnaise and vinegar.

For a typical southern lunch, collard greens, black-eyed peas or green beans are seasoned with bacon or fatback, simmered for hours and served alongside crispy fried chicken, catfish or ham. In Georgia, look for sweet **Vidalia onions** and fried green tomatoes. The South Carolina Lowcountry is the place to order **shrimp;** try the popular shrimp and grits, or Frogmore stew, a heady boil of shrimp, sausage and corn. Be sure to sample she-crab soup (a dollop of sherry is optional) in Charleston, South Carolina, and the state's beach towns.

Fresh Gulf of Mexico seafood—Apalachicola Bay oysters, amberjack, grouper, pompano, red snapper and stone crab—headline menus in Florida and along the southern Gulf Coast. End a meal here with a slice of tart **key lime pie.** International influences are evident in Miami in the paring of grilled fish with tropical-fruit salsa, and Cuban fare including black beans with rice, and *arroz con pollo* (chicken with yellow rice). Visitors go to New Orleans expressly to indulge in spicy **Cajun and Creole** (see NEW ORLEANS) specialties such as crawfish etouffée, jambalaya, seafood gumbo, and red beans and rice.

Smithfield ham tucked inside velvety homemade biscuits is another Virginia treat.

In the Pennsylvania Dutch region of Lancaster County, German culinary traditions inspire hearty dishes, served family-style in many restaurants: **snitz and knepp** (boiled cured ham, dried apples and dumplings), sauerkraut served with pork and mashed potatoes, **chowchow** (a pickled relish made with beans, peppers and corn) and sweet **shoofly pie,** a crumb-topped confection made with molasses and brown sugar.

HEARTLAND FARE

Midwestern cooking takes advantage of the abundant products of lake, garden, field and forest—wild rice from Minnesota, pecans and walnuts from Missouri, sour cherries from Michigan, fish from the Great Lakes, and beef, pork and lamb from the farms of Illinois. The northwest corner of Wisconsin ranks as the most productive dairy land in the nation, annually churning out two billion pounds of cheese.

In larger cities, search out steakhouses for thick cuts of corn-fed, aged **Midwestern beef**. Small towns often hold all-you-can-eat Friday-night fish fries, proffering piles of sizzling whitefish with tartar sauce on the side.

Immigrants who settled here in the late 19C originated such regional fare as Scandinavian fruit soups, Polish pierogi, German bratwurst, and the famed **deep-dish pizza** of Chicago. Distinctive

USA East History

Though each state cherishes its own history, statehood was fostered by the shared past of the eastern US, from its native beginnings to colonization and beyond.

Etowah Indian Mounds State Historic Site in Cartersville, Georgia
Georgia Department of Economic Development

Key Events

Key dates, events, characters, politics, society and cultural shifts in USA East's history: from the earliest inhabitants, the colonial period, the Revolutionary and Civil wars, through two World Wars to the New Millennium of the 21C.

THE FIRST AMERICANS

The first inhabitants of the Eastern US were Asians who arrived some 28,000 years ago via the Bering Strait on the land bridge then connecting Siberia with Alaska. Evolving into separate tribes, these early inhabitants are thought to have numbered 1.5 million to 2 million in the continental US by the time the New World was discovered. The **Adena** and **Hopewell** cultures established sizable populations in the Ohio Valley as early as 1000 BC. These advanced cultures were characterized by the conical or dome-shaped burial mounds they built. The rich soil of southeastern riverbeds fostered the master farmers and skilled artisans of the **Mississippian** culture, who settled in villages where they raised corn, squash and other crops. Remains of a number of Mississippian sites (AD 800-1600)—which feature huge temple mounds—are scattered in the east, from Ocmulgee and Etowah in Georgia to Cahokia in Illinois. Artifacts unearthed at their sites suggest complex societies, with well-developed economic, governmental and religious systems.

At the time of European settlement of the US, various groups of **Eastern Woodland Indians** occupied the vast land stretching the length of the Atlantic seaboard south to the Gulf of Mexico, west across the Appalachians to the Mississippi Valley and north to the Great Lakes. These hunter-gatherers were also fishermen and farmers who found food as well as material for shelter, tools and fuel in the dense forests that blanketed the east. Within two basic language groups—the Algonquian speakers who lived in communal wooden longhouses, and the Iroquoian speakers who lived in wigwams—the Woodland Indians comprised many smaller tribes. Settlers in the northeast met such tribes as the Massachuset, Pequot, Mohawk, Oneida and Delaware; in the Midwest and Great Lakes regions, Europeans encountered the Shawnee, Illinois, Sauk, Ottawa, Fox and Potawatomi. The Powhatan, Secotan, Cherokee, Chickasaw, Creek, Seminole and Natchez tribes, among others, held sway in the south. Unfortunately, the Europeans brought with them a host of diseases that took their toll on Native American populations, who had no immunity to such previously unknown plagues.

COLONIAL PERIOD

Some historians believe the Vikings explored North America as early as AD 1000, but the evidence is murky. What is known is that beginning in 1492, when Columbus discovered the Caribbean, Spanish, Dutch, French and English adventurers explored the Americas, laying claim to various areas. The Spanish, then the dominant European military power, concentrated on Florida, the Gulf Coast and California, while the English emphasized the eastern seaboard and the French gained a foothold in Canada and along the Mississippi River. In 1565, the Spanish established the first permanent US settlement at St. Augustine, Florida, and soon after established a garrison across the state at Pensacola. The English followed 22 years later with an unsuccessful attempt at **Roanoke Colony** in present-day North Carolina. Undaunted, the English founded **Jamestown** a bit farther north in 1607. By 1624 Jamestown was a thriving settlement, with flourishing crops of a plant called tobacco and even a fledgling legislature. Meanwhile, some 600mi up the coast, an English religious sect called the Puritans had established the **Plymouth Colony** in 1620. Others followed in 1629, settling the area around present-day Boston.

The 1660 restoration of Charles II to the English throne launched a frenzy of new colonization. The colony of **Connecticut** was chartered in 1662, Carolina in 1663, and New York—colonized by the Dutch as New Amsterdam in 1624—was claimed for England in 1664. **Pennsylvania** and **Delaware** followed. The 13th and last colony, **Georgia,** was chartered in 1732 as a refuge for English debtors.

1565	Pedro Menéndez de Avilés founds St. Augustine, Florida, the first permanent European settlement in North America.
1607	Captain John Smith founds **Jamestown** on the coast of Virginia, the first permanent English settlement in the New World.
1619	First African slaves arrive in the colonies.
1620	English Puritans establish **Plymouth Colony** in Massachusetts.
1626	Peter Minuit purchases Manhattan Island from Native Americans.

LIFE IN THE COLONIES

From 1700 to 1775, the colonial population increased almost tenfold, aided by massive immigration of German, Dutch, Irish and Scotch-Irish farmers and laborers seeking a better life. In 1700 approximately 250,000 colonists inhabited the mainland; by 1800 that number had reached 5.3 million.

Vibrant cities emerged, among them New York, Boston, Philadelphia and Charleston. Although not as populous as their European counterparts (mid-18C Philadelphia, for example, had a population around 25,000, compared to more than a half-million in London), these burgeoning cities were not only lively centers of business and trade, but also seats of learning and culture.

At the beginning of the 18C, the colonists looked to England to set the tone in fashion, architecture, religion and the arts; but by mid-century, cultural patterns were assuming a distinctly "American" flavor. Before the Revolutionary War, seven colleges were founded, including the northern Ivy League institutions of Harvard, Yale, Princeton and Brown, and William and Mary in Virginia.

Most notably, an independent spirit was beginning to blossom among the colonists—many of whom were beginning to chafe under English rule.

1718	Jean Baptiste Le Moyne, sieur de Bienville founds New Orleans.
1754	**French and Indian War** begins.

REVOLUTIONARY WAR

Tensions between the colonists and the Crown escalated during the 1760s. Britain's decision to maintain troops in the colonies after the end of the French and Indian War (1754-63) infuriated many settlers. A further alienating factor was the British Parliament's decision in 1763 to forbid settlement beyond the Appalachian Mountains. The final straw was the passage of a series of taxes— including a tax on tea—levied on the colonists, who lacked representation in Parliament. In late 1773 a group of Patriots boarded cargo ships in Boston Harbor and tossed cases of tea overboard. The incident, today known as the **Boston Tea Party,** prompted the English to clamp down even harder on the rebellious citizens. Sixteen months later, in April 1775, colonists clashed with English soldiers at Lexington, Massachusetts in the first battle of the American Revolution.

During the first months of the war, the English held the advantage, winning most of the battles and laying siege to Boston. Still, the colonists persevered, meeting in Philadelphia in July 1776 to adopt the **Declaration of Independence,** formally severing ties with England. Written by **Thomas Jefferson,** the declaration relied on the Enlightenment-era idea of government as a social contract.

In December of 1776, the war's tide turned when Gen. George Washington repelled British general William Howe at Trenton, New Jersey. Although Howe returned to take Philadelphia the following summer, Washington's triumph galvanized the colonists. Their cause was further bolstered in 1778 when Britain's old enemy, France, came to the aid of the Colonial army.

In 1781 Revolutionary and French forces managed to trap Gen. Charles Cornwallis on the narrow peninsula at Yorktown, Virginia. Cut off from the British navy, Cornwallis surrendered. The 1783 **Peace of Paris** granted the young nation independence from Britain and established its western boundary at the Mississippi River. Only parts of Florida remained under Spanish rule.

1763	**Treaty of Paris** ends the French and Indian War. England gains Canada and Louisiana east of the Mississippi River from France, and Florida from Spain.
1764-67	Britain imposes a series of taxes on colonists.
1770	British soldiers kill three colonists in the Boston Massacre.
1773	Irate Bostonians stage the **Boston Tea Party,** throwing cargoes of tea into Boston Harbor to protest British taxation.
1775	**Revolutionary War** begins as Minutemen clash with British troops at Lexington and Concord, Massachusetts. Daniel Boone blazes a trail across the Cumberland Gap, opening the way for settlement of the west.
1776	Colonists declare their independence from England when they adopt the **Declaration of Independence** in Philadelphia on 4 July.

THE NEW NATION

In 1781 colonial delegates had met in Philadelphia, adopting the formal name of the **United States of America** and issuing the **Articles of Confederation.** That document set up a Congress charged with carrying out the country's foreign relations. But after the war, it soon became clear the Articles were much too weak to govern the infant country. The confederation had no control over the states, no taxing power and no ability to stabilize currency.

These limitations led to the Constitutional Convention of 1787 in Philadelphia, where the **US Constitution** was drafted, establishing a centralized, democratic government with executive, legislative and judicial branches. In gratitude for his war service, convention delegates elected **George Washington** (1732-99) as the first president of the young Republic.

1781	British troops surrender to colonists at Yorktown, Virginia.
1783	**Peace of Paris** formally ends the Revolutionary War, declaring American victory and setting the western US boundary at the Mississippi River.
1793	Eli Whitney invents the cotton gin.

FEDERAL PERIOD (1800-1850)

From 1800 to 1850 three major themes dominated the American experience: westward expansion, the coming of industry and massive strides in transportation. By 1800 the new union boasted 16 states; Vermont was added in 1791, Kentucky in 1792 and Tennessee in 1796. The republic's 5.2 million citizens were almost evenly divided between North and South, most inhabiting a narrow coastal strip stretching along the Atlantic from New England to the Florida border.

As the population increased in the East, these coastal residents came to view the West as the land of opportunity. In 1775 frontiersman **Daniel Boone** (see WESTERN KENTUCKY) blazed a trail through the Cumberland Gap, a natural passage in the Appalachians leading from Virginia into Kentucky and the fertile lands beyond. Twenty years later, the **Wilderness Road,** which traced Boone's trail, was opened to covered-wagon and stagecoach traffic. Between 1775 and 1810, more than 300,000 Americans crossed the Cumberland Gap to begin new lives in the West. Westward expansion got a further boost in 1803 with the **Louisiana Purchase,** orchestrated by President Thomas Jefferson. In this $15 million deal that doubled the country's size, Congress purchased the French-owned territory—bounded by the Mississippi River, the Rocky Mountains, Canada and the Gulf of Mexico—from Napoleon. Jefferson's sponsorship of the scientific expedition of **Meriwether Lewis** and **William Clark** a year later underscored the importance of the historic purchase. However, as the settlers moved west they usurped more and more of the Indians' land. This led to mounting tensions and, eventually, to armed conflict. Looking for a permanent solution to the "Indian problem," President **Andrew Jackson** engineered the **Indian Removal Act** in 1830. By the terms of this law, eastern tribes were to be relocated to a designated area west of the Mississippi River; they would be paid for their land in the east and would hold perpetual title to their new territories in the west. The Cherokees were the last group to leave on the infamous **"Trail of Tears,"** ushered westward on a cruel trek by US soldiers.

TRADE AND TRANSPORTATION

The nation's economy expanded along with its geographical horizons. **Eli Whitney's** 1793 invention of the **cotton gin** pushed the South's production and export of cotton from 10,000 pounds to 8 million pounds annually between 1790 and 1800. As the nation pushed westward, the Midwest became the leading producer of pork, corn and wheat.

This outburst of industrial activity was facilitated by enormous strides in transportation. Begun in 1811, the first **National Road** covered the distance from Cumberland, Maryland, to Vandalia, Illinois, by 1838. The success of the first commercial **steamboat,** launched by Robert Fulton and Robert Livingston in 1807, opened the way for increased trade on the Mississippi River and spurred the growth of great port cities such as New Orleans. Back east, the 363mi-long **Erie Canal,** completed in 1825, made New York State the conduit of trade and migration between the eastern seaboard and the Great Lakes.

The first steam-powered **railroad** began operations in England the same year the Erie Canal opened. By 1854 more than 17,000mi of rail lines crisscrossed the eastern US, and an additional 12,000mi of track were under construction. These advances drastically reduced the time and money needed to move raw materials to factories and finished goods to market.

By 1850 Americans could justifiably feel smug about their country. The population stood at an all-time high of 23 million, the country had expanded to 30 states (California became the 31st on September 9, 1850), industrial production was at its peak, and literacy rates were higher than those in Europe. But looming over all this optimism was the dark cloud of slavery. Of all the issues dividing North and South, the institution of slavery provoked the strongest emotion.

THE SLAVERY QUESTION

Slaves were first imported by the British from Africa around 1619, primarily to work plantations in the South (Northerners used slaves as well, although to a far lesser extent). As the South's fertile soil and mild climate fostered its lucrative plantation economy, the practice of slavery steadily increased. The Constitution banned the importation of slaves after 1808, but illegal importation continued until the Civil War. By 1860 there were four million slaves in the US, the majority of them in the South.

Numerous moves to ban this "peculiar institution" were introduced in both the Congress and state legislatures as early as the 1780s, supported by those who felt slavery was tyrannical and immoral. But after cotton gained ascendancy, that support withered. Southern delegates knew that abolishing slavery would mean the end of their economic mainstay and affluent lifestyle.

With westward expansion the controversy grew increasingly rancorous and an active **Abolitionist movement** emerged. The Abolitionists, who wanted slavery abolished by law, operated an **Underground Railroad** system by means of which they helped slaves flee the South. In Congress, Northerners argued that slavery should be banned from the western territories, and a series of compromises narrowly averted armed conflict. John Brown's failed raid on the US arsenal at Harpers Ferry, Virginia, in 1859 crystallized Southern paranoia. With the election of Republican president Abraham Lincoln in 1860, conflict seemed inevitable.

1803	Congress completes the **Louisiana Purchase**, thus securing a vast stretch of more than 800,000sq mi lying between the Mississippi River and the Rocky Mountains.
1804	President Thomas Jefferson sends Meriwether Lewis and William Clark out to explore the Louisiana Purchase lands.
1807	Robert Fulton invents the steamboat.
1812	The **War of 1812** with Britain begins.
1825	The **Erie Canal** is completed, linking the Great Lakes with New York City.
1827	The first US railroad, the Baltimore and Ohio (B&O), is chartered.
1838-39	Cherokee Indians are removed from their southeastern lands and forced by the US government to march west to reservations in Oklahoma.
1844	First telegraph message is sent from Washington, DC, to Baltimore, Maryland, by inventor Samuel Morse.

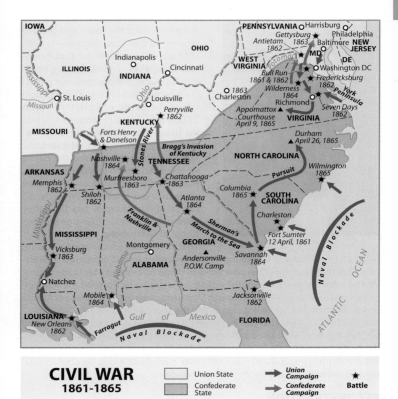

CIVIL WAR
1861-1865

Union State

Confederate State

Union Campaign

Confederate Campaign

Battle

1848

The first **Women's Rights Convention** is held at Seneca Falls, New York. Their Declaration of Sentiments calls for educational and professional opportunities equal to those of men, and the right to vote.

CIVIL WAR

On the eve of the Civil War, the North and South, roughly equal in population, were two separate and radically different societies. The North was dominated by trade and manufacturing, the South by agriculture. Since large-scale cultivation of crops such as cotton, rice, indigo and tobacco depended on slavery for its huge profits, most Southerners supported the practice, while most Northerners abhorred it. Northerners also favored a strong, centralized government; Southerners preferred leaving governing to the states.

No longer able to compromise by 1861, the separate regions became separate nations. South Carolina was the first state to secede from the Union in December 1860. In February 1861, the **Confederate States of America** was formed, with **Jefferson Davis** as its president and Montgomery, Alabama, as its capital (the Confederate capital was moved four months later to Richmond, Virginia). By March six more southern states had seceded. On April 12, the Civil War began when Confederates fired on Fort Sumter, in Charleston, South Carolina's harbor.

Abraham Lincoln

National Park Service

In the beginning, the South won decisive victories at **Bull Run,** Virginia—in both 1861 and 1862—and in the **York Peninsula Campaign** of 1862. Pushing north into Maryland that September, Confederate general Robert E. Lee's forces held fast at the **Battle of Antietam**—with 23,000 men killed or wounded, it was the bloodiest one-day battle in American history. Although Lee retreated, the fact that his army survived the battle emboldened him to push farther north. But when Confederate forces under Lee made their way toward the Pennsylvania capital of Harrisburg in July 1863, they were trounced by Gen. George Meade's troops at **Gettysburg.**

That same year, on the western front, Ulysses S. Grant's siege of **Vicksburg,** Mississippi, ended with a Confederate capitulation. With the Mississippi River now firmly in Union control and a blockade against southern Atlantic ports, the South began to suffer from a lack of food and supplies. In 1864 Union general William Tecumseh Sherman's conquest and burning of Atlanta on his "March to the Sea" campaign sealed the secessionists' fate.

In April 1865 Lee surrendered at **Appomattox Courthouse,** Virginia. An estimated 600,000 men had been killed and several thousand more injured in what remains the highest casualty rate for any war ever fought by Americans. The war's legacy left the South in physical and economic ruins. It would be a long time before relations between North and South were cordial again.

RECONSTRUCTION

To add insult to injury, certain political voices emerged urging strict punishment of the South. Although Lincoln's plan was to welcome the former Confederacy back into the Union without imposing harsh penalties, his plan died along with him when he was assassinated by actor John Wilkes Booth five days after Lee's surrender.

Instead, the vindictive voices of the Radical Republicans won out. The 1867 **Reconstruction Act** placed the southern states under martial law. Federal troops patrolled the streets and the Radical Republicans ran corrupt state legislatures. By the time Reconstruction was over in 1876, white Southerners were even more alienated than they had been at war's end.

The situation was not a whole lot better for blacks. Lacking education or skilled training, many had no jobs: those who did, often worked as tenant farmers for the masters who had once owned them. Although Lincoln's **Emancipation Proclamation** had technically granted slaves in the Confederate states their freedom in 1863, the passage of the 13th and 14th Amendments furthered their cause by banning slavery (1865) and guaranteeing civil rights (1868). All men—not women—were granted the right to vote per the 15th Amendment (1870), regardless of "race, color or previous condition of servitude."

1861	**Confederate States of America** are organized; opening shots of the Civil War are fired at Fort Sumter, South Carolina.
1863	Union forces win the Battle of Gettysburg. President Lincoln issues his **Emancipation Proclamation,**

	declaring all slaves in the Confederate states to be free as of 1 January 1863.
1865	Civil War ends. Congress passes the 13th Amendment to the Constitution, outlawing slavery. Abraham Lincoln is assassinated at Ford's Theatre in Washington, DC.
1869	The **New York Stock Exchange** is established. Rail service spans the continent as the Union and Central Pacific lines are joined by a golden spike at Promontory, Utah.

THE GILDED AGE: 1870–1912

The Gilded Age was a time of unprecedented invention and capitalism that did not see its equal until the high-tech revolution of a century later. Not unlike the unfettered individualism of the 1990s, the Gilded Age glorified the entrepreneur and the worship of materialism. It was during this era that America's captains of industry came to power—the great railroad barons, steel and oil tycoons and shipping magnates (Cornelius "Commodore" Vanderbilt, John D. Rockefeller, Andrew Carnegie). Achieving enormous wealth (there was as yet no federal income tax), they built lavish homes in places like Newport, Rhode Island, New York City and Palm Beach, Florida.

In 1870 the US population stood at 38.6 million, up 15 million from 20 years earlier. Many of the additions were immigrants, lured to eastern US cities by the prospect of industrial jobs. As their ranks swelled, so did the cities. By 1900 almost 40 percent of the country's population were urban dwellers.

After the Civil War, industrialization spread rapidly and oil, coal, copper and steel production soared. While this upsurge began in the Northeast, within a decade it was spreading westward. After 1880, the discovery of iron in northern Minnesota and Alabama expanded the steel industry westward into Minneapolis and south to Birmingham. Meatpacking became a major US enterprise after 1875, centered in Chicago and St. Louis. Flour milling, brewing and the manufacture of farm equipment also found bases in the Heartland.

Factories operating at full speed spelled employment for the thousands of immigrants and others streaming into the cities east of the Mississippi River. But vast discrepancies in income and lifestyle separated the ultra-rich industry titans from those who toiled for them. Cities became crowded and dirty as workers poured in and factories filled the air with smoke and noxious fumes. Low factory wages meant workers could not afford decent housing, and slums appeared. Finally, these inequalities erupted into full-blown labor hostilities as workers fought for their rights against an unsympathetic political establishment.

Things began to change with the dawn of the **Progressive Era** (1890 to 1920). Prompted in part by the writings of authors such as Upton Sinclair (*The Jungle*, 1906), who brought the horrors of Chicago's meatpacking industry to the fore, several states passed laws regulating wages, hours and workplace safety.

In 1901 **Theodore Roosevelt** became president, following the assassination of President William McKinley. Although born to wealth, Roosevelt believed the monopolistic practices of industrial tycoons were counter to the public good. After breaking up a railway monopoly in 1903, he established the Department of Commerce and Labor as a federal regulatory agency to oversee business and industry. Concerned that industrialization was squandering the nation's natural resources, he set aside large tracts of land as forest preserves and national parks. He also pushed through legislation regulating the drug and meatpacking industries.

The end of the Gilded Age was marked by the passage of the **16th Amendment** in 1913. This amendment, which established a federal income tax, put an end to the era's outrageous excess.

1870	The **15th Amendment** passes, granting "all men" the right to vote.
1879	Thomas Edison invents the lightbulb.
1883	The Brooklyn Bridge opens.

WORLD WAR I AND THE ROARING TWENTIES

The sinking of another luxury liner a few years later precipitated US entry into World War I, which had been raging in Europe since 1914. When German U-boats attacked the British passenger ship Lusitania, killing 124 Americans, German-American relations deteriorated, leading to President **Woodrow Wilson's** decision to enter the war in 1917. Fighting against the **Central Powers** (Germany, Austria, Turkey) on behalf of the **Allies** (Britain, France, Belgium, Russia, Italy) were 4.7 million Americans. In March 1918 the first Americans served in battle in France. Six months later, the war was over, 116,000 American lives had been lost, and the US teetered on the brink of the greatest era of prosperity in its history.

By 1920 the country's transformation from an agricultural economy into an industrial power was complete. The population stood at over 100 million and for the first time ever, more people lived in cities of 2,500 or more than in rural areas. Efficiencies of production and economies of scale had made items formerly reserved for the elite—such as automobiles, refrigerators and telephones—affordable for the masses.

New inventions proliferated—radio, motion pictures, the airplane—bringing the outside world to formerly isolated areas. The first commercial passenger flights began in 1925 when Congress authorized the US Post Office to contract private carriers for airmail routes. By mid-decade, unemployment stood at 2 percent, and the average American enjoyed a higher quality of life than ever before.

The decade soon earned the name "Roaring Twenties," not only because of its prosperous economy, but also owing to the sudden, massive societal changes that transformed the culture. The **19th Amendment** finally granted women the right to vote in 1920, unleashing other new freedoms. Bobbing her hair and donning shocking knee-length dresses, the "flapper" became the icon for feminism.

Even though the US had legally banned liquor with the adoption of the **Prohibition Amendment** in 1919, alcohol flowed freely in clubs known as speakeasies—to the tune of a sultry new sound called jazz. Since distillers were outlawed from manufacturing spirits—except for a few who gained exemption for "medicinal manufacturing"—a new, illegal liquor industry arose. Called "bootlegging," the business soon came under the auspice of powerful gangsters, such as Al Capone and Charles "Bugs" Moran, who controlled its manufacture and distribution.

One of the wildest parties of all, though, was on Wall Street. During the 1920s, for the first time, average Americans began buying common stocks, entering what had once been the sole province of the wealthy. As the good times continued, investors grew giddier, bidding stocks up to dizzying heights. Even though construction and factory production began to decline in 1927, few heeded the warning. Finally, on 29 October 1929, the bubble burst and the market collapsed, wiping out fortunes overnight and erasing $75 billion in market value.

1913	The **16th Amendment** passes, establishing a federal income tax.

1917	The US enters World War I on the side of the Allied Powers.
1919	The 18th, or **Prohibition Amendment** is adopted, banning the sale of alcoholic beverages.
1920	The **19th Amendment** grants women the right to vote.
1927	Charles Lindbergh completes the first solo transatlantic flight from New York to Paris.

THE GREAT DEPRESSION

The 1929 crash was followed by a surge of bank failures the next year, ushering in the greatest period of economic peril the country has ever known. By 1932 nearly a quarter of Americans were unemployed, industrial production was at 40 percent of capacity and the median national income had been cut in half. Compounding the misery, a drought across the Great Plains decimated crops and turned the area into a dust bowl. It was a disaster of epic proportions.

A young New Yorker named **Franklin D. Roosevelt** was elected president in 1932 (he would serve an unprecedented three terms in office) and immediately launched a massive program to turn the country around. Roosevelt's **New Deal** expanded the federal government's ability to shore up the economy by setting the price at which the government would buy gold, increasing the money supply, and instituting price controls and farm price supports. It also put into place agencies to regulate the stock exchanges and insure individual bank deposits.

The other part of the New Deal aimed to create jobs and prevent exploitation of the workforce. Its most important elements were a system to provide pension payments to aged and disabled Americans (the Social Security Administration); a public works program to provide government jobs for the unemployed; and enactment of minimum-wage, collective bargaining and child-labor laws.

1929	US stock market crashes, precipitating the Great Depression.
1931	The Empire State Building, tallest in the world, opens in New York City.
1933	President Franklin D. Roosevelt's initiates his **New Deal** policy.

WORLD WAR II

During the late 1930s, a series of totalitarian governments had come to power around the globe: now they were threatening Europe and Asia. Americans became increasingly alarmed as Adolf Hitler's armies marched through Europe; the isolationism spawned by World War I was crumbling.

On December 7, 1941, the Japanese bombed the American naval base at **Pearl Harbor,** Hawaii. The following day, Congress declared war on Japan. That same week, the two other **Axis Powers** (Germany and Italy) declared war on the US.

Within the space of one mind-boggling week, the US had committed to defensive war on two fronts. In the European theater, the Americans and their allies (Great Britain, France, and the Soviet Union) invaded North Africa, defeating the German army at El Alamein.

Meanwhile, the Japanese were making steady headway in the Pacific. They were finally stopped at the **Battle of Midway,** a three-day contest between the Allies

THE CIVIL RIGHTS MOVEMENT

"I have a dream that one day on the red hills of Georgia the sons of former slaves and the sons of former slaveowners will be able to sit down together at the table of brotherhood."
Martin Luther King, Jr., from his speech at the Civil Rights March on Washington, DC, August 28, 1963

As every American child learns in school, President Abraham Lincoln signed the Emancipation Proclamation abolishing slavery in 1863, in the middle of a terrible Civil War. Why, then, did Americans of African descent need a "civil rights movement" 100 years later?

The answer, complex and painful, can be summed up in a few phrases: a white Southern terrorist group known as the Ku Klux Klan, state-by-state "Jim Crow" laws enforcing racial segregation in all aspects of everyday life, and an 1896 Supreme Court case, *Plessy v.Ferguson,* declaring segregation legal as long as blacks and whites had schools and other public facilities that were "separate but equal." In reality, the public facilities and protections for black citizens—from public water fountains to voter registration to tax distributions for black schools—were never equal to those for whites.

By the 1930s and 40s, black citizens were moving north in search of factory jobs and fewer racial restrictions. After World War II, organizations such as the **Congress for Racial Equality** (CORE) and the **National Association for the Advancement of Colored People** (NAACP) began calling on President Harry Truman to eliminate segregation as the law of the land.

A 1954 Supreme Court decision on a Kansas case *(Brown v. Board of Education)* helped change everything. The case challenged an 1879 Kansas law that permitted racial segregation in elementary schools. Headed by McKinley Burnett, the state NAACP brought a suit by 13 parents on behalf of their 20 children. Thurgood Marshall, later the first African American to serve on the Supreme Court, was one of the lead lawyers in the case. The US Supreme Court ruled unanimously that racially segregated schools were "inherently unequal." This landmark case—and the Southern states' deliberate slowness in following its requirements—is generally viewed as the beginning of the modern civil rights movement.

Over the next 15 years, "the movement" involved thousands of activists, both black and white, and took many forms: boycotts, sit-ins, street marches and giant rallies. Beginning in December 1955, black citizens boycotted segregated buses in Montgomery, Alabama, for more than a year, until the Supreme Court outlawed the practice of making blacks give up their seats for whites. The **Southern Christian Leadership Conference** (SCLC), organized by the Reverend Dr. Martin Luther King, Jr. (see ATLANTA), a Baptist minister, helped black churches and communities all over the South organize nonviolent protests (based on the example of India's Mahatma Gandhi) and raise funds for a widespread, continuing fight against segregation. In 1957 nine black teenagers successfully integrated a Little Rock, Arkansas, high school, but they had to be accompanied by federal troops.

Soon hundreds of young black people were staging sit-ins and protests against segregated restaurants, parks, swimming pools, libraries and theaters in more than 100 Southern cities. Many of these activities, conducted in the face of escalating violence from whites, were organized by a new group, the **Student Nonviolent Coordinating Committee** (SNCC). Within a year, some

© UPPA/Photoshot

John Foreman, Martin Luther King, Jr., C.T. Vivian and Reverend Douglas march on the outskirts of Montgomery, Alabama, on March 7, 1965

70,000 people had participated in such protests, and at least 3,600 had been arrested.

Still the movement continued to gain momentum. "Freedom Riders" tested interstate bus integration in Alabama and Mississippi; schoolchildren faced down police dogs and fire hoses in Birmingham, Alabama, and 250,000 people marched on Washington, DC, inspired to further action by Dr. King's famous words: "I have a dream." When four young black girls were killed by a terrorist bomb in a Birmingham church in 1963, the public outcry led Congress to pass the comprehensive **Civil Rights Act** of 1964, outlawing racial discrimination in any form. By 1965 movement leaders had begun concentrating on another egregious legacy: "poll taxes," literacy tests, and other roadblocks to prevent blacks from registering to vote. After violent clashes in Selma and Montgomery, Alabama, the US Congress passed the 1965 **Voting Rights Act.** With the "Black Power" movement of the mid-1960s, civil rights protests took a more militant tone. A series of destructive, violent riots, primarily in impoverished black urban neighborhoods, led Dr. King to begin planning a "Poor People's March" on Washington for the summer of 1968.

But Dr. King's dream of uniting poor blacks and whites in peaceful civil protest never materialized. On a trip to Memphis, Tennessee, to speak on behalf of striking garbage workers, the nation's foremost civil rights leader was assassinated while standing on a balcony of the Lorraine Motel.

To millions of mourners, much of the optimism and the promise of the civil rights movement died with him on April 4, 1968. The movement never again had a leader of the stature and influence of Dr. Martin Luther King, Jr. But the cause he and thousands of others worked for—with extraordinary and heroic success—continues to be a profound and far-reaching theme in American political, social and economic life. The United States' first black president, Barack Obama, was inaugurated the day after Martin Luther King Day in January 2009, 41 years after Dr King's assassination.

and the Japanese fought almost entirely by air over 2sq mi Midway Island in the Pacific Ocean.

Back in Europe, the invasion of Normandy on the west coast of France began on June 6, 1944. On what became known as **D-Day,** Allied soldiers stormed the beaches, and by the following April, the Allies had breached German lines and were fast closing in on Hitler. As Allied troops approached Berlin later that month, Hitler committed suicide and Germany surrendered.

A few months later, Japan finally capitulated, following President **Harry S Truman's** decision to drop atomic bombs on Hiroshima and Nagasaki, Japan. By mid-August 1945 the war was over; more than 400,000 American lives had been lost.

1941	Japanese attack Pearl Harbor in Hawaii; US enters World War II.
1944	Allies land on Normandy beaches in France.
1945	World War II ends. President Roosevelt dies in office.

THE POSTWAR YEARS

The years immediately following World War II were marked by domestic prosperity. Returning war veterans began promising corporate careers or went into business for themselves. Housing developments sprang up overnight and the birthrate increased so dramatically that the generation born during these years earned its own moniker—the "Baby Boomers."

While the Soviet Union had been an ally to the US in World War II, conflicting political ideologies—Western free-market democracy versus the controls of Communism in the Soviet Union—culminated in a 40-year standoff known as the **Cold War.** This era was marked by constant tension, exacerbated by military buildups, covert operations, nuclear-weapons testing and propaganda campaigns on the part of both countries.

Although **Dwight D. Eisenhower,** elected president in 1952, was not politically progressive, his tenure was highlighted by an activist Supreme Court. Presided over by Chief Justice Earl Warren, the court outlawed racial segregation, spelled out the rights of criminal defendants, and laid down the "one man, one vote" rule, stipulating that all citizens must be represented equally in their state legislatures.

1947	Jackie Robinson becomes the first black player in major-league baseball when he joins the Brooklyn Dodgers.
1954	Supreme Court outlaws school segregation in *Brown vs. Board of Education*.

A DECADE OF REVOLUTION

The 1960s were tumultuous, distinguished by violence and profound social change. It began on a hopeful note with the election of **John F. Kennedy** (1917-63) who, at 44, was the youngest president ever to occupy the White House. It continued with the movement for full racial equality. Then, in quick succession, President Kennedy, his brother Attorney General Robert Kennedy, and civil rights leader **Dr. Martin Luther King, Jr.** were all assassinated by gunfire. Their deaths, coupled with an unpopular war in Vietnam, angered and alienated America's youth. There was growing discontent with the country's big government, big business and materialistic culture. By the mid-60s, a youth revolt was in full swing. Groups such as Students for a Democratic Society (SDS), formed by two University of Michigan students, were spawning anti-war demonstrations on college campuses across the US. Gradually, violence replaced passive civil disobedience as draft resisters and Black Power activists became more militant—and the "establishment" became less tolerant. Driven away from radical politics by the violence of the late 60s, members of the youth "counterculture" heeded Harvard professor Timothy Leary's invitation to "tune in, turn on, and drop out." Known as "hippies," these disaffected young people grew their hair long, wore blue jeans and tie-dyed shirts, listened to rock music, and experimented with mind-altering drugs and communal living arrangements. "Free sex" was rampant, with the introduction of the birth-control pill allowing women control over their reproductive lives.

Punctuated by the long and costly Vietnam War and the Watergate scandal, which led to the resignation of President **Richard Nixon** in 1974, the decade from 1965 to 1975 generated widespread distrust of political officials. **Watergate,** which took its name from the Washington, DC apartment building where its most famous offense occurred, included a number of administration officials involved in instances of burglary, illegal cover-ups, use of government agencies to harass political opponents, and illegal use of campaign contributions. Several officials were tried and convicted of criminal activities.

The 1980s were marked by a number of movements aimed at achieving personal and spiritual fulfillment.

1960	Black students stage the first sit-in of the civil rights movement at a lunch counter in Greensboro, North Carolina.
1961	Astronauat Alan Shepard makes the first American space flight aboard *Freedom 7* on May 5.
1962	President John F. **Kennedy** begins sending military advisers to **Vietnam** in an effort to contain Communism.
1963	President Kennedy is assassinated in Dallas, Texas. Civil-rights demonstrations in Montgomery, Alabama, are broken up by local police.
1964	Congress passes the landmark **Civil Rights Act** of 1964. US air strikes begin against North Vietnam.
1965	Congress passes the Voting Rights Act of 1965. President Lyndon Johnson commits combat troops to Vietnam.
1968	Martin Luther King, Jr. is assassinated in Memphis, Tennessee.
1969	Astronaut **Neil Armstrong** takes man's first steps on the moon.
1972	Richard **Nixon** becomes first American president to visit China.
1973	Last US troops leave Vietnam, ending the nation's longest war to date; American death toll: 57,685.
1974	President Nixon resigns for the illegal cover-up of a break-in at Democratic headquarters—a scandal known as Watergate.
1976	Supreme Court upholds death penalty in *Gregg vs. Georgia.*
1979	The first major nuclear power plant accident occurs at Three Mile Island in Pennsylvania.

| 1986 | Space shuttle *Challenger* explodes in Florida, killing seven passengers, including first US civilian selected for space travel. |
| 1989 | Hurricane Hugo strikes the coast of the Carolinas, inflicting more than $7 million in damages. |

END OF A MILLENNIUM

Two major trends underscored the 1990s—an increasingly diverse population mix and the technological revolution. By 1990 ever-faster computers and fax machines made global communication instantaneous and, in some cases, rendered offices obsolete, as increasing numbers of workers began to "telecommute" from home. Portable devices such as cellular phones, pagers and laptop computers enabled workers to perform their duties anywhere. By the mid-90s, widespread use of the Internet was revolutionizing traditional ways of doing business.

The other trend with wide-ranging cultural ramifications involved the sudden rise in ethnic diversity as Hispanic and Asian immigrants added to the existing mix of European and African stock. In the decade from 1980 to 1990, Asians increased their presence in the population by an astounding 107 percent; Hispanics increased by 53 percent. In 2010 the Hispanic population displaced blacks as the country's largest minority group.

1990	US troops engage Iraqi forces in the Gulf War called Operation Desert Storm.
1992	Hurricane Andrew devastates Miami and the Florida Keys.
1996	The **Centennial Olympic Games are held** in Atlanta, Georgia.
1999	President Bill Clinton becomes the first elected president in US history to be impeached by the House of Representatives for lying in a federal proceeding and obstructing justice. He was acquitted by the Senate.

A NEW MILLENNIUM

The new century started with less of a bang than was expected. Fears about Y2K, a glitch that may have made computers not recognize the new date caused concern that everything electronic would stand still. Instead, the transition from 1999 to 2000 went off without a hitch. The smooth sailing of the new century quickly ended. A close election between presidential candidates George W. Bush and former vice president Al Gore necessitated recounts, the first formal contest in the history of a presidential election and a trip to the US Supreme Court. In January 2001 Bush was sworn in as the 43rd president of the United States.

On the morning of September 11, 2001 (known as 9-11), two airplanes piloted by Islamic extremists terrorists hit New York's World Trade Center, causing the towers to fall and killing nearly 3,000 civilians. Another plane hit the Pentagon in Washington, D.C., while a fourth crashed in a Pennsylvania field. As a result of the attacks, security at airports, high-rises, public facilities and government buildings changed, in some cases dramatically. Despite the difficult foreign relations that 9-11 begat, the eastern US continued to thrive. Faster, more efficient technology further increased incidence of telecommuting, as well as distance learning.

At the turn of the second millennium, the eastern US remains America's core, with the majority (9 out of 15) of the country's most populous urban complexes lying east of the Mississippi River. New York City still ranks as the country's financial and commercial nerve center and remains its undisputed leader in the arts. Similarly, Washington, DC is America's political epicenter—the city that world leaders uniformly look to in time of crisis. And Chicago, center of the Midwest, reigns as a major transportation hub, with 19 rail lines linking it to every major American and Canadian city, as well as O'Hare International Airport, the nation's second-busiest. But, in many ways, America is a nation divided.

In 2008, the country elected its first African American president, Barack Obama. Formerly a junior United States Senator from Illinois, Obama rose quickly in prominence in the Democratic party. Known for his oratory skills and his passion for ideas, he was reelected in 2012 to a second term as US president.

2000	Former vice president Al Gore receives more popular votes, but Texas governor George W. Bush receives more electoral votes in the US presidential election. The US Supreme Court halts recounts and declares Bush the winner of the election.
2001	George W. Bush is sworn in as the 43rd president of the United States. Bush is the son of George H.W. Bush, the 41st president.
2001	Terrorists fly hijacked jumbo jets into New York's **World Trade Center,** felling the two skyscrapers and killing 2,979 people.
	President Bush sends US troops to **Afghanistan,** with international support, to destroy Al-Qaeda terrorist camps and depose the Taliban government.
2002	The **XIX Winter Olympic Games** are held in Salt Lake City, Utah.
2003	US troops engage in a coalition military operation in Iraq, code-named Operation Iraqi Freedom.
	The space shuttle *Columbia* disintegrates over Texas during re-entry.
2004	George W. Bush is re-elected to a second term as president.
2005	Hurricane Katrina, the third-strongest hurricane to make landfall in the US, hits the Gulf Coast. The city of New Orleans was one of the hardest hit cities.
2006	The US population passes the 300 million person mark.
2007	Gerald Ford: 38th president's state funeral in Washington, DC.
2009	Barack Obama sworn in as 44th president of the USA, the first African American elected to the position.
2010	Congress passes Health Bill.
2011	US Space Shuttle program ends.
2012	Barack Obama reelected for second presidential term.
2013	Terrorist bombing in Boston kills 3 and injuries 260 people. New York City's 911 Memorial is completed. Detroit files for bankruptcy.

USA East Art and Culture

The states of the eastern US encompass a wide spectrum of architecture, arts and performance venues, much to the delight of residents and visitors.

Art Deco Buildings, Miami Beach, Florida © Nick Tzolov/iStockphoto.com

Architecture

Punctuated by the skyscraper, America's great contribution to architecture, the built environment of the eastern US reveals influences from the nation's many immigrant groups. Technological and aesthetic innovations that originated here have also played a role. They have combined to result in some of the world's foremost examples of building artistry.

There were no trained architects among the European colonists who arrived in America in the 16C-17C; survival was initially more important than aesthetics. Settlers raised their own simple structures according to building traditions from their homelands, using locally available materials such as hardwood timber in New England, fieldstone in the mid-Atlantic states and cypress planks in Florida. In the southern colonies and along the Gulf Coast, raised cottages utilized opposing windows, wide porches and detached kitchens to combat heat and humidity, while on some New England farms, houses were linked to barns, sheds and other dependencies to eliminate the need for going outside in cold weather. Similar considerations of material, climate and culture gave rise to the saltbox house in New England; the Creole cottage in New Orleans; the shotgun house of the Gulf Coast, the coquina structures of St. Augustine, Florida, and other forms of vernacular residential architecture throughout the fledgling eastern US.

18TH CENTURY

As settlement increased and cities took shape, colonists began to create structures that were visually pleasing as well as functional. Amateur architects and skilled builders armed with English pattern books spread the **Georgian** style throughout the colonies. The symmetrical façades, Classical ornamentation, ample scale and geometric proportions of Georgian buildings at the new capital of Williamsburg reflected colonial determination.

After the American Revolution, the **Adam** style—a British Neoclassical tradition based on Roman villas and houses—was adopted by a growing merchant class in seaport towns along the coast. Called the **Federal** style in the US, it displayed clarity and simplicity of form, and restraint, delicacy and refinement. Garlands, urns and festoons decorated wall surfaces, fireplace mantels and entryways, and circular or oval-shaped rooms were common.

Builders of public structures turned to Roman Classical orders for inspiration. Thomas Jefferson's Virginia State Capitol (1798) in Richmond was based on the Maison Carrée, a Roman temple in Nîmes, France, giving rise to the Classical Revival, or **Jeffersonian,** style.

One of the first trained professional architects to work in the US was **Benjamin Henry Latrobe,** who arrived from England in 1796. An admirer of architectural forms of ancient Greece, Latrobe patterned the Bank of Pennsylvania (1800) in Philadelphia after an Athenian temple, pioneering the **Greek Revival** style for public buildings in America. The Greek temple front with Classical orders became so prevalent for banks, government buildings, churches and eventually residences—particularly plantation houses in the antebellum South—that the style was dubbed the "National style." **Charles Bullfinch's** design of the Massachusetts State House, with its central dome and columned frontispiece, served as the model for state houses across the country.

19TH CENTURY

The commercial availability of good-quality nails and lumber in uniform sizes brought about the invention in the 1830s of the light, inexpensive and speedily constructed "balloon frame." Other mass-produced components included pressed brick, cut stone, plate glass, cast iron and jigsawed wood. Houses were built rapidly, and, as the country entered the Victorian age in the latter half of the 19C, were designed and embellished in a plethora of eclectic substyles that quickly rose and fell in popularity. **Gothic Revival**-style structures sported pointed-arch windows, steep cross-gables and dormers decorated with intricately cut-out bargeboards. The architecture of Italy inspired the more formal **Italianate** style, characterized by square towers, shallow roofs, wide eaves with imposing cornices supported by brackets, and rounded windows and doors with hooded moldings. More elaborate still, **Second Empire**-style buildings sported Italianate features, with the addition of an imposing mansard roof and Classical ornamentation. Some clapboard or board-and-batten homes displayed post-and-beam structural members or diagonal braces as part of the exterior ornamentation in a variant known as the Stick style. The immensely influential New York architectural firm of **McKim, Mead & White** initially rose to popularity with their **Shingle**-style homes, in which a continuous flow of variously patterned shingles covered walls, dormers and trim. The most eclectic and picturesque of the Victorian substyles, however, is the **Queen Anne**. Homes in this fanciful style were laid in irregular plans of projecting wings, bays, towers, turrets and cross axes, lavishly ornamented with latticework, shingles, scrollwork, spindles and balusters, and painted in eye-catching colors. Toward the end of the 19C, Boston-born, Paris-trained architect **Henry Hobson Richardson** adapted Romanesque forms from France and Spain in a distinctly American style known as **Richardsonian Romanesque**. Characterized by heavy, rounded arches, rusticated stone surfaces and deeply inset doors and windows, the style was popular for public structures including churches and railroad terminals. Commercial architecture underwent a revolution following the Civil War as iron mills previously devoted to the war effort turned to production of cast-iron building components. By the 1870s structures framed entirely in iron, hung with prefabricated cast-iron façade panels and equipped with improved passenger elevators rose to heights not possible with masonry construction. Cast-iron façades were especially popular in New York, St. Louis, Charleston and New Orleans. In 1893 a team of architects including **Daniel Burnham** and **Frederick Law Olmsted,** America's most influential landscape architect, created a "White City" of classically ornamented buildings for the **World's Columbian Exposition** in Chicago, stimulating a national taste for the illustrious past in public architecture and city planning. Domes, pedimented porticoes and sweeping staircases characterized **Neoclassical** federal buildings in Washington, while **Richard Morris Hunt** and other practitioners of the more ornate **Beaux-Arts** style adorned courthouses, libraries, museums and mansions with paired columns, wreaths, swags, festoons, cartouches and statuary.

Turning away from the past, Chicago architect **Louis Henri Sullivan** espoused instead the notion that architectural design should be of its time. Sullivan and colleagues William Le Baron Jenney, Dankmar Adler, William Holabird and Martin Roche formed the **Chicago school** in the 1880s, and set about utilizing new advances in construction technology to create ever-taller commercial buildings in which non-load-bearing "curtain" walls were draped on a steel framework. The skeleton was visible on the façade in the horizontal spandrels and vertical piers separating windows of unprecedented size, and the shaft, rising from a defined base at entry level, was capped by an emphatically decorated cornice. Chicago school buildings achieved heights of up to 20 stories, prefiguring the modern **skyscraper** (see CHICAGO, infobox).

20TH CENTURY

In the boom decade following World War I, developers in Manhattan latched onto the concept of the vertical city as a means of multiplying the profits of small building sites by creating rentable space out of the air. New technologies pushed buildings higher, necessitating a 1916 city ordinance requiring architects to create set-backs at the upper levels to allow sunlight to reach the street. By the 1930s, a number of European architects working in America, including **Ludwig Mies van der Rohe,** and **Walter Gropius**—founder of the Bauhaus design school in Germany—introduced Bauhaus principles of minimalism and functionalism in what became known as the **International** style.

Influenced by the simple forms and austere surfaces of the International style, coupled with the ideas displayed at the 1925 Paris Exposition des Arts Décoratifs et Industriels Modernes, **Art Deco** adopted the sleek lines, cubic massing and new materials of the technology-oriented modernist aesthetic. Deco's geometric, abstracted motifs such as chevrons, sunbursts and lightning bolts worked in sleek, reflective materials were wildly popular throughout America for corporate headquarters, theaters and hotels—the latter particularly in Miami Beach, Florida. Pyramidal Art Deco skyscrapers such as New York City's Chrysler Building and the Empire State Building came to symbolize American power and ingenuity.

In the Midwest, **Frank Lloyd Wright** (&see CHICAGO, infobox) led a group of architects known as the **Prairie school** in development of a new style incorporating the natural environment into planning and design. Remaking the concept of horizontality, Wright's Prairie-style houses—typified by his **Robie House** in Chicago—hugged the flat Midwestern landscape; movable room partitions created flexible interior spaces and flat or shallow roofs surmounted long bands of windows.

In the mid-20C, the **Seagram Building** (1958, Ludwig Mies van der Rohe) in New York City, a rectangular skyscraper sheathed in glass and set amid a large plaza, strongly influenced the "glass box" look of office buildings in urban centers such as Boston, Detroit, Atlanta and Miami. The advent of rigid-tube construction in the 1970s allowed the soaring height of Chicago's 110-story **Sears Tower** by the prolific architectural firm of **Skidmore, Owings & Merrill**. Contemporary architects such as **Philip Johnson, I.M. Pei, Michael Graves** and **Robert Venturi** have since broken from the strict functionalism of International school design, altering the urban landscape with **Postmodern** structures that honor the past through free interpretations of historical motifs while utilizing new technologies and materials.

21ST CENTURY

As the 21C took hold, one trend led the way: green building. As Americans became more devoted to cutting their carbon footprints, architects and builders began to push their green plans as a way to cut energy inefficient and to market to a population increasingly dedicated to the sustainable lifestyle.

A prized term for a new building project is LEED-certified. Developed by the U.S. Green Building Council, this program provides "verification that a building or community is designed and built using strategies aimed at improving performance...in energy savings, water efficiency, CO2 emissions reduction, improved indoor environmental quality, and stewardship of resources...."

Each year the American Institute of Architects' Committee on the Environment announces the "Top Ten Green Projects." Recent US winners include the **Jewish Reconstructionist Congregation** in Evanston, IL and the **Yale University Sculpture Building and Gallery** in New Haven, CT. The new 104-story **One World Trade Center** in New York City, on the site of the 911 terrorist attack, met LEED Gold certification standards. Incorporating the latest advances in energy efficiency and safety measures, the building uses reclaimed rainwater in its cooling systems and waste steam to aid electricity generation.

The Arts

With New York City as the visual-art capital of the country, as well as being a vital center for music production, opera, dance and, naturally, the Broadway show, many are unaware of the contribution to the nation's cultural life made by the wider region. But with thriving performance scenes in cities both large and small, and many fine collections maintained at colleges and universities, the eastern US affords abundant opportunities to absorb the grand scope of the American cultural experience.

ART
Painting, Sculpture and Photography
18th Century
Sometimes called the father of American painting, New Englander **Benjamin West** spent the latter part of his career in London after touring Europe to absorb the works of the Old Masters. Artists who trained in his London studio included **Charles Willson Peale**, the first American resident history painter; and **Gilbert Stuart**, known for his oil sketch of George Washington. Bostonian **John Singleton Copley** became famous for his portraits of political and social leaders.

19th Century
America's first landscapist, **Thomas Cole** arrived in Philadelphia from England in 1818 and set out to record the unspoiled reaches of the Hudson River Valley and the Catskill Mountains. He and other artists of the **Hudson River school** such as **Frederic Edwin Church** (who rendered the period's definitive portrait of Niagara Falls) presented a romanticized view of nature imbued with moral overtones. Other important artists of this period include **John James Audubon**, whose studies in art and ornithology produced *The Birds of America* (1827-38); American marine painter Fitz Hugh Lane; Martin Johnson Heade, a Pennsylvania landscape artist; and Missourian **George Caleb Bingham**, the first significant American painter from the Midwest.
The works of Lane, Heade and Bingham all display characteristics of **Luminism**, an aspect of mid-19C painting concerned with the study and depiction of light.

Sculptors **Augustus Saint-Gaudens** and **Daniel Chester French** broke from the Neoclassical tradition of American sculpture to create bold, naturalistic memorials and monuments throughout the eastern US.

Massachusetts-born **James Abbott McNeill Whistler**, who settled in Paris in 1855, inspired a sea change in American art with his philosophy that art should exist for its own sake and not to convey a moral or narrative. **John Singer Sargent**, also active in Europe, is best known for his exquisitely rendered portraits of the wealthy.

America's finest Impressionist painter was Philadelphian **Mary Cassatt**, who lived most of her life in Paris. **William Merritt Chase**, who founded his own art school in New York in 1896, became one of that city's preeminent society portraitists. In Boston, **Winslow Homer** produced genre scenes of American life that focused on the sea. **Henry Ossawa Tanner**, the first black American painter to achieve renown outside the US, eschewed the stylistic traditions of his day, expressing his experiences as an African-American through his deeply spiritual works.

Postimpressionist painters **Maurice Prendergast** and **Thomas Eakins** favored a return to realism over academic theory. Eakins' work influenced **Robert Henri**, who, with followers **George Luks**, **John Sloan** and **George Bellows**, turned to the harsh realities of everyday life in New York as subject matter; their gritty style was dubbed the **Ash Can school**.

20th Century

Photographer **Alfred Stieglitz** likewise rebelled against academism. His 291 Gallery in New York City, which he cofounded in 1909, mounted works by new American artists such as **Marsden Hartley** and **Arthur Dove** (America's first abstract painter), and became a center for the city's artistic avant-garde. The 1913 International Exhibition of Modern Art, known as the Armory Show, presented new works by European Postimpressionists, Fauvists, Pointillists and Cubists to a shocked American public. The show also established New York City as the art capital of the nation.

The environment and life of the nation fueled the Depression-era works of American scene painters **Stuart Davis** and **Edward Hopper**. Black life in 1930s Harlem inspired African-American painter **Jacob Lawrence**, who fused bold forms and primary colors to create eloquent social statements—exemplified by his famed 60-panel narrative of the black migration from the rural South to the industrial North. Also during this period, **American scene painting** flowered in the Midwest, where artists such as Missouri native **Thomas Hart Benton** and Iowan **Grant Wood** sought to depict rural America in the face of encroaching industrialization. Wood is perhaps best known for *American Gothic* (1930), a hard-edged portrait of a Midwestern farmer/preacher and his daughter.

The onset of World War II brought a wave of European artists such as Max Ernst, Ynes Tanguy and Salvador Dalí to New York City. Along with Armenian émigré Arshile Gorky and German-born Hans Hofmann, they inspired a new avant-garde that gave rise in the 1940s to **Abstract Expressionism** (see NEW YORK CITY, infobox). Practitioners of this radical American art movement include "Action" painters **Willem de Kooning**, **Jackson Pollock** and **Franz Kline**; "Color Field" painters **Mark Rothko** and **Barnett Newman**; as well as **Clyfford Still**, **Helen Frankenthaler** and **Robert Motherwell**. Meanwhile, artists **Andrew Wyeth** and magazine illustrator **Norman Rockwell** reacted to the effect of modernization on regional culture through their nostalgic depictions of American folkways.

Mass commercialism enabled by new advances in media and communications gave rise in the 1960s to **Pop Art**. **Andy Warhol**, **Roy Lichtenstein**, **Jim Dine**, **James Rosenquist** and sculptor **Claes Oldenburg** embraced the commonplace with works based on commercial products, comic strips and billboards. American iconography also proved integral to works by collagist **Robert Rauschenberg** and painter/printmaker **Jasper Johns**. The 1960s also saw the rise of Conceptualism, a movement based on the notion that ideas take precedence over form. Raised in Harlem, **Romare Bearden** was a political cartoonist before beginning to paint in the 1950s; his innovative use of collage gained him renown by the 1970s.

Folk Art

Throughout the history of the eastern US, artists and craftspeople have created paintings, textiles, sculptures, furniture, pottery, glasswork and aesthetically pleasing objects for everyday use that fall under the broad category of folk art. Like a local accent, folk art is region-based, the product of non-academically trained artists working within provincial traditions to produce objects for their communities.

Native American cultures in the east produced objects for artistic, ritual and utilitarian purposes, including intricately woven and painted baskets, pottery vessels and effigy jars; cornhusk and leather dolls and masks; and carved wooden ware and figures. Tribes of the eastern woodlands were particularly known for their fine beadwork and body ornaments of metal and mica.

Folk art traditions in the eastern US include **Fraktur** (from the German *Frakturschrift*, or "fractured writing"), a type of illuminated calligraphy used by

German immigrants in Pennsylvania to illustrate formal documents; **quilting**, a practical art that peaked in eastern Amish communities in the late 19C; and **furniture making**, typified by the simple designs crafted in the Shaker communities of New York, Kentucky and New England.

Well-known folk painters include itinerant portraitist **Ammi Phillips** (1788-1865); **Joshua Johnson** (1764-1824), the first African-American painter to create a recognized body of work; and **Grandma Moses** (1860-1961), who at the age of seventy-six began painting realistic scenes of her early rural life in New York.

MUSIC AND DANCE
Music
Musicians of the eastern US have created and refashioned an astonishing variety of musical styles. Cutting-edge and traditional forms can be heard live in concert halls, nightclubs and outdoor music festivals. Most cities of even modest size support a symphony or chamber orchestra as well as a club scene that nurtures local pop artists. Although New York City has traditionally been the home of music production facilities in the East, today one of the largest segments of the US recording industry is based in Nashville, Tennessee.

Muddy Waters performing in 1950

© Tom Copi/Michael Ochs Archives/Getty Images

Classical composers in Europe and the US have been inspired by American hymns and folk songs. New England businessman and part-time composer **Charles Ives** (1874-1954), for example, borrowed dance tunes, church music and the raw sounds of bells and parades, mixing them into complex scores using 20C innovations of dissonance and contrasting rhythms. Pennsylvania native **Samuel Barber** (1910-81), best known for his serenely beautiful "Adagio for Strings," chose a more melodic approach. No composer embodied the American frontier spirit more than Brooklynite **Aaron Copland** (1900-90), who based his "Appalachian Spring" on a Shaker song. **George Gershwin** (1898-1937), also from Brooklyn, captured an urban electricity with "Rhapsody in Blue" and "Piano Concerto in F," both strongly influenced by jazz techniques.

Singin' The Blues
Along the Mississippi delta from the late 1890s, a style of music called **"the blues"** (see MEMPHIS) evolved primarily among African Americans playing guitars, harmonicas and other simple instruments. Sung by performers such as **Muddy Waters, B.B. King** and **Etta James**, the blues have become one of America's most enduring music genres, inspiring countless musicians including Eric Clapton, Bob Dylan and other rock-and-roll greats. The music flourishes in Memphis, New Orleans, Chicago and Kansas City, where blues artists have thrived since the days of speakeasies—bars where alcohol was sold illegally during Prohibition.

All That Jazz
The amalgam of styles known as **jazz** has many roots, including blues. **"Ragtime,"** the earliest form of jazz to have a wide appeal, began its long period of popularity in the 1890s. A piano style, ragtime emphasized syncopation and polyrhythm, best interpreted by composer **Scott Joplin**.

New Orleans is widely accepted as the birthplace of jazz. Its earliest influences might have been slave dances held in

THE AMERICAN MUSICAL

With roots in burlesque, comic opera and vaudeville, the musical rose to popularity early in the 20C and thrives today in theaters across the country. In the 1920s and early 30s, the bright productions, comedic plots and frivolous song-and-dance numbers by composers Jerome Kern, Irving Berlin, Cole Porter and George and Ira Gershwin provided a welcome escape from the cares of daily life. Richard Rodgers and Oscar Hammerstein II's *Oklahoma!* changed the direction of the genre in 1943 by integrating musical numbers with the plot line and featuring serious ballet. Jule Styne, Frank Loesser, Leonard Bernstein and Alan Jay Lerner and Frederick Loewe all followed this trend. The complex lyrics and innovative plots of shows such as Stephen Sondheim's *A Little Night Music* broke new ground in the 1970s. This decade also saw the rise of inventive new work by director/choreographers Jerome Robbins, Bob Fosse, Tommy Tune and Michael Bennet, whose musical, A Chorus Line, enjoyed one of the longest Broadway runs (1975-90). The six-year run of *The Producers* (2001-07) reinvigorated the genre. The longest-running Broadway show to date is *The Phantom of the Opera*, with more than 10,000 performances.

Congo Square, but the style grew up in the Storyville prostitution houses, riverboats and social clubs in the early 20C. Small ensembles of cornets, clarinets, trombones and, later, saxophones played standard and improvised melodies backed by lively, mixed rhythms. As the style evolved, colorful **Dixieland** music added banjo beats and a wild mix of instrumental solos played at once in a magical blend.

New Orleans pianist **Jelly Roll Morton** and clarinet player **Sidney Bichet** were two of the greatest influences of early jazz. The most famous jazzman of all, trumpet player **Louis Armstrong**, grew up in New Orleans but left in 1922 to join his mentor, King Oliver, in Chicago. The second great city of jazz, Chicago harbored many musicians who, like Armstrong, sought to escape the South's racial restrictions.

Closely following the development of jazz was the **Big Band** movement, large ensembles of horns that, with the help of radio, flourished from the 1920s to World War II. **Glenn Miller, Benny Goodman** and **Artie Shaw** were among its greatest proponents. Swing bands brought a more jazzy big-band sound that introduced energetic swing dancing, popular from 1930 to 1945 and recently revived. **Duke Ellington** was a giant on the music scene for years as a band leader, composer and performer

from the time he worked at New York's famous Cotton Club (1927-32) until his later years writing religious music (he died in 1974). Crooners like New Jersey-born **Frank Sinatra** got their start singing with big bands.

Around the mid-1950s, **rock and roll** exploded on the American popular music scene as several artists, including **Fats Domino, Little Richard**, and especially Memphis-based **Elvis Presley**, began combining jazz and blues influences with electrically amplified guitars, intricate bass lines and hopped-up rhythms. Wildly popular with teenagers, the pounding beat of rock came to represent a culture of sex, drugs and youthful rejection of societal norms. Guitarist Chuck Berry, vocalist **Buddy Holly** and pianist **Jerry Lee Lewis** all claimed huge followings, and Elvis Presley's theatrical sex appeal catapulted him to international fame.

Pickin' and Grinnin'

By far the most popular music in America is **country & western**, or simply Country (see NASHVILLE). The music's performance and recording capital is still Nashville, where the Grand Ole Opry was once the undisputed hall of fame for country music artists. Taking its roots in pioneer folk music, country is epitomized in the singing style of **Hank Williams**. A variant of country music, **bluegrass music** grew up in the Appalachian region, highlighted by the virtuoso guitarist **Doc Watson** and bluegrass legend **Earl Scruggs**.

Traditions and Trends

Regions in the eastern US lay claim to several musical traditions. Detroit, known as Motown (short for Motor Town) for its auto-making industry, is famous for its **Motown Sound**, a mix of gospel, pop, and rhythm and blues. **Smokey Robinson, the Temptations, Gladys Knight** and **Diana Ross and the Supremes** were some of Motown's greatest stars. The lyrics of American folksingers **Woody Guthrie, Pete Seeger** and **Bob Dylan** were inspired by civil rights and societal protest from the 1930s through the 60s.

Popular American music today reflects myriad styles and influences. **Alternative rock** bands have for the most part succeeded the heavy-metal and acid-rock groups that formed during the 1970s and 80s. The sound of urban protest, **rap** features hard-driving rhythms, booming bass and raging lyrics often laced with profanity. And the bouncing beats of Latin music, much of it based in South Florida, are leaving a growing mark on the American music scene. Recent trends include genres Hip-Hop, Electronica, Rap, Rock and Pop. The growth in the digital music market via portable media (downloads to iPods, smartphones, tablets, etc.) continues to skyrocket, impacting retail outlets such as Virgin Megastores, which closed its New York stores in 2009.

Dance

The rise of dance as a performance art came relatively late to the US. Since the 1940s, the American dance environment has nurtured preeminent classical ballet companies such as New York's **American Ballet Theater** (ABT) and the distinguished **New York City Ballet**, which flourished for years under the guidance of artistic director **George Balanchine**. Choreographers **Agnes de Mille** and **Jerome Robbins**, both associated with ABT, transferred their talents to Broadway; de Mille's use of traditional folk themes in musicals such as *Oklahoma!* inspired distinctively American ballet forms.

In America began **Isadora Duncan**, in the 1890s, introduced her revolutionary belief that the body should be free to improvise and express personal feelings. **Ruth St. Denis** and her husband **Ted Shawn** laid the foundations for modern dance in America with their influential Denishawn School, founded in 1915. But it was innovator **Martha Graham** who made America the center of modern dance in the mid 20C. Her studies of physical structure and movement, coupled with the belief that energy originates in the center of the body and not in its extremities, made for a stark, percussive style that was at first derided by critics and audiences. Her work influenced nearly every important modern choreographer, including **Merce Cunningham, Paul Taylor** and **Twyla Tharp**, all of whom founded their own companies in New York. Scottish, English and Irish jigs and reels inspired American folk-dance forms, including the **square dances** and **contra dances** that grew to popularity in rural areas. Irish clog dances were combined with elements of African step dances and the rhythms of jazz music to form the basis of complex **tap dances** seen in Broadway musicals and Hollywood film. Adapted by music-hall performers, tap

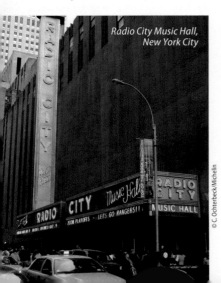

Radio City Music Hall, New York City

© C. Ochterbeck/Michelin

was performed on vaudeville stages by greats such as Bill "Bojangles" Robinson and John Bubbles, and has enjoyed a recent revival.

THEATER AND FILM
Theater

Theatrical fare in the eastern US indulges virtually every taste. Companies throughout the US stage timeless explorations of the human condition by mid-century dramatists **Eugene O'Neill, Arthur Miller, Tennessee Williams, Thornton Wilder** and **William Inge** as well as the sparkling comedies of prolific playwright Neil Simon. Avant-garde works by **Edward Albee, Lanford Wilson** and South African **Athol Fugard** are taking their place in the modern repertoire, as are contemporary works by New Yorker **Wendy Wasserstein**, Chicago-born **David Mamet** and Iowan **David Rabe**. Inspired by the ground-breaking work of **Laurie Anderson**, performance artists create genre-bending works combining music, dance, poetry and visual art.

Currently claiming some 240 venues, New York City has always been the theater capital of the US. Mainstream professional theater here is synonymous with **Broadway**, the renowned entertainment district in Manhattan. The first theaters were established here around the turn of the 20C, and the rise of the musical comedy in the 1920s catapulted the area to worldwide prominence. Today Broadway boasts some 40 legitimate theaters, most of them presenting big-budget musicals that can run for many years. Smaller **Off Broadway** theaters mounting lower-budget productions also flourish in the city. And nonprofit **Off-Off Broadway** theaters favor experimental works by emerging playwrights.

Elsewhere in the East, performance halls frequently host traveling companies of major Broadway productions, and many large cities support their own professional theaters and repertory troupes. Minneapolis, for example, boasts more theaters per capita than any American city besides New York, and Chicago's Steppenwolf Theater Company and Second City Theater are famous for spawning the careers of numerous actors and comedians.

Stars of stage, screen and television frequently can be seen performing in summer festivals and regional theater companies such as Maine's Ogunquit Playhouse, Flat Rock Playhouse in North Carolina, and the Red Barn Playhouse in Saugatuck, Michigan.

Film

Although California has long been the filmmaking capital of the world, the American film industry got its start in New Jersey, where **Thomas Edison** perfected the mechanisms for making and projecting 35mm movies in 1893. As cinema progressed from novelty to industry during the first decade of the 20C, American movie studios set up shop in New Jersey, Connecticut and Philadelphia, with the most important companies headquartered in Chicago (Selig and Essanay) and New York (Edison, Vitagraph and Biograph). Rural New Jersey even served as the exterior location for Edison's *The Great Train Robbery* (1903), and other early Westerns. Several studios also established facilities in Jacksonville, Florida, to take advantage of year-round filming opportunities as well as lush tropical backdrops.

The early movie-going public paid a nickel for admission to films screened in small theaters known as **nickelodeons**. In 1913 New York entrepreneurs erected the first "movie palaces"—large, fantastically decorated theaters where live vaudeville shows preceded movie screenings. Even after the film industry headed west in the 1920s, "underground" films by Shirley Clarke, John Cassavetes and Andy Warhol in the 1960s and 70s signaled the presence of an avant-garde film movement in New York. Today, Orlando, Florida, brings Hollywood back east with its theme parks/production facilities like Universal and Disney studios. Many cities offer guided tours of locations that played a role in popular films.

Literature

With its beginnings in the writings of early Virginia and New England settlers, American literature has reflected the development of the US through nationhood, expansion, industrialization, war and urbanization. In colonial times, publishing was confined mostly to sermons, journals, religious writings, political treatises and almanacs. In 1732 Benjamin Franklin began writing his *Poor Richard's Almanack*, a compendium of calendars, proverbs, practical information, popular science and humor. Various newspapers, broadsheets and political tracts disseminated opinion during the years leading up to the American Revolution. Englishman Thomas Paine turned the tide of colonial opinion toward a break from Great Britain with his pro-independence pamphlet *Common Sense* (1776).

19TH CENTURY

Popular literature in the early 19C found its way to readers via newspapers and chapbooks and inexpensive digests of moral musings. **James Fenimore Cooper** charted the disappearing wilderness of the American frontier with his *Leatherstocking Tales*, which included the novel *The Last of the Mohicans* (1826). The first American author to achieve international fame was **Washington Irving**, author of *Rip Van Winkle* (1820) and *The Legend of Sleepy Hollow* (1820). The poems and short stories of romantic Gothicist **Edgar Allan Poe** ("The Fall of the House of Usher," 1839) chilled readers with their themes of horror.

By the 1840s the **transcendentalist movement** (see BOSTON) leaders, **Ralph Waldo Emerson** and **Henry David Thoreau**, settled in the Boston area, establishing New England at the forefront of American thought and literary expression. In Boston, James Russell Lowell helped found the *Atlantic Monthly*, a literary periodical whose contributors included **Henry Wadsworth Longfellow**, the most widely read poet of his day. **Nathaniel Hawthorne** explored Puritan ethics with novels such as *The Scarlet Letter* (1850). In Amherst, Massachusetts, reclusive poet **Emily Dickinson** penned more than a thousand short lyric verses, most of them undiscovered during her lifetime. Elsewhere in the northeast, **Herman Melville** wrote *Moby-Dick* (1851), his epic novel of the sea, after spending 18 months on a whaler; and **Harriet Beecher Stowe** fanned the flames of abolitionist sentiment with *Uncle Tom's Cabin* (1852). Poet **Walt Whitman** published the first edition of *Leaves of Grass* in 1855. As the nation expanded in the last half of the 19C, a literary movement known as regionalism sought to preserve awareness of regional differences in scenery and speech. Humorist **Mark Twain** (né Samuel Clemens) captured the era of his boyhood in a Mississippi River town in *The Adventures of Tom Sawyer* (1876). In the South, **Joel Chandler Harris'** Uncle Remus stories rank among the greatest in black folk literature; **Richard M. Johnston** penned humorous sketches of life in rural Georgia; and **George Washington Cable** described the Creole society of New Orleans.

20TH CENTURY

A preponderance of writers, artists and thespians made New York City's **Greenwich Village** the bohemian capital of the US in the first decades of the 20C. The cultural ferment there produced a number of literary magazines whose contributors included experimental poet **e.e. cummings** and novelist **Floyd Dell**. The Greenwich Village productions of the plays of **Eugene O'Neill** (*Desire Under the Elms*, 1924) brought him recognition as the period's preeminent American play-wright. And **F. Scott**

Fitzgerald (*The Great Gatsby*, 1925) established himself as the foremost chronicler of the jazz age.

In Chicago, the aftermath of the 1893 World's Columbian Exposition spawned a literary renaissance in that city, which served as the backdrop for social realists **Henry Blake Fuller** (*The Cliff Dwellers*, 1893), **Theodore Dreiser** (*Sister Carrie*, 1900), **Frank Norris** (**The Pit**, 1903) and **Upton Sinclair** (*The Jungle*, 1906). Rural New England formed the subject for the poems of **Robert Frost**, who lived most of his life in the region, while works by **Sherwood Anderson** (*Winesburg*, Ohio, 1919), **Sinclair Lewis** (*Main Street*, 1920) and playwright **Thornton Wilder** (*Our Town*, 1938) explored the nature of small-town America.

A number of writers fled the political upheaval of America in the aftermath of World War I for Paris. There, the literary salon of Gertrude Stein nurtured young American writers, among them **Henry Miller, William Carlos Williams** and **Ernest Hemingway**, who described the intellectual atmosphere of Paris in the 1920s in *A Moveable Feast* (1964).

In the 1930s, Mississippi native **William Faulkner** fictionalized the setting of his boyhood in a series of tales that explored societal, racial and moral tensions in the South. Faulkner's work began a revival of Southern literature by **Marjorie Kinnan Rawlings** (*The Yearling*, 1938), **Carson McCullers** (*The Heart Is a Lonely Hunter*, 1940), **Robert Penn Warren** (*All the King's Men*, 1946), **Eudora Welty** (*Delta Wedding*, 1946), **Flannery O'Connor** (*Wise Blood*, 1952) and playwright **Tennessee Williams** (*Cat on a Hot Tin Roof*, 1955).

The celebration of black culture, the struggle for integration and civil rights, and the experiences of African Americans in both the South and the North have provided the themes of African-American writing in the 20C.

The **Harlem Renaissance** of arts beginning in the 1920s drew black writers from around the eastern US, including poet **Langston Hughes** (*Shakespeare in Harlem*, 1942), **Ralph Ellison** (*Invisible Man*, 1952) and **Zora Neale Hurston**

F. Scott Fitzgerald c. 1930

© UPPA/Photoshot

(*Their Eyes Were Watching God*, 1937). Chicago's slums formed the backdrop for works by **Richard Wright** (*Native Son*, 1940) and poet **Gwendolyn Brooks** (*The Bean Eaters*, 1960).

Contemporary African-American writers include **Maya Angelou** (*I Know Why the Caged Bird Sings*, 1969), who delivered her poem at President Clinton's 1993 inauguration; poet **Rita Dove** (*Thomas and Beulah*, 1986) and authors **Toni Morrison** (*Beloved*, 1987) and **Alice Walker** (*The Color Purple*, 1982).

Although New York City is considered the nation's literary capital, contemporary writers flourish all over the eastern US. Recognized figures include novelists **Tom Wolfe** (*The Bonfire of the Vanities*, 1987) and **John Updike** (the *Rabbit* series, ending with *Rabbit at Rest*, 1990); and playwrights **Wendy Wasserstein** (*The Heidi Chronicles*, 1988) and **Edward Albee** (*Three Tall Women*, 1994).

21ST CENTURY

Contemporary American authors who won a Pulitzer Prize for their work in the first decade of the 21C include **Jhumpa Lahiri** (*Interpreter of Maladies*, 2000); **Michael Chabon**, (*The Amazing Adventures of Kavalier & Clay*, 2000); **Junot Diaz** (*The Brief Wondrous Life of Oscar Wao*, 2007); and **Elizabeth Strout** (*Olive Kitteridge*, 2008). The most recent winner for fiction is **Adam Johnson** (*The Orphan Master's Son*, 2013).

Sports and Recreation

For exercise, for entertainment, for drama and for fellowship, Americans love to play sports and watch sports. Almost no event inspires more patriotic spirit than the quadrennial Olympic Games, and a year-round slate of professional, collegiate and amateur competition keeps the fever pitch high. Collegiate sports, particularly football and basketball, attract the excited attention of fans and alumni nationwide, especially during the annual college football "bowl games" in January and the "Final Four" basketball tournament in March.

TOP BALL GAMES

Sometimes called the "national pastime," **baseball** originated in 1845 in New York City, when the New York Knickerbockers Base Ball Club set down the rules that eventually developed into the modern game. Played on a diamond-shaped field, the corners of which are marked by three bases and a home plate, baseball inspires legions of devoted fans who follow teams with religious intensity. Although it may appear slow-paced, the game can be fraught with suspense, the outcome often resting on a final confrontation between pitcher and batter—when victory can vanish with a ball thrown just off-center or a bat swung seconds too late. Following **spring training**, which many teams spend at practice facilities in Florida, the professional season runs from April to October, culminating in the **World Series**, a best-of-seven-games match between the American and National League champs.

Fast-paced **basketball** draws participants and spectators from every walk of life. Players in this sport score goals by successfully throwing a ball through hoops suspended at either end of an indoor court. The National Basketball Association (NBA) organizes some 29 professional teams throughout the US, all competing for a berth in the **NBA Finals** held in June. Founded in 1997, the 12-team Women's National Basketball Association (WNBA) brought women's basketball to the professional level. Appealing for its potent combination of brute force and skilled maneuvering,

American **football** demands strength, speed and agility from its players in their quest to carry, pass and kick the football down a 300ft-long field to the goal.

The National Football League (NFL) oversees some 32 teams in two conferences: the American and the National Football Conference. Football season begins in late summer and culminates in late January with the annual **Super Bowl** contest between the conference champions; the game draws more viewers each year than any other televised event.

OTHER PRO SPORTS

Though **ice hockey** was born in Canada, it was in the US that the sport rose to the professional level. In this breakneck sport, skated players use sticks to maneuver a hard rubber puck into a goal at either end of an ice arena. The 29-team National Hockey League (NHL) pits Canadian and American teams in an annual race for the coveted **Stanley Cup**, with finals held in June.

Golf originated in Scotland; however, the US now ranks as the preeminent golf nation. Public and private courses abound, especially in the Southeast, where the climate allows play nearly year-round—Florida alone claims more than 1,000 golf courses. Audiences flock to important international tournaments, such as the annual **Masters** in Augusta, Georgia. America also hosts the **US Open**; held in Flushing Meadow, New York, this tournament ranks among the top four in the world.

New York Knicks vs. Milwaukee Bucks at Madison Square Garden, New York City

© Y. Saito/Michelin

The world's largest single-day sporting event, the annual **Indianapolis 500** (⟳see INDIANAPOLIS) pits 33 top international contenders against each other, while Florida's **Daytona 500** attracts diehard stock-car fans.

An aura of romance surrounds the annual **Kentucky Derby** (⟳see LOUISVILLE) horse race at Churchill Downs in Louisville; the race marks the first contest in the famed **Triple Crown** series of thoroughbred horseracing.

Though not a professional event, the prestigious **Boston Marathon** footrace, which celebrated its hundredth anniversary in 1996, numbers among the world's important marathons, attracting runners from around the globe.

RECREATION HEAVEN

From skiing in New England's White Mountains to surfing off the coast of Florida, from white-water rafting on Pennsylvania's Youghiogheny River to hiking the 2,050mi **Appalachian Trail** (⟳see PLANNING YOUR TRIP), the eastern US offers countless opportunities for recreation. Seekers of physical fitness and natural beauty take full advantage of the East's wealth of mountains, forests, rivers and oceanfront, as well as urban parks and bike and running paths. In-line skating, snowboarding and mountain biking are all relatively recent additions to the panoply of popular recreational sports. In recent years thrill-seekers ever in search of a new challenge have popularized **extreme sports**, riskier versions of already established pursuits, with names like big-air snowboarding, skysurfing, and downhill skating.

OFFBEAT ADVENTURES

Americans are best known for following and playing sports like baseball and football but across the nation's towns and cities, there are plenty off quirky and offbeat adventures to be had (or to watch).

Though the US's biggest dog mushing event, the Iditarod, takes place in Alaska, eastern residents in colder climates also enjoy the sport. Visitors can give it a try in states throughout most of the northeast, including Pennsylvania, New Jersey, New York, Vermont, New Hampshire and Maine. For those who prefer a super quirky (and dogfree) take on dog mushing, there is the annual Iditarod in New York City, where teams race shopping carts along a route.

Other offbeat American sports opportunities to play and watch include curling; duckpin bowling, a version of the game popular in New England as well as Baltimore, which uses smaller balls than traditional ten-pin bowling; and stock car racing.

Nature

From north to south, the eastern United States offers a wealth of opportunities to observe—and play in—nature.

Great Smoky Mountains National Park, North Carolina © Matej Krajcovic/iStockphoto.com

Landscapes

A sojourn in the eastern US is a glimpse into the heart of what most travelers agree is one of the most diverse, overwhelming and contradictory lands on earth. This most populous part of the US offers visitors incomparable opportunities for scenic, recreational, historical and cultural excursions in an epic landscape of contrasts: rocky outcroppings on Maine's chilly shore and suffocating heat in the Mississippi delta, concrete canyons on Manhattan Island (New York City) and isolated "hollers" (small secluded valleys) in deepest Appalachia.

The sheer size of the country can be astonishing: the distance from New York City to Miami is 1,291mi; from New York City to Chicago is 831mi. Indeed, visitors seeking a sense of "how America lives" are often surprised at the distances ordinary citizens travel daily to work or school. For tourists, most of this travel occurs on the road. For better or worse, the US is a country best viewed by chartered tour bus or private automobile, along the nation's vast interstate highway system (45,000mi spanning the 48 contiguous states), which links every state, large metropolis and region.

The highways and byways of the eastern US lead through vistas of great beauty, both natural and man-made. A car trip through New England coasts past a rugged shoreline and bucolic farms. Farther south, the spires of New York City crown an elongated metropolis running southward to Washington, DC. Heading west, the urban centers of Chicago and St. Louis anchor a vast midwestern agricultural region rippling with "amber waves of grain." In Kentucky, thoroughbred horses graze on the "bluegrass," while in the Deep South, the broad Suwannee River joins a meandering network of streams winding their way through moss-draped live oak, cypress and palmetto trees to the sea. In some respects the sheer size of the country and the American spirit of free enterprise has not always been kind to the land. Relentless commercialization plagues the landscape: farms have been replaced by mega-malls and parking lots; roads are lined with strips of shops, monotonous suburbs and the blinking neon signs of fast-food restaurants and gas stations.

Still, beneath the surface clutter lies a fascinating country with distinct regional differences, each offering unique environmental and ecological features. The eastern US has thousands of miles of coastline; a climate that ranges from bitter cold to tropical; an ancient, 1,500mi-long mountain range; five of the world's largest freshwater lakes and one of its longest rivers; and vegetation ranging from boreal forests to mangrove swamps.

The observant traveler will find insights into the United States' immense variety with every new bend in the road, as the roots of the country's art, music, literature and history spring vividly to life.

GEOLOGY

Scientists theorize that parts of the North American continent date back almost four billion years. The stable crust underlying the Canadian Shield, the continent's north central portion, was formed around 1.8 billion years ago; millions of years later, during the Paleozoic Era, this existing plate collided with other land masses to form the supercontinent of **Pangaea**. Geologic evidence indicates that the Appalachian Mountains resulted from folds in the earth's crust caused by repeated collisions during the formation of Pangaea. With a birth date of sometime between 435 million and 250 million years ago, these heavily forested, relatively low-lying eastern mountains (rising about

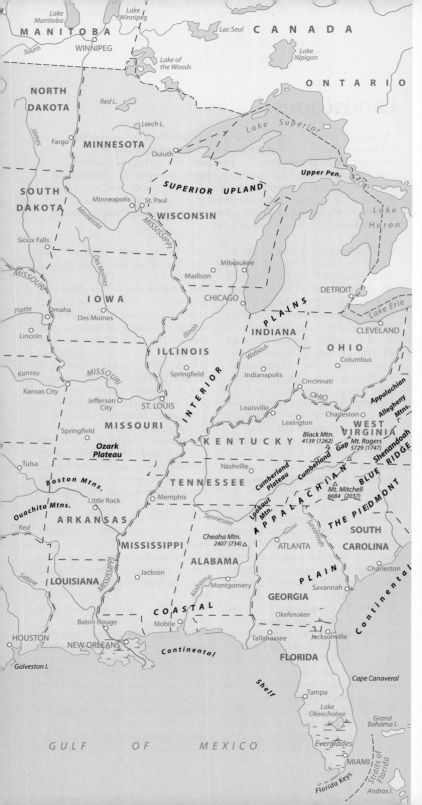

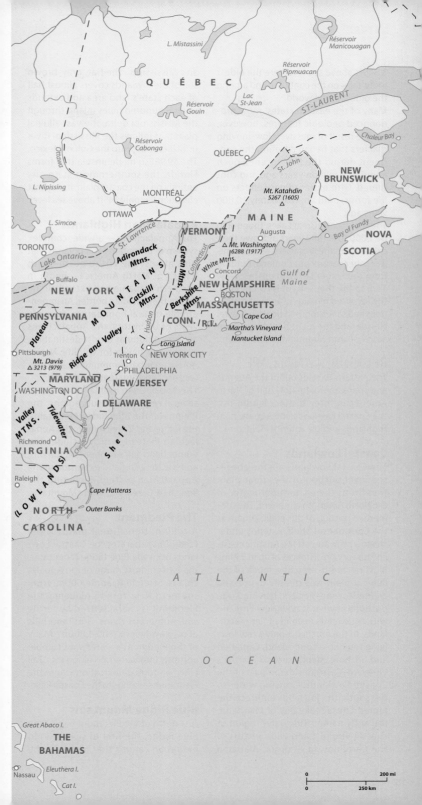

3,500ft above sea level) are the oldest mountains on the continent and among the oldest in the world.

Many of the eastern states' most pronounced geologic features, however, are the result of massive, slow-moving **glaciers** that began covering the continent during the Pleistocene Epoch about one million years ago and continued, with extraordinary effects on life forms, until approximately 10,000 years ago.

The spectacular Great Lakes, thought to be 7,000 to 32,000 years old, owe their existence to these glaciers, as do countless other natural phenomena, ranging from the Finger Lakes of upstate New York to the thin soils of New England, the fossilized remains of ancient mastodons and saber-toothed tigers in coastal Florida, and the giant boulders strewn atop Lookout Mountain in Tennessee.

REGIONAL LANDSCAPES

The eastern US rises out of the Atlantic and spans approximately half of North America in three distinct landforms: the Coastal Lowlands, the Appalachian Highlands and the Interior Plains.

Coastal Lowlands

The Coastal Lowlands are the above-sea-level portion of the great plain that forms the eastern perimeter of the North American continent. The submerged portion of this plain, known as the **Continental Shelf**, extends under shallow seawater off the Atlantic coastline for varying distances of up to 250mi. In its northern stretches, much of the coastal plain was deeply depressed by Pleistocene glaciers, leaving large portions of what is now New England with rocky cliffs instead of flat marshlands. In the northeast only a few low-lying regions—Long Island, Cape Cod and offshore islands such as Martha's Vineyard—are considered part of the Coastal Lowlands. Growing wider to the south, the lowlands embrace the famed Chesapeake Bay of Maryland, the aptly named Tidewater region of coastal Virginia, and wide swaths of the Carolinas. In Georgia, Alabama

and Mississippi, the flat, gray-brown soil of the lowlands covers almost half of each state's land area and extends several hundred miles inland through the Mississippi delta, the vast alluvial plain that follows the Mississippi River until it empties into the Gulf of Mexico. The 59,988sq mi peninsula that forms Florida, the southernmost state, sits entirely on the coastal plain; its highest elevation lies only 345ft above sea level.

Appalachian Highlands

The Appalachians—a wide, complex system of mountains and uplands that runs almost the entire north-south length of North America—begin in northern Alabama and extend all the way to the Canadian border. An impenetrable natural boundary in the early years of US history, the Appalachians are now a popular tourist destination, as well as a haven for wildlife, Native American tribal communities, and professional and amateur naturalists.

The Appalachian Highlands consist of several regions and subregions: the Piedmont; the Blue Ridge Mountains; the Ridge and Valley region; the Appalachian Plateau, which includes the Cumberland and Allegheny Mountains; and the New England extension of the Appalachian system, including the Berkshire, Green, and White Mountains.

The Piedmont

A rolling, transitional plateau, the Piedmont separates the Coastal Lowlands from the Blue Ridge Mountains, the easternmost range of the Appalachians. Stretching some 600mi from southern New York to Alabama, the Piedmont is characterized by fertile soil, numerous rivers, and long hills of modest height (300-1,800ft). Many of the Piedmont's waterways tumble abruptly into waterfalls along the "Fall Line," a rough demarcation where the Piedmont descends to the Coastal Plain.

Blue Ridge Mountains

Just north of the Piedmont begins the Blue Ridge, the first of several long mountain ranges that make up the

Appalachian Mountain system. So named because its dense forests appear bluish from a distance, the Blue Ridge starts in northeast Georgia and includes Great Smoky Mountains National Park and the highest peak in the eastern US—**Mt. Mitchell**—which towers 6,684ft near Asheville, North Carolina. Although the southern Blue Ridge includes multiple rows of mountains, its northern end is easily identifiable as the long narrow ridge—traversed by the scenic Blue Ridge Parkway—forming the eastern border of Virginia's Shenandoah Valley.

Ridge and Valley Region

West of the Blue Ridge, the Ridge and Valley region divides the broad middle of the Appalachian Highlands into long northeast-southwest ridges and wide, fertile valleys. The Great Valley, a 20-80mi-wide limestone-based trench, runs almost the entire length of the Appalachians. It begins in the north as the valley of Vermont and extends through the Hudson River Valley to become the Cumberland, Lebanon, and Lehigh valleys of Pennsylvania, the Shenandoah in Virginia, the Valley of East Tennessee, Rome Valley in Georgia, and the Great Valley in north Alabama. The ridges in this region rise to 1,000ft and may run unbroken for 10-20mi.

Appalachian Plateau

Immediately west of the Ridge and Valley region is a high, ridged plateau ribboned by the Tennessee River and its tributaries and marked by several additional mountain ranges, notably the Cumberland Mountains of Tennessee and the Alleghenies, which run northeasterly through Virginia and Pennsylvania to southern New York State.

On the southern edge of the plateau lies the famed **Cumberland Gap** (◔see EAST TENNESSEE), a major east-west route for 18C pioneers. In its northern stretches, the Appalachian Plateau is a land of thin soil and rocky terrain, and enormous deposits of bituminous coal. Known as Appalachia—once a synonym for impoverished, exploited mountain communities—these coal-mining regions of eastern Kentucky, southwest Virginia, West Virginia, and Pennsylvania fueled the early railroads and stoked the furnaces of steel mills, automobile manufacturers and other industries in cities such as Pittsburgh and Detroit for generations—often at great environmental and human cost. The region remains an important source of coal for industry and electricity generation.

New England Region

Although separated from the main expanse of the Appalachians by the Hudson River Valley, the numerous small mountain ranges of New England are generally considered part of the Appalachian Plateau. These landforms echo certain patterns of the southern Appalachians: the ridges and valleys around New England's Berkshire and **Green Mountains** look remarkably like the Ridge and Valley region of Virginia. The highest peak, **Mt. Washington** (6,288ft), in New Hampshire's White Mountains, strongly resembles the Blue Ridge range.

By contrast, the **Adirondacks** of northern New York State are younger, more rugged, and more closely related, geologically speaking, to the Superior Uplands of northern Wisconsin and Michigan.

THE INTERIOR PLAINS

West of the Appalachian Mountain system lies the great heartland of America—the Interior Plains. The eastern portion of this enormous landlocked area is distinguished by three striking features: the Great Lakes, which connect the Interior Plains via the St. Lawrence River to the Atlantic Ocean; the upper Mississippi River system, which provides a transportation link, via the Chicago and the Illinois rivers, from the Great Lakes to the Gulf of Mexico; and an abundance of rich, dark soil, ideal for growing corn and grain and raising cattle.

Great Lakes

Taken together, the five Great Lakes have a combined area of 94,510sq mi and are the largest group of freshwater lakes in the world. In order of size, **Lake Superior** is largest, at some 32,000sq mi; next are **Lake Huron** and **Lake Michigan**, each around 23,000sq mi; then **Lake Erie**, markedly shallower than the others; and the smallest, **Lake Ontario**, about as large as the state of New Jersey.

Spanning the border between the US and the Canadian provinces of Ontario and Quebec, these five giant lakes form a vast inland water system that affects not only climate, flora and fauna, but human activity as well. Along with recreational and scenic benefits, the Great Lakes and their eastern outlet, the **St. Lawrence River**, have long served as a vital trade route for the region.

Mississippi River System

Nicknamed "the Big Muddy," the slow-moving Mississippi River is a mile wide in some places, usually looks opaque and murky brown, and is navigable by barge for almost 1,200mi—virtually the entire north-south length of the central US, from Minneapolis south to the Gulf of Mexico. The Mississippi and its tributaries, the Illinois, Wabash and Ohio rivers, drain the eastern portion of the Interior Plains and are largely responsible for the rich alluvial soils that support the farm belts of Wisconsin, Indiana and Illinois.

CLIMATE

Situated between 25 and 50 degrees latitude, the eastern US is divided between the **humid subtropical** and **humid continental** climate zones. Although great differences exist between northern and southern states in terms of winter temperatures, length of summers and types of precipitation, the terrain east of the Rockies is subject to high humidity and summer temperatures of at least 75°F; the coastal plain as far north as New York City, frequently suffers temperatures well into the 90s. Southern states—Louisiana, Mississippi, Alabama, Georgia, Florida, and North and South Carolina—are legendary for oppressively hot and humid

summers, which while ideal for mosquitoes, can cause heat stroke in the unwary. Only along the Great Lakes, in the Appalachians, and in New England are summer temperatures comfortable without air-conditioning. The southern half of the eastern US and the East Coast generally get between 40 and 80 inches of precipitation per year, while the drier northern portion receives between 20 and 40 inches.

In much of **New England**, winter temperatures routinely hover in the low to mid-teens (10-20°F) and snow may blanket the ground for weeks, making downhill skiing a popular pastime in the mountains of upstate New York, New Hampshire and Vermont. Although the Great Lakes temper the climate in the Midwest, Chicago is famous for its cold, windy winters, and the inland farming regions endure much snow. In contrast, from the **Appalachian Plateau** southward to the Piedmont, winter temperatures often dip below freezing at night but rise to 35-40°F during the day. While the mountain peaks may be dusted with snow, the valleys get snow only intermittently. In the **Piedmont**, where snow is rare, freezing rain is a winter hazard. Along the **Coastal Lowlands**, winters are rainy and mild (often 50-60°F), enabling farmers to grow abundant winter crops of vegetables. Off the southern tip of Florida, Key West ranks as the nation's hottest city with an average year-round temperature of 77.4°F.

The eastern states are also subject to violent storms. Intense tropical cyclones called **hurricanes** (⚓ see PLANNING YOUR TRIP, Nature and Safety), with winds ranging from 74 to 200mph, can pound the Gulf and Atlantic coasts between June and October. Powerful **"northeasters"** roar off the North Atlantic into New England in winter, dropping up to 10 inches of snow. And summer thunderstorms can spawn the vicious winds of funnel-shaped **tornadoes** that spiral at speeds of up to 300 mph—most commonly through the central and southern plains. The Mississippi River Valley, for example, endures more tornadoes than any other region on earth.

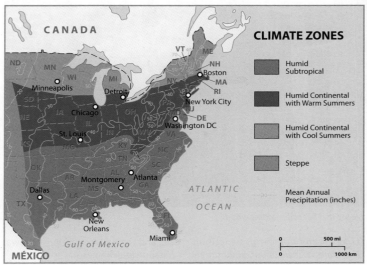

CLIMATE ZONES

Humid Subtropical

Humid Continental with Warm Summers

Humid Continental with Cool Summers

Steppe

Mean Annual Precipitation (inches)

0   500 mi
0   1000 km

After Glenn T. Trewartha "*Elements of Physical Geography*", 1957.

Flora and Fauna

The eastern US enjoys a great diversity of vegetation and wildlife, as might be expected in so large a region. In fact, the Southern Appalachians are generally considered to hold greater biological diversity than any other region of the world, with the possible exception of certain tropical rain forests. On one three-hour Appalachian hike from the lower to the uppermost elevations, observant visitors will note that 98 percent of the vegetation changes from bottom to top, representing nearly every kind of habitat common in eastern North America.

FLORA

A small sliver of **boreal forest**—the northernmost, highest-altitude forest type on the continent—runs down the spine of the Appalachians from Canada to Georgia. Consisting primarily of tall conifers—pine, hemlock, spruce and fir—the dense, moist boreal forest also accommodates an undercover of flowering **rhododendrons**, wildflowers such as trilliums, and forest-floor mosses, mushrooms and lichens.

Hiking at slightly lower elevations, visitors will likely encounter a band of **transitional forest**, a combination of conifers (hemlocks, firs) and regionally distinct species of deciduous trees: yellow birch (*Betula alleghaniensis*) and

sugar maple (*Acer saccharum*) in New England, or American basswood (*Tilia americana*) and quaking aspen (*Populus tremuloides*) along the Great Lakes. Speckled with patches of sunlight, the transitional-forest floor supports a lively undergrowth of ferns, smaller trees and shrubs.

In broad outline, the transitional forest extends westward from Maine to Minnesota, surrounding the Great Lakes and covering much of New York and Pennsylvania. A narrow band runs southward along the Appalachians.

By far the largest proportion of existing forests in the eastern US, however, are of the **mixed deciduous** type: broadleaf hardwoods such as yellow poplar

Moose and her calf in Maine woods

(*Liriodendron tulipifera*), sweetgum (*Liquidambar styraciflua*), and numerous species of oak and hickory mixed with evergreens, primarily pines (eastern white, loblolly, pitch, shortleaf, Virginia), magnolias, and smaller trees such as the American holly (*Ilex opaca*). Interspersed with cleared fields and natural meadows, this variegated habitat extends south and west through the heartland, stretching from Massachusetts to Ohio, Indiana, Illinois, Wisconsin, and the eastern portions of Iowa, Missouri and Minnesota.

In the Ozark Highlands of Arkansas, the distinctive **oak-hickory forest** represents the westernmost manifestation of deciduous forests in the US.

At higher elevations, especially in New England and the Appalachians, these forests attract millions of visitors every fall during "**leaf season**," when the hardwoods' leaves change from green to brilliant red, yellow, orange and gold.

The **Southern pinelands** describes the varied landscapes of the Piedmont and coastal plain. Extending for some 3,000sq mi from New Jersey's Pine Barrens to Florida and westward along the Gulf of Mexico to Louisiana, the pinelands cover most of the Deep South.

In northern areas, pines (longleaf, loblolly, shortleaf, slash, sand) commingle with deciduous trees; close to the coast, pinelands include live oaks draped with Spanish moss, hardwood hammocks, cypress swamps, maritime forests, bogs and bayous.

The Florida peninsula's dominant vegetation type is essentially **subtropical forest**, in a temperate zone. Boasting several hundred species of palm trees (only 15 of which are native), this vacation paradise encompasses not only beaches, but also slash-pine forests with saw-palmetto floors, air plants, glades, and mangroves—the only trees known to survive in saltwater.

Bald Eagle

FAUNA

Were it not for human intervention, the wonderfully rich and diverse environment of the eastern US would support an extraordinary wildlife population. Some 200 years ago, the land was well-stocked with large game (bear, moose, deer, mountain lion); the skies full of songbirds and soaring raptors (eagles, falcons, hawks); the waters full of beaver, otter, brown and speckled trout; and the meadows sheltered myriad smaller animals such as foxes, wolves, bobcats, raccoons, opossums, rabbits and shrews.

However in 21C America, habitat destruction and an increasingly intrusive human presence have pushed larger animals into ever-smaller, more isolated high-country regions. Only a few large mammals—notably, black bears (*Ursus americanus*) and white-tailed deer (*Odocoileus virginianus*)—have adapted to human co-habitation. Meanwhile, the reduction of natural predators has boosted stocks of grazing animals; deer bounding along roadsides are a common hazard to rural drivers. In state and national forests, park rangers repeatedly warn hikers to protect their foodstuffs and refrain from feeding the bears.

Orchestrated breeding and restoration efforts have reestablished viable populations of bald eagles (*Haliaeetus leucocephalus*), golden eagles (*Aquila chrysaetos*) and peregrine falcons (*Falco peregrinus*); the banning of chemical substances such as DDT has helped improve songbird and fish populations; and coastal areas strictly prohibit interference with endangered sea turtles' nests or human interaction with wild dolphins. On the other hand, an attempt by federal wildlife experts to reintroduce the gray wolf (*Canis lupus*) to its original eastern habitats has met with opposition from farmers and hunters.

In populated areas, casual visitors are unlikely to glimpse any but the most common birds and small mammals—blue jays, robins, mourning doves, rabbits, chipmunks and squirrels. For the more watchful, sightings of humming-birds, pileated woodpeckers (*Dryoco-pus pileatus*), red-tailed hawks (*Buteo jamaicensis*) and raccoons (*Procyon lotor*) are quite possible. The coastal and mountainous areas offer variety and accessibility for viewing greater numbers of wildlife, especially in protected areas such as Great Smoky Mountains National Park and designated national forest preserves. Florida's 1.5 million-acre Everglades National Park, supports more than 350 species of birds, both year-round and migratory, and 600 species of fish, alligators, snakes, mammals and sea turtles. Ranging from the large, black and easily recognized anhinga (*Anhinga anhinga*) to little blue herons (*Egretta caerulea*), elusive American bitterns (*Botaurus lentiginosus*), and endangered wood storks (*Mycteria americana*), the Everglades' winged wildlife draws bird-watchers from around the globe. In addition to birds, the world's last remaining Florida panthers (*Felis concolor coryl*) prowl the Everglades, and the endangered American crocodile (*Crocodylus acutus*) thrives here—as does its cousin the American alligator (*Alligator mississippiensis*), now plentiful in swamps throughout the South.

Like native species in many highly developed areas of the world, the indigenous flora and fauna of the eastern US fight a constant battle against not only human encroachment, but importation of nonindigenous species. For example, the glorious American chestnut trees (*Castanea dentata*) that once reigned throughout the Appalachians were decimated by a blight caused by an accidentally imported fungus first identified in New York City in 1904. By 1945 the species was all but wiped out, though sprouts continue to grow from old roots. Kudzu (*Pueraria thunbergiana*), a hardy vine introduced from Japan in 1911 to help control erosion, now twines its way over millions of acres in the Southeast, suffocating native pines and shrubs in its greedy grip. In the animal kingdom, imports like the European wild boar (*Sus scrofa*) have had a profound negative impact on native plants and animals.

Discovering
USA East

Louisiana Cajun Country
© Eric Lucas/Michelin

New York
New Jersey
Pennsylvania

Hall of Saurischian Dinosaurs, American Museum of Natural History, New York City

New York City Area

New York is arguably the most stimulating and sophisticated urban center in the US, and its environs, north along the Hudson River Valley, among the most beautiful. The 301sq mi city proper consists of five boroughs: Manhattan, Brooklyn, Queens, the Bronx and Staten Island. They spread over miles of mainland, scattered islets and a chunk of western Long Island. "The island" itself ranks as the biggest land mass adjoining the continental US, covering an estimated 1,377sq mi as it stretches eastward opposite the Connecticut coast almost as far as Rhode Island. The area of Long Island that sits close to the city features densely-populated suburbs, but the relatively quiet forked "tail" at the eastern end of the island offers an unforgettably lovely seaside landscape of bluffs, dunes and salt ponds.

Highlights

1 The view from inside the **Statue of Liberty's** crown (p128)
2 Chinese New Year parade (p132)
3 The **Tenement Museum** (p133)
4 Ice skating on Central Park's **Wollman Rink** (p138)
5 Hudson River Valley **mansions** (p141-143)

New York City

New York Harbor with the Statue of Liberty and Manhattan skyline

©Terraxplorer/iStockphoto.com

GETTING THERE

John F. Kennedy International Airport (JFK): ☎718-244-4444; 15mi southeast of Midtown. Information counters in all terminals. **LaGuardia Airport (LGA):** ☎718-533-3400; 8mi northeast of Midtown. Information counter between Concourses C and D on departure level. **Newark International Aiport (EWR):** ☎973-961-6000; 16mi southwest of Midtown. Information counter in terminal B, lower level.

For further information on all three airports, including ground transportation options (car rental agencies, the AirTrain from JFK, taxis, car and van services, and buses) contact: Port Authority of New York & New Jersey ☎212-435-7000, www.panynj.gov. Rental car agencies are located at the airports.

Pennsylvania Railroad Station (32nd St. & Seventh Ave.) provides national and regional rail service by **Amtrak**, ☎800-872-7245, www.amtrak.com; **Long Island Railroad**, ☎718-217-5477; and **New Jersey Transit**, ☎973-275-5555. **Grand Central Railroad Terminal** (42nd St. & Park Ave.) provides local service by **Metro-North**, ☎212-532-4900. **Port Authority Bus Terminal** (42nd St. & Eighth Ave.) provides bus service by **Greyhound** (☎800-231-2222; www.greyhound.com) and **Peter Pan** (☎800-343-9999 www.peterpanbus.com).

GETTING AROUND

Bus and **subway** maps and timetables are available on buses, at subway stations and visitor information centers, or online (www.mta.info/nyct/maps/index.html). The Travel Information Center (☎718-330-1234) offers route and fare information. Foreign language information: ☎718-330-4847. All fares $2.25 one-way. **Taxi:** Yellow Medallion cabs www.nycgo.com/articles/nyc-transportation-getting-around).

VISITOR INFORMATION

For a free visit planner, maps and information on accommodations, shopping, entertainment, festivals and recreations, contact **NYC & Company,** the city's convention and visitors bureau, 810 Seventh Ave., New York NY 10019, ☎212-484-1222, www.nycgo.com; or **Times Square Information Center**, 1560 7th Ave. between 46th & 47th Sts., ☎212-452-5283, www.timessquarenyc.org.

A City for All Seasons

North of the city, a succession of historic houses and Revolutionary War sites advances up the Hudson River Valley in a living catalog of American history and architecture. This landscape, immortalized by the artists of the Hudson River school, ranks among the most spectacular in the Northeast. The valley, the city and Long Island offer every imaginable diversion and recreational pastime. Because of the beaches, summer is a great time to visit Long Island, but it is also the busiest. Many people favor the fall for exploring the greater New York City region, when nature explodes in a blaze of color as Indian summer arrives. Temperatures (usually) range from the 50s to the 70s making autumn the ideal time of year to visit the Hudson River Valley.

Great Hall, Metropolitan Museum of Art

Courtesy The Metropolitan Museum of Art. © Brooks Walker 2002

ADDRESSES

🛏️STAY

$$$$$ New York Palace – 455 Madison Ave., New York City. ✗♿🅿️☎️212-888-7000. www.newyorkpalace.com. 909 rooms. The entrance to this 55-story skyscraper is the 19C Villard House opposite Midtown's St. Patrick's Cathedral. Just inside, you'll see the mansion's original molded ceilings before descending the grand staircase into the marble-columned lobby. The rooms are pricey but for NYC, quite large. Maloney and Porcelli serves American classics with a twist.

$$$$ Castle Hotel & Spa – 400 Benedict Ave., Tarrytown, NY. ✗♿🅿️☎️914-631-1980 or 800-616-4487. www.castlehotel andspa.com. 31 rooms. Resembling a medieval fort—with towers and arched windows—this mansion sits on a hilltop overlooking the Hudson River 25mi north of New York City. Inside, stained-glass windows, Oriental rugs and period tapestries soften beamed ceilings and stone walls. Hand-carved four-poster beds (tower suites only) draped in goose-down comforters, and custom-made chandeliers decorate the rooms. Dinner at **Equus** is memorable.

$$$$ Washington Square Hotel – 103 Waverly Pl., New York City. ✗☎️212-777-9515. www.washingtonsquarehotel. 152 rooms. Across Washington Square Park in Greenwich Village, this intimate 1910 property is introduced by the small, green-and-white marble lobby, with hand-painted tile murals of wildflowers. Rooms have Art Deco furniture and complimentary wired high-speed Internet access.

$$$$ W New York – 541 Lexington Ave., New York City. ✗♿🅿️☎️212-755-1200. www.wnewyork.com. 688 rooms. Earth, wind, fire and water are the cardinal elements that inspired this hotel's Zen-like ambience. Relaxing earth tones, fluffy feather beds and top amenities compensate for the small bedrooms.

$$$ Casablanca Hotel– 147 W. 43rd St., New York City. 🛏️♿ ☎️212-869-1212. www.casablancahotel.com. 45 rooms. This small and cozy Midtown hotel offers complimentary continental breakfast, free afternoon tea and complimentary wine and cheese reception in the evening. The staff is friendly and helpful and Wi-Fi is free.

$$ 380 Inn – 380 Montauk Hwy., Wainscott, NY. 🅿️ ☎️631-527-7000. www.380inn.com. 19 rooms. Free Wi-Fi is a perk at this East Hampton area motel located conveniently to the beach (2mi away) and a golf course. Rooms have hardwood floors and some have kitchenettes. A swimming pool is open in warm weather.

🍽️EAT

$$$ Park Avenue Cafe – 100 E. 63rd St., New York City. ☎️212-644-1900. www.parkavenyc.com. **American.** As the seasons change, so does this Upper East Side restaurant; from one season to the next, even the decor becomes a whole new experience. The menu is heavy on fresh seafood and modern takes on American classics like burgers and chicken and waffles. Try its signature chocolate cube dessert, filled with caramel mousse.

$$$ The Boathouse – 72nd St. & Park Dr. N., New York City. ☎️212-517-2233. www.thecentralparkboathouse. Lunch and brunch year-round; dinner from April-November only. **Contemporary.** At the Loeb Boathouse in Central Park, the lakeside eatery offers delicious respite from the cold during colder months and, when NYC heats up, one of the best outdoor seating areas in the city.

$$ Gramercy Tavern – 42 E. 20th St., New York City ☎️212-477-0777. www.gramercytavern.com. **Contemporary.** This cozy Gramercy Park spot wins rave reviews for contemporary fare that's more about comfort than panache—and the incredibly knowledgable (and service-oriented) staff.

$$ Carnegie Deli – 854 7th St., New York City ☎️212-757-2245. www.carnegiedeli.com. **Delicatessen.** A Big Apple fixture since 1937, this New York institution with the bright yellow sign and red awning is famous for salty service and among other delights, mile-high pastrami sandwiches, pot roast, bagels, and cheesecake. Open daily from 6:30am, the Deli offers a breakfast, lunch and dinner menu for dine-in or take-out.

New York City★★★

New York City is a world unto itself thanks to its dynamic economic activity, cultural life and the sheer number of people who live there. It's also a million different worlds—every visitor can experience it in their own way. The area, once wooded and wild, was the province of Native Americans until Giovanni da Verrazano began the influx of Europeans in 1524. First a Dutch colony, then British by 1664, New York blossomed as an important trading post. The city was among the first British targets during the Revolution; British troops occupied the area for the duration of the war.

▶ **Population:** 8,363,710
◔ **Michelin Map:** p115 and p123.
▤ **Info:** ✆212-484-1222; www.nycgo.com.
ℙ **Parking:** Parking in NYC is expensive and difficult; save your time and money and take the subways and buses, or hail a cab.
◕ **Timing:** Plan gallery hopping mid-week: most art galleries and museums are closed on Mondays.
▲▲ **Kids:** The gold vault in the Federal Reserve Bank of New York will wow youngsters.

A BIT OF HISTORY

Between 1785 and 1790, New York served as US capital and hosted the inauguration of George Washington, the first president. By 1820, the city was the most densely populated in the nation, growing steadily as the flow of European immigrants accelerated. A prosperous shipping and banking center, New York established itself as a cultural mecca and home to a burgeoning upper class following the success of America's first world's fair held in the city in 1853. Commercial and industrial growth perpetuated a rush of immigration that ebbed and flowed into the 20C. In 1898, the five boroughs were bundled into Greater New York City, creating a metropolis of three million people, the largest in the world.

At the dawn of the 20C, the city grew skyward as architects developed new ways to construct ever-taller buildings. Theater and the arts flourished, fueled by a large contingent of avant-garde writers, poets, thespians and artists who lived in Greenwich Village and other enclaves. In Harlem, African-American arts, letters and music flowered. While the trials of the stock market crash in 1929, the ensuing depression, gangster activity and World War II took their toll, New York endured to solidify its international position in industry, commerce and finance in the late 1940s. New immigrants from Puerto Rico and Asia contributed to the melting pot, and a controversial group of poets—known as "the Beats"—and modern artists redefined New York's bohemian character. A haven for refugee intelligentsia from post-World War II Europe, the city emerged as the center of modern art. **Abstract Expressionism**, America's first radical artistic movement, rose from the studios of New York's painters.

Racial and labor tensions beset the city in the 1960s. The 1964 **Harlem Uprising** marked the first major northern black unrest of the civil rights era. In 1975 an economic downturn forced the city government to default on its debts. (That year, after President Gerald Ford refused to help the city with its fiscal woes, the *New York Daily News* ran the infamous headline "Ford to City: Drop Dead.") The city's budget was balanced by 1981, and soon an upswing in the world economy led to massive expansion on Wall Street. The events of September 11, 2001, forever changed the landscape of downtown Manhattan, but today New York City continues to cope with urban challenges on a grand scale as it moves forward in the new century.

MANHATTAN

This tongue-shaped island, flanked on the west by the expansive Hudson River and on the east by the Harlem and East rivers, measures 13.4mi in length and 2.3mi at its widest point, making it the smallest borough. It is, nonetheless, the best-known—and the residents of the "outer boroughs" say (some more grudgingly than others) that they're going "into the city" when they head to Manhattan. The name Manhattan was derived from an Algonquin Indian word meaning "island of the hills." The island was acquired from the Algonquins by Dutch governor Peter Minuit in 1626. The purchase price? Trinkets valued, during that period, at a mere $24. The Dutch settlement of Nieuw Amsterdam developed on the island's southern tip. After British occupation, the town expanded northward, following a neat grid of numbered streets and avenues that eventually predominated throughout most of the island.

Some of the most historic sections are found in the areas south of 14th Street, occupied by "Lower Manhattan" and "Downtown." Manhattan's commercial core is "Midtown," the vicinity between 34th and 59th Streets. "Uptown," or anything above 59th Street, offers a broad cross-section of cultural and educational institutions, fashionable residential blocks and well-entrenched neighborhoods. For all its sophistication, Manhattan retains a remarkably diverse physical and social makeup, epitomizing the melting pot that makes New York so fascinating to explore. The famous landmarks should not be missed, but visitors will be best served if they remember that the city is also a collection of neighborhoods. Brownstones, bodegas and the average activities of people living their lives are as much a part of the urban fabric as skyscrapers and Saks Fifth Avenue.

LOWER MANHATTAN★★

Crowded onto the southernmost tip of Manhattan below Chambers Street, cathedrals of commerce, religion and government comfortably coexist in the **Financial District★★** and **Civic Center★★**. The first site of 17C Dutch settlement, Lower Manhattan still bears the imprint of Nieuw Amsterdam's winding streets. The most famous, **Wall Street★★**, so-called for a defensive stockade built by the Dutch in 1653 between the Hudson and East Rivers to discourage attacks, symbolizes the nation's financial power. At the corner of William Street in 1792, 24 brokers met to found the forerunner of the **New York Stock Exchange★**, today located in a 17-story building (1903) at 11 Wall Street. The visitor center has been closed to the public since 9/11. **Trinity Church★★**, a striking Gothic Revival presence at the head of Wall Street at Broadway, was the tallest building in the city in 1846. Northeast of the Financial District, the Civic Center includes **Foley Square**, surrounded by the monumental **New York State Supreme Court**, Cass Gilbert's 1936 **U.S. Courthouse**, and the colossal **Municipal Building★**. In the midst of a shady park several blocks south along Centre Street stands handsome **City Hall★★**, completed in 1811.

World Trade Center Site★★

This site of the former World Trade Center Twin Towers, destroyed in the terrorist attacks of September 11, 2001, is bounded by Liberty, Church, Barclay and West streets. It has been totally revitalized with the **One World Trade Center** skyscraper, a memorial plaza and a museum. Designed by David Childs of the architectural firm Skidmore, Owings & Merrill, the 104-story tower rises 1,776ft and incorporates the latest technology in safety measures and energy efficiency; an observation deck occupies floors 100 to 102.

The 8-acre tree-filled **911 Memorial**, dedicated to the nearly 3,000 victims of the attack, centers on two immense reflecting pools with waterfalls. Expected to open in 2014, the **911 Museum** will display artifacts, photos, memorabilia, audio tapes, video recordings and other items associated with the tragedy. (212-266-5211; www.911memorial.org).

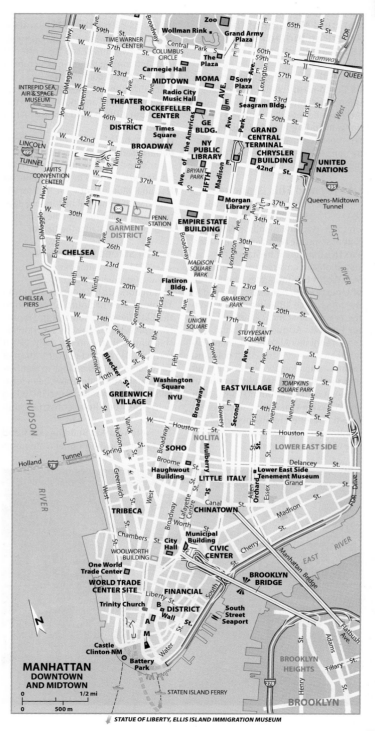

Zoo
Wollman Rink
Grand Army Plaza
TIME WARNER CENTER
COLUMBUS CIRCLE
The Plaza
Carnegie Hall
MIDTOWN
MOMA
Sony Plaza
INTREPID SEA, AIR & SPACE MUSEUM
Radio City Music Hall
THEATER
ROCKEFELLER CENTER
Seagram Bldg.
DISTRICT
Times Square
GE BLDG.
GRAND CENTRAL TERMINAL
LINCOLN TUNNEL
BROADWAY
NY PUBLIC LIBRARY
CHRYSLER BUILDING
JAVITS CONVENTION CENTER
Bryant Park
42nd St.
UNITED NATIONS
Queens-Midtown Tunnel
Morgan Library
GARMENT DISTRICT
PENN. STATION
EMPIRE STATE BUILDING
CHELSEA
MADISON SQUARE PARK
CHELSEA PIERS
Flatiron Bldg.
GRAMERCY PARK
UNION SQUARE
STUYVESANT SQUARE
Holland Tunnel
HUDSON RIVER
Washington Square
GREENWICH VILLAGE
NYU
EAST VILLAGE
TOMPKINS SQUARE PARK
Houston St.
NOLITA
LOWER EAST SIDE
SOHO
Haughwout Building
LITTLE ITALY
Lower East Side Tenement Museum
Delancey St.
Grand
TRIBECA
CHINATOWN
Canal
WOOLWORTH BUILDING
City Hall
Municipal Building
CIVIC CENTER
One World Trade Center
WORLD TRADE CENTER SITE
FINANCIAL DISTRICT
BROOKLYN BRIDGE
Manhattan Bridge
EAST RIVER
Trinity Church
Wall St.
South Street Seaport
Castle Clinton NM
Battery Park
BROOKLYN HEIGHTS
STATEN ISLAND FERRY
BROOKLYN

MANHATTAN
DOWNTOWN AND MIDTOWN

0 ——— 1/2 mi
0 ——— 500 m

STATUE OF LIBERTY, ELLIS ISLAND IMMIGRATION MUSEUM

National Museum of the American Indian★★

1 Bowling Green. ♿ ✆212-514-3700. www.nmai.si.edu.

Cass Gilbert's former Beaux-Arts **US Custom House★** (1907) makes a splendid setting for this Smithsonian museum. Beautifully displayed collections, including masks, weapons and ceremonial garments, represent the history and culture of indigenous peoples of the Americas.

Liberty and Ellis Islands★★★

Ferry departs from Battery Park South. ✕♿ ✆212-363-3200. www.nps.gov/stli.

On these two tiny islands in New York Harbor stand the twin symbols of America's rich immigrant heritage.

Listed on the coveted roster of UNESCO World Heritage sites, the **Statue of Liberty★★★**, her torch upraised in welcome since 1886, was a gift from the people of France. Alsatian sculptor Frédéric-Auguste Bartholdi and French engineer Alexandre Gustave Eiffel created the 225-ton, 151ft colossus. American architect Richard Morris Hunt designed the base, which contains an observation deck affording spectacular **city views★★★**. In 2009, Lady Liberty's crown reopened to visitors willing to climb the 354 steps it takes to take in one of NYC's best views.

Buildings on nearby **Ellis Island★★** served as a gateway for 12 million immigrants between 1892 and 1954. After 30 years left empty, the main structure in the 33-building complex was returned to its 1920s appearance during a massive restoration, and now houses the poignant **Ellis Island Immigration Museum★★**.

Ferries to both Liberty and Ellis Islands depart from Battery Parka, a 21-acre greensward at the water's edge. Ticket booths are located in **Castle Clinton National Monument★**, an 1811 fortification with a colorful history of adaptive reuse. Walks through the park offer splendid views across the harbor

South Street Seaport★★

✆212-732-7678 (visitor center). www.southstreetseaport.com.

This historic district encompasses an 11-block area of South Street along the East River, just south of the Brooklyn Bridge. Hub of the city's worldwide shipping activities in the early 19C, it contains the largest concentration of early commercial buildings in Manhattan. Many of the oldest have been rehabilitated for commercial use, including **Schermerhorn Row**, constructed in 1811-12.

The **Fulton Market Building** (1983) and the **Pier 17 Pavilion★** offer restaurants

Great Hall, Ellis Island Immigration Museum

©PhotoDisc

South Street Seaport

© Peter Wrenn/Michelin

and shops in the heart of former Fulton Fish Market, which relocated to a new facility in the Bronx in 2005. The **South Street Seaport Museum**★★ (𝒫212-748-8600) maintains a variety of historic attractions, including a fleet of **historic vessels**★ dating from 1885 to 1935. Begin in the visitor center (12 Fulton St.) for an introductory exhibit on seaport history.

Brooklyn Bridge★★★

The pedestrian walkway can be reached by crossing Park Row from City Hall Park, or from the Brooklyn Bridge-City Hall subway station. A link between Manhattan and Brooklyn, this elegant 5,989ft bridge is one of the oldest suspension bridges in the US and ranks among the great engineering triumphs of the 19C. German-born designer John Augustus Roebling began work in 1869, succumbing shortly thereafter to a gangrenous injury. His son Washington took over, but was stricken with the bends while working in the deep underwater construction caissons and had to supervise the construction from his bed until the bridge was completed in 1883.

A sunset stroll across this enduring landmark offers magnificent **views**★★ of the city. Finish on the Brooklyn side with a stop at Grimaldi's Pizza (𝒫718-858-4300; www.grimaldis.com).

DOWNTOWN AND THE NEIGHBORHOODS★★

In the patchwork of neighborhoods below 34th Street abides much that is quintessential New York. Shaped by rich and poor, immigrants and bohemians, these districts include such enduring residential communities as Gramercy Park and Murray Hill, along with the fabled Villages and the ethnic enclaves of Chinatown and Little Italy.

On the Lower East Side, once teeming with Jewish immigrants, **Orchard Street**★ still bustles with merchants and street hawkers—though the area is also

Cushman Row, Chelsea

© Peter Wrenn/Michelin

129

BUILDING MANHATTAN

American author Edith Wharton once wrote that New York would become "as much a vanished city as Atlantis or the lowest layer of Schliemann's Troy." On the crowded island of Manhattan, the architectural strata are especially deep. The oldest layers are now visible only in isolated outcroppings; the more recent define entire city blocks. From the long-gone step-gable roofs of Nieuw Amsterdam to the new skyscrapers to be built at Ground Zero, the Manhattan skyline now more than ever is a work in progress. And though much here changes, the city leads the nation in protecting thousands of buildings and historic districts that illustrate its development.

Only one 18C Dutch Colonial-style farmhouse, **Dyckman Farmhouse**, still stands in Manhattan (4881 Broadway at 204th St.; ✆212-304-9422; www.dyckmanfarmhouse.org). The English introduced the Georgian style, which emphasized the symmetry and decorum of Classical architecture, well-illustrated by the handsome **Morris-Jumel Mansion** (65 Jumel Terrace between W. 160th St. & Edgecomb Ave. ✆212-923-8008. www.morrisjumel.org) in Harlem. After the Revolution, Americans adapted Classical forms to suit the new nation, and the elegant results became known as the Federal style. New York's 1811 **City Hall★★** (between Centre St. & Broadway at Chambers St.), despite the influence of its French architect, makes an exquisite example. That same year the city released the Randel Plan for Manhattan, a monotonous grid of streets that divided the city into narrow east-west blocks and provided a framework upon which Manhattan could grow.

Two serious fires in 1835 and 1845 accelerated the building process, and the growth of public transportation helped ferry people north. Slums grew along with the city, and shantytowns filled the still-vacant lands in Central Park and upper Manhattan.

Throughout the 19C, a flurry of Revival styles—drawing on Greek, Gothic, Italian Renaissance, Romanesque and even Egyptian design motifs—left an ever more eclectic imprint on the city. By mid-century, the vertical, rectangular façades of the Renaissance-inspired Italianate style proved ideal for the narrow lots of the booming city. It became the basis for the brownstone and the cast-iron commercial warehouse—both quintessential

Detail of Flatiron Building

© Peter Wrenn/MICHELIN

Pinnacle of Chrysler Building at dusk

© Y. Saito/Michelin

New York innovations. The elegant **E.V. Haughwout Building★** (488-92 Broadway) boasts the oldest complete cast-iron façade in the city (1857), as well as the first safety elevator, an invention that would help push civilization skyward.

In 1893 the success of Chicago's World's Columbian Exposition created a rage for Beaux-Arts architecture, and the New York firm of **McKim, Mead and White** led the way. They modeled their incomparable Pennsylvania Station (demolished) on the ancient Baths of Caracalla. Daniel Burnham's 1902 **Flatiron Building** (junction of Broadway & Fifth Ave.) made the style popular for skyscrapers.

In 1916 the city passed the nation's first zoning law to ensure that adequate light and air reached the deepening street-level canyons. Zoning required buildings to set their façades back from the street as they grew higher, and soon there sprouted a profusion of ziggurat-shaped towers. The zoning laws, new technologies such as field riveting (a more efficient method of connecting steel pieces on site) and the streamlined aesthetics of modern art inspired the Art Deco skyscraper, which achieved its greatest expressions in New York. By the late 1920s and 1930s, landmarks like the **Chrysler Building★★★** (1930, William Van Alen), at 405 Lexington Avenue, with its zigzag steel conical crown, and the muscular **Empire State Building★★★** (350 Fifth Ave.) best exemplified the modern style.

After the Depression the International style emerged. Its ultra-sleek look rejected ornament and setbacks for boxlike slabs set in open plazas. The new technology of the glass-curtain wall attained its clearest expression in the 1958 **Seagram Building★★** (375 Park Ave.) by Ludwig Mies van der Rohe. Before long, however, architects began another round of embellishment, applying historical elements and materials to modern steel-frame buildings. The former **AT&T Headquarters** (1982, Johnson & Burgee), in Sony Plaza, introduced this Postmodernism with its whimsical "Chippendale" roofline. In the 21C, the flash of Postmodernism will likely yield to a new range of practical possibilities. It has already begun.

The city recently began experimenting with new ways to create more public spaces. Times Square, which was always a crazy snarl of cars, was turned into a traffic-free pedestrian zone. Though very little permanent street furniture was created for the change, do expect it in the future. But one of NYC's greatest architectural triumphs in recent years was dreamt up by people outside city government. Once an abandoned elevated subway line, the **High Line** park (www.thehighline.org), which runs from Gansevoort St. to 34th St. between 10th and 11th, was an instant hit with residents when it opened in June 2009. Those projects, along with a renewed focus on neighborhoods and waterfront development along the rivers all signal a city ready to reinvent itself, again.

New Art from New York

As Europe staggered under the overlapping tragedies of two world wars, political oppression and economic depression in the first half of the 20C, a host of her most gifted artists sought refuge in New York City. They came steeped in Surrealism and Expressionism and imported an intense interest in the new science of psychoanalysis. Many had been influenced by Picasso, whose expressionistic masterpiece *Guernica* (1937) took the city by storm upon its arrival in 1939. As émigrés like **Willem de Kooning, Hans Hofmann, Max Ernst** and **Arshile Gorky** mixed and mingled with New York artists, the avant-garde cauldron began to boil. At the end of World War II, it combusted into a full-blown movement called **Abstract Expressionism**, and New York City emerged as a cultural mecca and world leader in the production and promotion of modern art. Painters of the New York school found it impossible to reconcile traditional subjects and styles to the "moral crisis of a world in shambles," as artist Barnett Newman later described the postwar dilemma. "We actually began ... from scratch ... as if painting never existed." The results combined a subjectless abstraction with the expression of raw emotion. Large-scale works emphasized the picture plane and spontaneous brushwork while ignoring bounds imposed by the physical canvas. Considered by many to be the first truly influential American movement, Abstract Expressionism reflects something of the national psyche in its monumental canvases.

home to some of the hippest stores and eateries in all of NYC. Trendy neighborhoods like **TriBeCa★** (an acronym for Triangle Below Canal) and **Chelsea★** epitomize the late-20C urban flair for adapting warehouses for residential and mercantile use.

Elsewhere, 19C brownstones mark the blocks once favored by New York's elite before the more remote uptown neighborhoods became fashionable. In between, peaceful squares and small parks punctuate the built-up landscape with greenery and open space.

Chinatown and Little Italy

These adjacent enclaves rank as the most famous (and most touristy) of New York's immigrant neighborhoods. While once distinct, their borders have blurred as **Chinatown★★** expands. Throughout the entire area, narrow streets lined with colorful shops selling souvenirs at rock-bottom prices, produce stands and restaurants bustle with locals and visitors, particularly on weekends.

New York's first Chinese came from the American West, where they had worked as laborers before 1880. Today, the majority of Manhattan's nearly 150,000 Asians and Asian-Americans live in the area around Canal, Mott, Bayard and Pell Streets, the heart of Chinatown. The neighborhood comes alive with a bang during the **Chinese New Year** (*first full moon after 19 January*) with traditional parades and fireworks.

Little Italy★, roughly bounded by Canal, Lafayette, Houston Streets and the Bowery, was the destination for thousands of Italian immigrants between 1880 and the 1920s. Its hub lies along **Mulberry Street★**. The corridor throngs with visitors during the **Feast of San Gennaro** in mid-September.

East Village★

Defined by Houston and 14th Streets east of Broadway, this neighborhood may be best known as the haven of the Beat writers of the 1950s who gravitated to its low rents and romantic seediness and, later, as the center of the city's punk scene. Though the low rents are long gone, the neighborhood remains a favorite of younger visitors (and residents) for its atmospheric bars, restaurants and coffeehouses. Shopping abounds west of Avenue A. Though once a center of the punk scene, St.

Mark's Place (between 2nd & 3rd Aves.) has been cleaned up in recent years—a change that didn't thrill many locals.

Greenwich Village★★

West of Broadway, venerable Greenwich Village wears well its reputation as New York's historic bohemia. A country village into the 19C, "the Village," as locals call it, still retains a small-town feeling in its narrow, bending streets and alleys, where owner-operated shops outnumber chain stores, and private art galleries proliferate. Rising to become the political, artistic and literary center for New York's intelligentsia in the early 1900s, the neighborhood still offers a diversity of lifestyles.

New York University (NYU), the largest private university in the US, makes **Washington Square★★** its unofficial campus. This plaza at the foot of Fifth Avenue serves as the district's hub and can be instantly identified by its emblematic arch designed by Stanford White in 1892.

For another taste of the Village, stroll down **Bleecker Street★**, famed for its pastry shops and coffeehouses, as well as for the small cabarets, music clubs and bars that flourished in the 1960s.

SoHo★★

The site of the first free black community on the island, this area was settled in 1644 by former slaves of the Dutch West India Company. Today, Soho (an acronym for South of Houston Street) mixes up a lively blend of chain emporiums, art galleries and bargain outlets, particularly along West Broadway and **Broadway★**.

Here also is the largest concentration of 19C **cast-iron warehouses** in the US, a legacy of the district's history as a thriving industrial dry-goods center between 1850 and 1890. The oldest, built in 1857 and known as the **E.V. Haughwout Building★**, stands at 488-92 Broadway. **Greene Street★** boasts a rich assortment of these buildings, most converted to modern uses.

ALONG THE WAY
Lower East Side Tenement Museum★★

103 Orchard St. 🚇Visits by guided tour only. ☏212-982-8420. www.tenement.org.

The museum's tour guides introduce visitors to the true stories of the people who lived—and often, worked—in the building. While most of the tours are kid-friendly, small ones will really love the living history Confino family tour featuring a costumed interpreter.

Macy's★

Bounded by Broadway, Seventh Ave., 34th & 35th Sts. ☏212-494-3827. www.visitmacysnewyork.com.

The "world's largest store" was built in two parts: the 1901 Classically inspired eastern section and the western wing, built in the Art Deco style in 1931.

MIDTOWN★★★

New York City has long been famous for its hectic go–go–go pace—and it has Midtown (and the movies) to thank for that. Everybody in Midtown is going somewhere; there's very little dawdling. Situated between 34th and 59th Streets, the area is as famous for its avenues and cross-streets as for its skyscrapers and shops. **Fifth Avenue★★★**, Midtown's backbone, separates the East and West Sides. Known in the late 19C as "Millionaires' Row" (home to the Goulds, Astors and Vanderbilts), the Avenue is now bordered by famous department and jewelry stores.

West one block, an imposing line of 1960s skyscrapers creates a dramatic canyon of glass and steel along the **Avenue of the Americas★** (Sixth Ave.). A block east of Fifth, **Madison Avenue★**, once a choice residential address, now ranks among the city's most exclusive shopping thoroughfares. One more block east, **Park Avenue★★★** boasts some of New York's architectural gems. New York's major crosstown thoroughfare, **42nd Street★★** features a line-up of distinguished Art Deco structures at its eastern end. Ongoing revitalization efforts aim at returning its western length to its former splendor as a byway of the **Theater District★★**. The most famous New York street, however, may be **Broadway**, which runs the length of Manhattan and lends its name to the entertainment district between 40th and 53rd Streets. At Broadway and Seventh Avenue, **Times Square★★** marks the epicenter of that district, where some 40 theaters cluster. The **nighttime illuminations★★★** in the square pulse the rhythm of the city, as they have since the early 20C when the sign industry moved here.

👥 Empire State Building★★★

350 Fifth Ave. Consult a visibility chart before buying tickets to the observatory. ✕♿ 𝄢 212-736-3100. www.esbnyc.com. Completed in 1931, this Art Deco masterpiece remains the most distinctive feature of the Manhattan skyline. The needle-nosed tower, rising to 1,454ft, was the world's tallest for four decades. The top floor was intended as a mooring platform for dirigibles until a near-catastrophic trial run in 1932. Enjoy the 80mi view from the 86th-floor **observatory** by both day and night, or visit the glass-enclosed circular observatory on the 102nd floor. From afar, notice the

Bas-relief and glass screen by Lee Lawrie, GE Building

Empire State Building

© Stephen Brake/iStockphoto.com

colors of the tower lights, which change to honor seasons, holidays and special events.

Rockefeller Center★★★

Between Fifth & Seventh Aves. and 47th & 52nd Sts.
This "city within a city" ranks among the most vital and cohesive design complexes in America. Brainchild of oil magnate John D. Rockefeller, Jr., the center's 19 buildings, which cover 22 acres, were erected between 1932 and 1973. Among the first, the Art Deco **GE (General Electric) Building★★★** (30 Rockefeller Plaza), formerly the RCA Building, soars 70 stories up and houses both the **NBC Studios★** (👁 visit by 1hr 10min guided tour only; 𝄢212-664-3700; www.nbcstudiotour.com) and the legendary restaurant and ballroom, the **Rainbow Room. Radio City Music Hall★★** was the largest theater in the world when it was erected in 1932, seating 6,000 people. It remains a must-hit for throngs of tourists who come to see the Radio City Christmas spectacular with the Rockettes each year. Outside, lovely **Channel Gardens★★** incorporate six pools and lush seasonal flower beds. The annual lighting of the Christmas tree here is one of the city's most beloved holiday traditions. A promenade leads

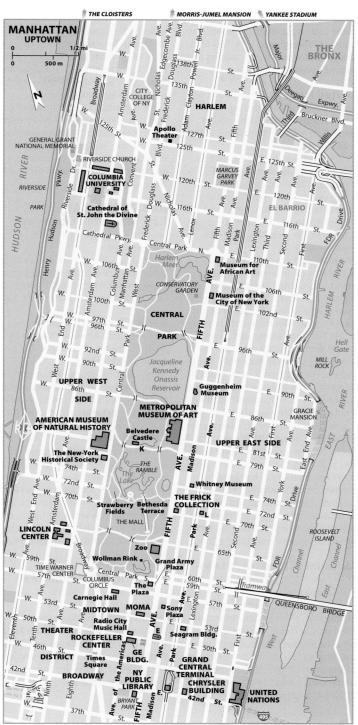

THE CLOISTERS   MORRIS-JUMEL MANSION   YANKEE STADIUM

MANHATTAN
UPTOWN

0   1/2 mi
0   500 m

THE BRONX

CITY COLLEGE OF NY

HARLEM

Apollo Theater

GENERAL GRANT NATIONAL MEMORIAL

RIVERSIDE CHURCH

COLUMBIA UNIVERSITY

RIVER

MARCUS GARVEY PARK

EL BARRIO

Cathedral of St. John the Divine

RIVERSIDE PARK

HUDSON

Harlem Meer

CONSERVATORY GARDEN

Museum for African Art

Museum of the City of New York

CENTRAL

PARK

HARLEM RIVER

Hell Gate

MILL ROCK

Jacqueline Kennedy Onassis Reservoir

UPPER WEST SIDE

Guggenheim Museum

AMERICAN MUSEUM OF NATURAL HISTORY

METROPOLITAN MUSEUM OF ART

Belvedere Castle

UPPER EAST SIDE

GRACIE MANSION

The New-York Historical Society

THE RAMBLE

EAST RIVER

The Lake

Whitney Museum

Strawberry Fields

Bethesda Terrace

THE FRICK COLLECTION

THE MALL

ROOSEVELT ISLAND

LINCOLN CENTER

Zoo

Wollman Rink

Grand Army Plaza

TIME WARNER CENTER

COLUMBUS CIRCLE

The Plaza

Carnegie Hall

MIDTOWN

MOMA

Sony Plaza

THEATER

Radio City Music Hall

ROCKEFELLER CENTER

Seagram Bldg.

QUEENSBORO BRIDGE

DISTRICT

GE BLDG.

Times Square

BROADWAY

NY PUBLIC LIBRARY

GRAND CENTRAL TERMINAL

CHRYSLER BUILDING

UNITED NATIONS

BRYANT PARK

I-495

to the sunken plaza where the reclining figure of **Prometheus** (1934, Paul Manship) presides over winter skating and summer dining.

United Nations★★★

Visitor Center relocated to Dag Hammarskjöld Library Building (42nd Street & 1st Avenue) effective mid-2013 until 2015.

First Ave. between E. 42nd & E. 48th Sts. ✈Visit by guided tour only; children under 5 not admitted on tours. Tours in a language other than English require reservations (212-963-7539) after 9:30am the day of the visit. ✈Tours are conducted Mar–Dec. ✖& 212-963-4440. www.un.org.

The four buildings of the UN, designed in 1946 by an international group of architects, occupy 18 acres overlooking the East River. Here 192 member states, whose flags flutter in English alphabetical order from north to south at the buildings' front, work to resolve global problems and disputes. In the low-slung **General Assembly Building★★**, the UN's main body holds its annual three-month session, beginning in September. Constructed of white Vermont marble and glass-and-aluminum panels, the striking **Secretariat Building★★** houses UN offices on its 39 floors. The five-story **Conference Building** connects the two and provides meeting and council chambers.

Located on the southwest corner of the grounds, the **Hammarskjold Library** is dedicated to the second secretary-general who was killed in a 1961 plane crash while on a peace mission to the Congo.

Museum of Modern Art★★★

11 W. 53rd St. ✖& 212-708-9400. www.moma.org.

One of the world's preeminent cultural institutions, MOMA offers an unparalleled overview of all the modern visual arts. The original 1939 marble and glass building was one of the first examples of the International style in the US; it underwent extensive renovations in 2002-04, and reopened after heavy

redesign by Japanese architect Yoshio Taniguchi. The museum itself dates to 1929 when three benefactors—Abby Aldrich Rockefeller, Lillie P. Bliss and Mary Quinn Sullivan—launched a show of Postimpressionists.

Since the initial 1931 bequest of 235 works, holdings have grown to encompass more than 150,000 pieces including painting, sculpture, photography; decorative, graphic and industrial art; architectural plans and models; and video and film.

ALONG THE WAY
New York Public Library★★

476 Fifth Ave. & 917-275-6975. www.nypl.org.

Housed in a 1911 Beaux-Arts masterpiece, this facility is the second-largest research library in the US (after the Library of Congress in Washington, DC).

Radio City Music Hall★★

1260 Ave. of the Americas. ✈Visit by guided tour only. 212-247-4777. www.radiocity.com.

Since 1932, this fabulous Art Deco music hall has hosted live musical spectaculars and the world's finest precision dance team, the **Rockettes**.

Carnegie Hall★

156 W. 57th St. ✈Visit by guided tour only. & 212-903-9765. www.carnegiehall.org.

Opened in 1891 and later named after its benefactor, steel magnate and philanthropist Andrew Carnegie, this majestic structure is regarded as one of the world's most prestigious music halls.

St. Patrick's Cathedral★★

Fifth Ave. between E. 50th & 51st Sts. & 212-753-2261. www.saintpatrickscathedral.org.

Designed by renowned architect James Renwick and consecrated in 1879, St. Patrick's is the city's major Roman Catholic cathedral. Its services and concerts are open to the public.

Grand Central Terminal★★★

Park Ave. & 42nd St.
www.grandcentralterminal.com.
Opened in 1913, the sumptuous Beaux-Arts "gateway to the city" is among New York's great civic monuments. The main concourse's "sky ceiling" is one of the city's best reasons to look up. Not just a transportation hub, Grand Central also houses shops and restaurants.

Morgan Library and Museum★★

29-33 E. 36th St. ✆212-685-0008.
www.themorgan.org.
This venerable institution houses an outstanding collection of books, prints and rare manuscripts assembled by 19C industrialist J. Pierpont Morgan.

UPTOWN★★

Northern Manhattan above Midtown comprises many vibrant and interesting neighborhoods. The best known include the Upper East Side, the Upper West Side and Harlem. The **Upper East Side★★** covers the blocks between Central Park and the East River, from 59th Street to 97th Street.

The area remained rural until the mid-19C, when high society began migrating uptown, extending **Fifth Avenue★★** northward with lavish mansions. New York's most prestigious addresses still border the avenue along Central Park north of the **Grand Army Plaza★★**. Two blocks east, **Park Avenue★** makes its way north, lined with dignified apartment buildings.

Across Central Park, the **Upper West Side★★** extends north from Columbus Circle to 125th Street. The area has attracted an eclectic blend of residents over the years, evidenced by its mix of luxury apartment buildings, stylish row houses, artists' studios and urban renewal projects. The presence of **Columbia University★** (main entrance at W. 116th St.) adds a large student population.

Northern Manhattan hosts **Harlem★**. It became world-famous during the 1920s Harlem Renaissance as a center for black arts and culture. The **Apollo Theater** (253 W. 125th St.; ✆212-531-5300; www.apollotheater.com), legendary for its all-black revues of the 1930s, still offers variety shows. Harlem encompasses some outstanding architecture, several landmark historic districts and renowned churches and institutions. **Harlem Spirituals** (✆212-391-0900; www.harlemspirituals.com) offers gospel and jazz tours of the neighborhood.

Grand Central Terminal

©Mario Savoia/iStockphoto.com

Gondola on the Lake in Central Park

© Peter Wrenn/Michelin

Central Park★★★

℘212-310-6600.
www.centralparknyc.org.
Manhattan swirls around this lush 843-acre sanctuary, which provides refuge and recreation for millions of people annually. Construction began in 1857, interpreting the "picturesque" designs of Frederick Law Olmsted and Calvert Vaux; Central Park opened 19 years later as the first large-scale recreation space in America. Favorite park destinations include the **Central Park Zoo★** ♣♟ (200-800 Fifth Ave.; ℘212-439-6500; www.centralparkzoo.org), which includes creatures from penguin to red pandas in replications of their natural habitats and the **Children's Zoo**, a petting zoo with farm animals. **Bethesda Terrace** and the lake beyond spanned by its famous Art Deco bridge, is perfect for people-watching on a warm, sunny day, and the **Henry Luce Nature Observa-**tory, which occupies two floors of fanciful **Belvidere Castle**, has microscopes and all manner of exhibits. **Strawberry Fields**, once a favorite park spot of John Lennon, is now a memorial to the musician. In winter, one of the most popular park spots is **Wollman Rink**, where ice skaters take advantage of prices that are a fraction of those at the Rockefeller Center Ice Rink. In summer, the place to be is the **Delacorte Theater**, where The Public Theater (and the big name talent it pulls in) stages the free Shakespeare in the Park events (℘212-539-8500; www.publictheater.org).

The New-York Historical Society★★

2 W. 77th St. ℘212-873-3400.
www.nyhistory.org.
The collections of the city's oldest museum (founded in 1804) cover three centuries of Americana—including a superb assemblage of Hudson River school paintings, Audubon watercolors and Tiffany lamps.

♣♟ American Museum of Natural History★★★

Central Park West at 79th St. ✕&
℘212-769-5100. www.amnh.org.
The holdings of this venerable institution (1869) include more than 30 million specimens related to all facets of natural history. The museum is best known for having the largest collection of fossil vertebrates in the world, and their display in six **fossil halls★★** on the top floor represents a visual and intellectual tour de force.

Yankee Stadium

Located in the Bronx, the new **Yankee Stadium★** (161st St. & River Ave; ℘718-293-6000 ticket office) opened in 2009 and has, by no means, been a rousing success—especially if you count long-time fans amongst the critics. But, grousing is all part of the fun when you're a New Yorker. They'll keep going to the games but, of course, will never stop talking about the old stadium, "the house that Ruth built."

The Frick Collection★★★

1 E. 70th St. Children under 10 not admitted. ♿ ℘212-288-0700. www.frick.org.

A Pittsburgh coke and steel industrialist, Henry Clay Frick (👆 see PITTSBURGH), commissioned this 40-room mansion in 1913 to display his outstanding collection of 18C English paintings, sculpture, drawings and decorative arts.

Metropolitan Museum of Art★★★

1000 Fifth Ave. at E. 82nd St. ✕♿🅿 ℘212-535-7710. www.metmuseum.org.

Founded in 1870 by members of New York's Union League Club, this monument to world culture has occupied its present location since 1880. The building itself has grown in stages over the years, with contributions by an impressive roster of architects, including Calvert Vaux, Richard Morris Hunt and McKim, Mead and White. Its three million objects dating from prehistory to the 20C make it the largest museum in the western hemisphere.

The Met's assemblage of **Ancient Art★★★** encompasses four wellsprings of civilization (Egypt, Greece, Rome and the Near East); impressive installations like the magnificent Egyptian **Temple of Dendur★** give the museum a breathtaking scale. **European Sculpture and Decorative Arts★★★** emphasizes French and English furniture, and porcelain from Germany and France.

A superb assemblage of **Impressionists and Postimpressionists★★★** takes in works by Cézanne, Manet, Monet, Renoir, Gauguin and Seurat.

Re-opened in early 2012 after a two-year renovation, the **New American Wing★★★** features sculpture and stained glass in the open and airy Charles Engelhard Couter, and 19 full-scale American period rooms that span nearly 250 years.

Primitive art from Africa, Oceania and the Americas include masks, clay vessels and mosaic jewelry.

The **Medieval collection★★** comprises more than 4,000 works from the early Christian, Byzantine, Romanesque and Gothic periods.

Pieces from this collection are exhibited farther up at **The Cloisters★★★** (Fort Tryon Park; 🅿 ℘212-923-3700), the museum's lovely re-created hilltop monastery devoted to the art and architecture of Medieval Europe.

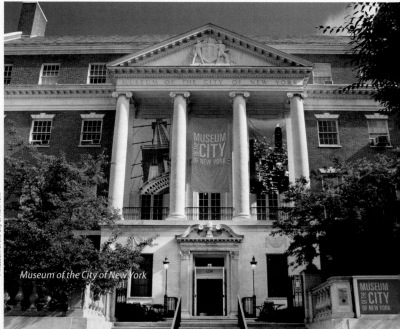

Museum of the City of New York

© Museum of the City of New York

Solomon R. Guggenheim Museum★★

1071 Fifth Ave. ✕🅖 ℘212-423-3500.
www.guggenheim.org.

In 1943, art patrons Solomon R. Guggenheim and his wife, Irene Rothschild, commissioned architect Frank Lloyd Wright to design a permanent home for their collection of modern art, which today numbers more than 7,000 works, dating from the late 19C to the present. The building is as much a work of art as the masterpieces it contains, and Wright considered it his crowning achievement.

Indeed, few public spaces in New York rival the drama of the main gallery, encircled by the famous spiral ramp, more than a quarter-mile long.

👥 Museum of the City of New York★★

1220 Fifth Ave. at 103rd St. 🅖
℘212-534-1672; www.mcny.org.

Founded in 1923 as America's first institution dedicated to the history of a city, this museum chronicles the changing face of New York through its rich collections of decorative arts, furnishings, silver, prints and paintings. Especially beguiling are the doll houses★, which were all owned or made by locals.

Whitney Museum of American Art★★

945 Madison Ave. ✕🅖 ℘212-570-3600.
www.whitney.org.

The Whitney, which grew from the collections of Gertrude Vanderbilt Whitney in the early 1930s, is dedicated to the advancement of contemporary artists and is known for largely its provocative exhibits.

Its outstanding collection of 20C American art includes more than 10,000 works by such artists as Hopper, de Kooning, Nevelson and Calder.

Held for about three months every year, The Whitney Biennial is an exhibition of recent art mostly by young, lesser-known artists that is considered trend-setting.

ALONG THE WAY
The Plaza★

Southeast corner of Central Park at Fifth Ave. ℘212-759-3000.
www.fairmont.com/theplaza.

The elegant Plaza has been a bastion of New York society since 1907. The hotel has long played a role in children's imaginations: it was the setting for the children's book, Eloise at the Plaza.

Asia Society and Museum★

725 Park Ave. 🅖 ℘212-288-6400.
www.asiasociety.org.

The society provides an elegant setting for Indian bronzes, Chinese and Japanese ceramics, exquisite screen paintings and other works of Asian art.

Museum for African Art★

Currently closed for renovation. 1280 Fifth Ave. & 110th St. 🅖 ℘212-444-9795.
www.africanart.org.

The museum is one of only two in the US devoted to African art (the other is part of the Smithsonian Institution in Washington, DC). The 100,000sq ft building includes gallery space and an interactive educational center.

Lincoln Center★★

On Broadway between W. 62nd & 67th Sts. ✕🅖 🅿 ℘212-875-5350.
www.lincolncenter.org.

Though concerts and other events continue in its midst, this 16-acre cultural complex—home of the New York City Ballet, New York Philharmonic, The Metropolitan Opera and many other arts organizations—completed a 1.2 billion renovation in 2012 to improve the facilities and visitor experience.

Cathedral of St. John the Divine★★

Amsterdam Ave. at W. 112th St.
℘212-316-7540. Tours: 212-932-7347.
www.stjohndivine.org.

The seat of the Episcopal Diocese of New York is reportedly the largest Gothic-style cathedral in the world. it houses one of the country's busiest conservation laboratories to conserve the Cathedral's textiles.

Hudson River Valley★★★

Originating high in the Adirondacks, the Hudson River passes through a rich landscape of hills, highlands and history. At Albany★, New York's state capital, the river becomes navigable, connecting upstate New York to the world. Named for explorer Henry Hudson, the first European to navigate the river in 1609, the majestic waterway has been widely celebrated in literature and art. Honored in 1996 as a Heritage Area by the National Park Service, the valley itself is also notable for its man-made environment.

Info: ✆800-232-4782; www.travelhudsonvalley.com.

Location: The Hudson River flows 315mi to the Atlantic Ocean. The following sights lie within a day's drive of New York City, and are organized traveling up the East Bank and down the West Bank.

Don't Miss: The ancestral home of Franklin Delano Roosevelt.

Timing: Leave plenty of time to pull over and take photos of this breathtaking landscape.

THE VALLEY TODAY

A remarkable concentration of historic homes reflects the centuries-old Dutch settlement pattern that carved feudal estates from the lands flanking the river. The Vanderbilts, Goulds, Rockefellers and other latter-day barons flocked to the river's edge to add their mansions to the mix.

Along the East Bank, Route 9 links these historic homes with quaint villages such as **Cold Spring★** and **Garrison-on-Hudson**. Dia: Beacon houses large-scale works of contemporary art, and farther north, Vassar College, founded as a women's college in 1861, is now co-ed. West of the river, Route 9W connects a variety of sights—many related to the Revolutionary War, as well as the US military academy West Point.

Beyond Kingston, the velvety blue-green **Catskill Mountains★★** loom on the western horizon. Seven bridges, including the George Washington, which Le Corbusier, one of the founders of modern architecture, called "the most beautiful bridge in the world," cross the river, while two tunnels—the Lincoln and the Holland—go under it.

An American Aristocracy

It's hard to get far in New York without encountering the names J.P. **Morgan**, Cornelius **Vanderbilt**, Andrew **Carnegie**, Jay **Gould** and John D. **Rockefeller**. Members of America's first generation of self-made millionaires, these men built American industry in the boom years after the Civil War. Until then, New York's high society revolved around established and modestly wealthy Dutch and colonial families whose inheritance came from early land holdings and trade.

By the 1870s, however, expanded markets, a growing labor force and laws favoring big business spawned a brash new breed of American entrepreneur.

Constructing empires around oil, railroads, banking and steel, these capitalists accrued an unprecedented bundle of personal wealth. Befitting the domestic requirements of America's new "aristocracy," Fifth Avenue between 42nd and 92nd Streets blossomed with French "chateaux" and Rhine "castles." And, lest there be any doubt of their royal aspirations, scores of young heiresses sought out European dukes and princes to marry for their titles.

In 2013 preconstruction work began on a twin-span replacement for the Tappen Zee bridge near Tarrytown.

SIGHTS
Washington Irving's Sunnyside★

W. Sunnyside Lane, off Rte. 9, Tarrytown. ☞ Visit by guided tour only early May–mid-Nov. 🅿 ✆914-631-8200 (914-591-8763 Sat–Sun). www.hudsonvalley.org. Focal point of "Sleepy Hollow Country," this quaint riverside hideaway still evokes the storybook setting cultivated by its owner, **Washington Irving** (1783-1859), America's first internationally famous author. Its fanciful architecture and lovely views embody the essence of the 19C Romantic landscape. Built around an existing farmhouse in 1835, this "snuggery" blends English, Dutch, Spanish and Scottish elements.

Lyndhurst★

635 S. Broadway, off Rte. 9, Tarrytown. ☞ Visit by guided tour only. ✖ 🚻 🅿. ✆914-631-4481. www.lyndhurst.org. An astonishing Gothic Revival castle, Lyndhurst was designed in 1838 by Alexander Jackson Davis, the most prolific architect of Gothic country houses in America. The manse represents one of the finest residential examples of this style, associated more often in the US with churches and universities. Tiffany stained glass and a dark-wood Gothic interior complement its picturesque exterior.

Kykuit★★

☞ Visit by guided tour only, early May –mid-Nov. Tours begin from Philipsburg Manor Visitor Center, Rte. 9, Sleepy Hollow. ✖ 🚻 🅿 ✆914-631-8200. www.hudsonvalley.org. One of the last grand homes to be built in the Hudson River Valley, Kykuit (Dutch for "lookout;" pronounced KYE-cut) offers a glimpse into the lives of four generations of Rockefellers. Original construction was begun in 1906 by John D. Rockefeller, Jr., for his father, patriarch of Standard Oil; the present Beaux-Arts façade was added during a later redesign. Rooms date to the residency of New York State governor Nelson Rockefeller, beginning in 1963. By then the house brimmed with antique furniture, Chinese ceramics and Rockefeller's burgeoning modern **art collection★**. Spectacular **views★** across the Hudson blend with gardens and art into painterly tableaux.

Boscobel House and Gardens★★

1601 Rte. 9D, 4mi north of the junction with Rte. 403. ☞ Visit by guided tour only, Apr–Dec. 🅿 ✆845-265-3638. www.boscobel.org. Fastidiously appointed and furnished, this crisply elegant restoration embodies the essence of the American Federal style. Originally built 15mi to the south in 1804, the house was rescued from destruction, moved to this site, and opened to the public in 1961. Federal architecture with its light and delicate aspect represents the "antique taste" made popular in the 18C by archaeological study of the ancient world. Indoors and out, note Boscobel's slight columns, narrow windows and dainty, shallow ornament.
Restrained and slender period furniture fills the home, some of it the work of New York's virtuoso craftsman Duncan Phyfe.

Home of Franklin D. Roosevelt National Historic Site (Springwood)★★

On Rte. 9, Hyde Park. ☞ Visit by guided tour only. 🅿 ✆800-337-8474. www.nps.gov/hofr. Ancestral home of **Franklin Delano Roosevelt** (1882-1945), Springwood offers an exceedingly personal encounter with the 32nd president of the US. Born in the house in 1882, Roosevelt took his bride, Eleanor, there in 1905 and soon launched his political career. He enlarged the house over the years, designing the present field-stone wings. Stricken with polio in 1921, FDR convalesced here. He and Eleanor are buried side by side in the rose garden. The Roosevelt presence remains palpable in the rooms, furnished comfortably and filled with family mementos. Also on the property is Roosevelt's "Top Cottage," which he built as a personal getaway—and a place to discuss politics with advisors and allies. Springwood is also home to the first US presidential library, the **FDR Library and Museum**, which features extensive exhibits about the family.

A short drive away on Route 9G stands the **Eleanor Roosevelt National Historic Site★** (👣visit by guided tour only; 🅿 🖉845-229-9422; www.nps.gov/elro), a cozy complex of buildings known as "Val-Kill" (named after the nearby stream). It started taking shape in 1925, when Franklin built a stone cottage on the grounds of Springwood as a retreat for Eleanor. She used the space to think about and work on her plans for social change. After FDR's death, she took up permanent residence in the cottage. She lived there until her death in 1962.

Vanderbilt Mansion National Historic Site★★

4097 Albany Post Rd., on Rte. 9, Hyde Park. 👣Visit by guided tour only. 🅿 🖉845-229-9115 ext 2010. www.nps.gov/vama.

Commissioned by Frederick (grandson of Cornelius Vanderbilt) and Louise Vanderbilt in 1898 for fall and spring entertaining, this mansion epitomizes the extravagance of the Gilded Age nouveau riche. The 50-room Beaux-Arts edifice designed by McKim, Mead and White overflows with art and furniture befitting America's self-styled "nobility" and ranging from Renaissance to Rococo in style. When visiting, leave time to explore the 211 acres of park land surrounding the mansion; they feature Italian Gardens, as well as views of the Hudson River and, to the north, and west, the Catskill Mountains.

West Point★★

On Rte. 218, Highlands. Visitor center and museum open to the public. 👣Visit of academy grounds by guided tour only (🖉845-446-4724; www.westpointtours.com). ✕🖉🅿 🖉845-938-2638. www.usma.edu.

Fortress West Point was established in 1778 to protect the strategically important Hudson River at its most defensible location. After the Revolution, the grounds became a repository for trophies and captured equipment. In 1802, Congress installed the US Military Academy at West Point, and it remains the nation's oldest continuously occupied military post. Today this sprawling campus can easily fill a day of walking and driving from point to point.

West Point offers layers of history to peel away at leisure, beginning at the **visitor center**. The **military museum★★** presents a thorough examination of martial history. At mid-campus, **Fort Putnam★** (🖉845-938-3590), the historic heart of West Point, affords commanding views 500ft above the river. In fall and spring, the **Parades**—troop reviews famous for their precision—are held. (Call for schedules: 🖉845-938-2638.)

Vanderbilt Mansion

Washington's Headquarters State Historic Site★

Corner of Washington & Liberty Sts., Newburgh. 🐾Visit by guided tour only Apr–Oct; rest of the year by appointment 🅿 ☎845-562-1195. www.nysparks.state.ny.us.

Of the many Revolutionary War "Washington's Headquarters" in the Northeast, this site is of particular importance as the one he occupied the longest. Even with peace imminent, Gen. George Washington distrusted the British and chose to watch the river from this simple Dutch farmhouse.

Storm King Art Center★

Off Rte. 9 West on Old Pleasant Hill Rd., Mountainville. ✕🅿Open Apr –Dec 1. ☎845-534-3115. www.stormking.org. Begin a visit to this stunning outdoor sculpture park at the Normandy-style museum building (1935). From there, set off in any direction across the rolling landscape to seek out more than 100 works by masters of modern sculpture. Founded in 1970, the collection includes works by David Smith, Alexander Calder, Henry Moore and many others. Visitors are encouraged to bring a picnic to enjoy on the grounds.

EXCURSION

National Baseball Hall of Fame and Museum★★

◗ 25 Main St., 70mi west of Albany in Cooperstown, NY. Take US-20 West to Rte. 80 South. ☎888-425-5633. www.baseballhall.org.

Dedicated in 1939, this shrine to baseball covers its subject with encyclopedic thoroughness. Steeped in history, personalities and statistics, bright and imaginative galleries cover every aspect of the sport from the evolution of equipment and uniforms to records made and broken. The **Hall of Fame** honors 300 baseball greats and inducts new members every year.

Long Island★★

Claiming some of the finest beaches and best-protected harbors on the Atlantic seaboard, Long Island is New York State's oceanside vacationland. Along the North Shore, wealthy New Yorkers built vacation homes among the rocky necks and beaches, thick woodlands and steep bluffs that overlook Long Island Sound.

🄸 **Info:** ☎877-386-6654. www.licvb.com.

◗ **Location:** The island extends 125mi into the Atlantic, and 20mi separate the North and South shores at its widest point.

☺ **Don't Miss:** The popular resorts of the Hamptons.

ISLAND DELIGHTS

The picturesque town of **Oyster Bay** typifies the "Gold Coast" with its historic landmarks and quaint shops. **Cold Spring Harbor** preserves its history as a 19C whaling center at the **Whaling Museum**★👥👤 (301 Main St.; ☎631-367-3418; www.cswhalingmuseum.org). The idyllic rural hamlet of **Stony Brook**★★ is noted for its historic planned business district (1941), as well as for its complex of museums. Farther east, the unspoiled village of **Cutchoque** and the hardworking port of **Greenport** occupy the North Fork, which culminates at Orient Point. Beachy barrier islands—32mi-long **Fire Island**★ the most famous among them—line the scenic South Shore. The exclusive "Hamptons" dominate the South Fork, and the charming whaling village of **Sag Harbor**★ is a living museum of Colonial and 19C architecture. For peaceful biking and hiking, **Shelter Island**★ lies a short ferry ride from Sag Harbor.

Long Island **wineries** on both forks enjoy an ever-increasing reputation for their Merlots and Chardonnays, and local steamer and quahog (pronounced KOE-hog) clams, oysters, scallops and lobsters are not to be missed. Visitors can enjoy all the waterfront perquisites, along with tennis, golf, horseback riding, touring and other holiday pleasures, between the din and congestion of the island's western end, and its remote eastern tip, which splits into the North and South forks.

SIGHTS
Planting Fields Arboretum State Historic Park★★

1395 Planting Fields Rd., Oyster Bay.
&🅿✕ (Sat–Sun only) 🖉516-922-8600. www.plantingfields.org.
Formerly the private estate of financier William Robertson Coe, the 409 acres of planting fields include 160 acres that have been developed as an arboretum; the remaining have been kept as a natural habitat. In their midst stands **Coe Hall**, a fine example of the Tudor Revival style.

▲▲ Long Island Museum of American Art, History & Carriages★

1200 Rte. 25A at Main St. &🅿🖉631-751-0066. www.longislandmuseum.org.
Explore Long Island's history with a visit to this nine-acre complex, which includes gardens, a 20-ton Beaux-Arts fountain and a former one-room schoolhouse. The permanent collection consists of 40,000 items that date back to the late 1700s. The art museum displays the work of 19C artist **William Sidney Mount**, who settled in Stony Brook.

▲▲ Old Bethpage Village Restoration★★

Round Swamp Rd. ✕🅿🖉516-572-8400. www.discoverlongisland.com.
It's always the mid-19C at this 209-acre village. Blacksmiths, cobblers, tailors, farmers and other workers ply their trades among the 51 historic buildings that have been moved to the site.

The Hamptons★★

Beginning at **Westhampton Beach**, the Hamptons form a 35mi chain of vacation colonies. Once a seafaring community, this chic summertime retreat is now favored by the rich and famous who escape New York City on the weekends. Dune Road, though narrow and sometimes impassable after a storm, offers a lovely drive along the beach. The largest of these villages, **Southampton★** boasts superb estates and the nearby **Parrish Art Museum** (279 Montauk Hwy., Water Mill; 🖉613-283-2118; www.parrishart.org), which focuses on American art in a newly constructed building. Quaint **East Hampton** has long attracted artists and writers, and among the magnificent elms on **Main Street** stand a number of historic structures.

Jones Beach State Park★★

1 Ocean State Pkwy., Wantaugh. 🖉516-785-1600. www.nysparks.state.ny.us.
Ocean, bay and pool fans will all find satisfaction at Jones Beach State Park. The park includes the well-known **Jones Beach Theater**, a nautical stadium, heated pools, sports fields and play areas.
Be sure to take the beautiful **coastal drive** along Ocean State Parkway between Jones Beach and **Robert Moses State Park★** on neighboring Fire Island.

Fire Island Lighthouse
©Kenneth C. Zirkel/iStockphoto.com

Upstate New York

Though New York City cuts a bold silhouette on the state's landscape, much that is beautiful about New York's 47,000sq mi lies upstate. Bisected by the Mohawk River that flows between Troy and Rome, this region's varied terrain includes the ancient Appalachian Plateau south of the river and the heavily wooded Adirondack Mountains to the north. As recently as 10,000 years ago, glaciers provided the details, carving out lakes and valleys, bedecking the land with moraine deposits and melting into rushing streams and rivers.

A Bit of History

Fertile soil, abundant wildlife and ample natural resources made the region hospitable to early humans, and there flowered the mighty **Iroquois Confederacy**. These five Indian nations, the Seneca, Mohawk,

Oneida, Cayuga and Onondaga (the Tuscarora joined the confederacy in the early 18C, making it six tribes), occupied and controlled much of upstate New York from AD 1300 until the American Revolution. After siding with the British in that conflict,

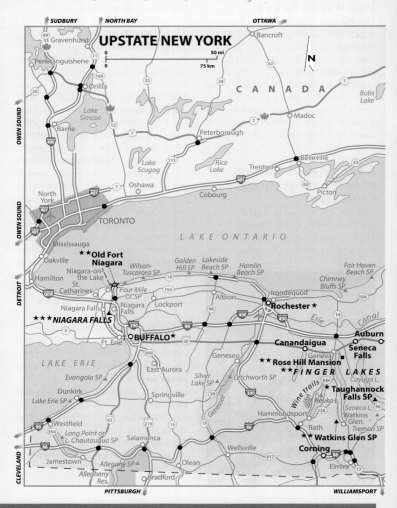

Upstate New York

the confederacy faltered, only to be decimated by the Continental Army. A highly sophisticated society, the Iroquois created

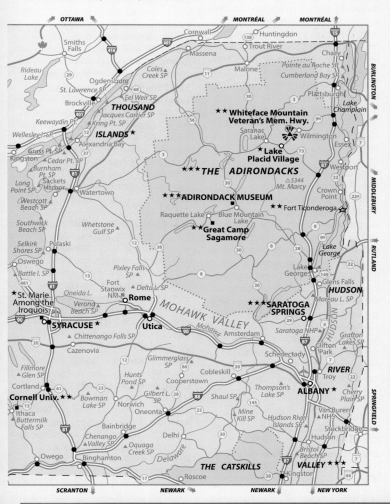

America's first representative democracy, which inspired Benjamin Franklin and James Madison as they crafted the bylaws of the American Republic in the mid-1700s. The Erie Canal, which linked Albany and Buffalo by 1825, and later the railroad, brought people and industry west, expedited the transport of goods and crops east, and sealed the economic good fortune of the Empire State. A deeper and wider barge canal replaced the Erie Canal in 1918, and commercial and recreational boaters still ply the 524mi of New York's artificial waterways. Most modern upstate travelers, however, take the New York State Thruway (I-90) across the state from Albany to Buffalo through the Mohawk Valley. The crossroads of the region lies at **Syracuse★** (where I-81 and I-90 intersect), once the central meeting place of the Iroquois nations. Upstate's other cities—**Albany★, Utica, Rome, Rochester★** and **Buffalo★**—lie mostly along the Mohawk River-Erie Canal corridor. Near the canal's end, spectacular Niagara Falls has been wowing visitors since at least 1678, when French missionary Father Louis Hennepin saw the roaring waters and proclaimed: "The Universe does not afford its Parallel."

North of the Mohawk River, the wilderness of the Adirondacks prevails despite threats from logging and development. Autumn provides perfect weather to explore and sample all that's grown on the state's farmland and vineyards. The season's incomparable foliage provides a stunning backdrop to hiking and camping, as well as visits to the historic lakeside settlements and country villages that punctuate the rolling hills to the south and west. Abundant winter snow means good skiing and a range of cold-weather sports. The wide-ranging geography also provides respite from extreme summer heat when visitors enjoy the cool Adirondack forests and the refreshing waterfalls of the Finger Lakes.

ADDRESSES

🏠 STAY

$$$$$ Mirror Lake Inn Resort and Spa – 5 Mirror Lake Dr., Lake Placid, NY. ✕⚐🅿⚒ ✆518-523-2544. www.mirrorlakeinn.com.

131 rooms. This elegant 19C mansion has been operating as an exclusive retreat since 1925. Choose a Colonial-style bedroom or superior suites with views.

$$$ The Red Coach Inn – 2 Buffalo Ave., Niagara Falls, NY. ✕🅿 ✆716-282-1459. www.redcoach.com. 31 rooms. This guesthouse is modeled after an English inn and combines home comforts with top service. Apartment-size quarters, have full kitchens and views of the Upper Rapids.

$$$$ Geneva on the Lake – 1001 Lochland Rd., Geneva, NY. ✕⚐🅿⚒ ✆315-789-7190. www. GenevaontheLake.com. 29 rooms. A 1910 estate, modeled after Rome's Villa Lancellotti, sits on 10 acres of labyrinthine gardens. Most guest quarters are one-bedroom suites that look onto Seneca Lake. The resort is located on Seneca Lake Wine Trail, near Hobart and William Smith colleges.

$$$$$ The Sagamore Resort on Lake George – 11 Sagamore Rd., Bolton Landing, NY. ✕⚐🅿⚒ ✆518-644-9400. www.thesagamore.com. 382 rooms. The 70-acre private island resort is just as luxurious as when it started out as the playground of America's millionaires in 1883. Guests stay at the hotel (c.1883) or The Lodges in rooms with fireplaces.

🍴 EAT

$$$ Edgar's at Belhurst Castle – Rte. 14, Geneva, NY. ✆315-781-0201. www.belhurstcastle.com. **Steakhouse.** This 1885 mansion and hotel, which sits on Seneca Lake about a mile outside town, has been everything from a casino to a speakeasy. Today all six luxurious dining rooms, featuring mahogany paneling and mosaic tile fireplaces, attract regulars from as far away as Rochester.

$$ Anchor Bar – 1047 Main St., Buffalo, NY. ✆716-884-4083. www.anchorbar.com. **Classic American. $$ Duff's** – 3651 Sheridan Dr., Amherst, NY. ✆716-834-6234. www.duffsfamouswings.ca. **Classic American.** Though both restaurants claim they created Buffalo wings, that's where the similarities end. Anchor Bar is an old downtown tavern, while Duff's is a hipper spot in a suburban area.

The Adirondacks★★★

One of the best-protected wilderness areas in the nation, Adirondack Park comprises some 6 million acres (9,400sq mi) of public and private land, or one-fifth of New York State's total area. It is bigger than Yellowstone, Grand Canyon and Yosemite national parks combined and encompasses more than 3,000 ponds and lakes; 2,000 peaks in five mountain ranges (the highest is Mt. Marcy at 5,344ft); and 31,500mi of rivers, brooks and streams. More than a billion trees shelter its abundant wildlife. The park is bounded on the east by Lake George and Lake Champlain (named after the area's first European explorer), where Fort Ticonderoga★★ (Rte. 74, 1mi east of Ticonderoga; ✕&🅿 🖉518-585-2821; www.fortticonderoga.org) offers views and a strong dose of history from both the French and Indian, and Revolutionary wars. About 29mi south, the spa town of Saratoga Springs★★★, an elite 19C vacation mecca, makes an interesting gateway to the Adirondacks. To the northwest, the St. Lawrence River forms the backbone of the scenic Thousand Islands★ region along the Canadian border.

A BIT OF HISTORY

Long considered a "dismal wilderness," by 1850 the area's rich timber reserves had made New York the biggest logging state in the Union. To protect the watershed, the state created a forest preserve, and in 1894 amended its constitution to ensure that all such lands, including Adirondack Park, would remain "forever wild." Since then, an often tense blend of preservation and development has succeeded in balancing pristine wilderness with public and private use. Today, some 10 million visitors and 130,000 year-round residents enjoy the beauty of Adirondack Park. In late

🛈 **Info:** 🖉518-846-8016. www.visitadirondacks.com.

😊 **Don't Miss:** Winter pleasures at Lake Placid resort.

🕐 **Timing:** Winter travelers can encounter delays due to the weather.

2013, about 21,000 acres of Adirondack forest preserve purchased by the state from Nature Conservancy opened to the public, giving access to land that was off limits for more than 100 years.

SIGHTS

Lake Placid Village★

On Mirror Lake. 🖉518-523-2445. www.lakeplacid.com.

A winter sports resort since the 1850s, this tiny village sealed its reputation as the "birthplace of winter sports in America" by hosting the 1932 and 1980 Winter Olympics. Today the village bustles with athletes who come to train at the state-of-the-art sports facilities, as well astourists who come to ski and hike in winter, and mountain bike and take scenic gondola rides in summer. Upscale restaurants and shops line Main Street, and the hulking **Olympic Center** (2634 Main St.; 🖉518-523-1655; www.whiteface.com) offers visitors the chance to take a bobsled run or, for a calmer experience, visit the Olympic Museum. You can also visit the **Olympic Jumping Complex** (2mi south of downtown on Rte. 73; 🖉518-523-2202), where ski jumpers practice on a special surface.

Whiteface Mountain Veterans Memorial Highway★★

From Lake Placid take Rte. 86 to Rte. 431 in downtown Wilmington; continue 3mi to toll booth. May be closed during inclement weather. ✕🅿 🖉518-946-2223. www.whiteface.com.

A notable exception to the 1894 "forever wild" clause, this two-lane road was built in 1927 as a memorial to

Saranac Lake and Whiteface Mountain

© Gwen Cannon/MICHELIN

World War I veterans. Climbing 8mi, it provides the only automobile access to a summit in the High Peaks. Park at the top and scale the final .2mi on foot from Whiteface Castle (or by elevator from the parking lot) to the summit of Whiteface Mountain (4,867ft), where the 360-degree **view★★★** extends 110mi on a clear day.

Adirondack Museum★★★

Intersection of Rtes. 30 & 28, Blue Mountain Lake. Open late-May–mid-October. ✕&🅿️ 𝒫518-352-7311. www.adkmuseum.org.

Commanding a picturesque **view★** of Blue Mountain Lake, this 32-acre compound of historic buildings, galleries and exhibit halls explores all aspects of the region's history. On the grounds, explore stunning examples of **Adirondack architecture★**, including rustic twig **Sunset Cottage★** and whimsical **Bull Cottage★**, where examples of the area's famed Adirondack furniture are on display.

The acclaimed exhibit on **Boats and Boating in the Adirondacks★★** is highlighted by an entire room devoted to Adirondack **guideboats★★**—developed around 1849 to transport wilderness guides and their clients. The **Roads and Rails Exhibit★** focuses on the challenge of transportation in this rugged region. Vehicles of all descrip-

tions include an exquisitely restored 1890 **Pullman railroad car★★**.

Great Camp Sagamore★★

4mi south of the town of Raquette Lake, off Rte. 28. 🕿 Visit by guided tour only. Memorial Day weekend–third weekend in October. ✕🅿️ 𝒫315-354-5311. www.sagamore.org.

"Wilderness playground" of the wealthy Vanderbilt family for more than 50 years, Sagamore represents the passion among America's turn-of-the-century nouveau riche for getaways in the Adirondacks. Built by developer William West Durant in 1897, this "great camp" was once a 1,500-acre self-contained village, providing its owners an "haute rustic" lifestyle.

Today the 19-acre National Historic Landmark comprises 27 buildings, including the **upper camp** of servants' and workers' quarters and other outbuildings. In the **lower camp**, the **Wigwam★** was once used as a men's lodge, and the **main lodge★★** typifies Durant's Swiss-chalet-meets-Adirondack-rustic aesthetic, a style he is credited with inventing.

The famous outdoor **bowling alley★** (1913) functions to this day. Camps and workshops focusing on everything from sports to culture are available to all age groups. Also, local artisans showcase their handicrafts each weekend.

Finger Lakes★★

At the heart of upstate New York hang the 11 Finger Lakes. Viewed from above, the lakes appear suspended, like slender pendants on an invisible chain. Each one a jewel in its own right, these narrow lakes form the framework for landscape, leisure and life in this region. The Finger Lakes region encompasses 14 counties. A happy blend of history, natural beauty and viticulture attracts millions of visitors to the Finger Lakes each year.

- 🕒 **Michelin Map:** p134.
- **Info:** ℘315-536-7488; www.fingerlakes.org
- ▶ **Location:** The Finger Lakes region covers 9,000 acres from Lake Ontario south to Pennsylvania, east to Syracuse and west to Rochester.
- ☺ **Don't Miss:** The views from Watkins Glen State Park.
- ♣ **Kids:** Glass-blowing demonstrations at the Corning Museum of Glass entertain kids of all ages.

A BIT OF HISTORY

The area's stunning features—precipitous glens and gorges and their boisterous waterfalls—are scenic by-products of ongoing water erosion, a process that began during the last Ice Age when glaciers carved up the surrounding terrain. Since 1300 the Iroquois tribes—later organized into the powerful six nations of the Iroquois Confederacy—have inhabited these lands. To learn about the Iroquois and the French missionaries who lived in the area during the 17C, visit **Sainte Marie Among the Iroquois★ ♣♣** (on Onondaga Pkwy./Rte. 370; ℘315-453-6768; www.ongov.net) just outside of Syracuse in Liverpool.

In 1825 the Erie Canal cut its swath north of the lakes bringing settlers, commerce and industry; the **Erie Canal Museum★** (318 Erie Blvd. E. at Montgomery St.; ℘315-471-0593; www.eriecanalmuseum.org) in Syracuse explores its history.

ALLURING LAKES

Among the lakes, Cayuga is the longest at 40mi, and Seneca the deepest, reaching down more than 600ft in places. Tiny Canadice Lake, only 3mi long, is highest in elevation at 1,099ft above sea level. Each lake hosts quaint communities at its north and south ends, and temperate microclimates in between make the Finger Lakes the second-largest winemaking region in the US after California's Napa Valley (🕒see On the Trail infobox).

SIGHTS
Cornell University★★

Main campus at intersection of Ithaca Rd. & Hoy Rd., Ithaca. ♿🅿 ℘607-254-4636. www.cornell.edu.

Cornell was chartered in 1865 as New York's land-grant university to provide an education in both liberal and practical arts. Ezra Cornell, who had made his fortune in the telegraph business, donated 300 acres and a generous endowment to found the college.

Today the 745-acre campus educates more than 21,000 students in more than 100 fields. Its lovely site above Cayuga Lake encompasses Sage Chapel, where Ezra Cornell is buried; and "Old Stone Row," which contains the oldest structures on campus.

A good way to visit the campus is to follow one of the trails that originate at **Cornell Plantations★** (One Plantation Rd.; 🅿 ℘607-255-2400; www.cornellplantations.org), a laboratory of local and non-native flora. If you're a bird-lover, don't miss **Sapsucker Woods**, a 230-acre sanctuary overseen by the university, with trails, boardwalks and a visitor center (℘800-843-2473; www.birds.cornell.edu).

Watkins Glen State Park★★

Rte. 14/Franklin St., Watkins Glen. Gorge Trail open May–mid-Nov. △ 🅿 ℘607-535-4511. http://nysparks.com/parks.

At the tip of Lake Seneca and about 25mi west of Ithaca, Watkins is perhaps the most spectacular glen in the Finger Lakes. The 1.5mi hike into the narrow gorge ascends 832 steps and 700ft in elevation alongside Glen Creek as it dances down the canyon through 19 waterfalls into crystal-clear plunge pools and over well-worn rock formations. Climb Jacob's Ladder (a steep staircase) at the end and return along one of the upper trails. Then take in the view from the 85ft suspension bridge that crosses the gorge and connects the Indian and South Rim trails.

Sonnenberg Gardens & Mansion State Historic Park★

151 Charlotte St., Canandaigua. Open the day after Memorial Day–early October. 🕭🅿 ℘585-394-4922. www.sonnenberg.org.

Set on 50 beautifully landscaped acres 20mi southeast of Rochester, this 40-room Queen Anne mansion was begun in 1885 for the founder of the First National Bank of New York. The gardens and the mansion's interior reflect the height of Victorian taste. The park's wine center offers a good introduction to products from more than 40 partner wineries and farms.

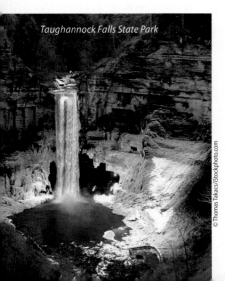
Taughannock Falls State Park

© Thomas Takacs/iStockphoto.com

Granger Homestead and Carriage Museum★

295 N. Main St., Canandaigua. Jun–Oct. 🕭🅿 ℘585-394-1472. www.granger homestead.org.

After a guided tour through the homestead, including an 1816 Federal-style mansion and Victorian gardens, visitors will be well-versed in local history. Other highlights include a carriage museum, housed in two barns, that showcases more than 100 antique carriages and sleighs.

Rose Hill Mansion★★

3mi east of Geneva on Rte. 96A. Open May–Oct. ℘315-789-3848. www.genevahistoricalsociety.com.

Find this charming 1839 Greek Revival mansion at the top of Lake Seneca, with a lovely view of the lake from its porch. Passed through many hands over the years, the mansion has been beautifully restored, from its temple-like exterior to the meticulously researched plasterwork, wall colors, floor coverings and furniture inside. An introductory 7min video and knowledgeable guides enhance the visit.

Women's Rights National Historical Park★★

136 Fall St., Seneca Falls. 🕭🅿 ℘315-568-2991. www.nps.gov/wori.

Seneca Falls, at the northern end of Lake Cayuga, is best known today as the historic center of the Women's Rights Movement. Inspired by the movement to abolish slavery, the first Women's Rights Convention met here in 1848 in an attempt to extend equal rights to women.

Today, a national historic park comprises several diverse sites important to the history of women's rights, including the home of movement leader Elizabeth Cady Stanton. The visitor center stands at its heart, offering detailed and thoughtful exhibits about historic and contemporary women's issues.

On the Trail

With four different wine trails—and more than 200 wineries—it would be a mistake to dismiss Finger Lakes Wine Country. Make no mistake; there is some very good wine being produced in upstate New York. Wine Spectator magazine recently proclaimed that the Finger Lakes are turning out some "impressive Rieslings and ambitious reds." Those new to the Finger Lakes should consider a trip along one of the established trails: Canandaigua Lake Wine Trail (℘585-223-4210 x.121; www.canandaiguawinetrail.com); the Cayuga Lake Wine Trail (℘800-684-5217; www.cayugawinetrail.com); the Keuka Lake Wine Trail (℘315-536-5056; www.keukawinetrail.com); or the Seneca Lake Wine Trail (℘877-536-2717; www.senecalakewine.com).

Seward House Museum★★

33 South St., Auburn. ⟍Visit by guided tour only. ♿℘315-252-1283. www.sewardhouse.org.

Built in 1816, this fine Federal-style home reflects the full and rich life of its gregarious 48-year occupant, statesman William Henry Seward (1801-72). Because five generations of the family lived here over the years, the house, which is surrounded by gardens, is remarkably appointed with personal possessions.

The guided tour—a must—includes several rooms of artifacts relating to the attempt on Seward's life in 1865 and the Alaska Purchase, which he helped bring about.

Corning Museum of Glass★★

1 Museum Way, Corning. ✗♿🅿℘607-937-5371. www.cmog.org.

This huge, stunning museum introduces visitors to the art and craft of glassmaking through its collection—the world's largest—of more than 45,000 art and historical glass objects, plus hands-on exhibits about the science and technology involved in the process.

There are daily glass-blowing demonstrationsand a studio that offers in-depth courses year-round.

A new building, slated for completion in late 2014, will hold a 26,000sq ft contemporary gallery and a 500-seat venue for glassmaking demonstrations.

The museum is also home to the Rakow Research Library, the largest library dedicated to the art, history and craft of glass. Visit the GlassMarket to see more than 15,000 glass objects that are all just waiting for a visitor to fall in love with them and take them home.

Rockwell Museum of Western Art★

111 Cedar St., Corning. ℘607-937-5386. www.rockwellmuseum.org.

Housed in the restored 1893 Romanesque Revival City Hall, the museum showcases American western and Native American art that was amassed by local department store scion Robert F. Rockwell, Jr. Featured artists include Remington, Russell, Bierstadt and Moran. The museum's galleries are divided by subject: Visions of the West, Wilderness Gallery, Buffalo Gallery, Appeal to the Great Spirit, and more. An extensive calendar of events will appeal to the whole family.

ALONG THE WAY
Taughannock Falls State Park★

Rte. 89, Ulysses between Trumansburg and Ithaca. Trail closed in winter. ⚠♿🅿 ℘607-387-6739. www.nysparks.com/parks/62.

Impressed by Niagara Falls? Consider adding in a visit to Taughannock; at 215ft tall, it's more than 30 ft higher than its famous cousin.

In addition to the falls, this 783-acre state park has something for everyone, including a beach on Lake Cayuga, hiking trails and picnic grounds.

Niagara Falls★★★

Near Buffalo, New York's second-largest city, the Niagara River suddenly plunges almost 180ft, creating one of the world's greatest natural spectacles: Niagara Falls. These three sets of falls straddle the US/Canada border—American and Bridal Veil Falls on the American side, and Horseshoe Falls on the Canadian side. Today, with a crest length of 2,200ft (1,000ft flank-to-flank), Horseshoe Falls channels more than 90 percent of the water at Niagara—some 315,000 to 675,000 gallons per second in the summertime, depending on how much water is being diverted for hydroelectric power. American Falls has a crest length of about 1,100ft; Bridal Veil Falls, a ribbon-like 40ft. Together these two funnel between 60,000 and 75,000 gallons of water over their edges every second.

A BIT OF HISTORY

The falls began their evolution about 10,000 years ago when the young Niagara River flowed out of Lake Erie and tumbled over the Niagara Escarpment 7.5mi to the north. The river waters slowly eroded their way backward to the present-day location of the falls. Since Native Americans first laid eyes on them, the falls have been a source of wonder to all who view them, not for their height, but for their panoramic breadth, powerful roar and scenic beauty. Drawn by their tumult and spray, explorers, painters, daredevils, hucksters, honeymooners and sightseers have flocked to their banks. Niagara is still one of the most popular tourist destinations in the world, attracting more than 22 million visitors a year. The water's forceful flow has long been exploited by hydroelectric power plants, and today, upstream power projects divert half to three-quarters of the falls' water.

▶ **Population:** 49,722
◔ **Michelin Map:** p134.
▯ **Info:** ✆800-283-3256; www.visitbuffaloniagara.com
◖ **Location:** These majestic falls are just 20mi from Buffalo.
◌ **Don't Miss:** The world-famous Maid of the Mist Boat Tour.

SIGHTS
Niagara Falls State Park★★
Prospect St. ✕♿▯✆716-278-1796. www.niagarafallsstatepark.com.
This strip of green—America's oldest state park, landscaped by Frederick Law Olmsted in the 1880s—stretches 3.5mi along the Niagara River and over the five islands located at the top of the gorge. Within it lie all the attractions on the US side. The park provides something of a refuge from nearby hotels and thick crowds. **Prospect Point** affords a bird's-eye view of American Falls, and a glass elevator descends to its craggy base from the **New York State Observation Tower**. From the tower's top, walk to the outdoor deck for a panoramic view of all of Niagara Falls.
A tree-lined pedestrian path follows the American bank of the Niagara River to bridges that lead to tranquil Goat Island, which separates Horseshoe from American Falls. **Terrapin Point**, on the west end of the island, affords the best view of Horseshoe Falls from the US.

♙♙ Maid of the Mist Boat Tour★★★
Departs from Niagara Falls State Park. Open Apr–Oct, depending on ice conditions in the river. ♿▯✆716-284-8897. www.maidofthemist.com.
Launched in 1846, the first Maid of the Mist was a wooden-hulled, coal-fired steamboat. Today four all-steel, diesel-powered boats chug from the base of Prospect Point (*accessible via Observation Tower elevator*) past American and Bridal Veil Falls to bob at the tumultuous base of Horseshoe Falls. Visitors are

given plastic hooded rain ponchos to protect them from the fantastic spray.

Cave of the Winds★★

Goat Island. Open May–Oct. ✕ 🅿
𝒫716-278-1730. www.niagarafalls statepark.com.

This walking tour passes within a breathtaking 25ft of roaring Bridal Veil Falls. Outfitted with heavy-duty slickers and special sandals, visitors descend an elevator 175ft into the Niagara Gorge and then follow a path to the base of the falls. The boardwalk culminates on the Hurricane Deck, pounded brutally with water when the wind comes from the east and lifts the mist off the falls.

Observation Point, Niagara Falls

© Wally Stemberger/iStockphoto.com

Old Fort Niagara★★

In Fort Niagara State Park off the Robert Moses Pkwy. (Rte. 18), Youngstown. ♿🅿𝒫716-745-7611; www.oldfortniagara.org.

Situated on a scenic promontory where the Niagara River feeds into Lake Ontario about 15mi north of the falls, this 22-acre complex has alternately served as a French, English and American military stronghold over the centuries. Because it controlled water access from Lake Ontario to the four other Great Lakes, the fort commanded one of the most strategic—and therefore contested—locations in western New York.

Its 18C buildings have been returned to their original appearance, and each is marked with a heraldic plaque identifying the country that erected it.

France, first to occupy the site in 1679, built the crown jewel of the complex, called the **French Castle★** (1726).

On clear days it affords a stupendous **view★★** of Toronto across the lake.

The British captured the fort in 1759, but surrendered it to the Americans in 1796. Except for a brief stint of British rule during the War of 1812, Fort Niagara has been maintained by the US ever since. It is both a National Historic Landmark and a New York State Historic Site.

Daredevils

Niagara has always posed a tempting challenge to adventurers. The first to tumble over **Horseshoe Falls**—the preferred "stunt" falls, because there are no rocks at the bottom—was an assembly of animals and birds aboard a wooden schooner pushed to certain demise in a publicity stunt in 1827. The most famous of Niagara's "rope dancers" was Jean-François Gravelet, also known as "the Great Blondin," who traversed Niagara Gorge on a tightrope for the first time in 1859. In later feats, he rode across the rope on a bicycle and made the trek carrying his manager. Another daredevil toted a small stove onto the tightrope, lit a fire, cooked two omelets, and lowered them down to passengers on the *Maid of the Mist*. Braving the falls in a barrel, though illegal, has been often attempted.

In 1901 schoolteacher Annie Edson Taylor became the first to survive the ordeal by encasing herself in an oak barrel. Subsequent daredevils devised all manner of contraptions to brave the drop and survive, but most remarkable was the plunge of Roger Woodward. In 1960 the 7-year-old managed to escape serious injury when he was swept over the falls clad in only a life jacket.

Philadelphia Area

One of America's most historic pockets is solidly anchored in the Middle Atlantic region. Philadelphia, along with neighboring Bucks County, Brandywine Valley and, farther afield, Lancaster County and Gettysburg, preserve a rich store of monuments to the past. Nearby New Jersey attracts visitors not only to try their luck at the glittering Atlantic City casinos, but to soak up the sun on the state's Atlantic Ocean beaches.

Highlights

1. Tour **Elfreth's Alley**, America's oldest residential street (p162)
2. Learn about Maurice Sendak's art and writing at the **Rosenbach Museum and Library** (p165)
3. See Thomas Eakins' *The Gross Clinic* at the **Philadelphia Museum of Art** (p167)
4. Walk in George Washington's footsteps at **Valley Forge National Historical Park** (p168)

Philadelphia

A Region Rich in History

Long before any white man admired these landscapes, the Lenni Lenape Indians inhabited the area. It was from this peaceful tribe that William Penn (1644-1718) purchased tracts in the late 17C. Penn's city of Philadelphia gave birth to the American Revolution in 1776 when Thomas Jefferson read the Declaration of Independence here. Eleven years later, the framers of the Constitution reconvened in Philadelphia to form a new government for the fledgling United States of America.

During the Revolutionary War, the region became contested ground, now famous as the site of George Washington's Valley Forge encampment and his crossing of the Delaware River. Nearly a century later, one of the most important battles of the Civil War raged 124mi west of Philadelphia in Gettysburg. The three-day battle in the summer of 1863 turned out to be a pivotal but hard-won Northern victory.

Hub of the region, Philadelphia offers a rich history, myriad culture and an ethnic diversity that guarantee the visitor a fascinating stay. When you tire of the city's bustle, bucolic Lancaster County, an hour's drive west, beckons 21C travelers back to a simpler time: Amish inhabitants of the Pennsylvania Dutch Country eschew modern conveniences such as electricity, and travel in horse-drawn buggies as they have for decades. Just beyond Philadelphia's southwestern boundary lies the verdant Brandywine Valley, whose beauty and hospitality attracted 19C industrialists and 20C artists. Tony Bucks County, just east of the city, is heralded for its artsy ambience.

Elfreth's Alley

© Walter Bibikow/AWL Images

ADDRESSES

🏨 STAY

$$$$$ The Virginia Hotel – 25 Jackson St., Cape May, NJ. ✕ ♿ 🅿 ✆800-732-4236. www.virginiahotel.com. 24 rooms. Service is key at this historic downtown inn, known for the wedding-cake trelliswork on its porch and balconies. Unlike most local Victorians, the 1879 building is designed in soothing beige and green tones. Furnishings blend period reproductions with contemporary overstuffed sofas. Luxury is the rule of the day at The Virginia, where the sheets are from Belgium and the bathroom amenities are from Bulgari. The hotel's acclaimed **Ebbitt Room** lures diners from near and far. Guests receive a complimentary continental breakfast.

$$$$$ Inn at Bowman's Hill – 518 Lurgan Rd., New Hope. 🅿 ⚏ ✆215-862-8090. www.theinnatbowmanshill.com. 6 rooms. A Certified Wildlife Habitat, this lovely inn sits on five manicured acres including a forest and pond. Rooms are individually decorated in soft colors with luxuries such as king-size feather-beds, whirlpool tubs, fireplaces and private decks. A made-to-order gourmet breakfast is served either in the privacy of your room, in the fireside dining room or on the terrace. Eggs come from the inn's own flock of free-range chickens.

$$$ The Inn & Spa at Intercourse Village – 3542 Old Philadelphia Pike., Intercourse, PA. 🅿 ✆717-768-2626. www.inn-spa.com. 12 rooms. Sit on the front porch of this 1909 Victorian house and watch Amish buggies trot by. Original dark woodwork is the backdrop for early-20C furnishings and lace curtains. Suites in the homestead buildings out back have a more rustic feel, with sloping beamed ceilings and handmade quilts, evoking the romance of past times. Need room to breathe and a jacuzzi? Book a grand suite.

$$$ The Latham Hotel – 135 S. 17th St., Philadelphia, PA. ♿ 🅿 ✆215-563-7474. www.lathamhotelphiladelphia.com. 139 rooms. Doormen welcome you in English riding habits at this boutique property. One block from Rittenhouse Square, the building hasn't changed much since 1907 when it opened as a high-rise apartment. Free wireless high-speed Internet access adds a nice business-friendly touch to the rooms, which were renovated in 2012 in a sophisticated contemporary style. The Latham's restaurant, **Urban Enoteca**, hones in on Italian classics.

$$ Fairville Inn – 506 Kennet Pike, Chadds Ford, PA. 🅿 ✆610-388-5900. www.fairvilleinn.com. 15 rooms. Two miles from Longwood Gardens, the Federal-style house (c.1857) has loads of country charm. Behind the sunny yellow façade,

Independence Hall, Philadelphia

Chippendale reproductions, handmade pierced lampshades, and Winterthur-inspired wallpaper decorate the rooms. A tempting assortment of home-baked cookies is laid out with afternoon tea.

$$ Penn's View Hotel – Front & Market Sts., Philadelphia, PA. ✕&🄿 ℘215-922-7600. www.pennsviewhotel.com. 51 rooms. An Old City gem inside two connecting 19C warehouses overlooking the Delaware River. Individually decorated accommodations—reproduction Chippendale, delicate floral wallpapers and hardwood floors—recall bedrooms at Grandma's house. Downstairs, the bar at the Italian trattoria-style **Ristorante Panorama** features a custom-made, 120-bottle, wine-dispensing machine.

ⴼ/EAT

$$ Sampan – 124 S. 13th St., Philadelphia, PA. ℘215-732-3501. www.sampanphilly.com. **Asian Fusion.** In Center City, Sampan offers big flavor on its small-plate dishes. Though many of the dishes will, at first, seem familiar, most veer off in a slightly different (and far more delicious) direction than expected. As a starter, crispy rock shrimp comes with pickled radish, yuzu and chile aioli, while Pekin duck served with scallion buns and hoisin sauce makes a delicious entrée. Finish with a trio of tiny ice cream cones in the flavor of the day.

$$ Fork – 306 Market St., Philadelphia, PA. ℘215-625-9425. www.forkrestaurant.com. **Contemporary.** This bustling Old Citybistro offers comfort food with a creative edge. The menu makes mouths water with dishes like home-made agnolotti stuffed with Jersey rabbit and Sicilian pistachios, and branzino "en croute" with spiced tamarind broth. Need a place to take a shopping break? Grab a window (or bar) seat at Fork and order one of the restaurant's crafted cocktails.

$$ The City Tavern – 138 S. 2nd St., Philadelphia, PA. ℘215-413-1443. www.citytavern.com. **Colonial.** This Old City eatery re-creates the original 1773 tavern where Revolutionary War heroes, including George Washington and John Adams, dined and strategized. Waiters dressed in period costume serve Thomas Jefferson's favorites: cornmeal-coated fried oysters and clover-honey-glazed roast duckling. The house ale is brewed using Jefferson's own formula. Parents need not worry; there are plenty of kid-friendly choices on the children's menu, including turkey pot pie, fish and chips, and a grilled ham and cheese sandwich.

$$ Supper – 926 South St., Philadelphia, PA. ℘215-592-8180. www.supperphilly.com. **Contemporary.** The first thing to notice about Supper is how much there is to notice about its interior; the design is elegant but casual, playful but sophisticated. The locally sourced food is even better. The fingerling potatoes fried in duck fat with black truffle mayo are a must. On Tuesday nights, pastrami fried chicken comes with Thousand Island dressing, house-made pickles, a scratch biscuit and a side for $25.

$ Pizzeria Stella – 420 S. 2nd St. at Lombard St., Philadelphia, PA. ℘215-320-8000. www.pizzeriastella.net. **Pizza.** Owned by Stephen Starr, one of Philadelphia's best-known restaurateurs. Pizzeria Stella has been a great surprise for the city. It's been touted by critic after critic as some of Philly's best pizza. One of the menu's most interesting flavor combinations is a pistachio, red onion, rosemary and fontina cheese pizza. The house-made gelati are a very good way to end a day.

$$$ Dilworthtown Inn – 1390 Old Wilmington Pike, West Chester, PA. ℘610-399-1390. www.dilworthtown.com. **Contemporary.** Fifteen intimate dining rooms with fireplaces, gaslit chandeliers and handmade chestnut tables take you back to colonial days, when this tavern fed Revolutionary heroes. Though the menu offers plenty of classic dishes, including chateaubriand for two, there are plenty of modern choices as well. The menu changes weekly but might include pistachio-crusted sea scallops with strawberry-grape gastrique, and roasted smoked duck with green curry and turmeric coconut stewed onions. Choose from an 800-bottle wine list. Extend the Dilworth experience by signing on for a wine or cooking class at the restaurant's cooking school, the Inn Keeper's Kitchen. Two-hour classes range from $65 to $85.

Philadelphia★★★

Cradle of US history, William Penn's "City of Brotherly Love," marks the country's earliest strides toward nationhood. The city's history has been shaped by religious freedom seekers, immigrant success stories, industrialist robber barons, and the creative genius of Benjamin Franklin. Although skyscrapers now pierce the skyline, the spirit of industry and culture, which has been Philadelphia's legacy since Franklin walked these streets, still prevails, making Philadelphia one of America's great destinations.

- **Population:** 1,547,607
- **Michelin Map:** P148.
- **Info:** ✆215-599-0776; www.visitphilly.com.
- **Parking:** Train service makes Philadelphia accessible without a car.
- **Don't Miss:** The sounds of freedom of the Liberty Bell.
- **Kids:** Take a walk through the Giant Heart at The Franklin Institute.

A BIT OF HISTORY

Beginning in the mid-17C, Swedes, British and Dutch began settling along the banks of the Delaware River. A power struggle ensued, with each side vying for control of the Delaware River Valley. Britain prevailed, and, in 1681, **William Penn** (son of British naval hero Admiral Sir William Penn) began his "holy experiment" in the New World. Escaping religious persecution in England, Penn established a peaceful Quaker colony along a stretch of land bounded by the Delaware and Schuylkill rivers. Penn's new settlement thrived, and by 1700 ranked second largest in the New World after Boston, populated not only by Quakers, but also by European immigrants of every stripe.

As the 18C drew to a close, the independent-minded colonies were beginning to chafe against British rule. As the most populous and wealthiest city in the colonies in 1774, Philadelphia was an obvious place for the First Continental Congress to discuss the colonists' strained relations with the Crown. A year later the Second Continental Congress set an irrevocable course for separation from Great Britain.

For the last decade of the 18C, Philadelphia served as interim capital of the newly formed United States, until the nation's capital relocated to Washington, DC, in 1800. Fueled by the engines of the Industrial Revolution, the economy boomed and immigrants flocked to Philadelphia to keep the wheels of industry turning. The city generally prospered until the end of World War II, after which time Philadelphia drifted rudderless for several decades and finally declared bankruptcy in the late 1980s. As of the 1990s, the "City of Brotherly Love" underwent a rebirth thanks to a revitalized Center City.

THE CITY TODAY

Today the economy of the nation's sixth-largest city is bolstered by health care and service industries. Philadelphia boasts a vibrant arts and theater scene, a wealth of fine museums and myriad upscale restaurants. Three major universities—University of Pennsylvania, Drexel and Temple—add a lively student flavor. The **University of Pennsylvania Museum of Archaeology and Anthropology★★** (3260 South St.; ✕♿ ✆215-898-4000; www.penn.museum) shouldn't be missed.

On the sports front, Philly boasts four national sports teams (the Eagles, Phillies, Flyers, and Sixers) and some of the most dedicated fans in the country.

William Penn still looks down on all he has wrought from his unassailable position atop City Hall; he once said: "And thou, Philadelphia ... what love, what care, what service, and what travail has there been to bring thee forth."

Liberty Bell

© Comstock, Inc.

INDEPENDENCE NATIONAL HISTORICAL PARK★★

Encompassing roughly 12 blocks (*bounded by 2nd & 6th Sts. on the east and west, and Market & Walnuts Sts. on the north and south*), the historic heart of Philadelphia witnessed the turbulent birth of the United States. Now juxtaposed against modern architecture, the historical park includes the country's most revered icons of liberty: the Independence Hall and the Liberty Bell. Events surrounding America's quest for independence come alive at the modern **Visitor Center** (6th & Market Sts.; ♿ ✆800-537-7676; www.phlvisitorcenter.com) through interactive computer stations and two short films: Independence and Choosing Sides.

For more details while touring the park, take advantage of the free Independence National Park cell phone tour, called Ring Up History. At each of the 23 stops on the tour, including the Old City Hall, Declaration House and the Merchants Exchange Building, dial the stop's phone number and code listed on the printout at www.nps.gov/inde/planyourvisit/ cell-phone-programhtm.

Independence Hall★★★

520 Chestnut St. between 5th & 6th Sts.
One of only a handful of works of architecture on the UNESCO World Heritage List, the steepled Georgian brick building (completed in 1756) was constructed as the Pennsylvania State House. In May 1775, delegates of the Second Continental Congress met in the Assembly Room here to determine the colonies' response to increasing British hostility. In reaction to the colonists; appointment of George Washington as commander-in-chief of the Continental Army later that summer, George III declared the colonists to be in "open and avowed rebellion." The following year, the Congress adopted the Declaration of Independence in this hall on July 4, 1776; the Revolutionary War had begun. The first public reading of the Declaration of Independence took place behind the Hall in **Independence Square** on July 8, 1776. When independence finally seemed imminent in 1781, Independence Hall saw the adoption of the Articles of Confederation. Six years later, the Constitutional Convention conceived a new government here and ratified the US Constitution on September 17, 1787. Today the building has been restored to its 18C appearance, with much of its original woodwork.

Flanking the west side of Independence Hall is **Congress Hall★**, the meeting place for the House of Representatives and Senate of the fledgling United States from 1790 to 1800. On the east side, **Old City Hall★** housed the US Supreme Court from the building's completion in 1791 until 1800.

Second Bank of the United States/National Portrait Gallery★★

420 Chestnut St.
This columned marble structure (1819, William Strickland) is a superb example of Greek Revival architecture. Opened in 1824, the bank was one of the world's most powerful financial institutions until Congress let the charter expire in 1836.

Since its restoration in 1974, the building has provided a permanent home for **"People of Independence."** Prominent among the paintings in this exhibit are more than 100 Charles Willson Peale

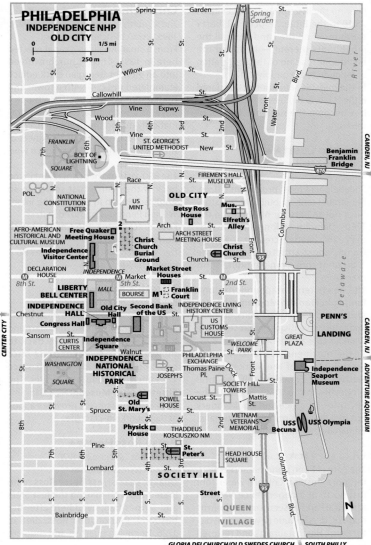

PHILADELPHIA
INDEPENDENCE NHP
OLD CITY

portraits of delegates to the Continental Congress, signers of the Constitution and officers of the Revolutionary War.

Liberty Bell Center★★★

526 Market St., across Chestnut St. from Independence Hall (between 5th & 6th Sts.).&

The glass-fronted pavilion on Independence Mall, completed for the US Bicentennial in 1976, enshrines the revered **Liberty Bell★★★**. Crafted in London's White-chapel Foundry in 1751, the (mostly) copper and lead bell developed a crack soon after its arrival in Philadelphia and had to be recast by local metalsmiths John Pass and John Stowe. Beginning in 1753, the 2,000-pound bell hung in the State House belfry for almost 100 years. The bell—

bearing the inscription from Leviticus 25:10 in the Bible: "Proclaim Liberty throughout all the Land unto all the inhabitants thereof"—heralded the first public reading of the Declaration of Independence on July 8, 1776.

In the mid-19C, abolitionists declared it the "Liberty Bell"; ever since, the bell has become the national symbol of freedom.

Franklin Court★★

Entrance on Market St. between 3rd & 4th Sts. &

Philadelphia's most prominent citizen, Benjamin Franklin, built a three-story brick house here for his family in the 1760s. Demolished long ago, the residence has been re-created as a steel-frame "ghost structure," as has the 1786 print shop Franklin built for his grandson.

The newly renovated, underground **Benjamin Franklin Museum★** houses an ingenious array of exhibits, artifacts and interactive displays that celebrate Franklin's life and genius.

At the north end of Franklin Court, reproductions of the **Market Street Houses** that Franklin built as rental properties in the 1780s re-create the 18C printing office and bookbindery run by Franklin's grandson, journalist Benjamin Franklin Bache.

OLD CITY★★

The core of Penn's original settlement, this once bustling Colonial waterfront just north of Independence National Historical Park has seen a revival from its mid-20C decrepitude (www.oldcitydistrict.org). Hip restaurants and restored historic buildings—many housing performing arts groups, artists' studios and galleries—now punctuate the area. The strong Quaker presence in early Philadelphia is preserved in the 1783 Free **Quaker Meeting House** (5th & Arch Sts.). On **First Fridays** (the first Friday of every month year-round, 5pm–9pm; ℘215-625-9200, www.visitphilly.com/events/philadelphia/first-friday), Old City galleries, showrooms and theaters extend their hours.

Christ Church★★

2nd St. north of Market St. & ℘215-922-1695. www.christchurchphila.org.

From a small Anglican chapel erected here in 1695, Christ Church evolved into an elegant Georgian brick edifice (completed in 1754) with a tower and "Philadelphia steeple." The church's Royalist congregation changed dramatically during the Revolution, when George Washington and 15 signers of the Declaration of Independence worshipped here.

The 600-year-old **baptismal font** in the back of the church first served in an Anglican church in London; the infant William Penn was baptized in it.

Four blocks west, the **Christ Church Burial Ground** (N. 5th & Arch Sts.; Mar–Dec weather permitting) includes Benjamin Franklin's grave.

Elfreth's Alley★★

Between N. 2nd & Front Sts.

Named after its mid-18C owner, blacksmith Jacob Elfreth, this charming block-long alleyway dates back to the early 18C. Several of its 32 brick row houses have stood here since 1725 and today house urbanites. The **Elfreth's Alley Museum★** (℘215-574-0560; elfrethsalley.org) provides a look at daily working-class life.

Betsy Ross House★

239 Arch St. ℘215-629-4026. www.betsyrosshouse.org.

Quaker seamstress Betsy Ross, who is credited with making the first Stars and Stripes flag, lived here after her husband, Patriot John Ross, died in 1776. Her living quarters and shop are preserved in the brick, gable-roofed home (c.1740).

PENN'S LANDING AND SOCIETY HILL★

Set along the Delaware River just east of Independence National Historical Park, the area now known as **Penn's Landing** sheltered Penn's first settlers in caves they dug in its riverside cliffs. The waterfront between Vine and South Streets has been recast as a recreational area with jogging paths, a skating rink, an amphitheater and the seaport museum. Dominating its northern end, the **Benjamin Franklin Bridge** spans the Delaware, while South Street's restaurants and nightclubs anchor its south side.

Constructed during the turbulent years that surrounded the nation's quest for independence, 18C churches and homes grace the Society Hill section that abuts Penn's Landing from Independence Hall to Lombard St.

Now restored to its historic glory, **Society Hill** contains some of the city's most venerable churches: 1761 **St. Peter's Church** (313 Pine St.); 1763 **Old St. Mary's Church** (252 S. 4th St.); and **Gloria Dei Church/Old Swedes Church★** (Columbus Blvd. & Christian St.), Philadelphia's oldedest (c.1700), founded by Swedish Lutherans.

👥 Independence Seaport Museum★

211 S. Columbus Blvd.; pedestrian access via Walnut St. walking bridge. ♿🅿 𝄢215-413-8655. www.philly seaport.org.

Covering 100,000sq ft, this contemporary waterfront facility comprises several permanent maritime exhibits, including "Home Port Philadelphia," which traces the transatlantic crossing of early-20C immigrants. Docked just to the museum's south, two National Historic landmark ships are berthed side by side: the **USS Olympia★**, Admiral Dewey's 1892 cruiser, and the **USS Becuna**, a World War II Guppy-class submarine.

Across the Delaware River from Penn's Landing, **Adventure Aquarium** 👥 contains denizens ranging from baby sharks to giant sea turtles (1 Riverside Dr., Camden, NJ; ✖♿𝄢856-365-3300; www.adventureaquarium.com; access via Riverlink ferry from Penn's Landing, 𝄢215-925-5465; www.riverlinkferry.org).

Physick House★★

321 S. 4th St. 𝄢215-925-7866. www.philalandmarks.org.

Purchased in 1815 by the "father of American Surgery," Dr. Philip Syng Physick, this stately home (1786) was occupied by the Physick family until 1940, when it was willed to the Pennsylvania Hospital. In the 1960s, philanthropists Walter and Lenore Annenberg purchased the property and funded the renovation that turned the house into a Federal-period showpiece. The fine collection of furnishings reflects the Federal and Empire styles.

South Street★★

Forming the southern border of Society Hill, trendy South Street has been a mecca for the counterculture since the 1960s. The blocks between the waterfront and 10th Street are lined with myriad shops, hip restaurants and cutting-edge clubs. **Jim's Steaks** (400 South St.; 𝄢215-928-1911; www.jimssteaks.com), which serves up some of the best Philly Cheesesteaks around, is also in the neighborhood.

CENTER CITY★★★

Bound on its north-south axis by Vine and South Streets, this historic area has been Philadelphia's main commercial district from the 1870s, when the current City Hall was built. Nearly 100 years later new construction began in an effort to revitalize the area from its mid-20C malaise. The first structure to exceed the height of Penn's statue atop City Hall's dome, **One Liberty Place** (1650 Market Pl.), inspired new growth. A boon to the city's finances, the **Pennsylvania Convention Center** (1101 Arch St.; 𝄢215-418-4700; www.paconvention.com) opened in 1993 and covers 1.3 million sq ft. Incorporated into its design is the Victorian-era train shed whose head house now contains the lively food bazaar of **Reading Terminal Market** (N. 12th St. & Arch St.; 𝄢215-922-2317; www.

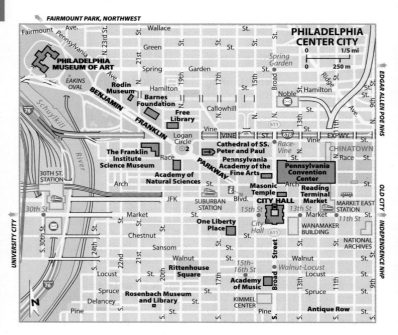

FAIRMOUNT PARK, NORTHWEST

PHILADELPHIA CENTER CITY

readingterminalmarket.org). Performing-arts venues abound along South Broad Street; chief among them is the 1850s Baroque-style **Academy of Music** (1420 Locust Ave.; 215-893-1935; www.academyofmusic.org), the winter quarters of the Philadelphia Orchestra. Art and commerce meet in the antique shops

that line **Antique Row** (Pine St. between S. 9th & S. 12th Sts.; www.antique-row.org). Respite from Center City's bustle can still be found in the eight acres of parkland in **Rittenhouse Square**, one of the public parks laid out in Penn's original city plan.

City Hall★★★

Broad St. & Market St. Interior rooms accessible by 12:30pm guided tour only. (except tower). 215-686-2840. www.visitphilly.com/history/philadelphia/city-hall/.

Centerpiece of downtown, this 700-room French Second Empire structure designed by John McArthur Jr. is the largest municipal building in the country. Upon its completion in 1901, the enormous structure with its solid masonry walls was almost obsolete, and in the early 20C there was talk of demolishing it. The very cost of demolition saved it, and City Hall still functions as Philadelphia's ceremonial "palace." Its 548ft tower is crowned by a statue of William Penn. Below the statue, an **observation deck** provides panoramic views of the city. Notable interior cham-

City Hall

© Natalia Bratslavsky/Bigstockphoto.com

Benjamin Franklin

The 15th child of an English soapmaker who immigrated to Boston in the early 18C, Benjamin Franklin (1706-90) only had two years of formal schooling before he was apprenticed to his brother James to learn the printing business in 1718. At age 17 Franklin headed to Philadelphia, where he established himself as a successful printer. To engage his creative restlessness, in 1732 Franklin began publishing his popular *Poor Richard's Almanack*, with homilies on such virtues as thrift and industry. Gradually he became a city leader and helped set up Philadelphia institutions such as the Library Company of Philadelphia, Pennsylvania Hospital and the Philadelphia Academy—precursor to the University of Pennsylvania. Franklin took great delight in his scientific endeavors; his experiments with electricity earned him fame in Europe. In his fifties Franklin was elected to the Pennsylvania Assembly, and thereafter much of his life was dominated by politics and the fight for nationhood. While the nation now reveres him as a Founding Father, Philadelphians proudly claim Franklin as their own "uncommon citizen."

bers include the **Mayor's Reception Room**, with its mahogany wainscoting, and the **Conversation Hall**, with its plaster and aluminum-leaf ceiling.

Masonic Temple★★

1 N. Broad St., on north side of City Hall. ✪Visit by guided tour only. ✆215-988-1900. www.pagrandlodge.org.
Considered one of Freemasonry's most magnificent temples, this Medieval Norman-style granite structure (1873) marked by spires and towers was conceived by Masonic brother James Windrim. Elaborate interior rooms— designed by George Herzog—are decorated in motifs reflecting the orders of Masonry: Moorish, Gothic, Ionic, Egyptian, Romanesque, Renaissance, and Corinthian.

Pennsylvania Academy of the Fine Arts★★

Broad & Cherry Sts. ♿✆215-972-7600. www.pafa.org.
Portraitist Charles Willson Peale founded the country's first art school and museum in 1805. Housed in an ornate brick and limestone Victorian structure (1876, Frank Furness and George Hewitt), the museum exhibits three centuries of artistic styles. Arranged in chronological order, galleries display works from the 18C "Grand Manner" tradition, 19C American sculpture, early-20C Modernism and post-

World War II Abstract Expressionism. Free tours begin in the lobby twice a day (1pm & 2pm) and feature highlights of the permanent collection.

Rosenbach Museum and Library★

2010 Delancey St. ✆215-732-1600. www.rosenbach.org.
The museum occupies an 1865 town house that was once home to book dealers Philip and Abraham Rosenbach. A fine group of decorative arts complements the library's 30,000 books and 300,000 manuscripts; a prize among the latter is James Joyce's handwritten ***Ulysses* manuscript★**.
Also of note is the oldest Hebrew bible in North America, which is on exhibit here, and the Maurice Sendak collection. ✪For access to Dr. Rosenbach's rare book library, join a guided tour of the house.

BENJAMIN FRANKLIN PARKWAY★★★

Modeled after the Champs Elysées, the parkway cuts a broad swath from City Hall to the Philadelphia Museum of Art. Designed by architects Jacques Gréber and Paul Cret in 1917, this avenue encompasses Logan Circle (*southeast end*), marked by Alexander Stirling Calder's elegant **Swann Memorial Fountain**. Facing Logan Circle at 19th and Vine Streets, the **Free Library of**

Philadelphia (1927, Horace Trumbauer) models the twin palaces that grace the Place de la Concorde in Paris.

Bordering the art museum, **Fairmount Park**★ became a reality in 1855. Sweeping across 9,200 acres northwest along the Schuylkill River, Fairmount ranks as one of the largest city parks in the world. Encompassed within its borders are the Beaux-Arts **Memorial Hall** (42nd St. & N. Concourse Dr.), one of 250 structures built in the park for the 1876 US Centennial Exposition; a spring-blooming **Azalea Garden** (off Kelly Dr.); and the **Horticulture Center** (N. Horticultural Dr. & Montgomery Dr.), with its serene Japanese **Pine Breeze Villa**★.

One of Philadelphia's most picturesque landmarks is **Boat House Row**★ (off Kelly Dr. along the Schuylkill River north of the Azalea Garden). For more than 150 years amateur rowing clubs have headquartered in this row of Victorian cottages, outlined in white lights at night.

Cathedral Basilica of Saints Peter and Paul★★

Benjamin Franklin Pkwy. & N. 18th St. ✆215-561-1313. www.cathedralphila.org. The design of this copper-domed Italian Renaissance cathedral (1846) was inspired by Rome's Church of San Carlo al Corso. Highlights of the interior include a coffered, barrel-vaulted ceiling overarching the transept and nave, and a dome oculus painted by Constantine Brumidi, producer of the frescoes in Washington, DC's Capitol Building.

♟ The Franklin Institute Science Museum★★

222 N. 20th St. ✖♿🅿 ✆215-448-1200. www2.fi.edu.
Founded in 1824 to teach science to artisans and mechanics, the Franklin Institute and its museum have made science entertaining. Enter the cavernous 300,000sq ft museum through the domed Benjamin Franklin National Memorial, dominated by a 122-ton likeness of a seated Franklin.

Inside, three floors of exhibits treat subjects from communications and transportation to computer technology

and geology. Kids never tire of walking through the nearly two-story tall **Giant Heart**.

♟ The Academy of Natural Sciences of Drexel University★

1900 Benjamin Franklin Pkwy. at Logan Circle. ✖♿ ✆215-299-1000. www.ansp.org.
Dating from 1812, the Academy is one of the oldest science research institutions in the Western Hemisphere.

On the first floor, the acclaimed **Dinosaur Hall**★ exhibit displays skeletons and details the rigors of uncovering fossils. Lifesize dioramas throughout the facility showcase native animals from North America, Asia and Africa.

The Barnes Foundation's Galleries and Arboretum★★

2025 Benjamin Franklin Pkwy.
♿✖🅿 ($15/4hrs). ✆215-278-7200. www.barnesfoundation.org.
Doctor, businessman and art connoisseur, **Dr. Albert C. Barnes** (1872-1951) believed all people were entitled to education and an appreciation of fine arts, and to that end he established the Barnes Foundation in 1922. Several years later he commissioned architect Paul Cret to design an Italianate gallery in nearby Merion to house his collection of more than 2,000 paintings. In May 2012, the collection moved to a striking new two-story, 93,000sq ft building in Center City. The contemporary limestone-faced structure, designed by Todd Williams and Billie Tsien Architects, is set amid landscaped grounds that recall the Barnes Arboretum in Merion. In the new Collection Gallery, Barnes' wealth of **Impressionist and Postimpressionist works**★★—including 181 pieces by Renoir, 69 by Cézanne and 59 by Matisse—are set off by natural light and an intelligent lighting control system that regulates the amount of illumination that falls on the art. Outside, at one end of the reflecting pool, stands The Barnes Totem, a 40ft sculpture made of bead-blasted stainless steel by American artist Ellsworth Kelly.

South Philly

Immigrants have long flocked to this section of Philadelphia, which takes its cue from the Italian community that has provided the dominant culture in the 20C. Today the action centers around the boisterous **Italian Market** (9th St. between Christian & Wharton Sts.; ℘215-278-2903; www.italianmarketphilly.org), where a panoply of vegetable stalls, and meat, fish and poultry markets offer everything from dried bakala (salt cod) to Parmigiano-Reggiano cheese to Sicilian olives.

South Philly's signature **Mummers Museum** (1100 S. 2nd St. at Washington Ave.; ℘215-336-3050; www.mummersmuseum.com) holds the glittering costumes worn in the annual January 1 Mummers parade, which traces its roots to the area's Swedish settlers. Today this Philadelphia frolic taps the creativity of the area's myriad ethnic groups.

Rodin Museum★

N. 22nd St. & Benjamin Franklin Pkwy.
♿ 🅿 ($12/4hrs) ℘215-568-6026.
www.rodinmuseum.org.
The small 1920s Beaux-Arts structure and its surrounding gardens, designed by Paul Cret and Jacques Gréber, house 124 sculptures by French artist **Auguste Rodin** (1840-1917). The recently renovated museum holds the largest collection of Rodin's works to be found outside France.

Philadelphia Museum of Art★★★

N. 26th & Benjamin Franklin Pkwy.
✕♿🅿 ℘215-763-8100.
www.philamuseum.org.
Anchoring the north end of the parkway, this stately Greek Revival building (1928, C. Clark Zantzinger, Horace Trumbauer and Charles L. Borie, Jr.) ranks among the most significant art museums in the US. The museum's roots trace back to the late 19C, when the state legislature called for the building of a permanent structure to serve as an art gallery during the 1876 Centennial Exposition. Today the museum houses a superb collection comprising more than 225,000 objects. In one first-floor wing is an outstanding collection of **European Art 1850-1900★★**, ranging from pieces by Courbet and Whistler to works by Cézanne (*The Large Bathers*, 1905). The adjoining section of **Modern and Contemporary Art** houses an extensive collection of Cubist, Expressionist and Surrealist works. Noteworthy 19C Philadelphia artist Thomas Eakins figures prominently in the **American Art** wing, along with Colonial silver, Shaker furniture and Pennsylvania-German decorative arts.

Philadelphia Museum of Art

Courtesy of Philadelphia Museum of Art

Take the **Great Stair Hall** to the second floor, which is devoted to European art. Earliest examples are found in **European Art 1100-1500★**, housing a rare group of architectural details from monasteries and chapels, and a host of religious paintings and sculpture. The Renaissance is represented in **European Art 1500-1850**, which includes re-created period rooms from French, English and Dutch homes. The **Asian Art★★** wing exhibits exquisite Thai Buddhist pieces and a stone **temple hall** from India. Chinese and Japanese art includes a 17C Chinese nobleman's **reception hall** and an early-20C **Japanese ceremonial tea-house**.

The museum is far too small for its ever expanding collection. In 2007, some of the space pressure was alleviated with the opening of the Art Deco **Perelman Building** across Pennsylvania Ave.

FAIRMONT PARK

👪 Philadelphia Zoo★

3400 W. Girard Ave., in Fairmont Park. ✕👤🅿️🖉215-243-1100. www.philadelphiazoo.org.
Covering 42 acres, this is the oldest zoo (1859) in the country. Modeled on a Victorian pleasure garden, the grounds feature paths that ramble past more than 1,300 animals from around the globe. Be sure to see the rare Amur **leopards at First Niagara Big Cat Falls**, the Primate House, and some of the world's most endangered species in the Rare Animal Conservation Center. Children, from toddlers to teens, will love the new KidZooU. Look overhead to see monkeys and lemurs running through the zoo's new Treetop Trail.

Fairmount Park Houses★

🖉215-683-8100. www.philadelphia museum.org/parkhouses.
In the 18C and early 19C, well-heeled Philadelphians built rural retreats on the bluffs above the Schuylkill River. Today the seven elegant homes open to the public provide fine examples of domestic period architecture. Among them is the oldest, 1746 **Cedar Grove★**, a fieldstone farmhouse (off Lansdowne

Dr.); the 18C Neo-classical gem **Lemon Hill★** (off Kelly Dr.); elegant **Mount Pleasant★** (off Fountain Green Dr.) with its elaborate interior woodwork; and the 1756 late-Georgian-style **Woodford★** (off Dauphin St.), noted for its fine **Colonial furnishings**.

EXCURSIONS

Valley Forge National Historical Park★★

❯ 20mi northwest of Center City via I-76 West. Take Exit 26B and continue 1.5mi in King of Prussia, PA. 👤🅿️🖉610-783-1099. www.nps.gov/vafo.
Initiated into the national park system for the 1976 US Bicentennial, the 3,620-acre park preserves the fields and ridges where George Washington's exhausted and poorly provisioned 12,000-man Continental Army camped from 19 December 1777, to June 19, 1778. Begin at the **visitor center** to view the 18min film dramatizing the travails of Washington's men, and to see artifacts used by the encamped army. Then take the 10mi self-guided **driving tour★** past earthworks and historic stone buildings, including **Washington's Headquarters**, where George and his wife, Martha, spent that stark winter; a free cell phone tour (🖉484-396-1018); or a self-guided tour on the park's 18mi of trails.

Bucks County★★

❯ Northeast of Philadelphia bordering the Delaware River.
Named for William Penn's birthplace of Buckinghamshire, England, Bucks County occupies 625sq acres beyond Philadelphia's northern border. With the prosperity that infused the new country after independence, the **Delaware Canal** was built in 1832, extending 60mi between Bristol and Easton. Although boats no longer "lock through" the canal, the towpath that runs along its length still attracts bikers and hikers. You can best experience the region's rural ambience by driving along lovely **River Road★**. Be sure to spend some time relaxing in the fine inns and restaurants of such towns as **Doylestown★** and **New Hope★**, or hunting for treas-

ures in the trove of antique shops that line Route 202.

Washington Crossing Historic Park★★

On Rte. 32 South between New Hope and Yardley. ♿🅿 ☎215-493-4076. www.ushistory.org/washingtoncrossing. This park, which is in two separate parcels, preserves sites connected with George Washington's famous crossing of the Delaware River in the winter of 1776 to launch a surprise attack on Britain's Hessian forces encamped across the river in Trenton, New Jersey. The **Lower Park** (7mi south of New Hope) contains the visitor center and a row of restored buildings from the 18C ferry-crossing town of Taylorsville.

The **Upper Park** (3.5mi north of visitor center) preserves the 1702 fieldstone house, called the Thompson-Neely House, that served as the Continental commander's headquarters during December 1776.

Pennsbury Manor★★

400 Pennsbury Memorial Rd., via US-1 or US-13 to Tyburn Rd. ☎215-946-0400. www.pennsburymanor.com.

The 43-acre site on the Delaware River 26mi north of Philadelphia was the personal summer estate of Pennsylvania's founder, William Penn. The stately Georgian **manor house★★** (👁visit by guided tour only) that stands today is a re-creation of the manse Penn began building in 1683; its brick façade overlooks formal English gardens and the river beyond. Filled with fine 17C and 18C English and Dutch furnishings—including several Penn family pieces—the interior rooms illustrate Penn's upper-class social status, which belied his Quaker beliefs.

A lively calendar of events runs throughout the year, featuring cookery demonstrations, hands-on gardening activities, sheep-shearing, cider-making, and, in winter, candlelit Holly Nights, with a Yule log bonfire, carolers and craftspeople selling their wares.

Brandywine Valley★★

The narrow Brandywine Creek (locally known as the Brandywine River) creates in its wake a valley so charming that it has spurred industrialists to build elaborate mansions, and artists to immortalize its verdant countryside on canvas. Situated between the metropolises of Philadelphia and Wilmington, Delaware, the Brandywine Valley retains a rural, yet tony, atmosphere.

A BIT OF HISTORY

The area's rolling hills saw action during the Revolutionary War when General Howe outmaneuvered George Washington's Patriot forces here in September 1777. Today **Brandywine Battlefield Historic Site** (on US-1 just east of the village of Chadds Ford; ✕♿🅿 ☎610-459-3342; www.ushistory.org/Brandywine) preserves the battlefield and two Quaker farmhouses used during the fighting as headquarters for the Marquis de Lafayette and General Washington. Realizing the river's potential as a source of hydroelectric power, French immi-

> 🛈 **Info:** ☎484-770-8550. www.brandywinevalley.com.
> ◖ **Location:** The valley weaves its way through Chester County, Pennsylvania and into Delaware.
> ☺ **Don't Miss:** An American decorative arts gem at the Winterthur Museum.

grant **Eleuthère Irénée (E.I.) du Pont** established a black-powder mill here on the banks of the Brandywine in the early 19C. Du Pont's mill community, called Hagley, became one of the world's largest manufacturers of black powder and begot a family of philanthropists who immeasurably enriched the region.

SIGHTS
Longwood Gardens★★★

Located off US-1 just west of Rte. 52 in Kennett Square, PA. ✕&🄿 𝒫610-388-1000. www.longwoodgardens.org.

Pierre S. du Pont (1870-1954), great-grandson of E.I. du Pont, created this world-renowned 1,050-acre horticultural masterpiece despite a demanding career as chairman of the board of both Du Pont and General Motors. After purchasing the initial 200-acre core in 1906 as a way to keep its trees from being turned into lumber, Du Pont added significantly to the property over the next 30 years.

As you enter the garden, follow signs for the **Peirce-du Pont House★**, the 1730 brick farmhouse built by Quakers Joshua and Samuel Peirce and later used by du Pont as a country home. The "Heritage Exhibit" discusses the lives and work of those—including Pierre S. du Pont—who developed the gardens. Behind

Longwood Gardens

Chester County Conference and Visitors Bureau

the house, a path leads through the original arboretum to the **Italian Water Garden★★**. The enormous Beaux-Arts **Conservatory★★★** to the northwest houses spectacular floral plantings that are changed seasonally. Below the conservatory is the **Main Fountain Garden**, a five-acre electric fountain.

On summer evenings during the **Festival of Fountains★★**, the fountain is illuminated by 674 colored lights.

Winterthur Museum & Country Estate★★★

On Rte. 52, 5 mi south of US-1, in Winterthur, DE. ✕&🄿 𝒫800-448-3883. www.winterthur.org.

A premier showcase of American decorative arts, the 1,000-acre former home of collector **Henry Francis du Pont** (1880-1969) occupies a green swale on the outskirts of Wilmington, Delaware. Built in the 1830s, the original three-story Greek Revival structure forms the core of the current mansion. The property now includes the du Pont mansion, 60 acres of **gardens★**, a research library and a gift shop.

Guided tours of **Winterthur** mansion showcase some of the 175 re-created **period rooms★★★** and du Pont's unsurpassed **decorative-arts collection★★★**. Consisting of more than 90,000 objects, the collection represents the best in American porcelain, furniture, pewter and silver, and portraiture from 1640 to 1860.

The **Galleries** have their own specific focus, from design styles popular in America between 1640 and 1860 to textiles and needlework. On the second floor, don't miss Winterthur's **furniture study collection★★**.

Children will take special delight in the three-acre "Enchanted Woods" garden featuring the Tulip Tree House and a Faerie Cottage.

Brandywine River Museum★★

On US-1, just south of intersection with Rte. 100 in Chadds Ford, PA. ✕&🄿 𝒫610-388-2700. www.brandywine museum.org.

Set on the banks of the Brandywine River, this Civil War-era gristmill has been converted into a three-story museum. Renowned for its collections of paintings by illustrator Newell Convers (N.C.) Wyeth (1882-1945), his son **Andrew** (b. 1917) and Andrew's son **Jamie** (b. 1946), the museum also features work by Howard Pyle, Maxfield Parrish, Charles Dana Gibson and Rockwell Kent in the first-floor **Brandywine Heritage Galleries★**.

The third floor houses the **Andrew Wyeth Gallery★★**, a collection of compelling watercolor, dry brush and tempera paintings that illustrate his career beginning in 1938. During warmer months, take time to wander through the Brandywine Conservancy's Wildflower and Native Plant Gardens at the museum.

Tours of **N.C. Wyeth's family house and his studio**, a National Historic Landmark, depart from the museum. Wyeth painted in the studio, which is still filled with his furniture and easels, until his death in 1945. Tours of **Kuerner Farm**, which appeared in many of Andrew Wyeth's paintings, also leave from the museum via shuttlebus.

Hagley Museum and Library★★

On Rte. 141 between Rtes. 100 & US-202 in Wilmington, DE. ✗ 🅿 ℘302-658-2400. www.hagley.lib.de.us.

Tucked into the forested banks of the Brandywine River, the old granite buildings of this early-19C factory were part of a mill complex that became the largest producer of black gun powder in the world. Founded in 1802 by French immigrant and chemist **Eleuthère Irénée (E.I.) du Pont** (1771-1834), Hagley gave rise to the Du Pont Company, an industrial behemoth that still thrives today.

Begin at the visitor center housed in the 1814 Henry Clay Mill. From here you can catch a tram to tour the grounds (cars are not permitted past the orientation center), where the day-to-day activities of factory workers are interpreted through a host of historic mills, waterwheels and a machine shop.

Crowning a hilltop upstream from the factory stands the stately Georgian **Eleutherian Mills★**, home to E.I. du Pont and his descendants from 1803 to 1890, when a powder explosion forced an evacuation of the premises.

Gettysburg★★★

Rolling farmland and forest surrounding this crossroads town witnessed the worst carnage of the Civil War in July 1863 and four months later, one of the greatest oratories in the nation's history.

▶ **Population:** 7,645

🛈 **Info:** ℘717-334-6274; www.gettysburg.travel.

☺ **Don't Miss:** The permanent home of President Dwight D. and Mamie Eisenhower, which served as their second White House.

A BIT OF HISTORY

Capitalizing on recent losses suffered by Union forces in the spring of 1863, **Robert E. Lee** (1807-70), commander of the Confederate Army of Northern Virginia, made a strategic decision to invade the North, hoping to capture the Pennsylvania state capital at Harrisburg. To counter Lee, Union commander Maj. Gen. Joe Hooker moved his Army of the Potomac north. Neither general anticipated the impact of the battle that began on that drizzly July 1st morning. Just before the battle caught fire, Hooker was replaced by Maj. Gen. George Meade, who would command the 93,000 Union troops against the 75,000 Confederates during the three-day confrontation.

At the end of the first day of fighting, the Confederates had the upper hand. By July 3rd, however, the tide of the battle had turned, and Lee realized that desperate action was necessary to regain the strategic high ground now held by the Union soldiers. That afternoon, 12,000 Confederates led by Gen. George Pickett attacked the Union center on Cemetery Ridge. As the Rebels surged across the open field, they were mowed down by Union fire. **Pickett's Charge** cost the Confederacy 6,000 men. The following day, Lee ordered his troops to retreat; it was the beginning of the end of the Southern cause.

In all, the Battle of Gettysburg claimed some 27,000 Confederate and 24,000 Union casualties, and left the town and surrounding countryside in shambles. Two local lawyers realized the need to preserve the battlefield and create a national cemetery to give the dead proper recognition. At the dedication on November 19, 1863, President Abraham Lincoln was invited to "add a few appropriate remarks" to Edward Everett's two-hour oration. Lincoln's two-minute speech was met with weak applause at the time, but his **Gettysburg Address** (⚲ See sidebar) is considered one of the nation's most inspirational statements to this day.

GETTYSBURG NATIONAL MILITARY PARK★★★

🅿 ☎717-334-1124. www.nps.gov/gett. Preserving the landscape where the Battle of Gettysburg erupted in 1863, this 5,900-acre park was declared a National Military Park by Congress in 1895. The visitor center—expanded in 2008—displays portions of the Rosensteels' collection of 4,000 artifacts, including uniforms and firearms, in the **Gettysburg Museum of the Civil War★★**. Also in the visitor center, an interactive exhibits and an electric map traces the movement of troops during the battle. Don't miss the circular concrete Cyclorama Center, which displays the 360ft-by-26ft circular **painting★★** titled *Pickett's Charge*. Completed in 1884 by French artist Paul Philippo-

teaux, the painting is the focus of the **Cyclorama Program★**, a narrated sound and light show that traces the battle's action while the painting revolves.

The Soldiers' National Cemetery★★

Across Taneytown Rd. from the visitor center.
More than 3,500 Union casualties are interred in this 17-acre plot where President Lincoln delivered his famous Gettysburg Address in November 1863. Graves form concentric semicircles around the towering **Soldiers' National Monument**.

Driving Tour★★★

24mi; allow 2hrs. Maps available at visitor center, where tour begins.
Trace the steps of Civil War soldiers along this self-guided driving tour, which recounts the events of the three-day battle in chronological order. The first stop is McPherson Ridge, where the fighting began. Nearby, the **Eternal Light Peace Memorial** (N. Confederate Ave.) commemorates the Union dead. Continue past such well-known areas of action as **Big Round Top**; the **Wheatfield**, where heavy fighting left more than 4,000 soldiers dead and wounded; and the **High Water Mark**, ground held by the Union center that repulsed Pickett's men. Conclude your tour at the East **Cavalry Battlefield Site** (off US-30, 4mi northeast of visitor center) where Lee's cavalry commander, Gen. "Jeb" Stuart withdrew in defeat. Throughout the battlefield stand more than 1,300 monuments memorializing soldiers from the North and the South.

Eisenhower National Historic Site★★

Access via shuttle bus from Gettysburg National Military Park visitor center.
☎717-338-9114. www.nps.gov/eise.
Set on 690 acres of rolling pastureland, this farm was the permanent home of President **Dwight D. Eisenhower** (1890-1969) and his wife, Mamie. When Eisenhower became the 34th president of the US in 1953, the Pennsylvania farm

The Gettysburg Address

President Abraham Lincoln delivered the following address at the dedication of the National Cemetery in Gettysburg on November 19, 1863. Today, his words are some of the most revered in American history.

"Four score and seven years ago our fathers brought forth, upon this continent, a new nation, conceived in Liberty, and dedicated to the proposition that all men are created equal. Now we are engaged in a great civil war, testing whether that nation, or any nation so conceived, and so dedicated, can long endure. We are met here on a great battlefield of that war. We have come to dedicate a portion of it as a final resting place for those who here gave their lives that that nation might live. It is altogether fitting and proper that we should do this. But in a larger sense, we can not dedicate—we can not consecrate—we can not hallow this ground. The brave men, living and dead, who struggled here, have consecrated it far above our poor power to add or detract. The world will little note, nor long remember, what we say here, but can never forget what they did here. It is for us, the living, rather to be dedicated here to the unfinished work which they have, thus far, so nobly carried on. It is rather for us to be here dedicated to the great task remaining before us—that from these honored dead we take increased devotion to that cause for which they here gave the last full measure of devotion—that we here highly resolve that these dead shall not have died in vain; that this nation shall have a new birth of freedom; and that this government of the people, by the people, for the people, shall not perish from the earth."

served as a second White House, where he and Mamie entertained such dignitaries as Nikita Khrushchev and Charles de Gaulle. After two terms as president, Eisenhower retired here until he died at the age of 78. Mamie lived at the farm until her death ten years later.

After a short orientation given by park service personnel, a self-guided tour or the new cell phone tour (☎717-253-9256) leads visitors through the home, which is decorated exactly as it was during the Eisenhowers' tenure here. After the tour, stroll around the grounds for a look at the barns, outbuildings and the herd of black Angus cattle grazing the pastures of the farm. The reception center has a short video about Eisenhower's career. Kids 7 to 12 will enjoy the Junior Secret Service Agent Program.

Gettysburg National Military Park

Pennsylvania Dutch Country★★★

Set amid rolling farmlands, Pennsylvania Dutch Country is centered in Lancaster County. Claiming the world's largest population of Mennonites and the second-largest community (after Holmes County, Ohio) of Amish, Lancaster County beckons visitors to experience a culture seemingly forgotten by the press of modern life. Here a flourishing cottage industry of handmade quilts and crafts, as well as the friendly ambience of family-style restaurants lure motorists to pause and experience a simpler time.

▶ **Population:** 523,594

Info: ℰ800-723-8824. www.padutchcountry.com.

P **Parking:** Horse-drawn buggies are a common site on the roads; drive with extra caution.

Don't Miss: Shopping for handmade quilts.

A BIT OF HISTORY

Beginning in the early 1700s, Protestant groups, including Pietists, Quakers, Brethren and Moravians, emigrated from Switzerland and the Rhineland (now southern Germany) seeking religious freedom in Pennsylvania. They found it in the fertile piedmont in and around present-day Lancaster County. Swiss **Mennonites** established the first permanent colony in Pennsylvania around 1700; German Mennonites followed. The sect that became known as the **Amish** began arriving in the 1720s. The Amish and Mennonites grew out of the Anabaptist movement (whose members believe in adult baptism) that arose during the Reformation in 16C Europe. Followers of **Menno Simons** were called Mennonites; those who went with bishop **Jakob Amman** when he split with the Mennonites in 1693 became known as the Amish. Amman believed the Mennonites were not strict enough in their rule regarding excommunication; transgressors, he held, should be shunned in social and business interactions, as well as in religious ones.

THE AMISH TODAY

Lancaster County is home to the oldest group of Old Order Amish in the US, numbering 16,000-18,000 people. The most conservative Amish sect, Old Order followers, eschew telephones, electricity and motorized vehicles. (Yet teenagers can drive and own cars since they do not become members of the church until they join freely as adults.) The Amish embrace values that stress

Amish School

family and community, humility and separation from the world. Men, women and children dress simply in plain, solid-color fabrics. Women wear long dresses, black bonnets and no makeup.

Men dress in trousers with suspenders and hats of straw or felt. Married men grow beards (mustaches are considered unsanitary and martial). Amish children attend school up to eighth grade; a more formal education is not considered necessary for their agrarian lifestyle. Today many Amish still speak a dialect that combines German and English called Pennsylvania Dutch— the name evolved as a corruption of Deutsch ("German").

LANCASTER★★

Seat of Lancaster County, this Colonial burg (69mi west of Philadelphia on US-30) anchors one of the richest farming areas in the country. Main roads lead like spokes on a wheel into the heart of Lancaster, market center for farmers and magnet for tourists. From its modest beginnings in 1721, the town of Lancaster grew to serve as the state capital from 1777 to 1778, and again from 1799 to 1812.

Today visitors to the area enjoy its historic heritage, as well as its bucolic charm. Three centuries of architecture are evident from the downtown's central **Penn Square** (King & Queen Sts.): the 1797 Old City Hall, the 1889 Central Market and the 12-story Griest building (1924). Soaring 195ft, the Colonial tower and steeple of the 1761 **Trinity Lutheran Church★** (31 S. Duke St.; 🅿 ✆717-397-2734; www.trinitylancaster.org) are visible from all over town.

Central Market★

Northwest corner of Penn Square. ♿🅿 ✆717-735-6980.

Long heralded for its architecture, Central Market's 1889 Romanesque-style brick structure now houses more than 60 vendors who ply a brisk trade in quilts, shoofly pie (filled with molasses and brown sugar), scrapple (made of pork scraps and cornmeal), sausages, pepper cheeses and other local specialties. It is America's oldest continuously-operating farmers' market.

Lancaster Campus of History

230 N. President Ave. ♿🅿 ✆717-392-4633. www.lancasterhistory.org.

Bounded by North President and Marietta avenues, the new Lancaster Campus of History encompasses the Lancaster County Historical Society and Wheatland within a sprawling, park-like campus. The 19,755sq ft addition to the Historical Society's headquarters contains new research facilities, an archival library, learning centers and an auditorium. The building's exhibition galleries display part of the collection formerly housed in the Lancaster Quilt & Textile Museum (now closed).

Located in the Old City Hall, the **Heritage Center Museum of Lancaster County★** is closed to the public indefinitely while the 1797 building is being restored.

Hans Herr House★★

1849 Hans Herr Dr. 🅿 ✆717-464-4438. www.hansherr.org.

Led by Hans Herr, the county's first white settlers were a group of 27 Mennonites escaping religious persecution in Germany in the early 18C. In 1719 Herr's son Christian built this two-story Medieval German-style house, the oldest homestead in the county. Inside the restored stone house, rooms are furnished with simple pre-1750 pieces.

Landis Valley Museum★

2451 Kissel Hill Rd. ♿🅿 ✆717-569-0401. www.landisvalleymuseum.org.

This 16-acre living-history village includes some 20 restored or re-created buildings that accurately interpret 18C and 19C Pennsylvania German rural life. Craftspeople demonstrate trades such as shoemaking, quilting and weaving.

Wheatland★★

1120 Marietta Ave. ⬫Visit by guided tour only. Tours depart from Ware Commons at the Lancaster County Historical Society building. ♿🅿 ✆717-392-4633. www.lancasterhistory.org.

Ephrata Cloister

Built in 1828 for Lancaster lawyer and banker William Jenkins, this Federal-style mansion was home to **James Buchanan** (1791-1868)—15th US president and the only one from Pennsylvania—from 1848 until his death. Buchanan bought the estate while serving Secretary of State under President James Polk. Furnishings reflect Buchanan's tenure as Head of State, and a number of the decorative pieces were gifts from foreign dignitaries.

LANCASTER COUNTY★★★

An hour west of Philadelphia, Lancaster County's landscape paints a pastoral tableau of market towns and patchwork fields. In the tiny burgs of Bird-in-Hand, Ephrata or Intercourse, you'll get a taste of the Amish culture and lifestyle through a variety of museums, historic villages, quilt shops and the like.

Though the main roads are often clogged with traffic, particularly on summer weekends, visitors who venture off the beaten path may be rewarded with rare glimpses of an Amish farmer plowing his fields with a team of six, or Amish children riding their homemade scooters along the roadside.

Stop at some of the area's plentiful **farmers' markets** to sample the bountiful fresh local produce, and regional treats such as shoofly pie.

The Ephrata Cloister★★★

632 W. Main St., Ephrata. ✎ Visit of buildings by guided tour only.
♿ℙ ℘717-733-6600.
www.ephratacloister.org.
One of the oldest religious communities in the country flourished in the northeast corner of the county from 1732 until 1813 under the leadership of German Pietist Conrad Beissel (1691-1768). Practicing Beissel's doctrine of hard work and self-denial, celibate members—known as brothers and sisters—worked 18 hours a day and slept on narrow wooden benches. The community ran one of the country's first printing presses, produced more than 1,000 hymns and made a fine art of the illuminated script called "Frakturschriften." After enjoying prominence in the mid-18C, the cloister declined steadily following Beissel's death.

Tours include a 15min introductory video and visits to the austere **Saal**, or meetinghouse (1741), used for worship services. Next to it, the **Saron** (1743) housed the sisters and included a kitchen, a workroom and sleeping cells on each of three floors. Low doorways forced members to stoop in humility and reminded them of the narrow way to heaven.

Bird-in-Hand★

℘800-665-8780.
www.bird-in-hand.com.
This village on Route 340 east of Lancaster drew its name from a local 18C tavern. For a closer look at Amish culture, take in the **Amish Experience Theater★** at the **Plain & Fancy Farm** (3121 Old Philadelphia Pike/Rte. 340; ✕♿ℙ ℘717-768-8400; www.amishexperience.com). The theater screens a 40 min multimedia show, Jacob's Choice, which dramatizes an Amish youth's struggle to stay true to his Amish ways.

Intercourse★

This quaint village, east of Bird-in-Hand on Route 340 in the heart of Amish farmland, draws visitors to its antique and quilt shops, and locals to its feed and hardware stores. On the second floor of the Old Country Store, **The Quilt Museum at The Old Country Store★** (3510 Old Philadelphia Pike; 🅿 ℘800-828-8218) displays quilted works of art.

Lititz★

North of Lancaster at the intersection of Rtes. 501 and 722. ℘717-626-6332. www.lititzpa.com.

This small industrial town was founded in 1756 by **Moravians**, a Protestant sect from Moravia and Bohemia (in the present-day Czech Republic), whose persecuted members escaped to southeastern Pennsylvania in 1741.

Named for the barony in Bohemia where the Moravian church originated in the 15C, Lititz came under the rule of the Moravian church for nearly a century.

The town's **Main Street** is lined with specialty shops and restaurants. On the second Friday of every month, downtown Lititz turns into a family-friendly party.

Southern New Jersey★

Lenni Lenape tribes introduced pottery and farming here a millennium ago, but it was Quaker John Fenwick who established the first permanent English-speaking settlement in the Delaware Valley in 1675. From the bright lights of coastal Atlantic City to the vegetable farms of the fertile Delaware River Valley, southern New Jersey offers a range of natural and cultural attractions.

A BIT OF HISTORY

By the 1770s strife with England was fomenting talk of war. Southern New Jersey proved logistically critical during the Revolution and saw the action of two key battles at **Trenton**—today New Jersey's state capital—and Princeton. Sitting atop a 17-trillion-gallon-aquifer, the 1.4 million acres of sandy, semi-forested land comprising the **Pine Barrens★** provided bog iron that was used in the manufacture of the Revolutionary War's munitions. One of the first bog-iron furnaces in the Pine Barrens was constructed at **Batsto Village★★**

- 🕭 **Michelin Map:** 583 T 8.
- 🚻 **Info:** ℘856-757-9400; www.visitsouthjersey.com.
- 😊 **Don't Miss:** Victorian charm in Cape May.

(on Rte. 542 in Wharton State Forest, Hammonton; ♿🅿℘609-561-0024; www.batstovillage.org), which today provides a glimpse of an intact 19C rural industrial settlement. The late 19C saw the advent of blueberry and cranberry farming; the latter is still a flourishing industry.

Today southern New Jersey suggests the rural charms of colonial life and early-19C settlement while providing a restful retreat for city dwellers.

CAPE MAY★★

The location of this lovely seaside town, situated at the southern tip of New Jersey bordered by the Atlantic Ocean on the east side and the Delaware Bay on the west, is what first lured New England fishermen to its shores in the 1680s. That same seaside location, which later turned Cape May into a popular 19C bathing resort, is what continues to draw vacationers today.

A series of 19C fires destroyed many early buildings, and Cape May was rebuilt on a smaller scale, forsaking giant hotels for affordable cottages. Homes built at the turn of the 20C favored the High Victorian style, in vogue at the time.

Designated a National Historic Landmark in 1976, Cape May has been revived as a tourist mecca, attracting visitors with its fine Victorian architecture, sandy beaches and a full calendar of events: April's **Spring Festival**; the May-June **Cape May Music Festival**; and **Victorian Week** in October. (For information on these and other local events, contact the Chamber of Commerce of Greater Cape May; 609-884-5508; www.cape maychamber.com.)

Downtown★★

Cape May's Victorian charm is concentrated in the downtown area, between Congress and Franklin Streets, and Beach Avenue and Lafayette Street, and is best explored on foot. You can find detailed information and walking-tour maps at the **Welcome Center**, housed in a restored church (609 Lafayette St.; 609-884-9562) one block north of Washington Street Mall.

For a sampling of Cape May's most noteworthy architecture, stroll along **Hughes Street★**; colorful **Jackson Street★**, and **Columbia Avenue★**, off which you'll find the 1876 Chalfonte Hotel (301 Howard St.), an American Bracketed Villa and Cape May's oldest operating hotel.

Take the time to drink in the fanciful ornamentation such as fish-scale shingles and cut-out balustrades that adorn the cottages in this historic district.

Emlen Physick Estate★★

1048 Washington St. Visit by guided tour only. 609-884-5404. www.capemaymac.org.

Noted Philadelphia architect **Frank Furness** designed this mansion (1878) for Dr. Emlen Physick Jr.

An Academy of Fine Arts design, the interior features a square staircase in the Victorian foyer. Walls throughout the house are trimmed in reeded oak and covered with lincrusta, a combination of paper and linseed oil. Physick never practiced medicine; he owned two tenant farms and kept livestock on the estate property.

Cape May Lighthouse★

3mi south of Cape May in Cape May Point State Park. 609-884-5404. www.capemaymac.org.

Dating from 1859, the lighthouse still guards the access to Philadelphia via the Delaware River. Climb the 199 steps to view exhibits about the lighthouse and admire the vistas from each landing. Before making the climb, visit the orientation center at the Oil House.

Historic Cold Springs Village★★

On US-9, 3mi north of Cape May. 609-898-2300. www.hcsv.org.

Victorian Architecture, Cape May
© Anne Culberson/MICHELIN

Atlantic City

Founded as a resort in the 1820s by Dr. Jonathan Pitney to promote the sea's healing benefits, **Atlantic City★** has defined American recreation for over a century and a half. Hotel proprietor Jacob Keim and railroad executive Alex Boardman opened the first boardwalk to keep sand out of the hotel lobbies.

By 1900 the resort had become an entertainment mecca with diversions including amusement parks and circus stunts. The first **Miss America** was crowned in AC in 1921. Though the city has struggled over the years, entertainment remains the city's charter at the glitzy casino resorts on, or near, the 4.5mi-long **Boardwalk★**, which rebounded after devastation by Hurricane Sandy in October 2012, but suffered a fire in 2013 that gutted 30 businesses. Atlantic City is also home to **Absecon Lighthouse**, the tallest in NJ and the third tallest in the US. (Contact the Atlantic City Convention & Visitors Authority, 2314 Pacific Ave., Atlantic City, NJ; ☏609-348-7100; www.atlanticcitynj.com.)

This outdoor living-history museum consists of more than 25 restored 19C buildings. The 1894 **Welcome Center** provides an orientation video on 19C life. Demonstrations of period crafts are among the many planned events on this 20-acre wooded site.

PRINCETON UNIVERSITY★★

Sheltered by lush, rolling countryside, Princeton University moved to its present site in 1756. This prestigious Ivy League university was founded in 1746 by a group of Presbyterian ministers as the College of New Jersey. Since then, the student body—which claims US presidents James Madison and Woodrow Wilson as alumni—has grown to 5,000 undergraduate students.

Princeton's shady, 500-acre campus (visitor assistance and maps available at the Frist Campus Center welcome desk; ☏609-258-1766) comprises more than 180 buildings in a variety of styles. Built in 1756, Neoclassical **Nassau Hall★** boasts a paneled **Faculty Room★** modeled on the House of Commons. Behind Nassau Hall, the Georgian quadrangle originally included East College (now demolished) and West College, both built in 1836.

In the early 20C, noted Gothicist Ralph Adams Cram crafted a new campus plan, including his triumphant **University Chapel★** (1928), inspired by King's College in Cambridge, England. Bordering the university to the north-

west, **Nassau Street** is the main thoroughfare of the surrounding town of **Princeton★**. Here Colonial and Federal buildings dominate the modest downtown along with Tudor Revival structures.

Princeton University Art Museum★★

In McCormick Hall, off Nassau St., in the center of the Princeton campus. ♿ ☏609-258-3788. www. artmuseum.princeton.edu.

Started in 1882 to collect objects for teaching, the museum houses a collection of considerable range and diversity. Among the highlights from the 80,000-piece collection are the pieces found in the **American Painting and Sculpture gallery**, including works by Augustus Saint-Gaudens and Frederic Remington; a substantial group of ancient Greek ceramics; the **Roman gallery**, with its sepulchral friezes; the **Asian galleries**, which trace four millennia of culture through bronzes, prints and calligraphy; and the **European Art** galleries, which feature a **Medieval** room.

Lewis Center for the Arts at Princeton University

185 Nassau St., Princeton. ♿ ☏609-258-1500. www.princeton.edu/arts.

The heart of Princeton's arts program, many of the Lewis Center performances and exhibitions are open to the public.

Pittsburgh and Southern Alleghenies

Defined on the west by the Ohio border and on the east by the Allegheny Mountains, this region of Pennsylvania is a fascinating intersection of natural beauty, natural resources and historic destiny. The southern Alleghenies and their rolling western foothills, the Laurel Highlands, are lush forested hills cut by swift-running mountain streams and covered with wild mountain laurel and delicate trillium. The mountains descend gradually toward Pittsburgh, where the Allegheny and Monongahela rivers join to form the Ohio River. In 1753 a 21-year-old George Washington scouted the future site of Pittsburgh, knowing the strategic importance of this tiny triangle of land for the westward expansion of the British colonies. The French and Indian War (1754–63) secured the land for the British, and Pittsburgh became a launching pad for thousands of pioneers who had set their sights on the fertile lands to the west.

Highlights

1 The **Strip District's** outdoor markets (p186)

2 The dinosaur exhibit at the **Carnegie Museum of Natural History** (p188)

3 **The Frick Art and Historical Center**, the former home of Henry Clay Frick (p189)

4 **Fallingwater**, one of Frank Lloyd Wright's most unusual designs (p190)

5 The rapids of the **Youghiogheny River** (p191)

Pittsburgh and Southern Alleghenies

Steady Evolution

During the early 19C, this region saw Conestoga wagon trails replaced with the nation's first National Road; in 1834 the **Main Line canal** system—a series of canals linked by portage railroads to haul canal boats over the mountains—was established as a transportation route between Philadelphia and Pittsburgh. Twenty years later, this system was supplanted by the **Pennsylvania Railroad**, which cut the travel time across Pennsylvania from five days to 12 hours.

By the mid-19C, the settlers began to profit from the rich local deposits of coal, oil and limestone, which formed the basis for Pittsburgh's legendary iron, steel and glass works. Supported by immigrant labor, these industries set the tone for the area's great productivity.

The Area Today

Today, the region moves ahead with a mix of manufacturing, high-tech industries and tourism, and its major city, Pittsburgh, has maintained its high-achiever image with a spruced-up modern skyline.

History buffs will enjoy exploring the wealth of historic sites here, while skiers and other outdoor enthusiasts will find a wide range of recreational activities. Hikers can attack Pennsylvania's highest point, 3,213ft **Mt. Davis**, and white-water rafters can pit their skills against the challenging rapids of the Youghiogheny River. Nature lovers will appreciate a drive along the mountains' scenic back roads—especially in the fall, when the foliage is stunning.

ADDRESSES

🛏 STAY

$$$$ Omni William Penn – 530 William Penn Pl., Pittsburgh, PA. ✕ ♿ 🅿 ☎412-281-7100. www.omniwilliampenn.com. 597 rooms. Modeled after France's Fontainebleau, the lobby of this downtown historic landmark (1916) features ornate molded ceilings and arched doorways. Oversized rooms have traditional cherry furnishings and framed botanical prints. The Grand Ballroom boasts 120-year-old crystal chandeliers made of Baccarat crystal.

$$$$ Renaissance Pittsburgh – 107 6th St., Pittsburgh, PA. ☎412-562-1200. www.renaissancepittsburghpa.com. 295 rooms. In the heart of the city's Cultural District and overlooking the Allegheny River, this chic hotel is housed in the classic Fulton Building, positioned among five acclaimed theaters and near famed PNC Park. Thoughtful attention to detail blends seamlessly with charming accommodations to create an inviting experience.

$$ The Georgian Inn of Somerset – 800 Georgian Place Dr., Somerset, PA. ✕ 🅿 ☎814-443-1043. www.thegeorgian innofsomerset.com. 16 rooms. You'll think you've returned to the Gilded Age as you approach the circular driveway to this 1915 mansion, 30mi north of Fallingwater. Rooms are done in rich jewel tones and period reproductions that include brass beds and wicker depicting the Georgian period.

🍴 EAT

$$$ Grand Concourse – Station Square, Pittsburgh, PA. ☎412-261-1717. www.muer.com. **American.** Across the Smithfield Street Bridge from downtown on the South Side, the 19C Pittsburgh & Lake Erie Railroad station's former waiting room has been transformed into an elegant restaurant that seats 500 people. Barrel-vaulted ceilings with stained-glass panels and wrought-iron dragon light fixtures are highlights of the main dining room. Locals crave traditional favorites like cedar-planked salmon, and garlicky shrimp scampi. The brunch is one of Pittsburgh's best.

$$ Church Brew Works – 3525 Liberty Ave., Pittsburgh, PA. ☎412-688-8200. www.churchbrew.com. **American.** A restored early-20C church is the setting for the city's hottest beer hall, where scaled-down versions of the old pews serve as banquettes, and copper beer tanks stand at the former altar. Try pierogies or buffalo meatloaf with stuffed mushrooms and roasted pesto potatoes.

Fort Pitt Bridge, Pittsburgh

© Steven M Deschenes/SXC

Pittsburgh★★

More than 700 bridges link Pittsburgh, a hardworking city of modern skyscrapers, magnificent churches and ethnic neighborhoods, which is spread over the hills and flats of the Monongahela and Allegheny rivers. The triangle of virgin timber that George Washington first spied in 1753 changed hands several times during the French and Indian War until the British took final control in 1768. There they built the largest battlement in the New World, Fort Pitt, named for William Pitt, England's Secretary of State and later Prime Minister.

▶ **Population:** 306,211
▫ **Info:** ☎800-359-0758; www.visitpittsburgh.com.
☺ **Don't Miss:** 15 minutes of fame at the Andy Warhol Museum.
Kids: Nearly 90 years old, the Carnegie Science Center's miniature railroad continues to chug along.

A BIT OF HISTORY

Situated near the natural resources needed to produce iron and the rivers necessary to transport it, Pittsburgh claimed 46 foundries, 50 glass factories and 53 oil refineries by 1868.

All this commerce provided fertile ground for great industrialists to thrive. Among the most renowned are **Andrew Carnegie** and **Henry Clay Frick**, who joined their steel-making and coal-producing enterprises to create the giant Carnegie Steel Company; the **Mellon** family with their banking and oil interests; **H.J. Heinz**, whose food-processing works revolutionized the concept of prepared foods; and **George Westinghouse**, known for his work in electrical systems.

To sate local industry's appetite for labor, thousands of immigrants from Italy, Poland, Austria-Hungary, Russia and the Balkans poured into the city, bringing with them a rich assortment of ethnic customs that continues to enliven Pittsburgh's neighborhoods today. These early immigrants endured poor wages and harsh conditions: unsanitary water led to epidemics of typhoid fever, and smoke from the mills blackened the sky to the point where day was sometimes indistinguishable from night. By the 1880s, industrial

Pittsburgh had become such a dismal, polluted city that one English journalist proclaimed it: "Hell with the lid taken off."

Beginning to decline before World War II, Pittsburgh's steel industry rallied for the war effort.

After the war, this worn-out city began the **Pittsburgh Renaissance** program to reinvent itself. Beginning with smoke and flood controls set in place during the 1950s, the plan encompassed two decades of new skyscraper construction tallying $500 million.

The original site of Fort Pitt was freed from a tangle of industrial buildings to become **Point State Park★** (601 Commonwealth Pl. at the western end of Liberty Ave.☒ ♿🅿 ☎412-471-0235; www.pointstatepark.com), Pittsburgh's inviting green welcome mat, which was completely renovated in 2013.

Today Pittsburgh ranks among the nation's most livable cities and Pittsburgh International Airport numbers among the nation's top airports. With its low crime rate and close-knit neighborhoods, its thriving service and high-tech businesses and rich tradition in the arts, Pittsburgh is poised to prosper as never before in the 21C.

DOWNTOWN AND SOUTH SIDE★★

Wrapped in rivers and wedged in by the Appalachian foothills, Pittsburgh's downtown is located on a compact sector of land known as the **Golden Triangle**. Less than a mile long, the Golden Triangle is easily covered on foot.

Senator John Heinz History Center

Several bridges, for motorists and pedestrians alike, link downtown to the North and South sides. A clean, easy-to-use subway stops at central locations downtown and crosses the Monongahela River to Station Square. Historically and topographically, Pittsburgh rolls out neatly from **Point State Park**, the site of the city's first settlements. East of the park, Pittsburgh's cultural district is home to two major performing arts centers: **Heinz Hall★** (6th St. & Penn Ave.; ℘412-392-4900; www.pittsburghsymphony.org), a 1926 vaudeville movie palace renovated as an opulent showcase for the Pittsburgh Symphony Orchestra; and **The Benedum Center★** (7th St. & Penn Ave.; ℘412-456-2600; www.trustarts.org/venues/benedum.aspx), where the walls are gilded with aluminum.

Formerly known as Pittsburgh's "Wall Street," **Fourth Avenue★** cradles some of the city's finest 19C and 20C architecture. At the intersection with Stanwix Street, **PPG Place★★** (Pittsburgh Plate Glass), a Gothic tower of reflective glass, was designed by Philip Johnson and John Burgee, and completed in 1984. **Grant Street★★** boasts Henry Hobson Richardson's 1888 Romanesque Revival masterpiece, **Allegheny County Courthouse and Jail★★** (at Forbes Ave.), and the exposed skeletal steel I-beams of the city's tallest structure, **U.S. Steel Tower** (at 6th Ave.).

For the best city perspectives, ride the **Monongahela Incline★★**, which rises

an elevation of 369ft during a 635-ft ride (W. Carson St. opposite Station Square; ♿℘412-442-2000; www.portauthority.org/paac/RiderServices/inclines.aspx), or the **Duquesne Incline★★**, which rises to an elevation of 800ft over a 400-ft span (W. Carson St., west of Fort Pitt Bridge; ℘412-381-1665; www.duquesneincline.org). These two late-19C funiculars once transported factory workers up and down Pittsburgh's steep hills. Today both provide unparalleled **views★★★** of the rivers converging at the triangle of land that holds downtown Pittsburgh.

Senator John Heinz History Center★★

1212 Smallman St. ✕♿🅿℘412-454-6000. www.heinzhistorycenter.org.

This massive renovated 1898 ice warehouse with its vaulted brick ceilings, heavy wooden beams and iron braces opened as the history center in 1996. Illustrating western Pennsylvania history through artifacts, photographs, interactive videos, model structures and live theater, the center's excellent long-term exhibit—Pittsburgh: A Tradition of Innovation (2nd & 3rd floors)—which looks at Pittsburgh's contributions to the world through history, and, now, in medicine, education and robotics. In assocation with the Smithsonian Institution, the center also houses the Western Pennsylvania Sports Museum, which features more than 70 interactive exhibits and 20 audio-visual programs.

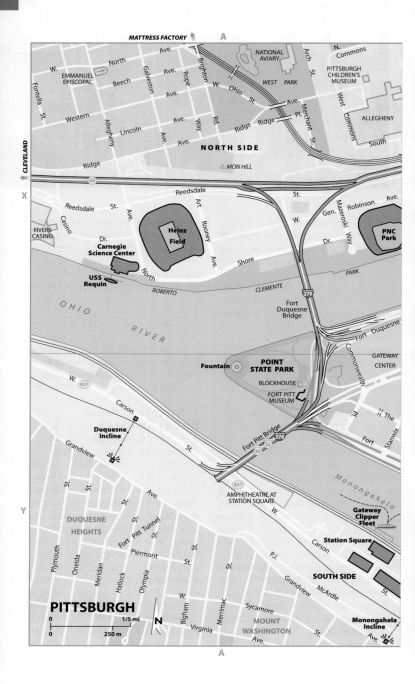

MATTRESS FACTORY

NATIONAL AVIARY

WEST PARK

N. Commons

PITTSBURGH CHILDREN'S MUSEUM

Arch St.

Merchant St.

West Commons

ALLEGHENY

South

EMMANUEL EPISCOPAL

North Ave.

Beech Ave.

Brighton Rd.

W. Ohio St.

Ridge Ave.

Ridge Pl.

Galveston Ave.

Rope Way

W. Fontella St.

Western Ave.

Allegheny Ave.

Lincoln Ave.

Ridge Ave.

NORTH SIDE

MON HILL

CLEVELAND

Reedsdale St.

Reedsdale St.

Casino Dr.

RIVERS CASINO

Art Rooney Ave.

Heinz Field

Carnegie Science Center

USS Requin

North Shore Dr.

ROBERTO

CLEMENTE

W. St.

Gen. Robinson St.

Mazeroski Way

Robinson Ave.

PNC Park

PARK

Fort Duquesne Bridge

Fort Duquesne Blvd.

OHIO RIVER

Fountain

POINT STATE PARK

BLOCKHOUSE

FORT PITT MUSEUM

Commonwealth Pl.

GATEWAY CENTER

The

Fort Pitt Bridge

Fort Stanwix

Duquesne Incline

Carson St.

W. Carson St.

Grandview

St.

AMPHITHEATRE AT STATION SQUARE

Monongahela

Gateway Clipper Fleet

Station Square

SOUTH SIDE

DUQUESNE HEIGHTS

Plymouth St.

Oneida St.

Meridan St.

Hallock St.

Olympia St.

Fort Pitt Tunnel

Piermont St.

W. Bigham St.

Virginia Ave.

Merrimac St.

Sycamore St.

MOUNT WASHINGTON

Carson St.

Grandview

McArdle

P.J.

Monongahela Incline

PITTSBURGH

0   1/5 mi
0   250 m

N

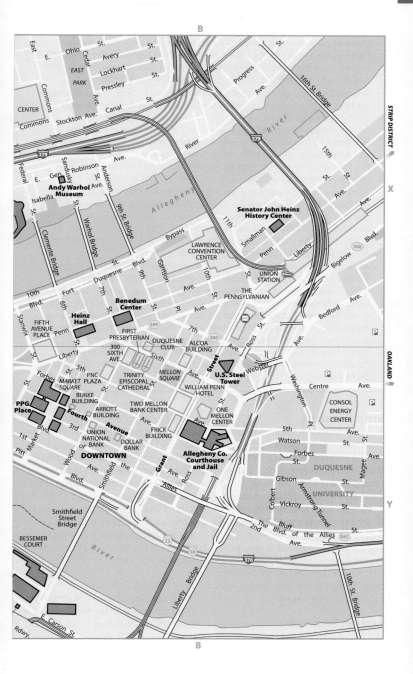

Captains of Industry

Of the 86 millionaires who resided in Pittsburgh in the late 19C, Andrew Carnegie and Henry Clay Frick were among the most legendary. From humble beginnings in the railroad, coal and steel industries, Carnegie and Frick created one of the most comprehensive industrial dynasties in the country.

Poor economic conditions forced the Carnegie family to come to America from Scotland in 1848. To help support his family, 13-year-old **Andrew Carnegie** (1835-1919) found his first job in a cotton factory. It was when he started working for the Pennsylvania Railroad in 1853 that he began climbing the ladder of success. He had already amassed a small fortune in railroads and oil by 1873 when he decided on steel as his future. Fifteen years later, Carnegie was the chief owner of Homestead Steel Works, which he consolidated—along with other steel interests—into the Carnegie Steel Company in 1899.

Born into a middle-class family near Pittsburgh, **Henry Clay Frick** (1849-1919) was borrowing money by the age of 21 to start a company to produce coke— coal that is "baked" in ovens to burn out impurities—to supply to the growing steel industry. During the financial panic of 1873, Frick began buying up coal fields, and by the age of 30 he was a millionaire. In 1889 Frick teamed up with Andrew Carnegie, becoming chairman of Carnegie Steel.

As partners, Carnegie and Frick controlled every aspect of the steel industry from mining coal to producing coke. They owned the barge companies that transported raw materials on Pittsburgh's rivers as well as the steel mills that devoured these resources. Together they unified their holdings and talents to create a dynasty, but their personal relationship was troubled. Both strong-willed, disciplined and opinionated men, Frick and Carnegie's relationship soured over the years. Shortly before his death, Carnegie reputedly sent a message to Frick asking for a reconciliation. "Tell Mr. Carnegie," Frick replied, "that I'll meet him in Hell." Fourteen years his junior, Frick died the same year as his former partner.

Strip District★

Smallman St. & Penn Ave. from 16th St. to 22nd St. www.neighborsinthestrip.com. Former location of the city's turn-of-the-century iron forges, this area was named for the 1.5mi flat "strip" of land it occupies on a flood plain between the Allegheny River and the extension of Grant's Hill. Since the 1920s, the Strip District has been better known as a streetside smorgasbord of wholesale-produce shops, bustling outdoor markets, flower stalls and ethnic food vendors. Shopping the Strip on Saturday mornings is a local tradition.

Station Square★

W. Carson St. ✕ ♿ 🅿
www.stationsquare.com.
An easy walk from downtown across the Smithfield Street Bridge (the city's oldest, 1883), Station Square is a 1970s redevelopment of a 19C railroad passenger terminal and freight yard. The 52-acre complex encompasses some 60 shops and restaurants including the **Grand Concourse**, which occupies the former passenger terminal for the Pittsburgh & Lake Erie Railroad Company and retains its splendid stained-glass, barrel-vaulted ceiling. Station Square is also the headquarters for the **Gateway Clipper Fleet**, which offers cruises on Pittsburgh's rivers.

NORTH SIDE★

The North Side's handful of attractions constitute some of the highlights of a Pittsburgh visit. Before it was annexed by the city in 1907, this area was known as the industrial center of Allegheny, where riverside factories churned out iron, textiles, pottery and brassware. The neighborhood's shoreline is currently dominated by **PNC Park** and **Heinz Field**, home of the city's professional baseball and football teams, the Pirates and the Steelers.

👥 Carnegie Science Center★

1 Allegheny Ave. ✕🐾🅿 ✆412-237-3400. www.carnegiesciencecenter.org.

Set on the north bank of the Ohio River, this slick science museum's contemporary design offers expansive views of the river and the Pittsburgh skyline. Much of the first floor is devoted to the **OMNIMAX Theater★**. On the second floor, be sure to visit the **Buhl Digital Dome planetarium★** and see the **Miniature Railroad and Village** with its 100 animated pieces.

See dazzling science demonstrations in **The Works Theater** multimedia lab, and visit roboworld, where interactive exhibits illustrate how robots sense, think and explore. Moored in the river behind the museum is the **USS Requin**, a World War II submarine.

Andy Warhol Museum★★

117 Sandusky St. ✕🐾 ✆412-237-8300. www.warhol.org.

Opened in 1994, this comprehensive single-artist museum sprawls over seven floors. On display at any one time are more than 500 works of art and archival artifacts, a fraction of the museum's total collection of more than 12,000 paintings, drawings, sculptures, films, and photographs.

Born of Eastern European immigrant parents, **Andy Warhol** (1928-87) grew up in Pittsburgh's Oakland neighborhood. After graduating from the Carnegie Institute of Technology's College of Fine Arts, he moved to New York and began creating the provocative persona that earned him an enduring place in the 20C art world. Start on the first floor for an introduction to Warhol's art, then take the elevator to the seventh floor and continue down through galleries that depict the diversity of Warhol's work. The museum also houses archives that include Warhol's famous Time Capsules.

Mattress Factory★

500 Sampsonia Way; entrance to parking lot at 505 Jacksonia St. 🐾🅿 ✆412-231-3169. www.mattress.org.

This late-19C warehouse is one of the few site-specific installation galleries in the US. A handful of artists is chosen each year and given carte-blanche to create their own *chefs-d'œuvre*. The results can be capricious, brilliant or ridiculous but are never boring.

An outdoor sculpture garden designed by Winifred Lutz recalls an archaeological dig.

OAKLAND★★★

Packed onto a 700-acre plateau 3mi east of the Golden Triangle, Oakland developed as Pittsburgh's alter ego. While the city labored beneath its blast-furnace and blue-collar reputation, Oakland developed as the city's cultural and academic center. First settled as farmland, the area was well on its way to becoming another blue-collar district in 1889 when expatriate Mary Schenley gave the city 400 acres on the eastern border of Oakland for the creation of **Schenley Park★** (access via Schenley Dr. or Panther Hollow Rd.). Andrew Carnegie followed suit and built his museum/ library/music-hall complex, the **Carnegie Institute** (now known simply as The Carnegie), on the park's border.

Carnegie's philanthropy extended into education. In the early 1900s, he built the Carnegie Technical Schools, which have evolved into Carnegie-Mellon University, widely known for its computer science, engineering and drama departments. In the 1900s the **University of Pittsburgh** relocated to Oakland and built one of the district's most visible landmarks, the 42-story Gothic-style **Cathedral of Learning★** (on the Quadrangle at Forbes Ave. & Bigelow Blvd., use Fifth Ave. entrance; ✆412-624-6000; www.nationalityrooms.pitt.edu/tours). Its 26 **Nationality Classrooms★** reflect the cultures of Pittsburgh's many immigrant groups.

On Forbes Avenue, the **Carnegie Library of Pittsburgh** (entrance on Schenley Dr.) contains more than four million items.

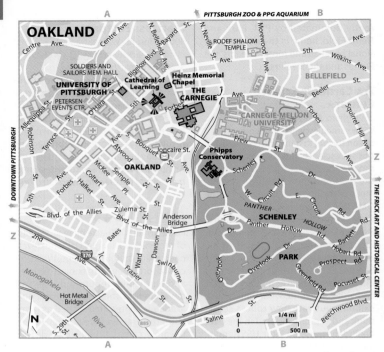

Adjacent to the library, **Carnegie Music Hall★** (entrance on Forbes Ave.) is home to the Pittsburgh Chamber Music Society and the River City Brass Band. It boasts the grandest interior in the complex with green marble columns and a 45ft-high gilded ceiling.

Carnegie Museum of Art★★

4400 Forbes Ave. ✕&🅿️ ☎412-622-3131. www.cmoa.org.

In keeping with Carnegie's wishes, the museum concentrates on European and American art from the late 19C to the present.

Based on the Mausoleum at Halicarnassus (one of the Seven Wonders of the Ancient World), the **Hall of Architecture★** (west side of 1st floor) holds more than 140 plaster casts of architectural masterpieces. Bathed in sunlight, the adjacent **Hall of Sculpture★** displays copies of statues from ancient Greece arrayed around the loggia.

On the second floor, the **Sarah Scaife Galleries★** were renovated in 2012. Besides being organized chronologically beginning with art from ancient

Egypt to early-19C Europe, the galleries now incorporate the large Gallery One space that displays works on paper and photography. The middle of the Scaife Galleries consists of a free-flowing maze of more than 20 large rooms. Browse through the works of Tintoretto and Rubens, and Impressionists such as Monet, Pissarro, van Gogh and Renoir. Contemporary art is well represented with a series of bold canvases by Pollock, de Kooning and Rauschenberg.

👥 Carnegie Museum of Natural History★★

4400 Forbes Ave. ✕&🅿️ ☎412-622-3131. www.carnegiemnh.org.

Long recognized as having one of the world's best collections of dinosaur skeletons, the Carnegie Museum of Natural History premiered the new exhibit, Dinosaurs in Their Time, in 2007. The expanded exhibit displays dinosaurs in scientifically accurate surroundings that replicate the Mesozoic Era in which these creatures lived. Other highlights include the Walton Hall of African Wildlife and the Alcoa Foundation Hall of

Ancient Egypt, which features adult and child mummies. The Hall of American Indians displays an impressive collection of some 1,000 native artifacts.

The Frick Art and Historical Center★★

7227 Reynolds St. (at S. Homewood Ave.). ✕&🅿 ℘412-371-0600. www.thefrickpittsburgh.org.

Situated at the eastern end of Pittsburgh, this six-acre estate and elegantly appointed 23-room Victorian mansion was the home of industrialist **Henry Clay Frick** from 1882 to 1905. Today the site includes the Frick Art Museum, the Car and Carriage Museum, and a cafe serving lunch and afternoon tea.

The home, **Clayton★★**, was willed to Frick's daughter Helen upon his death. Her greatest wish was that, one day, it be opened to the public.

Built just before the Civil War, the mansion was redesigned for the newly married Fricks in the 1890s by Pennsylvania architect Frederick Osterling. The Fricks lived in the house until the early 1900s, when the family moved to New York City. However, Frick's daughter, Helen, maintained the residence until her own death in 1984. Tours include the small but opulent **dining room**, with its tooled-leather friezes and built-in buffet, the family bedrooms upstairs and a richly furnished **library** and **sitting room**, hung with paintings by Childe Hassam and Monet. A multiphase expansion of The Frick will begin with the opening of a new Orientation Center in 2014.

Frick Art Museum★

7277 Reynolds St. ✕&🅿 ℘412-371-0600. www.thefrickpittsburgh.org.

Helen Frick built this intimate Italian Renaissance-style museum in 1969. It houses early-16C Flemish tapestries, works by Rubens and Boucher, and a French salon adorned with early-18C decorative arts. The museum also showcases several of Henry Clay Frick's early purchases, including Pittsburgh artist George Hetzel's *Landscape with River*.

👥 Pittsburgh Zoo & PPG Aquarium★

Off Butler St. near Highland Park Bridge. ✕&🅿 ℘412-665-3640. www.pittsburghzoo.org.

First opened in 1898, the 77-acre zoo now houses more than 400 species. A paved trail takes visitors past exotic exhibits, including the **Asian Forest**, featuring snow leopards and Amur tigers; the **Tropical Forest**, populated by monkeys and gorillas; **Kids Kingdom**, which adds interactive play to the day; and the Bear Dens, which showcase the zoo's oldest exhibits. Fans of the deep should head straight to the **PPG Aquarium**, which features a crawl-through stingray tunnel, a two-story shark tank and a host of playful penguins. The tram stops at eight locations throughout the zoo. A super kid-friendly menu at the on-site restaurants makes it easy to spend a full day on-site.

Phipps Conservatory and Botanical Gardens★

1059 Shady Ave., in Schenley Park. &℘412-622-6914. www.phipps. conservatory.org.

This 13-room Victorian glass house, which opened in 1893, is a delightful refuge filled with exotic flora, an impressive bonsai collection and a hands-on children's garden. Sign up for a tour (daily at 1pm; $2) of the Phipps' stunning new **Center for Sustainable Landscapes**, an award-winning, LEED-certified educational and research facility that boasts zero net energy and water.

Heinz Memorial Chapel★

5th & S. Bellefield Aves. &℘412-624-4157. www.heinzchapel.pitt.edu.

An elegant French Gothic memorial to H.J. Heinz from his children, this chapel's majestic, 73ft-high stained-glass windows are among the tallest in the world. Don't be surprised if you see a bouquet get tossed while you're there; it's a popular wedding spot for Pittsburgh residents.

Southern Alleghenies★★

Centering on 2,700ft Laurel Hill in the Allegheny Mountains, this broad swath of rolling, forested peaks, west of Pittsburgh, forms a recreational paradise. Its steep slopes challenge skiers in winter and the tumultuous currents of the Youghiogheny River attract whitewater rafters when the waters run high in the spring. The area preserves its history with re-created 18C forts, monuments to the almighty railroad, and architectural masterpieces, such as Frank Lloyd Wright's Fallingwater.

- **Michelin Map:** 583 R 7, 8
- **Info:** 📞800-842-5866; www.alleghenymountains.com.
- **Location:** These gems are nestled in southwestern Pennsylvania.
- **Don't Miss:** Frank Lloyd Wright's masterpiece, Fallingwater
- **Timing:** Set aside a full day to go river rafting.

A BIT OF HISTORY

Sparsely populated but alive with wildlife, this portion of the Alleghenies has supported both agriculture and industry since the 18C. From 1754 to 1763, the area was studded with forts built during the French and Indian War, including George Washington's hastily constructed Fort Necessity (1754). The **Fort Necessity National Battlefield★** (on US-40 in Farmington, 11mi east of Uniontown; ♿🅿📞724-329-5512; www.nps.gov/fone) is the site of the only surrender Washington experienced during his military career. After the British emerged victorious, the southern Alleghenies became a gateway to the West. Bountiful supplies of lumber, oil and coal created booming steel towns such as **Johnstown**, perhaps better known for the deadly flood of 1889 that killed more than 2,000 people.

Completed in 1834, the Allegheny Portage Railroad used a series of stepped inclines and steam locomotives to physically haul canal boats over the 2,400ft Allegheny Mountain range. Today the **Allegheny Portage Railroad National Historic Site★★** (off US-22, 10mi west of Altoona; take Gallitzin Exit and follow signs; ♿🅿📞814-886-6150; www.nps.gov/alpo) pays homage to this inventive railroad-canal system that survived for some 20 years before railroads replaced it. A renowned 19C railroad-engineering feat, the 220-degree, 2,375ft curve of track at **Horseshoe Curve National Historic Landmark★** (on Rte. 4008 in Altoona; 🅿📞814-941-0834; www.railroadcity.com) ascends 2,300ft Allegheny Mountain in the tightest curve on Pennsylvania's Main Line railroad.

SIGHTS
Fallingwater★★★

9mi north of US-40 on Rte. 381; between the villages of Mill Run and Ohiopyle. 👀Visit by guided tour only; reservations required. Closed Jan–Feb; hours vary seasonally. ♿🅿📞724-329-8501. www.fallingwater.org.

Balancing over a 20ft waterfall, this spectacular house was built for Edgar J. Kaufmann, a Pittsburgh department-store owner who hired renowned architect Frank Lloyd Wright (♿see CHICAGO) to design a weekend retreat

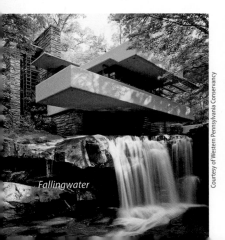

Fallingwater

Courtesy of Western Pennsylvania Conservancy

Whitewater Rafting

Leave the beaten path for a day and raft down the roiling waters of the famed **Youghiogheny River**. Cutting through the dramatic Youghiogheny Gorge (average depth 1,000ft), "the Yough" offers rafting opportunities for novices and experts alike. The most popular trip (*5-6hrs; minimum age 12*) leaves from scenic Ohiopyle State Park overlooking Ohiopyle Falls (from the PA Turnpike, take Exit 9 and follow Rte. 381 South to Ohiopyle). **Ohiopyle-based outfitters offer guided trips** (information and reservations: Ohiopyle State Park; ℘724-329-8591; www.cometoohiopyle.com).

on his rural property 75mi southeast of Pittsburgh.

From the visitor center a meandering path leads to the house, where visitors can see Wright's ideas in action. The unusual design is based on the use of cantilevers that extend out from the main structure well beyond the point of direct support. The effect is a series of terraces flowing from the natural sandstone formation upon which the home rests. The 1,800sq ft **living room★** is Fallingwater's most spectacular space and is almost entirely enclosed by glass, allowing uninterrupted views of the woods outside. Feel the "compression and release" philosophy at work on the narrow cave-like passageways that lead to brightly lit bedrooms.

In the decades following Fallingwater's completion, Wright's ebbing career was relaunched with a host of new commissions, including nearby **Kentuck Knob★★** (south of Fallingwater on Chalk Hill-Ohiopyle Rd., 6mi north of US-40; visit by guided tour only, reservations required; ℘724-329-1901; www.kentuckknob.com). Fashioned of red cypress and 800 tons of sandstone, and furnished with Wright pieces, Kentuck Knob was completed in 1956. Just east of the house, the "knob"—crouched 2,000ft above sea level—affords a fabulous **view★★★** of the Youghiogheny River Gorge.

Johnstown Flood Museum★★

304 Washington St., in Johnstown. &℘814-539-1889. www.jaha.org/floodmuseum.

The tragic story of the infamous 1889 flood is told inside a former Carnegie Library (1891). Built in the Gothic Revival style, this library-turned-museum offers three floors of outstanding exhibits and a film about the flood. Called the worst natural disaster of the 19C, the flood was caused by a 36ft wall of water that thundered down this valley at speeds of up to 40mph from a burst dam on Lake Conemaugh, 450ft above Johnstown. On May 31 1889, the murderous wave uprooted trees, boulders and freight cars, and claimed the lives of more than 2,200 citizens. Scandal heightened the tragedy: several years earlier, wealthy Pittsburgh industrialists had purchased land around Lake Conemaugh to build an elite hunting club, but had failed to maintain the lake's dam.

Museum highlights include a three-dimensional wall of wreckage and an animated relief map showing the path of the floodwater. Flood victims rest among the nearly 60,000 headstones at **Grandview Cemetery** (on Millcreek Rd.), including 777 unidentified bodies buried in the cemetery's centerpiece, the Unknown Plot.

Johnstown Flood National Memorial★★

Off US-219, 10mi northeast of Johnstown; take St. Michael/Sidman Exit and go east on Rte. 869. Follow signs to memorial. ℘814-495-4643. www.nps.gov/jofl.

Overlooking what was once Lake Conemaugh, this red barn-like structure houses displays that illustrate the damage done to Johnstown with dramatic before-and-after photographs.

New England

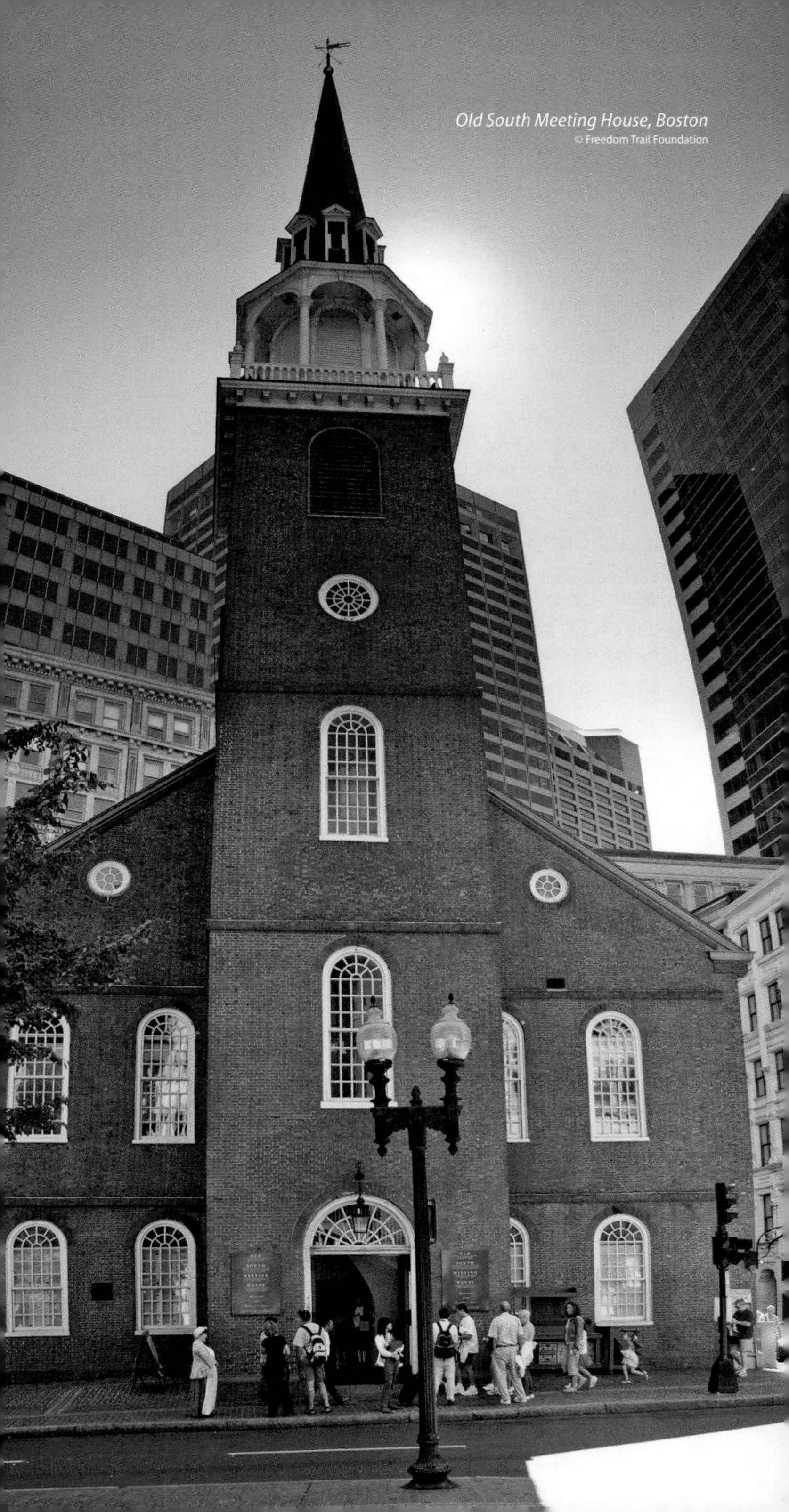

Old South Meeting House, Boston
© Freedom Trail Foundation

Boston and Southern New England

The three states that make up Southern New England—Massachusetts, Connecticut and Rhode Island—offer some of the most diverse attractions in the US. The area's greatest asset is its strong sense of history, which is preserved in its museums, tiny villages and architecturally significant neighborhoods. Massachusetts' capital, Boston, is southern New England's largest and most dynamic urban center. Although only about 636,400 people live within the 46sq mi city proper, a little more than 6 million occupy the metropolitan area. It was here that the American Revolution first started. The city's legacy is revealed in centuries-old cemeteries, twisting brick streets, and historic sights linked by a brick path called the Freedom Trail. The Boston area is also a cultural mecca, claiming several major universities along with a host of world-class museums.

Highlights

Boston and
Southern New England

1 Walk Boston's iconic **Freedom Trail** (p200)

2 Visit glorious **Cape Cod National Seashore** (p209)

3 Time-travel to the past at Mystic Seaport in **Mystic, CT** (p211)

4 Visit the opulent Gilded Age mansions of **Newport, RI** (p213)

5 Take an artsy escape to the **Berkshires in MA** (p217)

Excursions

History buffs will get their fill in the Boston area, from the Revolutionary War battlefields of Lexington and Concord and on to **Plymouth★★** (40mi south of Boston), where 102 Pilgrims came ashore in 1620. The English colonists' original settlement comes to life at 👤👤 **Plimoth Plantation★★** (2.5mi south of downtown Plymouth via Rte. 3A; 📞508-746-1622; www.plimoth.org). For beach lovers, southern New England has 400mi of coastline, including Cape Cod, plus the offshore islands of Martha's Vineyard and Nantucket in summer, but it is in the autumn that New England really shows its colors. Blazing fall foliage transforms the inland countryside into a palette of vivid gold, orange and scarlet.

Along the Cape Cod shore, Massachusetts

ADDRESSES

🖙 STAY

$$$$$ Cliffside Inn – 2 Seaview Ave, Newport, RI. 📞401-487-1811. www.cliffsideinn.com. 16 rooms. **No children under age 13.** Located steps from Cliff Walk (near First Beach), this antique-filled Victorian inn is one of America's top tea rooms, thanks to its decadent afternoon tea service. Guest rooms, oozing romance, have fireplaces and four-poster beds; some have big, share-able tubs. More than 100 self-portraits by mysterious beauty Beatrice Turner, who lived here for several years, grace the walls.

$$$$$ Mayflower Inn – 118 Woodbury Rd. (Rte. 47), Washington Depot, CT. 📞860-868-9466. www.mayflowerinn.com. 30 rooms. Set in the Litchfield Hills, this New England inn has been dramatically reinvented as a grand English-style country house, leading it to acceptance into the prestigious Relais & Chateaux group. Inside, you'll be surrounded by fine art and antiques; outside, you'll discover a Shakespearean garden, bocce court and pool, set on 58 wooded acres. The property includes a restaurant and a full-service spa.

$$$$$ XV Beacon – 15 Beacon St., Boston, MA. ✕🅿📞617-670-1500. www.xvbeacon.com. 63 rooms. Beacon Hill's most stylish hotel offers unsurpassed luxury. Past the intimate lobby's "living room" alcove, the Beaux-Arts building's original cage elevator (1903) takes guests up to oversized studios and suites, all of which are outfitted with canopy beds, gas fireplaces and mahogany paneling. Amenities include personalized business cards and air purifiers.

$$$$ Fairmont Copley Plaza – 138 St. James Ave., Boston, MA. ✕🅿📞617-267-5300. www.fairmont.com/copley-plaza-boston. 383 rooms. Back Bay's palatial property has been home base for visiting US presidents and foreign dignitaries since 1912. A look at the lobby's gilded coffered ceilings, crystal chandeliers and ornate French Renaissance-style furnishings may explain why Elizabeth Taylor and Richard Burton spent their second honeymoon here. A $20-million guest room renovation has mixed in modern amenities with classic fabrics and Louis XIV reproductions.

$$$$ The Porches Inn – 231 River St., North Adams, MA. 📞413-664-0400. www.porches.com. 44 rooms. Fashioned from six 1890s row houses, the inn sits directly across the street from MASS MoCA. Eclectic brightly painted, and located near great Berkshires hiking trails, this inn pumps up the fun level with a year-round outdoor heated pool, hot tub and bonfire pit.

$$$ A Cambridge House Inn – 2218 Massachusetts Ave., Cambridge, MA. 🖥🅿📞617-491-6300. www.acambridgehouse.com. 16 rooms. You'll never go hungry at this 1892 Greek Revival inn. Bowls of M&Ms and homemade cookies are set on antique side tables and credenzas all day. Pastel floral wall coverings, plush canopied beds, and jewel-tone chaise lounges create a cheerful Victorian ambience. Parking and a continental breakfast are included in the rate.

$$$ Steamboat Inn – 73 Steamboat Wharf, Mystic, CT. 🖥🅿📞860-536-8300. www.steamboatinnmystic.com. 11 rooms. Originally a ship's store, this luxury B&B is set on the Mystic River, downtown. Each guest room is unique in decor; all are designer decorated and outfitted with whirlpool baths (some with baths for two). Most rooms have fireplaces and river views. The pretty common room is open for serve-yourself "continental-plus" breakfast, afternoon tea, and evening sherry.

$$ Providence Biltmore – Kennedy Plaza, Providence, RI. 📞401-421-0700. www.providencebiltmore.com. 292 rooms. An institution since 1922, the Biltmore is the grande dame of Providence hotels. Stylish guest rooms are spacious (most measure 600sq ft); amenities include a 24hr fitness center and Elizabeth Arden Red Door spa. But the hotel's main claim to fame is its soaring, gold-leaf-painted lobby, with a centerpiece glass elevator and marble staircase, recalling a more gracious era (even though the Providence Place Mall is a short walk away).

♀/ EAT

$$$$ O Ya – 9 East Street Pl., Boston, MA. Closed Sun–Mon. Dinner only. ☎617-654-9900. www.oyarestaurantboston.com. **Japanese.** Tucked away on a side street near South Station, O Ya is devilishly hard to find, but that hasn't stopped local foodies from discovering it—and raving about the swoon-worthy sushi and other small plates ($8-$39). Chef/co-owner Tim Cushman served as an apprentice to Nobu Matsuhisa of Nobu fame, and it shows. Little tastes of Wagyu beef, sea urchin and Arctic char are artfully presented and wildly tasty. Cushman's wife, Nancy, serves as sake sommelier in this small (10 tables) restaurant.

$$$ B& G Oysters – 550 Tremont St., Boston, MA. ♿☎617-423-0550; www.bandgoysters.com. **Seafood.** At this sleek, subterranean restaurant, servers describe briny bivalves with the same reverence sommeliers have for wine. Nobody cares if you ultimately order the lobster roll instead! Chef Barbara Lynch of No. 9 Park, brings her magic touch to fresh seafood here, where the room is as sparkling as the food. It's all white marble, black stools, and silvery candlelight that evokes the inside of an oyster shell.

$$$ Bondir – 279A Broadway, Cambridge, MA. Closed Tue. Dinner only. ☎617-661-0009. www.bondircambridge.com. **Regional New England.** Inside this intimate farmhouse-style restaurant, with its simple bench banquettes and pale-green wainscoting, acclaimed chef Jason Bond spotlights the best of New England's edible bounty. Working in concert with a network of local farmers and fishermen, Bond seeks out uncommon vegetables and rare breeds of livestock for his symphony of creative, globally inspired dishes. A Massachusetts beef striploin might harmonize with a fricassee of wild mushrooms, while Scituate scallops sound Asian notes with dashi broth and roasted shishito peppers. The likes of cucumber Calabrese sherbert and buttermilk thyme ice cream make a fitting finale.

$$$ Harvest – 44 Brattle St., Cambridge, MA. ☎617-868-2255. www.harvestcambridge.com. **Contemporary.**

Pepper-colored banquettes accent the corn-yellow walls in this elegant eatery, a Cambridge mainstay. The seasonal menu reflects Northeastern bounty; you might find dishes like braised Vermont rabbit, Scituate striped bass, and smoked Gouda and lobster mac n' cheese. Milk chocolate banana crème brûlée makes a great ending to any meal.

$$ Brick Alley Pub & Restaurant – 140 Thames St., Newport, RI. ☎401-849-6334. www.brickalley.com. **American.** With its unique decor—a fire truck on the roof, a 1937 truck as a room divider—this affordable pub is a lively hang-out for tourists and locals alike. Start with portobello fries, jumbo crab cakes or ahi tuna sliders, followed by, perhaps, by a baked, stuffed fillet of sole. Choose a table on the shady patio in season.

$$ La Laiterie Bistro – 184-188 Wayland Ave, Providence, RI. Closed Mon. ☎401-274-7177. www.farmsteadinc.com/lalaiterie. **Regional New England.** This award-winning restaurant specializes in local, seasonal food, or "haute farmhouse cusine," such as marinated beets, a Berkshire pork tasting and Kate's rustic biscuits.

$$ Front Street – 230 Commercial St., Provincetown, MA. Closed Tue and Mon & Tue after Labor Day. ☎508-487-9715. www.frontstreetrestaurant.com. **Italian.** Brick walls, antique wooden booths, and lacquered handmade tables give this dining room a romantic appeal. The menu—American food with Mediterranean accents—changes every Friday. Specials may include filet mignon stuffed with crab, but herb-crusted rack of lamb and tea-smoked duck are always available.

$ Louis' Lunch – 261-263 Crown St., New Haven, CT. ☎203-562-5507. www.louislunch.com. Closed Sun, Mon, and month of Aug. **American.** One of New Haven's main claims to fame—after Yale—Is this tiny eatery. Louis' is considered the birthplace of the hamburger and is on the National Register of Historic Places. The burger is served today as it was 100 years ago: straight up, on toast, with cheese, tomatoes, and onions—no fries, no ketchup. Cash only.

Boston★★★

A bright, chaotic melding of old and new, modern Boston bears little resemblance to the spindly peninsula the Indians called Shawmut prior to the 17C. The first colonists, about 1,000 Puritans led to the area by John Winthrop, initially named the region Trimountain because of the three hills that defined its topography. Soon thereafter, the town's name was changed to Boston, after the town in Lincolnshire, England, from which many of the Puritans hailed. The colony quickly became the New World's largest, its ports bustling day and night with ships from Europe and Asia.

A BIT OF HISTORY

Though many Bostonians remained loyal to the Crown, tensions mounted when the Crown began enforcing previously uncollected taxes on imported goods after the costly French and Indian War. Colonists opposed "taxation without representation" because, although they were British citizens, they had no voice in Parliament. England made some concessions, but in general bore down harder on the colonists.

The 1770 **Boston Massacre**, during which Redcoats shot into a crowd of demonstrating colonists, killing five, marked the first act of overt British aggression. Patriots used this event to rile Bostonians toward revolution. To protest a tax on tea in 1773, colonists dumped the cargo of tea-laden British ships into Boston Harbor. In 1775 the War of Independence was under way.

The famous **Battle of Bunker Hill** took place in Charlestown, north of Boston, in June 1775. Although the British succeeded in taking the fort that colonists had built during the night, the Redcoats were seriously weakened. In early 1776, Patriots used supplies captured at Fort Ticonderoga in New York to drive the British out of Boston.

▶ **Population:** 636,479.
Info: ℰ617-536-4100 or 888-733-2678; www.bostonusa.com.
Parking: Driving in Boston is a wild ride, and not always for the better. Leave the car and hail a cab or take public transportation instead.
🕐 **Timing:** Allow plenty of time for the Freedom Trail.
Kids: The Boston Children's Museum.

Over the course of the 19C, Boston's population skyrocketed from 18,000 in 1790 to more than half a million at the turn of the 20C; its landmass also quadrupled with a series of ambitious landfill projects.

Near the end of the 19C, Frederick Law Olmsted designed the swath of greenery—now known as the **"Emerald Necklace"**—around the city. Beginning at **Boston Common★** (bounded by Charles, Beacon, Park, Tremont & Boylston Sts.), a 50-acre park that dates back to the 1630s, it stretches west on

©Liz Leyden/iStockphoto.com
Beacon Hill

GETTING THERE

Logan International Airport (BOS):
📞800-235-6426; www.massport.
com; 2mi northeast of downtown.
Taxis (*$25-$45*), water taxis (*$10*) and
commercial shuttles (*$20*) provide
transportation to downtown. Major
rental car agencies are located near
the airport. **Massachusetts Bay
Transportation Authority** (MBTA) Blue
Line services the airport, connecting
to North Stationand its free Silver Line
rapid transit bus service connects to
South station. Rowes Wharf Water
Transport (📞617-406-8584; www.
roweswharfwatertransport.com)
runs between the airport and
Rowes Wharf.

North Station (135 Causeway
St. at Canal St.) and **South Station**
(700 Atlantic Ave.) link national and
regional rail service. **Greyhound**
(📞800-231-2222; www.greyhound.
com) and **Peter Pan** (📞800-343-9999;
www.peterpanbus.com) **bus lines**
both depart from South Station, as
do **Amtrak trains** (📞800-872-7245,
www.amtrak.com).

MBTA suburban commuter trains
(📞617-722-3200; www.mbta.com)
depart from both North and South
stations.

GETTING AROUND

For information on road closures and
area traffic, call 📞617-986-5511 or 511
from a cell phone.

Boston Harbor Cruises (📞617-227-
4321) provides commuter **ferry**
service between Long Wharf and
Charlestown Navy Yard.

The **MBTA** operates underground and
surface transportation in the greater
Boston area. Stations are indicated
by the 'T' symbol at street level.
Most lines operate Mon-Sat 5:15am-
12:30am, Sun 6am-12:30am.

Subway fare is $2; **bus** fare is $1.50
with a Charlie Card, available at
station vending machines. MBTA
LinkPass (available at some stations
and hotels) are good for one (*$11*) or
seven (*$18*) days of unlimited travel on
all MBTA subway and local bus lines.
Subway maps are available at main
stations; MBTA system maps can be
downloaded at www.mbta.com.

Taxi: City Cab, 📞617-536-5100; Boston
Cab Association, 📞617-536-3200;
Metro Cab, 📞617-782-5500; Top Cab,
📞617-266-4800.

**Visitor Information – Greater Boston
Convention and Visitors Bureau**,
2 Copley Place, Suite 105, Boston MA
02116, 📞617-536-4100 or 888-733-
6278, www.bostonusa.
com; **Boston Common
Visitor Center**, Tremont
& West Sts., 📞888-733-
2678.

**Accommodation –
Reservation services**:
Boston Reservations Inc.,
📞781-547-5427, www.
bostonreservations.
com. Host Homes of
Boston, 📞617-244-1308
or 800-600-1308, www.
hosthomesofboston.
com. Bed & Breakfast
reservations: Bed and
Breakfast Association
Bay Colony, 📞617-720-
0522 or 888-486-6018,
www.bnbboston.com.

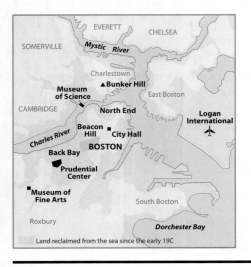

Land reclaimed from the sea since the early 19C

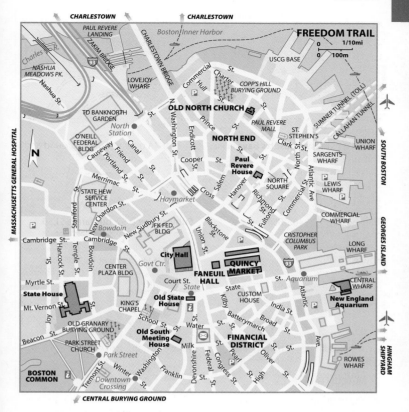

tree-shaded walkways from Commonwealth Avenue to Franklin Park. Today the city is a product of the twin poles of the Boston psyche: Puritan preservationism and Patriot progressivism. While pockets like the North End and Beacon Hill retain a distinguished Old World ambience, Boston politicos

Cool Ways to Sightsee in Boston

Sure, you can walk Freedom Trail, but you can also explore Boston by Segway, duck boat or rickshaw bike. On a Segway adventure by Boston By Segway (www.bostonbysegway.com; $60–$90 per person), they'll give you a quick lesson and then guide you on a zippy, one- or two-hour tour of city sites, including Harbor Walk and the Seaport District. (The longer version includes Freedom Trail landmarks.) Those crazy, colorful, tank-like vehicles you've seen on Boston streets? They're the World War II-style amphibious landing craft, piloted by kazoo-blowing guides from Boston Duck Tours (www.bostonducktours.com). These narrated tours (60min or 80min, $30.99–$33.99) feature the State House, Bunker Hill, Boston Common, and Newbury Street—the highlight is a plunge into the Charles River. If it's a nice day, and you're headed to, say, Fenway Park, skip the cab and hire a Boston Pedicab (www.bostonpedicab.com). On these environmentally friendly rickshaw-style bikes, it's pay-as-you-please. Other ways to ride: by trolley and horse-drawn carriage. Most of these are seasonal operations; check www.bostonusa.com for details.

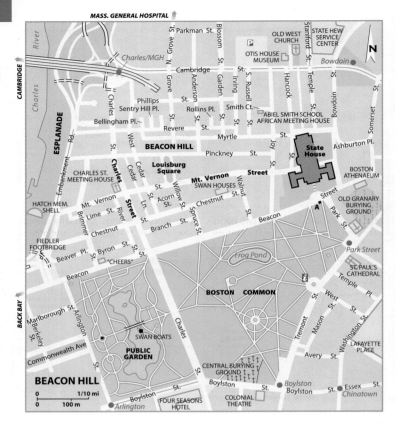

and architects are relentlessly trying to update what they consider "blighted" districts and link the city's fragmented neighborhoods. Visitors who dare to drive it find the city a nightmare to navigate, with its European-style tangle of narrow streets and traffic-clogged highways. But a good map, sturdy shoes and a Charlie card for the "T" will help uncover Boston's seemingly untouched Colonial landmarks, gleaming Postmodern skyscrapers, sylvan parks and top-notch museums.

FREEDOM TRAIL★★★

Boston Common Visitor Center: Tremont & West Sts.; ℘617-536-4100; Boston Historical Park Visitor Center: 15 State St.; ℘617-242-5642; www.thefreedomtrail.org.
The popular 2.5-mi walk, beginning at **Boston Common★** and ending at

Bunker Hill Monument in Charlestown, includes 16 sites related to Boston's 18C and 19C history, particularly those that played major roles in the Revolution. Marked by a painted red line or red bricks embedded in the sidewalk, the trail wends through several distinct neighborhoods: the "Old Boston" of Beacon Hill, the dense and bustling **Financial District**, the Faneuil Hall shopping complex, the twisting streets of Italian **North End★**, and **Charlestown★**, an Irish residential enclave.

Old South Meeting House★★

310 Washington St. ♿ Open daily. ℘617-482-6439.
Built in 1729, plain brick "Old South" remains a cherished Boston landmark. It was from the pulpit here that noted orators Samuel Adams and James Otis inspired the colonists to take arms

against the British. Sparse decoration, compass windows, box pews and a balcony (for the poor) characterize this 18C New England meeting-house.

Old State House★★

Washington & State Sts. &
Open daily. 617-720-1713.
www.bostonhistory.org.
Boston's oldest public building (1713), this stately brick edifice headquartered British officials until the Revolution. The **Boston Massacre** took place outside the building in 1770, and on 18 July, 1776, the Declaration of Independence was read from its balcony. Inside, two floors accessed by a spiral staircase feature excellent historical **exhibits**.
The Boston Society is launching a major restoration of the Old State House for the site's 300th anniversary in 2013.

Faneuil Hall★★★

Dock Sq. & Second-floor meeting hall and market-level information desks open daily. National Park Service rangers present historical talks every 30min, except when Hall is in use for special events. 617-242-5642;
www.thefreedomtrail.org.
Built and donated to the city of Boston in 1742 by the merchant Peter Faneuil (pronounced FAN-yul), this revered landmark was enlarged by preeminent

Boston architect Charles Bulfinch in 1806. It was called "the cradle of liberty" because of the protests against British policy voiced in its second-floor **Great Hall** (accessible via the grand staircase facing Quincy Market).
The third floor holds the museum and armory of the **Ancient and Honorable Artillery Company** (& 617-227-1638) of Massachusetts; the first floor has always been a market. Atop the roof, the 1742 **grasshopper weather vane** symbolizes the port of Boston.

Behind Faneuil Hall stands a trio of long, two-story buildings. Officially called Faneuil Hall Marketplace, it is often referred to as **Quincy Market★★**, the name of its 1826 Greek Revival centerpiece. This complex of restaurants, outdoor cafes and shops now ranks among the city's most popular attractions.

Paul Revere House★

19 North Square. 617-523-2338.
www.paulreverehouse.org.
A small clapboard house (1680) famed as the starting point of the historic ride of Patriot Paul Revere (1735-1818) to Lexington on 18 April, 1775 to warn Revolutionary troops that the British were coming. Inside you'll find Revere family furniture and personal effects.

Old State House

There She Blows!

Spotting whales, the largest mammals on earth, has been a New England preoccupation since the heyday of the whaling industry, immortalized in Herman Melville's 1851 novel Moby Dick. Today humpback, finback and minke whales can be seen on their plankton-filled migration route from the Caribbean to Greenland and Newfoundland from early spring to mid-October, primarily along the **Stellwagen Bank Marine Sanctuary** (27mi east of Boston) in the Gulf of Maine. About a dozen companies offer narrated whale-watching excursions from major New England harbors. Most companies guarantee sightings and recommend advance reservations. The popular three- to four-hour trip sponsored by the New England Aquarium (☏617-973-5200; www.neaq.org) departs from Boston on a high-tech boat staffed by naturalists and aquarium educators. **Hyannis Whale Watcher Cruises** (☏508-362-6088; www.whales. net) run their state-of-the-art vessel from Barnstable Harbor on Cape Cod to the bank and back in three-and-a-half hours. From Gloucester, **Yankee Whale Watch** (☏800-942-5464; www.yankeefleet.com) sponsors four-hour excursions. For a list of whale-watching tours, contact the visitor bureau in Boston, Gloucester or Cape Cod.

Old North Church★★★

193 Salem St. ♿ ☏617-523-6676. www.oldnorth.com.
Built in 1723, "Old North" earned its place in history during the Revolution. Here, on the evening of April 18, 1775, the sexton displayed two lanterns in the steeple to signal the departure of the British from Boston to Lexington by boat, thus prompting the ride of Paul Revere and igniting the American Revolution. The original bronze name plaques, dating from the 1720s, remain on each of the box pews.

> ● Freedom Trail crosses the mouth of the Charles River and continues in Charlestown. The following sights are located within .5mi of the North End.

Bunker Hill Monument

Monument Square, Charlestown. Visitor lodge and exhibits Open daily. ☏617-242-5641. www.thefreedomtrail.org.
The 221ft granite obelisk (1842), which actually stands on Breed's Hill where the 1775 battle was fought, is Charlestown's most prominent landmark. A 294-step staircase leads to the top of the monument, where the **view**★ includes Boston and the harbor.

♟ USS Constitution★★

Constitution Rd., Charlestown. ☛Visit by guided tour only. 🅿 ☏617-242-5670. www.history.navy.mil/ussconstitution.
Completed in 1797, this beloved 44-gun frigate is the oldest commissioned warship afloat. Undefeated in 33 battles, she earned her nickname "Old Ironsides" during the War of 1812 against the British, when enemy fire seemed to bounce off her wooden planking without causing damage. Entertaining tours, led by US Navy personnel, detail the intricate workings of this massive ship.

BEACON HILL★★

Bounded by Beacon Street, Bowdoin Street, Cambridge Street and Storrow Drive, Beacon Hill started off as the province of Boston's high society, known as the Boston Brahmins, as well as the first community of African Americans. Virtually undisturbed by the passage of nearly two centuries, the "Hill" today remains one of the city's most prized neighborhoods.
The best way to appreciate Beacon Hill is to stroll its charming cobblestone streets, where block after block of 19C town houses recalls Federal-era Boston. Be sure to take in lovely **Mt. Vernon Street**★★; **Louisburg Square**★★, a private park surrounded by Greek Revival

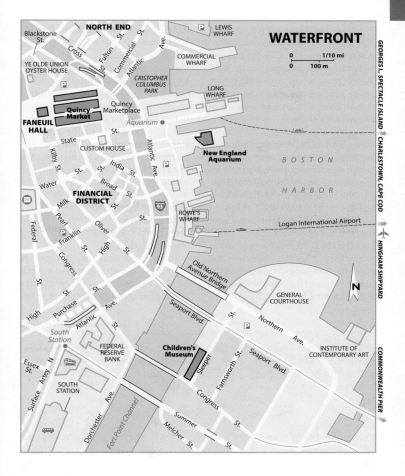

bowfront houses; and **Charles Street★**, the main shopping thoroughfare.

Massachusetts State House★★

Corner of Park & Beacon Sts. ♿☕Free tours available on weekdays. ✆617-727-3676. www.sec.state.ma.us.trs.

Two centuries ago, the golden dome of Massachusetts' capitol building took the place of the original beacon that lit up this historic hill. The monumental brick structure (1798, Charles Bulfinch) endures as a sparkling Boston landmark. The **interior** is embellished with murals, stained glass, columns, mosaic floors and carved Honduran mahogany paneling. Note the Hall of Flags and the oval House of Representatives chamber, where you'll find the wooden **Sacred Cod**, a symbol of Boston's fishing prosperity.

👥 Museum of Science★★

Just north of Beacon Hill off O'Brien Hwy. between Charles St. & Commercial Ave. ✗♿🅿✆617-723-2500. www.mos.org.

A kaleidoscopic array of exhibits in this mammoth structure overlooking the Charles River range from a 65-million-year-old Triceratops to cutting-edge, hands-on displays that encourage kids and adults to think through thorny scientific problems. Here, you can solve engineering problems in Innovative **Engineers**; play with fun-house-mirror effects at The Light House; and use your body as a unit of measurement in **Math Moves**. The **Charles Hayden Planetarium** and **Mugar Omni IMAX Theater** present larger-than-life shows. Opened in late 2013, the new **Hall of Human Life** takes a close-up view of human biology.

WATERFRONT★

The locus of Boston's long period of maritime prosperity, the waterfront fell on hard times in the first half of the 20C with the decline of the shipping business and the construction of a highway overpass that severed the waterfront from the rest of the city.

Since the 1960s the area has rebounded with a flurry of hotel construction and adaptive reuse projects, as well as the establishment of the popular New England Aquarium.

♟♟ Children's Museum★★

300 Congress St. at Museum Wharf.
✕⟨⟩ ℰ617-426-6500.
www.bostonkids.org.

Housed in a brick warehouse with timbered ceilings, Boston's popular children's museum features four levels of fun interactive displays, many with a multicultural twist (in the **Japanese House** visitors explore family life and customs in Japan). On the first-floor **Science Playground**, kids can experiment with physics.

♟♟ New England Aquarium★★

Central Wharf. ℰ617-973-5200.
www.neaq.org.

In this colossal aquarium, interpretive panels, demonstrations and special exhibits foster understanding of some 600 species of fish, invertebrates, mam-

HATCH MEMORIAL SHELL ⟩⟩⟩ CHEERS

ISABELLA STEWART GARDNER MUSEUM, MUSEUM OF FINE ARTS, THE FENWAY

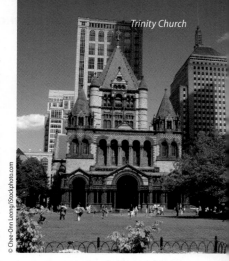
Trinity Church

mals, birds, reptiles, and amphibians. Fronted by a shimmering stainless-steel entry, the original 1969 structure centers on the spectacular four-story, cylindrical **Giant Ocean Tank**. Encircled by a graded ramp, the 200,000-gallon tank was recently renovated from top to bottom with new viewing windows that look out at a stunning coral reef swimming with sea turtles and blacknose sharksThe penguin exhibit contains more than 150,000 gallons of filtered Boston Harbor seawater and is home to three colonies of penguins. **Sea-lion shows** are offered daily aboard the floating pavilion Discovery. At the new **Blue Planet Action Center**, visitors can explore the challenges facing the world's oceans via interactive exhibits.

BACK BAY AND THE FENWAY★★

Built entirely on landfill, the Back Bay neighborhood occupies a massive trapezoid defined by Massachusetts Avenue, the Charles River, Arlington Street and Columbus Avenue. Within these boundaries visitors will find everything from the chic thoroughfare of **Commonwealth Avenue★★** to the sprawling indoor shopping malls of **Prudential Center** (access from Boylston St.) and **Copley Place**. At the northeast end of Commonwealth Avenue, the stunning 24-acre **Public Garden★★**, with a pond plied by beloved **swan boats**, continues to be Boston's prettiest public space. Eight-block-long **Newbury Street★**, lined with open-air cafes and high-end boutiques, is the place for Boston's fashion elite.

Bordering Back Bay to the west, the swampy greensward known as the Fens (part of the city's Emerald Necklace of parks) is home to students, the **Boston Symphony**, two world-class museums, and venerated **Fenway Park★** (4 Yawkey Way at Brookline Ave.; tickets: ☎877-REDSOX9; tours: ☎617-226-6666; www.boston.redsox.mlb.com), home field of the Boston Red Sox.

Trinity Church★★

206 Clarendon St. (Copley Square). ↝Guided tours vary daily. ☎617-536-0944. www.trinitychurchboston.org.
Recognized as the masterpiece of architect **Henry Hobson Richardson** (1838-86), this imposing granite and sandstone pile (1877) initiated the popular style known as Richardsonian Romanesque. A massive central tower dominates the church, but it is the **west porch** that catches the eye with its carved statues and biblical friezes. The church's cool, dark **interior** is brightened by lavish stained glass and murals by John La Farge.

Boston Public Library★★

700 Boylston St. ♿☎617-536-5400. www.bpl.org.
Widely cosidered the epitome of the Renaissance Revival style, this handsome edifice (1895, McKim, Mead and White) influenced the design of countless public buildings in the US. The granite façade is adorned with **wrought-iron lanterns**, and relief panels by Augustus Saint-Gaudens. Inside, the vaulted **grand entry** is faced with yellow Siena marble, and barrel-vaulted **Bates Hall** (2nd floor) is a paean to learning.

John Hancock Tower★★

200 Clarendon St. ☎617-663-3000. www.thejohnhancocktower.com.
More a sculpture than a building, this gleaming blue 60-story edifice,

sheathed in 10,344 units of half-inch-thick mirrored glass, was designed by I.M. Pei. Since its completion in 1976, the tower has reigned as New England's tallest skyscraper. A walk around the building reveals one of the iconic views of Boston: the reflection of Trinity Church in the tower's mirrored surfaces.

Christian Science Center★★

175 Hunting Ave. &617-450-2000. http://christianscience.com.

This stunning ensemble houses the world headquarters of the Christian Science Church. Founded by New Hampshire native Mary Baker Eddy in 1866, the Christian Science religion is based on the teachings of Christ Jesus. The original Romanesque-style edifice dates to 1894; today church services are held in the Extension. The Reflection Hall and two high-rise buildings were designed by I.M. Pei. The gardens and fountain are especially popular with the public in summer.

Museum of Fine Arts★★★

465 Huntington Ave. ✕&🅿 &617-267-9300. www.mfa.org.

One of the country's leading museums, the massive Museum of Fine Arts (MFA) houses an encyclopedic collection of treasures from prehistoric times through the present representing nearly all cultures of the world. Private collections, together with works from the Boston Athenaeum and Harvard University, formed the core of the museum's holdings in the years following its founding in 1870. A need for more exhibition space prompted construction of the present Neoclassical structure in 1909. The modern West Wing (I.M. Pei) was added in 1981, containing a small permanent collection of 20C art and traveling exhibits. Today the MFA's labyrinthine interior covers some 616,937sq ft of gallery space, and the collection comprises 500,000 objects.

The stellar collection of **Asian art★★★**, which includes rare works from China, India, Southeast Asia, the Himalayas and Japan, is widely considered to be one of the most comprehensive in the

US. **Ancient Egyptian, Nubian and Near Eastern art★★** comprises sculpture, tombs and jewelry.

The museum's holdings of **American art★★** include 60 portraits by John SingletonCopley and 50 by Gilbert Stuart. A massive renovation project, completed in 2010, includes a new wing for **Art of the Americas** and a glass-enclosed Family Courtyard.

Isabella Stewart Gardner Museum★★★

280 The Fenway. &617-566-1401. www.gardnermuseum.org.

Daring and vivacious, Isabella Stewart was born in New York City in 1840, and became part of Boston's high society when she married financier Jack Lowell Gardner in 1860. After her husband's sudden death in 1898, she poured her energy into the construction of **Fenway Court**, the current museum building, to house her formidable collection of art and artifacts. Completed in 1903, the museum—which resembles a 15C Venetian palazzo—houses 2,500 objects, including furnishings, textiles, paintings and sculpture.

Arranged as Gardner wished, in a setting that would "fire the imagination," the works are not chronological and many are unlabeled. Among the priceless paintings here are works by John Singer Sargent (El Jaleo, 1882) and Manet (Mme Auguste Manet, 1870); Raphael (Pietà, c.1504) and Rembrandt (Self-Portrait, 1629); Titian (Europa, 1562) and Botticelli (Madonna of the Eucharist, 1475). The second and third floors are illuminated by light from the stunning central **courtyard**, which brims with seasonal blooms.

CAMBRIDGE★★

Chosen as the Bay Colony's capital in 1630, Cambridge is now thought of as one of the most literate municipalities in the US. Named after the English university town, Boston's brainy little sibling is home to both Harvard University and **Massachusetts Institute of Technology★** (&617-253-4795; www.mit.edu), one of the nation's premier science

Transcendentalism

Concord found its way into history again in the 19C thanks to **Ralph Waldo Emerson** (1803–82), a Concord native who spearheaded his Transcendentalism movement—a philosophy built on the belief that God exists in both man and nature—here. Another follower of the movement, **Henry David Thoreau** (1817–62) spent two years in a primitive cabin he built in the woods at **Walden Pond**, now a nature preserve (1.5mi south of Concord on Rte. 126); he recorded his experiences in his 1854 book Walden. Philosopher **Amos Bronson Alcott** (1799-1888) and his daughter, Little Women author **Louisa May Alcott** (1832-88), also lived in town. Many of these literary figures are buried on Author's Ridge in tranquil **Sleepy Hollow Cemetery** (Rte. 62, Concord), and several of their homes can be toured (contact the Concord Visitor Center for information: 58 Main St., ℘978-369-3120).

and research universities (1861), which straddles Massachusetts Avenue along the Charles River. The campus, host to roughly 10,000 students from 117 countries, includes the **MIT Museum★ 🧑🦽** (265 Massachusetts Ave.; ℘617-253-5927; www.mit.edu/museum), which displays stop-motion photographs, kinetic sculptures and holograms. Opened in late 2013, the **5,000 Moving Parts** exhibit examines kinetic art.

Harvard University★★★

Harvard Information Center located in Holyoke Center 1539 Massachusetts Ave. (off Auburn St.). ℘617-495-1000. www.harvard.edu.

The first college established in America, Harvard has been one of the nation's most prominent educational institutions since it was founded in 1636. Its enrollment has grown from 12 men to 21,000 male and female degree candidates in its undergraduate college and 10 graduate schools. Boasting a $32 billion endowment, it is the richest university in the world. Today the campus sprawls along Massachusetts Avenue from Harvard Square to the Charles River. The oldest part of the university, **Harvard Yard★★** forms the core of the campus.

In addition to its renowned academic programs, Harvard has seven fine public campus museums. Harvard's longstanding art institutions, the **Fogg Art Museum**, the **Busch-Reisinger Museum** and the **Arthur M. Sackler Museum**,

are now united in a new single facility designed by acclaimed Italian architect Renzo Piano, which opens fall 2014 (www.harvardartmuseums.org).

Natural wonders of the world collected by Harvard researchers fill the **🧑🦽 Harvard Museum of Natural History** (26 Oxford St.; ℘617-495-3045; www.hmnh. harvard.edu) and its newly renovated Earth & Planetary Sciences Gallery.

EXCURSIONS
Salem★★

❯16mi north of Boston via Rte. 1A. Visitor center at 2 New Liberty St. ℘978-744-3663. www.salem.org.

Founded in 1626, the port of Salem derives its name from the Hebrew word shalom ("peace"). Ironically, intolerance and violence dominated the early days of this Puritan village, culminating in the notorious **witch trials** in the 1690s. Salem captures this gruesome chapter in its history with such attractions as the **Salem Witch Museum** (19 Washington Square; ♿ ℘978-744-1692; www.salem-witchmuseum.com) and the **Witch Dungeon Museum** (16 Lynde St.; 👣visit by guided tour only; ℘978-741-3570; www.witchdungeon.com).

Salem's rise and fall as a seaport is detailed at the **Salem Maritime National Historic Site★** (193 Derby St.; ℘978-740-1680; www.nps.gov/sama). Fans of writer **Nathaniel Hawthorne** (1804-64) won't want to miss the 1678 **House of the Seven Gables★** (54 Turner St.; 👣visit by guided tour only Jul-Oct;

*☎*978-744-0991; www.7gables.org), immortalized in his 1851 novel of the same name.

Peabody-Essex Museum★★★

East India Square. ✗&*☎*978-745-9500. www.pem.org.

Salem's premier museum's collections include more than 2.4 million works of art and culture with an emphasis on seafaring and international trade. The largest department is **Maritime Art and History**, which includes a fascinating collection of 19C carved ships' **figureheads** and an expansive exhibit on Yankee **whaling**. The **Asian Export Art** collection is the world's biggest collection of decorative art made in Asia for export to the West. One of the highlights of the museum is a tour of Yin Yu Tang: A Chinese House from the Anhui province. The house, more than 200 years old, has been reassembled here, on the museum's campus. (**☜**tours by reservation only; **☜**additional fee). And check out the new, expanded **Art & Nature Center**, which reopened in fall 2013. Temporary exhibitions cover a wide spectrum, ranging from the art of the ancient Maya to portraits of the Kennedy family by Richard Avedon.

Note that the Peabody-Essex Museum in in the process of executing a 75,000sq ft expansion project. Until it is completed in 2019, some galleries may be closed; visit the museum's website for updates.

♟♙ New Bedford Whaling Museum★★

18 Johnny Cake Hill. &*☎*508-997-0046. www.whalingmuseum.org.

A fascinating array of artifacts, photographs, paintings and displays outline the history of whaling, from harpooning, lancing and flensing a whale, to the cultural works the industry inspired— most notably Herman Melville's *Moby Dick* (1851). Exhibits revolve around the half-scale model of the 1826 whaling bark **Lagoda** and include **scrimshaw** (carved whalebone), harpoons, whale oil and riches brought back from the Orient on whaling expeditions.

Concord and Lexington★★

❯20mi northwest of Boston. Take Massachusetts Tpk. (I-90) to I-95/Rte. 128 North; exit at Rte. 2A West and follow signs to Lexington. Concord is 5mi west of Lexington via Rte. 2A. *☎*978-459-6150. www.merrimackvalley.org.

On 18 and 19 April 1775, these two towns became the crucible for the American Revolution. Setting out from Boston for Concord to confiscate a cache of colonists' weapons, British troops were intercepted on **Lexington Green★★** by colonial **minutemen** thanks to the warning brought by **Paul Revere** and **William Dawes**. It's not certain which side first fired the "shot heard round the world," but at the end of the skirmish five revolutionaries lay dead.

Spread over Lexington, Lincoln and Concord, the 750-acre **Minute Man National Historical Park★** (visitor center 3mi west of Lexington Green on Rte. 2A; &*☎*978-369-6993; www.nps.gov/mima) commemorates the events that took place on April 19, 1775, and includes a replica of the **Old North Bridge★** where colonists advanced on the British. Centered on Lexington Green, Historic Lexingtonaa preserves several buildings that played important roles in the battle.

In the **Concord Museum★** (200 Lexington Rd., Concord; &*☎*978-369-9763; www.concordmuseum.org) artifacts and documents survey the city's rich history.

♟♙ Lowell National Historical Park★★

246 Market St., Lowell. ✗&*☎*978-970-5000. www.nps.gov/lowe.

The history of Lowell, as told through the excellent exhibits housed in this complex of 19C mill buildings, illustrates the successes and failures of industrialization. In the early 19C, a group of investors affiliated with the late New England merchant **Frances Cabot Lowell** chose this spot on the Merrimack River for a large textile mill. By the mid-19C, Lowell ranked as the nation's largest cotton textile producer.

At the visitor center in Market Mills, view the multi-image **Lowell: The Industrial**

Revelation, as well as a riveting labor-oriented film strip, **Wheels of Change: The First Century of American Industry**. Built in 1873, the imposing brick factory complex **Boott Cotton Mills** (French & John Sts.) is the park's main attraction.

Cape Cod★★★

❯ 55mi southeast of Boston via Rte. 3 and US-6. Visitor information at the junction of US-6 & Rte. 132 and on Rte. 3 in Plymouth (Exit 5). ℘508-362-3225. www.capecodchamber.org.

Shaped like a muscular arm curled in a flex, celebrated Cape Cod, the area's beloved summer and fall getaway spot, is fringed with 300mi of sandy beaches, white-washed fishing villages, towering sand dunes and salt marshes. It was named in 1602 by explorer Bartholomew Gosnold, who was impressed by its cod-filled waters.

The first colonial settlement on Cape Cod, **Sandwich★**, founded in 1637, became known in the 19C for its colored-glass production. Today the quaint downtown, arrayed around the village green, includes the **Sandwich Glass Museum★** (129 Main St./Rte. 130; ℘508-888-0251; www.sandwichglassmuseum.org). The active port of **Chatham★** on the south shore successfully blends commercialism with historical preservation on its charming main street.

Occupying the northern tip of Cape Cod, **Provincetown★★** attracts throngs of summer visitors—many gay and lesbian—to its white-sand beaches, galleries and clubs. Despite its popularity, the Cape nonetheless retains vast stretches of unspoiled beach along the **Cape Cod National Seashore★★★**, which stretches from Chatham north to Provincetown along the Atlantic Ocean (main Salt Pond Visitor Centers located at Nauset Rd. and US-6 in Eastham; ℘508-255-3421;www.nps.gov/caco).

Nantucket Island★★★

❯ Accessible by ferry from Hyannis, MA. Visitor Center located at Zero Main St., Nantucket Village. ℘508-228-1700. www.natucketchamber.org.

Lying 28mi south of Cape Cod, Natucket forms a triangular patch of land 14mi long and 3.5mi wide. The island of Nantucket (the name derives from an Indian word meaning "distant land") includes the eponymous main village, situated on a magnificent harbor protected by a long narrow barrier of beach. With its Colonial architecture, wharfside shopping and cobblestone streets, **Nantucket Village★★★** reigns as one of the most charming, well-preserved towns on the East Coast. Shaded by venerable elms, **Main Street★★★** has preserved its colonial atmosphere despite the upscale boutiques and galleries that fill its storefronts.

Explore the island's whaling heritage at the **Whaling Museum★** ♟♟ (Broad & S. Beach Sts.; ℘508-228-1894; www.nha.org/sites); or bike the 7mi from Nantucket Village to the 17C fishing village of **Siasconset★** on the southeast side of the island.

© William DeSousa-Mauk/Cape Cod Chamber of Commerce

Chatham Harbor, Cape Cod

Connecticut★★

This rectangle of land bears the name of the river that divides it almost in half. Called Connecticut, after an Indian word meaning "beside the long tidal river," the state was first settled by staunch Puritans who arrived in 1633, after finding Boston too liberal. By 1639 they had adopted the Fundamental Orders of Connecticut—the first formal statutes of government in the New World—thus earning the official designation, the Constitution State.

▶ **Population:** 3,580,709.
◔ **Michelin Map:** 583 T, U 6, 7
▤ **Info:** ℰ888-288-4748; www.ctvisit.com.
◖ **Location:** This is a small state, just 90mi from east to west and 55mi from north to south.
◉ **Don't Miss:** Mystic Seaport.

A BIT OF HISTORY

Throughout the 18C and 19C, Connecticut thrived by virtue of its "Yankee ingenuity," manufacturing everything from clocks to firearms and then selling them across the colonies. Among the best-known Connecticut inventions are the **Colt .45 revolver**, the **Winchester rifle**, and Eli Whitney's **cotton gin**, though items such as hats, brass and silverware were more common. Hit hard by English raids, Connecticut was nonetheless an important provider of munitions to the Patriots during the Revolutionary War. While continuing to manufacture such military supplies as jet engines and nuclear submarines, the state today is a study in diversity. Connecticut's major industrial cities—Hartford, Stamford, Bridgeport and New Haven—all suffered economically in the 20C, but its southwestern suburbs (suburbs of New York City, that is) rank among the wealthiest in the nation. That said, Connecticut remains predominantly rural, with attractive colonial villages scattered throughout the hilly woodlands of the interior and along the picturesque southeastern coast.

MYSTIC

The village of Mystic, on the Mystic River in southeastern Connecticut, has been a shipbuilding center since the 17C. Today it is known for Mystic Seaport, a museum-village that occupies the former site of shipyards along the waterfront, and for its excellent aquarium.

Mystic Seaport

©PhotoDisc, Inc

👫 Mystic Seaport★★★

From I-95, take Exit 90 and follow Rte. 27 1mi south. 75 Greenmanville Ave. ✆860-572-0711. www.mysticseaport.org.

Located at the mouth of the Mystic River, this 17-acre complex pays homage to America's 19C maritime past. Over 60 buildings in the **village** house shops and businesses typically found in a 19C seaport, containing workshops where visitors can watch demonstrations of the lost art of wooden shipbuilding.

Three vessels are moored at the waterfront, including the 1841 *Charles W. Morgan*★★, the last surviving wooden whaling ship from America's 19C whaling fleet. The **Children's Museum** allows kids to participate in games and shipboard activities that were popular during the sailing era (try to get them to swab the deck), the three-story **Stillman Building** contains outstanding collections of **ship models** and **scrimshaw** (intricately carved whale bone and teeth), and the **Wendell Building** houses an array of painted wooden **ship's figureheads**, gorgeous folk-art talismans used for good fortune at sea.

👫 Mystic Aquarium★★

55 Coogan Blvd. (Exit 90 from I-95). ✆860-572-5955. www.mysticaquarium.org.

More than 6,000 sea creatures make their home in one of the nation's largest aquariums. Meet some cool cold-blooded creatures at the aquarium's new reptile encounter area, **Scales & Tails**. The **Arctic Coast** encompasses a one-acre outdoor beluga whale display, and you can watch endangered Stellar sea lions frolic in the **Pacific Northwest** exhibit.

EXCURSION

Mashantucket Pequot Museum and Research Center★★

▶7mi northeast of Mystic. From I-95, take Exit 92, then Rte. 2 West and follow signs. ✆800-411-9671. www.pequotmuseum.org.

This tribally owned and operated museum is devoted to the history and culture of the Mashantucket Pequot Indians, a southeastern Connecticut tribe who has lived continuously on the 3,000-acre reservation granted to them by the Connecticut Colony in 1666. Inside the museum, dioramas, videos and recorded bird songs create a multi-sensory experience that details the Pequot's day-to-day life from prehistoric times to the present. A highlight is **Pequot Village**, a re-creation of a 16C native dwelling site.

NEW HAVEN★★

✆203-777-8550. www.visitnewhaven.com.

Home of illustrious Yale University, New Haven was founded by Puritans in 1638. New Haven's downtown centers on the 1638 **New Haven green**, a 16-acre public park. Visitors can stroll the serene residential streets—including **Whitney Avenue, Hillhouse Avenue** and **Prospect Street**—and the quaint commercial district along College and Chapel Streets.

Yale University★★★

Mead Visitor Center at 149 Elm St., across from New Haven green. ✆203-432-2302. www.yale.edu.visitor.

One of the eight prestigious "Ivy League" schools, Yale was founded as the Collegiate School in Saybrook, Connecticut in 1701 by a group of Puritan clergymen. It was moved to New Haven in 1716 and renamed for the school's benefactor, wealthy merchant **Elihu Yale**. Today Yale enrolls more than 11,800 students.

Designed in the Gothic tradition after England's Oxford University, Yale was given a Postmodern facelift beginning in the 1950s thanks to architects Louis Kahn, Eero Saarinen and Philip Johnson.

Yale University Art Gallery★★

1111 Chapel St. ✆203-432-0600. www.artgallery.yale.edu)

Founded in 1832 with a gift of about 100 works of art from American artist **John Trumbull** (1756-1843), today the gallery comprises two interconnected units—a 1928 building in the Gothic style and a 1953 addition by Louis Kahn. The museum's 85,000-piece collection emphasizes American decorative arts, and 19C and 20C European painting and sculpture.

Across the street, the **Yale Center for British Art**★★ (1080 Chapel St.; ✆203-432-2800; www.britishart.yale.edu) is housed in a concrete, steel and glass building (1977, Louis Kahn) that allows natural light to filter down three- and four-story open courts to display areas. The holdings—the most comprehensive collection of British art outside the UK—revolve around Paul Mellon's bequest to the university in 1966.

HARTFORD★★

Hartford Visitor Center: in the Old State House, 800 Main St. ✆203-522-6766. www.enjoyhartford.com.

Nicknamed "the Insurance Capital of the Nation," Connecticut's capital city hosts the headquarters of myriad insurance companies. The city's downtown long suffered from urban blight, but more than $2 billion in public and private funds have been invested in revitalizing the city's core.

A new convention center, upscale hotels, retail shops, restaurants, and housing are breathing life into the historic city once again. Lively bars and cafes line the streets around the award-winning **Hartford Stage Company** (50 Church St.; ✆860-527-5151; www.hartfordstage.org), as do several landmarks by

noted architects. Designed in 1792 by Charles Bulfinch, the Federal-style **Old State House**★ (800 Main St.; ✆860-522-6766; www.oldstatehouse.org) contains graceful touches inside and out; while the completely unrestrained 1879 Connecticut **State Capitol**★ (210 Capitol Ave.; weekday tours; ✆860-240-0222; www.cga.ct.gov/capitoltours), a whimsical pile of turrets, finials, gables and towers by Richard Upjohn, was the talk of the town when it was built.

Wadsworth Athenaeum★★

600 Main St. ✆860-278-2670. www.thewadsworth.org.

Founded in 1842, this formidable art museum—the oldest public art museum in the US—has grown to include 50,000 works of art spanning more than 5,000 years. The structure is made up of five connected buildings of varying architectural styles. An ongoing renovation project has resulted to date in the reopening of the Morgan Great Hall, with 10 new clerestory windows to admit natural light. The Hall now contains large-scale contemporary works by the likes of Frank Stella, Willem de Kooning and Helen Frankenthaler. Other highlights include a spectacular collection of **Hudson River school landscapes**; the distinguished **Wallace Nutting collection** of early American Colonial furniture; 19C European paintings; and **American portraiture** (Copley, Eakins, Peale).

Mark Twain House★★

351 Farmington Ave. ☛Visit by guided tour only. Closed Tue and the month of Jan. ✆860-247-0988. www.marktwainhouse.org.

This memorial to the well-known author was commissioned by Twain in 1874. Its exterior sports a profusion of open porches, balconies, towers, brackets and steeply pitched roofs. Inside, the splendid 1881 decor has been restored. A high-spirited individualist, **Samuel Clemens** (1835-1910), under the pen-name Mark Twain, wrote seven of his most famous works here, including *The Adventures of Huckleberry Finn* (1884).

Mark Twain House

Rhode Island★★

The smallest state in the nation is not an island at all, but a largely flat, mostly rural trapezoid whose defining feature is Narragansett Bay. Rhode Island retains intriguing glimpses of all eras of its past, from its main cities, Providence and Newport, to the quaint Colonial villages of Jamestown and Wickford on Narragansett Bay, to pristine Bristol★ and Warren (both accessible via Rte. 114), which are great for antiquing. The white-sand beaches of South County, which stretch 6mi between the resort town of Narragansett to Point Judith, are some of the finest in New England, attracting a mix of families, sun worshipers and surfers.

- ▶ **Population:** 1,050,292.
- ⊙ **Michelin Map:** 583 U, V 6
- 🗊 **Info:** ✆800-556-2484; www.visitrhodeisland.com.
- ▶ **Location:** Rhode Island measures only 48mi long and 37mi wide.
- ☺ **Don't Miss:** Touring the opulent historic mansions in Newport.

A BIT OF HISTORY

The first European to navigate the bay was Giovanni da Verrazano in 1524, but Rhode Island was not formally colonized until the 1630s, when the liberal-minded Reverend **William Blackstone** and **Roger Williams** came here seeking religious freedom from the Puritans in Boston and Salem. Other religious exiles followed, including Jews and Quakers, earning the state the disdain of the Puritans, who called it "Rogues Island." Throughout the 17C and 18C Newport and Providence prospered as centers for maritime trade. Fortunes were made from the unsavory Triangle Trade (in which rum was exchanged for slaves, who were in turn exchanged for molasses in the West Indies to make more rum), as well as from trade with China.

NEWPORT★★★

Visitor information: 23 America's Cup Ave.; ✆800-326-6030. www.gonewport.com.
A resort once devoted exclusively to the wealthy, Newport is today a major sailing center and home to three renowned music festivals: the 17-day

Newport Music Festival in July (www.newportmusic.org), during which classical concerts are given in the sumptuous mansions; and the **Newport Folk Festival** (July; www.newportfolk.org) and the **Newport Jazz Festival** (August; www.jewportjassfest.net), both held at Fort Adams State Park.

Centered on Thames Street, the structures of **Colonial Newport★★** constitute one of the nation's great architectural treasures. Handsome Colonial mansions, including the elegant, fully furnished **Hunter House★★** (54 Washington St.; ➹visit by guided tour only; ✆401-847-7516), a 1754 Georgian home partially crafted by famed 18C cabinetmakers Townsend and Goddard, crowd Newport's side streets.

MANSIONS

World-famous for their mammoth size, decor and ostentation, Newport's "cottages" were built in the late 1800s and early 1900s by some of America's richest families. Several designs were based on the castles of Europe, while others were idiosyncratic monuments to personal whims and hubris. Taken together (nine remain open to the public) they provide a fascinating picture of the excesses of the gilded age.

A number of the mansions may be seen by driving along **Bellevue Avenue★★★** and **Ocean Drive★★**. The 3mi pedestrian **Cliff Walk★★** (Memorial Dr. to Bailey's Beach), is kept open to the public thanks to the protests of 19C fishermen and runs along the rocky shoreline, offering stunning **views** of the ocean and of the back sides of several estates. The mansions may also be visited by guided tour (mansions generally open Apr–Dec) combination tickets available for up to five houses; 401-847-1000; www.newportmansions.org). Below is a selection of the most popular homes.

The Breakers★★★
44 Ochre Point Ave.
Newport's grandest and most visited mansion, The Breakers is an opulent 70-room Italian Renaissance-style palace (1895), designed by Richard Morris Hunt. Outfitted with French and Italian stone, marble and bronze, red alabaster and gilded plaster, it was used as a summer retreat for the family of shipping magnate **Cornelius Vanderbilt II**.
The two-story-high **Great Hall** displays a spectacular array of creamy French Caen stone pilasters. In the airy **Morning Room**, four corner panels representing the Muses are painted in oil on silver leaf. The Breakers' most richly embellished room is the formal **Dining Room**, which boasts rose alabaster columns; a vaulted ceiling ornamented with carving, oil paintings and gilt; and two 12ft-high Baccarat-crystal chandeliers.

Marble House★★★
596 Bellevue Ave.
Renowned architect Richard Morris Hunt used 500,000 cubic feet of American, African and Italian marble in the lavish

1892 "cottage" that he designed for millionaire yachtsman **William K. Vanderbilt**. The Classical portico is supported by four marble Corinthian columns. Inside, two 17C Gobelins tapestries greet visitors in the two-story Siena marble entrance hall. The **Gold Ballroom**—Newport's most ornate—decked with gilt chandeliers, panels and mirrors, is modeled after the Hall of Mirrors at the Palace of Versailles in France. Don't miss the **Chinese Teahouse** at the rear of the property, where the Vanderbilts hosted small receptions and tea parties.

Rosecliff★★
548 Bellevue Ave.
Designed by Stanford White to resemble the Grand Trianon at Versailles, this H-shaped manse faced with white-glazed terracotta was completed in 1902 for one of Newport's most celebrated hostesses, **Theresa Fair Oelrichs**. Its grand 80ft-by-40ft **ballroom** was the scene for some of Newport's most spectacular events.

The Elms★★
367 Bellevue Ave.
Inspired by the Château d'Asnières near Paris, architect Horace Trumbauer designed this dignified country estate (1901) for coal "king" **Edward J. Berwind**. Decked out in the French classical style, the entrance hall and dining room are hung with monumental 18C Venetian paintings.

The Breakers, Rhode Island © sphraner/iStockphoto.com

Take time to stroll around the 12 acres of elaborate landscaped **grounds**, including a lavish lower garden featuring marble pavilions, fountains and a sunken garden.

PROVIDENCE★★

Visitor information: One Sabin St. ☎401-751-1177 or 800-233-1636. www.goprovidence.com.

Small as it is, Providence is nonetheless a cultural hub and architectural showcase. Downtown features the landmark Art Deco **Fleet Building** (111 Westminster St. at Fulton St.) as well as the 1828 **Arcade Providence**, a sort of ancestor to the modern shopping mall, whose skylit interior is lined with shops between Weybosset and Westminster Streets. Theaters, music clubs and bars are following the lead of the venerable **Trinity Repertory Theater Company** (201 Washington St.; ☎401-351-4242; www.trinityrep.com), Rhode Island's largest arts organization and one of the most respected regional theaters in the country. Once paved over, the Providence River now flanks the downtown core, crossed by bridges and lined with footpaths.

Directly west of downtown lies the lively Italian district **Federal Hill**, centered on Atwells Avenue, where the city's best European-style eateries are located. To the north, the 1901 McKim, Mead and White Neoclassical **Rhode Island State House★** (82 Smith St.; ☎401-222-3983; tours weekdays) looms above the city from its hilltop perch. Its freestanding **dome** is the second-largest in the world.

Rhode Island School of Design Museum★★

224 Benefit St. ☎401-454-6500. www.risd.edu.

Collections of art from various periods and civilizations are presented here. The annual RISD's Apparel Design Collection allows students to showcase their clothing designs to an admiring public at the Veterans Memorial Auditorium, a restored 1920 theater. Selected pieces then go on sale. Adjoining the museum is **Pendleton House**, built in 1906 for the **Charles Pendleton collection** of 18C American furnishing and decorative arts.

John Brown House Museum★★

52 Power St. at Benefit St. 🐾Visit by guided tour only, Apr-Nov. ☎401-273-7507. www.rihs.org.

This three-story brick mansion (1788) was designed for financier John Brown by his brother Joseph. From the outside it is a model in Georgian restraint. Within, the carved doorways, columns, fireplaces, cornices, wood trim and plasterwork provide an appropriate setting for the treasured collection of Rhode Island **furnishings**.

Western Massachusetts★★

Western Massachusetts extends to the border with New York state. The region's prime topography is the tree-covered Berkshire Hills that gradually slope down to the Connecticut Valley. You'll also find industrial towns (Springfield, Worcester, Pittsfield); seven liberal-arts colleges (including Amherst, Mt. Holyoke and Smith) situated around hip, counter-cultural Northhampton; and miles of land cut by rivers, as one travels west. This westernmost portion of the state, just south of green Vermont and north of urban New York, is a popular playground. Pristine colonial villages abut thick woods, and mountains provide ample opportunities for recreation.

AREA ASSETS

Running from Millers Falls (east) to the New York border (west), the **Mohawk Trail**★★, as the scenic 63mi stretch of Route 2 through northwestern Massachusetts is known, meanders along the banks of the Deerfield and Cold rivers through tiny mountaintop hamlets, sheer gorges and dense forests.Hikers and outdoor enthusiasts enjoy spectacular **views** of the region from the highest point in the state—3,491ft **Mount Greylock**★★ (5mi south of North Adams).

- **Michelin Map:** T, U 6
- **Info:** ℘617-973-8500; www.massvacation.com.
- **Don't Miss:** The romantic nights at the Tanglewood Music Festival.
- **Timing:** Plan your days so you have time to enjoy the living-history attractions that dot the landscape in Western Massachusetts.

OLD STURBRIDGE VILLAGE★★★

59mi west of Boston via I-90 (Massachusetts Tpk.). Take Exit 9 (I-84) and follow signs to village in Sturbridge, MA. ℘508-347-3362. www.osv.org.
One of the area's best-known attractions, this living-history museum authentically re-creates life c.1790-1840 in a rural New England community. Interpreters wearing 19C dress farm the land, cook, make tools, sew and celebrate according to traditional customs. The result, enhanced by the beauty of the village's woodsy site, is a glimpse into the everyday lives of early New Englanders.
Architecture ranges from the modest clapboard **Friends Meetinghouse**

Old Sturbridge Village

(1796) to the generously proportioned, Federal-style **Salem Towne House** (also 1796), with attic rooms adorned with Masonic symbols. Several exhibition halls display period antiques, such as glass, firearms and clocks. However, the fascinating **demonstrations** of trades such as blacksmithing, bookbinding, printing, coopering, weaving, and working an 1820 **water-powered sawmill** are the real draw here.

THE BERKSHIRES★★★

Tourist information: ☎413-743-4500; www.berkshires.org.

Blessed with a pastoral landscape virtually unrivaled in New England, the Berkshires have long been a haven for city folk and naturalists, artists and writers. These undulating foothills, arrayed along the fertile **Housatonic River Valley** on the western edge of Massachusetts, are set against the dramatic backdrop of the **Taconic** and **Hoosac** ranges, creating scenery that is idyllic, especially in the fall.

The **Mohegan** tribe lived peacefully in the area until the arrival of explorers and colonists. Bent on Christianizing the few Native Americans who remained after centuries of disease and warfare, the English established a mission at Stockbridge in the early 18C. Farming dominated the region through the early 19C, when milling gained prominence. The advent of the railroad brought on a golden age of estate building ended by tax reform and the Great Depression. Today the Berkshires harbor numerous luxurious second homes along with such charming villages as **Great Barrington, Tyringham** and **Lenox★**.

In summer, culture mavens flock to the world-renowned Tanglewood Music Festival (☎617-266-1492; www.bso.org), the **Berkshire Theatre Festival** (☎413-298-5576; www.berkshiretheatre.org), and the international **Jacob's Pillow Dance Festival** (Jun-Aug ☎413-243-0745; www.jacobspillow.org).

👥 Norman Rockwell Museum★★

2.5mi from Stockbridge center, 9 Glendale Rd., Rte. 183. ☎413-298-4100. www.nrm.org.

Occupying a 36-acre estate overlooking the Housatonic River Valley, the museum is the repository of the largest collection of original works by America's premier 20C illustrator. A Stockbridge resident from 1953 until his death, **Norman Rockwell** (1894-1978) is best known for the hundreds of homespun covers he illustrated for the Saturday Evening Post.

The museum's nine galleries display Rockwell works culled from a collection of some 570 paintings and drawings. The collection includes large-scale oil paintings such as *Stockbridge Main Street at Christmas* (1967) and *Girl at Mirror* (1954). Also on the grounds is Rockwell's simple **studio**.

Massachusetts Museum of Contemporary Art★★

87 Marshall St., North Adams, MA. On Rte. 8, .25mi north of Rte. 2. ☎413-662-2111. www.massmoca.org.

This modern art museum (1999) uses the vast wood-floored interiors of renovated brick factory buildings to display huge contemporary works largely unseen elsewhere owing to their size and weight. Works by such artists as Robert Rauschenberg, Mario Merz and Joseph Bueys come from studios and

Just Zip It

Now here's a way to see fall color—if you're brave enough to keep your eyes open! Zip-lining has come to Massachusetts, thanks to Deerfield Valley Canopy Tours, run by long-time outfitter Zoar Outdoors. Located in Charlemont (20mi southeast of North Adams) the three-hour forest canopy tour features 11 zip lines, 2 bridges, and 3 rappels, with views of the Deerfield Valley and northern Berkshires (☎800-532-7483; www.deerfieldzipline.com).

museums around the world and change on a regular basis. With its 27-building complex also hosting sound-art installations and theatrical, dance and music performances, MASS MOCA is considered one of the world's top contemporary art museums.

👥 HANCOCK SHAKER VILLAGE★★★

In Pittsfield, at junction of US-20 & Rte. 41, 9mi north of I-90 (Exit 1). 📞413-443-0188. www.hancockshakervillage.org.

Made up of 20 Shaker structures and 1,200 acres of farm, meadow and woodland, Hancock Shaker Village is a living-history museum that commemorates and describes the active Shaker community located here from 1790 to 1960. An offshoot of a group of Quakers in Manchester, England, the Shakers got their name from the whirling and shaking of their heightened spiritual states. Moving to America to avoid religious persecution, they established 19 communities between Kentucky and Maine from 1778 to 1836. Though considered the most successful of the communitarian groups established in the late 18C, the Shakers' emphasis on celibacy limited their longevity.

Today the complex interprets their life through some 10,000 objects, and demonstrations of such daily tasks as milking cows, spinning yarn and cooking. That the Shakers put their "hands to work and hearts to God" is evident in the simplicity and functionalism of their **furniture** and architecture. The 1826 **Round Stone Barn** is a classic Shaker design, and the **Brick Dwelling** (1830) contains living quarters for nearly 100 members.

WILLIAMSTOWN★★

This beautiful colonial village (at the junction of US-7 & Rte. 2; www.williams townchamber.com) nestles in the northwest corner of the state, bordering Vermont and New York, where the scenic Mohawk Trail enters the Berkshires.

In 1753 the early settlement of West Hoosuck was established here by soldiers from Fort Massachusetts. Later, one of the soldiers, Col. Ephraim Williams, Jr., bequeathed part of his estate for the founding of a free school in West Hoosuck, provided the town be renamed in his honor. Soon after the colonel's death, West Hoosuck was renamed Williamstown.

The Berkshires' verdant rolling hills provide a lovely setting for prestigious liberal arts **Williams College**, chartered in 1793 and home to the **Williams College Museum of Art★**, and for the renowned **Williamstown Theatre Festival** (📞413-597-3400; www.wtfestival. org). The well-regarded festival has taken place in Williamstown for more than half a century, drawing top talent and emerging artists to the area each year. The festival includes plays on two stages, held throughout the summer, June through August.

Sterling and Francine Clark Art Institute★★★

225 South St. 📞413-458-2303. www.clarkart.edu.

The works of art amassed by Robert Sterling Clark and his wife, Francine, between World War I and 1956 deserve comparison with some of the world's finest collections. Surrounded by hills and meadows, the original white marble building (1955) suggests a private residence in scale, natural light and architectural detail. The couple chose Williamstown for its idyllic setting and its location far from urban centers (most likely to be threatened in wartime).

The museum remains open as it continues a campus expansion project, which will add 2,300sq ft of space to the original museum building and add a new Visitor Exhibition and Conference Center.

At the heart of the collection are paintings, prints and drawings by the **Old Masters** and **19C French and American artists.** More than 30 canvases by Renoir are presented along with works by Europeans Corot, Millet, Degas, Monet and Toulouse-Lautrec, and Americans Frederic Remington, Winslow Homer and John Singer Sargent.

Northern New England

Composed of the states of Vermont, New Hampshire and Maine, northern New England boasts tracts of wilderness seldom associated with the densely populated eastern seaboard. Stacked on top of Massachusetts, the adjacent triangles of Vermont and New Hampshire fit together to form a tall rectangle of land. Maine extends north and east from New Hampshire toward Canada and into the Atlantic Ocean. Its landmass totals that of the other five New England states combined, though its population is smaller than many of them.

Highlights

1 Taking a lighthouse tour along the **Maine Coast** (p222)

2 Views from the top of Cadillac Mountain in Maine's **Acadia National Park** (p223)

3 Riding the rails to the summit of **Mount Washington** (p227)

4 Cruising around the **Isles of Shoals** (p227)

5 Discovering the American Folk Art collection at the **Shelburne Museum** (p229)

A Bit of History

Although the coast of Maine was explored as early as the 11C by the Vikings, European settlement in northern New England did not take place in earnest until the early 17C, when French and English towns started cropping up along the coast. Battles were frequent between the two colonial powers until the Treaty of Paris of 1763, which formally ended the American Revolutionary War and ceded control of the area to the British. Inland settlement proceeded slowly due to the enormity of the Appalachian ridge (the White and Green Mountains) that forms the region's backbone. Vermonter Ethan Allen and his Green Mountain Boys were typical of those farmers who did penetrate the rugged wilderness. Such freethinkers turned out in droves to fight the British, guerrilla-style. Later, many rebelled against government encroachment of any kind—including statehood. To this day, New Hampshire's motto, "Live Free or Die," describes the state's virulently anti-taxation stance, while Vermont continues to resist large-scale development with batteries of lawsuits and legislation.

Despite these differences, both states draw large numbers of visitors year-round: the eye-popping reds, yellows and oranges of the leaves in early October turn the forests into a brilliant wonderland, while the mountains beckon hikers, campers and cyclists during the other temperate months (May–Sept). Winter is ski season, when enthusiasts frequent the snowy slopes of Vermont and New Hampshire.

Maine's chief attraction is its 3,500-mi coastline, one of the most dramatic in the US. Rugged cliffs, fjords and rocky offshore islands offer stunning vistas, and cozy seaside towns provide ample opportunities to sample the state's richest delicacy: lobster. Maine is referred to as Down East because of the winds that carry sailing vessels eastward along this section of the coast.

Skiing, hiking, scenic drives, historic houses, the beach, regional seafood, a lively pier at Maine's Old Orchard Beach, and funky art at the Shelburne Museum in Burlington, Vermont—the area has it all..

Sledding and snowshoeing in Mad River Valley, Waitsfield, Vermont

Vermont Department of Tourism & Marketing/Dennis Curran

ADDRESSES

🛏 STAY

$$$$$ The Equinox – Rte. 7A, Manchester Center, VT. 🅿 ☎800-362-4747. www.equinoxresort.com. 195 rooms. The largest full-service resort in Vermont, the Equinox claims some unusual activities—a falconry program, an off-road driving school, shooting and fly-fishing instruction. Rooms in the white-columned main building all have modern amenities.

$$$$$ Omni Bretton Arms Inn – 173 Mt. Washington Rd., Bretton Woods, NH. ♿🅿 ☎603-278-3000. www.omnihotels.com. 34 rooms. Built as a private home in 1896 and host to the Conference Secretariat during the Bretton Wood Monetary Conference in 1944, this sprawling, white manse now operates as a country inn. The inn's wraparound verandah invites relaxation, while the surrounding slopes provide adventure galore for skiers. Classically decorated rooms come with private baths and access to the spa and other facilities of its nearby sibling, the Omni Mt. Washington Resort.

$$$$$ The Pitcher Inn – 275 Main St., Warren, VT. ♿🅿 ☎802-496-6350. www.pitcherinn.com. 11 rooms. This tiny gem is one of the top inns in the country. Each of its 11 exquisite guest rooms is decorated with original art and antiques representing some facet of Vermont: the Trout Room turns the interior into an actual log cabin, while in the School Room, a huge slate blackboard covers the wall behind the bed. More than half the rooms are outfitted with fireplaces and whirlpool tubs; others boast wet bars and steam rooms. The inn's acclaimed restaurant crafts international dishes from the bounty of local farms.

$$$$ Black Point Inn – 510 Black Point Rd., Prout's Neck, Scarborough, ME. 🅿 ☎207-883-2500. www.blackpointinn.com. 25 rooms. A classic Maine seaside resort, the updated c.1873 Inn features a large wrap-around sun porch, heated pool, and close proximity to golf courses and beaches. Guest rooms are spacious and decorated in an attractive beach-house style.

$$$ The Captain Lord Mansion – 6 Pleasant St., Kennebunkport, ME. 🅿 ☎207-967-3141. www.captainlord.com. 20 rooms. This regal, three-story Federal-style house holds a mix of historic opulence and modern comforts. Filled with period antiques, the romantic guest rooms have charm and amenities to spare, including heated bathroom floors, whirlpool tubs, marble baths, gas fireplaces and free Wi-Fi.

🍴 EAT

$ The Clam Shack – 2 Western Ave., Kennebunkport, ME. ☎207-967-3321. www.theclamshack.net. **Seafood.** Don't drive past Kennebunkport without stopping at this famous roadside eatery next to the Kennebunkport Bridge. There's always a line for the fried clam strips and luscious lobster rolls.

$$$$ White Barn Inn – 37 Beach Ave., Kennebunk Beach ME. Dinner only. Jackets required. ☎207-967-2321. www.whitebarninn.com. **Contemporary.** Housed in two handsome, restored barns, the splurge-worthy restaurant is appointed with country antiques and floor-to-ceiling windows with garden views. The prix-fixe menu changes weekly but an almond-crusted local halibut on black trumpet mushroom purée, and a farm-raised veal filet with sautéed sweetbreads will give you the idea. Don't let the magic end; book one on the 26 luxurious rooms in the inn.

Maine Coast★★

The Maine coast measures more than 3,500 miles; along the way, long, scenic peninsulas jut out into the Atlantic Ocean. Coastal cities along Route 1 are the biggest draw in summertime, when windjammer cruises, beaches and lobster shacks lure crowds. Visitors looking for art galleries, quaint inns and fine dining head to picturesque seaport towns like Ogunquit and Camden. Most visitors put Maine's spectacular Acadia National Park, on Mt. Desert Island, on their must-see list. Hikers and campers enjoy miles of trails, with views of mountains, ocean, lakes and ponds, while old carriage roads invite cyclists. This region of "Downeast" Maine frames postcard views of rocky shoreline-meets-frothy surf for which the state is famous.

- **Michelin Map:** p207
- **Info:** ℘888-624-6345; www.visitmaine.com.
- **Location:** The coast of Maine defines the eastern edge of the state, stretching 3,500mi from Kittery north to the border of New Brunswick, Canada.

A BIT OF HISTORY

In 1604 Pierre du Gua, Sieur de Monts and Samuel de Champlain established a small colony on an island in the St. Croix River from which they set out the following year to found the Acadian territory. An English settlement, the **Popham Colony**, was established at the mouth of the Kennebec River in 1607; then in 1635 English monarch Charles I gave the region of Maine to Sir Ferdinando Gorges. From that time on, the coast was the scene of constant battles between the French and the English. In 1677 the Massachusetts Colony bought Maine from the descendants of Sir Ferdinando Gorges. Maine was granted statehood under the conditions of the Missouri Compromise in 1820.

Vestiges of the Maine coast's 19C shipbuilding heyday can be glimpsed in sights such as **Maine Maritime Museum★★** (243 Washington St., Bath; ℘207-443-1316; www.mainemaritimemuseum.org) and the **Penobscot Marine Museum★** (5 Church St., just off Rte. 1, Searsport; ℘207-548-2529; www.penobscotmarinemuseum.org). Fishing, especially lobstering, is a major industry here; more than 50 percent of the nation's lobster catch comes from Maine.

KITTERY TO PORTLAND

US-1 traces the entire length of the Maine coastline, which begins just north of Portsmouth, New Hampshire, at the town of Kittery. Maine's first incorporated city, Kittery is now known for its retail outlet stores (US-1; t888-548-8379; www.thekitteryoutlets.com).

Colonial York★★

Along US-1A in York Village, just off US-1. Museum buildings are open Jun-mid-Oct. ☞Tours are also available. Purchase tickets at the Visitor Center, 3 Lindsay Rd, in York Village. ℘207-363-4974. www.oldyork.org.

Several 18C structures flanking the village green here recall colonial times. Across US-1A from the **Town Hall** is the **Old Burying Ground**, noteworthy for its 17C tombstones. Surrounding the cemetery you'll find cozy **Jefferds Tavern**, the 1740 **Emerson Wilcox House** and the **Old Gaol**, which held prisoners from 1719 to 1860.

Ogunquit★

16mi north of Kittery on US-1.

Christened Ogunquit ("beautiful place by the sea") by the local Indians, this beach town is a haven for artists and writers, as well as a large gay population. At the end of Shore Road, dozens of shops and seafood restaurants hug the man-made anchorage of **Perkins Cove★**. From the cove, stroll out along

Marginal Way★, a coastal footpath that leads around the windswept promontory called Israel's Head, for **views★**.

Kennebunkport★

17mi northeast of Ogunquit via US-1 and Rte. 99 East.

A seaside resort since the 19C, Kennebunkport is known as the summer home of **George Bush**, 41st president of the US (1989-93). The Bush family estate is visible from Ocean Drive. The town's commercial center, **Dock Square**, harbors a variety of charming shops set along the tidal Kennebunk River.

Old Orchard Beach★

20 miles via Rt. 1 to Rt 98.

Seven miles long, fun-loving Old Orchard Beach bustles with summer crowds. Its wooden pier along the beachfront is dotted with clam shacks and tourist shops, and a stretch of sandy beach.

PORTLAND TO BAR HARBOR

Largest city in Maine, Portland sits on Casco Bay, known for its picturesque **Calendar Islands** (cruises depart from Portland's Maine State Pier; Casco Bay Lines, ☎207-774-7871, www.cascobaylines.com). An important oil and fishing port, the city is also the financial, cultural and commercial center of northern New England.

Just 18mi north of Portland, the town of **Freeport** is a favored shopping spot along the coast. This popular town is the home of **L.L. Bean** (95 Main St. at Bow St.; open 24hrs/day year-round; ☎207-373-2700; www.llbean.com), the famous mail-order sporting-goods enterprise,

as well as some 120 retail outlets (on Main St./US-1).

Portland★★

Portland began as an English trading post in 1658. Called Falmouth in its early days, the village was shelled by the British in 1775 owing to the anti-Loyalist sentiments of its residents. Following the Revolutionary War, the few hundred colonists who remained in Falmouth rebuilt the city, renaming it Portland. From 1820 to 1832, Portland served as the state capital. The city prospered as a shipping center until 1866, when a fire swept through the downtown area, leveling the business district. From those ashes rose the revitalized Victorian structures that remain today in the **Old Port★★** (along Exchange, Middle & Fore Sts. downtown), where art galleries, craft shops and restaurants now occupy many of the 19C warehouses.

Portland Museum of Art★

7 Congress Square.✕&☎207-775-6148. www.portlandmuseum.org.

Maine's oldest (1882) and largest public museum is known for its collection of **19C and 20C American art**—in particular the **Maine Art** paintings by the likes of Winslow Homer, Andrew Wyeth, Edward Hopper and other artists who drew their inspiration from the striking Maine landscape.

Wadsworth-Longfellow House

489 Congress St. Ticket includes admission to Maine Historical Society Museum on-site. ☎207-774-1822. www.mainehistory.org.

The 1785 brick dwelling was the childhood home of poet **Henry Wadsworth**

Beacons of the Maine Coast

While not all of the 60-some **lighthouses** on the coast of Maine are still active, these venerable beacons played a key role in New England's maritime history. Below is a selection of some of the more prominent Maine lighthouses.

Cape Neddick "Nubble" Light★ (York Harbor). Take Nubble Rd. to the tip of Cape Neddick; **Portland Head Light★** (10mi south of Portland in Fort Williams Park, 1000 Shore Rd. Cape Elizabeth); and **Pemaquid Point Lighthouse★** (12mi south of Damariscotta via Rtes. 129 & 130 in Pemaquid Point).

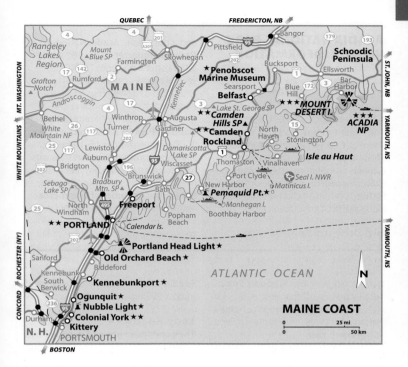

Longfellow (1807-82)—the first American to be memorialized in the Poet's Cor-ner of London's Westminster Abbey.

Farnsworth Art Museum★★

352 Main St., Rockland (44mi north of Bath on US-1). &♿ 207-596-6457. www.farnsworthmuseum.org.
The Farnsworth is a nationally acclaimed center for the study of Maine artists—notably three generations of Wyeth painters: **Newell Convers** (1882-1945), **Andrew** (b.1917) and **Jamie** (b.1946). The museum's main galleries contain works by Fitz Hugh Lane, George Inness, Thomas Eakin and Rockwell Kent.
In the adjacent **Wyeth Center** wing hang study drawings by the Wyeths. The white clapboard Methodist church on Union Street at Elm Street has been reborn as the **Wyeth Center★★**, showcasing hundreds of canvases by all three Wyeths. Next to the main museum on Elm Street, the 1850 **Farnsworth Homestead** was home to the family who provided seed money for the art museum. Nearby, in the town of Cush-

ing, the Olson House is now part of the museum. Andrew Wyeth depicted the **Olson House** in numerous works, including his 1948 painting Christina's World.

Camden★★

8mi north of Rockland on US-1.
Surveying the island-speckled waters of Penobscot Bay at the foot of the Camden Hills, Camden rates as one of the loveliest towns on the New England coast. Spend a day here exploring the shops and galleries in the village center, having a leisurely meal in a waterfront restaurant, or driving up to the top of Mt. Battie in **Camden Hills State Park★★** (off US-1 just north of Camden; ⚠♿ 207-236-3109, www.maine.gov) for a spectacular **view★★★** of Camden harbor and Penobscot Bay.

ACADIA NATIONAL PARK★★★

Located primarily on **Mount Desert Island★★★**, with smaller sections on **Isle au Haut** (off Deer Isle; access by boat

223

ACADIA NATIONAL PARK VISITOR INFORMATION

170mi north of Portland via US-1 North & Rte. 3 South. The park is open daily year-round, although snow and ice close most park roads in winter (Dec–Apr). Temperatures range from the 70s in summer to well below freezing in winter. From May through October, there's a $20 per vehicle park entrance fee, good for seven days. The Hulls Cove Visitor Center is located on Rte. 3 before entering Bar Harbor and offers a free audiovisual program about the park in several languages. There are also guided tours and a bookstore. **Acadia National Park Headquarters** is located on Rte. 233 west of Bar Harbor (△✕Open year-round daily, call for seasonal hours; ☎207-288-3338; www.nps.gov/acad). For information on camping and recreational activities, contact **Acadia National Park Headquarters** (P.O. Box 177, Bar Harbor, ME 04609). There are several accommodations, restaurants, tour operators, and activities available in Bar Harbor; contact the **Bar Harbor Chamber of Commerce** for information (1201 Bar Harbor Rd., Trenton, ME; ☎207-288-5103; www.barharborinfo.com).

from Stonington) and **Schoodic Peninsula** (across Frenchman Bay; access via US-1 North to Rte. 186 South), Acadia National Park welcomes some 4 million visitors each year.

More than one-third of the park's 40,000 acres (33,000 of which fall on Mount Desert Island) were donated by John D. Rockefeller, Jr., who created the 45mi of carriage paths that web the eastern side of the island. Bordering the temperate and subarctic climate zones, Acadia harbors 1,100 plant species and almost 300 types of birds.

Loop Road★★★

The park's main attraction, Loop Road (20mi) parallels a spectacular section of open coast with myriad scenic overlooks affording vistas from sweeping seascapes of island-studded waters. Many observation areas have benches from which to enjoy the breathtaking views of the Atlantic.

Isle au Haut, Acadia National Park

© National Park Service

New Hampshire★

Southern New Hampshire contains the state's largest cities—Manchester, Concord, (the state capital), Nashua and Keene—where politicians flock to pound the pavement every four years, vying for top ranking in the country's presidential primaries. Site of the biggest textile mill in the world in the 19C, Manchester ranks as New Hampshire's largest city. The state's only port town, Portsmouth, lies at the northern tip of New Hampshire's 18mi of shoreline. To the north, the White Mountains rise majestically in a north-south ridge passable via U-shaped valleys called notches.

▶ **Population:** 1,320,718.
ⓖ **Michelin Map:** 583 T, U 5, 6
ⓘ **Info:** ✆603-271-2665; www.visitnh.gov.
◗ **Location:** Northern New Hampshire is dominated by the dense forests that cover more than 80 percent of the state's land.

A BIT OF HISTORY

Known for its militant Revolutionary War-era motto, "Live Free or Die," New Hampshire has long been a land of uncompromising extremes. Although a settlement, **Strawbery Banke**, took hold at Portsmouth as early as 1623, the dense forests and rugged mountains in the state's interior rebuked intrusion well into the 19C, when the Industrial Revolution gave entrepreneurs a foothold in southern New Hampshire. Mills harnessing the power of the Merrimack River fueled the state's burgeoning economy, which was based at the time on granite quarrying and lumbering. At the turn of the 19C, the area's natural beauty began to draw thousands of tourists to **Mount Washington**, the Northeast's highest peak.

Today vigorous hiking, fall-foliage driving tours and winter skiing all enjoy tremendous popularity, as do quaint New England villages such as **Franconia★** and **New London★**.

Up near the Canadian border, more placid diversion can be found fishing or camping in the **Connecticut Lakes** region. New Hampshire also claims one of the nation's prominent Ivy League schools, **Dartmouth College★** (6016 N. Main St., Hanover; ✆603-646-1110; www.dartmouth.edu), which offers its 6,100 students top-quality instruction in the arts and sciences.

Canterbury Shaker Village

©David Shafer/The New Hampshire Division of Travel and Tourism Development

New Hampshire Coast

Sandy beaches, rocky ledges and state parks line New Hampshire's short 18mi coastline. Skirting the shore, Rte. 1A runs from Seabrook to Portsmouth passing resort areas, elegant estates. and fine views of the ocean. Be sure to visit **Odiorne Point State Park** (℘603-436-1552; www.nhstateparks.nh.us).

The ragged promontory of Odiorne Point was the site of the first settlement in New Hampshire. You'll have sweeping ocean views throuhout the park's 135 undeveloped acres. Be sure to visit the Seacoast Science Center at the park, with exhibits, aquariums and a touch tank (fee).

CANTERBURY SHAKER VILLAGE★★

13.7mi north of Concord. From I-93 take Exit 18 and follow signs (7mi) to Shaker Village, 288 Shaker Rd. ✗. Open late-May–mid-Oct daily. ☜Guided and self-guided tours available. ℘603-783-9511. www.shakers.org.

Attracted by the serene countryside and the gift of a large tract of land in Canterbury, the Shakers established a community near the village of **Canterbury Center★** in the 1780s. As in other Shaker communities, residents here made their own clothing, tools and furniture. The 26 original buildings—including the **Dwelling House**, the well-equipped **Schoolhouse**, and the 1792 **Meeting House**, which contains Shaker products—still stand on 694 acres.

PORTSMOUTH★★

New Hampshire's only seaport, Portsmouth lies at the mouth of the Piscataqua River across from the southern border of Maine. Settlers arrived here as early as 1623, after which time Portsmouth thrived as a center for maritime commerce.

Today many grand mansions remain, and the site of the original Strawbery Banke settlement has been preserved. The city boasts a thriving art scene and is well-known for its number and variety of top-notch restaurants. Historic brick buildings, housing art galleries, restaurants and boutiques surround and fan out from Market Square in the center of town.

Strawbery Banke Museum★★

420 Court St. ✗. Open May–Oct daily. ℘603-433-1100. www.strawberybanke.org.

This 10-acre restoration project remains a living model of the techniques used to rehabilitate an entire district. Slated for the wrecking ball in the 1950s, 42 buildings spanning three centuries have been preserved, showing the town's growth from a 1623 farming community to a prosperous port. Fifteen homes and period gardens are open to the public, ranging from the 17C timber **Sherburne House** to the elegant 1811 **Goodwin Mansion**. In September 2013, the expanded visitor center opened with its new cafe.

Historic Houses★★

Sprinkled throughout Portsmouth are nine furnished dwellings illustrating the decorative and architectural styles and high-quality craftsmanship that reigned in Portsmouth in the 18C and 19C. Of note are the **Warner House★★**, a 1716 Georgian mansion (150 Daniel St.; ℘603-436-5909; www.warnerhouse.org), the 1763 **Moffatt Ladd House★** (154 Market St.; ℘603-436-8221; www.moffattladd.org), the **Wentworth-Gardner State Historic Mansion** (50 Mechanic St.; ℘603-436-4406; www.wentworthgardnerandlear.org), a 1760 Georgian-style mansion, and the **Governor John Langdon House** (143 Pleasant St.; ℘603-436-3205; www.historicnewengland.org). Generally, the houses are open June through mid-October. Call for tour times and fees.

The Presidential Range in autumn
NHDTTD/Dale Lary

EXCURSIONS

Cruise to the Isles of Shoals★

Departs from Market St. dock mid-Jun–Labor Day daily. Limited schedule spring & fall. Round-trip 2hrs30min. Commentary. Reservations recommended. Fees & schedules vary; call for information: Isles of Shoals Steamship Co.: ℘603-431-5500 or 800-441-4620; www.islesofshoals.com.

The 10mi boat trip to this group of nine islands follows the banks of the Piscataqua River for 5mi before heading out to sea. There are good views of sights along the river, Fort McClary (Kittery, Maine), Fort Constitution, and the lovely homes in the island town of New Castle. In the 19C the islands were popularized by author Celia Thaxter and other writers who gathered at her home on Appledore Island each summer.

White Mountains★★★

Spreading across northern New Hampshire and into Maine, the White Mountains boast the highest peaks in New England, as well as some of its most spectacular scenery. Named for the snow that blankets the area during most of the year, these massifs, dominated by Mt. Washington (6,288ft) of the Presidential Range, are characterized by rounded summits and deep, U-shaped notches. Scenic roads, including the magnificent **Kancamagus Highway★★★**, pass through breathtaking notches such as **Pinkham★★**, **Crawford★★** and **Franconia★★★**.

Much of the area is protected as the 772,000-acre **White Mountain National Forest**, renowned for its 1,200mi of hiking and cross-country skiing trails. Down-hill skiing dominates the winter months at resorts including Attitash, Loon, Mt. Cranmore, Black Mountain, Wildcat Mountain, and Waterville Valley (trail conditions & information: ℘603-745-9396; www.skinh.com).

Mount Washington★★★

Off Rte. 16. ℘603-356-2137. www.mountwashington.org

Highest point in New England, Mt. Washington (6,288ft) experienced some of the strongest winds recorded on earth (231mph) in 1934. A subarctic climate—characterized by bitter cold, wind and ice—predominates in the higher altitudes of this peak. Snow falls on this peak during every month of the year. Fog-bound at least 300 days each year, the summit with its group of mountaintop buildings, has been dubbed the "City Among the Clouds." The mountaintop is accessible via the Auto Road, four strenuous hiking trails, and the 👥 **Mount Washington Cog Railway★★** (departs from Marshfield Base Station 6mi east of Rte. 302; call or check online for schedule: ℘603-278-5404; www.thecog.com).

Built in 1869, the railway offers passengers a thrilling 3.5mi ride to the summit for a 240mi **panorama★★★** of the entire region.

Vermont★★

Vermont offers a delightful blend of historic charm, quiet villages, pastoral and mountainous landscapes, smart resorts and thriving arts and culinary hot spots.

▶ **Population:** 620,811
Michelin Map: 583 T 5, 6
Info: ℘877-686-5253; www.vermont.org.
Location: Most of the state is a five hour drive from Boston.
Don't Miss: The American folk art collection at Shelburne Museum.

A BIT OF HISTORY

An Independent State – In 1777 Vermont declared itself independent, and a constitution was drawn up outlawing slavery and eliminating property ownership. Denied admission to the Union because of land claims by New York, Vermont remained independent for 14 years, coining its own money and negotiating with foreign powers. After the dispute with New York was settled, Vermont joined the Union in 1791 as the 14th state.

Today Vermont remains strikingly old-fashioned and picturesque. White clapboard Colonial architecture reigns in its small town centers, such as **Manchester Village★**, while larger towns such as **Burlington★**, the state's most populous city, have ingeniously adapted old buildings for modern use. Burlington also claims the **Ethan Allen Homestead★** ▲ (Rte. 127, 2mi north of downtown ℘802-865-4556; www. ethanallenhomestead.org), believed to have been the final home of the enigmatic folk hero.

Along the scenic country roads, used bookstores and antique shops are more common than gas stations. Autumn is the most popular time to explore Vermont, when the leaves take on blazing hues and apples are ripe for picking. In winter, more than 40 ski resorts draw thousands to the steep slopes (trail conditions & information: ℘802-223-2439; www.skivermont.com).

BENNINGTON★

In the southwest corner of Vermont at the intersection of US-7 and Rte. 9. ℘802-447-3311. www.bennington.com. Situated 2mi west of Bennington Center's shops and cafes, **Old Bennington★** is a small historic district known for its role in the Revolutionary War.

In May 1775, **Ethan Allen** and the **Green Mountain Boys** gathered here before they marched north to attack Fort Ticonderoga. Two years later, in August 1777, a British plan to seize munitions from a local supply depot was thwarted by colonial troops in the **Battle of Bennington**.

Today a 306ft dolomite obelisk, the **Bennington Battle Monument** (2mi west of Bennington Center on Monument Ave.; ℘802-447-0550, www.historicsites. vermont.gov) commemorates the battle and offers a sweeping mountain view★★ from its observation deck.

Ben and Jerry's Ice Cream Factory

▲ 1281 Waterbury-Stowe Rd., Waterbury, 15mi northwest of Montpelier via I-89 & Rte. 100. Open year-round, daily; call for seasonal hours. ℘802-882-1240. www.benjerry.com. When native Vermonters Ben Cohen and Jerry Greenfield signed up for a $5 correspondence course in ice-cream-making and opened a tiny scoop shop in Burlington in the late 1970s, they didn't know that their venture would grow into a multimillion-dollar global operation. Tours of their small factory, now owned by Unilever, conclude with free samples.

The Ticonderoga, Shelburne Museum

Courtesy of Shelburne Museum

Bennington Museum★

75 Main St. (Rte. 9). ♿ ☏802-447-1571. www.benningtonmuseum.org.
Grandma Moses (1860-1961), the beloved American folk artist who began to paint when she was 75, is the star attraction here. The museum contains 30 of her canvases, as well as extensive collections of Vermont-made art objects, including pressed and blown glass, furniture, and the country's largest collection of 19C Bennington pottery. The museum has a regularly changing temporary exhibition program, and runs events and classes for children and adults throughout the year.

👥 SHELBURNE MUSEUM★★★

12mi south of Burlington on US-7. ♿ Open mid-May–late-Oct, daily. ☏802-985-3346. www.shelburnemuseum.org.
"I was anxious to create something in arrangement and conception that had not been tried," wrote **Electra Havemeyer Webb** (1889-1960) of her life project, the Shelburne Museum. Indeed, this sprawling 45-acre complex, comprising 39 historic buildings, blends a formal art museum and a living-history museum into a "three-dimensional collage" whose 150,000-piece collection of art spans 300 years.
Architecturally the museum embraces a panoply of vernacular styles, ranging from the mansard-roofed Colchester

Reef Lighthousea (1871) to the rare wooden **Round Barn★★** (1901).
The eye-catching **Ticonderoga★★**, a luxurious 1906 side-wheeler steamship, now sits in a scooped-out basin in the middle of the grounds.
The new Pizzagalli Center for Art and Education with two galleries, a classroom and an auditorium and the Museum Store are open year-round.

WOODSTOCK★★

On US-4, 10mi west of I-89 Exit 1. ☏802-457-3355. www.woodstockvt.com.
One of the most pristine villages in Vermont, Woodstock was established in 1761. Today, art galleries, restaurants and a general store occupy historic storefronts along Central and Elm Streets, and the elegant Woodstock Inn borders the oval village green.

Marsh-Billings-Rockefeller National Historical Park★★

Across the street from **Billings Farm & Museum★★** (Rte. 12 and River Rd.; ♿ ☏802-457-2355; www.billingsfarm.org). Grounds open daily year-round. The Billings Farm & Museum is open May–Oct, daily. ☏802-457-3368. www.nps.gov/mabi.
Opened in June 1998, Vermont's first national park centers on a meticulously preserved, art-filled Queen Anne-style mansion and the conservation efforts of three of its residents: 19C environmen-

talist George Perkins Marsh; Frederick Billings, founder of Billings Farm; and Billings' granddaughter Mary French Rockefeller. Visit a working dairy farm, participate in hands-on 19C games and activities, and try your hand at churning butter, among other activities.

🚗 DRIVING TOUR

Villages of Southern Vermont★★

This scenic drive on the back roads of southern Vermont leads to classic, step-back-in-time villages, mountain resorts and farms.

▶ Leave Manchester Village by Rte. 7A. At Manchester Center take Rte. 30 East and continue on Rte.11.

🚹 Bromley Mountain

The Bromley ski area has become popular during the summer season because of its **alpine slide, zip line, water slide, mini-golf,** and more (🍴♿🖉802-824-5522; www.bromley.com). Bromley's summit (3,260ft) can be reached by hiking trails or a scenic chairlift ride and offers views of the Green Mountains.

Long Trail to Bromley Summit

🚹 From the Bromley ski area, follow Rte. 11 approximately 2mi east. A small sign indicates the Long Trail. 🅿 Parking is on the right.
From the parking lot, a dirt road leads to the trail (🚹 5.6mi round-trip), which

is a segment of both the Long Trail and the **Appalachian Trail**. After gently ascending through forest for 2mi, the trail climbs steeply, then crosses open meadowland. A **panorama★★** of Stratton Mountain (to the south) and the surrounding Green Mountains can be seen from an observation tower at the summit.

▶ Two miles after Bromley, take the road on the left through Peru. At the fork bear left and continue through North Landgrove, turning left in front of the town hall. After passing the Village Inn, bear right at the fork and continue to Weston.

Weston★

www.weston-vermont.com.
With its attractive village green, craft shops and general stores, Weston is a popular tourist stop on Rte. 100. Looking out on the green is the **Farrar-Mansur House**, a late-18C tavern that serves as the local history museum (🅿🖉802-824-5294).

▶ From Weston follow Rte. 100 past the green, then bear right at the sign for Chester. Continue through Andover, then east on Rte. 11.

Chester

www.chestervermont.org.
The wide main street of this community is lined with lodgings and shops, several of which are housed in historic build-

Maple Sugaring

With an annual average yield of over a million gallons, Vermont is the leading producer of maple syrup in the US. From early March to mid-April, when the nighttime temperature still drops below freezing, but the days get steadily warmer, more than a million hard-rock, or sugar-maple, trees in the state are tapped with small metal spouts. Under these spouts, buckets are hung to collect the 10 to 15 gallons of sap each tree is liable to produce. The sap is then taken to a ventilated sugar house to be boiled down to the desired thickness, filtered through layers of cloth, and jarred. Each gallon of syrup is the product of some 40 gallons of sap. Some 60 outfits tvhroughout the state invite you to witness the maple-sugaring process in early spring, and to sample their wares. Syrup comes in three grades: delicate light amber, all-purpose medium amber and robust dark amber.

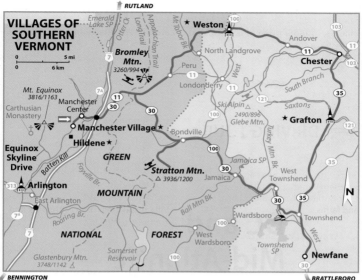

VILLAGES OF SOUTHERN VERMONT

ings (a walking-tour brochure is available from the information booth on the village green Jun-Oct).

▶ From Chester take Rte. 35 to Grafton.

Grafton★

www.graftonvermont.org.
Tucked into the mountains of southern Vermont, Grafton is one of the state's most picturesque villages. While you're in town, check out the Grafton Village Cheese Company (☏ 800-472-3866; www.graftonvillagecheese.com) to see how Vermont's favorite cheddar is made and for an opportunity to try samples. And don't miss a visit to the 1801 **Old Tavern** (☏ 802-843-1801, www.graftonin-nvermont.com), one of the oldest operating inns in America. Once frequented by such luminaries as Ulysses S. Grant, Oliver Wendell Holmes and Rudyard Kipling, the three-story brick tavern now welcomes guests as the historic 30-room Grafton Inn.

▶ In Grafton turn right, cross the bridge and turn left before the tavern. Follow this road to Rte. 35, which leads to Townshend, then take Rte. 30 South to Newfane.

Newfane

www.newfanevermont.com.
Nestled deep in the Green Mountains, this town has grown little since the 18C, when it was selected as the Windham county seat. Newfane's village **green★**, with its white Congregational church **Windham County Courthouse** and two old inns, is pretty at any time of the year, but it becomes a spectacular sight in the fall.

▶ Take Rte. 30 back through Townshend. Between Townshend and West Townshend you will pass a covered bridge on the left. Continue through Jamaica into Bondville, where Stratton Mountain Rd. to the left leads to the Stratton Mountain Ski Area.

Stratton Mountain

Off Rte. 30; from Bondville, follow Stratton Mountain Rd. 4mi to resort.
☏ 802-297-4000 or 800-STRATTON.
www.stratton.com.
With 94 trails accessible by a gondola and 14 chairlifts, this mountain (3,936ft) is one of the major ski areas in Vermont, as well as a popular summer playground.

▶ Return to Manchester via Rte. 30.

DC and Mid-Atlantic

Smithsonian Institution Building
The Castle - Washington, DC
© Gwen Cannon/Michelin

Washington, DC Area

Conceived as a national showplace, Washington, DC, embodies the spirit of American idealism in its Neoclassical monuments, its grand museums and its sweeping vistas. Today it is a truly international city, hosting world-class performing artists as well as offering fine shopping and dining. Lying 90mi inland from the mid-Atlantic seaboard, the city rises from low bottomland along the Potomac riverfront and covers 67sq mi carved out of Maryland. Though some restrictions have been put in place since the terrorist attacks of 9/11, the United States capital remains remarkably accessible. The doors of Congress, the White House and other federal institutions are open to the hosts of visitors who come to witness democracy in progress.

Highlights

1 **US Capitol Building** (p238)
2 **Library of Congress** (p239)
3 **The Mall** and its **Monuments** (p239)
4 **National Air and Space Museum** (p240)
5 **The White House** (p246)

Washington DC

A Capital Location

The Washington metropolitan area fans out in densely settled suburbs reaching north toward Baltimore, Maryland; south toward Fredericksburg, Virginia; east across the broad estuarine expanse of Maryland's Eastern Shore (&see BALTIMORE); and west toward the Blue Ridge Mountains. The rumblings that preceded the Civil War began in the mountains west of Washington. Once the war exploded, some of its most noted battles were fought in the countryside within an hour's drive of DC.

East of Washington on the Chesapeake Bay, Annapolis celebrates its 18C seafaring heritage at its bustling marina and at the US Naval Academy. Across the Potomac in Old Town Alexandria, Virginia, Colonial architecture and contemporary shops dot brick-paved sidewalks.

Neighboring Arlington, Virginia, is home to the **Pentagon** (I-395 at Washington Blvd.; visit by guided tour only; &703-695-1776; www.pentagontours.os.mil), the five-sided building targeted on 9/11 that houses the US Department of Defense.

City for All Seasons

With its rich history and world-class museums, the nation's capital holds events year-round. Come in spring for the **Cherry Blossom Festival** and celebrate the famous pink trees along the Tidal Basin.

Visit in summer to watch Fourth of July fireworks explode above the Washington Monument. Free military band concerts by US armed services are held Memorial Day to Labor Day at various locations. June-July brings the DC Jazz Festival and the Smithsonian Folk Life Festival.

Arrive in autumn to enjoy the bright foliage (Oct) that lines the towpath along the Chesapeake and Ohio (C&O) Canal. Come here in winter to see the President light the **National Christmas Tree** on the Ellipse.

&See CALENDAR OF EVENTS for above-mentioned festivals and events.

GETTING THERE

Ronald Reagan Washington National Airport (DCA): ℘703-417-8000, www.metwashairports.com; 4.5mi south of downtown DC. Airport information booths on the baggage-claim level of all terminals. Free shuttle buses operate daily to and from all terminals, parking lots and garages and the Metro station.

Dulles International Airport (DIA): ℘703-572-2700, www.metwashairports.com; 26mi west of downtown DC. Airport information booth on lower level of Main Terminal.

Baltimore-Washington International Airport (BWI): ℘410-859-7111, www.bwiairport.com; 28mi north of Washington. Airport information booth at entrances to piers C and D on upper level of terminal. Rental car agencies are located at the airports.

Union Station (Massachusetts & Delaware Aves.) provides **Amtrak** and other **rail service** to major destinations in the Northeast, Midwest and South. Reservations are recommended: ℘800-872-7245 or www.amtrak.com; **Bus** travel provided by **Greyhound** at the main bus terminal: in DC: 1005 1st St. N.E.; ℘202-289-5154.

GETTING AROUND

Washington Metropolitan Area Transit Authority (WMATA) operates **Metrorail**, Washington's rapid-transit system (runs daily until midnight; maps & tickets available at all Metro stations; ℘202-962-2733), and **Metrobus** (runs daily until midnight; ⊜$1.45 base fare purchased on bus, exact change required; ℘202-637-7000). Daily and weekly passes available for Metrorail and Metrobus. For additional fare information and schedules, access WMATA's website: www.wmata.com. DC **Streetcar**: scheduled to begin late 2013; ℘855-413-2954; www.dcstreetcar.com. **Taxi** service: DC Taxicab Commission, ℘202-645-6018.

VISITOR INFORMATION

For a free visit planner, contact **Destination DC**, 901 7th Street N.W., 4th Floor, ℘202-789-7000, http://washington.org/. The **Smithsonian Information Center** (1000 Jefferson Dr. S.W.; ℘202-633-1000) can help you plan your visit to Smithsonian museums. Most museums on the Mall are open daily and are free-of-charge. Many have cafeterias; food kiosks are usually open along the sidewalks.

ADDRESSES

🏨 STAY

Hotel reservation services:
Washington, DC Accommodations ℘202-289-2220, www.dcaccommodations.com.

Washington International Youth Hostel: ℘202-737-2333, hiwashingtondc.org.

$$$$$ The Hay-Adams Hotel – 800 16th st. N.W., Washington, DC. ♿🅿 ℘202-638-6600. www.hayadams.com. 145 rooms. Across from the White House, this Italian Renaissance-style property has been the first choice for the visiting elite since 1928. The posh lobby features walnut paneling edged with golden eagles and hand-carved fruit moldings (representing abundance) on the ceiling. Bedrooms are clad in pale, buttery colors and early 20C furnishings.

$$$$$ Inn at Perry Cabin – 308 Watkins Lane, St. Michaels, MD. ✖♿🅿🛁 ℘410-745-2200. www.perrycabin.com. 80 rooms. On the banks of the Miles River, this early-19C cabin has expanded into a luxury 25-acre resort surrounded by landscaped gardens. Bedrooms are designed as relaxing retreats. Some have private patios or cathedral ceilings. Furnishings range from antique armoires to simple oak pieces.

$$$$$ The Willard Washington – 1401 Pennsylvania Ave. NW, Washington, DC. ✖♿🅿🛁 ℘202-628-9100. http://washington.intercontinental.com. 335 rooms. Long a favorite of DC lobbyists hashing out deals, the Willard is also an historic landmark, loved for its Beaux-Arts architecture. Rooms in this **InterContinental** hotel are decorated in soft colors and boast modern amenities. Many have picturesque views overlooking Pennsylvania Avenue.

$$$ Morrison-Clark Inn – Massachusetts Ave. & 11th St. N.W., Washington, DC. ✖️♿️🅿️ 📞202-898-1200. www.morrisonclark.com. 54 rooms. This turn-of-the-century mansion, built in 1864 and composed of two townhouses, seems misplaced in the middle of downtown's business district. Past the antiques-filled parlor, with lace curtains and burgundy wall coverings, you'll find three styles of accommodation. Choose from neutral-toned Neoclassical, opulent Victorian, and country-style distressed woods and wicker. The restaurant's Southern-style specialties have made it a national favorite.

$$$ Morrison House – 116 S. Alfred St., Alexandria, VA. ✖️♿️🅿️📞703-838-8000. www.morrisonhouse.com. 45 rooms. There's no way of knowing that this Federal manor in Old Town, now a Kimpton property, was built in 1985. Butlers escort guests up the columned entrance's double staircase. The cheerful parlor is filled with framed Audubon prints, topiaries and rosy period couches. Guest rooms are fitted with early American-style four-poster beds and brass chandeliers.

$$ Celie's Waterfront Bed & Breakfast – 1714 Thames St., Baltimore, MD. ♿️🅿️ 📞410-522-2323. www.celieswaterfront. com. 9 rooms. This charming Fell's Point inn offers extras like whirlpools, plush down comforters and fresh flowers. Bright and tastefully decorated, guest quarters have wicker furnishings and antiques, as well as harbor or courtyard views. Other in-room features include balconies, separate seating alcoves and skylights.

🍽️ EAT

$$$$ The Caucus Room – 401 9th St. N.W., Washington, DC. 📞202-393-1300. www.thecaucusroom.com. **American.** This restaurant is the consummate Washington steak house, where power players disappear into the dark wooded interior to tuck in to a tender steak and a glass of merlot. Truly a bipartisan venture, The Caucus Room boasts a William Woodward mural of a donkey and elephant (respective symbols of the Democratic and Republican parties) amicably enjoying a lavish feast. Generous portions and impeccable service justify the high prices.

$$$ Bistro St. Michaels – 403 S. Talbot St., St. Michaels, MD. Closed Tue & Wed. 📞4410-745-9111; www.bistrostmichaels. com. **Contemporary.** Set in a Victorian house on the town's main thoroughfare, this casual eatery prepares comforting modern dishes with local produce and seafood. Vintage 19C French food ads in the bi-level dining room will spark your appetite for seasonal specials such as corn and crab chowder, sautéed soft-shell crabs, and mustard-crusted chicken paillard with orange honey.

$$$ Restaurant Nora –2132 Florida Ave. N.W., Washington, DC. 📞202-462-5143. www.noras.com. **Contemporary.** America's first certified organic restaurant, Nora is housed in an updated 19C grocery store off Dupont Circle. Nora Pouillon's menu reflects what is in-season and what is fresh each day, and may feature such delights asslow roasted rose veal with rye berries, or the grass-fed beef tartare with local truffles. DC diners have praised her innovative organic creations for 20-plus years.

$$$ Vidalia – 1990 M St. N.W., Washington, DC. 📞202-659-1990. www.vidaliadc.com. **Contemporary.** Cheerful yellow walls and antique-filled china cabinets decorate this downtown favorite. Chef Jeffrey Buben looks to the South for inspiration. Winning dishes on the seasonal menu include sautéed shrimp and grits in a sweet-onion ragu, duck breast with hot and sour baby beets and frogmore stew, made with shellfish and sweet corn.

$$ Georgia Brown's – 950 15th St. NW. 📞202-393-4499. www.gbrowns.com. **Southern.** This well-appointed restaurant pushes Dixie cooking to new heights by combining standard Southern ingredients in unusual ways. Try the she-crab soup as a starter, then the "head-on" shrimp with spicy sausage and grits or the Southern-fried chicken as your entrée. Peach cobbler à la mode is the yummy signature dessert.

Washington, DC★★★

Unique among most of the world's capital cities, Washington, DC, had its beginnings not as a monarchy, but as a democracy. Its broad avenues and regal monuments serve as visual paeans to the democratic ideal. Its heroes include George Washington, Thomas Jefferson, Abraham Lincoln and, more recently, John F. Kennedy Franklin Delano Roosevelt and Martin Luther King, Jr. The city abounds with tributes to these titans of American history. In recent decades Washington has emerged from its strictly political associations with its flagship John F. Kennedy Center for the Performing Arts★★ (New Hampshire Ave. at Rock Creek Pkwy.; ℘202-416-8000; www.kennedy-center.org), which houses four theaters and the resident National Symphony Orchestra. Culturally, the idealism of democracy is alive in the collection of outstanding museums that are open to the public all at no cost.

- ▶ **Population:** 599,657
- **Info:** ℘202-789-7000; http://washington.org.
- **Location:** DC is located on the north bank of the Potomac River.
- **Timing:** Leave time to tour the monuments at night when they are illuminated.
- **Kids:** A day at the Air and Space Museum will thrill young aviation enthusiasts.

A BIT OF HISTORY

Following the euphoria that resulted from winning independence from Britain, President **George Washington** (1732-99) chose a tract of land near the prosperous port of Georgetown in which to locate the seat of power for the new nation. Washington knew this area well, for his own plantation, Mount Vernon, lay just 16mi to the south along the Potomac River.

French major **Pierre Charles L'Enfant** (1754-1825) was appointed to design the new capital, a diamond-shaped federal district that measured 10mi long on each side and encompassed portions of Maryland as well as the County of Alexandria on the Potomac's west bank. L'Enfant situated the new Capitol building on Jenkins Hill, which commanded a striking view of the Potomac River. Along this east-west axis, he planned a 400ft-wide "Grand Avenue" (now the Mall) to be lined by foreign ministries and cultural institutions. The avenue would connect on a north-south axis with the "President's house," which

U.S. Capitol dome

©Zain Deane/Michelin

would link back to the Capitol via a mile-long commercial corridor (present-day Pennsylvania Avenue).

Despite numerous setbacks—including L'Enfant's dismissal in 1792 and the loss of Alexandria back to Virginia—by the mid-19C Washington was well on its way to becoming a city. In 1871 the District of Columbia incorporated Georgetown, and improved transportation spurred the growth of suburbs in nearby Virginia and Maryland.

Today, Washington's population is about 60 percent African-American and 40 percent white. Despite periods of racial unrest, this diversity has helped the city mature as an urban center boasting some 10 colleges and universities. Washington also owes a debt of gratitude to former First Lady "Lady-bird" Johnson, who began landscaping efforts in the 1960s that turned green spaces into showplaces bright with flowers. Washington's development is closely monitored to ensure that the monumental capital retains its reputation as "the City Beautiful." Continued improvements and expansion of The Mall are underway (see The Mall), and streetcars are being reintroduced to the city: in late 2013, the initial H Street/Benning Road line is scheduled to open between Union Station and the Anacostia River.

CAPITOL HILL★★★

Crowned by great stone buildings that house the legislative and judicial branches of the federal government, the city's high eastern ground was known as Jenkins Hill in 1791 when L'Enfant selected it as the future site of Congress. Now called Capitol Hill, the area incorporates residential neighborhoods of 19C row houses that reflect a true cross section of Washington's population.

Convenient to Congress members, the 1907 Beaux-Arts **Union Station★** (40 Massachusetts Ave. N.E.; ✕ ♿ 🅿 ✆202-371-9441; www.unionstationdc.com) was renovated in the 1980s to house shops, eateries and a cinema. The coffered, barrel-vaulted ceiling in its main

hall was inspired by the Roman Baths of Diocletian.

US Capitol Building★★★

Capitol Hill, National Mall. ✕ ♿ ✆202-226-8000. www.visitthecapitol.gov. ➥Visit by guided tour only daily except Sun and holidays. Photo ID is required. Tours begin from the Visitor Center beneath the Capitol East Front Plaza (1st & E. Capitol Sts.), which includes orientation theaters, exhibit space and a 550-seat cafeteria.

Characterized by city designer L'Enfant as "a pedestal waiting for a monument," the rising ground known as Capitol Hill is crowned by the massive Capitol building that has housed the US Congress since 1800. The original low-domed central section was designed by Dr. William Thornton to resemble Rome's Pantheon. Over the ensuing decades, the dome was enlarged and adjoining wings were added.

Above the **rotunda**, the ornate Capitol **dome★★**—180ft high and 98ft across—displays an allegorical fresco, *The Apotheosis of Washington* (1865), by Constantino Brumidi. Bordering the rotunda on the main floor, semicircular half-domed **Statuary Hall** appears (unfurnished) as it did in 1857 when it served as the House Chamber; on the other side of the rotunda is the restored **Old Senate Chamber** that housed the Supreme Court from 1860 to 1935. The ground floor holds the **Crypt**, the vaulted **Old Supreme Court Chamber**, and the intersecting **Brumidi Corridors,** which is embellished with the artist's murals. On the third floor (gallery level) the **House Chamber** holds the seats of the 435-member House of Representatives (Democrats to the right of the Speaker of the House; Republicans to the left). Across the hall in the **Senate Chamber**, the Vice President presides before 100 Senators (two from each of the 50 states).

Supreme Court★★

1st & E. Capitol Sts. N.E. ✕ ♿ ✆202-479-3000. www.supremecourtus.gov. Sessions are open to the public on a first-come, first-served basis. Consult the court's website for the daily schedule of arguments. Visitors can also tour the court building, view exhibits relating to its history, and attend free films and lectures about the court.

Across the street from the Capitol, the highest court in the land exercises its mandate to protect and interpret the spirit of the Constitution, and serve as a counterbalance to the legislative and executive branches of government. The broad staircase in front of this cross-shaped marble structure (1935, Cass Gilbert) is flanked by two James Fraser sculptures, representing the *Contemplation of Justice* (left) and the *Authority of Law* (right). Carved in the building's pediment are the words "Equal Justice Under Law."

Within the **courtroom**, justices sit on a raised bench ringed by massive columns. Dominating the main hall on ground level is the **statue** of John Marshall (1755-1835), the "Great Chief Justice" who held the post from 1801 to 1835.

Library of Congress★★

101 Independence Ave. S.E. ♿ Open Mon–Sat. Buildings, research centers, exhibits and reading rooms all keep different hours. ✆202-707-5000. www.loc.gov.

Established in 1800 (and housed in the Capitol) for the use of Congress, the Library of Congress ranks as the largest library in existence. A richly ornamented Beaux-Arts landmark, the original library building (1897) holds more than 16 million books, 46 million manuscripts, 4 million maps and atlases, and 8 million musical items. Noteworthy for its gold-leaf ceiling and vaulted corridors, the two-story **Great Hall** holds a copy of the mid-15C Giant Bible of Mainz, one of the last hand-illuminated manuscript versions of the Bible. An elaborately sculpted grand staircase leads to the second-story colonnade, where a visitors' gallery overlooks the **Main Reading Room**—a vast rotunda under the library's dome (160ft from floor to lantern) ringed by Corinthian columns and arched windows that are embellished with stained-glass state seals.

Folger Shakespeare Library★

201 E. Capitol St. S.E. ♿ ✆202-544-4600. www.folger.edu.

Established by Henry Clay Folger and his wife, Emily Jordan, in the 1930s, this library conserves 275,000 Renaissance-related books and manuscripts, including 79 of the 240 first editions of the collected works of Shakespeare known to exist. Designed by Paul Cret, the Art Deco structure's marble façade includes bas-relief under-panels featuring scenes from Shakespeare's plays. The interior features a Tudor-style **Great Hall** and an **Elizabethan theater**. The library is known for its public programs, including plays, concerts, school programs and literary readings.

THE MALL★★★

Focal point for such national events as the annual **Independence Day celebration** and the summer **Smithsonian Folklife Festival**, this sweeping greensward links the country's most revered monuments and museums. The Mall was developed in the mid-19C when ground was broken for the Washington Monument and the Smithsonian Castle. Today the **Smithsonian Institution**, founded through the generosity of Englishman James Smithson in 1835, operates nine museums on the **East Mall** between Capitol Hill and 15th Street. The Smithsonian's first building, a Romanesque Revival structure known as **The Castle** (Jefferson Dr. at 10th St. S.W.), serves as a visitor center. The **National Museum of the American Indian** opened on the Mall in 2004; its collections represent more than 1,000 indigenous cultures spanning 10,000 years of North, South, and Central American history. In 2006 the Smithsonian Institute announced plans for its newest museum on the Mall, the **National Museum of African American History and Culture**, devoted to African-American art, history and culture, and slated for completion in 2015. The first of several projects of a

$700 million plan to transform the Mall into a world-class urban park is scheduled for completion in 2016; projects include gardens, recreational facilities and landscaping.

The **West Mall** stretches from 15th Street to the Potomac River and is the site of monuments to past presidents and memorials to war veterans (&see Memorials below).

👥 National Air and Space Museum★★★

6th & Independence Ave. S.W. ✗ ℰ 202-633-1000. http://airandspace.si.edu.

Established in 1946, Washington's most popular museum contains hundreds of authentic artifacts commemorating man's aeronautical and astronautical achievements. Gyo Obata designed the marble-faced structure that opened for the nation's bicentennial in July 1976.

Within the building's four massive rectangles are an **IMAX® theater**, a **planetarium** and 21 galleries displaying hundreds of aircraft and spacecraft, rockets, guided missiles and satellites, as well as exhibits that trace the history of flight from its earliest days through to World War II. Topics such as the prin-

Eleanora O'Donnell Iselin (1888) by John Singer Sargent, National Gallery of Art

© National Gallery of Art

ciples of flight and aerial photography are also addressed. In the **Milestones of Flight** hall in the central part of the building hang such epoch-making aircraft as Charles Lindbergh's Ryan NYP *Spirit of St. Louis*, and John Glenn's *Friendship 7* space capsule. In the **At the Controls** gallery, you can test your skills in a flight simulator. In **Space Race** you'll see, among other displays, a replica of the Hubble Space Telescope and the *Apollo-Soyuz* spacecraft used for a joint docking-in-space experiment with the Russians in 1975.

Visitors can walk through the Skylab Orbital Workshop (accessible from the 2nd floor).The centerpiece display in the Wright Brothers gallery (2nd floor) is their *1903 Flyer*.

National Gallery of Art★★★

4th and Constitution Ave. N.W. ✗ & ℰ 202-737-4215. www.nga.gov.

Tracing Western art from the Middle Ages to the present, the National Gallery houses 3,000 paintings, 2,000 pieces of sculpture, 560 pieces of decorative art and over 47,000 works on paper.

In the 1920s, financier, industrialist and statesman **Andrew Mellon** (1855-1936) funded the stately marble **West Building** that graces the Mall today, and started the collection with 126 paintings and a group of fine 15C-16C Italian sculptures.

Arranged in chronological order, galleries on the main floor of the West Building progress from **13C Italian Painting** through Spanish, German and Flemish masterpieces to **19C French Painting**. Thomas Gainsborough and J.M.W. Turner are included among the collection of **British Painting**, while the portraiture of Benjamin West, Charles Willson Peale and Gilbert Stuart highlight the American Painting galleries. The ground floor displays sculpture and decorative arts.

In the 1970s the Mellon family again came forward to endow the museum's acclaimed **East Building**★★ (1978, I.M. Pei), which is devoted to 20C art. Considered the most impressive example of modern architecture in Washington, the East Building opens into a soaring skylit **atrium** dominated by an immense mobile by Alexander Calder. Galleries showcase the work of Pablo Picasso, Wassily Kandinsky, Mark Rothko, Georgia O'Keeffe and other prominent artists.

The **National Gallery of Art Sculpture Garden** (on the Mall at 7th St. & Constitution Ave. N.W.) is an urban oasis filled with contemporary sculptures by the likes of Alexander Calder, Claes Oldenburg and Joan Miró. Its dramatic circular fountain becomes an ice-skating rink in winter and the venue for free jazz concerts (Fri evening) in summer.

National Archives★★

Constitution Ave. between 7th & 9th Sts. N.W. ✕♿ ℰ866-272-6272. www.archives.gov..

This Classical Revival temple (1937, John Russell Pope) safeguards the nation's official and historical records, including 5 billion paper documents, 9 million aerial photographs, 6 million still photographs, and 300,000 video, film and sound recordings. Inside the cavernous rotunda, a dais enshrines the nation's **Charters of Freedom★★★**: the **Declaration of Independence**, two pages of the **Constitution**, and the **Bill of Rights**. The National Archives also functions as a major source of historical material for both domestic and foreign researchers.

👥 National Museum of Natural History★★

Constitution Ave. at 10th St. N.W. ♿ ℰ202-633-1000. www.mnh.si.edu. M2 on map.

Completed in 1911 to hold the Smithsonian's rapidly expanding collection of artifacts, this Classical Revival granite structure conserves more than 126 million specimens and provides laboratory facilities for scientists.

Dominating the first-floor rotunda is a great 13ft-tall **African bush elephant**. Exhibits on the first floor encompass mammals; sea life, including a model of a 45ft **whale** and a living **coral reef**; and dinosaurs, showcasing a 90ft **Diplodocus skeleton**.

The second floor displays a fabulous **gem collection★★**, which counts the Hope Diamond among its treasures; a creepy-crawly **insect zoo**; and the**Discovery Room**, which offers hands-on exhibits. The museum also houses an IMAX 2D-3D theater, three cafes and a gift shop.

👥 National Museum of American History★★

Constitution Ave. between 12th & 14th Sts. N.W. ✕♿ ℰ202-633-1000. http://americanhistory.si.edu.

Repository for such national treasures as a 1913 Model T Ford and various first ladies' gowns, this museum, with its more than 3-million-object collection, captures the essence of America's material and social development.

Highlights include advertising campaigns of iconic American brands such as Nike and Federal Express; artifacts from popular culture (the ruby slippers from *The Wizard of Oz* and a Kermit the Frog puppet); gloves worn by Muhammad Ali, Teddy Roosevelt's chaps and Bill Clinton's saxophone,as well as the original flag that inspired America's national anthem, "The Star-Spangled Banner".

Hirshhorn Museum and Sculpture Garden★★

Independence Ave. at 7th St. S.W. ✕♿ ℰ202-633-4674. www.hirshhorn.si.edu.

Although Gordon Bunshaft's cylindrical "doughnut" invited criticism when it was completed in 1966, the structure nonetheless houses one of the finest collections of modern art in the country. Latvian-born art collector **Joseph Hirshhorn** (1899-1981) started the ball rolling with his initial donation of 6,000 contemporary works.

Today the Hirshhorn contains some 5,000 paintings, 3,000 pieces of sculpture and mixed media, and 4,000 works on paper.

Small figurative works adorn the sunken **Sculpture Garden** located in front of the museum on the Mall side. The plaza on which the building stands is a show-

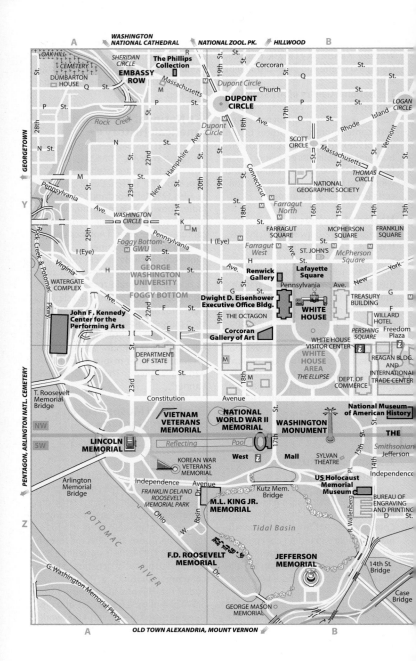

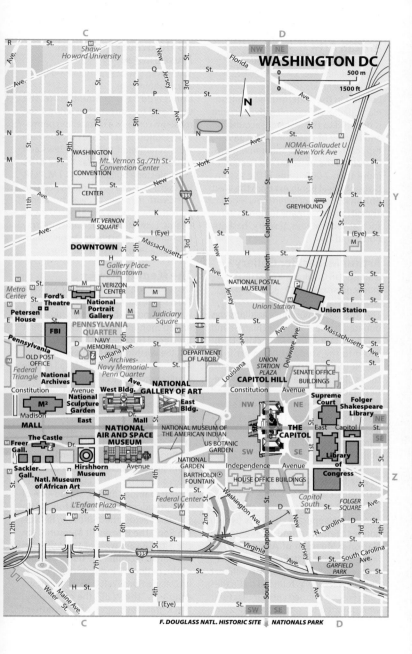

WASHINGTON DC

0   500 m

0   1500 ft

N

R St.

Shaw-Howard University

Q St.

P St.

O St.

N St.

7th St.

9th St.

5th St.

11th

Ave.

New Jersey

3rd St.

Florida

Ave.

NW   NE

New York

New York

Ave.

NOMA-Gallaudet U
New York Ave

1st St.

GREYHOUND

WASHINGTON
CONVENTION
CENTER

Mt. Vernon Sq./7th St.-
Convention Center

MT. VERNON
SQUARE

DOWNTOWN

Massachusetts

5th St.

3rd St.

New

Jersey

Ave.

Capitol

St.

North

Capitol

St.

I (Eye) St.

I (Eye) St.

G St.

2nd St.

3rd St.

4th St.

F St.

Y

Metro
Center

Ford's
Theatre

Petersen
House

FBI

Gallery Place-
Chinatown

VERIZON
CENTER

National
Portrait
Gallery

Judiciary
Square

NATIONAL POSTAL
MUSEUM

Union Station

Union Station

PENNSYLVANIA
QUARTER

Pennsylvania

OLD POST
OFFICE

Federal
Triangle

National
Archives

Constitution

NAVY
MEMORIAL

Indiana Ave.

Archives-
Navy Memorial-
Penn Quarter

DEPARTMENT
OF LABOR

Louisiana

Ave.

Delaware Ave.

UNION
STATION
PLAZA

Massachusetts

St.

SENATE OFFICE
BUILDINGS

CAPITOL HILL

Ave.

MALL

National
Sculpture
Garden

West Bldg.

NATIONAL
GALLERY OF ART

East
Bldg.

Constitution

Avenue

NW   NE

Supreme
Court

Folger
Shakespeare
Library

The Castle

Freer
Gall.

Sackler
Gall.

Natl. Museum
of African Art

East

Madison

Dr.

NATIONAL
AIR AND SPACE
MUSEUM

Hirshhorn
Museum

Mall

NATIONAL MUSEUM OF
THE AMERICAN INDIAN

US BOTANIC
GARDEN

THE
CAPITOL

SW   SE

East

Capitol

1st

St.

NE

SE

Library
of
Congress

Z

L'Enfant Plaza

12th

NATIONAL
GARDEN

BARTHOLDI
FOUNTAIN

Federal Center
SW

6th

2nd

4th

St.

Independence

HOUSE OFFICE BUILDINGS

Washington Ave.

Avenue

Capitol
South

FOLGER
SQUARE

N. Carolina

3rd

St.

395

7th

4th

I (Eye)

H St.

Maine Ave.

Water St.

St.

Virginia

Ave.

South

Capitol

St.

Jersey

Ave.

F St.

South Carolina
Ave.

GARFIELD
PARK

SW   SE

F. DOUGLASS NATL. HISTORIC SITE   NATIONALS PARK

C   D

place for monumental contemporary sculpture.

National Museum of African Art★★

Smithsonian Quadrangle at 950 Independence Ave. S.W. ♿ ✆202-633-4600. www.nmafa.si.edu.

Located in the underground Smithsonian Quadrangle complex, the museum is devoted to the research, acquisition and display of traditional African arts, especially of the sub-Saharan regions. Of note in the museum's collection of more than 7,000 items is the assemblage of **Royal Benin Art** from the West African kingdom of Benin (now Nigeria). The gift shop has many tempting items such as fabrics, toys, jewelry, baskets, books and CDs.

Arthur M. Sackler Gallery★★

Smithsonian Quadrangle at 1050 Independence Ave. S.W. ♿ ✆202-633-1000. www.asia.si.edu

The core of this museum's holdings was donated by New York psychiatrist and Asian art buff Arthur M. Sackler. Dedicated to the study of Asian art from the Neolithic period to the present, the facility boasts a fine group of **Chinese jades** (dating from 3000 BC) and **Ancient Near Eastern gold and silver** ceremonial objects. The gallery's collection of 11C-19C Islamic manuscripts, miniatures and calligraphy ranks as one of the world's finest.

Freer Gallery of Art★★

Jefferson Dr. at 12th St. S.W. ♿ ✆202-633-1000. www.asia.si.edu.

These two separate galleries (which connect underground) make up the **National Museum of Asian Art**. The Freer Gallery is an Italian-Renaissance-inspired building designed by architect Charles Watt. It was founded by Charles Lang Freer, a railroad car manufacturer who donated his personal collections and funds for a building to house them. Today it contains an exquisite Chinese collection that includes objects from the Ming (1368-1644) and Qing (1644-1911) dynasties, as well as one of the

world's largest collections of works by American-born artist **James McNeill Whistler** (1834-1903).

US Holocaust Memorial Museum★★

100 15th st. S.W. ✗♿ ✆202-488-0400. www.ushmm.org.

Conceived "to commemorate the dead and to educate the living," the museum contains a compelling permanent exhibit that focuses on the Nazi extermination of millions of Jews and others during World War II. The brick and limestone building (1993, I.M. Pei & Partners) evokes a Postmodern penitentiary, with its series of "watchtowers," and interior of glass and exposed metal beams. Exhibits present a moving array of photographs, artifacts, archival films and voice recordings of survivors.

The Memorials★★★

Offset by the Potomac River and the Tidal Basin, the Mall west of 15th Street is the setting for the country's most venerated monuments. Dedicated to first president George Washington (1789-97), the **Washington Monument** (on the Mall at 15th St. N.W.) is a 555ft-tall marble obelisk whose apex affords visitors one of the city's best panoramic **views★★★**. On the basin's south shore, the colonnaded **Jefferson Memorial** memorializes third president Thomas Jefferson (1801-09) with a 19ft-tall bronze statue by Rudolph Evans in its open interior. From inside the **Lincoln Memorial** (on the Mall at 23rd St. N.W.) Daniel Chester French's famous marble **statue★★★** of 16th president Abraham Lincoln (1861-65) stares across the 350ft-long Reflecting Pool. The **Roosevelt Memorial** (on the Tidal Basin, west of the Jefferson Memorial) recounts the terms of office of the nation's 32nd president, Franklin Delano Roosevelt (1933-45). Known simply as "the Wall," the compelling black granite expanse of the **Vietnam Veterans Memorial** (Constitution Ave. & 22nd St. N.W.) bears the names of the 58,195 men and women killed or missing in the Vietnam War (1959-75). The **Korean War Veterans Memorial**, south of the Reflecting Pool, honors US armed forces who served in the Korean War (1950-53). Completed in 2004, the **National World War II Memorial** pays tribute to veterans and the more than 400,000 Americans who lost their lives in the Second World War (1939-45). The latest monument, erected in 2011 on the Tidal Basin's shoreline, memorializes **Dr. Martin Luther King, Jr.**, the African-American pastor and Nobel Laureate, who was the driving force behind the 1960s civil rights movement.

DOWNTOWN★★

Conceived by planner Pierre L'Enfant to link the White House and the Capitol, **Pennsylvania Avenue** was the city's first thoroughfare and gave rise to the commercial heart of DC. At the avenue's center sits the White House, surrounded by manicured parks and grand public structures, including the 1888 Second Empire-style **Dwight D. Eisenhower Executive Office Building★** (17th & G Sts. N.W).

Just east of the White House, Downtown is a conglomeration of retail complexes, hotels, museums, office towers and restaurants, where top-dollar lawyers and politicos take power lunches. Recent attractions include the **International Spy Museum★★** (9th & F Sts.; ☏202-393-7798; www.spymuseum.org) with the likes of a lipstick pistol and an Aston Martin with rotating license

Martin Luther King, Jr. Memorial

©Gwen Cannon/Michelin

plates; the six-floor **Newseum★** (555 Pennsylvania Ave N.W; ☏202-292-6100; www.newseum.org), chronicling the news via ancient cuneiform tablets up to today's global digital media; and the **Crime and Punishment Museum** (575 7th St. NW, between E and F Sts.; ☏202-621-5550. www.crimemuseum.org), with displays ranging from implements of Medieval torture to Al Capone's comfortable prison cell.

Northwest of the White House at the intersection of Connecticut, Massachusetts and New Hampshire Avenues, **Dupont Circle★** harbors restored mansions along with many fine boutiques, galleries, restaurants and bars.

Embassy Row

Embassy Row is the popular name for the 2mi portion of Massachusetts Avenue between Scott and Observatory Circles where some 50 diplomatic embassies are concentrated. Beaux-Arts architecture is a favorite here, since many of the early-20C architects retained by wealthy Washingtonians had trained in Paris. Following the Great Depression in 1929, the luxuriant Beaux-Arts mansions were sold to foreign governments seeking a diplomatic presence in the District.

The most noteworthy part of Embassy Row begins at 22nd Street and Massachusetts Avenue, where the **Embassy of Luxembourg** is ensconced in the former home of lumber magnate and politician Alexander Wilson. Continuing up the avenue past the embassies of Togo and the Sudan, Sheridan Circle is home to the grandiose **Embassy of Turkey/Everett House** (1606 23rd St.). The procession of embassies continues to 24th Street, ending at the sprawling **British Embassy** (3100 Massachusetts Ave.), designed by prominent architect Sir Edwin Lutyens to resemble an early-18C English country estate.

Georgetown

A coveted Washington address, **Georgetown★★** is an amalgam of popular nightspots, restaurants and trendy boutiques concentrated along Wisconsin Avenue and M Street N.W. Surrounding this commercial core are quiet residential streets lined with restored Federal-style town houses. Settled by Scots in the 1700s, Georgetown became a thriving port in the late 18C owing to its location at the head of the Potomac River's navigable waters. In 1789 the first Catholic institution of higher learning in the country, now **Georgetown University**, was founded at the neighborhood's western edge. On the district's northern border, **Dumbarton Oaks★★** (1703 32nd St. N.W.; ☏202-339-6401; www.doaks.org) is renowned for its outstanding collections of **Byzantine★★** and **pre-Columbian art★**. The estate's lovely **gardens★★** (entrance at 31st & R Sts. N.W.) comprise 10 acres of formal, flowered terraces punctuated by fountains and pools.

The White House★★★

1600 Pennsylvania Ave. N.W. ♿
☏Free timed tickets for self-guided tours must be requested from your member of Congress up to 6 months in advance. ☏202-456-1111; www.whitehouse.gov. White House Visitor Center at Pennsylvania Ave. between 14th and 15th Sts. N.W.

Designed by Irish builder James Hoban in 1792, the three-story stone Georgian manor has been the home of America's presidents and their families beginning with John Adams in 1801. Theodore Roosevelt began restoring the mansion to its original appearance during his tenure in office (1901-09), and succeeding presidents followed his lead. Set amid 18 landscaped acres, the White House fronts Pennsylvania Avenue. Its south portico overlooks the Ellipse—an open expanse that serves as a ceremonial ground. The colonnaded north portico faces the seven-acre park named **Lafayette Square** in honor of the Marquis de Lafayette, America's ally in the Revolutionary War.

Visitors tour the mansion's first and ground floors only; upper floors are reserved for the First Family. Adorned with Bohemian cut-glass chandeliers, the **East Room** hosts White House ceremonies, concerts and dances. The **Green Room** is adorned with green watered-silk wall coverings and furnishings from the 19C workshop of Duncan Phyfe. Classical motifs in the elliptical **Blue Room** include seven of the original Bellange gilded armchairs that James Monroe ordered from Paris. Site of official dinners, the **State Dining Room** can seat 140 people.

Corcoran Gallery of Art★★

17th St. & New York Ave. N.W. ✕♿
☏202-639-1700. www.corcoran.org.
This private gallery was begun in 1859 by philanthropist **William Wilson Corcoran** (1798-1888), who donated a $900,000 endowment, his collection, the grounds and the original building—now the **Renwick Gallery★** (1661 Pennsylvania Ave. N.W.; ☏202-633-7970; http://americanart.si.edu/renwick)—"for the purpose of encouraging American genius." Today the Corcoran Gallery is housed in a larger, ornate 1897 Beaux-Arts building comprising an art school and fine collections of **European and American paintings**. Its collection of

The White House

©PhotoDisc, Inc

19C American art is considered among the best in the world; it also has an impressive selection of contemporary art from the likes of Andy Warhol, Ellsworth Kelly and Frank Stella.

National Portrait Gallery★★

Old Patent Office Building at 8th & F Sts. N.W. ✕&♿ ✆202-633-8300. www.npg.si.edu.

The "nation's family album" conserves some 15,000 paintings, sculptures, photographs, engravings and drawings of "men and women who have made significant contributions to the history, development and culture of the people of the United States."

The building is also home to the **Smithsonian American Art Museum** (✆202-633-1000; www.americanart.si.edu), a vast collection ranging from 18C to contemporary works by American artists.

Ford's Theatre★

511 10th St. between E & F Sts. N.W. ✆202-347-4833. www.fordstheatre.org.

Site of the assassination of President Abraham Lincoln on 14 April 1865, Ford's Theatre was opened by John Ford in 1863. After being shot by John Wilkes Booth, Lincoln was carried across the street to **Petersen House★** (516 10 St.; ✆202-347-4833), where he died the following morning. The restored Victorian theater reopened in 1968 as a playhouse, as well as a memorial to Lincoln's tragic slaying.

Adjacent, at no. 514, the new **Center for Education and Leadership** (2012) has exhibits on Lincoln's legacy and leadership; a stack of books written about him towers 34ft.

ADDITIONAL SIGHTS
The Phillips Collection★★

1600 21st St. N.W. ✕&✆202-387-2151. www.phillipscollection.org.

With his family's art collection, Duncan Phillips founded the nation's oldest museum of modern art as a memorial to his father and brother. He and his wife, painter Marjorie Acker, expanded the collection; today it contains nearly 2,500 works, including all the major French Impressionists, Postimpressionists, Cubists and 17C and 18C masters, among them Goya, El Greco and Chardin. The Goh Annex showcases the museum's renowned Renoir painting Luncheon of the Boating Party (1881) as well as the popular Bonnard Collection.

Frederick Douglass National Historic Site★

1411 W St. S.E. &♿ ✆202-426-5960. www.nps.gov/frdo.

Known as Cedar Hill, this quaint Victorian set above the Anacostia River was the last residence of black statesman, orator and abolitionist Frederick Douglass (1818-95). The two-story house is decorated with Victorian furnishings and Douglass family memorabilia, including a rare portrait of Douglass by Sarah James Eddy. Behinthe house, a small reconstructed stone building served as a second study, which Douglass called "the Growlery."

Washington National Cathedral★★

Massachusetts & Wisconsin Aves. N.W. &♿ ✆202-537-6200. www.nationalcathedral.org.

Dominating the skyline of northwest Washington with its 301ft-high **Gloria in Excelsis Tower**, this imposing Gothic edifice—replete with flying buttresses, vaulting, gargoyles and stained-glass windows— overlooks the city from its perch on Mount St. Alban. The final stone of the Cathedral of St. Peter and St. Paul—its official name—was set in place in 1990, 83 years after the foundation was laid. Look for the Darth Vader sculpture on St. Peter's Tower.

Hillwood★★

4155 Linnean Ave. N.W. ✕&♿ ➡Visit of mansion by guided tour only. ✆202-686-8500. www.hillwoodmuseum.org.

Above Rock Creek Park, the 25-acre estate of Post cereals heiress and art collector **Marjorie Merriweather Post** (1887-1973) holds the most extensive collection of **Russian imperial arts★★★** outside Russia.Don't miss the more than 50 Fabergé **Easter eggs**.

The Civil War in Northern Virginia

The decision to move the Confederate capital from Montgomery, Alabama, to Richmond, Virginia, determined that much of the Civil War would be fought between DC and Richmond, 90mi south. These two parks help tell the story.

Located 29mi southwest of Washington, DC, **Manassas National Battlefield Park★** (6511 Sudley Rd., Manassas, VA; ♿🅿 open daily; ☎703-361-1339; www.nps.gov/mana) marks the site of the first major land battle of the war. On 21 July 1861, the 35,000-man Confederate force beat back the 32,000-man Union Army at a stream called Bull Run in Manassas, Virginia. It was during this battle that Stonewall Jackson got his nickname. As the story goes, an officer, seeing Confederate general Thomas J. Jackson sitting tall in the saddle, shouted, "There stands Jackson like a stone wall! Rally behind the Virginians!"

Fredericksburg and Spotsylvania National Military Park★ (50mi south of DC via I-95; 120 Chatham Lane, Fredericksburg, VA; ♿🅿 Open daily; ☎540-654-5121; www.nps.gov/frsp), dubbed "the bloodiest landscape in North America" commemorates four major Civil War engagements. Occupying the midpoint between Washington and Richmond, Fredericksburg lay in the way of the Union Army's attempts to capture the Confederate capital.

♟♟ National Zoological Park★★

3001 Connecticut Ave. N.W.
✖♿🅿 ☎202-633-2614.
http://nationalzoo.si.edu.

Situated on 163 acres above Rock Creek Park, this Smithsonian "biopark" (more commonly known simply as the "National Zoo") exhibits more than 2,000 wild animals and serves as a research institution devoted to the study, preservation and breeding of threatened species. Most famous among them are the **giant pandas** on loan until 2015 from China.

EXCURSIONS
Arlington National Cemetery★★

▶ 3mi west of DC on the Virginia side of Arlington Memorial Bridge. ♿🅿 ☎703-235-1530. www.arlingtoncemetery.mil.
This vast military cemetery holds the remains of more than 300,000 people, including presidents, astronauts, explorers, and of course, military personnel, on 612 acres of rolling hills. During the Civil War, 200 acres surrounding Confederate General Robert E. Lee's mansion **Arlington House★** (on the cemetery grounds; ☎703-235-1530) were appropriated for the burial of fallen sol-

Mount Vernon

diers; in 1883 these lands became the official US national cemetery. Don't miss the eternal flame that marks the grave of assassinated president **John F. Kennedy** (1917-63), and the **Tomb of the Unknowns** (behind Memorial Amphitheater), where an elaborate changing of the guard ceremony is conducted throughout the day.

Old Town Alexandria★★

◗ 8mi south of DC via George Washington Memorial Pkwy. Ramsey House Visitor Center is located at 221 King St. ℘703-746-3301; www.visitalexandriava.com.

This area traces its beginnings to the early 1700s. Modern Old Town is a walkable enclave of shops, restaurants, historic homes and churches set on the banks of the river. A day in Alexandria might include a stroll along brick-paved **Gentry Row★** (200s block of Prince St.) and cobbled **Captain's Row★** (100s block of Prince St.) where 18C townhouses recall Alexandria's early seafaring days. When you're ready for lunch, sample colonial fare at **Gadsby's Tavern Museum★** (134 N. Royal St.; ☛visit of museum by guided tour only; restaurant open to the public; ℘703-838-4270) which dates to 1770. Nightfall finds Old Town bustling with bar patrons and diners.

Mount Vernon★★★

◗ 16mi south of DC in Alexandria, VA, via George Washington Memorial Pkwy. ☛Visit of mansion by guided tour only. ✕🅿℘703-780-0011. www.mountvernon.org.

Occupying a grassy slope overlooking the Potomac River south of Washington, this plantation estate was the beloved home of the nation's first president, **George Washington** (1732-99), who was also a successful Virginia planter. The Georgian farmhouse, with its hallmark columned piazza facing the river, is set off by curving colonnades that connect the flanking wings. Inside, a large central hall opens onto the piazza and four first-floor rooms. The lavishly appointed **dining room** features an

ornate marble mantel that Washington considered "too elegant and costly... for [his] republican style of living." Upstairs, five simply furnished bedrooms are arranged off a central hall. The **master bedroom** contains the mahogany four-poster bed in which Washington died. The estate's **grounds** comprise 40 acres of forests and landscaped gardens, including 12 small dependencies; the graves of George and his wife, Martha; and a **pioneer farm** that demonstrates 18C animal husbandry and crop cultivation.

In the fall of 2013, a new library devoted to the study of George Washington was opened amid fanfare adjacent to the estate. The Fred W. Smith National Library for the Study of George Washington is open to researchers by appointment only; it contains rare books, documents, maps and many other valuable materials in its collections.

Harpers Ferry National Historical Park★★

◗ 55mi northwest of DC in Harpers Ferry, WV. From DC take I-270 north to Frederick, MD; then head south on US-340. ♿🅿℘304-535-6029. www.nps.gov/hafe.

Located in the northeastern corner of West Virginia at the junction of the Shenandoah and Potomac rivers, Harpers Ferry is forever connected with the name **John Brown** (1800-59). On 16 October 1859, abolitionist Brown led his 21-man "army of liberation" into town, hoping to capture weapons to wage guerrilla warfare against slavery from the nearby mountains. Although the raid failed—Brown was captured and later hanged—the incident inflamed tensions between the North and South. Stop by the **Information Center** (Shenandoah St.), where exhibits outline the town's history, and pick up a copy of the trail guide to 24 key sites clustered on Shenandoah, High and Potomac Streets. Take time to discover the heritage of this 19C manufacturing village, shop its many boutiques, and take in great **views** of the rivers as you stroll Harpers Ferry's narrow, hilly streets.

Baltimore★★

Baltimore, Maryland's largest city, underwent a dramatic renaissance in the last quarter of the 20C; shedding its image as a decrepit Chesapeake Bay industrial port for that of a thriving metropolis. Gleaming skyscrapers designed by some of the nation's most noteworthy architects spike the skyline. A wide brick and asphalt sidewalk lines 5mi of the Patapsco River shoreline, linking several well-defined nearby neighborhoods: Little Italy, renowned for its Old World restaurants; the 18C shipbuilding center of Fells Point (these days a charming shopping and popular night spot); and Federal Hill, a great vantage point for wonderful views★ of the revitalized Inner Harbor.

▶ **Population:** 621,342
▢ **Info:** ✆410-659-7300; http://baltimore.org.
◖ **Location:** A major U.S. seaport, Baltimore is located in central Maryland.
◕ **Timing:** Leave time to explore Baltimore's many diverse neighborhoods.
👪 **Kids:** The dolphin show at the Baltimore National Aquarium.

A BIT OF HISTORY

Baltimore was officially established as a town—named after Maryland's Irish proprietors, the Lords Baltimore—on the Patapsco River in 1729. Blessed with a deep-water harbor, Baltimore thrived in its early years as a grain-shipping port and shipbuilding center (the fast schooners known as **Baltimore Clippers** were produced here in the late 18C and early 19C).

During the War of 1812, British troops came perilously close to capturing Baltimore. On 13 September 1814, English warships bombarded **Fort McHenry** in Baltimore's harbor for 25 hours, but failed to capture the battlement now a national monument (south end of Fort Ave., off Lawrence St.; open daily; ✆410-962-4290; www.nps.gov/fomc).

The next day, **Francis Scott Key** (1779-1843), a young Washington lawyer who witnessed the battle, immortalized the fighting in the now-famous verses of **"The Star-Spangled Banner"**—officially designated as the US national anthem in 1931. Fragments of the original banner that Key described as "so gallantly streaming" over the fort in 1814 are displayed in the **Star-Spangled Banner Flag House★** (844 E. Pratt St.; ✆410-837-1793; www.flaghouse.org).

Baltimore's development after the war was boosted by the establishment of the Baltimore and Ohio Railroad in 1827, which eventually gave the city's growing number of manufacturers access to myriad new markets. In 1904 a fire ravaged the majority of the downtown's 18C and 19C structures. One of the few pre-Revolutionary buildings to survive is **Mount Clare Museum House**, built

Blue Crabs

When summer settles into the Mid-Atlantic, there are few things more dear to a Marylander's heart than eating blue crabs. The small crustacean is the state's single most valuable fishery resource. Watermen harvested more than 53 million pounds of crabs in 2009. Although found as far north as Cape Cod, the blue crab (*Callinectes sapidus*) thrives in greatest abundance in the Chesapeake Bay. In season (Jun–Oct) you can sample it in several forms: by **picking crabs**, a messy but fun process of cracking the shell open and extracting the meat; as **soft shells**, a blue crab that has molted and not yet formed its new shell (available May-Sept); or made into Maryland's justifiably famous **crabcakes**.

in 1760 (1500 Washington Blvd. in Carroll Park; ✆410-837-3262; www.mountclare. org). Today the invigorated city claims such attractions as the ever-popular Inner Harbor, as well as the internationally known medical school of **Johns Hopkins University**. Part of the Hopkins campus is located on the grounds of the estate once owned by prominent Marylander Charles Carroll, a signer of the Declaration of Independence. Carroll's stately red-brick Georgian **Homewood House**★ dates to 1802 (3400 N. Charles St.; 👣visit by guided tour only; ✆410-516-5589; www.museums.jhu.edu).

THE INNER HARBOR

Rescued from its downtrodden state in the 1960s, Baltimore's harbor now shines as a waterfront complex of shops, restaurants, museums and hotels. Bounded by East Pratt and Light Streets, the Inner Harbor is anchored on the northeast and southwest corners by the National Aquarium and the **Maryland Science Center** 👥 (601 Light St.; ✆410-685-2370, www.mdsci. org) respectively. In between, the twin glass pavilions of **Harborplace** overlook the brick pier where the 1854 "sloop-of-war" USS Constellation is docked. Inside Harborplace's pavilions you'll find a festival of eateries and shops.

Views★ of the city and surrounding countryside are unbeatable from the 27th floor of the **World Trade Center**★ (1978, I.M. Pei), making the **Top of the World**★ observation deck an excellent place to begin a visit (401 E. Pratt St.; ♿✆410-837-8439; www.viewbaltimore.org).

A few blocks west of the waterfront, the city's beloved Orioles play in **Camden Yards** (333 W. Camden St.; ✆410-685-9800, http://baltimore.orioles.mlb.com), one of the nation's most beautiful baseball stadiums.

👥 National Aquarium★★

Pier Three, 501 E. Pratt St. ✕♿✆410-576-3800. www.aqua.org.

More than 17,000 creatures occupy the habitats within this 209,000sq ft aquatic museum. Housed in two imposing buildings crowned with glass pyramids, the aquarium is Baltimore's most popular attraction. Most of the exhibits are displayed in the five-story Main Aquarium. You can walk down through four stories of sharks, corals and other reef denizens in the **Atlantic Coral Reef**. The **Amazon Rain** features colorful creatures such as the **emerald tree boa** and **giant leaf frog**.

The **Animal Planet Australia** exhibit mimics a river running through a gorge with crocodiles, turtles and even a black-headed python. And save time for the **dolphin show** that takes place in the Lyn P. Meyerhoff 1,300-seat amphitheater (showtimes appear on admission ticket).

👥 Baltimore Maritime Museum★

Piers 3 and 5, Inner Harbor. Ticket booth on Pier Three next to the aquarium. ✆410-539-1797. www.historicships.org.

Baltimore Inner Harbor

©Aimin Tang /iStockphoto.com

Maryland's Eastern Shore

Just across the Chesapeake Bay Bridge from Annapolis (50mi east of Washington, DC) is Maryland's Eastern Shore, a peninsula that lies between the bay and the Atlantic Ocean. Characterized by sleepy fishing villages and small farms, the low-lying coastline here is a conglomeration of quiet coves and lonely marshes. You can easily wile away a couple of pleasant days exploring historic waterside villages such as **St. Michaels★** and **Chestertown**, staying in some of the fine bed-and-breakfast inns, poking through antique shops, bird-watching, and sampling the region's bountiful seafood—especially the famous **blue crabs** and oysters.

One of the shore's most celebrated events takes place each summer on the southern end of **Assateague Island National Seashore★** (29mi east of Salisbury, MD, via US-50 & Rte. 611; △ & 🅿 ℘410-641-2120; www.nps.gov/asis). This part of the 37mi-long barrier island harbors several hundred **wild ponies** that roam **Chincoteague National Wildlife Refuge**. The offspring of horses brought here by 17C settlers who wanted to avoid penning and taxation laws, the ponies are rounded up annually on Assateague Island and herded across the narrow channel (at slack tide) to the town of **Chincoteague** (across Chincoteague Bay on Rte. 175). Here the annual **Pony Penning★**, the public round-up and sale of foals, is held on the last Wednesday and Thursday of July (for information, call ℘757-336-6161; www.chincoteague.com).

Visitors to this partially floating museum begin their tour on the decks of the lightship Chesapeake (1930).

Adjacent to it is the **USS Torsk** (1945), a 311ft submarine that established a naval record of 11,884 dives. Docked at Pier Five, the US Coast Guard cutter Taney (1936) is the last remaining survivor of the Japanese attack on Pearl Harbor. **Seven Foot Knoll Lighthouse** on Pier Five is Maryland's oldest "screwpile" building (1855), so called as it was attached to nine cast-iron pilings "screwed" into the bay floor.

ADDITIONAL SIGHTS

👥 Port Discovery★

35 Market Pl. ✕ & ℘410-864-2700. www.portdiscovery.org.

A few blocks northeast of the Inner Harbor, Baltimore's late-19C fish market has been transformed into a three-floor museum geared to children between the ages of two and ten.

The permanent exhibits are **Harvest Hill**, where kids can sell their new products at a market; **Adventure Expeditions**, in which "time travelers" go back to ancient Egypt to search for the tomb of a lost pharaoh; and **Kick It Up!**, an indoor soccer stadium reserved for soccer, bike riding, dancing and electronic games.

American Visionary Art Museum★

800 Key Hwy. ✕ & ℘410-244-1900. www.avam.org.

The "visionary folk art" of self-taught artists from around the world is displayed, and their stories told, in a modern, elliptical building across from the waterfront. Large exhibits are on view in an adjacent former whiskey warehouse as well as a 55ft whirligig in the outside plaza.

Baltimore Museum of Industry★

1415 Key Hwy & 🅿 ℘410-727-4808. www.thebmi.org.

Recognizing Baltimore's industrial heritage is the mission of this well-kept, spacious museum housed in a former oyster cannery (c.1865) on the Patapsco River. After watching an informative 15min film, visitors tour a re-created cannery, machine shop, garment loft and print shop. On weekends, children can build an early 20C auto on an assembly line.

👥 B&O Railroad Museum★★

901 W. Pratt St. ✕♿🅿️ ☎410-752-2490. www.borail.org.

Beginning in 1830, the Baltimore and Ohio Railroad provided the first regular rail service in the US. Today more than 200 of the line's locomotives and cars are the star attractions of this 37-acre museum, located on the site of the railroad's Mount Clare station. About 40 rail cars and locomotives, including a c.1915 boxcar from the Paris-Lyon-Méditerranée line (a gift from France to the US), are displayed in a restored brick and wood **roundhouse** (1884). The rest of the collection, which features the Chesapeake and Ohio's Allegheny (1941), the most powerful steam locomotive ever built, fills the yard outside.

Walters Art Gallery★★

600 N. Charles St. ♿🅿️☎410-547-9000. www.thewalters.org.

With a collection of 30,000 works of art spanning 300 BC to the early 20C, this gem of an art museum—which comprises three buildings—is best known for its **Renaissance and Medieval art**, rare books and illuminated manuscripts. The manuscripts, as well as most of the ancient and Medieval pieces, are housed in a forbidding stone building on Centre Street. Renaissance masterpieces by such greats as Van Dyck and El Greco (*St. Francis Receiving the Stigmata,* c.1590) fill the original gallery, a 1909 Italianate palazzo commissioned by railroad magnate Henry Walters to showcase the artwork he and his father began collecting in the 1870s. Here, too, are European and American paintings and decorative arts from the 17C to 19C. The museum's impressive **Asian collection** is displayed in Hackerman House (1854), a stately brownstone attached to the main gallery.

Maryland Historical Society★

201 W. Monument St. ♿🅿️☎410-685-3750. www.mdhs.org.

The society's fine 20,000-piece collection of art, furniture and other memorabilia is contained in three buildings. In the **Heritage Wing**, which was a Greyhound bus garage until the early 1980s, you'll find a survey of the works of the **Peale** family, whose scion Charles Willson Peale and sons James, Titian, Rubens, Raphael and Rembrandt were among America's finest early painters. In the main building is the original draft of Francis Scott Key's **"The Star-Spangled Banner,"** and distinctive **painted furniture** made by 19C Baltimore craftsmen.

Washington Monument★

699 N. Charles. ☎410-396-0929.

Baltimoreans quickly point out that the nation's first memorial to the first president was built here, not in Washington, DC.

The 178ft marble and brick column (1829, Robert Mills) capped with a 30-ton statue of George Washington may be the city's best-known landmark. Climb the narrow flight of 228 steps for expansive **views** of the city.

Baltimore Museum of Art★★

10 Art Museum Dr., at N. Charles & 31st Sts. ✕♿🅿️☎443-573-1700. www.artbma.org.

Known for its collection of 20C art and American furnishings, this grand Neoclassical building (1929, John Russell Pope) and its light-filled 1982 and 1994 additions, house more than 85,000 objects from antiquity to the present. The **Cone Collection★★** is the museum's most famous. Local collectors Etta and Claribel Cone began buying the works of Matisse, Picasso and other Modernists (Cézanne, Degas, Monet, van Gogh, Gauguin) in 1898.

Today their collection of Matisse paintings (which includes Large Reclining Nude, 1935) and sculptures is one of the most comprehensive in the world. The museum has echoed the Cones' patronage of contemporary art by acquiring works by Andy Warhol, Jasper Johns, Frank Stella, Georgia O'Keeffe and Willem de Kooning.

The **American decorative arts** exhibits are displayed on all three floors of the museum. In addition to the Baltimore painted furniture (c.1800-10), Queen

Anne, Federal and American Chippendale pieces are showcased in galleries and reconstructed period rooms.

The Atrium Court on the main level is lined with priceless **mosaics** (5C-1C BC) from the ancient provincial Roman capital of Antioch.

Don't miss the pretty landscaped gardens.

Evergreen House★★

4545 N. Charles St. & 🅿 ☜Visit by guided tour only. ✆410-516-0341. www.museums.jhu.edu.

Former residence of Ambassador John Work Garrett and his wife, Evergreen (1858) is an elegant kaleidoscope of almost 100 years of trends in American architecture and interior design. The 48-room Italianate mansion includes a **Rare Book Library** that houses 8,000 volumes collected by the Garrett family. The adjoining former gymnasium was converted to a home theater in 1923 by Russian émigré set designer **Léon Bakst**, famed for the sets he created for the Ballets Russes.

EXCURSIONS

Hampton National Historic Site★★

3mi north of Baltimore in Towson, MD. From I-695, take Exit 27B/Dulaney Valley Rd. North and turn right on Hampton Lane; park entrance is on right. ☜Visit by guided tour only; check website for schedule. 🅿 ✆410-823-1309. www.nps.gov/hamp.

This yellow stone-and-stucco Georgian mansion tells the story of the people who lived and worked in it—the wealthy family members who owned it, the indentured servants who cast molten iron into cannons and ammunition for the Revolutionary army, and the enslaved people who once toiled here. The house itself was built as a country seat just after the Revolutionary War by a prominent Maryland family and the house and its immediate surroundings are just a small remnant of the vast Hampton estate of the early 1800s, which roughly equaled about half of current day Baltimore. Once owned by

Maryland's prominent Ridgely family, the house is decorated largely with their furnishings. After the house tour, visitors can explore the gardens and grounds.

Annapolis★

30mi southeast of Baltimore via I-97 South and US-301 East. ✆410-280-0445. www.visitannapolis.org.

Established on the banks of the Severn River by Virginia Puritans in 1648, Annapolis became the seat of colonial government in 1694, and subsequently grew to be a busy port. It is known as the home of the US Naval Academy.

The city's 1779 **State House★** (center of State Circle; ✆410-946-5400) served as the US capitol between 1783 and 1784. Today the shops and restaurants crowding the blocks around **City Dock** bustle with visitors year-round. A number of historic properties, including **Hammond Harwood House★★** (19 Maryland Ave.; ☜visit by guided tour only; ✆410-263-4683; www.hammond-harwoodhouse.org) and **Chase-Lloyd House★** (22 Maryland Ave.; ☜visit by guided tour only; ✆410-263-2723), typify the elegant Georgian-style residences built here in the 18C.

US Naval Academy★★

Armel-Leftwich Visitor Center at 52 King George St. ✕& 🅿 ✆410-263-8687. www.nadn.navy.mil.

Future officers in the US Navy and Marine Corps study on this peaceful, 338-acre campus established in 1850 along the Severn River and College Creek. The free guided tour around "the Yard," as the academy grounds are called, includes **Bancroft Hall**, the 1906 Baroque structure in the center of campus that covers 27 acres and boasts 5mi of corridors. Few buildings in Annapolis rival the glorious copper-domed **Navy Chapel★★** (1908, Ernest Flagg), modeled after the Hôtel des Invalides in Paris.

After the tour, be sure to visit the **US Naval Academy Museum** in Preble Hall, where you'll find a rare collection of dockyard **ship models★★**.

Richmond and The Tidewater

The first successful English settlement on the continent—Jamestown—was founded along the shores of the James and York rivers in 1607. Wealthy 17C tobacco planters later built their manor houses here, their opulent lifestyles often supported by the invidious institution of slavery. Here again, in the 18C colonial capital of Williamsburg, Virginia's patriots decried British tyranny and argued for independence from the Crown. With the Continental Army's victory at nearby Yorktown in 1781, that independence was won. In less than a century, the Virginia Tidewater again became a battleground. As the divided young nation fought against itself in the Civil War , the state capital of Richmond became the capital of a nation—the short-lived Confederate States of America.

Richmond and the Tidewater

Highlights

1 Historic **Richmond** (p257)
2 **Virginia Museum of Fine Arts** (p260)
3 Colonial National Historic Park at **Jamestown** (p262)
4 The **Colonial Parkway** (p262)
5 **Colonial Williamsburg** (p265)

The New South

Today, Richmond has risen again, to become a commercial center of the New South; but here and throughout Virginia's Tidewater area southeast of the capital city, the past remains a romantic overlay on the present. An endless procession of plantation manors, antebellum houses, historical museums, battlefields and re-created colonial villages parades across this low, marsh-saturated tidal land.

Virginia's Colonial Williamsburg ranks among the most extensive and authentic historic reconstructions in the world. The land itself, with its filigree of rivers, creeks, and pine and oak forests, has preserved the same timeless promise that first attracted adventuring Europeans to its shores.

Colonial Parkway

© Richard T. Nowitz/Corbis

ADDRESSES

🛏 STAY

$$$$$ The Jefferson – 101 W. Franklin St., Richmond, VA. ✖️♿🅿️🎧804-649-4750. www.jeffersonhotel.com. 262 rooms. Despite several fires and restorations since opening in 1895, this downtown landmark remains the city's most opulent "Southern belle." The palatial bi-level lobby showcases a stained-glass skylight, gold-leaf moldings and E.B. Valentine's sculpture of Thomas Jefferson. Renovated rooms feature mahogany furnishings and English country florals or deep hunt colors. Treat yourself to inspired contemporary cuisine in **Lemaire's** elegant dining room. On the weekends a popular afternoon tea is poured in the Tiffany stained-glass adorned Palm Court lobby. Alligators once lived in the Palm Court's fabled fountains.

$$$$$ The Williamsburg Inn – 136 E. Francis St., Williamsburg, VA. ✖️♿🅿️🎧757-220-7978. www.colonial williamsburg.com. 62 rooms. This elegant Neoclassical inn boasts the comfort of a private home, beloved by heads of state, royalty and celebrities since opening in 1937. The living room-style lobby is outfitted with Regency-style furniture, and lush pastel fabrics add a regal spark to the rich cherry and mahogany furniture in the guest rooms, which average a generous 500sq ft in size.

$$ Linden Row Inn – 100 E. Franklin St., Richmond, VA. ✖️♿🅿️🎧804-783-7000. www.lindenrowinn.com. 70 rooms. These six Greek Revival town houses were built on the site of Edgar Allan Poe's childhood rose gardens downtown. Traces of the past include plaster ceiling medallions and converted brass gasoliers. Rooms in the main house are furnished with Victorian antiques. A complimentary continental breakfast is served in the exposed-brick dining room. This charming boutique hotel is located within walking distance to many of Richmond's historic sites, restaurants and shops.

🍴 EAT

$$$ King's Arms Tavern – 416 Duke of Gloucester St., Williamsburg, VA. 🎧757-229-2141. www.colonialwilliamsburg.com. **American.** This tavern was reconstructed on the site of its mid-18C predecessor. Dine by candlelight in one of eleven Colonial-style rooms, where waiters in period dress serve 18C English classics including Colonial Game Pye filled with duck, rabbit and venison, and prime rib of beef with popovers. Try pecan pie or plum ice cream for dessert. The restaurant offers a children's menu both at dinner and lunch.

$$ Acacia – 2601 W. Cary St., Richmond, VA. 🎧804-562-0138. www.acaciarestaurant.com. **Contemporary.** An open, modern feel defines this popular restaurant in the Fan District. A glass-encased wine room displays the eatery's extensive wine collection and divides the restaurant. Che Dale Reitzer's menus change to reflect what is fresh and available and feature seafood dishes like local jumbo lump crab cakes with cheddar cheese grits and local asparagus, and bacon-wrapped apple-stuffed duck breat with ramp and English pea farotto. At under $25, the three-course prix-fixe menu is one of the best deals in town

$ Millie's – 2603 E. Main St., Richmond, VA. ✖️♿🅿️🎧804-643-5512.www.millies diner.com. **American.** There's often a line outside Millie's and for good reason. This diner with an attitude serves a variety of great dishes that use local ingredients but incorporate global influences. Written on a chalkboard, the menu here changes every three weeks and the vintage tabletop jukeboxes spin an impressive collection of 45s. The hip diner serves brunch, lunch and dinner and is closed on Mondays. Millie's does not accept reservations for parties smaller than six people, but the restaurant will let you order a drink to sip on while you wait In line for a table.

Richmond ★

Richmond offers an amalgam of antebellum nostalgia and New South vitality. Although founding fathers and Confederate generals are honored in preserved pockets of the contemporary city, these days Virginia's capital looks more to the future than to the past—and a bright future it appears to be.

- ▶ **Population:** 210,309.
- ⌖ **Michelin Map:** p242.
- ▤ **Info:** ✆804-783-7450; www.visitrichmond.com.
- ⊚ **Don't Miss:** The eclectic collection at the Virginia Museum of Fine Arts.
- ◷ **Timing:** Leave time to stroll by Richmond's stunning architectural treasures.

A BIT OF HISTORY

Prominent colonial planter William Byrd I, who owned this land, plotted the original village in the 1730s, convinced that its location at the fall line of the James River would ensure its growth. Though it did, in fact, grow slowly in its first decades, the city's fortunes altered dramatically and permanently in 1780, when it was chosen as the new capital of Virginia.

During the next century, Richmond—which was incorporated in 1782—became the industrial giant of the South. When the breakaway Confederate states formed their own union in 1861, Richmond soon replaced Montgomery, Alabama, as the Confederate capital. During the bloody and protracted Civil War, fighting swirled again and again around the beleaguered city, until April 1865, when both Richmond and the Confederacy fell. Throughout the next half century, even as the city recovered its prosperity, it never lost its cachet as cultural capital of the South. By the early decades of the 20C, Richmond boasted elegant department stores, elaborate Art Deco theaters, museums and fine Victorian homes. As the century progressed, tobacco and industrial giants Philip Morris and Reynolds brought financial vigor to the city, which began to spread west into the upscale neighborhoods that punctuate the West End.

DOWNTOWN ★

Anchored by the elegant Jeffersonian **Virginia State Capitol★** (bounded by 9th & Governor Sts. and Bank & Broad

Sts.; ✆804-698-1788; www.virginiacapitol.gov), Richmond's downtown long ranked as the most sophisticated in the American South. The downtown corridor (centered along Broad St.) has been revitalized with the addition of the 32-acre redeveloped **Riverfront** (at the foot of 5th St.).

A 19C canal turning basin is the focal point of the popular **Shockoe Slip** neighborhood (Cary St. between 12th & 15th Sts.), an area of renovated tobacco warehouses and cobbled streets that is now one of the city's liveliest nightspots. East of the central business district, Shockoe Bottom is evolving from an industrial area into another lively neighborhood for nightowls. At the west edge of downtown, the 1895 **Jefferson Hotel** (Franklin & Adams Sts.) remains the most elegant reminder of Richmond's gilded past.

Museum and White House of the Confederacy★

1201 E. Clay St. ♿ ▣ ✆804-649-1861. www.moc.org.

Confederate president Jefferson Davis and his family lived in this stucco 1818 mansion during the Civil War. The ornate Victorian interior reflects the mansion's appearance during the Davis years.

In the adjacent museum is an extensive collection of objects relating to the Confederate war effort, including the sword worn by Robert E. Lee at his surrender at Appomattox and E.B.D. Julio's monumental 1869 canvas *The Last Meeting of Lee and Jackson★* (lower level).

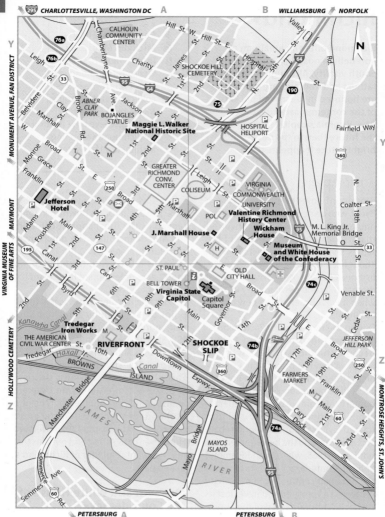

Valentine Richmond History Center★

1015 E. Clay St. ☎804-649-0711.
www.richmondhistorycenter.com.
Noted for its comprehensive archives on the capital city, the museum uses Richmond history to explore changing social themes in the fabric of American life through its permanent and changing exhibits.

The adjacent **Wickham House★★**, considered one of the finest examples of a Federal-style interior in the US, was the home of prominent attorney John Wickham and his family from 1812 to 1854. Noted for its cantilevered, mahogany spiral **staircase**, ornate plasterwork and rare Neoclassical wall paintings, the house interprets the life of both master and slave in early-19C Richmond.

John Marshall House★

818 E. Marshall St. ☎804-648-7998.
www.preservationvirginia.org.
The Federal-era brick residence was home to the third US Supreme Court

Richmond and the Civil War

As capital of the Confederacy and the only city to have been under long-term siege during the Civil War, Richmond is surrounded by many significant battle sites. Pivotal conflicts of Union general George B. McClellan's 1862 campaign to control the York-James Peninsula, and the final battles culminating in the siege of nearby Petersburg in 1864-65 took place in the countryside around Richmond.

Richmond National Battlefield Park★ (℘804-226-1981; www.nps.gov/rich) preserves 13 Civil War sites (1862 and 1864) that commemorate the battles for Richmond, organized as a self-guided, 80mi driving tour. Begin at the main park visitor center, located in part of the restored **Tredegar Iron Works** (at the base of 5th St. on Tredegar St. along the downtown Riverfront; ℘804-780-1865), where a large percentage of the Confederate armament was forged. Also part of the park complex is the **Chimborazo Medical Museum** (3215 E. Broad St.; ♿ 🅿 ℘804-226-1981), on a hilltop on the east side of the city that was the site of the Confederacy's largest hospital. The museum recounts the relatively barbaric state of Civil War-era medicine.

The 10-month siege (June 1864–April 1865) of Robert E. Lee's army by Union forces under Ulysses S. Grant, who were attempting to cut railroad supply lines to Richmond, is commemorated in the 2,460-acre **Petersburg National Battlefield**. A self-guided 37mi driving tour starts at the **visitor center** (20mi south of Richmond on Rte. 36; ℘804-732-3531; www.nps.gov/pete) and loops past elaborate earthworks erected by both armies. Grant's headquarters at City Point are also preserved.

The Civil War effectively ended 88mi west of Richmond in the tiny village of Appomattox Court House where Lee surrendered to Grant on April 9, 1865. The meeting took place in a plantation home preserved at **Appomattox Court House National Historical Park** (visitor center on Main St. in Appomattox, VA; ℘434-352-8987; www.nps.gov/apco).

chief justice, John Marshall (1755-1835). Known as the "Great Chief Justice" for the status he brought to the court during his 34-year tenure (beginning in 1801), Marshall lived here for much of his adult life, and his family furnishings still decorate the house.

Maggie L. Walker National Historic Site★

600 N. 2nd St.♿ ℘804-771-2017. www.nps.gov/mawa.
Located in the city's historic African-American neighborhood, Jackson Ward, this rambling brick Victorian row house was home to Maggie Walker (1867-1934), a pioneering black entrepreneur and the first American woman to found and preside over a chartered bank. Her St. Luke Penny Savings Bank opened in 1903; today it continues as the Consolidated Bank and Trust Company.

WESTERN RICHMOND★★

Fine old neighborhoods, gracious boulevards, parks and historic houses characterize the area that spreads west of the city center. Adjoining downtown, the **Fan District** is bounded by Monument Avenue on the north, Main Street on the south, Belvidere Street on the east, and Boulevard on the west. Named for its fan-like layout of streets, this lively district encompasses a wealth of restored 19C town houses, tucked-away cafes and the campus of Virginia Commonwealth University (VCU)—noted for its arts school. **Monument Avenue★**, punctuated by statues of Confederate heroes and noteworthy Virginians, links downtown with the Fan District. Confederate president Jefferson Davis and Confederate cavalry hero Jeb Stuart are buried at **Hollywood Cemetery★** (412 S. Cherry St.; ℘804-648-8501; www.

hollywoodcemetery.org), along with former US presidents James Monroe and John Tyler.

Small **galleries** stretch along West Main Street, from the 1300 to the 1800 block. On the west side of the Fan, **Carytown** (Cary St. between Boulevard & Thompson St.) harbors upscale boutiques, antique shops and restaurants. In the late 19C and early 20C, Richmond's aristocracy built elaborate country estates along the bluffs above the James River in Richmond's tony **West End**.

Virginia Historical Society★★

428 N. Boulevard. &🄿 ✆804-358-4901. www.vahistorical.org.

Built in the early 19C as the Confederate Memorial Institute, this stately structure now offers extensive historical exhibits, detailing the varied cultures and peoples involved in the making of Virginia. The permanent exhibit **"Story of Virginia: An American Experience"** chronicles the state's history through the 20C. In the Cheek Gallery, walls are lined with large murals painted in the early 20C by French artist Charles Hoffbauer and depicting the *Four Seasons of the Confederacy*.

Virginia Museum of Fine Arts★★

200 N. Boulevard. ✗&🄿 ✆804-340-1400. www.vmfa.state.va.us.

This eclectic gem reopened in 2010 after an expansion which added 165,000sq ft of space for major traveling exhibitions, the permanent collections and traveling exhibitions. The museum has grown considerably since 1919 when prominent Virginia judge John Barton Payne donated the first 100 objects. Today the light-filled facility boasts a permanent collection of more than than 23,000 items that span some 5,000 years. The museum houses an extraordinary collection of Impressionist, Post-Impressionist, American and British art, as well as the arts of China, Japan, Africa, Ancient Egypt, Classical Greece and Rome. Indian, Himalayan and Islamic religious art are also well represented. New galleries of 20C European art opened in 2013. Also note the decorative arts by Art Nouveau innovator Hector Guimard, jeweler René Lalique and Louis Comfort Tiffany. The museum's collection of Imperial Easter eggs and bibelots by Russian jeweler **Carl Fabergé** is one of the most extensive in the Western Hemisphere.

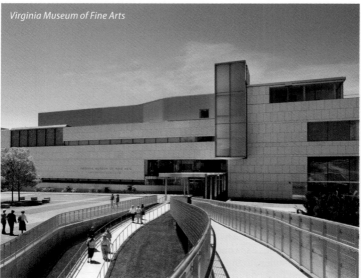

Virginia Museum of Fine Arts

© Bilyana Dimitrova

Story of Virginia, Virginia Historical Society

👥 Maymont★

1700 Hampton St. 🅿 ☎804-358-7166. www.maymont.org.

Topping bluffs above the James River, the former estate of late-19C railroad magnate James Dooley and his wife, Sallie May Dooley, has become a city showpiece. The Dooleys' stone Romanesque Revival Maymont Mansion, built in the 1890s, is decorated with the couple's extravagant Gilded Age furnishings, including a Tiffany-designed table of silver and carved narwhal tusks. Maymont's 100-acre grounds encompass formal gardens, a children's farm barn, a nature center and a cafe.

Virginia House★★

4301 Sulgrave Rd. ♿ Visit by appointment only. ☎804-353-4251. www.vahistorical.org.

The striking stone Tudor-style mansion was constructed from salvaged pieces of the 12C Priory of St. Sepulchre that stood in Warwick, England. In 1925 Richmond-born diplomat Alexander Weddell and his wife, Virginia, had the priory disassembled and commissioned architect Henry Grant Morse to reconfigure its stone facade and elaborate interior. The current design is modeled in part on Sulgrave Manor, ancestral home of George Washington in Northamptonshire, England. Acclaimed southern landscape architect Charles Gillette laid out the extensive grounds.

Agecroft Hall★★

4305 Sulgrave Rd. 🅿 ☎804-353-4241. www.agecrofthall.com.

The half-timbered walls and leaded windows of this home were originally part of an estate in Lancashire, England. Dating to the late 15C, the house was saved from demolition by Richmond scion T.C. Williams, who in 1926 had it dismantled and used its pieces to build a home in the Windsor Farms neighborhood.

Today the house is a museum. A permanent exhibit details how the house was dismantled, transported and reassembled in Richmond. The 23-acre site features five separate English-style gardens.

Virginia House

Colonial Parkway★★

One of the most picturesque coastal roadways in the East, the 23-mile aggregate-paved parkway sweeps past rivers and marshlands filled with birds and woodlands rich in color. Aside from its beauty, the parkway links the historic sites of Jamestown, birthplace of the English colonies, with those of Yorktown, where the colonies won their independence from England. The parkway was built in the 1930s by the Works Projects Administration and the Civilian Conservation Corps, both founded during Franklin Delano Roosevelt's tenure as president.

- **Michelin Map:** 584 S 9
- **Info:** ✆757-898-2410; www.nps.gov/colo/parkway.htm.
- **Location:** This is a 23mi drive along rivers and marshlands.
- **Timing:** Most of your time here will be spent in the car; plan for a leisurely drive.

A BIT OF HISTORY

In 1607 a group of 104 British colonists, led by Captain John Smith, anchored on a small island in the James River. Here, under a charter granted by James I to the Virginia Company in London, they established the colony of Virginia with Jamestown as its capital. Disease and starvation were rampant in the early years, claiming two-thirds of the settlement's population by the end of 1610. Nonetheless, the surviving colonists persevered, enduring Indian attacks, fires and numerous other setbacks over the ensuing decades. In 1699 the colony's government was moved to Williamsburg. Although Jamestown never became the "great cittie" envisioned by John Smith, the foundations that took root here helped mold the nation that would eventually become the United States of America.

Settled in 1631, nearby **Yorktown** developed into a prosperous colonial shipping center. But the town is best remembered for its part in the American Revolution. It was here in October 1781 that British general Charles Cornwallis surrendered to George Washington. Today the village's modest Main Street preserves several historic structures.

SIGHTS
Colonial National Historic Park at Jamestown★★

West end of Colonial Pkwy. &P
✆757-898-2410. www.nps.gov/colo.

In 1607 this 1,500-acre James River Island became the site of the first permanent English-speaking colony in America. Now administered by the National Park Service, most of the island has been returned to its natural state

Glasshouse, Colonial National Historic Park at Jamestown

© National Park Service

and 3- and 5mi loop drives weave across its bogs and woodlands.

On the northwest corner of the island, the **Jamestown Visitor Center** exhibits recovered artifacts. Behind the visitor center an excavated street grid outlines the foundations of the buildings from the former colonial capital. The brick tower from a church begun in 1639 is the only early structure remaining. East of the tower, the brick replica **Memorial Church** was built in 1907 on the cobblestone foundations of the 1617 church.

A 10min walk from the visitor center, the new **Jamestown Archaerium** tells the story of the early English settlers through objects unearthed at the Jamestown Fort site.

A causeway connects the island to the mainland, where the park maintains its popular **Glasshouse★** (take the first right after park entrance). Here you'll find the ruins of the original 1608 glass house and the replica where costumed artisans demonstrate colonial glassmaking.

Jamestown Settlement★★

Near the west end of Colonial Pkwy. at Rte. 31. ✕&🅿 ✆757-253-4838. www.historyisfun.org.

The state-run facility re-creates the life of both Native Americans and English colonists in early 17C Virginia. Visits begin at the **exhibit galleries★**, where a new 30,000sq ft gallery recounts the early efforts at colonization and the cultures of the coastal Powhatan Indians and the first known Africans in Virginia. A 30min documentary, **1607: A Nation Takes Root**, tells the story of the Virginia Company, which sponsored Jamestown Colony.

A palisaded reproduction of James Fort surrounds the kind of simple thatch-roofed structures that served as the only European foothold on the continent for several years. Adjacent to the fort is a re-creation of a Powhatan Indian village. Berthed in the river below the fort are reproductions of the three ships that brought the colonists to Jamestown in 1607. Costumed interpreters explain the difficult transatlantic crossing.

Pocahontas

The name of one of the most famous Native American women, Matoaka, has been changed in posterity to Pocahontas, "the playful one." Daughter of the powerful Powhatan chief Wahunsenacawh, the young girl was apparently fascinated by the English colonists and befriended their leader, John Smith. In 1614 Pocahontas married John Rolfe, the colonist who hybridized a smokable form of tobacco, and took the name Rebecca. Their marriage gave the colonists four strife-free years with the native Powhatans—years known as the Pocahontas Peace.

👥 Yorktown Victory Center★

Near the east end of Colonial Pkwy. at Rte. 238. &🅿 ✆757-253-4838. www.historyisfun.org.

Exhibits, a timeline and the 18min film A Time of Revolution explain the events leading up to the Revolution and the 1781 Siege of Yorktown, where the Continental Army won a victory that ensured America's independence from England. On the museum grounds, a Continental Army encampment and a post-Revolutionary farm are re-created.

Yorktown National Battlefield Park★

East end of Colonial Pkwy. &🅿 ✆757-898-2410. www.nps.gov/yonb. Encompassing some 5,000 acres on the bluffs above the York River, this park preserves earthworks from the 1781 **Siege of Yorktown**, several houses associated with the siege, and the Yorktown National Cemetery, where Union soldiers who fell in the Civil War are buried. The park visitor center features exhibits and the 16min docudrama Siege at Yorktown, detailing Gen. George Washington's crucial victory here over England's Lord Cornwallis in the early fall of 1781. A self-guided driving tour leads 7mi through the open battlefields to the

James River Plantations

Along the banks of the James, between Richmond and Williamsburg (a 22mi drive southeast of Richmond on Rte. 5; www.jamesriverplantations.org) stand the great estates of Virginia's illustrious colonial gentry. Built on the tobacco wealth that cemented the colony in the 17C, these superb Georgian manor houses symbolize the grandeur of that age, when Virginia's planters lived baronial lives at the edge of a vast continental wilderness. While only a handful of these houses are open to the public, a number of others are visible along Route 5 (John Tyler Highway), also known as the **Plantation Route.** (Combination tickets are available; inquire at the plantations. Visits to all plantation houses are by guided tour only.)

The first estate you'll come to as you drive south along Route 5 is **Shirley Plantation★★** (501 Shirley Plantation Rd.; ✕ 🅿 ✆804-829-5121). Virginia's oldest plantation has been owned by descendants of the Hill-Carter family since 1660. This Queen Anne manor (c.1720s) overlooking the James is justifiably famous for its square-rigged three-story **staircase** in the main entry hall.

Offset by towering boxwood hedges, **Georgian Berkeley Plantation★★** (off Rte. 5 at 12602 Harrison Landing Rd.; ✕ 🅿 ✆804-829-6018) served as the seat of the Harrison family. This lineage of respected national figures included Benjamin Harrison IV, who built the house in 1726, and his son Benjamin Harrison V, a signer of the Declaration of Independence.

Tenth US president **John Tyler** retired to the frame house on **Sherwood Forest Plantation★** (14501 Rte. 5; 🅿 ✆804-829-5377) after his tenure in office ended in 1845. Built c.1730, the house was lengthened by Tyler's wife, Julia. Only one room wide, it now measures 301ft long, making it the longest frame house in the US.

white clapboard **Moore House**, where terms of surrender were discussed, then on to **Surrender Field**, where the British capitulated on 19 October.

Rising on the river bluffs north of the visitor center, the **Yorktown Victory Monument** (1781) is an 84ft-high shaft topped by a 14ft statue of Liberty.

EXCURSION
Norfolk★

❯ 42mi south of Yorktown via I-64.
Occupying a broad peninsula bounded by the Chesapeake Bay, Hampton Roads and the Elizabeth River, Norfolk has been a shipping center since it was founded in 1608. Continuing its maritime traditions, the city is home to the **Norfolk Naval Station★★** (☚visit by guided tour only; tours depart from 9079 Hampton Blvd.; 🅿 ✆757-444-7955). The largest naval complex in the world sprawls across 8,000 acres edging the Elizabeth River and Willoughby Bay. The base is home port to ships (including aircraft carriers), aircraft and major naval commanders.

Aside from its working port, Norfolk is home to the **Chrysler Museum★★** (245 Olney Rd.; ✕ 🅿 ✆757-664-6200; www. chrysler.org; closed for renovation until 2014). Named for its benefactor, automobile scion and art collector Walter Chrysler, this art museum contains a renowned **glass collection★★★**, with pieces ranging from 100 BC to modern works by Dale Chihuly.

Horticulturists will love the **Norfolk Botanical Gardens★** (6700 Azalea Garden Rd.; ✕ 🅿 ✆757-441-5830; www. norfolkbotanicalgarden.org), which grace 155 acres with bountiful azaleas (Apr–mid-May), camellias (spring, fall and winter) and rhododendrons (May).

Colonial Williamsburg★★★

Virginia's 18C colonial capital has been painstakingly re-created on this 173-acre town site that includes 88 original shops, houses, and public buildings and hundreds of reconstructed colonial structures on their original sites. The restoration project, which was begun in the late 1920s, continues to this day.

- ◔ **Michelin Map:** 584 T 9
- 🗐 **Info:** ℘757-229-1000; www.colonialwilliamsburg.com.
- ▶ **Location:** Leave the car and plan to spend time on foot to get a sense of how folks did things in the 18C.
- ☺ **Don't Miss:** A glimpse of an era gone by wherever you look.
- 👤 **Kids:** With period costumes and hands-on exhibits, most of Williamsburg is interesting to kids.

A BIT OF HISTORY

The town's roots date to 1699, when colonial legislators decided to move their capital from Jamestown inland to Middle Plantation, where the College of William and Mary had been recently founded.

The new capital, Williamsburg, named after William III, centered around mile-long, unpaved Duke of Gloucester Street, anchored on the east by the colonial capitol, on the west by the college, and in the middle by Bruton Parish Church—a layout reflecting the spiritual, educational and governmental concerns of 18C Englishmen. The town rapidly grew into an important commercial, governmental and cultural center. Many prominent Virginians educated at the college (Thomas Jefferson among them) became proponents of the patriotic cause, and in the 1770s the town itself became a hotbed of Revolutionary zeal. From Virginia's House of Burgesses came some of the leading figures of the American Revolution, such as Peyton Randolph, George Washington, Thomas Jefferson and Patrick Henry. In 1780 the Virginia capital was moved to Richmond, and the town languished until 1926, when with generous funding from John D. Rockefeller, Jr., scholars and archaeologists began reconstructing the colonial town.

Today Colonial Williamsburg brings history to life with the help of well-versed costumed guides and strolling character interpreters who depict 18C citizens of Williamsburg going about their daily routines. Daily "Day in History" enactments re-create seminal events leading up to the Revolution.

VISIT

Begin at the **Visitor Center** (Lafayette St. near intersection with Colonial Pkwy.; ℘757-220-7645; www.colonialwilliamsburg.com), and view the 35min film,

---

Williamsburg in the 21C

Aside from the pleasures of the past available in the colonial village, visitors also flock to the Williamsburg area for more contemporary attractions. Chief among them is golf. Colonial Williamsburg itself boasts three courses, including the acclaimed Golden Horseshoe. Another draw is **Busch Gardens Williamsburg** 👤 (℘800-343-7946; www.buschgardens.com), a beautifully landscaped amusement park with thrill rides, games and live entertainment, all set within European-themed villages. An affiliated Busch attraction, nearby **Water Country USA** 👤 (℘800-343-7946; www.watercountryusa.com) offers water rides, slides and entertainment in a 1950s surf-culture setting. For shoppers, a seemingly endless string of **outlet malls** lines US-60, west of the historic area.

Colonial Williamsburg After Hours

Nighttime is one of the best times to experience Colonial Williamsburg, after the crowds have left. More than 27 houses and taverns here have overnight guest rooms for rent. All are decorated with reproduction antiques and offer the ambience of the past with all the comforts of the present. Take in the sunset flag-lowering ceremony, then enjoy dinner (reserve well in advance, ℘757-229-2141) at one of the four colonial taverns (King's Arms, Christiana Campbell's, Shields, Chowning's), where you'll be entertained by 18C storytellers and balladeers. After dinner, go for "Gambols" (whist and other card games) at Chowning's Tavern (Duke of Gloucester St).

Williamsburg: The Story of a Patriot, for a grounding in the town's historical significance. Stop in at colonial taverns and shops, including the **James Geddy House and Foundry** to see smithing techniques, and the **Pasteur & Galt Apothecary Shop**, where the healing techniques of "apothecary-surgeons" are detailed. At the newest reconstruction, **Anderson's Blacksmith Shop & Public Armoury,** you can see how weapons were forged for the American Revolution.

Capitol★★★

East end of Duke of Gloucester St. ⬤Visit by guided tour only.

Originally completed in 1705, the colony's capitol was destroyed by fire in 1747, rebuilt in 1753 and destroyed again in 1832. The current reconstruction faithfully depicts the first building in its layout and distinctive rounded walls. The two-story structure's H shape symbolizes the bicameral system of British colonial government, with the elected burgesses housed on the sparely decorated east side of the building and the royal governor and his council of 13 appointed men on the lavishly decorated west side. Here, in the impressive general court, the council sat in judgment on colonists accused of crimes. Most famous of the re-created capitol chambers is the **Hall of the House of Burgesses**, with its simple straight-backed pews. It was here in 1765 that patriotic firebrand **Patrick Henry** delivered his inflammatory lines: "Caesar... had his Brutus, Charles the First his Cromwell, and George the

Third may profit by their example. If this be treason, make the most of it."

The restored **public gaol** (north of the Capitol on Nicholson St.) depicts the harsh conditions under which accused persons were held until they came to trial—leg irons, sleeping mats on the floor and only a thin blanket were the norm. In contrast, the jailkeeper and his family enjoyed pleasant living quarters.

Raleigh Tavern★★

East end of Duke of Gloucester St., 1 block west of the capitol. ⬤Visit by guided tour only.

This reconstruction of the famous colonial tavern contains 18C gaming rooms, reception halls and "above-stairs" guest chambers. In its heyday, the tavern welcomed such illustrious regulars as George Washington, Thomas Jefferson and Peyton Randolph. When, owing to their outspoken patriotism, Virginia's elected burgesses (representatives) were "dissolved" by the Royal Governor, they typically reconstituted themselves by meeting unofficially at the Raleigh. The original building burned in 1859; the reconstruction relies on colonial drawings and inventories for its authenticity.

Courthouse★

Duke of Gloucester St.

Completed in 1771, the Georgian brick building, ornamented with "round-headed" windows and double doors served the community for more than 160 years. It is topped by an octagonal cupola bearing its original weathervane. Reenactments of colonial court cases are held here daily.

Governor's Palace★★★

North end of Palace Green.

Visit by guided tour only.

An elaborate reconstruction of the 1722 royal governor's palace that burned in 1781, the stately structure is deserving of its original status as the most impressive building of its era in the colonies. Elegant woodwork and period furnishings characterize its public reception rooms and grand ballroom; an incomparable ornamental display of 18C firearms hangs in its entrance **Hall of Armor** and along the broad paneled stairway leading to the second floor. The upper-floor private chambers feature delft-tile fireplace surrounds and finely wrought wall paneling; the **governor's office** boasts hand-tooled Moroccan leather wallpaper. Seven royal governors and Virginia's first two independent governors lived here, and during the decisive Siege of Yorktown, the palace served as a hospital for wounded Continental soldiers. The building is surrounded by 10 acres of formal gardens, including a **boxwood maze** that is as popular with contemporary children as it was with their colonial counterparts.

George Wythe House★★

West side of Palace Green.

Visit by guided tour only.

The starkly Georgian original brick home of Virginia's most respected jurist and the College of William and Mary's first law professor was considered one of the finest structures in Colonial Williamsburg. Here, George Wythe (1726-1806) mentored his students, some of whom (Thomas Jefferson and John Marshall) became the nation's founding fathers. Wythe himself was an outspoken Patriot, and many of his enlightened ideas still inform US law and government. The rich interior of the house reflects the 18C tastes of the Virginia gentry in its brightly painted paneling and wallpaper. Behind the house a row of dependencies reflect the operations necessary to sustain a well-heeled colonial household.

College of William and Mary★

West end of Duke of Gloucester St.

☏757-221-4000, www.wm.edu.

Predating Williamsburg itself, this lovely "university college" ranks as the second-oldest institution of higher learning in the US (after Harvard University in Massachusetts). King William and Queen Mary chartered it as a theological college for gentlemen in 1693, and in 1695 the foundations for the stately U-shaped **Wren Building★**, believed to have been designed by prominent English architect Sir Christopher Wren, were laid.

DeWitt Wallace Decorative Arts Museum

326 W. Francis Sts. ☏757-220-7554. www.history.org.

This gallery is renowned for its collection of English and American pieces from 1600 through 1830. The gallery was named for its premier benefactor, *Reader's Digest* magazine founder DeWitt Wallace.

The **Masterworks collection★** features rare decorative arts from the Colonial period. Highlights also include the **American Furniture** exhibit and an extensive silver collection.

The outdoor **garden** centers on a reflecting pool, offset with a reproduction of Augustus Saint-Gaudens' *Diana*.

EXCURSION
Carter's Grove

❯ 8mi southeast of Colonial Williamsburg on US-60. Private property. Once owned by Colonial Williamsburg, this imposing Georgian manor house on the James River was originally built in the 1750s for the grandson of wealthy Virginia planter Robert "King" Carter. In 2007 Colonial Williamsburg sold the property to a private investor. A 1930s restoration that happened here resulted in a hybrid of Colonial furnishings in a rich, comfortable setting. On the estate's extensive grounds a cluster of re-created **slave quarters** depicts the living conditions and cultural traditions of enslaved African Americans in the Tidewater area during the 18C.

Great Lakes

Aerial View of Chicago and Lake Michigan
©PhotoDisc

Chicago Area

Located in Illinois, less than an hour's drive from Indiana to the southeast and Wisconsin to the north, Chicago occupies a strategic position on the southern end of Lake Michigan. Stretching north and east over 22,300sq mi, this majestic lake is the fifth-largest body of freshwater in the world and the only one of the five Great Lakes whose borders lie entirely within the US. Its temperate breezes can turn a winter's day lovely; while an angry northerly can just as easily blow through a summer's afternoon. The Chicago River flows west from the lake, bisecting downtown and then forking north and south just over a mile inland.

Highlights

1 Gazing over Chicagoland from the **Willis Tower** (p275)

2 Outdoor concerts in **Millennium Park** (p276)

3 The treasures at the **Art Institute of Chicago** (p276)

4 Gazing up at those marvels of architecture and engineering, **Chicago's skyscrapers** (p277)

5 Sinking your teeth into a gooey slice of **deep-dish pizza** (p278)

City by the Lake

From its perch at water's edge, the city proper spills north, west and south to cover 228sq mi. Outranked in population size only by New York City and Los Angeles, this polyglot city of nearly 3 million prides itself on its neighborhoods, all 175 of them. While some are the stuff of developers' dreams, many trace their outlines around the historic ethnic enclaves from which the city was built.

Beyond city borders, suburbs, exurbs and collar counties encircle the Chicago like growth rings on a tree, adding another 4,400sq mi to "Chicagoland." Recent years have seen an explosion of suburban growth, as downtown employers opt for less expensive locations outside the city, creating thriving commercial and residential corridors in surrounding communities. For now, the city and its far-flung satellites seem to have struck a happy balance. Revitalization of urban spaces, inside and out, has reawakened an interest in city living and working. And, while thousands of suburbanites make the daily commute to work downtown, a growing number "reverse-commute" to work outside the city limits. Though many of Chicago's cultural gems cluster in the downtown neighborhoods, there is much to be seen slightly farther afield. To the west, **Oak Park★★★** is a trove of architectural treasures by Frank Lloyd Wright. The windswept dunes, marshes and forests of the Lake Michigan shore are best enjoyed at Indiana **Dunes National Lakeshore★** (𝄢 219-926-7561), which spreads along Highway 12 in Indiana less than an hour's drive from Chicago.

For those who wish to venture farther still, Indianapolis, 177mi to the southeast, hosts the famed Indianapolis 500 auto race each May. And several sights related to the life of the nation's 16th president, Abraham Lincoln, are located in the Illinois state capital of **Springfield**, approximately 200mi southwest of Chicago.

GETTING THERE

O'Hare International Airport (ORD):
☎773-686-2200, www.flychicago.com. Information booths located on lower level of terminals 1, 2 and 3, and on upper and lower levels of terminal 5. Free transit between terminals and parking lots; rental car companies have free shuttles to their offices.

Chicago Midway Airport (MDW):
☎773-838-0600, www.flychicago.com; 10mi southwest of the Loop. Information booths located on the lower level of the main terminal near baggage claim. **GO Airport Express** (☎888-284-3826, www.airportexpress.com) operates shuttles from both airports to downtown. CTA (below) Blue and Orange line trains run from O'Hare and Midway, respectively, to downtown. Rental car agencies are located at both airports.

Union Station (225 S. Canal St.) links national and regional rail service by **Amtrak**, (☎800-872-7245; www.amtrak.com) with **Metra** commuter trains. **Greyhound bus** station: 630 W. Harrison St., ☎312-408-5821 or 800-231-2222, www.greyhound.com.

GETTING AROUND

The Chicago rapid-transit system is officially nicknamed the 'L' although you'll also see it denoted as the 'El'. **Bus** and **rapid-transit** maps and the *Downtown Transit Sightseeing Guide* are available (free) at train stations, hotels, and visitor centers and downloadable at www.transitchicago.com. CTA fares are $2.25 one-way, no transfers when paying in cash (exact change required); $2.00 for the bus, $2.25 for the 'L' when paying with a Transit Card or a Chicago Card (available from www.transitchicago.com). **Taxi**: Checker Taxi Co., ☎312-243-2537, www.checkertaxichicago.com; and Yellow Cab Co., ☎312-829-4222, www.yellowcabchicago.com.

VISITOR INFORMATION

For free maps and information contact:, **Choose Chicago**, www.choosechicago.com; tourisminfo@choosechicago.com. **Choose Chicago Visitor Centers**: Chicago Cultural Center, 77 E. Randolph St. (Loop); Chicago Water Works, 163 E. Pearson St. at Michigan Ave (Magnificent Mile).

ADDRESSES

🏠 STAY

Bed & Breakfast reservations: Chicago Bed & Breakfast Association, www.chicago-bed-breakfast.com. **Hostels:** Hostelling International Chicago Hostel, ☎312-360-0300, www.hichicago.org.

$$$$ The Drake Hotel – 140 E. Walton Pl., Chicago, IL. ☎312-787-2200. www.thedrakehotel.com. 535 rooms, 74 rooms. Since 1920 the handsome Italian Renaissance-style building on the Magnificent Mile has been the stop for celebrities. The renowned Cape Cod seafood restaurant headlines multiple on-site dining options. Lobby highlights include the original mahogany ceiling inset with hand-painted tiles. Several rooms overlook Lake Michigan.

$$$$ Hotel Monaco – 225 N. Wabash Ave., Chicago, IL. ✕🚫♿🅿 ☎312-960-8500. www.monaco-chicago.com. 191 rooms. Two blocks from the Magnificent Mile, this boutique property was designed as the world-traveler's 1930s Art Deco-style living room. Whimsical amenities include an in-room pet goldfish delivered on request.

$$$ The Alexander – 333 S. Delaware St., Indianapolis, IN. ✕♿🅿 ☎317-624-8200. www.thealexander.com. 157 rooms, 52 suites. They take art seriously at this stylish hotel in Indy's CityWay neighborhood. Guest rooms and public spaces alike function as display spaces for commissioned artworks in every medium. Bedrooms are spacious and comfortable, and guests rave about the Midwestern dishes at Cerulean.

BP Bridge, Millennium Park, Chicago

©Steve Geer/iStockphoto.com

$$$ Hotel Allegro Chicago – 171 W. Randolph St., Chicago, IL. ✕&P ☎312-236-0123. www.allegrochicago.com. 483 rooms. Bold colors and contemporary prints have transformed the North Loop theater district's 1926 Bismarck Hotel, now a boutique property in the Kimpton hotel family. Fitness buffs enjoy on-site bike rental, a complimentary fitness center, and a yoga mat in every room.

$$$ Omni Severin Hotel – 40 W. Jackson Pl., Indianapolis, IN. ✕&P☒ ☎317-634-6664. www.omnihotels.com. 424 rooms. Located across from Union Station downtown, this 1913 high rise was the place to stay until the late 1930s. Guest rooms blend contemporary furnishings with warm, neutral tones.

⏲ EAT

$$$ Blackbird – 619 W. Randolph St., Chicago, IL. ☎312-715-0708. www.blackbirdrestaurant.com. **Contemporary.** In contrast to its spare decor, the food at this Market District hot spot is a feast for the eyes. Dig into gorgeously presented plates of aged pekin duck breast or grilled sturgeon.

$$$ Dunaway's Palazzo Ossigeno – 351 S. East St., Indianapolis, IN. Closed Sun. ☎317-638-7663. www.dunaways.com. **American.** On the edge of the Fletcher Place Historic District, this restaurant occupies a restored 1930 Art Deco gem. Menus change seasonally, but you can count on finding steakhouse-style comfort food such as veal chops and aged flank steak.

$$$ Grace – 652 W. Randolph St., Chicago, IL Dinner only; closed Sun. ☎312-234-9494. www.grace-restaurant.com. **Contemporary.** This Chicago's fine dining spot draws raves. Chef Curtis Duffy's elegant menu changes with the micro-seasons, bringing refined, of-the-moment flavors to diners' plates.

$$ Lula Café – 2537 N. Kedzie Blvd., Chicago, IL. Closed Tue. ☎773-489-9554. www.lulacafe.com. **American.** An early proponent of the farm-to-table movement, this Logan Square hotspot prides itself on artisanal cooking both adventurous and comforting. Menus vary, but look for seasonally inspired dishes like roasted eggplant with lamb pancetta; dry-aged sirloin steak and inventive vegetable preparations.

$$ Mikado – 148 S. Illinois St., Indianapolis, IN. ☎317-972-4180. www.mikadoindy.com. **Japanese.** Inside Downtown's oldest Japanese restaurant, you'll find a serene, contemporary interior, seafood dishes, plus traditional Japanese and fusion fare.

$$ Mindy's Hot Chocolate – 1747 N. Damen Ave., Chicago, IL. Closed Mon. ☎773-489-1747. www.hotchocolate chicago.com. **American.** Chef/owner Mindy Segal's desserts are legendary. But you can enjoy chicken, meat, fish dishes here for dinner as well.

$ The Original Gino's East – 162 E. Superior St., Chicago, IL. ☎312-266-3337. www.ginoseast.com **Pizza.** Try this 1966 landmark for the city's classic deep-dish pie. The thick, gooey slices layer cheeses, sauce and your choice of extras atop a signature cornmeal crust.

Chicago★★★

Fulcrum of modern American commerce, Chicago takes its name from the Potawatomi word *She-caw-gu*, meaning "stinking onion"—a reference to the garlic that grew wild in the area. The city, which today covers 228sq mi, began as a trading outpost on the swampy banks of the river in 1779. Its first permanent inhabitant, Jean-Baptiste Point du Sable, was a trader of African-Caribbean descent.

▶ **Population:** 2,714,856.
🛈 **Info:** ℘312-744-2400; www.choosechicago.com.
🅿 **Parking:** Always a challenge in Chicago. Garage the car and hop on the El instead.
🚐 **Don't Miss:** The Art Institute of Chicago.
👫 **Kids:** Hands-down, the Museum of Science and Industry.

A BIT OF HISTORY

When incorporated as a city in 1837, Chicago had a population of a mere 4,000; it would top 300,000 by 1871 and 1.5 million by the turn of the 19C. During that time, its central location straddling East and West, between the Mississippi River and the Great Lakes, became increasingly strategic as the hub of transportation and shipping, commerce and industry in an expanding America. Lumber, grain and livestock funneled through Chicago in monumental quantities. City fathers frantically constructed tunnels, bridges and sewers to accommodate the busy metropolis, and Irish and German laborers arrived in droves to do the work.

In October 1871, the **Great Chicago Fire** broke out, burning for three days and destroying the central city. Rebuilding began immediately and growth continued unabated; the population tripled in the decade following the fire. In spite of crowding, poor sanitation and grueling working conditions, Chicago rose above the miasma of its stockyards and steel mills. After 1880 the central city grew tall on the talents of a coterie of architects who pioneered the **Chicago School of Architecture** (ℂ see INTRODUCTION, Architecture).

By the 1890s, elite residents had enough leisure time and money to establish cultural institutions. The crowning achievement would be the staging of the **World's Columbian Exposition** in 1893 on the South Side lakefront. A showcase of Neoclassical architecture and modern technology, the fair established Chicago as a world-class city.

In the 20C, the Roaring Twenties left a permanent scar as bootlegging gangsters—**Al Capone** foremost among them—committed hundreds of murders in their attempts to control the illegal liquor business. Together with the fire and the fair, this gangster heritage still plays a leading role in defining the city's diverse urban personality. Reinforcing that diversity, Chicago's population today is 36 percent African American, 26 percent Hispanic and close to 4 percent Asian. Some 80 additional ethnic strains enrich the mix. Contemporary Chicago continues to navigate its urban hazards, ensuring the city's diversity, vitality and livability in the new millennium.

THE LOOP★★★

Looming large along the lakefront, Chicago's busy Loop and its environs have been fertile grounds for architectural innovation since the fire in 1871. Named for the elevated tracks that girdle them, these blocks bustle with workday energy as Chicagoans transact daily business in an array of office towers that catalog the city's growth skyward since the 19C. The **James R. Thompson Center★★** (bounded by Clark, LaSalle, Randolph & Lake Sts.; ✖ ♿), designed by Helmut Jahn in 1985, may be the Loop's quirkiest structure, its pastel panels enclosing a soaring atriuma. Representing the apex of the

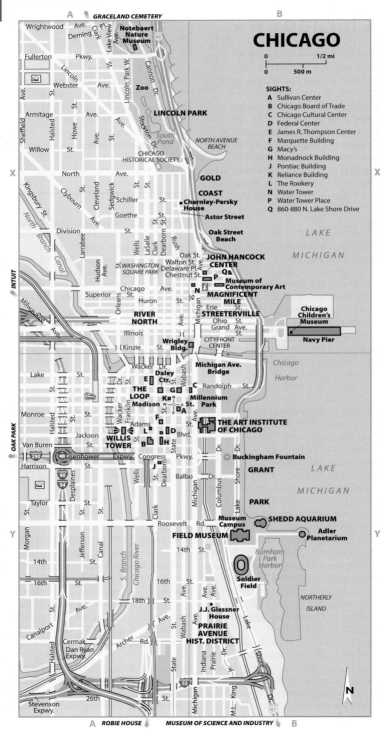

International style is Ludwig Mies van der Rohe's **Federal Center★★** (Dearborn St. between Adams St. & Jackson Blvd.), completed in 1974, and the 1965 **Richard J. Daley Center★★** (bounded by Washington, Randolph, Clark & Dearborn Sts.), by C.F. Murphy Associates. Both these buildings feature stunning (and famous) plaza sculptures: Alexander Calder's 1973 **Flamingo** adds a burst of red outside the Federal Center. From Daley Plaza rises an untitled work by **Pablo Picasso**.

Stretching between the river and Congress Parkway, State Street was once the city's grand retail concourse. Today, two late-19C landmark department store buildings endure: the **Macy's★** (between Randolph & Washington Sts.) building was designed by D.H. Burnham & Co. for Marshall Field & Co., which occupied it until 2006; the exterior corner clocks are Chicago icons. Until 2007 **One South State Street★★★** was home to the flagship store of Chicago retail giant Carson Pirie Scott; the structure is considered the greatest work of Chicago architect Louis Sullivan.

Willis Tower (former Sears Tower)★★★

233 S. Wacker Dr. www.willistower.com.
This 110-story feat of engineering cuts an unmistakable profile on the city's skyline. At the time of its construction (1968-74), the city did not require a zoning variance for the tower, allowing it to rise to a then-unsurpassed height of 1,450ft.

In 1996 architect Cesar Pelli's Petronas Towers in Kuala Lumpur, Malaysia, topped the Willis (then known as the Sears Tower) in height (today Dubai's Burj Khalifa tower reigns as the world's tallest structure at 2,717ft). Designed by architect Bruce Graham and chief engineer Fazlur Khan for Skidmore, Owings & Merrill, the Chicago landmark is solidly anchored into the bedrock hundreds of feet below ground; its structural skeleton required 76,000 tons of steel. Enter on Jackson Street for the **Skydeck** ▲▲ (& ☎312-875-9696) and soar 103 stories up to enjoy spectacular **views★★★** from the recently (2009) renovated glass balconies of the city and the lake.

Chicago Cultural Center★★

78 E. Washington St. ☎312-744-6630. www.cityofchicago.org.
This Neoclassical palazzo served as the city's first library when completed in 1897 after designs by Shepley, Rutan & Coolidge. Admire the inlaid-marble grand stairway that ascends from the Washington Street entrance to **Preston Bradley Hall★**, with its Tiffany stained-glass dome (free concerts are offered here ;check website). The **Choose Chicago Visitor Information Center** (☎312-744-6630) on the north side of the building makes a good place to start a Loop tour.

Chicago Board of Trade Building★

141 W. Jackson Blvd. ☎312-435-3590. www.cbotbuilding.com.
One of the city's finest Art Deco skyscrapers, this building, designed by Holabird & Root (1930), and its two annexes house the world's oldest and largest futures exchange, established in 1848 to regulate the trade of grain and commodities from Illinois and the Great

Willis Tower [former Sears Tower]

Plains through Chicago to the eastern seaboard. Trading-floor viewing galleries are closed to the public, but you can step inside the lobby.

GRANT PARK★

The city's 319-acre "front yard," located between Randolph Street on the north and **Soldier Field** (1929, Holabird & Roche) on the south, Lake Michigan on the east and Michigan Avenue on the west, marks roughly the midpoint in the swath of parks that trims Chicago's 28mi lakeshore. The park has been shaped by landfill, accretion, erosion and the human hand since 1835 when state commissioners set aside a thin strip of land along the shoreline to "remain forever open, clear and free." Sixty years later, mail-order magnate A. Montgomery Ward conducted a lengthy and successful battle with the city to clear the stables, railroad tracks and other eyesores that had rooted there in spite of the old edict. In 1909 Daniel Burnham's Plan of Chicago called for "a formal focal point," and the elegant landscaping of the park began to emerge as construction started in 1915. Though the automobile age sliced the green space with busy streets, the park still offers peaceful gardens, picnic spots and lovely vistas of the city and lake. Centerpiece of the park, 1927 **Buckingham Fountain★★** was modeled on the Latona Basin at Versailles. On summer evenings its waters are illuminated to spectacular effect.

At the south end of the park, the 10-acre **Museum Campus** unites in spirit and space to create Chicago's great triad of natural science museums: the Field Museum of Natural History, the Shedd Aquarium and the Adler Planetarium. And each July, the grounds come alive with the city's largest outdoor festival, **Taste of Chicago**.

Millennium Park★★★

201 E. Randolph St. ✆312-742-1168. www.millenniumpark.org.

Opened in 2005, this 24.5-acre park is quickly becoming Chicago's best-loved tourist attraction—even for locals.

Works of art, public concerts, free winter ice skating and bracing skyline views offer entertainment at every turn. On hot days especially don't miss a visit to water-spouting and wade-worthy **Crown Fountain★★** with its twin glass-block towers projecting an intriguing shifting array of video faces. From afar you'll spot the scrambled steel shapes of the Frank Gehry-designed **Jay Pritzker Pavilion★★★**, scene of outdoor performances in warm weather. Gehry also designed the **BP Bridge★★**, a 925ft span of sultry serpentine curves. Anish Kapoor's sculpture **Cloud Gate★★★**, affectionately known as "the bean," mirrors the sky, the city, and your face if you step close enough; the **Lurie Garden★** features native plants.

The Art Institute of Chicago★★★

111 S. Michigan Ave. at E. Adams St. ✗&✆312-443-3600. www.artic.edu.

With its flanking lions and marble lobby, the Michigan Avenue main building was once part of the World's Columbian Exposition. Designed by Shepley, Rutan & Coolidge, it opened as the Art Institute of Chicago on 8 December 1893. A world-renowned art museum has emerged in the past century, now housing one of the largest permanent collections in the United States. The continuously expanding collections have necessitated the addition of several new wings over the years, bringing its size to 275,200sq ft of gallery space. In 2009, the museum completed a three-story glass and limestone Modern Wing designed by Renzo Piano and featuring an eye-catching "flying carpet" roof and a bridge connecting it to Millennium Park across Monroe Street. New and refurbished gallery spaces for Japanese art, African and Indian art of the Americas, and textile arts were completed in 2011.

Spanning five millennia, the institute's collections cover a multitude of cultures, though its reputation is based largely on its cache of **Impressionist and Post-impressionist paintings★★★**, one of the largest and most important

SCRAPING THE SKY

It took a talented and energetic cohort of architects to rebuild Chicago after the 1871 fire. Within a year of the blaze, 10,000 new buildings rose up at a cost of $45 million. By 1890, the booming population increased the pressure on the downtown district to accommodate more people, more services and more offices. With no place to go but up, Chicago architects and engineers created the skyscraper. In traditional masonry construction, thick walls support the weight of the building. Architect **William Le Baron Jenney** reversed the formula by developing a skeletal steel frame on which to hang "curtain" walls, allowing buildings to grow taller. Based on this steel-frame construction, Jenney's 1884 nine-story Home Insurance Building, now demolished, is considered the first modern "skyscraper." At the same time, engineers mastered ways to anchor tall buildings in Chicago's swampy soil and to reduce the effects of high winds. Improvements to the elevator and telephone made vertical height practical. These innovations gave birth to the **Chicago School of Architecture**, recognized as the first significant new movement in architecture since the Italian High Renaissance. With it came a new aesthetic, and by 1894 most Chicago School architects had rejected historical ornament in favor of vertical sculptures made of piers, spandrels and windows. Their work would change city architecture around the world. Visitors on foot can still glimpse the scale of 19C Chicago. The **Monadnock Building★★** (53 W. Jackson Blvd.) combines the old load-bearing masonry style in its northern half (1891, Burnham & Root) with steel-frame construction in its southern portion (1893, Holabird & Roche). The **Reliance Building★★** (32 N. State St.), designed and completed by Charles Atwood and David Burnham in 1895, anticipated the glass skyscrapers of the 1980s. Built in 1891, 1895 and 1905 respectively, **Pontiac★** (542 S. Dearborn St.) the **Marquette★★** (140 S. Dearborn St.) and the **Chicago** (7 W. Madison St.) buildings by Holabird & Roche are masterpieces of Chicago school design. At the southeast corner of LaSalle and Adams Streets, the **Rookery★★** (1888, Burnham & Root) houses a rare commercial interior by Frank Lloyd Wright (1905).

Interior of the Rookery

© Mario Savoia/Bigstockphoto.com

A Sunday on La Grande Jatte - 1884 (1884-86) by Georges Seurat, The Art Institute of Chicago

outside France. This assemblage of painterly genius encompasses important works by Courbet, Manet, Monet, Cézanne, Renoir, Degas and Seurat.

Besides these treasures, the institute has a strong collection of **American fine and decorative arts★★**, ranging from Colonial furniture and silver to molded 20C chairs by Eero Saarinen and Charles Eames; as well as a fine collection of **Modern and Contemporary art** from Europe and the Americas. Covering 5,000 years from the Neolithic Age to the 20C, the institute's **Chinese, Japanese and Korean★★★** holdings rank among the finest in the US. A significant collection of 15,000 **Japanese woodblock prints★** and a fine group of **archaic Chinese jades★** constitute some of the highlights.

The 68 **Thorne Miniature Rooms★★** **👤👤** —delicately crafted and historically precise—are a perennial favorite.

Of local interest is the architectural collection, which includes fragments of demolished buildings and a re-installation of the **Trading Room of the Chicago Stock Exchange★★** (1894, Adler & Sullivan).

👤👤 Field Museum of Natural History★★★

1400 S. Lake Shore Dr. on the Museum Campus. ✖♿🅿 𝒫312-922-9410. fieldmuseum.org.

More than nine acres of exhibit halls and 25 million artifacts inhabit the vast Neoclassical edifice (1921, Daniel Burnham) that houses this world-class natural history museum.

Amassed for the World's Columbian Exposition in 1893, the collections acquired their permanent home here in 1921. Dinosaur bones are one of the museum's specialties, represented by **Sue★★**, the most complete Tyranno-

City of the Big Pizza

Chicago ranks as one of the country's greatest spots for pizza. Aficionados rave about the city's deep-dish variety, sometimes called thick-crust or pan pizza. This savory concoction of tomatoes, cheese, sausage and vegetables ladled over a thick, doughy crust was developed in the 1940s by restaurateur Ike Sewell, whose restaurants **Pizzeria Uno** (**now renamed Uno Chicago Grill**) (Ohio St. & Wabash Ave.) and **Pizzeria Due** (on Wabash at Ontario) still serve the genuine article to crowds of eager eaters. More than 2,000 restaurants in Chicago offer some permutation of this mouth-watering dish, with toppings ranging from mushrooms to clams and artichokes.

The Perfect Town

George M. Pullman was the founder of the Pullman Palace Car Company railcar company. But he is better known for instigating the country's first labor strike when he lowered Pullman's workers' wages in 1894. When he decreased wages, he did not lower the rents for the homes in which they were required to live.

What Pullman lacked in social policy know-how he had in urban planning acumen. The worker's town he created is now a landmark and oft-referred to as the "most perfect town." Expect to see blocks of preserved brick rowhouses and parks, and remnants of a shopping arcade and other public buildings. A fire ravaged the original 1880 Pullman Factory and Clock Tower in the 1990s, but preservationists have worked to keep the self-contained community vibrant.

Your first stop should be the **Historic Pullman Visitor Center** (11141 S. Cottage Grove Ave., open Tue-Sun. ✆773-785-8901. www.pullmanil.org) on the site of Pullman's handsome Arcade Building, where you'll find introductory videos and exhibits about Pullman and the community's unique history. Self-guided tour information is available, as are helpful docents. Then you can stroll the manicured streets, looking at Arcade Park and the historic home exteriors.

saurus Rex skeleton found to date, and the extensive exhibit **Evolving Planet**, which covers life on earth from the days before the dinosaurs to the Ice Age. The 15,000sq ft **Underground Adventure★** takes visitors through the subterranean world.

Other colorful, interactive exhibits explore **Africa★★** and **Ancient Egypt** (the latter features a **mastaba tomb★**, the largest full-size reconstruction of a tomb outside Egypt), while a number of quieter galleries present finely crafted animal taxidermy and wildlife dioramas. Superb ethnographic holdings thoroughly cover the cultures of the Americas and Oceania, and the hall of **Gems★** highlights the earth science collection. The Field Museum is renowned for its blockbuster temporary exhibitions; be sure to check the schedule to see what's on during your visit.

👥 Shedd Aquarium★★★

1200 S. Lake Shore Dr. on the Museum Campus. ✆312-939-2438. www.sheddaquarium.org.
The world's largest indoor aquarium, the Shedd includes some 32,000 aquatic animals comprising nearly 1,500 species, all presented in exhibits and programs that emphasize conservation and

Tyrannosaurus rex, "Sue", Field Museum of Natural History

© The Field Museum

Frank Lloyd Wright

From the fertile ground that nourished the creativity of Chicago's innovative skyscraper architects rose another master, whose best-known works revolutionized residential building design. Born in Wisconsin in 1867, Frank Lloyd Wright came early under the influence of Louis Sullivan, apprenticing in his studio until striking out on his own at the age of 25. Living and working in suburban Oak Park, he developed his distinctive Prairie style, its strong horizontal lines and overhanging eaves inspired by the flat Midwestern landscape. Wright's signature open floor plans allowed rooms to flow into one another, and he created furniture to complement his organic designs.

The quintessential Prairie school **Robie House★★** (5757 S. Woodlawn Ave.; visit by guided tour only; purchase tickets in advance online; ℘312-994-4000; www.gowright.org), on the University of Chicago campus, made Wright world famous in 1910 and helped "break the box" of traditional architecture. Today a large enclave of Wright-designed homes comprises the **Frank Lloyd Wright and Prairie School of Architecture Historic District** (bordered by Division, Lake, Ridgeland & Marion Sts.). At its heart, the **Frank Lloyd Wright Home and Studio★★** (1889-1909) makes an excellent place to begin a walking tour (951 W. Chicago Ave.; visit by guided tour only; ℘312-994-4000 ; www.gowright.org). Wright executed commissions elsewhere during this time, notably the c.1904 **Dana-Thomas House★★★** (301 E. Lawrence Ave., Springfield, IL; ℘217-782-6776; www.dana-thomas.org), renowned for its size, complexity and 250 art-glass windows and doors.

In 1909, Wright left his wife and six children in a scandal that effectively ended his practice in socially conservative Oak Park. His architecture became more expressionistic in the 1910s and 20s, and in 1931 he established Taliesin (👓 see MADISON) in his home state to train architects. Following construction of the stunning 1936 house called Fallingwater (👓 see SOUTHERN ALLEGHENIES) in Pennsylvania, Wright opened Taliesin West in Arizona and remained in the limelight until his death in 1959 at age 91.

the environment. One of the last Beaux-Arts buildings (Graham, Anderson, Probst & White) in Chicago, it opened in 1930. Today it houses fish, reptiles, amphibians, birds and marine mammals from around the world, including those in the **Caribbean Reef★**, home to some 500 tropical fish (don't miss the daily feedings narrated by scuba-diving animal caretakers). Added in 1991, the **Oceanarium★★**, with its sweeping views of Lake Michigan, houses marine mammals in a naturalistic Northwest coast setting. The Oceanarium's renovated amphitheater mounts a variety of multispecies live aquatic shows throughout the day; check daily schedules online or at the door.

Kids can suit up in penguin outfits to slip and slide through the **Polar Play Zone**, while fearsome-looking anacondas, piranhas and bird-eating spiders make their home in **Amazon Rising★**, complete with a flooded forest.

Wild Reef★★ features denizens of an Indo-Pacific reef system, including sharks, rays, eels and beautiful corals.

👥 Adler Planetarium★★

1300 S. Lake Shore Dr. on the Museum Campus. ✕&🅿 ℘312-922-7827. www.adlerplanetarium.org.

Occupying a beautiful vantage point, the planetarium offers commanding **views★★** of the lakefront. The oldest planetarium in the Western Hemisphere (1930), the Adler is renowned for its fine collection of historic astronomical instruments and its sky shows beneath the original dome. The 60,000sq ft Sky Pavilion houses colorful hands-on exhibits that explore the universe. The state-of-the-art **Definiti Space Theater** offers interactive virtual-reality sky shows; other immersive sky shows are presented in the Johnson Family Star Theater (3D) and the Grainger Sky Theater, the Adler's largest and most technically advanced dome theater.

MAGNIFICENT MILE★★★

The Champs Elysées of Chicago, this promenade along North Michigan Avenue is the city's most prestigious thoroughfare. Lined with exclusive boutiques and large retail stores, luxury hotels and premier residential and office high rises, the "Boul Mich" has come a long way from its beginnings as an ordinary city street. Its most distinctive relics survived the Great Fire in 1871: the castellated 1889 **Water Tower★** still stands toward the north end at Chicago Avenue. Across the street, the old pumping station (1866) houses a **visitor information center**. The opening of the **Michigan Avenue Bridge★** (Wacker Dr. & N. Michigan Ave.) joined the north and south sides of the city in 1920, catalyzing an incredible building boom that spawned most of the landmarks on the avenue. Among them, the French Renaissance **Wrigley Building★★** at nos. 400-410 may be most familiar, especially by night when floodlights illuminate its terracotta cladding.

The John Hancock Center and **Water Tower Place★** (no. 835) ushered in a new era of skyscrapers and retailing in the early 1970s, when Michigan Avenue displaced State Street as the city's shopping corridor.

Two busy neighborhoods flank the "Mag Mile." Between the lake and Michigan Avenue, **Streeterville** is the home of Northwestern University's Chicago campus and the residential towers at **860-880 N. Lake Shore Drive★★**, which established the high-rise influence of Ludwig Mies van der Rohe in the early 1950s. Nestled in the crook between the Chicago River east of Wabash Avenue is **River North★**, an eclectic district of **art galleries**, restaurants and trendy clubs.

John Hancock Center at night

John Hancock Center★★★

875 N. Michigan Ave. ✕ ♿ 🅿 ✆888-875-8439. www.hancockobservatory.com.
Muscular and monumental, the profile of "Big John" is a Chicago icon. Completed in 1970 by Skidmore, Owings & Merrill, the 100-story tower (Chicago's third-tallest) is a city unto itself, its 2.8 million square feet housing retail, restaurant, office and residential space. Its efficient obelisk-shaped design, distinguished by brawny cross-braces, includes 46,000 tons of steel that easily carry gravity and wind loads.

Soar to the 94th-floor **observatory** (✆312-654-5023) for spectacular **views★★★** of the lake and landscape some 1,127ft below. Step out on to the open-air Skywalk (additional charge) for a breathtaking outdoor experience.

Museum of Contemporary Art★

220 E. Chicago Ave. ✕ ♿ 🅿 ✆312-280-2660. www.mcachicago.org.
Founded in 1967, the museum presents a wide range of contemporary visual and performing arts by both well-established artists and those on the leading edge. The MCA presents works on loan and traveling exhibits along with installations from its 2,500-piece permanent collection, which includes post-1945 works by Marcel Duchamp,

Abraham Lincoln in Illinois

A revered figure in America, **Abraham Lincoln** (1809-65) began life in a Kentucky log cabin, attending less than a year of school, but reading avidly between hours of manual labor. A year after his family moved to Illinois in 1830, Lincoln—then 22—settled in the village of New Salem and held a variety of jobs including storekeeper, postmaster and surveyor. **Lincoln's New Salem State Historic Site★** (2mi south of Petersburg, IL on Rte. 97; ☎217-632-4000; www.lincolnsnewsalem. com) re-creates many of the buildings where Lincoln worked.

In 1837, Lincoln, now a lawyer, moved to Springfield—the Illinois state capital— where he set up his law practice. There Lincoln met and married Kentucky socialite Mary Todd and purchased a house. Today you can tour this two-story brown clapboard Greek Revival structure (the only home Lincoln ever owned) at **Lincoln Home National Historic Site★★** (426 S. 7th St., Springfield, IL; ➤visit by free guided tour only, whichdeparts daily from visitor center on-site; ♿🅿; ☎217-492-4241).

Lincoln rose quickly as an attorney in Springfield, and in 1858 he ran for Senate, debating Illinois' leading politician, Stephen A. Douglas, on the issue of slavery. Although Lincoln lost the election, he won a national following that garnered him the Republican nomination for US president in 1860. Within weeks of President Lincoln's inauguration, the Southern states seceded from the Union, foreshadowing the beginning of the Civil War in April 1861.

Author of the 1863 Emancipation Proclamation freeing Southern slaves, and the eloquent Gettysburg Address (👁see GETTYSBURG), Lincoln was elected to a second term in 1864. Although Lincoln promised «malice toward none" and "charity for all» in his inaugural speech, the president was assassinated by John Wilkes Booth on 14 April 1865, while attending a performance at Ford's Theatre in Washington, DC. General Robert E. Lee's surrender to Ulysses S. Grant at Appomattox, Virginia, had taken place just five days earlier. Back in the city, once Lincoln was brought home, 75,000 mourners filed past the president's coffin as he lay in state in the **Old State Capitol** (6th & Adams Sts., Springfield, IL). Today the man who became a myth is buried at **Lincoln's Tomb State Historic Site★** (Oak Ridge Cemetery, 1500 Monument Ave., Springfield, IL; ☎212-782-2717; www.lincolntomb.org). Springfield is located 210mi south of Chicago via I-55.

Alexander Calder, René Magritte, Joan Miró and Andy Warhol. Chicago artists represented in the collection include Ed Paschke, Leon Golub and Jim Nutt.

👥 Navy Pier★★
600 E. Grand Ave. at Lake Michigan.
✕♿🅿 ☎312-595-7437.
www.navypier.com.
Encompassing 50 acres of shops, eateries and entertainment, the pier is a bustling and festive place that draws throngs of visitors. Built in 1916 as a passenger and freight terminal, the pier also served as a naval training base and a university campus. The pier's most prominent feature is the 150ft Ferris wheel, which is illuminated at night. The **Chicago Children's Museum★** (☎312-527-1000; www.chicagochildrensmuseum.org), features interactive exhibits that invite children to have supervised fun. Local cruise and sightseeing vessels dock on the south side of the pier.

ADDITIONAL SIGHTS
Gold Coast★★
Between Oak St. & North Ave., Lake Michigan & LaSalle St.
This slice of Chicago's lakefront has been home to the city's elite for over a century. The park-like enclave is home to some of the most elegant and expensive residential property in Chicago.

While all but a few of the mansions that once lined Lake Shore Drive have been demolished, a strong late-19C ambience is well preserved along landmark **Astor Street**, where quaint Victorian town houses and graystones occupy tiny, beautifully cultivated lots.

Frank Lloyd Wright designed the **Charnley-Persky House★** (1365 N. Astor St.; ●❧visit by guided tour only; ℘312-915-0105..www.sah.org) in 1892. Chic **Oak Street Beach★★** lies at the doorstep of the Gold Coast (Lake Shore Dr. at Michigan Ave.).

© Steve Geer/iStockphoto.com

Graceland Cemetery

Lincoln Park★★

Along the lakefront, between North Ave. & Fullerton Pkwy.

This sweeping expanse is today one of Chicago's most compelling landscapes. Stretching 6mi and 1,200 acres along the shoreline, Lincoln Park trims the city's watery edge with a peaceful greenbelt, beaches, playing fields and picnic spots. Its most striking feature is **Lincoln Park Zoo★★** ♒♟ (2001 N. Clark St.; ✖&🅿 ℘312-742-2000; www. lpzoo.org), a wonderfully accessible zoo that houses more than 1,200 animals in recently renovated historic habitats and new exhibits.

Just north of Fuller-ton Parkway stands the park's newest addition, the **Peggy Notebaert Nature Museum★** (2430 N. Cannon Dr.; ℘773-755-5100; www. naturemuseum.org), an indoor-outdoor facility featuring a 2,700sq ft butterfly haven and exhibits that challenge visitors to connect with the natural world.

Graceland Cemetery★★

4001 N. Clark St. Site plan available at entrance. 🅿 ℘773-525-1105; www.gracelandcemetery.org.

One of Chicago's most beautiful and evocative sites, this 119-acre "Cemetery of Architects" (1860) contains Louis Sullivan's masterful **Getty Tomb★** (1890) as well as the Egyptian-style mastaba (1887) he designed for Martin Ryerson. Sullivan himself is buried here, as are the Potter Palmers, Marshall Field, Daniel Burnham and Ludwig Mies van der Rohe.

John Jacob Glessner House★★

1800 S. Prairie Ave. ℘312-326-1480. www.glessnerhouse.org.

Cornerstone of the **Prairie Avenue Historic District★**, Glessner House was designed for a wealthy farm-implement manufacturer by Henry Hobson Richardson in 1886. The house revolutionized domestic American architecture with its open floor plan and unadorned Romanesque facade. The **interior★** contains an abundance of Arts and Crafts detail, including a William Morris wall and tile patterns.

♒♟ Museum of Science and Industry★★★

57th St. at Lake Shore Dr.

✖&🅿(underground). ℘773-684-1414. www.msichicago.org.

This cacophonous hall of wonders is one of Chicago's most popular attractions. Since 1933, the "MSI" has occupied the only building left after the World's Columbian Exposition of 1893, designed in the grand Beaux-Arts style by Charles B. Atwood.

The complex space can be difficult to navigate efficiently, so pick up a floor plan in the Entry Hall. The museum is organized into thematic "zones" covering the human body, transportation, communication, energy and the environment, space and defense, and manufacturing.

Science Storms, Museum of Science and Industry

Among its huge vehicular treasures are the World War II German **U-505 Submarine★★★** (the only German submarine in the US), the 197ft **Pioneer Zephyr** train, and a cutaway **Boeing 727★** suspended from the second-story balcony.

On the first floor, guests "descend" into a **Coal Mine★★** for an "underground" tour. Of special appeal to children are the rides in authentic flight simulators in the **Transportation Gallery**. At **Toymaker 3000★★** you can watch a huge robotic assembly line manufacture 300 tops an hour. Furnished with more than 1,000 miniatures, the jewel-encrusted **Fairy Castle★** has running water and even electricity. Be sure to admire the **The Great Train Story★**, where a model railroad features 1,400ft of track.

New exhibits include the two-story **Science Storms**, offering the opportunity to uncover the science behind natural phenomena with the likes of a 40ft indoor "tornado," a giant movable avalanche disk, and a Tesla Coil that produces lighting charges. **You! The Experience** enables visitors to explore human health by transmitting their pulse to a 13ft virtual heart.

East of the main building, the **Henry Crown Space Center** houses an Omnimax theater as well as exhibits about space exploration, including the **Apollo 8 command module★**, the first spacecraft to circle the moon in 1968.

Intuit: The Center for Intuitive and Outside Art

756 N. Milwaukee Ave. ☏312-243-9088. www.art.org.

This was one of the country's first art institutions devoted to the works of outsider artists such as Henry Darger, Howard Finster and Sister Gertrude Morgan. Stop here to see the works of those who developed their talent independent of Classic art influences.

National Museum of Mexican Art

1852 W. 19th St. ☏312-738-1503. www.nationalmuseumofmexicanart.org.

Situated in the heart of Chicago's Pilsen neighborhood, this museum is the nation's largest Latino arts institution, boasting a collection of some 7,000 works. An interesting cross-section of temporary and permanent exhibitions gives insight into this tradition of art. A respected ethnic center as well, the museum is perhaps best known for its exhibits and programs focusing on Mexico's colorful celebration of the Day of the Dead.

Permanent collection highlights include significant works of ancient (Aztec and pre-Aztec) art, drawings by Carlos Cortez and Leopoldo Mendez, a stunning beaded mural called *New Awakening*, and an open-air plaza. Don't miss browsing in the gift shop.

Indianapolis★

The capital city of Indiana is equated in the minds of many with the Indianapolis Motor Speedway and its famous 500-mile auto race. In addition to state and federal government, the city's institutional base includes the combined campus of Indiana University/Purdue University Indianapolis. Long satirized as a boring backwater, the city today is vibrant and rich in cultural attractions.

▶ **Population:** 834,852.
◐ **Michelin Map:** 583 P 8
▌ **Info:** ☏317-639-4282; www.visitindy.com.
◖ **Location:** The city is located in the center of Indiana 185mi southeast of Chicago.
▲▲ **Kids:** Even big-city kids are impressed by the Children's Museum of Indianapolis.

A BIT OF HISTORY

The busy government and commercial center of Indianapolis had inauspicious beginnings. Named the state capital in 1825, its inaccessible location on the White River and failed Wabash and Erie Canal drew sparse settlement, even after the National Road was built, connecting Indianapolis with the East Coast before the railroads arrived in the 1830s. Railroads and the city's role as a staging point for the Civil War finally produced rapid growth after 1860.

Meat packing and agricultural trade lined the city's coffers, and in 1876 Civil War colonel Eli Lilly (1838-98) established a pharmaceutical company that remains a dominant economic and cultural force in the area. Lilly's company led the world in the production of penicillin, insulin and the polio vaccine, and the family helped create a major art museum and the nation's leading state historic preservation organization, the Historic Landmarks Foundation of Indiana.

In the early 20C, automobiles such as the Stutz, Cole and Duesenberg were made in Indianapolis. Beginning in 1911, the famed **Indianapolis 500★★★** (◐see sidebar) auto race has attracted, and continues to attract, hordes of fans to the city each year.

CITY PLAN

Conceived by Alexander Ralston, the city's original plan called for a series of streets radiating out from a central circle. Although the radial plan was never realized, **Monument Circle** still forms the focal point of downtown. Anchoring the west end of Market Street from Monument Circle, the 1888 Renaissance Revival **Indiana State House** (200 W. Washington St.; ☏317-233-5293; www.in.gov) was designed by Adolf Sherrer and Edwin May. Its restored interior features a rotunda with a **stained-glass dome.**

South of the circle, new retailers hide behind the historic façade of **Circle Centre** (49 W. Maryland St.). This two-block, four-story mall links via elevated walkways the **Indiana Convention Center** (100 S. Capitol Ave.; www.icclos.com) and the adjoining 67,000-seat **Lucas Oil Stadium,** home of the **Indianapolis Colts NFL football team.**

SIGHTS

Monument Circle★

At the intersection of Meridian & Market Sts.

Dedicated in 1902, the 284ft-high obelisk of the Indiana **Soldiers' and Sailors' Monument★★** forms the center of the circle. The limestone shaft, commemorating veterans of the Civil War, is surrounded by fountains and capped by a 38ft-high statue of Victory. Surrounding buildings curve in deference to the memorial, whose observation tower offers a **view** 231ft above the city. Others on the circle include the 1857 Gothic Revival **Christ Church Cathedral** (no. 125); the tiered wedding-cake roof of **Circle Tower;** and the temple facade of the 1916 **Hilbert Circle Theater**

Marmon "Wasp", the first car to win the Indianapolis 500, Hall of Fame Museum

Indianapolis Convention & Visitors Association; visitIndy.com

THE INDY 500

The largest single-day sporting event in the world, the Indianapolis 500 auto race was first run at the **Indianapolis Motor Speedway**★★ (4790 W. 16th St.; ✕ & 🅿 ☏317-481-8500; www.indy500.com) in 1911. Local automobile magnate Carl Fisher financed the construction of the track in 1909, and the initial race held on this 2.5mi oval (then paved with brick) consisted of two laps (5mi). A 24-hour competition was scheduled for 1910, but the following year Fisher and his partners agreed that 500mi was the ideal distance for a race. The winner of that first Indy 500 was Ray Harroun, who averaged a speed of 74.6mph (the current one-lap track speed record, set in 2007 by Tony Kanaan, is 217.728mph).

His six-cylinder Marmon Wasp along with more than 75 other racing cars are on display at the **Hall of Fame Museum**★★ (☏317-492-6784) located on the speedway infield. Classics in the collection, which are either displayed or in storage, include the 1964 Lotus, the 1969 STP Oil Treatment Special driven by Mario Andretti, and the 1977 Texaco Star driven by Janet Guthrie, the first woman Indy 500 racer. You'll also find rare and vintage cars like the 1935 Duesenberg Model JN (only three were built).

Having celebrated its 100th birthday in 2009, the speedway today attracts more than 400,000 avid fans every Memorial Day (last weekend in May) to watch 33 open-wheel racecars roar off at the sound of those famous words: "Gentlemen, start your engines."

⊙ *Grounds tours are scheduled throughout the year; information ☏317-492-6747.*

Indianapolis Motor Speedway

Eiteljorg Museum of American Indians and Western Art

(no. 45; ✆317-262-1100), home to the Indianapolis Symphony Orchestra.

Indiana War Memorials★★

From Monument Circle, a series of war memorials occupy five public plazas as you head north on Meridian Street to St. Clair Street. Beginning the procession, the square at **University Park★** (between New York & Vermont Sts.) was once a Civil War drilling ground. Just north, the **Indiana World War Memorial Plaza★★** (between Vermont & Michigan Sts.; ✆317-232-7615) centers on the Classical Memorial Building, its south steps graced by the 25ft-high bronze Pro Patria (1929, Henry Hering). Inside the building is the awe-inspiring Shrine Rooma; the lower concourse houses a military museum.

Just north, a black and gold obelisk marks **Veterans Memorial Plaza** (between Michigan & North Sts.). The last memorial on Meridian Street is the two-block-long **American Legion Mall★** (between North & St. Clair Sts.), which features a black granite cenotaph honoring Indiana's war dead. On the west side of Meridian, the massive, 1929 Gothic-style **Scottish Rite Cathedral★** (no. 650) is crowned with a 212ft tower.

James Whitcomb Riley Museum Home★★

528 Lockerbie St. ✆317-631-5885. www.rileykids.org.

Set amid the trim mid-19C Victorians of historic **Lockerbie Square** neighborhood, this never-restored 1872 home presents the actual finishes and furnishings of Magdalene and Charles Holstein. Indiana-born poet James Whitcomb Riley (1849-1916) was a houseguest here for the last 23 years of his life. The drawing room contains Riley's guitar and player piano; the library across the hall was Riley's favorite room. Upstairs, framed examples of Riley's poetry decorate the walls.

Canal Walk★

West of downtown, a residential and museum complex edged with a waterside promenade follows 1.2mi of the never-completed Wabash and Erie Canal. The canal's L shape follows West Street from St. Clair Street to Ohio Street, then angles west through **White River State Park**. The canal turns toward the White River at **Military Park** (bounded by Blackford, New York & West Sts.) and crosses a footbridge over the river to the **Indianapolis Zoo ♣♣** (1200 W. Washington St.; ✆317-630-2001; www.indyzoo.com).

Eiteljorg Museum of American Indians and Western Art★★

500 W. Washington St. ♿🅿 ✆317-636-9378. www.eiteljorg.org.

Rising above the canal like a cubic desert mesa, the contemporary 73,000sq ft museum is known for its collections of Native American and Western art.

On the first floor, the **Art of the American West Gallery** contrasts the work of early-19C artist-historians George Catlin and Albert Bierstadt with the more romantic views of Frederick Remington and Charles Russell. A highlight here is the large group of works by **Taos Society Artists** amassed by businessman and collector Harrison Eiteljorg. The Modernists Gallery contains works by Georgia O'Keefe, Robert Henri, Marsden Hartley and other modernists active in the western US in the early 20C. Second-floor galleries trace the **Art of Native America**, with strengths in Plains and Southwest Indian artifacts.

Benjamin Harrison Home★

1230 N. Delaware St. 🅿 ℰ 317-631-1888. www.presidentbenjaminharrison.org.
The nation's 23rd president, Benjamin Harrison (1833-1901) built this 1874 Italianate home during his legal career, campaigned from its front porch in 1888, returned to it in 1893 after serving one term, and died here eight years later. Harrison's office is reconstructed on the second floor. The third-floor ballroom holds changing exhibits relating to Harrison's life. A series of watercolors by Harrison's wife, Caroline, is displayed, and the museum mounts temporary historical exhibitions to round out the visit.

Indianapolis Museum of Art★★

4000 Michigan Rd. ✕ ⚷ 🅿 ℰ 317-923-1331. www.ima-art.org.
Founded in 1883, this fine institution incorporates the 1914 French Provincial **Oldfields-Lilly House & Gardens**, a 22-room mansion amid grounds landscaped by the Olmsted brothers. Inside the museum itself, three levels of galleries in three adjoining pavilions contain an impressive array of more than 54,000 works of European, American, Asian and African art dating from 600 BC to the present. The museum's main entrance brings you into the Krannert Pavilion, which displays **American art** and changing exhibits.

Upper floors hold pre-Columbian art and Asian art, 20C European art, decorative arts and Contemporary works. Highlights of the Hulman Pavilion include a collection of **Postimpressionist art★**, featuring works by Georges

Seurat, and an impressive group of 1,400-plus **African art★** objects. The Clowes Pavilion holds **Old Masters** and Renaissance art on its first floor. On the second floor, 19C English drawings and watercolors include a fine group of works by **J.M.W. Turner**, one of the largest outside of Great Britain. You won't want to miss a stroll in the adjacent **Virginia Fairbanks Art & Nature Park**, a 100-acre untamed expanse featuring site-specific works commissioned by the museum to explore the relationship between nature and contemporary art.

👥 Children's Museum of Indianapolis★

3000 N. Meridian St. ✕ ⚷ 🅿 ℰ 317-334-3322. www.childrensmuseum.org.
Exhibits in this massive, five-story structure explore myriad topics from dinosaurs to Egyptology, with plenty of spaces to create and play in. A special highlight is **ScienceWorks** (fourth floor), where kids can explore the worlds of biotechnology and scientific exploration in a fun-filled atmosphere .

EXCURSION
Conner Prairie Interactive History Park★★

◐ 6mi northeast of Indianapolis in Fishers, IN. From I-465, take Exit 35N (Allisonville Rd.). 13400 Allisonville Rd. ✕ ⚷ 🅿 ℰ 317-776-6000.
www.connerprairie.org.
A premier living-history museum, Conner Prairie comprises several distinct sections. Begin at the **Museum Center**, which displays dioramas, photos and artifacts that track 19C cultural, economic and environmental changes brought to the area by European settlers. Interpretation varies from the costumed actors at **Prairietown**, a composite 1836 Midwestern village, to the **1859 Balloon Flight**, exploring the excitement of the early days of flight with a trip up to 350ft above the prairie.. A guided tour of the Federal-style 1823 **Conner Homestead** focuses on Ohio fur trader William Conner, who lived among the local Delaware Indians for 17 years.

Detroit Area

If the lower peninsula of Michigan is shaped like a mitten, defined by lakes Erie, Huron, Michigan and St. Clair, then the Detroit metropolitan area lies at the base of the thumb, in the southeastern sector of the state. Detroit, whose name is derived from the French *d'étroit*, meaning "of the strait," spreads out in a flat semicircle from the Detroit River, which joins Lake Erie to picturesque Lake St. Clair. Across the river lies Windsor, Ontario, its huge neon casino signs reflected in the water.

Highlights

1 The microphone at the historic **Motown Records** studio (p295)

2 Architecture at **Cranbrook Educational Community** (p296)

3 Sampling rich, delicious fudge on **Mackinac Island** (p297)

4 Seeing how far we've come at the **Henry Ford Museum** (p299)

5 The pioneering **Arab American National Museum** (p299)

Motor City

Long known by the moniker "Motor City," Detroit is the birthplace of the automobile in America. **Henry Ford** (&see DEARBORN) implemented assembly-line production here, and suburban factories still crank out more cars than any other place in the US. In the early 1920s, the founding families of automobile history—among them, the **Fords**, the **Dodges** and the **Fishers**—built (or moved) their enormous mansions and factories outside city limits. In 2003 General Motors moved its corporate headquarters to the glittering Renaissance Center downtown.

Detroit Today

Today the suburbs—such as **Dearborn**, home to Ford's estate and production plants—thrive as mostly residential enclaves, while the city itself continues its efforts at revitalization, including an elevated light-rail loop (the People Mover), several large casino hotels and impressive new stadiums for the Detroit Tigers baseball team and the Detroit Lions football team. Yet, despite the concerted efforts of city officials, Detroit's economy continues to decline. In 2013, the city filed for bankruptcy (&see A BIT OF HISTORY).

The Detroit vicinity now extends north to Rochester, west to **Ann Arbor★**, home to the more than 41,000-student **University of Michigan** (founded in 1817), and east to the posh suburb of **Grosse Pointe**. Detroit proper forms the geographical center of the area: cultural attractions, ranging from the sumptuous auto-baron mansions to Henry Ford's Smithsonian-like museum to the sylvan Detroit zoo, may be up to 30mi away, and are best reached by car.

ADDRESSES

STAY

$$$$ Grand Hotel – Mackinac Island, MI. Closed Nov-Apr. ☎906-847-3331. ✕&♿☀☞ www.grandhotel.com. 385 rooms. The world's largest summer resort has been welcoming guests at the dock by horse-drawn carriage (*no cars are permitted on the island*) since 1887. The majestic white façade beckons visitors to relax on the expansive, columned front porch; strolling in the gardens and along the lakefront is sheer delight. Meals are included in several different rate packages. . Accommodations resemble summer cottages, with period antiques and cheery chintz fabrics. Tennis and golf facilities are on site; horseback riding is available nearby.

$$$ Courtyard Detroit Downtown – 333 East Jefferson Ave., Detroit, MI. ✕ 🚹 🅿 🗝 ✆313-772-7700. 260 rooms. A sleek, stylish star among downtown Detroit, Michigan hotels, the distinctive Courtyard by Marriott Detroit Downtown offers superior convenience and style opposite the GM Renaissance Center/mall and the People Mover tram. Amenities include complimentary high-speed Internet, 32-inch flat screen TVs, a state-of-the-art fitness center, indoor pool and outdoor running track.

$$$ Dearborn Inn – 20301 Oakwood Blvd., Dearborn, MI. ✕ 🚹 🅿 🗝 ✆313-271-2700. www.marriott.com. 229 rooms. A charming historic property built in 1931 on the grounds of the Ford Motor Company, this lovely brick inn has been tastefully renovated and updated with modern amenities such as flat-screen TVs, high-speed Internet access and comfortable beds. Stay in the main inn or choose one of the five Colonial-style guesthouses on the attractive grounds. If you're weekending here, don't miss brunch at the **Early American Tavern**, a favorite with locals.

$$ The Atheneum Suite Hotel – 1000 Brush Ave., Detroit, MI. ✕ 🚹 🅿 🗝 ✆313-962-2323. www.atheneumsuites.com. 174 rooms. A two-story lobby mural of Trojan War figures sets the scene for trendy Greektown's popular all-suite property. Contemporary armchairs, cherry side tables, and white ceramic urn lamps decorate the plush living quarters. Attentive service makes this the first choice for visiting celebs. Downstairs, **Fishbone's Rhythm Cafe** is a local hot spot for Cajun and Creole seafood.

⑂ EAT

$$ Streetside Seafood – 273 Pierce St., Birmingham, MI. ✆248-645-9123. www.streetsideseafood.com. **Seafood.** Fish, seafood and oysters from both coasts as well as fresh waters of the midwest headline the menu at this upscale-but-casual spot. Locals rave about the sesame-seared tuna loin, the pan-roasted salmon with lentils and especially the expertly prepared lake whitefish dishes. If fish isn't your thing, try one of the beautifully grilled steaks or chops. Save room for a slice of their famous walnut-bourbon pie.

$$$ The Hill – 123 Kercheval, Grosse Point Farms, MI. Closed Sun. ✆313-886-8101. www.thehillgrossepointe.com. **American.** This classy seafood and chophouse in upscale Grosse Pointe Farms features seafood specialties such as beautifully prepared scallops, swordfish, ahi tuna, Scottish salmon, whitefish and fresh lake perch. Alternatively, order the expertly cut, aged Midwestern steaks and chops, tantalizingly sauced and graced with imaginative vegetable sides.

$$ Slows Bar BQ – 2138 Michigan Ave., Detroit, MI. ✆313-962-9828. www.slowsbarbq.com **Regional American.** Tantalizing fragrances waft out the door of this hopping joint, where smokers turn out meats cooked Texas style (smoked brisket), Carolina style (pulled pork dressed with sauce), and St. Louis style (ribs dry-rubbed and smoked) plus baby backs, catfish and chicken. Traditional go-withs include coleslaw, mac n' cheese, blackeye peas, baked beans and potato salad.

$$ Vicente's Cuban Cuisine – 1250 Library St., Detroit. ✆314-962-8800. www.vicente.us. **Cuban.** It's a long way from Detroit to Havana, but this bustling downtown spot just blocks from Orchestra Hall shortens the distance with traditional salsa music and expertly prepared Cuban cuisine. Start with spicy empanadas or the Camarones Cubita Belle, a delectable appetizer of bacon-wrapped deep-fried shrimp, jalapeno peppers and cream cheese. The ropa vieja—seasoned shredded beef in a heady tomato sauce—and the marinated grilled pork leg are popular entrees, all served with delicious fried yucca, rice and sweet plantains.

Detroit★

Encompassing 143sq mi on the banks of Lake St. Clair, Detroit is home to a metropolitan population of 3.7 million spread over more than 6,000sq mi. Key to that growth is the automobile, Detroit's most revered product. Thanks to inventor-entrepreneurs such as Henry Ford, Ransom E. Olds, and John and Horace Dodge, the car has become the symbol of the Motor City, but Detroiters are quick to point out that despite their contributions, these men didn't build the place from scratch.

▶ **Population:** 701,745.
ℹ **Info:** ✆313-202-1800 or or 800-338-7648. www.visitdetroit.com
☺ **Don't Miss:** Detroit's remarkable public art and dramatic historic architecture; the historic Pewabic Pottery Tudor building and museum.
👪 **Kids:** Singing tour guides at the Motown Historical Museum.

A BIT OF HISTORY

There were about nine American Indian tribes in the northern Great Lakes area prior to European settlement. Detroit got its start in 1701 when **Antoine de la Mothe Cadillac** and a cadre of French soldiers, concerned about English incursions into the fur-trading industry, built a fort on the Detroit River. Indians laid siege to the fort in 1763, as part of an unsuccessful wave of attacks led by Ottawa chief **Pontiac** to regain control of North American lands. The area was placed under British rule by the Treaty of Paris until Americans claimed it at the end of the Revolutionary War in 1783.

In the early 19C, Detroit was a center of abolitionist activity, the last US stop (before Canada) on some of the **Underground Railroad** routes that conveyed escaped slaves from the South to freedom in Canada. After the Civil War ended in 1865, manufacturing became the city's chief activity. Trees, iron ore, plentiful water power and cheap trade routes made the area a choice industrial center. Beginning in 1896, Henry Ford put those resources to work building cars, and introduced assembly-line production in 1913.

During World War II, a huge influx of African Americans emigrated to Detroit from the South to work in factories converted to make war supplies. Racial tensions led to the first of the city's race riots in 1943. In July 1967, another riot resulted in 43 deaths and a fire that razed 1,300 buildings. Between 1950 and 2010 the city lost more than half its population (nearly a million people) to the suburbs. New urban renaissance projects—including major-league ballparks, gorgeously restored theaters and riverfront casinos—began to flank downtown on all sides, with the hope that they would regenerate the city center in coming years.

However in recent decades, Detroit has struggled economically due largely to

GM Renaissance Center

© Alexey Stiop/iStockphoto.com

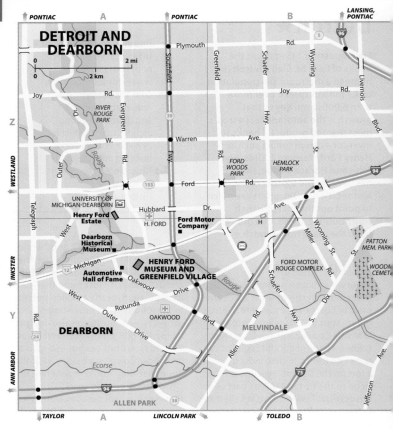

DETROIT AND DEARBORN

the withdrawal of auto production from the city, the population shift to the suburbs and resulting loss of tax revenue. In July 2013 the city filed for Chapter 9 bankruptcy protection (the largest city in US history to do so) in an effort to restructure an estimated $20 billion in long-term debt. The controversial action has left many city employees bereft of pension benefits, and will undoubtedly mire city authorities in prolonged legal proceedings for the foreseeable future.

ARCHITECTURAL ASSETS

The prosperity of the Roaring Twenties yielded several Art Deco masterpieces, including the 1929 **Guardian Building** (500 Griswold Ave.), decorated with locally made Pewabic tiles, and the 1928 **Fisher Building★** (2nd Ave. & W. Grand Blvd.) by Detroiter Albert Kahn, featur-

ing dramatic setbacks and an exquisite interior **arcade★**. Also from this era are two of the city's most prized theaters—the massive Byzantine **Fox Theatre★** (2111 Woodward Ave.; ✆313-471-3200; www.olympiaentertainment.com) and the Spanish Revival **Gem Theater** (333 Madison Ave.; ✆313-963-9800; www.gemdetroit.com)—as well as Cass Gilbert's Renaissance Revival **Detroit Public Library** (5201 Woodward Ave.; ✆313-481-1300; www.detroit.lib.mi.us). For good views of the city, ride the glass elevators to the top floor of the 73-story **Detroit Marriott Renaissance Center** (Jefferson Ave. between Brush & Beaubien Sts.).

Art admirers will find worthy works Downtown: Isamu Noguchi's doughnut-shaped *Dodge Memorial Fountain*; Marshall Frederick's *Spirit of Detroit*; and Robert Graham's *Joe Louis Fist*—at the

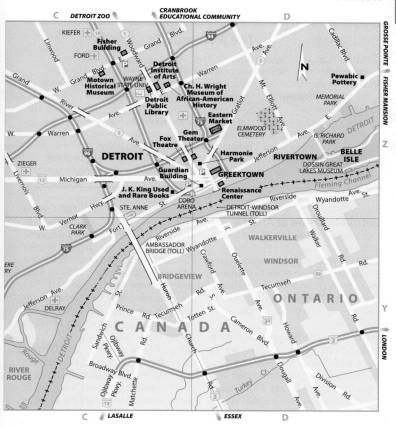

intersection of Woodward and Jefferson avenues.

Housed in a 1907 Arts and Crafts structure, **Pewabic Pottery** (10125 E. Jefferson Ave.; ✆313-626-2000, www.pewabic.org) was built for ceramicist Mary Chase Perry Stratton, whose signature iridescent-glazed architectural tiles still decorate many 1920s-era buildings. Today it's an active workshop and pottery museum with intriguing changing exhibits.

Crammed with 750,000 titles, **John K. King Used and Rare Books** (901 W. Lafayette Blvd.; ✆313-961-0622; www.rarebooklink.com) is Michigan's largest bookstore and a real treat for bibliophiles, who can spend hours in the converted former glove factory, or (for art and rare books) the old Otis Elevator building.

The **Eastern Market** (Gratiot Ave. & Russell St.; ✆313-833-9300; www.detroit-easternmarket.com), with its brightly painted Victorian sheds, draws green-grocers, craftspeople and musicians on Saturdays year-round. For nightlife, try **Greektown★** (Monroe St. between Randolph St. & I-375) with its festive cafes, restaurants and casinos. Adjacent **Harmony Park** hosts trendy restaurants.

For a diversion, drive out to **Belle Isle** (accessible via the MacArthur Bridge at E. Jefferson Ave. & E. Grand Blvd.). The latter is a 983-acre island park in the Detroit River that includes an 85ft carillon tower with computer-automated performances, a small branch of the Detroit Zoo, a, conservatory, Kids' Play Area and the Dossin Great Lakes Museum, with a fine collection of scale models of Great Lakes vessels.

The Automobile

"I think that cars today are almost the exact equivalent of the great Gothic cathedrals: I mean the supreme creation of an era, conceived with passion by unknown artists, and consumed in image if not in usage by a whole population which appropriates them as a purely magical object." *Roland Barthes, Mythologies, 1957.*

Long a symbol of freedom, style, sex appeal and wealth, the car is synonymous with the American identity. Americans own 30 percent of the world's passenger vehicles, while constituting only about 4 percent of its population. More than 90 percent of US households have at least one car; most have two. Traffic worsens and smog thickens, yet Americans persist in their love affair with the automobile.

SIGHTS
Detroit Institute of Arts★★

5200 Woodward Ave. ✗ & 🅿 ✆ 313-833-7900. www.dia.org.

Boasting a strong and meticulously displayed collection of works spanning the centuries from ancient times to the present, the Detroit Institute of Arts is one of the largest fine-arts museum in the country.

The central Renaissance Revival-style building opened in 1927; two wings were added in the 1960s and 70s, and the museum was renovated and expanded again in late 2007. Today the collection exceeds 65,000 objects spread over more than 100 galleries. Works of **American art** formed the core holdings when the institute was founded in 1883; today the American art collection forms a broad survey of paintings, sculpture, furniture and decorative arts as well as contemporary art. Other strengths of the permanent

collection include nine **18C French galleries**, which feature 200 paintings, pieces of sculpture and decorative art objects; and the General Motors Center for African American Art. In the third-floor European art galleries hang several large works by Rubens and Bruegel; the newly refurbished **modern and contemporary art galleries** contain excellent examples of nearly all the major 20C schools.

Diego Rivera's fresco cycle **Detroit Industry★★** remains the institute's pièce de résistance. Commissioned in 1932 to paint murals on two walls of what is now Rivera Court, the Mexican artist was so captivated by the grit and grace of Detroit's assembly plants that he ended up painting all four walls with a mesmerizing visual narrative exploring the relationship between humanity and technology, life and death, workers and bosses.

Detroit Industry, North wall, Diego Rivera, 1932-33, fresco

♟♙ Charles H. Wright Museum of African-American History★

315 E. Warren Ave. ✕♿🅿 ✆313-494-5800. www.thewright.org.

The world's largest institution of African-American history deals with the life and culture of African Americans from slave-trade days to the present. Wright, a local doctor, started the museum in three row houses in 1965; the present glass-domed structure was completed in 1997.

The moving, mutimedia exhibit "**And Still We Rise**" interprets 600 years of American history from an Afrocentric perspective while "**Inspiring Minds**" hones in on African-American achievements in science, technology and engineering. Art and temporary exhibits occupy other galleries.

Motown Historical Museum★

2648 W. Grand Blvd. ♿✆313-875-2264. www.motownmuseum.com.

In 1959, local African-American songwriter **Berry Gordy, Jr.** purchased this brick house and named it "Hitsville USA" in the hope that his record company, the Motown Record Corp., would make a dent in the charts. By 1966 Motown's offices occupied eight dwellings on the block and boasted performers such as the Temptations, the Supremes, Marvin Gaye, Stevie Wonder, Smokey Robinson, Gladys Knight and the Pips, the Jackson Five and others who merged gospel, pop, and rhythm-and-blues to create what became known as the Motown sound. Gordy's sister Esther transformed the house as a museum in 1985; today it contains a gallery charting Motown's success, and **Studio A**, the actual tiny recording studio where dozens of hits were made. Visitors get to test their vocal chords in that very studio, and tour guides often break into song.

Fisher Mansion

383 Lenox Ave. ✕🅿 ✆313-331-6740.

One of the few "auto baron" estates not to imitate the gray stone manors of England, this extravagant Mediterranean-style villa was designed in 1928 by C. Howard Crane for **Lawrence P. Fisher**, founder of the Fisher Body Co. and general manager of Cadillac Motors.

The mansion, now owned by the International Society for Krishna Consciousness, is filled with Vedic art.

EXCURSIONS

Edsel & Eleanor Ford House★

▶ 8mi east of Detroit in Grosse Pointe Shores. Take E. Jefferson Rd./Lake Shore Rd. to 1100 Lake Shore Rd. ✕🅿 ✆313-884-4222. www.fordhouse.org.

The only child of Henry Ford and Clara Bryant, Edsel Ford was an avid art collector and built this house for his family as well as their growing collection of fine artworks, most of which they later donated to the Detroit Institute of Arts. Completed in 1929, the dwelling was designed by Detroit architect Albert Kahn to resemble an English country manor. Its 60 richly appointed rooms feature dark wood paneling, decorative plaster ceilings and leaded glass. The Modern Rooms, however, were streamlined in the 1930s by Walter Dorwin Teague to include polished wood veneers and Art Deco furniture. Acclaimed landscape architect Jens Jensen designed the beautiful grounds fringing the shoreline of Lake St. Clair.

♟♙ Detroit Zoo★

▶ 10mi north of Detroit in Royal Oak. Take I-75 and I-696 to Exit 16 (Woodward Ave.) and follow signs to 8450 W. 10 Mile Rd. ✕🅿 ✆248-398-0900. www.detroitzoo.org.

This zoo was one of the first in the country to feature open, natural environments for its animals. Loop trails and a miniature train wind amid its 125 park-like acres, home to 3,300 mammals, birds and reptiles. Habitats include the four-acre **Arctic Ring of Life** (one of the largest polar-bear exhibits in the world) and the new **National Amphibian Conservation Center**. Inside a renovated 1928 glass-domed bird house, the **Wildlife Interpretive Gallery** incorporates

Arctic Ring of Life Polar Passage, Detroit Zoo

a butterfly garden, an aquarium, and the **Science on a Sphere** environmental phenomena display.

Cranbrook Educational Community★★

▶ 17mi north of Detroit in Bloomfield Hills. Take I-75 North to I-696 West. Exit Woodward Ave. North to 39221 N. Woodward Ave. ✕⎙🅿 ☏877-462-7262. www.cranbrook.edu.

Longtime art collectors and philanthropists George Gough Booth and Ellen Scripps Booth used the fortune they earned in the newspaper business to found this 315-acre multipurpose art community in the 1920s. The stunning campus was conceived as a "total work of art" by Booth and Finnish-American architect **Eliel Saarinen** (1873-1950), who presided over the Cranbrook Academy of Art. The campus has structures by Albert Kahn, Tod Williams and Billie Tsien; sculptor Carles Milles. Saarinen's bold **peristyle** (1942) forms the focal point of the campus. It joins the library with the **art museum★**, which contains works by generations of Cranbrook faculty and students and outstanding examples of 20C and 21C contemporary art and design. The **Saarinen House★★** (👁visit by guided tour only), designed in 1927 by the architect for his family, has been meticulously renovated to appear as it did during the architect's tenure here. Also on campus is the **Cranbrook Institute of Science★** 👥, a science and natural history museum with excellent temporary exhibits drawn from a permanent collection of some 200,000 artifacts.

Cranbrook House and Gardens★

380 Lone Pine Rd., adjacent to campus. ☏248-645-3147.

Designed for the Booths by Albert Kahn in 1908, this pristine English manor features excellent examples of decorative arts from the Arts and Crafts Movement. Don't miss the 40-acre **gardens★★**, with their formal terraces sweeping down toward the forested rim of the Cranbrook campus.

Meadow Brook Hall

▶ 25mi north of Detroit on the east campus of Oakland University in Rochester, MI. Take I-75 to Exit 79 East (University Dr.) to the university's main entrance; turn left at Squirrel Rd. Turn left on Walton Blvd., right on Adams Rd., then right at east campus entrance and follow signs. 480 South Adams Rd. ⎙🅿 ☏248-269-7672. www.meadowbrookhall.org.

This 110-room, 88,000sq ft Tudor Revival-style pile was completed in 1929 for **Matilda Dodge**, widow of automotive giant **John Dodge**, and her second husband, Alfred G. Wilson. Inspired by English country manors, it boasts 24 fireplaces, exquisite architectural detailing and original family furnishings. Within the grounds stands redbrick **Knole Cottage**, a playhouse for Matilda's daughter.

Dearborn★

A southwestern suburb of Detroit, Dearborn is best known as the former home of industrialist Henry Ford and as the headquarters and main assembly plants of the Ford Motor Company, which form the city's economic base.

▶ **Population:** 96,474.

▪ **Info:** Detroit Metro Convention and Visitors Bureau ℰ313-202-1800, 800-338-7648; www.visitdetroit.com

🅿 **Parking:** This is Motor City USA: there is plenty of parking wherever you go.

A BIT OF HISTORY

The area was inhabited by Wyandot Indians when European colonists settled here in 1701. Dearborn was the site of the US Arsenal from 1833 to 1875; two of the original buildings—the Commandant's Quarters and the McFadden-Ross House are now preserved as the **Dearborn Historical Museum** (21950 Michigan Ave. & 915 Brady St.; ℰ313-565-3000; www.thedhm.com). Incorporated in 1927, the city is home to many Ford workers and executives, and students who attend the University of Michigan at Dearborn, established in 1959 on 200 acres gifted by Ford Motor Company.

SIGHTS

Henry Ford Estate (Fair Lane)★

4901 Evergreen Rd., on University of Michigan-Dearborn campus. Mansion is closed for restoration. ✕🅿 ℰ313-593-5590. www.henryfordestate.org.

This 56-room, English-style mansion, made of rough-hewn Ohio limestone with a crenellated roofline and turret, set the opulent standard for "auto baron" dwellings. Built for Henry Ford and his wife, Clara, in 1915, the house is decorated with roseleaf mahogany paneling, silver chandeliers and hand-

Mackinac Island: Fudge and Gingerbread

From Detroit, a day's drive north along the shore of Lake Huron via Route 25 and US-23 brings you to tiny **Mackinac Island★**, which lies between Michigan's Upper and Lower Peninsulas where lakes Huron and Michigan meet. Only 8.3mi around, Mackinac (pronounced MAK-i-naw) has a remarkably rich history and flourishes today as a carefree retreat. Its location at the intersection of lakes and land made the MacKinac Island a gathering place for Native Americans who called it *Michilimackinack*, or "Great Turtle," for its shape. When the British built **Fort Mackinac** atop its bluff in 1779, the island eclipsed other nearby settlements as a center of fur trading and military importance.

A host of historic sites, including the fort and several museums, recall the island's early days, but it was the rush of tourism in the mid-1800s that really made it famous. Indeed, its lavish Victorian architecture, horse-drawn vehicles, and quiet ways still echo a bygone era. Venerable hostelries, the regal 1887 **Grand Hotel** (see Addresses) topping the list, and abundant bed and breakfasts occupy lovely gingerbread gems. The absence of cars on the island ensures a leisurely pace, and the north woods air is clear and clean. If at times the crush of summer day visitors—called "fudgies" after the island's scrumptious specialty—grows thick around the harbor, a bicycle ride to the island's breezy north shore or wooded interior makes an easy escape.

You can reach Mackinac Island by passenger ferry from Mackinaw City or St. Ignace (Arnold Transit Co., ℰ906-847-3351, www.arnoldline.com; Shepler's Mackinac Island Ferry, ℰ231-436-5023, www.sheplersferry.com; or Star Line, ℰ906-643-7635, www.mackinacferry.com). Mackinac Island Tourism Bureau, ℰ906-847-3783 or www.mackinac.com.

HENRY FORD

The man who revolutionized factory production was born one of eight children to an Irish immigrant farmer in Greenfield, Michigan, in 1863. At the age of 16, Ford dropped out of school and took a job as a machinist's apprentice in Detroit. Three years later, he returned to his family's farm and tinkered with building his own engines when not working part time for the Westinghouse Engine Company. Ford married Clara Bryant in 1888 and moved back to the city, where he secured a position as chief engineer at the Detroit Edison Company plant. Having completed his first "horseless carriage" by 1896, Ford and his backers started the Detroit Automobile Company in 1898. In 1903 he formed the Ford Motor Company, whose **Model T**—"a motor car for the great multitude," as Ford called it—was an instant success when it was launched in 1908.

In 1913 Ford incorporated an assembly-line method of production in his new plant that turned out a complete chassis every 93 minutes—a significant improvement over the 840 minutes previously required. Improvements in mass-production techniques eventually enabled Ford's plant to produce a Model T every 24 seconds. The societal revolution brought about by mass production of the automobile was buoyed by the fact that Ford offered his workers wages that were nearly double the industry standard, enabling his employees to purchase the very products they made. After Ford died at home in April 1947, his only child, Edsel Bryant Ford, assumed presidency of the company. Edsel's son, Henry Ford II, took over as company president in 1945 (he died in 1987). Today Henry Ford's great-grandsons Edsel B. Ford II and William Clay Ford, Jr. serve on the company's board of directors and his great-great-granddaughter Elena Ford is a company Vice President.

Edsel (left) and Henry (right) Ford with a Ford V8 engine

carved woodwork★. A tunnel containing 35mi of pipes connects the house to a six-story powerhouse★ contrived by Ford and his friend Thomas Edison (1847-1931) to make Fair Lane self-sufficient for electricity and heat. The 72-acre estate grounds contain fine examples of landscape art.

🧍‍♂️ Henry Ford Museum and Greenfield Village★★★

20900 Oakwood Blvd. ✕🚶♿🅿
☎313-982-6001. www.hfmgv.org.
Sprawled over nearly 100 acres, this complex constitutes the world's largest indoor-outdoor museum.
Ford founded the museum and village in 1929 to "show how far and fast we have come" in terms of technological advancement. Today holdings include more than a million objects and 25 million historic papers spanning three centuries.

Henry Ford Museum★★★

Fronted by a replica of Philadephia's Independence Hall, the museum resembles a colossal (12acres) automobile factory within and presents a veritable treasure trove of Americana. The museum's most popular exhibit, "The Automobile in American Life and Society"aa, tells the story of the car's evolution and how it has changed the world. More than 150 cars and trucks are displayed, from the last remaining 1896 Duryea (American's first production car) to the classic 1959 Cadillac Eldorado convertible. Another large exhibit, "With Liberty and Justice for All", explores the evolution of American freedom, and incorporates the bus upon which Rosa Parks made her famed stand for civil rights. Be sure to visit the newest permanent exhibit "Heroes of the Sky," honoring the entrepreneurs, explorers and inventors who launched air travel and adventure; original and replica aircraft include the Spirit of St. Louis and the Wright flyer.
Around these exhibits lie row upon row of fascinating objects, from the historic (the theater seat in which President Abraham Lincoln was assassinated) to the hilarious (the Oscar Mayer Wienermobile).

Greenfield Village★★

Henry Ford uprooted more than 83 historic structures from all over the country and plopped them down in his idealized village in an effort to preserve the way of life that, ironically, disappeared with the birth of Ford's Model T.
Among the buildings designed to illustrate the work of famous people are Ford's own humble birthplace; the Wright Brothers' home and one of their four bicycle shops from Dayton, Ohio, in which they performed experiments leading to the first successful airplane flight; Thomas Edison's Menlo Park laboratory★, where nearly 400 inventions originated in New Jersey; and the 1823 house where Noah Webster wrote the American Dictionary of the English Language. Don't miss the daily demonstrationsa by tinsmiths, glassblowers, printers and weavers; or the chance to ride in an authentic Model T.

🧍‍♂️ Automotive Hall of Fame

21400 Oakwood Blvd. ♿🅿☎313-240-4000; www.automotivehalloffame.org)
This showcase for the history of automobiles and the accomplishments of the automotive industry's movers and shakers boasts a welter of interactive exhibits, including a crankable Model T Ford and a hands-on assembly line.

Arab American National Museum

13624 Michican Ave. 🅿☎313-582-2266. www.arabamericanmuseum.org.
Opened in 2005, this Smithsonian-affiliated museum uses art, artifacts and documents in thoughtful displays to illustrate the history, culture and experiences of Arab Americans, and to promote understanding of this diverse ethnic group. The second-floor gallery features Making an Impact, an interactive permanent exhibit detailing the stories and contributions of prominent Arab Americans, including Ralph Nader, journalist Helen Thomas and racing legend Bobby Rahal.

Milwaukee Area

The hub of the US Socialist movement in the first half of the 20C, Milwaukee is a modern Midwestern city that bears the marks of its no-nonsense, hard-working German character—an industrial center that today prides itself on its clean streets and clean politics. The city is set on the shore of Lake Michigan in the southeastern corner of Wisconsin, 90mi north of Chicago.

Highlights

1 Milwaukee's triumverate of fine lakefront museums: **Discovery World**, the **Public Museum** and the **Art Museum** (p303)

2 Sampling cheese and sausage at **Usinger's** (p303)

3 Touring a **brewery** and then sampling some of its products (p304)

4 **Taliesin**—an architecture buff's utopia (p307)

Ancient Cultures

Ancient mound builders here decorated the land with effigies of birds, animals and human forms between 700 and 1300 AD. In more modern times, Menominee, Chippewa, Fox, Sauk, Winnebago and Potawatomi tribes wandered the area to hunt and fish. Searching for a Northwest Passage to Asia, French explorers combed Wisconsin in the 1600s, beginning with **Jean Nicolet**, who landed at Green Bay in 1634. Ceded to Britain under the terms of the Treaty of Paris in 1763, Wisconsin was largely ignored as "Indian country," until the American government organized these lands as part of the Indiana Territory in 1800. Wisconsin became the 30th state in 1848, with Madison as its capital and Milwaukee a budding center for grain trading.

Area Attractions

Today the Milwaukee area offers much beyond the cultural attractions of the city. To the north, Door County peninsula provides a waterside respite along its shores. Madison, 77mi west, combines the governmental bustle of a state capital with the college-town atmosphere created by the University of Wisconsin. North of Madison, **The Dells★** (52mi north via Rte. 12) are layered limestone cliffs carved by glacial melt into a 7mi section of the Wisconsin River. West of Madison in Spring Green sits Taliesin, Frank Lloyd Wright's famous home and studio.

ADDRESSES

STAY

$$$ The Pfister Hotel – 424 E. Wisconsin Ave., Milwaukee, WI. ✕⚐🅿️⚒ ☎414-273-8222. www.thepfisterhotel.com. 307 rooms. East downtown's oldest property (1893) remains the city's grande dame. A hand-painted mural of the azure sky, with cherubs and garlands, decorates the lobby's three-story ceiling. The world's largest hotel collection of Victorian paintings adorns the public areas. Bedrooms, updated in luxurious style, are done in florals, with walnut armoires and crystal lamps.

Milwaukee Art Museum

© Milwaukee Art Museumaa

$$ Hotel Metro – 411 E. Mason St., Milwaukee, WI. ✕♿🅿✆414-272-1937. www.hotelmetro.com. 63 suites. An all-suite Art Deco landmark in east downtown that offers loft-like, pet-friendly guest quarters averaging 640sq ft. Bamboo floors, hand-woven Tibetan rugs and contemporary furnishings update the look. Stylish **Metro** restaurant offers enticing breakfast and lunch specials; Friday brings a classic Midwestern fish fry.

$$ Knickerbocker on the Lake – 1028 E. Juneau Ave., WI. ✕🅿✆414-276-8500. www.knickerbockeronthelake.com. 67 rooms. This beautifully restored 1929 National Register hotel is located in a quiet residential area five blocks from the art museum. Each of the guest rooms and suites is uniquely decorated and come with a fully equipped kitchen or kitchenette, which includes a microwave, stove, refrigerator and coffee maker The hotel has retained much of the original charm in the lobby with vaulted ceilings, crystal chandeliers, and the original terrazzo floors; modern amenities include digital cable and high-speed Internet access. A number of suites provide panoramic views of Milwaukee and Lake Michigan. The **Knick** restaurant is critically acclaimed.

$$ Radisson Hotel Madison – 517 Grand Canyon Drive, WI. ✕♿🅿🛏☐ ✆608-833-0100. www.radisson.com/madisonwi. 153 rooms. Located in the heart of Madison's Westside shopping district, minutes from Madison city center, the newly renovated Radisson Hotel Madison offers facilities such as an indoor pool, fitness center and restaurant. Many rooms have Sleep Number beds, allowing guests to adjust air chambers in the mattress to find the optimum combination of comfort, firmness and support.

$$ White Lace Inn – 16 N. 5th Ave., Sturgeon Bay, WI. ♿🅿☐✆920-743-1105. www.whitelaceinn.com. 18 rooms. Four early-20C houses connected by winding garden paths make up this romantic B&B, just two blocks from downtown Sturgeon Bay. Accommodations are whimsically designed with Laura Ashley chintz,

and antique four-poster beds with lace canopies. Most rooms have whirlpools and/or fireplaces.

🍴/EAT

$$ Karl Ratzsch's Old World Restaurant – 320 E. Mason St., Milwaukee, WI. Closed Sun. ✆414-276-2720. www.karlratzsch.com. **German.** Family favorites have been served here since 1904. Dark walnut panels, beamed ceilings and stag-horn chandeliers make the downtown locale feel like a hunting lodge. Beer comes to the table in traditional steins. Perfectly turned-out German culinary stalwarts headline the menus here, including roast goose, sauerbraten with potato dumplings, and wienerschnitzel with spätzle. German apple pancakes and Viennese delights such as fruit and chocolate tortes headline the dessert menu.

$$ Sardine – 617 Williams St., Madison, WI. Dinner and Sat–Sun brunch only. ✆608-441-1600. www.sardinemadison.com. **French and American**. This spacious French bistro edges Lake Monona. The dining room's floor-to-ceiling windows and the outdoor patio provide patrons with splendid views of the water. Fish and meat dishes include entrées such as roasted sole and seared whitefish or steak frites and duck à l'orange. The menu's house-made cavatelli is a signature pasta here. The weekend brunch and restaurant bar are popular draws.

$ Elsa's on the Park – 833 N. Jefferson St., Milwaukee, WI. ✆414-765-0615. www.elsas.com. **American.** Milwaukee's people-watching haunt sits across from Cathedral Square. Visiting celebrities, sports pros and occasionally a former President stop in for pork-chop sandwiches and the specialty half-pound burgers with baskets of waffle fries (called "eight fries"). Choose from six exotic variations of burger or opt for the house favorite with American, Swiss, white Cheddar and Colby cheeses, large salads, hearty soups, or filling chicken sandwiches from the "Chicken Monday" menu. Cocktails are served until at least 2am every night in the bustling bar. The quirky decor changes every few months.

Milwaukee★★

Defined by the Milwaukee, Menominee and Kinnickinnic rivers, the city of Milwaukee was chartered in 1846. Before the Europeans arrived, Indians lived on the natural abundance of this area, with its fish-filled waters and hardwood forests, prompting the local Chippewa to name it *Millioki*, meaning "gathering place by the waters."

▶ **Population:** 598,916.

Info: Visit Milwaukee. ℰ414-273-7222; www.milwaukee.org.

Location: Less than two hours north of Chicago.

Don't Miss: The Pfister Hotel lobby, even if you have other accommodations.

Kids: See sea-lion shows and take camel rides at the Milwaukee County Zoo.

A BIT OF HISTORY

Nascent Milwaukee comprised three settlements divided by the Milwaukee River. In the 1830s Montreal fur trader **Solomon Juneau** and his partner, lawyer Morgan L. Martin, laid claim to most of the land on the east side of the river (Juneautown), while the west side (Kilbourntown) was secured by Connecticut engineer **Byron Kilbourn**. In 1849 Virginian **George Walker** purchased the land on the south side of the settlement, naming it Walker's Point. Today, **Historic Walker Point** includes a collection of late-19C landmarks on National Avenue (between 5th & 6th Sts.).

Rivalry between the early east- and westside settlements proved intense. Attempting to cut each other off from municipal services, Juneau and Kilbourn laid out their streets so that they did not meet at the river, thus posing an obstacle to bridge construction. The city's population increased between 1840 and 1860, bolstered mainly by immigrants—who made up half of Milwaukee's population by 1860.Germans became the dominant group in 19C Milwaukee, proving to be a significant political force into the 20C. German brewing traditions, supported by grain and hops from the state's central grain-growing region, made Milwaukee America's beer capital. By the late 19C, access to rail and water transportation and the availability of cheap and abundant raw materials catapulted Milwaukee to the forefront of industry.

Door County

120mi north of Milwaukee. For information, contact the Door County Visitor Bureau: P.O. Box 406, Sturgeon Bay, WI 54235, ℰ920-743-4456, www.doorcounty.com.

Consisting of a finger of land that separates Green Bay from Lake Michigan, Door County takes its name from French explorers, who called the treacherous water passage at the peninsula's tip "Death's Door." Anchored by **Green Bay** at the base of the peninsula and by Washington Island 6mi off the northern tip, Door County attracts a steady stream of tourists who transform the peninsula into a midwestern Cape Cod each summer. Routes 42 and 57 outline the peninsula, merging at **Sturgeon Bay** (38mi north of Green Bay), the commercial center of Door County. North of Sturgeon Bay, you can explore tiny scenic fishing villages with names such as Sister Bay, Egg Harbor, Fish Creek, Ephraim and Ellison Bay. Ferries (Island Clipper, ℰ920-854-2972; www.islandclipper.com; and Washington Island Ferry, ℰ920-847-2546; www.wisferry.com) depart from Northport on the tip of the peninsula for recreational **Washington Island**, settled by Icelandic fishermen more than a century ago. The Rock Island Ferry (ℰ800-223-2094) leaves Washington Island for secluded **Rock Island State Park** (ℰ920-847-2235), a 912-acre nature preserve.

THE CITY TODAY

Milwaukee nurtures the performing arts downtown, staging ballet, symphony and Broadway shows in a variety of venues, including the restored Renaissance Revival **Pabst Theater**★ (144 E. Wells St.; ☎414-286-3663; www.pabsttheater.org), designed in 1895 by Otto Strack.

Acres of parks ring the city, and west of downtown, **Marquette University** (Wisconsin Ave. & 11th St.) provides an institutional anchor.

Milwaukee's Miller Park is home to the National League **Brewers** baseball team. The city also claims the **Bucks** NBA basketball team, and the International Hockey League's **Admirals**.

Beginning in late June each year, the city hosts the renowned 11-day music festival called **Summerfest**, the world's largest music fest, in Henry W. Maier Festival Park on the shores of Lake Michigan, where nationally known acts draw thousands of music buffs (www.summerfest.com). The lakeshore is lined with several parks, all boasting glorious views of sparkling Lake Michigan.

DOWNTOWN

Historically the center of government and finance, the east side remains Milwaukee's business center. It is bounded on the south by the renovated warehouse lofts, design studios and antique shops of the **Historic Third Ward** (home to Milwaukee's 19C Irish immigrants) and on the north by the tony residential Yankee Hill and **Historic Brady Street**—a one-time Italian neighborhood that has evolved into a strip of boutiques, restaurants and coffeehouses. The 200 block of East Michigan Street reveals 19C Milwaukee in the Second Empire roofline of the **Mitchell Building** (no. 207) and the adjacent **Mackie Building**★ (no. 225). The second floor of the Mackie Building houses the nation's first trading pit, the ornate Grain Exchange Rooma. Farther east on Wisconsin Avenue, the 1899 **Federal Building**★ (nos. 515-19) is a landmark with its tall central tower and limestone facade. Atop the 1930 Art Deco **Wisconsin Gas Company Building** (no. 626), the flame

finial glows red for warm weather, gold for cold, and blue for no change; it flickers for rain or snow.

On the west side of the river, characterized by its cultural and commercial attractions, **Old World Third Street**★ (1000 & 1100 blocks of 3rd St.) preserves the city's German heritage (you can still select the best of the wurst at **Usinger's Famous Sausage shop**; 1030; ☎414-276-9105; www.usingers.com).

Milwaukee Art Museum★★

700 N. Art Museum Dr.; entrance on lake side. ♿🅿 ☎414-224-3200. www.mam.org.

The museum's original block-like concrete structure was designed by Eero Saarinen in 1957. In 2001 the gallery spaces were renovated and the museum added the eye-catching Quadracci Pavilion topped by a sail-like retractable sunscreen designed by Santiago Calatrava. Spanning civilizations from ancient Egypt to the present, its 25,000-piece collection shines in 19C European art, German Expressionism and 20C American painting and sculpture. The **Flagg Galleries** hold significant Medieval and Renaissance religious artworks. The mezzanine level displays a large collection of **Haitian art**. On the upper level, the Bradley Collection contains a prized group of **20C European and American art**★; nearby, cubical **lake overlooks** set with modern sculptures are framed by the lake's horizon.

Milwaukee Public Museum★★

800 W. Wells St. ☎414-278-2728. www.mpm.edu.

The 1963 Milwaukee Public Museum features excellent permanent exhibits including the walk-through Streets of Old Milwaukee, The Third Planet (which explores plate tectonics) and the Puelicher Butterfly Wing, both on the museum's first floor.

🧍‍♂️🧍 Discovery World★

500 N. Harbor Dr. ☎414-765-9966; www.discoveryworld.org.

Housed in a building on the lakeshore, the museum is jammed with interac-

BEER IN MILWAUKEE

The foundation of Milwaukee's early economy, beer has played a defining role in Milwaukee's history. Though the city is no longer the official brewing capital, brewing continues to define its cultural identity. Started in 1840 by three Welshmen, the city's first brewery produced ale and porter, both English-style top-fermentation beers. Light golden lager, a bottom-fermentation beer, was introduced to the city the following year. Milwaukee's port location, combined with a profusion of local barley and hops, fostered a vibrant beer industry, dominated by such giants as Blatz (1846-1959), Pabst (since 1844), Schlitz (1849-1981) and Miller (since 1855). By the 1880s, Milwaukee boasted more than 80 breweries.

Prohibition devastated the smaller breweries, however, and post-war consolidation left **Miller Brewing Company** (4000 W. State St.; ♿🅿️📞414-931-2337; www.millercoors.com) as the one large brewer in Milwaukee. Today merged with Coors Brewing Co., it still operates from the site its founder purchased in 1855. Tours begin in the visitor center and take in the bottling and packaging operations and the **brewhouse**, where rows of massive copper kettles boil hundreds of barrels at a time. Before leaving, visitors can sample the company's products in the 1892 Miller Inn or beer garden.

Begun in reaction to the mass-market approach of large beer companies, the modern microbreweries revive historic brewing methods and the distinctive quality of regional beer. **Sprecher Brewery** (701 W. Glendale Ave., Glendale; reservations required; ♿🅿️📞414-964-2739; www.sprecherbrewery.com) was the bellwether in Milwaukee (since 1985). Visitors here learn how the company's single brew kettle turns out products ranging from Imperial stout to root beer—although its output is literally a drop in Miller's bucket.

Located in a former power plant, **Lakefront Brewery** (1872 N. Commerce St.; ♿🅿️📞414-372-8800; www.lakefrontbrewery.com) offers informative and laid-back tours of their brewing process, which includes seasonal brews and such innovations as cherry beer (made with Door County cherries), organic beer and gluten-free beer.

Miller Brewing Company

© Milwaukee Convention & Visitors Bureau

tive exhibits that open up the worlds of science and technology, and incorporates an aquarium with a walk-through tank. Summer brings a replicated 1837 schooner to the harbor outside.

ADDITIONAL SIGHTS

Charles Allis Art Museum★

1801 N. Prospect Ave. ℘414-278-8295. www.cavtmuseums.org.

Housed in the 1911 Tudor-style mansion where Charles Allis, the first president of Milwaukee's Allis-Chalmers Company, once lived, this museum is known for its **Asian porcelains**, French and American painting, and original decorative arts displayed in the mansion's living spaces.

Villa Terrace Decorative Arts Museum★

2220 N. Terrace Ave. ℘414-271-3656. www.cavtmuseums.org.

This 1923 **mansion** was modeled after a 16C Northern Italian villa. Cypress-beamed ceilings and a courtyard adorn the interior, while outside, terraces cascade down toward Lake Michigan and end in a formal garden. The collection includes paintings, furnishings and decorative arts from the 15C to the 18C.

Pabst Mansion★★

2000 W. Wisconsin Ave. ⅌ 🅿 ℘414-931-0808. www.pabstmansion.com.

A remnant of Milwaukee's grand days as America's beer capital, the elegant 37-room Flemish Renaissance Revival-style mansion (1892), with its terra-cotta ornamentation, was the home of the German-born Great Lakes steamship captain **Frederick Pabst** (1836-1904). In 1864 Pabst joined the brewery business of his father-in-law, Phillip Best, and took over the operations nine years later. Tours begin on the east side of the house in the Neoclassical domed **beer pavilion**, a relic of the 1893 World's Columbian Exposition in Chicago, where Pabst won the blue ribbon that still serves as the logo for the company's beer. Inside the mansion, the French Rococo **ladies' parlor** is balanced by the masculine **music room** with its heavy oak furniture.

Mitchell Park Horticultural Conservatory★

524 S. Layton Blvd. 🅿 ℘414-257-5600. www.milwaukeedomes.org.

Three parabolic domes support plant life from a specific ecosystem. The **Desert Dome** shelters cacti, succlents and arid bulbs. The jungly **Tropical Dome** features exotic flora from rain forests on five continents. Colorful floral displays change seasonally in the **Show Dome**.

♁♁ Milwaukee County Zoo★★

10001 W. Bluemound Rd.
From downtown, follow I-94 West to US-45 North and take Exit 39/ Bluemound Rd. ✕⅌🅿 ℘414-771-3040. www.milwaukeezoo.org.

In this sprawling 200-acre zoo, more than 2,000 animals occupy layered outdoor environments that place predators behind prey: Jaguars and South American alpaca, Amur tigers and camels, African lions and zebras.

Harley Davidson Museum

400 W. Canal St. ✕ ⅌🅿 ℘414-343-7850. www.harley-davidson.com.

America's only remaining motorcycle maker began in a Milwaukee shed in 1903 and still assembles its distinctive "V" twin-cam engines north of the city. This museum highlights the role of Harley "hogs" in American pop culture, with vehicles and memorabilia galore.

EXCURSION

Annunciation Greek Orthodox Church★★

⊙ 9400 W. Congress St. 22mi northwest of Milwaukee in Wauwatosa, WI. Take I-94 West to US-45 North and exit at Capital Dr. East; follow Capital Dr. to 92nd St. North. 🅿 ℘414-461-9400. www.annunciationwi.org.

One of architect Frank Lloyd Wright's last works (1961), this blue dome rising above a ring of eyelid windows resembles a flying saucer. The arched entrance is fronted by a saucer-shaped fountain, and space age ornamentation fills the sanctuary.

Madison★

Considered one of America's most livable small cities, Madison owes its existence to Judge James Doty, who moved Wisconsin's capital to the mile-wide isthmus between lakes Mendota and Monona in 1836, thus enhancing his real-estate holdings. Today some 40,000 students who attend the University of Wisconsin at Madison, which covers 932 acres on the shore of Lake Mendota west of downtown, help support the capital city's vibrant arts and entertainment scene.

▶ **Population:** 240,323.
🛈 **Info:** ℘608-255-2537; www.visitmadison.com.
🅿 **Parking:** Scrap the wheels and walk the picture-perfect downtown streets.
😋 **Don't Miss:** Taliesin, the quintessential Frank Lloyd Wright.
👪 **Kids:** Learn a condiment song at the National Mustard Museum.

SIGHTS
Wisconsin State Capitol★★

2 E. Main St. ♿🅿 ℘608-266-0382. www.wisconsin.gov.
The capitol's towering Beaux-Arts-style white Vermont-granite dome, designed by New York architects George B. Post & Sons in 1906, is one of the largest in the world by volume. Four massive temple facades front the capitol building, the dome of which is capped at 200ft by Daniel Chester French's 15ft bronze, **Wisconsin**. Step inside for a breathtaking look at 43 types of stone, glass mosaics and the soaring rotunda. Guided tours take in the Venetian **Gov-**

Aerial view of Wisconsin State Capitol

© James Bushelle/Dreamstime.com

ernor's Conference Room, the marble **Supreme Court chamber★★** and the **Assembly chamber★**.
On the west side of Capitol Square, two museums commemorate the state's history: the **Wisconsin State Historical Museum★** (30 Carroll St.; ℘608-264-6555; www.wisconsinhistory.org) and the **Wisconsin Veterans Museum★** (30 W. Mifflin St.; ℘608-267-1799; www.wisvets-museum.com). **State Street★** (closed to automobile traffic), links the capitol to the university campus via restaurants, shops and galleries.
Two blocks from the capitol, John Nolen Drive follows smaller Lake Monona to the south, passing the curving white facade of **Monona Terrace Community and Convention Center★** (1 John Nolen Dr; www.mononaterrace.com). The center's Frank Lloyd Wright design was not realized until 1996, half a century after his death, by Anthony Puttnam and Taliesin Architects. Its curving terrace repeats the form of the windows while offering lovely lake **views★**.

Unitarian Meeting House★★
900 University Bay Dr. ♿🅿 ℘608-233-9774. www.fusmadison.org.
A triangular prow of glass slicing through a hillside on a residential street announces this late work (1951) by Frank Lloyd Wright. Metal roof overhangs cramp the entry, initiating a passage that sweeps dramatically upward into the sanctuary, suggesting "the wings of a bird in flight."

Chazen Museum of Art★★

750 University Ave. ♿ ℰ608-263-2246. www.chazen.wisc.edu.

This excellent collection is arranged on three floors around a central skylit court and in an adjacent, expanded facility completed in 2011. Holdings range from ancient Greek vases to 19C American and European paintings. There's also a wonderful selection of early-20C works (Georgia O'Keeffe, Grant Wood, Alexander Calder). Contemporary art is the focus of the bright fourth floor.

EXCURSIONS

♟♙ Circus World Museum★★

◑ 40mi north of Madison in Baraboo, WI. Take I-90/94 West and exit on Rte. 33 West toward Baraboo; in Baraboo, take Rte. 113 South and follow signs. ✕♿🅿 ℰ608-356-8341. www.circusworld. wisconsinhistory.org.

Fifty acres of exhibits surround the historic winter quarters of the Ringling Brothers, whose 1884 Baraboo circus became the nation's largest circus company—the "Greatest Show on Earth." The biggest collection of circus artifacts in the world conveys the bombast and showmanship of these traveling extravaganzas through circus posters, costumes and reconstructed spectacles.

Taliesin★★★

◑ 35mi west of Madison. Take US-14 West to Rte. 23 South through Spring Green and cross the Wisconsin River to 5607 County Rd. C. ✕♿🅿 ℰ608-588-7900. www.taliesinpreservation.org.

Renowned architect **Frank Lloyd Wright** (1867-1959), born in nearby Richland Center, returned in 1911 to build Taliesin (Welsh for "shining brow") as his home. Wright eventually began an atelier here, and the 600-acre complex still welcomes Taliesin fellows to study in the countryside that fostered the master. The horizontal sweep of limestone that Wright designed in 1953 as a restaurant now holds the **Frank Lloyd Wright Visitor Center**, where tours begin. His home, **Taliesin**, perches on a hill across from the visitor center. Wright began his famed Fellowship here and built and

rebuilt the original Prairie-style house over five decades. A small road leads to the tiny stone and shingle **Unity Chapel**, designed in 1886 by Wright's first employer, J.L. Silsbee. Around the bend, the broad eaves of Wright's **Hillside Studio and Theater** (1902), the office of Taliesin Architects, rise above the road.

♟♙ The House on the Rock

◑ 5754 State Rd.23, in Spring Green, WI. 60mi west of Madison, in Spring Green, WI. Take US-18 West to Dodgeville and go north on Rte. 23 to no. 5754. ✕♿🅿 ℰ608-935-3639. www.thehouseontherock.com.

This limestone house was built on a rocky outcrop as a weekend retreat by collector Alex Jordan in the 1940s. Today, buildings in the complex are filled with an eclectic collection of music machines, armor, weaponry, dolls—and the world's largest indoor carousel.

Effigy Mounds National Monument★★

◑ 100mi west of Madison. Take US-18 West 97mi to Prairie du Chien and cross the Mississippi River to Marquette, IA. Take US-76 North 3mi and follow signs. ♿🅿 ℰ563-873-3491. www.nps.gov/efmo.

Located on a 2,526-acre bluff overlooking the west bank of the Mississippi River, the monument contains some of the country's largest earthworks. Visible via a web of hiking trails, nearly 200 burial mounds lie within the park's borders. While most of these are conical, 29 are animal effigies—unique to the upper Mississippi River Valley. Archaeologists have dated the mounds as far back as 500 BC and as recently as AD 1300.

♟♙ National Mustard Museum

◑ 7477 Hubbard Ave., 5mi west of Madison in Middleton WI. ℰ608-831-2222. www.mustardmuseum.com.

This quirky museum displays more than 5,000 mustards and countless pieces of condiment memorabilia. The gift shop is packed with mustards of all kind and other culinary supplies.

Cleveland and the Western Reserve

When Ohio was opened for settlement after the Revolutionary War, the State of Connecticut reserved 3.5 million acres of land in northeastern Ohio, which became known as the Western Reserve. The reserve is bounded by Pennsylvania on the east, the Cuyahoga River on the west, Lake Erie on the north and Akron on the south; it was first surveyed in 1796 by Connecticut Land Company representative Moses Cleaveland. It was Cleaveland's job to establish townships east of the Cuyahoga River (lands to the west were under Indian control). He chose a plain on the east bank of the river, where it meets Lake Erie, for his settlement of Cleveland (the "a" was later dropped).

Highlights

Cleveland

OH

The Western Reserve

For two decades after its creation, this disease-ridden northern outpost floundered; settlers flocked instead to the fertile farmlands in the southern part of the reserve. Cleveland finally began to attract interest in 1827 when the city became the terminus

Cleveland Skyline from the Great Lakes Science Center

© www.positivelycleveland.com

for the Ohio and Erie Canal. In the 1850s, the railroad linked Cleveland to raw materials in the east and west, giving birth to the steel and oil-refining industries along the flats lining the river. Inspired by the city's economic growth during Cleveland's industrial heyday, Jeptha H. Wade consolidated a number of Midwest telegraph lines into the **Western Union Telegraph Company** in 1856, and industrialist **John D. Rockefeller** (1839-1937) founded the Standard Oil Company here in 1870.

European immigrants, the majority of them from Eastern Europe, swelled Cleveland's population in the late 19C and early 20C, drawn by the promise of jobs in the city's burgeoning industries. By 1920, Cleveland ranked as the nation's fifth-largest city; the Cleveland metropolitan area is now home to three and a half million people.

Outside the city, amid acres of peaceful farmland, historical sites commemorate the region's cultural diversity. About 85mi south of Cleveland, Berlin in Holmes County, Ohio, harbors the nation's largest population of Amish.

The first Christian mission in Ohio, started by Moravians in 1772, is preserved at **Schoenbrunn★** (90mi south on Rte. 259 in New Philadelphia, OH; ☎330-663-6610; www.ohiosfirstvillage.com). At **Zoar Village State Memorial** (75mi south of Cleveland in Zoar, OH; ☎330-874-3011; www.historiczoarvillage.com) you can learn the ways of German Separatists who sought religious freedom in a quiet Ohio valley in 1817. Near Sandusky, a cluster of Lake Erie islands makes a delightful day's excursion.

ADDRESSES

🏠 STAY

$$$ Renaissance Cleveland Hotel –
24 Public Square, Cleveland, OH. ✕&🅿 🛏 ☎216-696-5600. www.renaissance hotels.com. 491 rooms. Downtown's grande dame opened as the Hotel Cleveland in 1918. Guest rooms are large and have oversize marble bathrooms with TVs and jacuzzis. Fitness Center and indoor pool.

$$ Glidden House –
1901 Ford Dr., Cleveland, OH. ✕&🅿 🛏 ☎216-231-8900. www.gliddenhouse.com. 60 rooms. Located in University Circle, the 1910 French Gothic-style mansion retains its residential feel. Individually decorated rooms combine an inviting decor with modern amenities. Breakfast is served in the plant-filled sunroom on bistro tables. The restaurant is next door in the carriage house.

$$ The Tudor Arms Hotel –
10660 Carnegie Ave., Cleveland, OH. ✕&🅿 ☎216-455-1260. www.doubletree3. hilton.com. 157 rooms. This dignified, historic pile enjoys a fine location in Cleveland's East Side Cultural District, steps from several venues and just a few miles from downtown. Nicely updated rooms feature hardwood floors, pristine white duvets, deluxe bath products, and complimentary Wi-Fi.

🍴 EAT

$$$ Blue Point Grille –
700 W. St. Clair Ave., Cleveland, OH. ☎216-875-7827. www.bluepointgrille.com **Seafood.** This upscale Warehouse District eatery turns out foolproof seafood dishes. Crabcakes come with honey mustard, and sautéed grouper is served with lobster mash and spinach.

$$$ Lola –
2058 E. 4th St., Cleveland. ☎216-621-5652. www.lolabistro.com. Sophisticated ingredients meet expert technique at Michael Symon's bistro in the Euclid Corridor area. Try the melting pork shank with lentils or the excellent rib eye with blue cheese.

$ Melt –
14718 Detroit Ave., Lakewood, OH. ☎216-226-3699. www.meltbarand grilled.com. **American.** Comfort food at its finest, the menu headliners at the hip-but-casual joint (there are several other locations around the Cleveland area) feature a happy common denominator: melted cheese. Try any incarnation of grilled cheese sandwich piled high with delectable meats and add-ons, all on artisan breads. The beer selection invites experimenters.

Cleveland★

Beneath a modern skyline, Cleveland bills itself as the "New American City;" its conservative, hard-working citizens live up to the image. The city remains closely linked to the lake with a busy port and a dynamic set of lakefront attractions that have been tied together with a modern rapid-transit line.

▶ **Population:** 390,928.
🚗 **Michelin Map:** 583 Q 7
ℹ **Info:** ℘216-875-6680; www. positivelycleveland.com.
▸ **Location:** Cleveland's epicenter is at the mouth of the Cuyahoga River.
☺ **Don't Miss:** America's signature sound and celebrity royalty at the Rock and Roll Hall of Fame and Museum.
👪 **Kids:** The Great Lakes Science Center and its OMNIMAX theater.

A BIT OF HISTORY

Wedged between the Cuyahoga River and Lake Erie, Cleveland's downtown was originally laid out around a 10-acre village green now called Public Square. Industry eventually grew up in the **Flats** area on the east riverbank; immigrants settled across the river on the west bank. Today that area, an ethnically diverse enclave called **Ohio City**, features the **West Side Market** (1979 W. 25th St; ℘216-664-3387; www. westsidemarket.org), one of the largest indoor/outdoor markets in the country. The market continues to trade produce as it has since 1912.

Seat of Cleveland's cultural institutions, University Circle is flanked by Case Western Reserve University and the Cleveland Clinic, renowned for its work in cardiology. Encircling the city, 14 generous parkland reserves offer 60mi of paved trails and activities including golfing, fishing and sunbathing.

Modern Cleveland has recovered nicely from the economic nosedive the city took in the 1960s and 70s as industries began to leave the city; today it is the economic and cultural capital of the Western Reserve. Service industries, especially health care and business, have filled the vacuum left by heavy industry. Today, after more than 200 years of growth and change, Cleveland sparkles anew with its towering office buildings and a redeveloped lakefront area and trendy neighborhoods.

DOWNTOWN

Revitalized historic districts flank the downtown core. To the west, Cleve-land's oldest neighborhood, the **Ware-house District** (bounded by Superior Ave., W. 3rd St., Lakeside Ave. and W. 10th St.), bustles with trendy restaurants, jazz clubs and upscale condominiums. The **Gateway District** (south of Superior Ave. and east of E. 9th St.) boasts **Progres-sive Field** (2401 Ontario St.), home of the Cleveland Indians baseball team, and **Quicken Loans Arena** (1 Center Ct.; www.theqarena.com), which hosts basketball and hockey. To the east, the **Theater District** (east of E. 9th St. & south of Superior Ave.) centers on **Playhouse Square★** (1501 Euclid Ave.), the largest performing-arts center outside New York City. Its five restored early-20C theaters—the Allen, State, Ohio, Palace and Hanna—stage ballet, opera and Broadway productions. Restoration of Playhouse Square sparked redevel-opment efforts along Euclid Avenue, and the pedestrian-friendly area has boomed with trendy restaurants, shops, galleries and nightlife.

Public Square★★

Intersection of Ontario & Superior Aves.
Focal point of downtown, Public Square's four landscaped quadrants contain some of the city's finest archi-tecture. Looming over the square from the southwest corner, the **Tower City Center** originally contained the Union Railroad Station. Now a three-level shopping mall fills the former con-

course below the 52-story Beaux-Arts **Terminal Tower★** (1927, Oris and Mantis Van Sweringen), which connects to office buildings and hotels on either side. Dominating the southeastern quadrant is the 125ft-high granite shaft of the **Soldiers and Sailors Monument**, erected in 1894 as a monument to Civil War veterans. On the square's southeast corner, the eight-story atrium of the **BP America Building** (1985) showcases an elaborate water cascade.

Next door, the splendid 1890 stone-and-brick **Cleveland Arcade★★** (401 Euclid Ave.) reflects the exuberant optimism of the city's heyday. On the northern edge of Public Square stands a familiar Cleveland landmark, 1858 **Old Stone Church** (91 Public Square). East across Ontario Street rises the state's tallest building, 888ft **Key Tower** (1991, Cesar Pelli).

Cleveland Mall

Bounded by Lakeside Ave., E. 9th St., Rockwell Ave. & W. 3rd St.

Inspired by the 1893 Chicago Columbian Exposition, Cleveland's leaders conceived a plan in 1903 to erect a monumental grouping of public buildings. The plan was carried out by architects Daniel Burnham, John Carrère and Arnold Brunner. Their work, set on a T-shaped series of grassy malls, yielded some of the city's Beaux Arts and Renaissance Revival jewels. These include the 1912 **Cuyahoga County Courthouse** (1 Lakeside Ave.); the Neo-classical **City Hall** (601 Lakeside Ave.); the 1922 **Public Auditorium** (1220 E. 6th St.),

now part of the city's convention center; and the 1911 Old **Federal Building** (201 Superior Ave.).

NORTH COAST HARBOR

Site of the Port of Cleveland, the North Coast district borders the Lake Erie shore north of downtown at Erieside Avenue and East Ninth Street. Beginning at the western edge of the harbor is the **FirstEnergy Stadium** (100 Alfred Lerner Way), home to the **Cleveland Browns** football team. Clustered around the harbor to the east are the Rock and Roll Hall of Fame, a science museum and a lakefront park.

Two historic ships are docked on the eastern side of the pier; farther east lies Burke Lakefront Airport, home of the International Women's Air & Space Museum, Inc. (1501 North Marginal Rd.; ✆216-623-1111; www.iwasm.org).

Rock and Roll Hall of Fame and Museum★★★

1100 Rock and Roll Blvd. ✕ ♿ ✆216-781-7625. www.rockhall.com.

Like the music it represents, this museum's geometric design (1995, I.M. Pei) is bold and energetic. Focal point of Cleveland's renewed waterfront since its opening in 1995, the Hall of Fame encompasses six levels of exhibits ranging from the roots of rock and roll to regional music scenes and the careers of individual artists. Begin with the slick, two-part video presentation in adjacent ground-floor theaters. Then proceed to the permanent installment **Legends of Rock and Roll★**, which displays an

Rock and Roll Hall of Fame and Museum

impressive array of costumes and artifacts, supplemented by interactive stations featuring the music of more than 500 performers.

In a drum-shaped wing that opened in 1998, the **Hall of Fame★★** (level 3) honors over 279 rock legends (including 104 music groups)) with a multimedia production that incorporates music, film excerpts and taped interviews.

▲▲ Great Lakes Science Center

601 Erieside Ave. ✕&🅿 ✆216-694-2000. www.glsc.org.

Sitting next door to the Rock and Roll Hall of Fame, the center boasts an awesome main entrance comprising a concrete-metal-and-glass, nine-story atrium with views of Lake Erie. More than 400 hands-on exhibits occupy the west wing and are organized into major themes: science, environment, space exploration and technology. Don't miss the amazing shows in the OMNIMAX Theater or a visit to the historic steamship **William G. Mather**, moored outside the museum at Dock 32 west of the Ninth Street Pier. Referred to as "the ship that built Cleveland," the Mather carried iron ore and coal to Great Lakes factories and mills for nearly 55 years beginning in 1925. Visitors can walk through the restored freighter, with its oak-paneled **pilot house** and four-story **engine room**.

USS Cod

East of the pier off N. Marginal Rd. 🅿 ✆216-566-8770. www.usscod.org.

The last completely authentic World War II American submarine in existence today, the Cod completed her final patrol in 1945. Inside the sub's cramped quarters, the smell of diesel fuel and machine oil still lingers.

UNIVERSITY CIRCLE

Cleveland's cultural center, University Circle is located 4mi east of downtown near Case Western University. One square mile in size, it was laid out in 1895 to improve access to the "heights," a series of plateaus around the city that formed an enclave for Cleveland's affluent residents. Most famed of these, **Shaker Heights**, was laid out in the 1920s as a planned residential community. Edged by East Boulevard and Martin Luther King, Jr. Drive, **Wade Park** forms the hub of the circle. Here you'll find Cleveland's major cultural institutions and the Cleveland Botanical Gardens (11030 East Blvd.; ✆216-721-1600. www.cbgarden.org), all within easy walking distance.

Cleveland Museum of Art★★

11150 East Blvd. ✕&✆216-421-7340. www.clevelandart.org.

Recent expansions and renovations completed in 2013 have breathed new life into Cleveland's renowned art museum, showcasing its fine 40,000-piece collection to excellent effect. Don't miss the remarkable **Asian Collection** and a fascinating Armor Court showcasing 300 pieces of European arms and armor. You'll also find troves of American paintings, early Christian art and European paintings and sculpture.

▲▲ Cleveland Museum of Natural History★

1 Wade Oval Dr. ✕&✆216-231-4600. www.cmnh.org.

Designed as a quadrangle, the lobby of the museum is brightened by shafts of sunlight pouring in from the inviting Environmental Courtyard. In the Kirtland Hall of Prehistoric Life, you'll find full-sized replicas of a triceratops and a Tyrannosaurus Rex as well as a cast of the three-million-year-old skeleton named **Lucy★**, the most famous fossil of a human ancestor.

Or soar across the terrain of any planet in the solar system via an interactive computer station in multisensory "**Plantary Odyssey**." More than 1,500 precious gem-stones, jewelry and lapidary artworks sparkle in the **Wade Gallery of Gems & Jewels**.

Western Reserve Historical Society★★

10825 East Blvd. Entrance on Magnolia Dr. &🅿 ✆216-721-5722. www.wrhs.org.

This sprawling institution consists of two museums, a historic home and an adjoining research library. Founded in 1867, the Western Reserve's collection is housed in two adjoining Italian Renaissance mansions. The Bingham-Hanna mansion (1919) holds exhibits (first floor) relating to Cleveland's development and showcases portions of the society's collection of more than 30,000 pieces of 18C-20C clothing in the **Chisholm Halle Costume Wing★**.

The 1911 **Hay-McKinney Mansion** designed by Abram Garfield (son of President Garfield), contains furniture and decorative arts reflecting the lifestyles of Cleveland's elite in the Gilded Age. In a separate wing, the **Crawford Auto Aviation Collection★** displays selections of the society's collection of historic aircraft and some 200 vintage automobiles.

ADDITIONAL SIGHTS

♟ Cleveland Metroparks Zoo★★

3900 Wildlife Way. ✕♿🅿✆216-661-6500. www.clemetzoo.com.

Located 5mi south of downtown Cleveland, this 165-acre wooded zoo re-creates ecosystems for more than 600 animal species. Here you can see a sleek pack of Mexican wolves close-up in **Wolf Wilderness**, or visit the steamy **RainForest**, which brings together more than 6,000 plants and 600 animals from the jungles of Africa, Asia and the Americas beneath a glass biosphere.

EXCURSIONS

Hale Farm and Village★★

◖ 21mi south of Cleveland in Bath, OH. Take I-77 South to Exit 143 and turn right onto Wheatley Rd. At first stoplight turn left on Brecksville Rd., then left again on Ira Rd. to 2686 Oak Hill Rd. ✕♿🅿 ✆330-666-3711. www.wrhs.org.

Located in a quiet meadow, Hale Homestead was settled in 1810 by Connecticut farmer Jonathan Hale. An early19C Western Reserve village has been re-created as a living history museum on the original site of his farm. On one side of Oak Hill Road, which bisects the site,

artisans demonstrate crafts in the buildings around **Hale House** (1826).

South Bass Island★★

◖ 75mi west of Cleveland on Lake Erie. Take I-90 West (Ohio Tpk.) to Hwy. 2 West and follow Rte. 53 North to Catawba Point; or stay on Hwy. 2 to Port Clinton. Access via ferry from Catawba Point (Miller Boat Line, ✆419-285-2421) and Port Clinton (Jet Express, ✆419-732-2800). ⚠✕♿🅿 Information: ✆419-285-2832 or www.putinbay.com.

Cool breezes blowing across the lake and sunlight glittering off the water make the journey to this unpretentious little island a delight. Part of a cluster of Lake Erie islands that played a part in the War of 1812, South Bass is located northwest of Sandusky, Ohio.

The island's most prominent natural feature is its 30 **caves**, a result of the island's rock layers being eroded by water over millions of years. Two are open to the public: **Perry's Cave** (979 Catawba Ave.; ✆419-285-2405; www.perryscave.com), a 50ft-deep limestone cave that Admiral Perry is credited with discovering in 1813; and **Crystal Cave** (across from Perry's Cave at 978 Catawba Ave.; ✆419-285-2811), where blue-green crystals line the walls.

Perry's Victory and International Peace Memorial★★

93 Delaware Ave., Put-in-Bay. 🅿✆419-285-2184. www.nps.gov/pevi.

This 352ft-high pink granite column (1915) commemorates the victory of Commodore **Oliver Hazard Perry** (1785-1819) over the British during the War of 1812. Commander of the American fleet, Perry forced the surrender of six British vessels in September 1813 in the Battle of Lake Erie. With this victory, the Americans took control of Lake Erie and most of the Northwest. Perry's battle report to Gen. William Henry Harrison contained the now-famous words: "We have met the enemy and they are ours." The **view★** from the observation platform on a clear day reaches 10mi northwest to the battle site.

Cincinnati Area

Cradled by the Ohio River, which borders the state from the east and south before feeding into the Mississippi, south-central Ohio is a mostly rural enclave, with livestock, soybeans and corn adorning its gently rolling hills and fertile valleys. Prehistoric earthworks, including burial plots, enclosures and effigy mounds, attest to the presence of nomadic tribes in the region between 1000 BC and AD 500 . Two of its three main cities, Cincinnati and Dayton, grew up as trade centers, ferrying agricultural products via a network of rivers and canals. Columbus is the state capital and home to the massive Ohio State University.

Highlights

1 Exploring the Cincinnati **Museum Center** (p317)

2 Marveling at the ancients at **Serpent Mound State Park Memorial** (p317)

3 Making friends with manatees at the world-class **Cincinnati Zoo** (p318)

4 An afternoon at the **Dayton Art Institute** (p318)

Cincinnati

Gateway to the West

First explored around 1670 by Frenchman René Robert Cavelier de La Salle, Ohio remained the province of Native Americans well into the 18C. An increasing demand for furs, land and control of river trade made the region a bone of contention during the French and Indian War (1754-63). The loss of that war marked the end of French hopes to connect Canadian territories with the port in New Orleans. English victory brought about westward expansion and the settlement of the area through a series of broken treaties with—and ultimately the massacre of—local Indian tribes.

In 1803 Ohio became the first state to be chipped out of the Northwest Territory. Called the Gateway to the West, it was soon scored with roads, canals and finally railroads. River and canal traffic sparked the growth of Cincinnati and Dayton. Columbus was named state capital in 1816. Today these three cities remain the focal points of history and culture in the region. All boast excellent museums for cities of their size: art and science museums are especially strong in Columbus and Cincinnati, while Dayton's Air Force Museum showcases the largest collection of military airplanes in the world. Set

Center of Science and Industry, Columbus

© COSI, Photo by Brad Feinknopf

in clusters around the countryside, ancient earthworks now preserved as historic sites provide a rare window into the world of prehistoric North America.

ADDRESSES

🛏️STAY

$$$ The Cincinnatian Hotel – 601 Vine St., Cincinnati, OH. ✗♿🅿️✆513-381-3000. www.cincinnatianhotel.com. 147 rooms. This Second French Empire-style property downtown has welcomed guests since 1882. Beyond its limestone exterior is a luxury boutique hotel with modern decor and a skylit atrium, yet Old-World service remains a trademark. For American fine dining, head to the celebrated **Palace Restaurant**.

$$$ Hilton Cincinnati Netherland Plaza – 35 W. 5th St., Cincinnati, OH. ✆513-421-9100. www.hilton.com. 516 rooms. A downtown Art Deco jewel that's dazzled guests—from Elvis Presley to Winston Churchill—since 1931. The lobby looks like a Hollywood movie palace, with rosewood paneling and climbing-vine wall sconces in silver. The signature restaurant, **Orchids**, is just as opulent as the rest of the hotel and its inspired American dishes get raves.

$$$ The Lofts Hotel – 55 E. Nationwide Blvd., Columbus, OH. ✗♿🅿️✆614-461-2663. www.55lofts.com. 44 rooms. Located in downtown Columbus' most exciting neighborhood, the Arena District, a lively arts and entertainment community, nationally renowned dining, nightlife, live music venues, boutiques, and galleries are just steps from The Lofts. Sensitively converted from one of the city's last remaining warehouses, the hotel's designer interior offers clean, contemporary lines, dramatically juxtaposed against the strength of a historic building. Beyond its rich history and great beauty, guests rave about the personalized concierge service, 37" Flat Panel HDTVs, garden tub suites, and dramatic floor-to-ceiling windows.

$$ The Blackwell – 2110 Tuttle Park Place, Columbus, OH. ✗♿🅿️✆614-247-4000. www.theblackwell.com. 151 rooms. This comfortable, contemporary hotel run by the OSU School of Business boasts lots of amenities for business travelers, but its excellent location on campus within view of the stadium makes it an excellent choice for football weekends and leisure trips to Columbus.

$$ Symphony Hotel – 210 W. 14th St., Cincinnati, OH. ✗♿🛏️✆513-731-3353. www.symphonyhotel.com. 5 rooms. Sitting right across the street from Music Hall, this charming European-style hostelry began life as the elegant mansion of an ardent fan of the symphony. It features four comfortable guest rooms, each named after a classical composer and decorated with appropriate busts and sheet music. Expertly prepared four-course dinners are served before Music Hall performances.

🍴EAT

$$$ The Celestial – 1071 Celestial St., Cincinnati, OH. ✆513-241-4455. www.thecelestial.com. **American.** Perched on a hillside in trendy Mount Adams, this old-school restaurant plates excellent, perfectly grilled steaks and chops dressed with your choice of traditional accompaniments like Bernaise sauce, blue cheese or truffle butter. Start with a cold appetizer from the raw bar if you like, all while taking in the delightful views of the Cincinnati skyline.

$$ Local 127 – 413 Vine St., Cincinnati, OH. ✆513-721-1345. www.mylocal127.com. **American.** Acclaimed chef Steven Geddes includes "All Grandmothers" on his list of inspirations for seasonal, locally sourced versions of American classics like chicken with cheese grits and gremolata, russet potato soup with parsley oil and duck breast with rhubarb. Take a gander at the charcuterie selections, all housemade.

$$ Sage American Bistro – 2653 North High St, Columbus, OH. ✆617-267-7243. Closed Sun and Mon. www.sageamericanbistro.com. **American.** In his upscale brickfront restaurant in Columbus' University District, chef Bill Glover serves forth sophisticated twists on unpretentious American classics like salt cod fritters (with chorizo aioli), chicken and dumplings (with lavender-honey sauce and pheasant sausage) and cream of mushroom soup (with brie and truffle oil).

Cincinnati★

The downtown district is laid out on a grid and flanked by steep hills that harbor the University of Cincinnati, Eden Park★ and the quaint Mount Adams★ district, a warren of Victorian dwellings, shops and pubs along St. Gregory Street.

▶ **Population:** 296,550.
Ⓒ **Michelin Map:** 583 P 9
🄸 **Info:** Cincinnati Convention and Visitors Bureau. ℘513-621-2142; www.cincyusa.com
▶ **Location:** Cincinnati lies just across the Ohio River from picturesque Covington, Kentucky.
☺ **Don't Miss:** The National Underground Railroad Freedom Center.

A BIT OF HISTORY

Named after the Roman soldier and statesman Cincinnatus, the city was founded in 1788 and thrived as a center of river commerce—the "Queen City" of the Ohio Valley, it was called—until the 1850s, when the railroad diverted traffic through Chicago. Cincinnati continued to prosper, however, as a manufacturing and, more recently, white-collar business center. The first bridge to link Ohio with Kentucky, the 1867 **Roebling Bridge★** (Walnut St. & Mehring Way) is one of the city's most vigorous structures. It was a prototype for the Brooklyn Bridge in New York City.

Today the city is witnessing a spurt of architectural renovation and new development. Downtown, the **Aronoff Center for the Arts** (650 Walnut St.; ℘513-621-2787), designed by Cesar Pelli and completed in 1995, comprises three theaters and an art gallery. On the banks of the river, two massive sports facilities draw fans of the **Cincinnati Bengals** (Paul Brown Stadium) and the **Cincinnati Reds** (Great American Ballpark), the nation's first professional baseball team. Meanwhile, the **Over-the-Rhine** district (Main St. between 12th & 14th Sts.) is home to the 3,500-seat 1878 Gothic-style **Music Hall** (1241-43 Elm St.).

SIGHTS

Cincinnati Art Museum★★

953 Eden Park Dr. ✕🄳🄿 ℘513-639-2995. www.cincinnatiartmuseum.org. Opened in 1886, the hilltop museum in scenic Eden Park is one of the earliest art institutions in the nation and the first art museum west of the Alleghenies to have its own building. Over the years the collection has grown from a single Native American jar to more than

Cincinnati Museum Center

© Lauren Bishop/Cincinnati Museum Center

60,000 works covering 6,000 years of art making, and the original Richardsonian Romanesque museum structure has expanded accordingly. Today an eclectic melding of architectural styles (Beaux-Arts, International, Doric temple) echoes the impressive diversity of its collection, which is especially strong in European **Old Masters★★**, Native American art, non-Western art (including the only collection of **Nabataean art** outside Jordan) and American painting.

▲▲ Cincinnati Museum Center★★

1301 Western Ave. ✕ ♿ ☏513-287-7000. www.cincymuseum.org.

Formerly a train station capable of accommodating 17,000 passengers and 216 trains a day, the **structure★★** is a 1933 Art Deco masterpiece of awesome proportions. Designed by Alfred Fellheimer-Steward Wagner, it boasts the largest half-dome in the western hemisphere (180ft wide and 106ft high),

as well as gigantic, brightly colored mosaic murals depicting work, progress and history. Three full-size museums and an OMNIMAX theater fit easily within the multilevel building. Using multimedia walk-through exhibits, the **Cincinnati History Museum★★** brilliantly re-creates the city's history through the 1940s and includes a working model of the city, complete with trains and inclines. Both the **Museum of Natural History and Science** and the **Children's Museum** are geared to kids, full of hands-on exhibits and play areas.

▲▲ National Underground Railroad Freedom Center

50 E. Freedom Way. ♿ 🅿 ☏513-333-7500. www.freedomcenter.org.

A sobering yet inspirational experience, this $110-million facility uses the Underground Railroad, which traveled through this site on the banks of the Ohio River, as the backdrop for visi-

Ohio's Mound Builders

Southern Ohio has its share of rolling hills, but some of them are not what they seem. Under the surface of the fertile soil lie troves of prehistoric artifacts, mastodon bones and human remains. Before development, farming and erosion took their toll, some 6,000 conical mounds, enclosures and effigies dotted the countryside here—more than anywhere else in North America. Though not much is known about the mounds or the people who built them, ongoing archaeological research has revealed that three distinct groups once occupied the region: the **Adena** group (1000 BC to AD 100); the **Hopewell** group (200 BC to AD 500); and the **Fort Ancient** group (AD 900 to 1500).

Two hilltop enclosures, **Fort Ancient** (30mi northeast of Cincinnati on Rte. 350, Oregonia; ☏513-932-4421; www.fortancient.org) and **Fort Hill** (off Rte. 41, 3mi south of Cynthiana; ☏614-297-2630) are among the largest and most scenic of Ohio's prehistoric monuments. Both feature sloping earthen walls enclosing open spaces once used for ceremonies, as well as new visitor centers and networks of hiking trails. One of the best interpreted sights, **Hopewell Culture Historical Park★** (Rte. 104, Chillicothe; ☏740-774-1126; ww.nps.gov/hocu) is a "Mound City" consisting of an earthwork wall enclosing 13 acres and 23 substantial mounds. The best-known—and least understood—earthworks in Ohio can be found at **Serpent Mound State Memorial★★** (Rte. 73, 4mi north of Locust Grove; ☏937-587-2796). Here visitors will find a .25mi-long, 5ft-high earthen snake with a rippling body, a coiled tail and a hyperextended jaw ready to chomp down on an oval that could be an egg or a frog. The mound is thought to have been created around AD 1070 by the Fort Ancient people.

For more information, contact the Ohio Historical Society (1982 Velma Ave., Columbus, ☏614-297-2300, www.ohiohistory.org).

tors' exploration of past and present freedom issues from around the world. Opened in 2004, it features three pavilions full of interactive exhibits. Visitors can get a chilling feel for the stark reality of slave life in The Slave Pen, an authentic structure used to restrain as many as 75 slaves at a time. **From Slavery to Freedom** documents three centuries of slavery in America while **Invisible: Slavery Today** explores the ongoing issues of exploitation and human trafficking around the world.

William Howard Taft National Historic Site★★

2038 Auburn Ave.&🅿️ ☎513-684-3262. www.nps.gov/wiho.

The nation's 27th president, William Taft (1857-1930), lived in this handsome Greek Revival dwelling (1841) from his birth until he embarked on his political career 20 years later. The house today is split evenly between the Tafts' downstairs living spaces and upstairs **exhibit rooms★★** that trace the trajectory of Taft's life and times with personal mementos, photographs and even music. Happy to give up the cutthroat politics of the presidency, Taft became the 10th chief justice of the Supreme Court. He remains the only American to have held both positions.

Taft Museum of Art★

316 Pike St. ✕&🅿️ ☎513-241-0343. www.taftmuseum.org.

This Federal-style house (1820) was the home of Charles Phelps Taft (the president's half-brother) and his wife, Anna Sinton Taft, from 1873 until 1930. In 1931 the house opened as a museum to display the 600 works of art collected by the Tafts. Rembrandt, Gainsborough, Millet, Corot, Turner and Whistler are all represented in the current collection.

▲▲ Cincinnati Zoo and Botanical Garden★

3400 Vine St. ✕&🅿️ ☎513-281-4700. www.cincinnati.org.

Recognized among the leading zoos in the US, the Cincinnati Zoo houses more than 740 species of animals and 3,000 types of plants in its attractive garden setting. Don't miss the chimpanzees and orangutans in **Jungle Trails**, the newly completed **Africa** section featuring giraffes, flamingos and cheetahs or the zoo's popular inhabitants at **Manatee Springs**.

EXCURSIONS

Dayton

◗ 52mi north of Cincinnati via I-75.

Ohio's sixth-largest city sits on the Miami River floodplain, which fueled its industry in the late 19C. Dayton's most famous native sons are **Wilbur and Orville Wright**, whose experiments at their bicycle-repair shop (22 S. Williams St.) led to the first successful airplane flight in 1903 (💲see THE OUTER BANKS). The **Dayton Aviation Heritage National Historical Park** (☎937-225-7705; www.nps.gov/daav) tracks the Wrights' discoveries at various sites throughout the city.

Dayton Art Institute★★

456 Belmonte Park N. ✕&🅿️ ☎937-223-5277. www.daytonartinstitute.org.

A 1997 expansion added 35,000sq ft of gallery space to the existing structure, a 1930 Italian Renaissance-style landmark building with a red tile roof. Arranged chronologically on an octagonal floor plan, more than 10,000 works on two levels of galleries trace the development of both Western and non-Western art. Strengths to look out for are 17C-19C **European paintings★**, 20C **American paintings** and the fine collection of **Asian art★**.

National Museum of the US Air Force★★

1100 Spaatz St., Wright Patterson Air Force Base. ✕&🅿️ ☎937-255-3286. www.nationalmuseum.af.mil.

This gargantuan institution sprawls over 10 acres and features more than 400 aerospace vehicles, some of which visitors can climb aboard. The museum has announced plans for a major expansion, to be launched in summer 2014, to house new galleries for Presidential Aircraft and Space Exploration.

Columbus

Ohio's capital city, Columbus marks the approximate center of the state. Situated on the banks of the Scioto and Olentangy rivers 109mi northeast of Cincinnati, Columbus takes its name from explorer Christopher Columbus; a replica of his flagship, the *Santa Maria*, is docked downtown.

▶ **Population:** 809,798.
◔ **Michelin Map:** 583 Q 8
▤ **Info:** ℰ614 221-6623; www.experiencecolumbus.com
👥 **Kids:** The exhibits at Center of Science and Industry are made for curious kids.

THE CITY TODAY

Columbus is a lively place, combining a strong preservationist ethic with forward-thinking development. Completed in 1861, the Greek Revival **Ohio Statehouse★** (Broad & High Sts.) is one of the few state houses without a dome. Bordering the **Brewery District**, where old brick warehouses have been converted into clubs and brewpubs, **German Village** comprises 233 acres of mid-19C residences centered on Third Street. The **Short North** boasts hip galleries, cafes, restaurants and bars along High Street just north of downtown (from Goodale St. to 5th Ave.). A few blocks farther north sprawls **Ohio State University**; with nearly 57,000 students, it claims one of the largest enrollments of any residential university in the nation. Its celebrated **Wexner Center for the Arts★★** (1871 N. High St.; ℰ614-292-3535; www.wexarts.org) is the place in Columbus to see world-famous performers, contemporary art exhibitions and film.

SIGHTS

Columbus Museum of Art★★

480 E. Broad St. ✕🅰🅿 ℰ614-221-6801. www.columbusmuseum.org.
Founded in 1878, the museum has amassed an impressive collection that seeks not to give the usual broad overview of Western art, but to highlight specific schools and movements. American Precisionism, European Cubism, German Expressionism and the Ash Can school all merit their own galleries, as does **20C American art★**. Two blocks south of the museum (corner of Washington Ave. & E. Town St.), a fascinating **Topiary Park★** re-creates, with carefully pruned life-size shrubs, Georges Seurat's famous 1884 painting *Sunday Afternoon on the Island of La Grande Jatte.*

👥 Center of Science and Industry (COSI)★★

333 W. Broad St. ✕🅰 ℰ614-228-2674. www.cosi.org.
Ohio's premier science and industry museum moved into these spacious digs on the Scioto River in November 1999. Designed by the Japanese-born architect Arata Isozaki, the structure incorporates a 1924 Beaux-Arts high school and encompasses 320,000sq ft of space. Nestled within are a giant "Extreme Screen" theater, a Dome Theater, and seven state of the art "Learning Worlds" centered on the human body, gadgetry, progress, space, the oceans, big science, and digital technology. It's a kid's paradise.

Detail of The Rocket *(1909) by Middleton Manigault, Columbus Museum of Art*

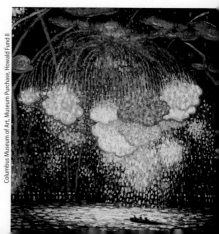

Columbus Museum of Art, Museum Purchase, Howald Fund II

Minneapolis
Iowa
Missouri

Minneapolis/St. Paul Area

Minneapolis/St. Paul, a metropolitan area of more than 3.3 million people, contains the lion's share of the state's cultural treasures—and many natural ones, too. Situated in the southeastern portion of Minnesota, less than 20mi from Wisconsin's western border, Minneapolis and St. Paul are often called the Twin Cities because of their close proximity. As siblings, they have much in common: both nurture the arts, especially music and theater; both value, and attempt to preserve, their historic architecture.

A Perfect Pair

The region served as stomping grounds for Native Americans for nearly 10,000 years before the French arrived in the early 18C to build a network of fur-trading posts. In 1763, after the French and Indian War, the land was relinquished to the English, and finally to the US, which acquired it in 1803 as part of the Louisiana Purchase. Only during the latter half of the 19C did the paths of the two cities diverge. Minneapolis became an industrial center; St. Paul formed the nexus of the area's steamship and railroad lines.

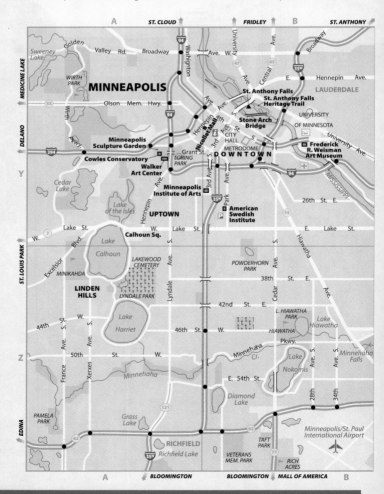

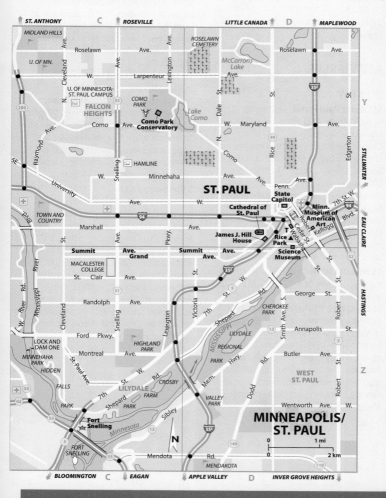

Highlights

1 Attend one of **Minneapolis' many theaters** (p326)

2 Tour the **Walker Art Center's** incredible contemporary art collection (p327)

3 Watch a live taping of *The Prairie Home Companion* (p330)

4 Walk in F. Scott Fitzgerald's footsteps on **Summit Ave.** (p330)

5 Kayak around the **Apostle Islands** (p332)

Today, Minneapolis is larger and more cosmopolitan, its skyline a glittering showcase of modern architecture. St. Paul remains more of a sleepy, European enclave, home to a quiet, well-preserved downtown; and the government seat, which in 1998 claimed the first professional wrestler to become a state governor, Jesse ("the Body") Ventura.

Twin Citians like to say that the two cities complement each other: St. Paul's staid traditionalism reveals itself in its historic mansions, landmark conservatory and century-old annual **Winter Carnival** (Jan–Feb), while Minneapolis' urban progressivism can be found in its contemporary art museums, sculpture garden and funky summer arts and music festival **Aquatennial** (Jul).

Located 150mi north of Minneapolis, **Duluth** anchors two scenic routes: north along US-61 and east along US-2 and Route 28. Here the remote Lake Superior shoreline reveals its breathtaking natural beauty.

ADDRESSES

🏨 STAY

$$$ Saint Paul Hotel – 350 Market St., St. Paul, MN. ✕♿🅿 𝒫651-292-9292. www.saintpaulhotel.com. 254 rooms. Downtown's 1910 landmark has hosted the likes of movie stars Sophia Loren and Bill Murray. Gold-leaf columns, a 20ft-wide antique mirror and vibrant Oriental rugs highlight the ornate lobby. Guest rooms, by contrast, claim warm earth tones and simple Colonial-style furniture; most overlook Rice Park and downtown. The **St. Paul Grill** is known for its regional American classic dishes.

$$ Nicollet Island Inn – 95 Merriam St., Minneapolis, MN. ✕♿🅿 𝒫612-331-1800. www.nicolletislandinn.com. 24 rooms. Located on a small island 2mi from downtown Minneapolis, this elegant guesthouse was built of locally quarried limestone in 1893. The lobby is set up like a cozy living room with two fireplaces flanked by wing chairs. Guest quarters, in subtle colors with antique canopy or four-poster beds, permit Mississippi River views.

🍽 EAT

$$$ La Belle Vie – 510 Groveland Ave., Minneapolis, MN. 𝒫612-874-6440. www.labellevie.us **American.** The elegant decor includes crystal chandeliers and museum-quality paintings and sculptures at this popular spot. Choose from prix-fixe tasting or à la carte menus in the formal dining room, or more casual but still outstanding selections in the adjacent lounge. Start with burrata with marinated tomatoes, followed by pan-roasted poussin with sweet corn, foie gras and mushrooms, and finish with blood orange tarte tatin with sesame ice cream and orange curd.

$$ Pazzaluna – 360 St. Peter St., Paul, MN. 𝒫651-223-7000. www.pazzaluna.com. Dinner only. **Italian.** This trattoria across from the Saint Paul Hotel specializes in regional Italian fare, serving pastas, risottos, gnocchi and an array of meat and fish dishes.

$$ Tavern on Grand – 656 Grand Ave., St. Paul, MN. 𝒫651-228-9030. www.tavernongrand.com. **American.** St. Paul's casual eatery prepares burgers, steaks and pasta, but its specialty is the "state fish" walleye, as in walleye cake appetizers, walleye sandwiches at lunch, or served with vegetables for "supper." The woodsy setting is welcoming.

$ Birchwood Cafe – 3311 E. 25th St., Minneapolis, MN. 𝒫612-722-4474. www.birchwoodcafe.com. **American.** Located in the Seward neighborhood among East Streets other eateries, this funky cafe serves breakfasts and hearty weekend brunches to University of Minneapolis students and the walkers, runners, bladers and cyclists from River Road. There's a variety of lunch and dinner specials with ingredients sourced locally, a kids' menu, art on the walls and a laid-back vibe.

Minneapolis★

While hosting a population of only about 392,000, making it the 47th-largest city in America, Minneapolis nurtures a wealth of diverse neighborhoods, from the warehouse district to the pristine neighborhoods that flank the verdant parkways of its 22 lakes. The city is also an urban mecca for visual and performing arts, boasting scores of theaters, a world-class symphony and several rock and pop bands (Prince; the Replacements) who have made it big in the music world. A handful of excellent museums rounds out the cultural scene.

A BIT OF HISTORY

The name Minneapolis derives from the Dakota word for water, *minne*, and the Greek word for city, *polis*—an appropriate moniker considering the huge role water has played, and continues to play, in the city's cultural and economic life. The last ice sheet retreated from present-day Minneapolis about 12,000 years ago, leaving behind a landscape covered with relatively small, but deep, craters. Glacial runoff filled the holes with water, creating today's lakes; it also carved out the Minnesota and Mississippi rivers, which connect at the southeastern corner of the city before the Mississippi jogs north through St. Paul. Initially it was at this intersection that St. Anthony Falls were located, but as water continued to wear away the limestone riverbed, the waterfall moved farther and farther up the Mississippi, leaving behind a dramatic gorge. Facilitator of the city's modern development—and the only waterfall on the entire 2,348mi-long Mississippi— **St. Anthony Falls** is now located 8mi upstream from its original location. In 1680 Franciscan missionary Father Louis Hennepin became the first white man to see the falls, which he named after his patron saint, Anthony of Padua. In 1819 the construction of Fort Snelling

> ▶ **Population:** 392,880.
>
> **Info:** ℘612-767-8000; www.minneapolis.org.
>
> **Location:** Minneapolis hugs the southwest bank of the Mississippi River, which makes a switchback here on its journey south.
>
> **Don't Miss:** The remarkable permanent collection at the Walker Art Museum.

marked the beginning of US rule in the region. Minneapolis was incorporated in 1872; it was the milling capital of the world. After World War II, Minneapolis began the process of converting to a white-collar, service economy. The city's success in doing so has provided an example that has been followed by cities of similar size nationwide.

SIGHTS
Downtown★★

Its distinctive skyline visible for miles around, downtown Minneapolis displays some architectural gems, from late-19C sandstone piles to glittering late-20C office towers. One of America's first pedestrian thoroughfares, 1mi-long **Nicollet Mall** (Nicollet Ave. between Washington & Grant Sts.) is the site of most of the town's outdoor retail activity in the summer months, while the celebrated 11mi-long **Skyway**

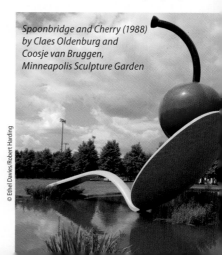

Spoonbridge and Cherry (1988) by Claes Oldenburg and Coosje van Bruggen, Minneapolis Sculpture Garden

© Ethel Davies/Robert Harding

Theater in Minneapolis

Boasting more theaters per capita than any other American city outside of New York, Minneapolis was, is, and may always be a thespian town, with dozens of plays—from absurdist comedies to wrenching dramas—on stage every night. While drama here dates back to the late 1800s, when immigrant groups such as the Swedes put on vernacular plays in social clubs, it was the founding of the **Guthrie Theater** (818 S. 2nd St.; ✕♿🅿 ℘612-377-2224; www. guthrietheater.org) in 1963 that really put the city on the map. The downtown theater scene is dominated by touring Broadway crowd-pleasers mounted in gorgeous old-fashioned jewel boxes such as the **Music Box Theatre** (1407 Nicollet Ave. (at the Nicolet Mall); ℘612-874-1100; www.musicboxtheatre. org), the **Orpheum Theatre** (910 Hennepin Ave.; ℘612-339-7007; www. hennepintheatretrust.org) and the **State Theatre** (805 Hennepin Ave.; ℘612-339-7007; www.hennepintheatretrust.org). Nearby stand two of the city's best black-box, or non-proscenium, theaters. In the Warehouse District, the intimate **Lab Theater** (700 N. 1st St.; ℘612-333-7977; www.thelabtheater.org) stages envelope-pushing world premieres.

Clustered in the artsy Calhoun Square district uptown are the well-respected **Jungle Theater** (2951 Lyndale Ave. S.; ℘612-822-7063; www.jungletheater.com), which stages American classics by playwrights such as David Mamet, John Guare and Tennessee Williams; the **Brave New Workshop** (824 Hennepin Ave. ; ℘612-332-6620; www.bravenewworkshop.org), specializing in satirical comedy revues since 1958; and the **Bryant-Lake Bowl Cabaret Theater** (810 W. Lake St.; ℘612-825-8949; www.bryantlakebowl.com), a space that manages to meld a diner, a bowling alley and a space for small-scale performances with ease.

system links up nearly 69 blocks and more than 100 downtown buildings with climate-controlled corridors lined with restaurants and shops that bustle year-round. A **visitor center** is located at the **Minneapolis Convention Center** (1301 2nd Ave. South).

At 821 Marquette Avenue, the 32-story obelisk **Foshay Tower** (1929) is one of the city's most recognizable landmarks, if only for the 10ft-high letters spelling out FOSHAY above its 31st-floor **observation deck**, where you'll also find a small but interesting museum (www.foshaymuseum.com). **IDS Center** (1973, Philip Johnson), at 777 Nicollet Mall, contains Minneapolis' tallest skyscraper, the octagonal blue-glass **IDS Tower** (51 stories), as well as the Plexiglass-enclosed **Crystal Court**, one of the city's most fetching public interiors. The second-tallest building, the **Capella Tower** (225 6th St. S.), renamed in 2008 for its largest tenant, Capella University, is easily distinguished by the semi-circular halo that crowns it.

Riverfront and Mill District★

Clustered around St. Anthony Falls, the multiuse district contains relics of Minneapolis' earliest industry. Soldiers at Fort Snelling (♿ see ST. PAUL) built the first mills on the falls in the early 19C. By the 1880s, two dozen gargantuan flour mills lined a three-block corridor surrounding the falls, and warehouses cropped up nearby. Recent gentrification has turned some of the old brick buildings into bars, restaurants and loft apartments. At **Salty Tart Bakery** (920 E. Lake St.; www.saltytart.com), cupcakes are made with locally brewed beer.

St. Anthony Falls Heritage trail (pedestrian and bicycle traffic only) loops 2mi along the riverfront and passes two important landmarks: the 1881 blue lime-stone **Pillsbury "A" Mill** (not open to the public), the largest flour mill in the world at the time of its opening; and the 1883 **Stone Arch Bridge**. Celebrated as an engineering marvel, the curving, 2,100ft-long span is the only stone bridge to cross the Mississippi River.

Walker Art Center★★

Vineland Pl. & Lyndale Ave. S. ✖&🄿
🖋612-375-7600. www.walkerart.org.
The award-winning Walker Art Center contains the most extensive—and most intelligently curated—collection of contemporary art in Minneapolis. Housed in a modern, angular building (1971, 1984, Edward Larrabee Barnes), selections from the museum's permanent collection—including works by Roy Lichtenstein, Andy Warhol, Joan Mitchell, Chuck Close and Jasper Johns—are displayed alongside thought-provoking traveling exhibits. A 2005 expansion added new galleries, educational areas, and a 385-seat theater. The Walker's performing arts department offers visitors the opportunity to see a wide variety of performances all under one roof.

The adjacent **Minneapolis Sculpture Garden★★** (&🄿 🖋612-375-7622) comprises 11 acres of lawns and hedges, and more than 40 modern artworks by such acclaimed artists as Henry Moore, Isamu Noguchi and Alexander Calder. The 29ft-high aluminum sculpture **Spoonbridge and Cherry★**, by Claes Oldenburg and Coosje van Bruggen (1988), has become one of Minneapolis' most playful landmarks. In glass-paneled **Cowles Conservatory★**, tropical plants surround Frank Gehry's massive Standing Glass Fish.

Frederick R. Weisman Art Museum★

333 E. River Rd., on the University of Minnesota campus. 🖋612-625-9494.
www.weisman.umn.edu.
Overlooking the Mississippi River is Frank Gehry's awe-inspiring stainless-steel and brick **building★★** (1993). His mission was to not build "just another brick lump," and he succeeded. The undulating metallic structure holds a collection of mostly 20C American art, including the world's largest groupings of work by **American Modernists** Marsden Hartley and Alfred Maurer.
The campus also houses an extensive public art collection, including sculptures and multi-media installations.

Minneapolis Institute of Arts★

2400 3rd Ave. S. &🄿 🖋888-642-2787.
www.artsmia.org.
Housed in a Beaux-Arts structure (1915) by McKim, Mead and White, the Minneapolis Institute of Arts focuses on seven curatorial areas: Arts of Africa and the Americas; decorative arts, textiles and sculpture; Asian art; paintings; contemporary art; photographs and new media; and prints and drawings. The 80,000-object collection, which covers more than 5,000 years, includes masterworks by Rembrandt, Van Gogh, Magritte and El Greco.
Chinese period rooms★ showcase art and architecture from the late Ming and early Ch'ing Dynasties (16C-18C).

American Swedish Institute★

2600 Park Ave. &✖🄿 🖋612-871-4907.
www.americanswedishinst.org.
The 33-room French Château-style mansion (1904) that houses the American Swedish Institute was built for Swedish entrepreneur Swan Turnblad. With its raucous assemblage of turrets, balconies, pillars and gables, the gray limestone structure resembles a fairytale castle. In 1929 the house became the headquarters of the American Swedish Institute, created to "foster and preserve Swedish culture in America." The interior of the house showcases intricately carved **woodwork★★** as well as 11 rare porcelain-tile *kakelugnar* (stoves), each of a different design. Upper floors contain Scandinavian artifacts ranging from a AD 5C pre-Viking drinking vessel to a 600-piece collection of contemporary glasswork.

Uptown and Chain of Lakes★

Confusingly, what locals refer to as uptown is actually located southwest of downtown Minneapolis. Roughly grouped around the city's in-town lakes (which are connected by parkways and paths that are perfect for in-line skating, jogging and cycling), these Uptown neighborhoods are the cherished places where Twin Citians live, play and eat.

St. Paul★

While Minneapolis has been called the first city of the West, and a sparkling paean to commerce and wealth, St. Paul is considered the last city of the East; close to its Old World roots, protective of its architecture, and like many European burgs, difficult to navigate without a map. The area around Rice Park epitomizes St. Paul's pristine elegance, and its science and children's museums are the finest in the state. Some of the best cafe-crawling and window-shopping in the Twin Cities can be done on Grand Avenue, where boutiques crowd into old Victorian structures.

▶ **Population:** 288,448.
🛈 **Info:** ℘651-265-4900; www.visitsaintpaul.com.
◉ **Location:** Contiguous St. Paul lies on the northeast bank of the Mississippi River.
👥 **Kids:** Bad weather doesn't bother little ones thanks to the convertible-dome IMAX Omnitheater.

A BIT OF HISTORY

Their city centers less than 10mi apart, St. Paul and Minneapolis were both part of Sioux territory before white settlers arrived. Their modern histories can both be traced back to the 1819 construction of Fort Snelling, which was key in promoting the mill industry that fueled the subsequent growth of Minneapolis. Initially called "Pig's Eye"—the nickname of one of its first residents—St. Paul became a trading and transportation hub. The city was named the Minnesota state capital in 1849 and received its charter five years later. Today, Minnesota's palatial **State Capitol★** (Aurora Ave., between Cedar St. & Constitution Ave.; ✕👤🅿℘651-296-2881; www.mnhs.org), severed from downtown by I-94, is the most famous local work of one-time St. Paul architect **Cass Gilbert** (1859-1934).

Throughout the latter half of the 19C, St. Paul thrived as the site of the Twin Cities' three main steamboat landings. After local railroad tycoon James J. Hill connected St. Paul with Washington State in 1893 via his Great Northern Railroad, the city became the most impor-

Minnesota State Capitol
©PhotoDisc

tant transportation hub in the upper Midwest. Dependent on Minneapolis' lumber and flour mills to provide the goods that fueled its transport-based economy, St. Paul crashed hard during the Great Depression. New downtown construction since the 1950s has met with mixed success, yet sensitive architectural renovations—such as the acclaimed 1904 Richardsonian Romanesque **Landmark Center**—have been hailed by preservationists nationwide. One of the newer projects, **Saint Paul RiverCentre**, brought 46 conventions to the city in its first year.

SIGHTS
Rice Park★★

Hemmed in by Fourth and Fifth Streets and Washington and Market Streets, Rice Park (1849) still holds sway as St. Paul's prettiest public space. Nestled in the center of so many St. Paul landscapes, it's easily one of the city's best spots to stop for an al fresco lunch. Though St. Paul winters are, most certainly, chilly, locals say it's the park's loveliest season, when, for months on end, it remains dressed up in snow.

Landmark Center★ rises to the north of Rice Park; its red-roofed, pink-granite assemblage of copper-topped turrets and gables features a soaring, six-story skylit **courtyard★★**. Inside you'll find the **Gallery of Wood Art** and the **Schubert Club Museum**.

East of Rice Park towers the 1910 **St. Paul Hotel** (350 Market St.).

South of the park, the ornate 1916 **James J. Hill Reference Library** (80 W. 4th St.), boasts a two-story **Great Reading Room** showcasing a soaring coffered ceiling and inlaid marble floors. The city's largest performing-arts venue, the **Ordway Center for the Performing Arts** (345 Washington St., ℘651-224-4222) looks like an upright tray of ice cubes, with its two-story, glass-paneled front lobby on the park's west side.

Farther afield, former Rice Park neighbor, the **Minnesota Museum of American Art** (332 N. Robert St.; ℘651-222-6080; www.mmaa.org) has moved to the **Pioneer Building** (4th and Robert St.); its 3,500 piece collection focuses on regional and Minnesota artists, and includes works by Grant Wood, Thomas

---

Mall of America

Located a 30min drive from the Twin Cities just south of I-494 and east of Rte. 77/Cedar Ave. in Bloomington, MN. ℘952-883-8800. www.mallofamerica.com. The mall's public-transit station is located outside the first-floor entrance to East Broadway. Express buses run between the Mall of America and the Twin Cities International Airport, Nicollet Mall, and downtown St. Paul. Call ℘612-373-3333 for fares and schedules.

If ever there was a place that epitomized the American maxim that bigger is better, this is it. The largest shopping and entertainment complex in the US, it encompasses—under a single roof—more than 400 stores, an indoor theme park, 20 restaurants, 30 fast-food joints, 14 movie screens, an aquarium and a wedding chapel. Drawing 35 to 40 million visitors a year, the mall is one of the most visited tourist attractions in Minneapolis.

Completed in 1992 at a cost of $650 million, the 4.2-million-square-foot mall is shaped like a giant three-story rectangle, with four department stores (Macy's, Bloomingdale's, Nordstrom and Sears) anchoring the corners. Besides a red-neon Mall of America sign on its exterior, the structure is hardly visible from the outside, due to the web of highways and the 13,000 parking spots (all within 300ft of an entrance) that surround it. Inside, massive corridors with the height and girth of airplane hangars are lined with every store imaginable. Although the atmosphere is especially chaotic during the Christmas season, at any time of year the mall affords a fascinating glimpse into the heart of American capitalism.

Hart Benton, Louise Nevelson and members of the Ash Can School.

Fitzgerald Theater

10 East Exchange St. ♿🅿
☎651-290-1200.
Named for onetime St. Paul resident F. Scott Fitzgerald, the 1910 Beaux-Arts Fitzgerald Theater is St. Paul's oldest. Here, well-known Twin Cities denizen **Garrison Keillor** broadcasts his famous weekly radio show, *The Prairie Home Companion*, in front of a live audience (tickets ☎651- 290-1221; in person from the box office; www.prairiehome. publicradio.org).

♟♟ Science Museum of Minnesota★

120 W. Kellogg Blvd. ✕♿🅿.
☎651-221-9444. www.smm.org.
Among the first-rate exhibits at this Mississippi riverfront facility are an expanded paleontology exhibit, an experiment gallery, a human-body gallery, an exhibit on the ecology and history of the Mississippi River, and a convertible-dome IMAX Omnitheater.

Summit Avenue★★

Sprawled across the highest ground in St. Paul, just west of downtown, this prestigious 4.5mi thoroughfare is one of the best-preserved Victorian boulevards in the country. Summit Avenue begins at the copper-domed **Cathedral of Saint Paul★**, which enjoys a commanding view over downtown from its bluff-top perch (♿🅿 ☎651-228-1766; www.cathedralsaintpaul.org).
Lined with more than 300 mansions, the avenue was the stomping grounds for the fin-de-siècle elite, and remains one of the city's toniest addresses. Author and St. Paul native **F. Scott Fitzgerald** (1896-1940) wrote *This Side of Paradise* in a third-floor apartment at 599 Summit in the summer of 1919.
Running parallel to Summit one block south, **Grand Avenue** may be the most interesting shopping district in the Twin Cities. Many of its boutiques and restaurants are tucked into quirky Victorian houses centered on the eastern end of Grand at Victoria Street.

James J. Hill House★★

240 Summit Ave. ♿🐾♿Visit by guided tour only. ☎651-297-2555. www.mnhs.org.
This 1891 Richardsonian Romanesque manse stands as a tribute to the work of Canadian-born railroad tycoon James Hill. Its 42 rooms contain 22 fireplaces, 13 bathrooms, the 2,000sq ft **Great Hall★**, a two-story skylit art gallery and a marvelous stained-glass window. Guided tours here showcase life in the Gilded Age.

Fort Snelling★

Rtes. 55 & 5. ☎612-726-1171.
www.historicfortsnelling.org.
Begun in 1819, Fort Snelling ranks as the westernmost fort built by the US government after the War of 1812. It was set on a bluff overlooking the confluence of the Minnesota and Mississippi rivers, allowing soldiers to control fur-trade routes. Soldiers at the fort helped build the first flour mills on St. Anthony Falls, while officers oversaw the "treaties" that wrested land from Native Americans. Today the re-created diamond-shaped fort encompasses a store, a hospital, a school and the original Round and Hexagonal towers.
A 20min film introduces the fort's history, and costumed guides (May–Oct) interpret what life was like here 195 years ago.

Como Park Conservatory★

1325 Aida Pl. Open daily.
☎651-487-8200.
Situated in 450-acre Como Park, one of the largest green spaces in the Twin Cities, this 1915 conservatory, made of aluminum, steel and glass, underwent a $12 million renovation in the 1990s. Six public areas within provide botanical delights for the senses, including a Japanese garden, frog pond, 18-hole Como Golf Course, amusement park, pool and picnic area.

Western Lake Superior★

Lovely coastal and forest landscapes occupy this remote corner of the US and provide a stunning setting for the jewel that is Lake Superior, the largest of the Greak Lakes. On its bottom lie 350 shipwrecks, many of them victims of the lake's infamous autumnal northeasters. Ancient volcanic and glacial activity along with wind and water erosion created the "sweetwater sea," trimming its edges with basalt cliffs, soaring escarpments, fine sand beaches and dunes, and multihued sandstone.

A BIT OF HISTORY

For the Ojibwa, the region's first inhabitants, Lake Superior and its surrounding forests provided sustenance and spiritual energy.

In the centuries after the Europeans arrived, commerce in furs, lumber, sandstone, copper, iron and fish brought settlers and entrepreneurs to the region. Today its rich harvest of natural beauty and historic sites supports tourism, the latest local industry. A visit here should, logically, begin in the small city of **Duluth★**, Minnesota, where the north and south shores of western Lake Superior converge to form the Great Lakes' largest and busiest harbor.

- **Info:** ℰ651-296-5029; www.exploreminnesota.com.
- **Location:** Covering 31,700sq mi, Lake Superior is the largest body of freshwater in the world and the deepest, cleanest, clearest and coldest of the Great Lakes.
- **Don't Miss:** The views on the Brockway Mountain Drive.

SOUTH SHORE★

Broad bays and sand beaches characterize much of Superior's southern coast, which spans Wisconsin and the Upper Peninsula of Michigan. Silent remnants of the 19C copper and iron mining booms—smokestacks, headframes and company towns—mark the landscape as well. Two scenic peninsulas are worth exploring. Route 13 leads around the Bayfield Peninsula in Wisconsin through small coastal towns, including quaint **Bayfield** itself, where you can kayak to sea caves or tour the lighthouses of the Apostle Islands by boat. Reminders of the copper rush linger in towns along Michigan's **Keweenaw Peninsula★**, where Route 26 and US-41 end in remote, beautiful **Copper Harbor**. East beyond the Huron Mountains lies **Marquette**, the region's largest city.

View from Brockway Mountain Drive, near Copper Harbor

© Danita Delimont / Alamy

Apostle Islands National Lakeshore

National Park Service

Porcupine Mountain Wilderness State Park★

S. Boundary Rd., Ontonagon, MI.
Visitor center located at 33303
Headquarters Rd, at S. Boundary Rd. &
Rte. M-107. △&P ℘906-885-5275.
www.michigan.gov/dnr.

Established in 1945 to preserve the last large stand of virgin hardwood between the Rockies and the Adirondacks, this lovely park includes 60,000 acres of deep wilderness and 100mi of rugged hiking and skiing trails.

The "Porkies" lie astride a 500ft-deep escarpment that parallels the lakeshore. From the beach, the gentle slopes resemble the hunched backs of porcupines covered in a dense, bristly forest. Stunning scenery abounds from such viewpoints as **Escarpment Lookout**a and the **Summit Peak Observation Tower**.

Brockway Mountain Drive★★

Off State Rte. M-26 between Eagle &
Copper Harbors.

The highest road between the Alleghenies and the Rockies, this 9mi stretch climbs the spine of the Keweenaw Fault through a drooping corridor of birch and hardwoods. There's a reason the area is nicknamed "Michigan's top of the world." The drive peaks at a windblown 1,337ft above sea level for a spectacular **view★** of Lake Superior and the forests below. When spring arrives, so do the hawks that migrate along the peninsula. Take extra care if making the drive during the area's very snowy winters; the road is not plowed. The **Keweenaw Convention & Visitors Bureau** (56638 Calumet Ave., ℘906-337-4579, www.keweenaw.info) provides more area information.

Pictured Rocks National Lakeshore★

Off County Rd. H-58, Munising, MI.
Visitor centers located at Munising (Rtes.
M-28 & H-58; ℘906-387-3700); Grand
Marais (E21090 County Rd. H-58; ℘906-494-2660); and Miners Castle (end of Miners Castle Rd., off H-58).
www.nps.gov/piro. △&P

Apostle Islands National Lakeshore★★

Visitor center is located in the
19C Bayfield County Courthouse,
Washington Ave. between 4th & 5th Sts.
in Bayfield, WI. △P ℘715-779-3397.
www.nps.gov/apis.

Though trapped, hunted, logged, fished, farmed, quarried and visited for 400 years, this cluster of islands off Wisconsin's Bayfield Peninsula remains unspoiled. Today accessible by private boat and a regular schedule of cruises run by the **Apostle Islands Cruise Service** (℘715-779-3925, www.apostleisland.com) out of Bayfield, these 21 islands were exposed by retreating glaciers during the last Ice Age.

Characterized by pink-sand beaches, dense forests, sandstone cliffs and sea caves, the Apostles offer sailing, hiking and kayaking in summer and a variety of winter pastimes for those adventurous enough to cross the ice. Six historic light stations built between 1857 and 1891 still mark the treacherous outer islands, and park staff conduct interpretive programs at several of them.

The park also includes 12 mainland miles along the northwest coast of the peninsula at Little Sand Bay (off Rte. 13 between Meyers Rd. and Little Sand Bay Rd.).

The Area's First Residents

The written and oral history of the Ojibwe people is clear—they were the first to call the area around the Apostle Islands home. Known for being a people who showed great reverence for the land—they let nothing go to waste—the lives of the Ojibwe people were forever changed in the 1800s when the United States government forced them onto reservations.

A 42mi shoreline foot trail runs the narrow length of this 72,000-acre park, which is famed for its multicolored sandstone cliffs. Paved or dirt roads access several of the park's features, including **Munising Falls; Miners Castle**, a natural rock outcrop; and **Sand Point** in the west.

Hikers should plan to spend time on the park's 100 miles of trails. For the best view of the "pictured rock" formations on the water's edge, take one of the **boat tours** that leave from Munising (Pictured Rocks Cruises, Inc., City Pier; 📞906-387-2379; www.picturedrocks.com). Another highlight: the Au Sable Light Station (drive 12 miles from Grand Marais to the Hurricane River Campground and walk 1.5 miles east), which began operation in 1874.

NORTH SHORE★

This rocky and rugged coast spans 150mi between Duluth and the Canadian border. Along the way, scenic **Highway 61** connects fishing villages, seven state parks, and an abundance of natural beauty. To the west lie Minnesota's iron ranges, a broad expanse of national forests, and the **Boundary Waters Canoe Area Wilderness**, which can be accessed by car along the **Gunflint Trail** out of Grand Marais. Some 18mi off Grand Portage lies wild **Isle Royale**, an island wilderness and national park accessible on a limited basis only by boat from May through October (Grand Portage-Isle Royale Transportation Line; 📞218-475-0024, www.isleroyaleboats.com). **Boats also depart from Houghton and Copper Harbor, Michigan.** For information, contact park headquarters at 800 E. Lakeshore Dr., Houghton, MI; 📞906-482-0984.

Split Rock Lighthouse★

3713 Split Rock Lighthouse Rd., Two Harbors, MN. ♿🅿 📞218-226-6372. www.mnhs.org/places/sites/srl.

Shipwrecks from a massive 1905 gale prompted the construction of this rugged landmark. From its rocky perch 130ft above treacherous Lake Superior southwest of the city of Silver Bay, sturdy Split Rock Lighthouse (1910) blinked its warning for nearly 60 years. Accessible only by water until 1924, the lighthouse required an elaborate system of derricks and tramways to construct and provision it, remnants of which remain today. Stop in the history center, then descend 171 steps to the beach below.

Grand Portage National Monument★

Off Hwy. 61, Grand Portage, MN. Stockade closed late Oct-mid May. 🅿 📞218-475-0123. www.nps.gov/grpo.

This remote compound once bustled with activity as the largest fur-trading depot on the Great Lakes. Hardy French Canadians called *voyageurs* were hired by fur-trading companies to paddle birch-bark canoes in the late 18C and early 19C. They set out from here, carrying their canoes past the rapids of the Pigeon River over the 8.5mi Grand Portage on their way to the Canadian interior for winter trapping. Each July, hundreds of *voyageurs* returned here to trade their furs.

Several buildings have been reconstructed on the site and are manned by costumed interpreters.

Every summer, the gathering of the fur traders is remembered today during Rendezvous Days (Aug), Minnesota's largest annual celebration.

Des Moines Area

Lying just south of the state's geographical center, Des Moines ranks as Iowa's capital and largest city. This Heartland hub boasts many of the state's finest cultural attractions, as well as the summertime **State Fair★★★**, a must for anyone wanting a hands-on experience of America's agricultural Midwest.

Highlights

1 Take in the 20C at the **Des Moines Art Center** (p335)

2 Eat food on a stick at the **Iowa State Fair** (p336)

3 Walk the Grand Staircase at the **State Capitol Building** (p336)

4 Imagine stenciling the ceilings at **Terrace Hill** (p337)

Des Moines

Where City and Farms Meet

The rugged Driftless Area in Iowa's northeast corner was the only landform in the state unaffected by glaciers: elsewhere, the landscape is characterized by uneven heaps of glacial drift, now covered with tallgrass prairie. Before the arrival of French and British fur traders in the 18C, the region was home to the Sauk and Mesquakie Indians, who called this area Moingonia, "river of the mounds." French explorers later translated the name as "La Rivière des Moines."

Permanent settlers began to arrive in the 1830s. In 1842 a sham treaty saw the Native Americans cede 10 million acres of land to the federal government and the removal of the resident tribespeople to a Kansas reservation.

Created in 1838, the Iowa Territory included present-day Iowa, part of Minnesota and the Dakotas. Iowa entered the Union as the 29th state in 1846. In the late 19C, agriculture thrived as steamboat and rail travel helped bring crops to mills and markets.

Iowa still depends on agriculture for the major portion of its revenues. It has been the nation's largest corn producer since 1890, and is covered by a blanket of corn and soybean crops.

Rolling farmland takes up 93 percent of the state's area. Here small towns still thrive among the fields, nurturing regional folk art and hearty stick-to-your-ribs cooking, influenced by the area's German heritage.

ADDRESSES

🛏 STAY

$$ Renaissance Des Moines Savery Hotel – 401 Locust St., Des Moines, IA. ✕🚻♿🅿🛎 ☏515-244-2151. www.marriott.com. 212 rooms. Listed on the National Register of Historic Places, this 1919 Greek Revival gem is directly linked to the 4mi climate-controlled Skywalk.

🍽 EAT

$$ Raccoon River Brewing Company – 200 10th St., Des Moines, IA. ☏515-362-5222. www.raccoonbrew.com. **American.** Soaring ceilings, dark wood booths and a pool hall give this downtown pub a welcoming feel. The food is a notch above your average beer hall. Niman Ranch pork medallians and a New York strip glazed with Bourbon set the standard. Five house-brewed beers are on tap at all times.

Des Moines★

Straddling the V of the Des Moines and Raccoon rivers, Iowa's capital city is also its economic and political seat. While the city's late-20C downtown skyline is somewhat bland, the excellent art museum and glittering capitol are anything but.

▶ **Population:** 206,599.

Info: Greater Des Moines Convention and Visitors Bureau. ☎515-286-4960; www.catchdesmoines.com.

Don't Miss: A day trip back in time at the Amana Colonies or the Palace of the Prairie and other examples of US Second Empire-style architecture, as well as modern architectural feats.

A BIT OF HISTORY

Responding to pressure for a more central location for the capital, the state government relocated from Iowa City (capital from 1838) to Des Moines in 1857. Through the late 19C, Des Moines' economy grew up around business and agriculture. Insurance became particularly important around 1867, when Connecticut native Frederick Hubbell helped found the Equitable Life Insurance Company here. Today the city ranks third in the world—after London, England, and Hartford, Connecticut—in the insurance industry.

Most of Des Moines' downtown activity happens in the **Court Avenue District** (Court Ave. from 5th Ave. to S.W. 1st St.), where 19C Italianate brick storefronts house nightclubs and cafes; on Saturday mornings from May to October, the **Downtown Farmers' Market★** (www.desmoinesfarmersmarket.com)—ranked among the top 10 in the US by Bon

Appétit magazine—fills the street with fresh produce, baked goods, music and crafts. The west side of town, including the **Sherman Hill Historic District**, contains beautiful Victorian residences and most of the city's best restaurants.

SIGHTS

Des Moines Art Center★★

4700 Grand Ave. ✕&🅿 ☎515-277-4405. www.desmoinesartcenter.org.

The Des Moines Art Center meanders through galleries designed by three great architects of the 20C. Architect **Eliel Saarinen's** original museum building (1948), a one-story U-shaped structure made of pale Lannon stone, hugs a hilltop perch and encircles a reflecting pool. Its galleries house the center's collection of late-19C and early-20C art,

Des Moines skyline

© Greater Des Moines Convention & Visitors Bureau

Iowa State Fair

👥 Grounds entrance at E. 30th & University Aves. For information, contact Iowa State Fair, State House, 400 E. 14th St., Des Moines, IA 50319-0198. 📞515-262-3111 or www.iowastatefair.org.

Known as America's Classic State Fair, the **Iowa State Fair★** epitomizes the rural Midwest: massive, friendly, wholesome, fattening and fun. A visual and culinary feast running for 11 days each August, it boasts everything from prize pigs and beauty pageants to a wide selection of delectable foods available on a stick.

The first Iowa State Fair was held in 1854; it moved to these 400-acre grounds in 1886 and has thrived here ever since as one of the oldest and largest fairs in the country. Lined with trees and old-fashioned lamp posts, as well as turn-of-the-20C structures for four-legged summer guests, the fairgrounds' **Main Street★** is a testament to the permanence of the event. Around it sprawl acres of rolling terrain used for arts and crafts displays, carnival rides, food tents and campgrounds. The 1909 **Grandstand**, a massive coliseum that forms the centerpiece of the fair, hosts concerts by top-billing country-music performers as well as tractor pulls, the prize-animal parade and a rodeo. But the main draw here instead is the quirky slices of American life that you won't find anywhere else—monster arm-wrestling contests, a bust of Elvis carved entirely out of butter, cutthroat baking competitions, and nearly every food you can imagine (pickles, ice cream, hot dogs, pretzels, dough) perforated with a stick for maximum portability.

with works by Americans Grant Wood and Edward Hopper, and Europeans Joan Miró, Paul Klee, Marc Chagall and Henri Matisse.

The first addition (1968), by **I.M. Pei**, was designed specially for large works of sculpture. Dark and echoey, it holds mammoth works by Claes Oldenberg, George Siegal and Frank Stella. It also offers wonderful views of Greenwood Park, the Art Center's home.

Richard Meier designed the most recent wing (1986), a curvaceous four-level pile of porcelain, glass and metal. One of the Art Center's newest off-site additions is the **John and Mary Pappajohn Sculpture Park** (Des Moines Western Gateway Park, bordered by Grand Ave. and Locust, 13th and 15th Sts.).

State Capitol Building★★

1007 E. Grand Ave. Tours available. ✕♿🅿📞515-281-5591. www.legis.iowa.gov.

Completed in 1886—the second capitol on this site—the Beaux-Arts Iowa State Capitol sparkles on its perch overlooking downtown. While its most recognizable feature is its glittering, 23-carat-gold-covered dome (modeled after Les Invalides in Paris), the structure boasts an interior that incorporates 29 types of marble.

The **Grand Staircase★★** is surmounted by stained glass and a gigantic mural depicting pioneers' arrival in Iowa. The stunning **law library★★** occupies the entire west wing of the second floor. Full-length windows let in copious light, illuminating the colorful ceiling fresco.

State of Iowa Historical Building★

600 E. Locust St. ✕ 🅿 🖉515-281-5111. www.iowahistory.org.

One block away from the State Capitol, the red granite and glass ziggurat contains eye-catching displays about various periods of Iowa history.

On the west side of the building, three levels of exhibits—which don't shy away from thorny topics such as the wresting of land from Native Americans, racism, and industry's deleterious effects on the environment—surround a bright, oak-floored atrium.

Terrace Hill★

2300 Grand Ave., 2mi west of downtown. 🖉515-281-7205. www.terracehilliowa.org.

Dubbed "Palace of the Prairie" upon its completion in 1869, 21-room Terrace Hill is considered one of the best-preserved examples of the Second Empire style in the US, designed by Chicago architect W.W. Boyington (also credited with Chicago's Water Tower, ⚲see CHICAGO). Restored to its 1880s appearance, the elegant red-brick manse, which sits above the Raccoon River Valley, now serves as the governor's residence. Highlights include 15ft stenciled ceilings, said to have taken 6,000 hours to paint. The building is filled with furniture built from the end of the Civil War up through the early 1900s.

Salisbury House & Gardens★

4025 Tonawanda Dr. From downtown, take I-235 West to 42nd St., and turn left on Tonawanda Dr. ●✑Visit by guided tour only. 🖉515-274-1777. www.salisburyhouse.org.

Nestled on 11 wooded acres stands what may seem an anachronism: a Medieval manor in a state that wasn't settled until the Victorian era. But cosmetics tycoon Carl Weeks was bent on re-creating the King's House, a royal-family retreat in Salisbury, England, in his native Iowa. The 42-room mansion, completed in 1928, incorporates three architectural styles—Gothic, Tudor and Carolean.

The house is filled with an eclectic 10,000 piece collection that includes paintings by artists Joseph Stella and Lillian Genth, both favorites of Carl and and his wife, Edith Weeks.

EXCURSION
Amana Colonies★

❯ 88mi east of Des Moines. Take I-80 East to Exit 225 (Rte. 151 North). A visitor center for the colonies is located at the junction of US-151 and Rte. 220 in Amana. 🖉319-622-7622 or 800-579-2294. www.amanacolonies.org.

This cluster of seven now-touristy villages marks the site where, in 1855, one of the largest communal enclaves in America was founded. Due to ideological conflicts, the group voted to end the commune in 1932, forming a profit-sharing corporation instead.

Today about one-third of the 1,700 residents of the villages (which together cover about 40sq mi) belong to the Church of the True Inspiration (a splinter group of the Lutherans). Architecture around the National Historic Landmark-designated site ranges from simple 19C brick, stone and frame structures to modern split-levels.

More than 70 shops, 12 restaurants, and bed-and-breakfast inns fuel a brisk tourist trade. Many of the shops sell crafts that have been produced in the area for generations, including quilts and furniture.

In the largest and oldest village, **Amana**, the **Museum of Amana History★** (4310 220th Trail; 🖉319-622-3567; www.nps.gov/history/nr/travel/amana/mah.htm) describes the religious beliefs and daily life of the Amanans through artifacts—including a schoolhouse and woodshed—and a slide show.

St. Louis Area

Tucked just south of the confluence of the Mississippi and Missouri rivers, the city of St. Louis and its environs fan out over 6,400sq mi. Encompassing 12 counties, the Greater St. Louis area includes the collar counties of Franklin, St. Charles and Jefferson, as well as the Illinois communities just east across the Mississippi. From downtown, the city unfolds westward to its border with St. Louis County just beyond Forest Park. Separate entities since 1876, the city and county are often lumped together as "St. Louis," even though communities outside the city limit are identified by their location in North, West, Mid or South County. With nearly 2.8 million people, this metropolitan area is the 19th-largest in the US.

Highlights

1 Ascend **Gateway Arch** (p341)
2 Stroll in **Forest Park** (p344)
3 Giggle over the kitschy delights of the **Museum of Mirth, Mystery, and Mayhem** (p344)
4 Take time to smell the flowers inside a **geodesic dome** (p345)
5 Explore the **largest prehistoric settlement** north of Mexico (p347)

St. Louis

MO

Beyond the Arch

From the north, the Mississippi River cuts its swath through little hills and floodplains, past farms and fields.

Missouri's Great **River Road**, Route 79 between St. Louis and **Hannibal**, parallels its course and affords several spectacular vantage points where the road climbs into the oak forests that blanket the limestone bluffs. South of the city, the Mississippi rolls past the German river town of **Kimmswick** and on to **Ste. Genevieve**, Missouri's oldest permanent settlement, founded in the 1730s by French lead miners.

Some 90mi west of downtown St. Louis, the state capitol building rises grandly from the riverbank at **Jefferson City**. Completed in 1918, the handsome edifice features a comprehensive state museum along with a remarkable room of murals wrought by Missouri artist Thomas Hart Benton in 1936. Southwest of the capital, **Lake of the Ozarks**, the state's largest lake, sprawls over 93sq mi. Created by damming the Osage River in 1929, the lake attracts fishing enthusiasts, boaters and campers to its 90mi of shoreline, while tourists swarm the area's outlet malls, fun parks and miniature-golf courses.

St. Louis and the Gateway Arch

©Photo Disc

ADDRESSES

🛏 STAY

$$$ Omni Majestic Hotel – 1019 Pine St., St. Louis, MO. ✕&🅿️ 📞314-436-2355. www.omnihotels.com. 91 rooms. Built in 1913, the Omni Majestic Hotel in downtown St. Louis occupies a restored National Historic Landmark that combines an atmosphere of timeless elegance with impeccable service. Spacious guest rooms capture the essence of European charm with Italian marble and 19C poster beds triple sheeted with luxurious linens. Contemporary comforts include dual phone lines and complimentary high-speed Internet access. The hotel is moments from attractions such as the Anheuser Busch Brewery, Busch Stadium and the St. Louis Gateway Arch. There's a $50 fee for pets (under 25 pounds) and the staff is very pet-friendly.

$$$ St. Louis Union Station Hotel – 1820 Market St, St. Louis, MO. ✕&🅿️ 📞314-621-5262. www.stlunionstation hotel.com. 562 rooms. Housed in one of the country's largest 19C railroad terminals, the opulent hotel lobby (formerly the station's Grand Hall) boasts six-story vaulted ceilings, stained-glass windows and bas-reliefs. Take a moment to take in the Tiffany allegorical window; it's been at the station since it was first built and has thankfully survived the renovations. An outdoor swimming pool and close proximity to the kid-friendly City Museum makes this an ideal spot for families.

$$ Seven Gables Inn – 26 N. Meramec Ave., St. Louis, MO. ✕&🅿️ 📞314-863-8400. www.sevengablesinn.com. 32 rooms. Built in 1926, this National Register-listed Tudor Revival apartment building in tony Clayton has been renovated and revamped as a countrified guest house. Subtle rose-and-beige-backed florals set the scene for 19C hardwood armoires and brass beds in the spacious rooms. Separate seating areas with overstuffed couches complete the picture. When the weather allows, enjoy the complimentary breakfast—baked goods and assorted quiches—at a table in the brick courtyard.

$$ The Roberts Mayfair – 806 St. Charles St., St. Louis, MO. ✕&🅿️ 📞314-421-2500. www.robertsmayfairhotel.com. 179 rooms. This 1925 downtown landmark's elegant lobby looks as glamorous as when Cary Grant stayed here in the 1950s. Rumor has it that the whole chocolates-on-pillows tradition at hotels started here as one of Grant's methods for wooing women.. The hotel's 179 smoke-free demi-suites and suites were recently renovated; business travelers will appreciate the Herman Miller Aeron ergonomic chairs and free Wi-Fi. Rooms are decorated with an elegant chocolate brown and blue color scheme.

🍴 EAT

$$$ Sidney Street Cafe – 2000 Sidney St., St. Louis, MO. Closed Sun & Mon. 📞314-771-5777. www.sidneystreetcafe.com. **Contemporary.** Exposed-brick walls and old-fashioned street lamps recall an outdoor courtyard, but this Benton Park restaurant is set inside a 19C storefront. Regulars and visitors dine by candlelight on updated classics like roasted scallops with red cabbage, and roasted leg of Missouri lamb with lemon aioli. Sweets fans will fall for the Snicker Bar cake.

$ Harry's Restaurant & Bar – 2144 Market St., St. Louis, MO. 📞314-421-6969.www.harrysrestaurantandbar.com. **American.** There are stunning views of Union Station and the Gateway Arch from almost any table at this chic downtown nightclub. Vibrant multicolored walls lined with local artwork offset the somber dark wood booths edged along 20ft-tall windows. The outside patio is the ideal place to enjoy hearty lunchtime salads or popular fish dishes.

$ Blueberry Hill – 6504 Delmar Blvd., St. Louis, MO. 📞314-727-4444. www.blueberryhill.com **American.** Residents come to this festive U-City Loop nightclub for the best burgers in town. The historic jukebox is an able stand-in when live bands aren't playing. The block-long venue is a wall-to-wall showcase of pop-culture memorabilia, including everything from Beatles dolls to Chuck Berry's Gibson guitar.

St. Louis★

Known for its unique city icon, the mammoth Gateway Arch, St. Louis is an important port city on the Mississippi River, long equated with riverboat traffic and Lewis and Clark. It was from the St. Louis area in May 1804 that explorers Meriwether Lewis and William Clark began their transcontinental Corps of Discovery expedition that reached the Pacific Ocean. Today, with a world-class symphony orchestra, Saint Louis and Washington universities, three professional sports franchises—the Cardinals (baseball), Rams (football) and Blues (hockey)—and some of the best jazz and blues music in the country, St. Louis offers the entertainment and educational variety of a much larger city. A little East, a bit of West; some North and a dash of South combine into a blend of American history, custom and culture that characterizes this "Gateway to the West."

- ▶ **Population:** 318,069.
- ◔ **Michelin Map:** p324.
- ▤ **Info:** ✆800-916-0040; 314-342-5036; www.explorestlouis.com.
- ☉ **Don't Miss:** The iconic Gateway Arch.
- ♟ **Kids:** The open enclosures of the St. Louis Zoo.

A BIT OF HISTORY

In the 17C, some 750,000 Native Americans inhabited this landscape embossed by the earthen mounds of their ancient ancestors. The French came next, and their influence still lingers in the architecture and atmosphere. In 1764 fur traders Pierre Laclede and René Chouteau named their riverfront trading post for Louis IX, French king and saint, and the Louisiana Purchase in 1803 established St. Louis at the edge of the frontier. Eager settlers funneled through the growing city, headed West in the wake of Lewis and Clark (see EXCURSIONS, St. Charles). As the steamboat age dawned in 1817, river traffic increased until 100 boats a day crowded the levee. The railroads arrived in 1857 bringing new waves of immigrants, many of them Germans, who built up the industrial city that would become "first in shoes, first in booze." When the first St. Louis bridge spanned the river in 1874, steamboats succumbed to railroads. The 1904 Louisiana Purchase Exposition, better known as the **St. Louis World's Fair**, buoyed civic spirits and gave St. Louis a new sense of culture and worldliness. Twentieth-century St. Louis shared difficult times with other industrial centers. Urban blight, suburban flight, racial tension, a declining tax base and a weakening of the manufacturing economy took their toll. Beginning in the 1960s, projects including the Jefferson National Expansion Memorial and several sports and convention venues have helped to revitalize the downtown, and a growing service sector provides jobs for upward of one-third of the labor force. Shipments of raw goods still flow through the city, which remains a major river crossing.

DOWNTOWN

Extending west from the riverfront for about 20 blocks, St. Louis' central business district is bounded on the north by Biddle Street and on the south by Chouteau Avenue.

Defining downtown's main east-west axis, Market and Chestnut Streets border a strip of public plazas and important buildings called **Gateway Mall**. Anchored at its western end by monumental Union Station and **Aloe Plaza**—where you'll find the frolicsome fountain *Meeting of the Waters* (1940) by Swedish sculptor Carl Milles—the strip abuts the Jefferson National Expansion Memorial to the east. Set about by convention centers and sporting arenas (Busch Stadium, Savvis Center, America's Center and Edward Jones

Dome), downtown also boasts Louis Sullivan's 1891 **Wainwright Building** (111 N. 7th St.), one of the earliest steel-frame skyscrapers. Another engineering wonder, **Eads Bridge**, the world's first steel-truss span (1874), crosses the Mississippi at Washington Avenue. Just north of the bridge, nine square blocks of 19C commercial warehouses have been converted into a dining and entertainment district known as **Laclede's Landing**. South of downtown lies the historic **Soulard** neighborhood.

Jefferson National Expansion Memorial★

Along the riverfront between Poplar St. & Washington Ave. ℘314-655-1700. www.nps.gov/jeff.

This rectangular greensward occupies the historic levee once alive with waterfront commerce. In 1939, some 40 square blocks of the then-decrepit area were razed to make way for a memorial to US President Thomas Jefferson and his vision of westward expansion. Within the 91-acre park, the soaring Gateway Arch and the Old Courthouse commemorate and document that vision.

Gateway Arch★★

Riverfront between Poplar & Washington Aves. ℘877-982-1410. www.gatewayarch.com.

This astonishing bend of steel is, at 630ft, the tallest man-made monument in the US. An early work by architect Eero Saarinen, it was completed with much fanfare in October 1965 and has since come to symbolize St. Louis. The arch astounds for its scale, its construction and, most of all, for its shimmering skin and crisp geometry.

Underground entrances at each foot access the visitor center, where the **Museum of Westward Expansion** (M2 on map) uses historic artifacts and photographs to trace the settlement of America. In the Tucker Theater, a spine-tingling 35min film called ***Monument to the Dream*★** documents the precarious construction process.

For those who wish to ascend the arch, small tram cars climb up inside the curve of each leg to the apex. Since by law no building in St. Louis may exceed the monument in height, small portholes at the top provide the best **view★** of the city. (To avoid crowds, purchase tickets early for timed entry to the tram and movies.)

The Old Courthouse★

11 N. 4th St. ℘314-655-1600. www.nps.gov/jeff.

To the west across Memorial Drive, St. Louis' historic Greek Revival courthouse was completed in stages by the 1860s with the addition of a cast-iron dome in the Italian Renaissance style. Within these walls slaves Dred and Helen Scott won their suit for freedom in 1850; overturned by higher courts, the Dred Scott Decision hastened the Civil War.

The Old Courthouse

© Shaun Clark/iStockphoto.com

Under its elegantly restored rotunda, the Old Courthouse now houses the site's National Park Service headquarters, as well as four compact **history galleries★**.

Basilica of St. Louis, King (The Old Cathedral)

209 Walnut St. ♿ 🅿 ✆ 314-231-3250. www.psichurch.com/churches/140stlouis.

Completed in 1834, the cathedral served a diocese that covered half the continent. Granted basilica status by the Pope John XXII in 1961 for its age and influence, the church was restored to its original appearance in 1963 and remains the seat of an active parish. The simple Neoclassical elegance of the mauve and blue **interior★** strongly reflects the church's French roots.

Union Station★★

Market St. between 18th & 20th Sts. ✗♿🅿 ✆ 314-421-6655. www.stlouisunionstation.com.

By every measure monumental, the Richardsonian Romanesque profile of Union Station rivals the Gateway Arch

for skyline honors. Architect Theodore Link took inspiration from the walled city of Carcassonne in France to design his 1894 masterwork. Restored in 1985, the station now houses a luxury hotel, restaurants and shops.

Informational panels mounted on the balustrades throughout the complex explain its history. Enter under the glass and iron porte cochere off Market Street for a breathtaking first impression of the magnificent vaulted **Grand Hall★★**. The lovely **art-glass lunette** above the entryway depicts the railroad muses of St. Louis, New York and San Francisco.

The station is also a top-notch family destination: kids will enjoy a paddle boat ride on the station's lake and the old-fashioned candy store inside the building.

🏃 City Museum★

701 N. 15th St. ✗♿🅿 ✆ 314-231-2489. www.citymuseum.org.

Mixing magic with the mundane, City Museum combines ordinary objects into a creative brew of art and ideas. The converted shoe warehouse con-

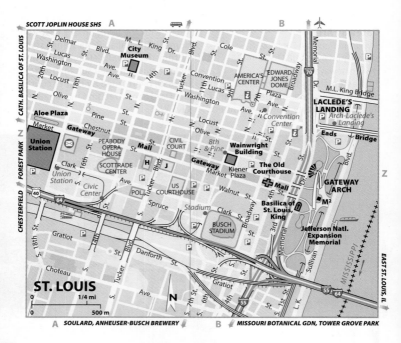

ST. LOUIS

MARK TWAIN OF MISSOURI

Among America's best-loved authors and humorists, Mark Twain (1835-1910) gave voice through his writings to the burgeoning culture of America's heartland. With an ear for dialect and a quick wit, Twain brought to life the people of the Mississippi River Valley and the very rhythms of the river he knew so well. Twain was born Samuel Clemens (his pen name comes from riverboat jargon for deep water) in Florida, Missouri.

Mark Twain

Today the **Mark Twain Birthplace State Historic Site** (37352 Shrine Rd.; ✆573-565-3449; www.mostateparks. com/twainsite.htm) preserves his tiny two-room home along with exhibits on the man and his work.

His father, a justice of the peace, moved the family to the Mississippi River town of Hannibal when Samuel was four. Laid out in 1819 between chunky limestone bluffs, the little town was swarming with riverboat traffic by the 1840s. River life and landscape bewitched the young boy and served, along with friends and family, as the inspiration for Twain's most famous works: *The Adventures of Tom Sawyer* (1876) and *The Adventures of Huckleberry Finn* (1885).

Hannibal (100mi north of St. Louis via US-61) still holds up to Twain's description of "a white town drowsing in the sunshine." Visitors can tour six historic sites and other attractions with one pass from the **Mark Twain Boyhood Home and Museum** (120 N. Main St.; ✆573-221-9010; www.marktwainmuseum.org). There are also riverboats to ride (Center Street Landing; ✆573-221-3222) and, outside of town, the **Mark Twain Cave** (Rte. 79 South; ✆573-221-1656; www.marktwaincave.com), where, like Tom Sawyer, young Twain no doubt enjoyed some boyhood adventures. Twain left Hannibal in 1853 to pursue printing, riverboat piloting, journalism and, finally, writing. He composed his Mississippi River sagas on the banks of the Chemung River in upstate New York, where he spent summers with his wife's family from 1870.

Tom Sawyer's House

Missouri's Weinstrasse

For a fun excursion from Defiance, take Route 94 West and enjoy lunch and an afternoon of wine tasting on the **Missouri Weinstrasse**. Along the banks of the Missouri River west of St. Louis, 19C German immigrants planted vineyards and established the first American wine district. Today, Route 94, Missouri's **Wine Route**, bends along the river for 20mi from Defiance to Dutzow past wineries that date to the mid-1800s. For maps and information, contact Missouri Wine and Grape Board ℰ800-392-9463 or www.moweinstrasse.com.

tains three floors plus a fantastical rooftop playground furnished largely with recycled materials—from conveyer belt spindles to laboratory mouse cages. Kids might even find they have a passion for architecture thanks to the museum's ever-changing stash of relics. Don't miss the kitschy delights in the Museum of Mirth, Mystery, and Mayhem on the third floor. Families with wee ones will appreciate Toddler Town, a shrunken version of many of City Museum's full-size exhibits.

ADDITIONAL SIGHTS
Forest Park
www.forestparkforever.org.
St. Louis' major green space occupies nearly 1,300 acres at the city's west end. Opened in 1876, it covers more ground than New York's Central Park and is famous for having hosted the Louisiana Purchase Exposition in 1904. This pleasant park today provides the setting for several of St. Louis' major cultural institutions including the city's art museum, zoo and science museum. A day spent here might include a stroll in nearby **Central West End**, the historic neighborhood at the park's northeast corner where elegant homes, trendy bistros and small shops share the tree-lined blocks.

Saint Louis Art Museum★
1 Fine Arts Dr. ✕ & 🅿 ℰ314-721-0072. www.slam.org.
Founded in 1879, the art museum took up residence here after the 1904 world's fair in the exposition's only remaining permanent building, the Beaux-Arts Palace of Fine Arts (1904, Cass Gilbert). With a collection of 33,000 pieces

spanning the gamut of world art from ancient to modern and Eastern to Western, the museum is particularly strong in German Expressionists, including the largest cache of works by **Max Beckmann** anywhere.

St. Louis Zoo★
1 Government Dr. ✕ & 🅿 ℰ314-781-0900. www.stlzoo.org.
The impetus for this fine zoo came from the huge wire mesh "flight cage" built by the Smithsonian Institution to house the US bird exhibit at the 1904 world's fair. A pioneer in the use of open enclosures, the zoo's 90-acres include the "River's Edge," where elephants hang out, "Historic Hill," a 1920s-inspired architecture showcase where primates also play, and, so kids can have a hands-on experience, a petting zoo. When wee ones are ready for a break, climb aboard the zoo's railroad for a 20min narrated tour of the animal exhibits.

St. Louis Science Center
5050 Oakland Ave. ✕ & 🅿 ℰ314-289-4400. www.slsc.org.
In the mold of many modern science museums, this bustling and colorful complex offers hundreds of hands-on science and technology exhibits, as well as an OMNIMAX theater. The "Discovery Room" caters to kids ages 3-7. A glass-enclosed bridge and an underground tunnel connect with **McDonnell Planetarium** across busy US-40/I-64, providing the perfect setting to explore high-speed roadway design.

Cathedral Basilica of Saint Louis★★

4431 Lindell Blvd. Guided tours available. ♿🅿℘314-373-8200. www.cathedralstl.org.

Several blocks east of Forest Park, the handsome, if reserved, Romanesque exterior of this Catholic cathedral belies the breathtaking riot of color inside. From narthex to sanctuary and up to the apex of the 143ft central dome, 41.5 million pieces of glass tesserae in 8,000 colors encrust 83,000sq ft. Byzantine in style, the spectacle represents the largest mosaic collection in the world. Construction began in 1907, and the mosaics took 20 artists more than 75 years to complete.

A museum about the church and its mosaics occupies the lower level.

Lavish interior of Cathedral Basilica of Saint Louis
© Diana Lundin/iStockphoto.com

Anheuser-Busch Brewery★

12th & Lynch Sts. 🐾Visit of interior by guided tour only. ♿🅿℘314-577-2626. www.budweisertours.com.

German immigrants used the cool depths of St. Louis' network of underground limestone caves to age their beer. On the south side, where caves were especially plentiful, Eberhard Anheuser established his brewery in 1860. Son-in-law Adolphus Busch launched the first national brand of beer with the debut of Budweiser in 1876; today Budweiser is the top-selling beer in the world and Anheuser-Busch is the largest brewery.

Hour-long walking tours of the 100-acre world headquarters begin at the **Tour Center** and take in the well-maintained brewing, aging and bottling buildings. One highlight are the pristine **stables**, built in 1885 to house the brewery's drafthorses, and today occupied by one of the famous Anheuser-Busch Clydesdale teams.

Missouri Botanical Garden★★

4344 Shaw Blvd. ✗♿🅿℘314-577-5100. www.mobot.org.

A labor of love by wealthy merchant Henry Shaw, the 79-acre Missouri Botanic Garden opened to the public in 1859. Paths wind through a variety of gardens, representing different historic styles, groupings of related plants, and theories of garden design. Highlights include the **Climatron®** conservatory, a half-acre area housed under a geodesic dome that houses an impressive tropical rainforest. Another favorite of visitors:, the **Japanese Garden★**, which, at 14 acres, is the largest of its kind in the US. **Tower Grove House**, Shaw's country estate, is the centerpiece of the Victorian District. The **Linnean House** conservatory (1882) has exhibited camellias for more than a century.

South of the garden lies the 276-acre **Tower Grove Park** (4255 Arsenal St.; ℘314-771-2679; www.towergrovepark. org). Also donated to the city by Henry Shaw, it survives as a rare unaltered example of Victorian park landscaping, complete with gazebos, pavilions and a bandstand. The park is a favorite of picnickers and joggers.

Scott Joplin House State Historic Site

2658 Delmar Blvd. 🐾Visit by guided tour only. ♿℘314-340-5790. www. mostateparks.com/ScottJoplin.htm.

African-American jazz musician Scott Joplin (1868-1917) composed some of

Historic Daniel Boone Home & Heritage Center

his best-known ragtime works during the two years he occupied this second-floor flat. Soon enough he was known as the "King of Ragtime."

The home is still lit by gaslight and features furnishings that popular in 1902, when Joplin and his wife, Belle, lived in the home.

EXCURSIONS
St. Charles★

◐ 22mi west of St. Louis. Take I-70 across Missouri River to the 5th St. Exit, then north to First Capitol Dr. Turn right on Main St. ℘636-946-7776. www.historicstcharles.com.

Just over the Missouri River lies this historic hamlet established by French-Canadian fur traders in 1769. Today St. Charles, the oldest settlement on the river, preserves its past in the **Frenchtown Historic District** (N. 2nd St. between Decatur & Tecumseh Sts.) and the **South Main Historic District★**, which stretches for 10 blocks south of Jefferson Street (walking-tour brochures for both districts are available at the visitors bureau, 230 S. Main St.; ℘636-946-7776). Lewis and Clark set off from here in 1804 to chart the unknown Louisiana Purchase; the **Lewis and Clark**

Boat House and Nature Center (1050 Riverside Dr.; ℘636-947-3199; www.lewisandclark.net) recounts their journey via artifacts, displays about the Missouri River ecosystem and replicas of the expedition's boats.

There's still plenty of trading to be done in the stores and antique shops of St. Charles. It's also well-known for its many festivals and events.

Historic Daniel Boone Home & Heritage Center

◐ 35mi west of St. Louis in Defiance, MO. Take I-40/64 West to Rte. 94 South, turn right on Hwy. F to no. 1868. ☞Visit by guided tour only. ℘636-798-2005. www.danielboonehome.com.

Nestled in Missouri's rolling farm country, this living-history village—and registered National Historic Site—focuses on the limestone home of legendary frontiersman Daniel Boone (◔ see WESTERN KENTUCKY), completed here in 1810.

Born in Pennsylvania, Boone (1734-1820) moved in 1799 with his family to what later became Missouri. He spent his old age in this house and died in his second-story bedroom in 1820.

Of note on the grounds is the lovely 1838 **Old Peace Chapel★**. The village tour walks visitors into a typical day in the early 1800s.

Cahokia Mounds State Historic Site★★

◗ 8mi from St. Louis in Collinsville, IL. Take I-55/70 East, get off at Exit 6, go right on Hwy. 111 for .25mi. then left on Collinsville Rd. for 1.5mi. Turn right on Ramey St. to Interpretive Center. ♿ 🅿 ✆618-346-5160. www.cahokiamounds.com.

This 2,200-acre UNESCO World Heritage Site was the largest prehistoric settlement north of Mexico, sustaining at its peak as many as 20,000 people.

Begin your visit at the **Interpretive Center** with a 15min slide show and an elaborate exhibit that explores life in Cahokia between AD 700 and AD 1400. Archaeologists believe the complex and sophisticated "schiefdom" was the center of a vast trading network supported by the rich agricultural bounty of the Mississippi floodplain.

Although the Cahokians mysteriously abandoned the site by the 1400s, the giant earth mounds they built for ceremony and burial remain. The largest, 100ft-high **Monk's Mound,** has a base of more than 14 acres.

National Winston Churchill Museum

◗ 100mi west of St. Louis on the Westminster College campus in Fulton, MO. Take I-70 West to US-54 South, then turn left on Rte. F to Fulton. 501 Westminster Ave. Open daily 10am-4pm. ✆573-592-5369. www.churchillmemorial.org.

A 17C Christopher Wren-designed English church cuts a surprising silhouette in this small Missouri college town of Fulton, Missouri, but St. Mary the Virgin, Aldermanbury, is indeed authentic. It marks the site where British statesman Sir Winston Churchill (1874-1965) gave his famous "Sinews of Peace" speech on March 5, 1946—in which he immortalized the phrase "Iron Curtain."

Churchill served as British Prime Minister during World War II. After defeat in the election of 1945, he traveled abroad, giving speeches and touring. In 1946, he and US President Harry Truman were invited to Westminster College, where Churchill delivered his speech on the campus.

The venerable **church** was moved here in 1969.

Enter through the museum, where a 12min video and exhibits will introduce you to Churchill's life and the restoration of the church.

Aerial view of Cahokia Mounds State Historic Site

© Jim Wark/Photolibrary

Mid-South

Elvis statue, Memphis, Tennessee
© Memphis Convention & Visitors Bureau

Memphis Area

Like the ancient Egyptian city for which it is named, Memphis, Tennessee, grew beside a great river to become a hub of trade, culture and population for the surrounding delta and beyond. The major urban presence on the Mississippi River between St. Louis and New Orleans, Memphis began as a 19C cotton exporting town and evolved into a distinctive business, transportation and tourism center with a wide-reaching regional identity—unusual for a US city. For those who wonder where "the South," "the Midwest," and "the West" merge (or collide) in the American imagination, the answer is "somewhere around here."

Highlights

1 Digging into a pit-barbecued slab of **pork ribs** (p251)

2 Strolling down **Beale Street**, home of the blues (p354)

3 Wandering **Graceland**, estate of the late Elvis Presley (p354)

4 Remembering at the **National Civil Rights Museum** (p356)

Memphis TN

Blues and Barbecue

Home of Elvis Presley and music called the blues, Memphis sits just across the river from Arkansas, birthplace of the quintessential "New South" Democrat, former US President Bill Clinton (whose Southern accent sounds remarkably like Elvis'). Yet in Memphis, Civil War and Old South sights are far less prominent than the city's African-American musical and civil rights legacies. Although Little Rock, the Arkansas capital,

Pork barbecue with typical sides

© Gwen Cannon/Michelin

is definitely Southern, the state is overrun with mountains and imbued with a pioneer sensibility that leans more westward than toward the Deep South.

A few hours' drive north lies historic Eureka Springs, a popular resort in the heart of the Ozark Mountains. Like Hot Springs National Park near Little Rock, Eureka Springs has been a tourist attraction offering "healing" waters for generations. From Eureka Springs, it's only 60mi to **Branson**, Missouri, an incongruously pioneer setting for big-production-style musical theater. In Branson, top country and Las Vegas performers offer mainstream middle-American entertainment (no edgy, experimental productions here) and draw crowds of thousands. From a vantage point high on the Memphis bluffs overlooking the Mississippi, it is easy to understand why westbound explorers, hardscrabble pioneers, cotton merchants, riverboat gamblers, and innumerable hopefuls toting harmonicas and guitars all began—or ended—their journeys in Memphis. For the modern traveler, an intriguing cultural question is where and how—somewhere between Memphis and Branson, a distance of 300mi—the South has irretrievably ended and the Midwest has begun.

ADDRESSES

🛏 STAY

$$$ The Capital Hotel – 111 W. Markham St., Little Rock, AR (ideal choice for the Ozarks). ✖♿🅿 📞501-374-7474. www.capitalhotel.com. 94 rooms. Since Bill Clinton's first presidential campaign, this landmark has been the headquarters of politicians and international media. The cast-iron facade was pre-assembled and bolted onto the original building back in the 1870s. A stained-glass skylight caps the two-story lobby. Guest rooms are spacious and plushly furnished and feature fine Frete linens and other luxurious amenties.

$$$ Palace Hotel and Bath House – 135 Spring St. Eureka Springs, AR. 📞479-253-7474. www.palacehotelbathhouse.com. 8 rooms. Behind its rustic limestone facade, this old-fashioned hostelry re-creates the bygone era of natural therapeutic spa resorts. Rooms are comfortably appointed with Victorian period antiques, and all feature in-room Jacuzzis; you can also make appointments for traditional spa treatments in the lower level.

$$$ The Peabody – 149 Union Ave., Memphis, TN. ✖♿🅿 📞901-529-4000. www.peabodymemphis.com. 464 rooms. The city's largest and oldest hotel (1925) remains the hub of downtown's social scene. Guests gather in the two-story lobby at 11am and 5pm to watch the resident ducks march down a red carpet to take their rightful place in the famous marble fountain. New Classic-style furnishings and pale pastel fabrics have polished the aging dowager's appearance.

$$ Talbot Heirs Guesthouse – 99 S. 2nd St., Memphis, TN. 📞901-527-9772. www.talbotheirs.com. 8 rooms. A favorite with celebrities, this intimate property sits across the street from the Peabody, and just a block from Historic Beale Street. Accommodations are mini-apartments ranging in style from retro 1960s to simple Shaker design. All come with separate living areas and full kitchens—stocked with groceries on request. Breakfast muffins, scones and fresh fruit are already in the pantry when you arrive.

🍴 EAT

$$ Red Door – 3701 Old Cantrell Rd., Little Rock, AR. 📞501-666-8482. www.reddoorrestaurant.net. **Southern.** Part southern roadhouse, part contemporary hotspot, chef Mark Abernathy's eclectic eatery serves up traditional southern favorites with a modern twist such as halibut with black rice and coconut beurre blanc, or to-die-for smoked ribs. Fans rave about the mac n'cheese.

$$ Blues City Cafe – 138 Beale St., Memphis, TN. 📞901-526-3637. www.bluescitycafe.com. **Southern.** This is the top jukebox joint on the downtown club strip. Aluminum chairs and worn Formica tables create the right atmosphere to down hefty portions of porterhouse steak, meaty pork ribs and fried catfish. Food served until 3am on weekdays and until 5am on weekends.

$ Gus's World Famous Fried Chicken – 310 S. Front St., Memphis, TN. 📞901-527-4877. www.gusfriedchicken.com **American.** As down-home as it gets, this bare-bones dining area with white-tile walls and checked oilcloth table covers dishes out sizzling portions of tender, juicy fried chicken. Don't forget the essential go-withs: fried dill pickles and fried green tomatoes.

$ The Rendezvous – 52 S. 2nd St., Memphis, TN. Closed Sun & Mon. 📞901-523-2746. www.hogsfly.com. **Barbecue.** Residents swear this basement restaurant off a downtown alley makes the best pit-barbecued pork ribs in town. The dry rub is a secret family recipe, so don't ask. Plates come with requisite baked beans and slaw.

Memphis★★

Known as "the home of the blues and the birthplace of rock and roll," this bustling Mississippi River port is a lively place with an appealing blend of Southern manners, cosmopolitan riches, and rough-and-tumble river blues; its most internationally famous resident, the late Elvis Presley, personified all these characteristics. Today, visitors to Memphis' legendary Beale Street find that the spirit of Presley's music—as well as that of bluesmen W.C. Handy, B.B. King and countless others—is alive and thriving in dozens of small clubs. On a more somber note, Memphis was also the site of the 1968 assassination of civil rights leader Dr. Martin Luther King, Jr.

▶ **Population:** 655,155.
Info: ☎901-543-5300. www.memphistravel.com
◖ **Location:** Memphis lives on the Mississippi, across the river from Arkansas.
⊘ **Don't Miss:** The American icon of Graceland and legendary Sun Studio, the birthplace of Rock 'n' Roll.
Kids: No one of any age can resist watching ducks walking the red carpet at the Peabody hotel.

A BIT OF HISTORY

Although French explorer René-Robert Cavelier, Sieur de La Salle claimed the area for France in 1682, this desirable property high on a bluff above the river delta was sought after by indigenous Chickasaw tribes, as well as by Great Britain and Spain.

After the Revolutionary War, the area came under control of the newly formed United States, and by 1819 military hero **Andrew Jackson** and others had organized and named the new settlement Memphis. The town became a center for merchants and slave traders who bought and sold cotton, slaves and supplies for plantations throughout the vast fertile delta, from Kentucky south to the port of New Orleans.

A strategic target during the Civil War, Memphis was held by Union forces from 1862 until the war's end. Three virulent yellow fever epidemics decimated the city between 1867 and 1878, with thousands dying (primarily the more susceptible white population) and thousands more fleeing the mosquito-infested terrain. In 1879 the city went bankrupt, had its charter revoked by the state legislature and officially ceased to exist for 12 years.

Steamboat trade revitalized the river port in the 1890s, and by the early 20C, Beale Street, the African-American commercial and entertainment district, was home to the nation's leading black-owned businesses. For a new generation of free Americans of color—former slaves, aspiring merchants and ambitious entertainers—Memphis became one of the most attractive destinations in the country.

Following a difficult period in the mid-20C—marked by the Great Depression,

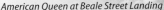
American Queen at Beale Street Landing

© Memphis Convention & Visitors Bureau

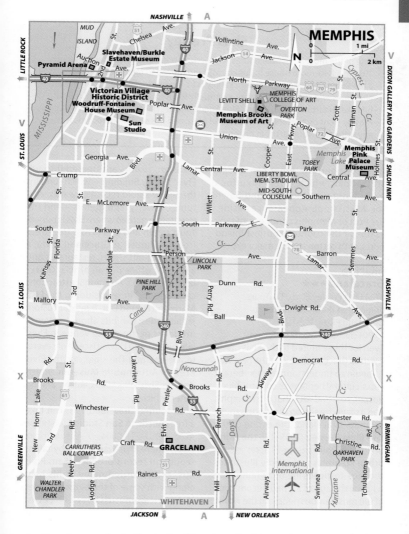

Jim Crow laws, and a decline in the US cotton market—the city has rebounded with the revival of Beale Street and the preservation of the surviving Adams Avenue mansions in the **Victorian Village Historic District**. The latter includes the nearby Second Empire-style **Woodruff-Fontaine House Museum** (680 Adams Ave.; ℘901-526-1469; www.woodruff-fontaine.com), built in 1871. Other promising signs of revival: the gleaming riverfront **Pyramid Arena** (1 Auction Ave.), a silver-and-glass former sports arena now occupied by a branch of the outdoor-gear retailer Bass Pro Shops, and the refurbished historic **Peabody Hotel** (149 Union Ave.), which parades its main attraction—a group of mallard ducks—on a red carpet across the lobby twice each day.

To the casual observer, the giant river that flows past Memphis seems oddly ignored, but it's possible to stroll down for a closer look at **Beale Street Landing**, home to restaurants, shops and the port of call for the **Memphis Riverboats** sightseeing paddlewheeler (45 Riverside Dr.; ℘901-527-2628; www.memphisriver

Elvis Presley

One of the most influential figures of American pop culture was born poor in 1935 in a two-room house in Tupelo, MS, and moved to Memphis when he was a teenager. Presley developed rockabilly, a fusion of African-American rhythm and blues and country music, but eventually focused solely on rock 'n' roll with hits like "Hearbreak Hotel" and "Blue Suede Shoes". Handsome and charismatic, Presley went on to star in 31 Hollywood films, and has sold more records than any other individual artist in history.

boats.net) and the American Queen steamboat, which offers luxurious multi-night excursions up and down the Mississippi. Appearances aside, the Port of Memphis continues to rank as one of the country's busiest inland ports, with cotton again a major export.

SIGHTS
Graceland★★★
3734 Elvis Presley Blvd. ☎Tours originate at the visitor center at Graceland Plaza. ✕&🅿
☏901-332-3322. www.elvis.com.
Even for those inured to the Elvis myth, a visit to Graceland is by far the best way to begin to understand the exuberant cross-cultural heritage of country, blues, gospel, soul and rock that put Memphis and its favorite son on the world's musical map. Graceland, the estate of the late **Elvis Presley** (1935-77), the "King of Rock 'n' Roll," sits on 13 acres in suburban Memphis and vividly illustrates the rags-to-riches life of a young man who, by the age of 22, had become one of the most famous people in the world. In 1957 the singer purchased Graceland, a Southern Colonial-style mansion built in 1939 for a wealthy Memphis doctor. Stepping through the doorway of Graceland—one of the few places where Presley could escape the incessant attention of media and fans—visitors immediately sense how much the singer became a prisoner of his own fame. Furnished in 1950s to 70s style—white plush carpeting, a themed den called "the Jungle Room," avocado and harvest-gold kitchen appliances—the house was equipped above all for music, with Elvis' sound system carrying music to every room. In addition to touring the

mansion, visitors are steered through **Elvis' Trophy Building**—which contains the singer's gold records, awards, costumes, jewelry, and guitars—and the meditation garden where Elvis is buried. Tours begin and end across the street from the house at Graceland Plaza, a complex of gift shops, restaurants and a US post office (for an official Graceland postmark). Additional attractions can be found here, including the **Lisa Marie** and **Hound Dog II JetStar** custom jet airplanes; exhibits about Las Vegas (frequent performance venue in Elvis' later years), and Hawaii (scene of several movies starring The King); and the **Elvis Presley Automobile Museum**, which displays Elvis' pink 1955 Cadillac, among other vehicles.
After touring Graceland, fans can take a free shuttle to **Sun Studio** (706 Union Ave.; ☏901-521-0664; www.sunstudio. com), where Elvis was signed by talent scout and record producer Sam Phillips, and recorded many of his hits, along with some of the biggest names in American music (Jerry Lee Lewis, Johnny Cash). The guided studio tour (40min) includes the chance to stand inside the recording room and listen to session outtakes.

National Civil Rights Museum★★
450 Mulberry St. &🅿☏901-521-9699.
www.civilrightsmuseum.org.
From the outside, this unusual museum looks exactly like what it once was—the 1950s-era Lorraine Motel, the finest lodging available for gen-erations of Jim Crow-era African Americans traveling through Memphis. The hotel hosted such luminaries as Cab Calloway,

SINGIN' THE BLUES

As Archibald MacLeish once versified, "a poem should not mean, but be," and so it is with the blues, as difficult to define as poetry.

While certainly descriptive of a state of mind, the term blues derives from what musicologists call a "blue note"—a technique of deliberately flatting (lowering) the third, fifth or seventh note of a major chord from time to time to give a minor or "bent" sound on certain phrases in a song.

In its most basic form, blues is a powerfully rhythmic, repetitive, guitar-based folk music with simple, often wry lyrics that mourn or mock the players' lives of hard labor, love and loss. With three-line stanzas of recurring phrases and chord progressions that are easy to follow, blues music is accessible for listeners and amateur musicians alike. In the hands of highly skilled blues artists such as the legendary **Robert Johnson** (1911-38), **Muddy Waters** (1915-83) or **B.B. "Blues Boy" King** (b.1925), the blues can be a spellbinding evocation of universal human emotions.

An amalgam of African slave chants, work songs and spirituals, this unique American musical form was born in the dusty cotton fields of the Mississippi River delta and traveled north on the "blues highway"—US-61—that ran alongside the river from Vicksburg to Memphis. By the early 1900s, the music was known as the Delta, Mississippi, or Memphis blues (as distinguished from the Chicago blues, a northern descendant with a more urban, amplified and less acoustic sound). In Memphis, this indigenous music was adapted and expanded upon—and published in precise musical scores—by classically trained African-American composer and bandleader **W.C. Handy** (1873-1958). Known as "the Father of the Blues," Handy composed hundreds of songs—the "Memphis Blues," the "St. Louis Blues," the "Beale Street Blues"—and popularized them among black and white musicians and listeners nationwide. His sophisticated tunes had a major impact on the development of American jazz and cabaret music as well as, of course, rock and roll.

Today, devoted blues fans from around the world can find first-rate live blues, both old and new, in dozens of clubs and outdoor venues in Memphis and smaller towns across the region. Memphis' **Beale Street** district draws thousands to blues festivals each year, including the annual **Beale Street Music Festival** (early May), the **Blues Music Awards** (formerly the **W.C. Handy Blues Awards**) weekend (late May), the **Memphis Music and Heritage Festival** (late summer).

Beale Street

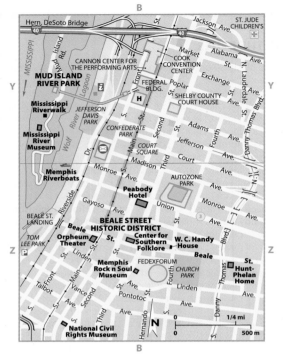

Aretha Franklin, B.B. King, and civil rights leader **Dr. Martin Luther King, Jr.**, who was assassinated on the balcony outside his room here on 4 April 1968. Today the former hotel is a 22,800sq ft memorial depicting key events of the US Civil Rights Movement in the 1950s and 60s. Visitors will be moved by the spectacle of life-size mannequins—Memphis' striking garbage workers—who bravely carried picket signs declaring "I AM A MAN" in front of police armed with bayonets.

By far the most emotionally wrenching space in the museum, however, is the **upstairs balcony** and **hotel rooms 306 and 307**, left as they were on April 4, 1968, as Dr. King's aides tried frantically to save him after the sniper's attack. In silent testimony to enduring grief, memorial wreaths adorn the balcony railing, and the two vintage Cadillacs used by the King entourage are still parked below.

Temporary exhibits host a diverse range of touring shows sympathetic to the museum's human rights ethos.

Beale Street Historic District★★

Beale St. between Main & 4th Sts. ✕ ◇
www.bealestreet.com.

A four-block-long, neon-lit midway of clubs, restaurants, record stores and souvenir shops (where automobiles are off-limits after dark on week-ends), Beale Street is a living museum that nurtures new talent for America's most distinctive musical genre: **Mississippi blues**. A stroll down Beale Street on a spring evening is a trip through a musical wonderland, with impossibly sweet guitar licks and bluesy voices emanating from every door.

Step a few blocks off Beale to the mustsee **Center for Southern Folklore** (119 S. Main St.; ✆901-525-3655; www.southernfolklore.com), a combination of blues club, soda fountain, folk-art and rare-records gallery, museum and archive. It's a blues fanatic's paradise, the sort of place where bluesman Gatemouth Moore or harmonica great Charlie Musselwhite may simply drop in to play. Another required stop is the small white-frame **W.C. Handy House** (no. 352; 🅿 𝒫901-522-1556; www.wchandymemphis.org), relocated from north Alabama in honor of the ban-dleader and composer of "Beale Street Blues" and countless other tunes.

Memphis Rock n Soul Museum

191 Beale St., in FedEx Forum
♿🅿 𝒫901-205-2533.
www.memphisrocknsoul.org.
Opened in 2000, this audio-based museum illustrates Memphis' role as a spawning ground of great American musical styles and sounds. The visit starts with a video presentation (12min); afterward, outfitted with an audioguide, you proceed through the exhibits at your own pace, accompanied by a vast selection of musical recordings. Jukeboxes from each period allow you to hear whatever songs strike your fancy on a musical walk through history.

Hunt-Phelan Home★

533 Beale St. ✕♿🅿 𝒫901-525-8225.
www.huntphelan.com.
Owned by the same family for 160 years, this elegant Georgian mansion designed by Robert Mills was occupied by Union forces during the Civil War, serving as headquarters for Union commander Ulysses S. Grant. During the occupation Mrs. Hunt (and much of the home's original furniture) took refuge in an elaborately fitted railroad boxcar. Today the mansion operates as an inn and special-events facility.

Mud Island River Park★

Accessible via monorail from the station at 125 S. Front St. ✕♿🅿 𝒫901-576-7241. www.mudisland.com.
A man-made island just offshore from downtown Memphis, this 52-acre entertainment complex includes a 5,000-seat amphitheater, a museum of river history, a topographically accurate scale model of the Mississippi River, and **Memphis Belle Pavilion**, featuring one of the most famous B-17 bombers of World War II. At the **Mississippi River Museum,** visitors can tour life-size

replicas of a Mississippi riverboat and an ironclad Civil War gunboat. Outside, wade in the half-mile-long **Mississippi Riverwalk**, which replicates in miniature the river's 1,000mi journey from Cairo, Illinois, to the Gulf of Mexico; each 30-inch stride covers one mile of the actual river. The Gulf is represented by a one-acre water enclosure where you can journey about by pedal-boat.

Slavehaven/ Burkle Estate Museum★

826 N. 2nd St. ♿🅿 𝒫901-527-3227;
www.slavehaven-undergroundrailroad museum.org.
This c.1850 bungalow on the edge of "the Pinch" district of Memphis—so named because of the poverty of its early immigrant settlers—is thought to have been a stop on the **Underground Railroad**, the secret network of abolitionists and sympathizers who helped slaves escape the Deep South. Built by German immigrant Jacob Burkle, the house has a trapdoor and a **cellar** where runaway slaves could hide on their route north.

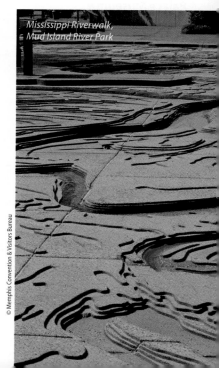

Mississippi Riverwalk, Mud Island River Park

© Memphis Convention & Visitors Bureau

Memphis Brooks Museum of Art★

1934 Poplar Ave., in Overton Park.
✕🅰🅿 🕿901-544-6200.
www.brooksmuseum.org.

Tennessee's oldest fine-arts museum, the Brooks houses more than 9,000 works, including pieces by Italian Renaissance and Baroque masters (Van Dyck, Manfredi); French Impressionists (Corot, Pissarro, Renoir, Sisley); 18C and 19C English and American artists (Stuart, Homer); and 20C and contemporary works (O'Keeffe, Wesley).

A special highlight is the museum's group of **English portraits**, the finest such collection in the South, featuring works by Gainsborough, Reynolds and Lawrence.

Exhibits in the original 1916 Beaux-Arts building range from Greek and Roman antiquities to the Renaissance, as well as a Medieval treasury of religious items in an alcove that evokes a stone-walled monastery.

The museum also boasts a noteworthy survey of vibrant works of African art.

👥 Memphis Pink Palace Museum★

3050 Central Ave. 🕿901-320-6320.
www.memphismuseums.org.

Opened in 1930 as the Memphis Museum of Natural History and Industrial Arts, the pink marble mansion houses an unusual mix of human history, anthropology and biological wonders that range from the scientific to the bizarre. The original structure was begun in 1922 as the home of Memphis entrepreneur Clarence Saunders, whose Piggly Wiggly stores became the first modern, serve-yourself grocery chain. Today the mansion contains exhibits highlighting Memphis history; the three-story entry hall boasts outstanding WPA murals by Memphis artist Burton Callicott. Exhibits in the expanded 170,000sq ft facility—which contains an IMAX theater and planetarium—include a replica of the first Piggly Wiggly store and other features of Memphis history.

Dixon Gallery and Gardens★

4339 Park Ave. 🅰🅿 🕿901-761-5250.
www.dixon.org.

Opened to the public in 1976, this first-rate art gallery is set among 17 acres of formal English gardens. Works of art by Braque, Utrillo, Cézanne, Chagall, Monet, and Renoir are displayed in two distinctly different settings: hung in the elegant living and dining rooms of the original Georgian-style **Dixon Residence** (built in 1941 for British-born cotton merchant Hugo Dixon and his Memphis-born wife), and arrayed gallery-style in a modern addition. The Dixons' decorative arts holdings include the 300 plus-item **Adler Pewter Collection**, which spans three centu-ries, and the stunning, nearly 600-piece Stout Collection of **18C German porcelain**.

EXCURSION

Shiloh National Military Park★

▶ 110mi east of Memphis. Take Hwy. 72 East to Hwy. 22 North to the park. 🅰🅿
🕿901-689-5696. www.nps.gov/shil.

Nearly 24,000 soldiers were killed, wounded or went missing after the two-day Civil War battle that raged here in 1862; it was one of the first major confrontations in the war's Western theater. Beginning with a Confederate surprise attack on Gen. Ulysses S. Grant's Army of Tennessee, the prolonged battle employed 62 cannons on a site called "the Hornet's Nest," and included gunboat fire from ironclads on the Tennessee River. At the battle's end, the Confederates, led by P.G.T. Beauregard, retreated.

Begin in the visitor center, where a film offers an account of the battle. After this orientation, take the self-guided, 9.5mi **driving tour** of the 4,000-acre battle-field that leads from the National Cemetery (where lie the remains of 3,584 Union solders) and Pittsburg Landing on the river past mass burial trenches, numerous state markers, "Bloody Pond" and the site of the Shiloh Meeting House—from which the battle took its name.

The Ozarks★

Strictly speaking, the Ozark Mountains define the region north of the Arkansas River including northern Arkansas, southern Missouri, northeast Oklahoma and part of southern Illinois. The mountains are actually an eroded sandstone and limestone plateau that uplifted out of the ocean some 285 million years ago, rather than a true mountain range. Rugged valleys, heavily forested hills, fast-flowing rivers, spectacular limestone caverns, and abundant springs (including Hot Springs National Park) characterize this region, providing enough outdoor activities to keep even the most energetic visitor busy.

🛈 **Info:** 📞501-682-7777; www.arkansas.com
⊚ **Don't Miss:** The William J. Clinton Presidential Library.
🕑 **Timing:** Save time for the soothing waters of the Hot Springs.

A BIT OF HISTORY

Traces of the region's earliest inhabitants can be found in the form of pictographs and petroglyphs etched into the walls of limestone caves. In 1686 Frenchman Henri de Tonti established the first permanent white settlement near the confluence of the Arkansas and Mississippi rivers. In 1819 de Tonti's post became the capital of Arkansas Territory. Two years later the territorial capital was moved upriver to centrally located **Little Rock** (🕭see opposite).The little town of **Mountain View** (104mi north of Little Rock at the intersection of Rtes. 9, 5 & 14) prides itself on its folk-music tradition, which draws country and folk musicians from far and wide to events such as the annual **Arkansas Folk Festival** in April. At the **Ozark Folk Center★** (1032 Park Ave., Mountain View, off Rte. 9; 📞870-269-3851; www.ozark-folkcenter.com), you can watch artisans woodworking, weaving and playing folk music.

Fans of a wider variety of music flock to **Branson**, just over the Arkansas state line in Missouri (168mi north of Little Rock; tourist information 📞417-334-4136; www.explorebranson.com), where a dazzling array of Las Vegas-style shows star performers such as the Oak Ridge Boys, Micky Gilley and Mel Tillis along with numerous tribute bands and performances. With more theater seats than Broadway, "America's live-entertainment capital" attracts millions of visitors each year to its strip of theaters along congested Route 76.

LITTLE ROCK

Arkansas' largest city (population 196,500), Little Rock is the state capital as well as the jumping-off point for sojourns to the Ozarks (Little Rock Convention & Visitors Bureau, 7 Statehouse Plaza, 426 W. Markham St.; 📞501-376-4781; www.littlerock.com). **President Bill Clinton** made his election-night victory speeches in both 1992 and 1996 at the 1842 Greek Revival **Old State House Museum★** (300 W. Markham St.; 📞501-324-9685; www.oldstatehouse.com). The compact downtown holds the grande dame **Capital Hotel**, a city landmark since 1870, host to President U.S. Grant, and the epitome of Southern hospitality. Within walking distance, the **River Market** (📞501-376-4781; www.rivermarket.info) and neighboring retailers include cafes, restaurants, bars, and shops served by a streetcar trolley. About a mile upriver, the sparkling, glass-enclosed **William J. Clinton Presidential Library** (1200 President Clinton Ave.; 📞501-374-4242; www.clintonlibrary.gov) opened its doors in 2004 above the Arkansas River, and offers an in-depth look at the times and accomplishments of the 42nd US president.

HOT SPRINGS NATIONAL PARK★★

58mi southwest of Little Rock (take I-30 South to US-270 West to

Rte. 7/Central Ave.). Visitor center located in the Fordyce Bathhouse on Central Ave. in Hot Springs, AR. ⚠&♿🅿 501-620-6715. www.nps.gov/hosp.

Hot Springs' therapeutic waters have been attracting visitors for hundreds,—perhaps thousands—of years, beginning with the early Indians who bathed here. Extraordinarily pure water from the springs is heated thousands of feet below the earth's surface, and bubbles up through faults in the underlying sandstone at a constant 143°F. The warm water flows from 47 springs at the average total rate of 850,000 gallons per day.

Famous 20C visitors have included presidents Franklin Delano Roosevelt and Harry Truman, and gangster Al Capone. Begin your tour at the visitor center on magnolia-lined Central Avenue, also known as **Bathhouse Row★**. The 1915 **Fordyce★** is the grandest of the eight remaining early-20C bathhouse structures, most of which went out of business when bathing declined in the 1970s. It has been completely restored and offers visitors a vivid look at what "taking the waters" once meant.

Today visitors can enjoy a traditional bathing experience along Central Avenue at the **Buckstaff Bath House** (no. 509; 𝒫501-623-2308), or a more modern, day spa experience at the **Quapaw Bathhouse** (no. 413; 𝒫501-609-9822; www.quapawbaths.com), the only two of the original bathhouses currently open to the public. Most of the springs have been capped, but the spring at the corner of Central Avenue and Fountain Street is easily accessible. It tumbles down the hillside like most springs originally did.

A short drive from town, the 216ft **Hot Springs Mountain Tower** (take Central Ave. to Fountain St. to Hot Springs Mountain Dr.; 𝒫501-623-6035; www.hotsprings.org) offers fine **views★** of the town and surrounding countryside.

NORTHERN ARKANSAS

Nestled among the mountains and deep valleys here is a host of historic sites, charming small towns, and the popular resort of Eureka Springs. For a lovely drive, take **Scenic Highway 7★** from Russellville (77mi northwest of Little Rock via I-40) and drive north to Harrison. This 88mi stretch traverses the **Ozark National Forest** and snakes through the mountains, past towns with names such as Marble Falls and Booger Hollow—"Population 7, Countin' One Coon Dog," reads the sign.

Blanchard Springs Caverns★

15mi northwest of Mountain View on Rte. 14. ⚠&🅿 𝒫870-757-2211. www.blanchardsprings.org.

Part of the Ozark National Forest, this cave, filled with flowstones, rimstone terraces and underground rivers, is among the most beautiful of America's cave systems. A guided tour (1hr; year-round) of the .4mi **Dripstone Trail** covers the older part of the caverns (240ft deep) and takes in the 1,150ft-long **Cathedral Room**. The more challenging 1.2mi **Discovery Trail** tour (1.5hrs; summer only) passes through a younger, deeper system (366ft deep) and requires visitors to navigate 700 steps. The **Wild Cave** tour (5hrs; advance reservation required) explores the undeveloped sections of the cave; it's great for amateur spelunkers prepared to crawl, climb and navigate red clay beds.

Eureka Springs★

42mi west of Harrison on US-62. Visitor Information Center is located at 516 Village Circle. 𝒫479-253-8737. www.eurekasprings.org.

Located just south of the Missouri border, Eureka Springs was long revered by Native Americans for the rejuvenating waters that flow from its 42 springs. A famed health resort in the 1890s, Eureka Springs now offers antique shops and crafts galleries (along Spring St.) as well as the splendidly preserved turn-of-the-19C buildings that line the steep, winding streets of the downtown **Eureka Springs Historic District**. The 1901 Palace Hotel and Bath House (135 Spring St.; 𝒫479-253-7474; www.palacehotelbathhouse.com) is one of several places in town that carry on the 19C bathing tradition.

Nashville Area

Tennessee's centrally located capital, Nashville anchors a sprawling state that extends almost 500mi from the Appalachian Mountains to the flat coastal plain along the Mississippi River. Between these extremes are ridge upon ridge of forests, divided by wide rivers and broad valleys supporting abundant wildlife and agriculture.

Nashville
TN

Highlights

1 Standing at the mike in **Studio B** (p366)

2 Music, history and live broadcasts at the **Grand Ole Opry House** or the **Ryman Auditorium** (p366)

3 Riding trains at the **Tennessee Valley Railroad Musuem** (p371)

4 Taking in the view from Lover's Leap at **Rock City Gardens** (p372)

5 Drinking in history and views at **Cumberland Gap** (p374)

Country Music Capital

Tennessee's fertile countryside shows traces of nomadic hunters as far back as the last Ice Age. Woodland and Mississippian Indians left burial mounds and structures such as the mysterious earthen walls of 2,000-year-old **Old Stone Fort State Archaeological Park** (732 Stone Fort Dr., Manchester; ✆931-723-5073; www.tn.gov/environment/parks/OldStoneFort). Long before the British and the French began staking claims in the 1700s, Cherokee, Chickasaw and other tribes had villages across the region. Because of the Cherokee opposition to white settlement in the area, both Nashville (founded 1779) and Knoxville (founded 1786) began as stockaded forts. The independent-minded Tennessee settlers, cut off from the eastern colonies by the mountains, created their own early governments: the Watauga Association (1772), the Cumberland Compact (1779-80) and the State of Franklin (1784). The area was declared a US Territory in 1789 and became the 16th state in 1796. By 1838, the last Cherokee families departed for Oklahoma on the infamous "Trail of Tears."

Tennessee was the last Southern state to secede from the Union and the first to rejoin it. Despite reluctance to affiliate with the slave-owners of the Deep South, Tennessee endured bloody battles of the Civil War at **Fort Donelson** (1mi west of Dover on US-79; ✆931-232-5706; www.nps.gov/fodo) and **Stones River** (3501 Old Nashville Hwy., Murfreesboro; ✆615-893-9501; www.nps.gov/stri) as Union troops advanced steadily southward.

Railroads, river traffic, roads and air waves eliminated any feelings of isolation by the early 1900s. In 1925 listeners nationwide began tuning in to the Grand Ole Opry, broadcast on Nashville radio station WSM. The US government established the Tennessee Valley Authority for electricity and flood control in 1933, and chose Oak Ridge for the government installation that developed materials necessary to build the first atomic bomb.

Today the **Grand Ole Opry** is more popular than ever, and Nashville reigns as the world's country-music capital.

ADDRESSES

🦉 STAY

$$$$$ Blackberry Farm – 1471 West Millers Cove Rd., Walland, TN. ♿🅿︎🖵 ☎865-984-8166. www.blackberryfarm.com. 58 rooms. Memorable views abound at this 4,200-acre retreat (17mi southeast of Knoxville airport) and working farm bordering Great Smoky Mountains National Park. Choose from rooms in the main house or cottage suites nestled among the trees. Hefty rates at this pastoral, luxurious facility include all meals, afternoon tea, and snacks stocked in several pantries. Bicycles are available for touring and canoeing or kayaking excursions can be arranged.

$$$$$ Hermitage Hotel – 231 6th Ave. N., Nashville, TN⛔ 🗙♿🅿︎ ☎615-244-3121. www.thehermitagehotel.com. 122 rooms. Four blocks from the downtown historic district, this Beaux-Arts beauty opened its doors to guests in 1910. A skylight lets sunlight stream into the ornate three-story lobby, featuring plaster-molded arches and huge floral arrangements. Guest rooms are unusually spacious, while suites boast separate living- and bedrooms, all stocked with top-notch creature comforts. Dine on updated Southern specials at the elegant **Capitol Grille** helmed by chef and farmer Tyler Brown, who creates his menus from seasonal goodies sustainably raised at the nearby Farm at Glen Leven.

$$$ Dancing Bear Lodge – 137 Apple Valley Way, Townsend, TN. 🖵 ☎865-448-6000. www.dancingbearlodge.com. 12 rooms and 8 cabins. The hand-hewn, rustic log construction of this lodge and surrounding cabins belies the superb ambience, service, accommodation and cuisine it offers at the southwest entrance to Great Smoky National Park. The restaurant's Southern Appalachian cooking—corn chowder, local pork and handmade sausage, Carolina rice—is hearty but sophisticated.

$$$ Sheraton Music City Hotel – 777 McGavock Pike, Nashville, TN. 🗙♿🅿︎🏊 ☎615-885-2200. www.sheratonmusic city.com. 410 rooms. Though built in 1978, this place resembles a Georgian mansion on its 23-acre estate 9 miles from downtown Nashville in Century City. The hotel offers abundant amenities including two swimming pools, flat-screen TVs and Bliss bath products. The cherry-paneled lobby overlooks the trellised veranda. Guest rooms are unusually large; those with balconies have courtyard or garden views.

🍴 EAT

$$ Bound'ry – 911 20th Ave. S., Nashville, TN. ☎615-321-3043. www. boundrynashville.com. **Contemporary.** Music moguls come to this Hillsboro Village spot for dishes that fuse global flavors with local staples. Tennessee trout, roasted on a cedar plank, comes with corn pudding. And the smoked double pork chop, glazed with bourbon cider sauce, is served with truffled macaroni and cheese.

$ Loveless Motel & Cafe – 8400 Highway 100, Nashville, TN. ☎615-646-9700. www. lovelesscafe.com. **Southern.** For more than 50 years, the neon sign on the Loveless Cafe has beckoned locals and country-music stars like Reba McEntire to breakfast in West Nashville. Heaping plates of country ham and eggs with red-eye gravy, country-fried steak, cheese grits, piping hot biscuits and homemade preserves are the standard. The cafe also hosts live radio broadcasts of roots music by up-and-coming artists Wednesdays at 7pm.

$ Marche Artisan Foods – 1000 Main St. Nashville, TN. ☎615-262-1111. www. marcheartisanfoods.com. **American.** Hipster central, where musicians dine on brioche and egg salad. Menus change with the seasons; weekend brunches are ever-popular, featuring fresh salads, egg dishes, crepes and decadent croissant French toast. You may see a music celebrity or two here.

Nashville★★

Set on the banks of the Cumberland River, Tennessee's capital is perhaps better known as "Music City USA." With a sports arena and restored 19C warehouses-turned-nightclubs drawing crowds to the waterfront, Nashville is a lively, upbeat tourist town with both historical and contemporary attractions. Home to Opryland, barbecue joints and Andrew Jackson's estate, it appeals especially to country-music lovers, foodies, and history buffs.

▶ **Population:** 624,496.
Ỗ **Michelin Map:** p344 and 345.
⧉ **Info:** Nashville Convention & Visitor Corp. ℘615-259-4730; www.visitmusic city.com.
🅿 **Parking:** Public transportation is limited, but parking is usually not a problem in the Music City.
☺ **Don't Miss:** How all genres of music come together at the Country Music of Hall of Fame.
👥 **Kids:** A giant sculpture of Athena delights kids of all ages at the Parthenon.

A BIT OF HISTORY

The city's history is evoked on the waterfront in a replica of the 1780 log **Fort Nashborough** (170 1st Ave. N., in Riverfront Park; ℘615-862-8400), the stockade built by James Robertson and his men after a journey of 400mi on foot through the Cumberland Gap. A few months later, John Donelson brought the men's wives and children by boat, a treacherous 1,000mi journey from the other side of the mountains.

Nashville grew rapidly with the opening of the West, attracting ambitious men including Andrew Jackson and James Polk—both of whom be-came US presidents. After the Civil War, the city emerged as an educational, reli-gious and cultural center, celebrating its rebirth with a Centennial Exposition in 1879. A full-sized replica of **The Parthenon** (2500 West End Ave. at 25th Ave., Centennial Park; ℘615-862-8431; www. nashville.gov/parthenon), complete with a 42ft statue of Athena, was built for this exposition. The lower floor now houses a city art museum with a small but qual-ity collection of works by Nashville art-ists, as well as American icons William Merrit Chase and Albert Bierstadt.

In 1916 a catastrophic fire destroyed more than 648 buildings in east Nash-

Guitar pick-shaped sign

© Jay Wright/Michelin

ville. Glimpses of the historic downtown remain along **Printer's Alley** (between Union & Church Sts. at 3rd & 4th Aves. N.) and in the glass-roofed 1903 **Arcade** (between 4th & 5th Aves.), which now houses shops and restaurants.

By the 1920s, Nashville had its own radio station, WSM, and the station's live broadcasts attracted guitar-pickers, fiddlers and singers from across the South. The Grand Ole Opry required its performers to be available every Saturday night—a restriction that, in those pre-airline days, meant that hundreds of professional musicians (and those who did business with them) found themselves living in Nashville.

THE CITY TODAY

Downtown Nashville is the home of the honkytonk. All along Broadway are bars where talented musicians play shows after the sun sets. Most of these bars do not have cover charges, so you'll pay nothing (except the cost of your beer) to hear these sounds. Pop your head in and see if there's someone playing who strikes your fancy and, if not, head to the next honkytonk. Favorites include the only-in-Nashville experience of **Robert's Western World** (416B Broadway, ☏615-244-9552; www.robertswesternworld.com), where you can buy cowboy boots while you drink and dance. Other options include a "holler and a swaller" at **Tootsie's Orchid Lounge** (422 Broadway, ☏615-726-0463; www.tootsies.net) and, for the edgier crowd, **The Stage** (412 Broadway ☏615-726-0504; www.thestageonbroadway.com).

These days "Music City USA" is home not only to the Opry and its parent company's myriad enterprises, but also to a large segment of the multibillion-dollar

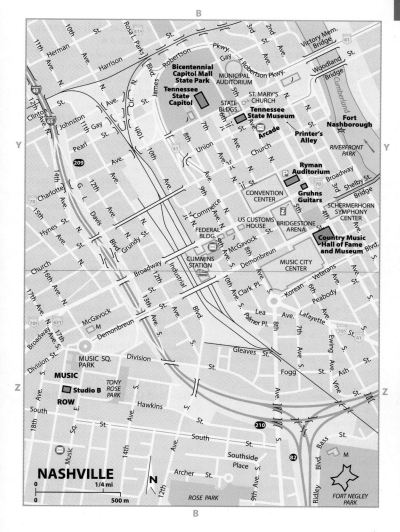

NASHVILLE

0 — 1/4 mi

0 — 500 m

N

US recording industry. **Music Row** (Division St. & Music Square E.) is a neighborhood of office towers harboring artists' agents; music publishing houses; offices for Arista Nashville, EMI, RCA and Warner Music; and signature buildings for ASCAP and BMI.

With world-class recording studios, specialty shops like the legendary **Gruhns Guitars** (400 Broadway; ✆615-256-2033; www.gruhn.com), and a resident population of skilled session musicians who readily "cross over" from country to rock and roll, gospel, soul and jazz, Nashville

ranks as the major recording venue for American popular music.

In early May 2010, a stalled storm system dumped more than 17 inches of rain in Nashville over three days, more than doubling the previous record set in 1979 and causing the Cumberland River to overtop its banks. River- and rainwater flooded areas of Nashville closest to the river, causing extensive damage to the Grand Ole Opry House, the Gaylord Opryland Resort, the Country Music Hall of Fame, Opry Mills Mall, and scores of other buildings. Damage to private property from the flood was estimated at $2 billion. Repair and remediation began immediately and continued for many months. Today, the recovered city bears few signs of the disaster.

SIGHTS

Tennessee State Capitol★

Charlotte Ave. between 6th and 7th Avenues. ♿ℰ615-741-0830. zwww.capitol.tn.gov.

The self-professed masterpiece of architect **William Strickland** (1788-1854), this Tennessee limestone Greek Revival "temple" sits high on a hill and boasts ancient Athenian models for its Ionic porticoes and towering cupola. Inside you'll find solid marble stairs, ceiling frescoes, and the restored library, where the balcony railing displays cast-iron profiles of famous figures.

Down the hill from the capitol, stop by the **Tennessee State Museum** (505 Deaderick St.; ♿ℰ615-741-2692; www.tnmuseum.org) to see the story of the state from its prehistoric beginnings through the 19C. The museum's strong collection of Civil War artifacts and weapons is well worth investigating. The Quilt Gallery shows off more than 300 traditionally patterned quilts.

Bicentennial Capitol Mall State Park

600 James Robertson Parkway. ♿🅿ℰ615-741-5280. www.tn.gov/environment/parks/Bicentennial/.

Built to honor the state's 200th birthday, this 19-acre outdoor park is in the shadow of the Tennessee State Capitol. Among the many interesting elements here are a granite wall with a timeline of the state's history, a granite map of the state, a landscaped replica of the changing foliage of the state from east to west and an amphitheater. Stop by the park visitor center to see exhibits chronicling Tennessee's struggles during the Civil War. A circle of bells plays (what else?) the *Tennessee Waltz* every hour.

The local farmers' market and a weekly flea market are located nearby off Rosa L. Parks Boulevard.

Country Music Hall of Fame and Museum★★

222 Fifth Ave. S. ✕♿🅿ℰ615-416-2001. www.countrymusichalloffame.com.

This jam-packed facility is generally considered the best of Nashville's numerous "museums" of country music and its stars. "Sing Me Back Home"— the museum's permanent exhibit— highlights the instruments and styles of country music and progresses to showy performers and their costumes (Vince Gill's shiny red baseball jacket, Loretta Lynn's dress); cars of the stars (Elvis' "Solid Gold" Cadillac); and the development of the Grand Ole Opry. The Hall of Fame itself is a room with more than 60 plaques honoring country-music artists and executives.

Admission includes a transportation to and tour of RCA's legendary **Studio B**, cradle of more than 35,000 songs. Elvis Presley and Patsy Cline played the 1940s Steinway grand piano here and guitarist Chet Atkins perfected a recording style that the world now recognizes as "the Nashville Sound."

ADDITIONAL SIGHTS

Gaylord Opry Entertainment Complex★★

2804 Opryland Dr. ♿🅿 ☺Advance reservations are required for all Opry and TV shows. ℰ615-871-6779; www.opry.com.

The world's longest-running live radio show, the **Grand Ole Opry** features the best in country, bluegrass and Cajun music. Its home is the **Grand Ole Opry House★★** — a 4,400-seat concert hall that forms the centerpiece of this mega-entertainment complex on the Cumberland River about 9mi northeast of downtown. In 1943 the Grand Ole Opry settled into the late-19C **Ryman Auditorium★** downtown (116 5th Ave. N.; ♿ℰ615-889-3060; www.ryman.com) and played to packed houses every weekend for the next 31 years. In 1974 the show moved here to this glitzy, high-tech performance venue outfitted with state-of-the-art lighting, broadcast and recording capabilities. The Opry House was severely damaged but quickly

Country Music Hall of Fame

TNVacation.com

COUNTRY MUSIC

"Country" music incorporates elements of bluegrass and Cajun and cowboy, gospel and honkytonk, rockabilly and western swing. Names associated with this musical genre include Loretta Lynn, Willie Nelson, Garth Brooks, Reba McEntire and Vince Gill. What was branded early on as "American folk tunes" (according to *Billboard* magazine in 1948), then "country and western," then "crossover country"—is now mainstream American music.

To purists, contemporary country music may seem homogenized and predictable. But the vast majority of country-music fans appear well pleased with Nashville's steady stream of catchy three-chord tunes and heart-warming lyrics, especially when delivered by Brad Paisley, Alan Jackson, Faith Hill, Carrie Underwood or Tim McGraw. Nomenclature aside, modern country music remains "folk" music—accessible, easy to imitate and adapt on various stringed instruments, and derived from English, Scottish and Irish folk-music traditions that came to the Southeast with white pioneers.

For performers just starting out, breaking into an entrenched multi-billion industry is much different from the early days, , when Roy Acuff might simply hear a nervous young singer and decide to put her on the Opry live. Yet difficult as it can be to make it big in Nashville today, aspiring guitar, mandolin and fiddle virtuosos, songwriters and singers inevitably head here. For visitors, this means that in any ordinary bar, the musicians before the microphone are probably superb.

The **Bluebird Cafe** (4104 Hillsboro Pike., Nashville; ✆615-383-1461; www. bluebirdcafe.com) is a hot spot to hear up-and-coming singers and songwriters, but live music crops up all over middle Tennessee. The fiddler in any small-town club may not be as polished as those in Nashville, but the tunes probably date back to his Scotch-Irish great-grandfather and the clogging (buck dancing) will be spontaneous and very, very good.

A few sights in the Nashville area achieve the admirable feat of presenting the wide-ranging story of this quintessential American music genre. Foremost among them is the **Country Music Hall of Fame** (p366). A visit here is a great way to precede an evening of live music.

Grand Ole Opry

© Grand Ole Opry/Chris Hollo/Hollo Photographics, Inc./TNVacation.com

restored in the 2010 Nashville flood. Today the gleaming new Opry continues to draw crowds for its Tuesday evening and weekend shows.

For a behind-the-scenes look at the Opry, take the midday backstage tour, which includes an opportunity to stand before the microphone on the grand stage itself. The four-deck **General Jackson** showboat (music and dining) plies the river.

The hotel at the **Gaylord Opryland Resort and Convention Center** (2800 Opryland Dr.; ✆615-889-1000; www. gaylordopryland.com) is a spectacle in itself, with nearly 3,000 rooms clustered around nine acres of gardens, rivers and waterfalls—all under glass. **Opry Mills** retail and entertainment complex includes many factory outlet stores, a movie theater and family-friendly restaurants.

Fisk University Galleries★

On the Fisk University campus, 1000 17th Ave. N. ♿ 🅿 ✆615-329-8720. www.fisk.edu/campuslife/FiskUniversityGalleries.aspx.

After the death of her husband (American photographer Alfred Stieglitz), painter Georgia O'Keeffe donated their personal art collection to this black institution. Today the **Carl Van Vechten Art Gallery** (Jackson St.) displays more than 100 paintings, drawings, photo-graphs and sculptures by outstanding artists from Stieglitz and O'Keeffe to Cézanne, Picasso and Rivera.

The **Aaron Douglas Gallery** (on third floor of the library, across from the Van Vechten Gallery) features work by African-American artists Aaron Douglas, Romare Bearden, and Henry Tanner, among others.

Belle Meade Plantation★★

5025 Harding Pike. ✖♿🅿 ✆615-356-0501. www.bellemeadeplantation.com.

Most antebellum plantation homes display portraits of family members in gilded frames, but at Belle Meade—a stud farm and breeding operation since 1816—the portraits are of Thoroughbred racehorses. For more than 80 years, racehorse owners worldwide came to look for promising yearlings at Belle Meade's annual sale. The 1853 Greek Revival mansion, which was faithfully restored in the 1980s to its 19C appearance, boasts 26ft limestone columns (quarried on the property), marbleized woodwork, and ornate furnishings (1840-60) by John Henry Belter, Duncan Phyfe and Joseph Meeks. The **carriage house and stable** (c.1890) show off 19C cabriolet carriages and luxurious horse stalls. A well-crafted film dramatization provides an overview of the plantation's history.

Cheekwood

1200 Forrest Park Dr. ✕ ♿ 🅿 📞615-353-8000. www.cheekwood.org.

This 55 acre-attraction is all about beauty, whether it grows in the garden or it hangs on the walls. The building itself is the former Cheek estate, a grand limestone mansion in the English style completed in 1932 for Leslie and Mabel Cheek and now listed on the National Register of Historic Places. The collection, the nucleus of which was formed by the donated holdings of the Nashville Museum of art, comprises more than 600 paintings and 5,000 prints, and photographs and works shown in temporary exhibitions.

The Hermitage★★

4580 Rachel's Lane. ✕ ♿ 🅿 📞615-889-2941. www.thehermitage.com.

Built for Tennessee military hero and seventh US president **Andrew Jackson** (1767-1845), The Hermitage in its heyday was a prosperous 1,100-acre plantation with cotton fields, fine horses and illustrious visitors. Jackson, a controversial personality nicknamed "Old Hickory" for his steadfast loyalty to his soldiers, was elected president for two consecutive terms (1828-36). Both Andrew and his wife, Rachel, are buried in the mansion garden.

Begun as a Federal-style home in 1819, The Hermitage was expanded in 1831, damaged by fire in 1834 and rebuilt in the Greek Revival style in 1836. Tours highlight exquisite original furnishings and daily activities in the kitchen, garden and slave quarters (where archaeologists are still uncovering new details). Tours begin and end at the visitor center, which has a theater, exhibits and a restaurant.

EXCURSION
Jack Daniel's Distillery★

◑ 75mi southeast of Nashville in Lynchburg. Take I-24 to Rte. 55, follow Rte. 55 South 30mi to distillery visitor center. ♿ 🅿 📞931-759-6357. www.jackdaniels.com.

The oldest registered whiskey distillery (1866) in the US, this rustic-looking establishment is the sole production facility for Jack Daniel's "Tennessee sipping whiskey," now sold in more than 130 countries. The fascinating tour (1hr 30min) covers the clear Cave Spring of iron-free water, essential to making good whiskey; the rickyard where native sugar-maple trees are burned into charcoal; the giant mash vats, where a golden-colored mixture of corn, rye and barley malt ferment pungently; and the charcoal filtering rooms, where 140-proof whiskey seeps slowly through 10ft of charcoal. A walk through one of the aromatic barrelhouses (the liquid's last stop before bottling) offers a glimpse of hundreds of oak barrels aging thousands of gallons of whiskey.

General Jackson Showboat

East Tennessee ★

East of Nashville, Tennessee's landscape is dominated by the Great Smoky Mountains, a section of the Appalachian range that runs along the state's eastern border with North Carolina. Both river towns, Knoxville and Chattanooga are the region's major cities.

- **Info:** ℘423-756-8687; www.chattanoogafun.com.
- **Don't Miss:** The combination of man-made and natural attractions at Ruby Falls.
- **Kids:** The ultimate kids' attraction is the Chattanooga Choo-Choo.

A BIT OF HISTORY

The peaks of the Great Smokies proved a daunting barrier for early settlers, until frontiersman Daniel Boone (see WESTERN KENTUCKY) discovered the Cumberland Gap (a passageway that breaches the mountains where Tennessee, Kentucky and Virginia meet) and led the way west in 1775. The gap remained the major westward route until the 1830s when steamboats and the Erie and the Pennsylvania Main Line canals gave travelers new alternatives. The first area of the state to be settled, East Tennessee developed a rich folk culture of handcrafts, music and dance that has passed down to the mountain people from the pioneers. Knoxville and Chattanooga, the region's largest cities, were both born in the late 18C. **Knoxville**, 100mi up the Tennessee River from Chattanooga and 40mi from Great Smoky Mountains National Park (see GREAT SMOKY MOUNTAINS NATIONAL PARK), served as the first capital when Tennessee became a state in 1796. (The capital moved several times before being permanently established in Nashville in 1826.)

Today its downtown is dominated by the 400-acre campus of the University of Tennessee and enlivened by restaurants and clubs in the restored **Old City** (W. Jackson Ave. & Central St. S.).

A popular tourist destination since the 1920s, Chattanooga offers a first-rate aquarium, fine arts, natural wonders and a fine selection of lodging and eateries.

CHATTANOOGA

Two distinct geographic features define Chattanooga: the wide bend of the Tennessee River and the hulking ridge of **Lookout Mountain**. Both have been pivotal in the city's history. The Cherokee

---

Davy Crockett, American Pioneer

Born into the rough life of a mountain pioneer, Davy Crockett (1786-1836) grew up to become a celebrated Indian fighter, bear hunter, trail blazer and US congressman before heading off to Texas to join the ill-fated fighters at the Alamo in present-day San Antonio. (All 187 Americans, including Crockett, were killed in this pivotal battle with Mexico for Texas' independence.)

Crockett's exploits and his legend are amply displayed at the visitor center at **Davy Crockett Birthplace State Park** (1245 Davy Crockett Park Rd., off Rte. 11 East near Limestone, TN; ℘423-257-2167; www.tn.gov/environment/parks/DavyCrockettSHP). A reconstructed log cabin here on the Nolichucky River represents the approximate location of the Crockett family's primitive dwelling. When Davy was six, his family moved farther west, eventually settling on the Knoxville-Abingdon trail and opening their rough-hewn home to travelers. The **Crockett Tavern Museum** (2002 Morningside Dr., Morristown, TN; ℘423-587-9900; www.crocketttavernmuseum.org) replicates the original inn.

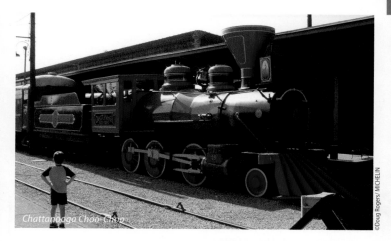
Chattanooga Choo-Choo
©Doug Rogers/ MICHELIN

splinter group called the Chickamauga settled in what is now Chattanooga around 1777, and in 1815 Cherokee chief John Ross built Ross's Landing, a trading post and ferry dock. Steamboats and railroads followed, and Chattanooga—an Indian name for Lookout Mountain—became a transportation hub. As such, Chattanooga was crucial to both sides during the Civil War. In 1863 the Battle for Chattanooga raged over Lookout Mountain and south to Chickamauga Creek in Georgia for nearly three months before Southern forces retreated.

Irving Berlin's 1941 song "The Chattanooga Choo-Choo" immortalized train travel in the early 20C. Visitors to Chattanooga can relive the experience by riding trains at the **Tennessee Valley Railroad Museum** ♿♦ (4119 Cromwell Rd.; ☎423-894-8028, www.tvrail.com) and the restored **Chattanooga Choo-Choo Terminal Station** (1400 Market St., ☎800-872-2529, www.choochoo.com), now an upscale Sterling Hotel with shops, guest rooms and restaurants in retired railroad cars.

Set high above the Tennessee River, Chattanooga's **Bluff View Art District** (High St.) is the site of the art museum as well as galleries, restaurants and a bakery-cafe.

Free electric shuttle buses geared to tourists make getting around Chattanooga a breeze.

♦♦ Tennessee Aquarium★★

1 Broad St. ♿ ☎423-265-0695. www.tnaqua.org.

This towering stone-and-glass structure dominates **Ross's Landing**, Chattanooga's restored riverfront, and opens onto a sunny plaza with fountains and rock-lined streams. Housing more than 10,000 fish, reptiles, amphibians, birds and mammals on four levels, the aquarium's major exhibits (River Journey and Ocean Journey) trace the course of the Tennessee River from its origins in the Smoky Mountains.

The excellent Penguins' Rock exhibit chronicles two cold-climate species of this water bird, while the nearby IMAX 3D Theater offers deep-sea themed film features.

Hunter Museum of American Art★

10 Bluff View. ♿ 🅿 ☎423-267-0968. www.huntermuseum.org.

This fine collection of American art from Colonial to contemporary times is housed in a two-part facility—the restored 1904 Hunter mansion and an attached 1975 modern wing. Arrayed above hand-carved fireplace mantels in the mansion are major Hudson River School paintings and examples of American Impressionists (such as Childe Hassam).

The modern wing offers contemporary sculptures and works by members

Sequoyah and his Alphabet

Scholars of the world's languages marvel at the achievement of a Cherokee silversmith named **Sequoyah** (1776-1843), who single-handedly created an alphabet for his native language and brought literacy to the Cherokee Indian nation. Born in the village of Tuskeegee (now underwater at the Tellico Reservoir near present-day Vonore), Sequoyah was the child of a Virginia fur trader and a Cherokee chieftain's daughter. At the **Sequoyah Birthplace Museum** (576 Hwy. 360, Vonore, TN; ♿ 🅿 ✆423-884-6246; www.sequoyahmuseum.org), owned and operated by the Eastern Band of Cherokee Indians, his life and accomplishments are vividly described.

Library of Congress

Se-Quo-Yah (1836), Lithograph by McKenney & Hall

of the Ashcan School (Robert Henri, George Luks, William Glackens).

Houston Museum of Decorative Arts

201 High St. 🅿 ✆423-267-7176.
www.thehoustonmuseum.org
Anna Safley Houston (1876-1951) spent her later years as an antiques dealer amassing an extensive collection of antique glassware, ceramics, furniture, textiles and music boxes. The assortment of stunning **American glassware**, includes pieces from Tiffany and Steuben to early Amberina. The collection, which includes rare Mettlach beer steins, and 19C English and American pewter, is crammed into a Victorian house a half-block from the Hunter Museum.

ADDITIONAL SIGHTS

▲▲ Rock City Gardens★

1400 Patten Rd. (Rte. 58), Lookout Mountain, GA. ✖🅿 ✆706-820-2531.
www.seerockcity.com.
Anyone who drove the rural South of yesteryear has seen "See Rock City" painted on barn roofs—and this kitschy 1932 tourist attraction still attracts hordes of visitors. Here a self-guided walking tour threads through a 14-acre expanse of windblown mountain veg-

etation amid giant boulders and cliffs, an ancient seabed carved into exotic shapes during the Ice Age. On a clear day, the **view★★** from Lover's Leap spans seven states.

▲▲ Lookout Mountain Incline Railway★

827 East Brow Rd., Lookout Mountain.
✖🅿 (at lower station, 3917 St. Elmo Ave.)
✆423-821-4224.
www.ridetheincline.com.
This cable-drawn railway, constructed in 1895 and modernized since, is both a National Historic Site and a National Historic Mechanical Engineering Landmark. And yes, the track is really steep—a 72.7 percent grade near the top, so that passengers feel almost perpendicular. From the top, drink in the views of Chattanooga and the Great Smoky Mountains. From here you can stroll to several points of interest related to the Civil War.

Ruby Falls at Lookout Mountain Caverns

1720 S. Scenic Hwy. ✖🅿 ✆423-821-2544. www.rubyfalls.com.
Like Rock City, Ruby Falls is a kitschy, old-fashioned tourist attraction built around a genuinely interesting natural

phenomenon. Entering through the brooding, ivy-covered stone Caverns Castle, visitors descend 1,200ft inside the mountain in an elevator and follow a long, narrow trail through stalactites and stalagmites to 145ft **Ruby Falls★**, an underground waterfall.

EXCURSIONS
Chickamauga and Chattanooga National Military Park★★
❂ Park visitor center is 9mi south of Chattanooga in Fort Oglethorpe, GA. From I-75, take Exit 350 West (Battlefield Pkwy.) turn left on Lafayette Rd., and go 1mi to park. ♿🅿 ✆706-866-9241. www.nps.gov/chch.

The nation's oldest and largest Civil War park (8,200 acres) commemorates the hard-fought 1863 campaign for Chattanooga, a key Confederate rail center. Begin at the park visitor center on the edge of the Chickamauga battlefield to view the film, The **Battle of Chickamauga**, and wander through the **Fuller Gun Collection of American Military Arms**. A 7mi automobile tour (map available at visitor center) of Chickamauga leads past some 1,400

monuments and markers that recall Confederate general Braxton Bragg's humiliating defeat of the Union Army in September 1863.

About 5mi north on Lookout Mountain is the Chattanooga section, **Point Park**. Here, two months later, General Grant routed Bragg's forces at Lookout Mountain, thus gaining control of East Tennessee.

The **Lookout Mountain Battlefield Visitor Center** (off Rte. 148 on E. Brow Rd.; ✆423-821-7786) features the mural-sized "**Battle of Lookout Mountain**," painted by James Walker in 1874; inside the park you'll find three batteries of cannon, the **New York Peace Memorial** and the **Ochs Museum and Overlook**. Farther down the mountain, **Cravens House**, the Confederate headquarters during the assault, is accessible by a steep hiking trail or by car.

Museum of Appalachia★★
❂ 2819 Andersonville Hwy., Clinton (16mi north of Knoxville at I-75 Exit 122). ✆865-494-7680. www.museumofappalachia.org.
Now affiliated with the Smithsonian Institution, this 65-acre collection of

---

The "Secret City" of Oak Ridge

In 1942 the US military bought 59,000 acres in an isolated valley about 24mi west of Knoxville, built a "secret city" of 75,000 people almost overnight, and began producing the fissionable material necessary for atomic weapons. The "**Manhattan Project**" came to fruition on August 6, 1945, when a US-made bomb destroyed the Japanese city of Hiroshima. The bombing of Nagasaki followed on August 9, and the Japanese surrender ended World War II just five days later.

Today, Oak Ridge's three gigantic, mysteriously named facilities from the war years—K-25, Y-12 and X-10—harbor more benign research under the US Department of Energy. The former K-25 is now a technology park, while Y-12 remains a high-security plant devoted to manufacturing technology. The former X-10 is now **Oak Ridge National Laboratory** (10mi west of Rte. 62 on Bethel Valley Rd.; ✆865-574-7199; www.ornl.gov), home to state-of-the-art research in fields including energy, supercomputers, neutron science and national security.. Guided tours depart from the American Museum of Science and Energy (below) and lead to the control room and catwalk just outside the massive Graphite Reactor, the world's first model nuclear reactor—decommissioned in 1963.

For an in-depth view of Oak Ridge, head for the **American Museum of Science and Energy** 🚹🚻 (300 S. Tulane Ave., in the Oak Ridge Convention and Visitor Center building; ✆865-576-3200; www.amse.org).

View of Cumberland Gap National Historical Park from Pinnacle Overlook

© Mike Briner / Alamy

weathered 19C log cabins and outbuildings (smokehouse, corn crib, hog house, corn mill) sits behind split-rail fences enclosing placid horses and sheep. Gobbling turkeys and clucking hens roam the grounds, and the occasional fiddler can be found sitting on a cabin porch. The provenance and estimated age of each structure is documented, usually through a story about its owners.

Self-guided tours start in the **Appalachian Hall of Fame**, a three-story edifice crammed with marvelous handcrafted items. The extensive collection of musical instruments ranges from fine examples owned by big-name artists to handmade guitars, fid-dles and banjos crafted by backwoods residents; and bears witness to the role of music in the life of rural Appalachia.

Events such as heritage days, sheep shearing and anvil throwing, and the annual Fall Homecoming, bring customs and music vividly to life.

Cumberland Gap National Historical Park★★

⊙ 60mi north of Knoxville at the border of KY, TN & VA. Take I-75 North to Rte. 63 North and follow US-25 East to the visitor center, 91 Bartlett Park Rd.,

Middlesboro. ⚠ &. 🅿 ℘606-248-2817. www.nps.gov/cuga.

A buffalo and Native American pathway for centuries, 800ft-high Cumberland Gap (half as high as nearby peaks) was discovered by white explorers in 1750 but became popular only after **Daniel Boone** (Ⓒ see WESTERN KENTUCKY) led the way through it in 1775.

Authorized as a national historical park in 1940, the 20,000-acre site encompasses the long, high ridge of Cumberland Mountain, offering spectacular vistas and 70mi of hiking trails.

For sweeping **views★★** of Virginia, Tennessee and Kentucky, take the steep, hairpin-curve drive from the visitor center up to **Pinnacle Overlook** (2,440ft). Visitors can take a half-day guided tour (reservations recommended) via park shuttle bus to the abandoned **Hensley Settlement**, a pioneer community whose last inhabitant left the mountain in 1951.

Ranger-led tours take visitors along some of the subterranean passages beneath the mountains, where you can glimpse plant and animal life especially adapted to underground survival (*appropriate hiking footwear required*).

Kentucky

Kentucky is largely rural, claiming only two cities with populations exceeding 200,000—Lexington and Louisville. Bordered by Tennessee, Missouri, Illinois, Indiana, Ohio, West Virginia and Virginia, the state's geography varies from the rugged Appalachian Mountains of the eastern coal country and the gentle terrain of the Bluegrass to the flatlands of the Mississippi River on its extreme western edge. A temperate climate and high annual rainfall render the central and western regions of the state ideal for agriculture.

Kentucky

Highlights

1 Sampling a mint julep made with fine **Kentucky bourbon** (p377)

2 The majestic Parade of Breeds at **Kentucky Horse Park** (p379)

3 Discovering **Shaker Village at Pleasant Hill** (p380)

4 Exploring underground at **Mammoth Cave** (p384)

Bluegrass and Bluebloods

As long as 12,000 years ago, Mississippian Indians roamed what is now Western Kentucky. Evidence of their presence can be found at **Wickliffe Mounds** (5mi northwest of Wickliffe, KY, on US-51/60/62; ☎270-335-3681; http://parks.ky.gov) and just over the Kentucky border at **Angel Mounds State Historic Site** (8215 Pollack Ave., off I-64 at Covert Ave. Exit; ☎812-853-3956; www.angelmounds.org) in Evansville, Indiana. Indian attacks were a constant threat when the first settlers arrived in the late 1700s, via the Wilderness Trail that explorer and folk hero **Daniel Boone** (☚see WESTERN KENTUCKY) had blazed through the Cumberland Gap. In 1775 only one settlement, Harrodsburg, existed in Kentucky. By the time Kentucky was granted statehood in 1792, settlers were raising hemp and tobacco, and breeding horses—giving rise to the state's modern Thoroughbred industry. Kentucky's fertile soil also nourished an abundance of corn, which ultimately sprouted the manufacture of bourbon whiskey (☚see BLUEGRASS COUNTRY). When war was declared between the states in 1861, Kentucky was a slave state, but it nonetheless had strong economic ties to the North. Although the state never

Mammoth Cave National Park

© National Park Service

seceded from the Union, a number of its young men fought for the Confederacy. Union victories at **Columbus-Belmont**, on the western fringe, and at **Perryville**, south of Harrodsburg, dashed Confederate hopes of winning control of Kentucky.

Coal mining began in the 1890s, and Kentucky soon led the nation in coal production. Today it ranks third (behind Wyoming and West Virginia), but the state's $4 billion coal industry still produces more than 108 million tons of "black gold" annually. Another significant part of Kentucky's revenue derives from distilleries and horse-racing, with agricultural crops of corn and soy being significant contributors to the economy. Kentucky is the country's second-largest tobacco producer (after North Carolina). Recent years have seen an expansion of the economic base with the introduction of auto manufacturers and corporate headquarters. Even so, the Bluegrass state remains timeless—a mélange of meadowlands and scenic winding roads threading pastoral towns.

ADDRESSES

🛏 STAY

$$$ The Brown Hotel– 335 W. Broadway, Louisville, KY. ✖♿🅿 ✆502-583-1234. www.brownhotel.com. 293 rooms. Equestrian artwork pays tribute to horse country in this downtown thoroughbred's English Renaissance-style lobby, complete with hand-painted coffered ceilings. Egyptian cotton linens and goose-down comforters grace pillowtop beds in the spacious, airy guest rooms. **The English Grill** offers classic fine dining in an elegant setting.

$$$ Lyndon House Bed & Breakfast – 507 N. Broadway, Lexington, KY. 🅿☕ ✆859-420-2683. www.lyndonhouse.com. 7 rooms. This charming brick residence built in 1883 is surrounded by a lovingly kept flower garden that makes for delightful wandering. The current restoration preserved the original crown moldings, cherry woodwork and white oak floors. Rooms are furnished with fine wood pieces and decorated in soothing florals. Sumptuous breakfasts are served in the dining room.

$$$ The Seelbach Hilton – 500 Fourth St., Louisville, KY. ✖♿🅿 ✆502-585-3200. www.seelbachhilton.com. 321 rooms. Frequent visitor F. Scott Fitzgerald set parts of The Great Gatsby (1925) in this Gilded Age downtown landmark. Guests are still swept away by the palatial lobby's hand-painted murals and imposing bronze staircase. In **The Oakroom**, chef Patrick Roney uses the best local and seasonal ingredients to whip up delicious classic American specialties.

🍴 EAT

$$$ Jack Frys – 1007 Bardstown Rd., Louisville, KY. ✆502-452-9244. www.jackfrys.com. **American.** A much-loved Louisville institution, Jack Fry's first opened in 1933. Steaks and chops (veal, pork and lamb) headline the menu, but also don't miss the chef's innovative fish preparations, such as rainbow trout with caviar and champagne aioli or pan-seared snapper in Parmesan pistou broth. Southern-style desserts include fruit cobblers, sweet potato beignets and chocolate souffle cake.

$$ Merrick Inn – 1074 Merrick Dr., Lexington, KY. ✆859-269-5417. www.themerrickinn.com. Closed Sunday. **Southern.** Located in residential Lansdowne, the city's most popular eatery was the manor house of a pre-Civil War horse farm. Prime rib and fried walleyed pike come with salad and fluffy homemade biscuits; the fried chicken ranks as some of the best in the area. Ask about the butterscotch pie.

$ Ramsey's – 496 E. High St., Lexington, KY. ✆859-259-2708. www.ramseysdiners.com. **American.** Local residents flock here for traditional diner fare at its finest, including the area's best "hot brown," an open-faced turkey sandwich topped with bacon and tasty gravy. The menu sticks mainly to the typical meant-and-three graced with special fillips like homemade ranch dressing. The summertime Corn Daze menu features local corn and tomatoes. Top it all off with a giant slice of Missy's pie.

Bluegrass Country★★

Named for the finely bladed native grass that takes on a faint bluish cast each spring, the Bluegrass roughly encompasses a seven-county area radiating outward from Lexington. It was the first region settled because it was easier to farm than the eastern mountains. Known as the center of the Thoroughbred industry, it is marked by rolling meadows dotted with horse farms outlined by white plank fences.

🔲 **Info:** ℰ502-564-4930; www.kentuckytourism.com

⊛ **Don't Miss:** The Old State Capitol, which made Gideon Shryock famous.

👪 **Kids:** Get up close and personal at the Kentucky Horse Park with the animal that made the region famous.

A BIT OF HISTORY

Many of the Bluegrass towns—such as Harrodsburg, Danville and Bardstown—date from the late 1700s and, except for Lexington—the second-largest city—have remained small and somewhat isolated. Even Frankfort, the capital, is small. Consequently, a large number of the early buildings survive, including many imposing Federal and Georgian houses.

In addition to its repository of antebellum structures, the Bluegrass is distinguished as the center of the nation's equine industry, which brings $5 billion into the state annually and accounts for a significant part of its tourism. In recent years, the Bluegrass economy has become more diverse with the migration of new industry to the area, including Toyota Motor Manufacturing and Lexmark International.

FRANKFORT★★

Tucked into the Kentucky River Valley, between Lexington and Louisville, Frankfort was established as Kentucky's capital in 1792. This small (population 27,590) city concerns itself primarily with governing the state. Best known for its grand 1909 Beaux-Arts **State Capitol**★ (Capital Ave.; ♿🅿 ℰ502-564-3449; www.capitol.ky.gov), Frankfort also features the **Kentucky Military History Museum** (E. Main St. at Capital

Bourbon

Whiskey-making was a favorite Kentucky pastime before Kentucky was a state. Many early settlers distilled their own, and soon discovered that the region's limestone-rich water gave their corn liquor a coveted flavor. But the invention of bourbon whiskey came about quite by accident in the late 18C when a fire accidentally charred the oak barrels in which Baptist minister and whiskey-maker Elijah Craig aged his stock. Craig used them anyway and the end result was a darker, mellower beverage. Folks called it bourbon after Bourbon County. By 1891 Kentucky boasted 172 distilleries and bourbon manufacturing was one of the state's largest industries. A century later, that number had dwindled to nine, the result of Prohibition, economic downturns and changing tastes. Today, 98 percent of all bourbon whiskey sold in the US comes from Kentucky's distilleries.

Most of Kentucky's bourbon whiskey is made within a 50mi radius of **Bardstown**, home to Jim Beam, Heaven Hill and Barton, with Maker's Mark located in nearby Loretto. Most of the distilleries offer free tours. **Maker's Mark** (3mi east of Loretto on Rte. 52; ℰ270-865-2099; www.makersmark.com), conducts one of the best.

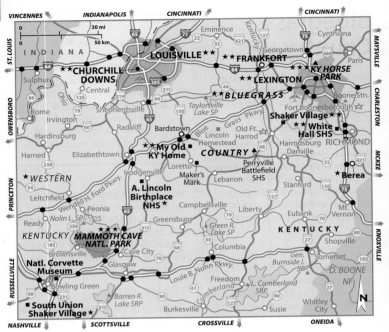

Ave.; 502-564-1792; www.history.ky. gov), showcasing firearms, artillery and uniforms dating from the Revolutionary War.

Old State Capitol★★

300 W. Broadway (corner of Broadway & Lewis Sts.). 502-564-1792. http://history.ky.gov.

This small gem of a building was designed by Kentucky's foremost antebellum architect, **Gideon Shryock**. Then relatively unknown, Shryock soon became famous for his flawless Greek Revival creation in Frankfort. Constructed in 1830, the building mimics the Greek Temple of Minerva with the addition of a cupola.

Inside, the rotunda features rust-colored floors crafted from Kentucky river-bottom marble. A freestanding spiral staircase leads from the rotunda to the second-floor legislative chambers, preserved as they were in the 1850s with several original desks. The structure served as Kentucky's capitol building until the early 20C. It has since housed the state's historical society.

👥 Thomas D. Clark Center for Kentucky History★★

100 W. Broadway. ♿🅿 502-564-1792. http://history.ky.gov.

This $29 million museum celebrates the state with a plethora of lifelike exhibits and state-of-the-art technology. The block-long, red-brick structure in the city's oldest district seeks to blend Palladian and Greek Revival details amid its blocky, contemporary styling.

Inside, the atrium's focal point is a sweeping spiral stairway, patterned after the one in Frankfort's Old Capitol. As you walk through the main exhibit, **A Kentucky Journey**, you'll feel the sway of the keelboat and hear the water lapping at an early river settlement.

LEXINGTON★★

The heart of the Bluegrass, Lexington was founded in 1779 and soon became a center of learning, wealth and culture. Transylvania University (300 N. Broadway), the oldest college west of the Alleghenies, was chartered in 1780, followed by the state's first lending library in 1795 and the University of

Kentucky (500 S. Limestone St.) in 1865. A group of the city's early-18C Federal and Georgian mansions are clustered in the 12-block **Gratz Park Historic District** (bounded by N. Broadway, Upper, 2nd & 3rd Sts.).

The combined Lexington-Fayette County area now has a population of 305,489, and contains a vibrant mix of educational, cultural and business interests. Despite recent economic diversification, the horse industry remains the backbone of the local economy. With 450 horse farms, two racetracks and two Thoroughbred auction facilities, the Lexington area still reigns as the "Horse Capital of the World."

Mary Todd Lincoln House★

578 W. Main St. ♿🅿 ☎859-233-9999. www.mtlhouse.org.

This 14-room brick house, just west of downtown, was the girlhood home of Mary Todd Lincoln (1818-82), later the wife of Abraham Lincoln, 16th president of the US. Surviving family furnishings include a mahogany table where Lincoln is believed to have played cards and a rare collection of coin-silver **mint-julep cups** crafted by local silversmiths.

Ashland★★

120 Sycamore Rd. ✖🅿 ☎859-266-8581. www.henryclay.org.

Known as "the great compromiser," **Henry Clay** (1777-1852) was Kentucky's pre-eminent 19C statesman. The US Senator, Speaker of the House of Representatives and three-time candidate for president made his home on a 600-acre estate he named Ashland. When the original 1806 structure was torn down in 1852, Clay's son rebuilt an 18-room brick Italianate villa on its foundation, using the same Federal floor plan. Later remodeling by a granddaughter reflects Victorian tastes. An octagonal entryway and dining room, beautiful inlaid wood floors and Sheffield silver doorknobs highlight the interior.

👥 Kentucky Horse Park★★★

4089 Iron Works Parkway. ✖♿ ☎859-233-4303. www.kyhorsepark.com.

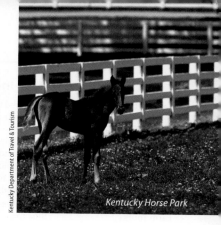

Kentucky Department of Travel & Tourism

Kentucky Horse Park

Set on the rolling pastureland of a former working horse farm, this facility is a paean to the state's best-loved domestic animal. Everywhere the horse is celebrated, whether it is in the excellent introductory movie, *Rein of Nobility*; amid the displays in the Smithsonian-affiliated **International Museum of the Horse** chronicling the animal's history and evolution; or at the twice-daily **Horses of the World Show**, where horses of every size, shape and pedigree strut their stuff. Envisioned as a facility to showcase part of Kentucky's heritage, the park became a reality in the 1970s when the state purchased the farm and turned it into a tourist attraction. It is also a premier exhibition center, staging numerous equestrian events annually. A statue of **Man O' War**, considered the greatest racehorse of all time, presides over the entrance. The acclaimed horse's remains were moved to the park in 1978 from nearby Faraway Farm where he died in 1947 at the age of 30. The adjacent **American Saddlebred Museum** (4093 Iron Works Pkwy.; ☎859-259-2746; www.asbmuseum.org) commemorates the Saddlebred, the only breed native to Kentucky.

EXCURSIONS
White Hall State Historic Site★★

▶ 19mi south of Lexington via I-75 at 500 White Hall Shrine Rd., Richmond. ☎859-623-9178. www.parks.ky.gov.

This brooding, Italianate-style house guarded by concrete lions was home to the "Lion of White Hall," the flamboyant abolitionist **Cassius Marcellus Clay**

Horse Industry

Early settlers in the Bluegrass discovered that the limestone strata underlying the region's rich soil fortified the water building strong bones, a requisite for winning racehorses. Horse farms sprang up around Lexington, and by 1789 the city claimed more horses than people. Today 450 horse farms dot the area. Although development has steadily encroached upon the farms as the area's population has soared, breeding champion racehorses remains a staple here. Here they can see their favorite steeds cavorting in a Bluegrass meadow, hard at work at the racetrack, or bought and sold.

A number of companies offer tours of the farms encircling Lexington: **Horse Farm Tours** (☎859-268-2906); **Blue Grass Tours** (☎859-252-5744); and **Thoroughbred Heritage Tours** (☎859-260-8687), to name a few. Or you can set out on your own driving tour with a special map provided by the **Lexington Convention and Visitors Bureau** (301 E. Vine St.; ☎859-233-7299; www.visitlex.com). If the bugle and the cry "they're off" get your blood pumping, you'll probably want to visit **Keeneland** (racemeets Apr & Sept; 4201 Versailles Rd., Lexington, KY; ☎859-254-3412; www.keeneland.com) or **Louisville's Churchill Downs** (&see LOUISVILLE).

(1810-1903). Scion of a wealthy family, Clay never realized his ambition to serve in Congress, but he was elected to the Kentucky General Assembly and later appointed ambassador to Russia.

His grand home consists of a house within a house: the simple 1798 Georgian residence built by his father and the elaborate overlay added after 1861. A notable feature is the indoor bathroom, which utilized rainwater collected from the rooftop.

Shaker Village of Pleasant Hill★★

◗ 3501 Lexington Rd., Harrodsburg (25mi southwest of Lexington on US-68). ✕&🅿 ☎859-734-5411.
www.shakervillageky.org.

The United Society of Believers in Christ's Second Appearing, also known as "Shakers" for their odd movements during worship, had two colonies in Kentucky—this one and a smaller group at South Union (&see WESTERN KENTUCKY). Simplicity, fine craftsmanship and celibacy were hallmarks of their way of life.

On 4,000 acres high above the Kentucky River, the Pleasant Hill community flourished from 1805 until 1910. Its 500 members farmed and sold the products of their cottage industries (brooms, wooden boxes, garden seeds) as far afield as New Orleans.

Today, costumed interpreters demonstrate typical Shaker activities in 14 of the 34 restored buildings that are open to visitors; original furniture and crafts are on display in the Centre Family Dwelling. Don't miss the daily performance of Shaker songs and dances.

Berea★

◗ 39mi S of Lexington (I-75).
www.berea.com.

The small city of Berea is primarily known as a folk art and craft center. **Berea College** (101 Chestnut St.), established in 1855 by wealthy landowner Cassius Clay, was founded to serve Appalachian youth. All students work for their tuition-free education. To sample the students' excellent crafts, visit the **Log House Craft Gallery** (200 Estill St.; ☎859-985-3220). Stroll through adjacent **Old Town Artisans' Village** to watch glassblowers, woodcarvers and weavers at work in their studios.

Louisville★★

Located in the eastern part of the state, near the Indiana border, Kentucky's largest city brings to mind the Kentucky Derby, Churchill Downs and mint juleps. Horse breeding and horse racing have long been traditions in this Bluegrass town, which held its first Derby in 1875. Situated at the falls of the Ohio River, the early settlement was destined to become a major inland port; cargo transport remains a significant source of revenue today, more so from Louisville's airport and the city's proximity to major freeways. As for two-legged transportation, Louisville is completing a 100mi bicycle loop around the community. More than 120 parks and the nation's largest urban wooded area, the Jefferson Memorial Forest, offer opportunities for walking and hiking.

A BIT OF HISTORY

The city was founded in 1778 by George Rogers Clark, the military hero whose campaigns secured the West. Given its location on the Ohio River, it was an ideal stopping point for westward travelers and soon became an important port and trading center. After the steamboat's demise, Louisville's central location made it a busy rail hub. Iron foundries sprang up to serve the railroad industry, and by the turn of the 19C Louisville produced much of the country's decorative ironwork.

DOWNTOWN

Louisville's downtown is a bustling blend of commerce, government and entertainment. Along the major thoroughfare, West Main Street, you'll find the Louisville Slugger Museum; the excellent **Kentucky Science Center** (727 W. Main St.; ℘502-561-6100; www.kysciencecenter.org); and the lofty headquarters of healthcare giant Humana (1985, Michael Graves), its pink granite entrance flanked by two 50ft waterfalls.

▶ **Population:** 605,110.
🄸 **Info:** Louisville Convention and Visitors Bureau. ℘502-584-2121; www.gotolouisville.com.
☺ **Don't Miss:** Churchill Downs, home of the world-famous Kentucky Derby.
👪 **Kids:** Little ones like to swing at bat at the Louisville Slugger Museum.

Across the street, steps lead down to the *Belle of Louisville*—one of the few steamboats still plying the Ohio—docked at 4th Street and River Road (℘502-574-2992; www.belleoflouisville.com). Also downtown is the restored 1928 **Palace Theater** (625 S. 4th St.), still used today for concerts; and the Greek Revival-style **Jefferson County Courthouse** (531 W. Jefferson St.), begun according to designs by Gideon Shryock and completed in 1860.

Long a cultural center, Louisville boasts the acclaimed Actor's Theatre, a respected symphony and ballet, and the Speed Art Museum. Well-known local pottery maker, **Louisville Stoneware** (731 Brent St.; ♿🅿 ℘502-582-1900; www.louisvillestoneware.com) offers tours of its facility.

SIGHTS
Speed Art Museum★

2035 S. 3rd St. ✕♿🅿 ℘502-634-2700. Currently closed for expansion and renovation; expected completion date: 2016. During closure, the museum will present "Speed About Town," a series of temporary exhibits at various sites around Louisville. Details available on the museum's website, www.speedmuseum.org.

Numerous artists are represented in this delightful Classically inspired building adjoining the University of Louisville campus. Although the museum, which opened in 1927, contains the work of numerous masters (Monet, Rembrandt, Rubens), two particular collections stand out: the **European Galleries** and the **Kentucky Room**. The former features tapestries and Medieval decorative arts; the latter showcases paintings, sculpture and decorative arts with a Kentucky connection.

Louisville Slugger Museum & Factory★

800 W. Main St. ♿🅿️✆502-588-7228. www.sluggermuseum.com.

It would be hard to miss this downtown attraction with the 120ft-high baseball bat (the world's largest) marking its threshold. Hillerich and Bradsby, manufacturers of the world-famous official bats of major league baseball, have been a Louisville mainstay since 1884, when they became the first company to mass-produce this baseball essential. The tour begins with an excellent movie introducing the sport of baseball. Visitors then walk through a baseball dugout to a full-size replica of Baltimore's Camden Yards stadium. The tour ends with a walk through the factory that turns out 2,000 white-ash and maple bats a day.

Farmington★

3033 Bardstown Rd. ⟿Visit of house by guided tour only. 🅿️ ✆502-452-9920. www.historichomes.org/Farmington/Welcome/tabid/1367/Default.aspx.

It's easy to see the Jeffersonian influence in this restored 1816 Federal home, with its secret stairway, wide central hallway, and many-sided rooms. The spacious, 14-room home was the centerpiece of a 550-acre hemp plantation operated from 1808 to 1865 by members of the Speed family. In addition to family objets d'art, the house contains a multimedia show and permanent exhibit highlighting John and Lucy Speed's friendship with Abraham Lincoln.

Locust Grove★★

561 Blankenbaker Lane. ⟿Visit of house by guided tour only. 🅿️✆502-897-9845. www.locustgrove.org.

Historically important as the last home of Louisville founder George Rogers Clark, this sweeping 1790s homestead (restored in 2010) was owned by his sister Lucy and her husband, William Croghan. Elderly and ill, Clark was cared for here by Lucy from 1809 until his death in 1818. It was here that William Clark, George's brother, and his partner Meriwether Lewis returned in 1806 after their historic expedition.

One of the first brick houses in the region, Locust Grove is distinguished by its paneled walls, unusual built-in cabinets and its **ballroom**, which boasts extravagant 18C French wallpaper.

👥 Falls of the Ohio State Park★

201 W. Riverside Dr., Clarksville, IN. ♿🅿️✆812-280-9970. www.fallsoftheohio.org.

The adjacent banks and bottom areas of this peaceful park, just across the Ohio River from downtown Louisville, contain some of the richest Devonian **fossil deposits** in the world.

The park's striking contemporary **Interpretive Center** is constructed of tiers of limestone and multicolored bricks, mirroring the fossil beds it interprets. Inside, a documentary traces their evolution, formed more than 350 million years ago.

👥 Churchill Downs★★

700 Central Ave. Racemeets April, May, Jun & Nov. ✗♿🅿️ (No parking available during racemeets). ✆502-636-4400. www.churchilldowns.com.

Perhaps no Kentucky landmark is more familiar than the twin spires of Churchill Downs, home of the famed **Kentucky Derby★★★**, the first contest (held in May) in the Triple Crown series (the other two are the Belmont Stakes in New York and the Preakness in Maryland). First run in 1875, the Derby is America's oldest continual sports event. Behind-the-scenes guided tours of Churchill Downs facilities are conducted in the off-season by the **Kentucky Derby Museum★★** (704 Central Ave; ✆502-637-7097; www.derbymuseum.org), which was renovated following flood damage in 2010. Interactive exhibits on the main floor cover the fan experience, a chance to test skills as a jockey, Derby

Daniel Boone

In the annals of Kentucky history, Daniel Boone (born in Pennsylvania in 1734) has achieved almost mythic status. Every Kentucky schoolchild knows how he carved his name and the words "killed a bar [bear]" into a Kentucky tree in 1760. But Boone's lasting legacy is his creation of a major transportation link to the West.

In 1775 Boone blazed the first trail through the natural pass in the Appalachians known as the Cumberland Gap (👆see EAST TENNESSEE) to the Bluegrass, opening the land route westward. That same year, he established Boonesborough, an outpost on the Kentucky River near present-day Richmond, Kentucky. Beset by Indian attacks and frequent flooding, the fort did not survive. Reconstructed in 1974, **Fort Boonesborough** (in Fort Boonesborough State Park on Rte. 627, 4375 Boonesborough Rd., Richmond, KY; ✆859-527-3131; www.parks.ky.gov) is now a living-history museum.

Boone spent his final years exploring, venturing as far west as present-day Yellowstone National Park. He died in Missouri; his remains and those of his wife, Rebecca, were moved to the **Frankfort Cemetery** (215 E. Main St., Frankfort, KY).

history and Derby-day fashion (including the winners of the annual fancy hat contest). The second floor focuses on behind-the-scenes aspects of the Derby, telling the stories of the horses and their owners, trainers and jockeys. The museum also possesses tapes of every Derby since 1918 and offers interactive exhibits where guests can test their wagering abilities.

EXCURSIONS
My Old Kentucky Home State Park★★

❯ 501 E. Stephen Foster Ave., 40mi south of Louisville via US-31 East in Bardstown. ⚠&🅿✆502-348-3502. http://parks.ky.gov.

The "Old Kentucky Home" immortalized in a ballad by composer **Stephen Foster** (1826-64) is actually Federal Hill, a Federal-style brick home built in 1818 by Foster's cousin, Judge John Rowan. It was on a visit here in 1852 that Foster composed what is now Kentucky's state song. In 1923 the home was officially renamed "My Old Kentucky Home" when it was bequeathed to the state by Rowan heirs.

Abraham Lincoln Birthplace National Historic Site★

❯ 58mi south of Louisville on US-31 East, 3mi south of Hodgenville. &🅿 ✆270-358-3137. www.nps.gov/abli.

Abraham Lincoln (👆see CHICAGO, infobox) spent the first two years of his life on this rocky land, known locally as the Sinking Spring farm.

Go outside to climb the 56 steps—one for each year of Lincoln's life—to the granite and marble **memorial** (1909, John Russell Pope) that encloses a replica of the cabin where Lincoln was born.

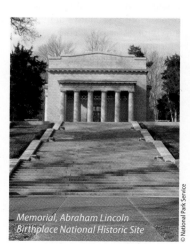

Memorial, Abraham Lincoln Birthplace National Historic Site

© National Park Service

Western Kentucky★

From the edge of the Bluegrass westward to the Mississippi River lies the region of Western Kentucky, an area of fertile farms, burley tobacco and barbecue. The region is home to the world's most extensive known cave system and the site of a Civil War battle at the strategic Mississippi River town of Columbus. Here Columbus-Belmont State Park (Rte. 58, in Columbus; ℘270-677-2327; http://parks.ky.gov) commemorates the February 1862 battle in which Union forces beat back the Rebels and gained control of the river.

Info: Kentucky's Western Waterland. ℘270-928-4411; www.kentuckylakebarkley.org.

Location: Once the unknown West, the area was a magnet for experimental communities such as the Shakers and Harmonists.

Don't Miss: Mother Nature's majesty at Mammoth Cave.

SIGHTS

Mammoth Cave National Park★★★

8mi west of Cave City via Rte. 70 (or 9mi northwest of I-65 from Exit 48 at Park City). ℘301-722-1257. △✕⚑🅿Park information; ℘270-758-2180. www.nps.gov/maca.

The world's longest cave (more than 350mi of the five-level labyrinth have been mapped), Mammoth underlies three Kentucky counties. Known to Woodland Indians over 4,000 years ago and rediscovered by frontiersmen in the late 18C, Mammoth Cave was established as a national park in 1941.

A wide variety of guided tours are offered into Mammoth's depths, taking visitors as far as 360ft below ground. Among the sights are the ruins of an 1810-12 saltpeter mining operation; a decorative stone formation called **Frozen Niagara**; and the underground **River Styx**, home of eyeless fish. Designated a UNESCO World Heritage Site and an International Biosphere Reserve, the cave is home to the world's most diverse cave ecosystem, including some life forms that cannot survive outside its walls. (👣Tours last 1-6 hours, with varying degrees of difficulty. Reservations recommended. Cave temperatures average 54°F year-round; bring a sweater or light jacket. Wear sturdy, comfortable shoes and be prepared to climb.)

National Corvette Museum

350 Corvette Dr. (off I-65 Exit 28), Bowling Green. ⚑🅿 ℘270-781-7973. www.corvettemuseum.org.

This unique museum was inspired by its neighbor across the road, the only plant in America where Corvettes are assembled (👣guided tours of the plant by reservation ℘270-745-8419; www.bowlinggreenassemblyplant.com).

In the low-slung building with brightly colored modules you can investigate more than 68,000sq ft of exhibits tracing the evolution of the first American sports car. Visitors over 16 years of age can test their driving skills during a 15min simulator ride (free; reservation required at admissions desk).

South Union Shaker Village★

Near the junction of US-68/80 & Rte. 1446 in South Union. 🅿℘270-542-4167. www.shakermuseum.com.

This community, though smaller than the Pleasant Hill group, was wealthier in land and property. Its 349 members owned 6,000 acres and more than 200 buildings—only a fraction of which remain. Like their Pleasant Hill counterparts, they sold a variety of products. The colony lasted from 1807 until 1922, when the Industrial Age and declining membership sealed its fate.

Birmingham Area

Alabama's largest city lies roughly in the middle of a state whose vigorous economy is based on agriculture, manufacturing, service industries and technology. Birmingham has a balanced mix of well-preserved 19C architecture interspersed with skyscrapers named after their Fortune 500 owners, yet its most important history is found in the Civil Rights District.

Birmingham

AL

Highlights

1 A slice of fried green tomato at the **Irondale Cafe** (p386)

2 Thought-provoking exhibts at the **Birmingham Civil Rights Institute** (p387)

3 The massive Saturn V rocket (indoors!) at the **U.S. Space and Rocket Center** (p391)

Early Settlers

Native Americans occupied Alabama's mountain forests and verdant river valleys for at least 9,000 years. Evidence of these native cultures, both early and late, lives on in scores of historic sites and mellifluous place names—including Alabama, derived from the Chickasaw word *Alibamu*, meaning "thicket clearers." One such site, **Moundville Archaeological Park★★** (72mi southwest of Birmingham off Rte. 69, 634 Mound Park, Moundville; ℘205-371-2234; http://moundville.ua.edu), was once home to the largest Native American settlement in the southeast during the Mississippian Period (AD 800-1600). Today, more than two dozen flat-topped earthen mounds remain, built as platforms for temples, council houses and homes of tribal leaders.

As settlers expanded westward in the early 1800s, a series of bloody battles with the Indians culminated in Gen. Andrew Jackson's crushing defeat in 1814 of the last remaining Creek Indians at Horseshoe Bend northeast of Montgomery. **Horseshoe Bend National Military Park★** (on Rte. 49 near the Georgia border, 12mi north of Dadeville, 11288 Horseshoe Bend Rd., Daviston; ℘256-234-7111; www.nps.gov/hobe) preserves the battle site where the decimated Creeks signed the Treaty of Fort Jackson on August 9, 1814, ceding some 20 million acres of land to the US—land that in 1819 became the State of Alabama.

Segregationist Past

The struggles of Alabama's African-American citizens made headlines around the world in 1955, as civil rights advocates boycotted the bus system in Montgomery for 381 days and emerged victorious with a 1956 order from the US Supreme Court outlawing bus segregation in Montgomery. Today the cruel reminders of Alabama's segregationist past are largely confined to historic markers and museums such as the excellent Birmingham Civil Rights Institute. Visits to three of the state's four largest cities—Birmingham, Montgomery and Huntsville (Mobile is second-largest, and growing rapidly; ⚓see GULF COAST)—offer thought-provoking and sometimes surprising juxtapositions of past and present in the "Heart of Dixie," as the state is nicknamed.

ADDRESSES

🏨 STAY

$$$ The Tutwiler – 2021 Park Pl. N., Birmingham, AL. ✗♿🅿️⌁ ℘205-322-2100. www.thetutwilerhotel.com. 147 rooms. Housed in a dignified 1913 red-brick landmark, this downtown hotel (now part of the Hampton Inn chain) has hosted everyone from Henry Kissinger to Stevie Wonder. Note the lobby's restored coffered ceilings. Guest rooms feature comfy bedding and flat-screen TVs. Breakfast is served in the 8th-floor lounge.

$$ Hotel Highland – 1023 20th St. South, Birmingham, AL. ✕ ♿ 🅿 ⬛ 🔎205-933-9555. www.thehotelhighland.com. 63 rooms. This boutique hotel fashioned from Birmingham's historic Medical Arts office tower (1931) is your best bet for a stay in the Five Points South area. Brazilian hardwood furnishings and a neutral decor are enlivened with jewel-tone accents in the sleek, if smallish guest rooms.

$$ Red Bluff Cottage – 551 Clay St., Montgomery, AL. 🅿 ⬛🔎334-264-0056. www.redbluffcottage.com. 5 rooms. This raised-cottage-style B&B overlooks the city and river plain in the historic Cottage Hill district. Antique pencil-post beds, handmade quilts and family photos make you feel right at home. Walk to the Civil Rights Memorial and Riverfront Park.

$$ The Redmont Hotel – 2101 Fifth Ave., Birmingham, AL. ♿🅿🔎205-324-2101. www.theredmont.com. 114 rooms. Conveniently close to the convention center, the Civil Rights Institute and downtown Birmingham, this boutique hotel offers updated accommodations in a nicely renovated historic property. Spacious guest rooms include comfy beds with premium linens; flat-screen TVs; and wireless Internet. Evenings bring live entertainment to **Above**, the hotel's rooftop bar.

🍴EAT

$$$ Highlands Bar & Grill – 2011 11th Ave. S., Birmingham, AL. 🔎205-939-1400. **American.** A national standout thanks to the chef Frank Stitt's creative take on Southern cuisine. Vintage French food ads decorate the romantic Southside dining room. Baked grits, bacon-wrapped rabbit, and upside-down peach cornbread cake highlight the daily menu.

$$ Bottega Café – 2240 Highland Ave. S., Birmingham, AL. Closed Sun. 🔎205-939-1000. www.bottegarestaurant.com. **Mediterranean.** Local foodies rave about this Southside hot spot housed in a historic Beaux-Arts building. Fine local ingredients go into mouthwatering Mediterranean-style dishes like Gulf red snapper with Sardinian couscous, grilled grouper, and homemade pappardelle with Louisiana rabbit. Have a seat out front in fine weather.

$$ Hot & Hot Fish Club – 2180 11th Court S., Birmingham, AL. 🔎205-933-5474. www.hotandhotfishclub.com. **American.** Devoted to the use of local ingredients in their Southern regional cooking, chef Chris Hastings mines a wide network of local suppliers. Menus change daily, but you'll always find his signature shrimp and grits or duck breats with dirty rice, along with simply sauced grilled fish. The charming dining room, housed in an updated burger joint, is furnished and decorated with whimsical works by regional artists The Libations cocktail menu changes seasonally.

$$ Jubilee – 1057 Woodley Rd., Montgomery, AL. Closed Sun–Mon. 🔎334-262-6224. www.jubileeseafood restaurant.com. **Seafood.** Just-caught fish from the Gulf of Mexico keeps folks waiting in line for a table at this casual Old Cloverdale eatery. Cobia, trigger fish and yellowfin grouper turn up on the often changing menu. Blackened red snapper, oysters on the half-shell, and barbecued bacon-wrapped shrimp are top sellers.

$ Irondale Cafe – 1906 1st Ave. N., Irondale, AL. Closed Sun-Mon. 🔎205-956-5258. www.irondalecafe.com. **Southern.** Seven miles from downtown Birmingham, the railway diner that inspired the novel *Fried Green Tomatoes at the Whistle Stop Café* is a lunchtime favorite. Freight trains rumble by while you eat fried chicken, boiled squash, and of course, fried green tomatoes. Save room for some peach cobbler.

Birmingham★

Presided over by the 56ft-tall, cast-iron Guiseppe Moretti sculpture of **Vulcan★★** (US-31 & Valley Ave., 1701 Valley View Dr.), **Birmingham is laid out in an orderly grid of numbered streets that crisscross the city's three interstate highways and climb up and down hills. Many of the star attractions in Alabama's largest city lie within walking distance of each other downtown.**

A BIT OF HISTORY

Unlike most of its southern sisters, Birmingham boasts no Civil War survival stories (because it dates back to only 1871, six years after the war ended). In the turbulent years of Reconstruction, industrialists mined Red Mountain and the adjacent hills to make fortunes from the land's rich deposits of coal, limestone and iron ore. The key role that iron played in the city's history is evident today at the **Sloss Furnaces National Historic Landmark★★** (20 32nd St. North, at 32nd St. & First Ave. N.; ℘205-324-1911; www.slossfurnaces. com), constructed in the early 20C, and at the **Tannehill Ironworks Historical State Park★★** (31.7mi southwest at 12632 Confederate Pkwy., in McCalla; ℘205-477-5711; www.tannehill.org), where Confederate soldiers produced up to 20 tons of pig iron a day for Rebel cannons and bullets.

Named after England's then-thriving industrial hub, the new Alabama town of Birmingham grew rapidly around two rail lines, the Alabama & Chattanooga and the South & North. The town was once heralded as the "Pittsburgh of the South," but by the 1960s, the US iron-and-steel industry was rusting, and Birmingham became known as "Bombingham," owing to the murderous bombings and beatings endured by the city's civil rights activists.

Today the city's racial strife has largely healed, and its economy depends far more on medicine, academia and the service industry than on metalwork.

▶ **Population:** 229,800.

Info: 2200 Ninth Ave., North; ℘205-458-8000; www.birminghamal.org.

Don't Miss: The sites detailing America's Civil Rights Movement.

Streets in **Five Points South★** (20th St. S. at 11th Ave. S.), the city's revitalized 1890s shopping and entertainment district near the University of Alabama campus, are lined with restaurants, bars and cafes. Adjoining the district is pedestrians-only **Cobb Lane**, a short brick-paved block with restaurants, art galleries and bars wedged into vintage Craftsman-style apartments at 13th Avenue South. Along First Avenue South (between 14th and 18th Sts.), Railroad Park is a green space across from Regions Field, home Birmingham's minor-league baseball team, the Birmingham Barons.

SIGHTS
Civil Rights District★

Bounded by 15th to 17th Streets and 3rd to 7th Avenues, the district commemorates sites where civil rights activists banded together and changed the face of America with their protests during the 1960s. Here you'll find soul-food restaurants as well as the **Sixteenth Street Baptist Church★** (1530 Sixth Ave. N. at corner of 16th St.; ℘205-251-9402). Designed by African-American architect Wallace Rayfield, this twin-towered church (1911) was bombed by white racists on Sunday, September 15, 1963.

Birmingham Civil Rights Institute★★★

520 16th St. N. ℘205-328-9696. www.bcri.org.

Anchoring the Civil Rights District, this interpretive center, research library and self-directed museum (1992, J. Max Bond, Jr.) guides visitors through a series of engrossing multimedia and three-dimensional exhibits that bring the drama and tumult of the American Civil Rights Movement to vivid, sometimes frightening, life. In chronological order, room-size exhibits detail the major confrontations, achievements and tragedies of the struggle, highlighting such pivotal events as the 1955 boycott of the Montgomery bus system sparked by Rosa Parks and Dr. Martin Luther King, Jr.'s "I Have a Dream" speech during the 1963 march on Washington, DC.

Beginning with the late-19C years of harsh segregation, the exhibit weaves first-person reminiscences with media accounts that immerse visitors in the sights and sounds of "the movement": film footage of snarling police dogs turned on black children, and eerie footage of a nighttime cross-burning by hooded members of the Ku Klux Klan. Visitors can view the burned-out shell of a bus ridden by the Freedom Riders, and the door of the cell where Dr. King wrote his "Letter from Birmingham Jail." Other displays focus on civil rights violations and landmark events such as the 1989 massacre of protesters in Tiananmen Square in the People's Republic of China.

Across from the Civil Rights Institute lies quiet **Kelly Ingram Park★** (Fifth Ave. & 16th St.), where sculptures by James Drake evoke some of the more horrific events that took place here. (audio-tour guides are available for the park from the Institute.)

Birmingham Museum of Art★★

2000 Rev. Abraham Woods Jr. Blvd.
✕⚭🅿 ✆205-254-2565.
www.artsbma.org.

Housed in a modern building near the convention district, Birmingham's art museum boasts a wide-ranging collection of some 24,000 works, one of the finest in the Southeast. Particular strengths include Native American and pre-Colombian art and artifacts (textiles and pottery are especially noteworthy and fun to look at); and the Kress Collection of Renaissance art, where you'll see works by Canaletto and Perugino. There are also several noteworthy works by British portraitists Thomas Gainsborough and Thomas Lawrence.

The Bohorfoush Gallery mounts changing exhibits from the museum's permanent collection of African-American art, which includes works by Romare Bearden, Henry Ossawa Tanner and James Van der Zee.

The museum houses an outstanding collection of **Wedgwood pottery★**, as well as French paintings (Courbet, Cassat and Corot) and decorative arts donated in 1991 by coal heiress and Birmingham native Eugenia Woodward Hitt.

The intriguing Folk Art Gallery features selections by Alabama quilters and other self-taught artists.

Birmingham Museum of Art

Montgomery ★

A pleasant, well-kept city on the banks of the Alabama River, this shiny modern-day capital bears little trace of its early history—a claim staked by Hernando de Soto for Spain in 1540; by French explorers as they established nearby Fort Toulouse in 1717; by the British at the end of the French and Indian War in 1763; and by the half-Scottish, half-Indian Alexander McGillivray for the Creek Indian Nation from 1783 to 1793. Montgomery was already a busy regional marketplace and transportation center when it became Alabama's capital in 1846.

- ▶ **Population:** 201,998.
- ⚅ **Michelin Map:** 584
- ▯ **Info:** 300 Water St; ☎334-262-0013; www.visiting montgomery.com.
- ⏱ **Timing:** Most of the Montgomery sights require thoughtful contemplation as they are not amusement parks. Plan accordingly.

A BIT OF HISTORY

Named as the temporary capital of the Confederate States of America in 1861, Montgomery survived the war years virtually unscathed. After Reconstruction, the city prospered again as a transportation center, shipping cotton to markets in the northeast and Europe. In the early years of the 20C, lumber and textile mills were established. Bolstered by the arrival of the **Alabama**

Shakespeare Festival★★ (⚅see below) in 1985, the city now hosts a lively performing arts community with a full slate of shows, plays and concerts.

From fanciful **Court Street Fountain** (corner of Court St. & Dexter Ave.) downtown, the **view** due east up Dexter Avenue is imbued with historical significance. On the right is the Italianate **Winter Building** (2 Dexter Ave.), from which the War Department of the Confederacy telegraphed orders to fire on Fort Sumter in April 1861, thus beginning the Civil War. Straight ahead is an impressive view of the Alabama State Capitol—the same view seen by black seamstress **Rosa Parks** when she boarded a bus here on December

Alabama Shakespeare Festival

Originally located in Anniston, this 200-person professional repertory theater relocated to Montgomery in 1985 after Montgomery-based industrialist Wynton M. Blount and his wife, Carolyn, pledged funds to build a new, $21.5 million performing-arts complex. The sixth-largest Shakespeare festival in the world, the Alabama troupe is the only American group invited by Britain's Royal Shakespeare Company to fly the Royal Shakespeare flag. The **Carolyn Blount Theatre**, housing the 792-seat Festival Stage and the 262-seat Octagon, occupies a lakefront English-garden setting on this 250-acre site. More than 400 performances—Shakespearean and contemporary dramas, musical revues and Broadway-bound tryouts—are mounted year-round. The **Shakespeare Garden and Amphitheatre** offers outdoor seating for 250; the Elizabethan garden features plants referred to in Shakespeare's plays (1 Festival Dr. ; ⚅▯☎334-271-5353 or 800-841-4ASF; www.asf.net).

The site is also home to the **Montgomery Museum of Fine Arts** (1 Museum Dr.; ☎334-240-4333; www.mmfa.org), which houses the Blount Collection of American Paintings, an excellent chronological survey of works on paper by important American artists including Copley, Peale, Church, Moran, Homer and Hopper.

Rosa Parks

Alabama native and seamstress Rosa Parks (1913–2005) led a quiet life in Montgomery until, in 1955, she refused to vacate her seat on a segregated city bus to make room for a white passenger. Parks' act of civil disobedience sparked a boycott of the bus system by civil rights activists that brought about the end of segregation on Montgomery's public transit system. Parks was arrested and fine $10. In 1999 at the age of 86, Parks received the Con-gressional Gold Medal, the highest civilian accolade awarded by Congress.

1, 1955, and was promptly arrested for refusing to yield her seat to a white passenger. Parks' arrest, which inspired the year-long Montgomery bus boycott, is considered the beginning of the Civil Rights Movement.

Today the round, table-like **Civil Rights Memorial★** (400 Washington Ave.; www.splcenter.org), designed by Maya Lin, pays homage to 40 civil rights martyrs, including Dr. Martin Luther King, Jr. Step inside the adjacent Civil Rights Memorial Center to take in exhibits about the center, the Wall of Tolerance, and exhibits about martyrs of Civil Rights cause.

SIGHTS

Alabama State Capitol★★

600 Dexter Ave. ℘334-242-3935; www.preserveala.org/capitoltour.htm.

A stunning Greek Revival building, Alabama's National Historic Landmark capitol was rebuilt in 1850-51 after a previous capitol on the site burned in 1849. Interior highlights include the restored c.1880s trompe l'œil **paneling** in the original suites belonging to the governor and the secretary of state. The **Old Senate Chamber** appears as it did in February 1861, when delegates from the seceding southern states met to form the Confederate States of America. Note the twin cantilevered staircases in the entry foyer, and the eight murals depicting Alabama history painted just below the rotunda's skylit dome.

Alabama Department of Archives and History★

624 Washington Ave. ℘334-242-4435. www.archives.state.al.us.

Three floors of research and exhibit space hold an eclectic collection of Alabama artifacts, ranging from prehistoric pottery shards to cheap glass beads manufactured in Venice for trade with 19C American Indians to Civil War paraphernalia. (Tours must be booked in advance.)

First White House of the Confederacy★★

644 Washington Ave. ℘334-242-1861. www.firstwhitehouse.org.

Jefferson Davis (1808-89), president of the Confederate States of America, used this 1835 wood-frame, Italianate house as his executive mansion during Montgomery's three-month reign (February–May 1861) as the CSA's capital. With well-preserved period furnishings and many Davis family belongings, the home feels as though Mrs. Davis may return momentarily to play the Chickering square piano.

Dexter Avenue King Memorial Baptist Church★

454 Dexter Ave.; ℘34-263-3970, www.dexterkingmemorial.org.

The Reverend Dr. Martin Luther King, Jr., was pastor here in 1955, when he and other civil rights leaders launched the 381-day Montgomery bus boycott in support of Rosa Parks' heroic refusal to yield her seat to a white passenger. The 1889 brick church features a basement mural chronicling the Civil Rights Movement.

Fitzgerald Museum★

919 Felder Ave. ℘334-264-4222 or 334-262-1911. www.fitzgeraldmuseum.net.

Fans of *The Great Gatsby* (1925) find memorabilia and an informative videotape in the former home of F. Scott and Zelda Fitzgerald. The couple shared this house—where Fitzgerald penned *Tender Is the Night*—from 1931 to 1932. Each Christmas the house is decorated by local schoolchildren; other events throughout the year commemorate dates such as the couple's birthdays and mark publication anniversaries of their work.

EXCURSION
Tuskegee Institute National Historic Site★★

◯ 49mi east of Montgomery in Tuskegee. Take I-85 North to Rte. 29 South; then right on US-80 to Tuskegee University campus. 1212 West Montgomery Rd. Visitor center is located in the Carver Museum. ♿ 334-727-3200. www.nps.gov/tuin.

Booker T. Washington (1856-1915) founded Tuskegee Normal School (now Tuskegee University) in 1881 to train African Americans as teachers, skilled laborers and farmers in the impoverished, segregated Reconstruction-era South. By 1899 Tuskegee was financially secure and internationally known, and Washington commissioned a Queen Anne-style home, **The Oaks** (Old Montgomery Rd.; guided tours depart from visitor center), for his family. Tours of the campus, designated a National Historic District, depart from the George Washington Carver Museum.

U.S. Space and Rocket Center★★★

Located 99mi north of Birmingham in Huntsville, the Smithsonian-affiliated U.S. Space and Rocket Center harbors the world's largest collection of spacecraft artifacts, along with a park, theater and interactive exhibits to make the history of manned space flight come alive for visitors. One of Alabama's top tourist destinations, the center lies on the perimeter of the US Army's legendary Redstone Arsenal, a 37,910-acre military post just southwest of the city center.

A BIT OF HISTORY

The former mill town of Huntsville changed abruptly during World War II when the US Army created Redstone Arsenal to make chemical weapons. Then, in 1950, the Army hired Dr. Werner von Braun and 117 other German rocket scientists to propel the US into the forefront of space exploration. With the creation of the National Aeronautics and Space Administration (NASA)

⚬ **Michelin Map:** 584 p11
🕐 **Timing:** If you are in town for long periods of time, check out the intensive space camps for both kids and grown-ups.

in 1958, the team of scientists became civilian rather than military employees, and the large NASA research site at Redstone was converted to **Marshall Space Flight Center**. The Space Flight Center ranks as the major research and testing arm for US space exploration.

Since Redstone Arsenal and the Marshall Space Flight Center are restricted, the state of Alabama opened "the world's largest space-travel attraction" nearby in 1970. Home to the popular children's **U.S. Space Camp®**, the U.S. Space and Rocket Center, NASA's first visitor center, is filled with interactive gadgetry, as well as complex and thought-provoking exhibits.

👥 VISIT

1 Tranquility Base, off I-565 in Huntsville. ⚠️✕♿🅿 256-837-3400. www.rocketcenter.com.
Begin your visit in the **Davidson Center for Space Exploration**, where a time

line tells the story of the space program, from its inception to the present. The chronology wends its way around the ground level beneath an awe-inspiring **Saturn V rocket**, fully restored to the era of the Apol-lo space program. Make your way to the upper level for intriguing exhibits highlighted by "The Challenge," tracing Huntsville's transformation to rocket capital of the US. On view here are test models from the Apollo 16 mission, including a command module, a lonar rover and a lunar lander. The Force exhibit simulates the firing of an F-1 rocket.

In the adjacent Rocket Park and Shuttle Park, artifacts and attractions include the **Space Shot** simulator, which blasts riders 140ft into the air and induces the sensation of weightlessness during the descent. A full-scale model of the *Pathfinder* space shuttle is complete with external tank and rocket boosters. The **Arium Building** houses large-scale temporary exhibits along with artifacts from the pre-Apollo era, including test-model artifacts from the Mercury and Gemini space programs. A Skylab mock-up used for astronaut training offers a fascinating glimpse into the human realities of long-term space travel—such as how to take a shower when the soap and water float.

U.S. Space and Rocket Center

© Jeff Greenberg / age fotostock

Just outside the main exhibit area, a giant curved-screen **Spacedome IMAX Theater** presents films hourly. 3-D films are shown on the Davidson Center's 3-D screen.

EXCURSIONS

Helen Keller Birthplace★

◗ 3000 N. Commons St. West, 75mi west of Huntsville in Tuscumbia. Take US-72 to N. Main St. in Tuscumbia; go north 2mi to Keller Lane. ♿🅿 ✆256-383-4066. www.helenkellerbirthplace.org.

The charming Virginia-style cottage called Ivy Green was the birthplace of Helen Keller (1880-1968), whose extraordinary life and achievements despite multiple disabilities have served as the inspiration for generations of the similarly afflicted. Stricken blind and deaf as a child, Keller learned to sign, speak and write with help from her devoted teacher, Annie Sullivan. The house showcases a custom-made Braille watch, writ-ing tools and other mementos of Keller's life. Helen Keller eventually graduated from the demanding Radcliffe College and went on to champion the cause of hearing- and sight-impaired people around the world.

Russell Cave National Monument★★

◗ 90mi north of Huntsville. Take US-72 North to Bridgeport Exit and follow Rtes. 98 & 75 northwest 8mi. 3729 County Road 98. ✆256-495-2672. www.nps.gov/ruca.

In the early 1950s, a team of archaeologists from the National Geographic Society and the Smithsonian Institution excavated human remains and tools in Russell Cave dating back at least 9,000 years. One of the oldest verified sites of human habitation in the southeastern US, the cave held tools of stone and bone, pottery and shell jewelry indicating occupation in the Paleo (10,000 BC), Archaic (7000 to 500 BC) and Woodlands (500 BC to AD 1000) periods. Visitors can follow a short path with self-guiding markers into the cave's shallow upper mouth and over-hang (👣guided tours available).

Mississippi Area

Named for and defined by the 2,348mi "Father of Waters"—an early Indian name for North America's longest river—the state of Mississippi extends 47,000sq mi from the Appalachian ridges of the northeast across to the delta (Mississippi River's broad alluvial plain) to the crumbly loess soil and pine trees of the East Gulf Coastal Plain. Along the way are some of the finest antebellum homes and most productive farmlands in the US, juxtaposed against some of the nation's most intractable poverty. Celebrated American writers and musicians, from author William Faulkner to blues musician B.B. King, hail from the Magnolia State.

Mississippi

Highlights

1   Spending the night in a restored antebellum-period plantation house (p394)

2   A soothing drive on the scenic **Natchez Trace Parkway** (p396)

3   Reliving the fall of Vicksburg at **Vicksburg National Military Park** (p399)

King Cotton

When Hernando de Soto first viewed the giant river near present-day Clarksdale in 1541, the Chickasaw, Choctaw and Natchez tribes occupied its fertile valleys amid ancient ceremonial mounds. The French settled at Natchez in 1716, and the first Africans arrived—as slaves—in 1719.

As the American colonies grew and attained independence over the next century, the region passed from French to British to Spanish control before becoming the 20th US state in 1817. By the 1840s, vast tracts of central and lower Mississippi were planted with cotton—tended by slaves—and these regions claimed more millionaires than any other part of the US except New York City.

Control of Mississippi's plantation wealth and port cities was critical for both sides in the Civil War. As a result, Mississippi's houses were burned, its imports and exports were blockaded, and thousands of acres of cotton and food crops were destroyed. The war's devastation and the struggles of impoverished former slaves haunted Mississippi for decades as cotton plantations gave way to sharecropping, with whites im-posing cruel restrictions on the civil rights of blacks. By the 1950s and 60s, however, public officials were working to revitalize the economy, and civil rights leaders were breaking down centuries-old barriers to public universities, government and employment.

Without question, the Mississippi of today retains visible reminders of its pre-colonial history and plantation past, as well as a genuine sense of optimism about the future. Visitors who venture beyond the coastal cities of Biloxi and Gulfport (⮐ see GULF COAST) will find an intriguing mix of modernity and old-fashioned Southern ruralism—such as glitzy casinos dishing up fried okra, cornbread and sweet iced tea.

Jackson, Mississippi's capital, is by far the largest city in the state today (with more than 175,000 people).

Every four years, it hosts the USA International Ballet Competition, a world-class gathering with sister events in Moscow and Varna, Bulgaria (the next competition is scheduled for June 2014).

In the smaller cities of Natchez and Vicksburg, a sense of the Old South prevails, despite contemporary commerce.

Great Mississippi River Balloon Race, Natchez

ADDRESSES

🏨 STAY

$$$ Dunleith – 84 Homochitto St., Natchez, MS. ✕♿🅿🛏 📞601-446-8500. www.dunleith.com. 26 rooms. After a day of touring Natchez antebellum homes, spend the night in one of the most romantic. This gorgeous 1856 Greek-Revival mansion sports a columned double gallery ideal for passing a slow summer evening. Spacious guest rooms have lovely period furnishings, fine fabrics and some have even Italian marble fireplaces and clawfoot tubs! For a treat, dine at the **Castle Restaurant** on the property.

$$$ Monmouth Plantation – 36 Melrose Ave., Natchez, MS. ✕♿🅿🛏 📞601-442-5852. www.monmouthplantation.com. 30 rooms. Framed by towering oak trees and 26 acres of landscaped grounds, this mansion is located just half a mile from downtown. Rooms are beautifully designed, with hand-carved period antiques and half-tester beds dressed with rich fabrics. Reserve ahead for

the five-course Southern-style dinner ($52) served in **1818**, the opulent dining room; there's also an à la carte menu if you choose.

$$ Cedar Grove Mansion Inn – 2200 Oak St., Vicksburg, MS. ✕♿🅿🛏 📞601-636-1000. www.cedargroveinn.com. 33 rooms. An antebellum estate, in the middle of town, surrounded by five acres of gardens with rose-covered arbors and gazebos. The Greek Revival-style inn is filled with marble fireplaces, French Empire gasoliers and gold-leaf mirrors. Posh bedrooms (some named for *Gone With The Wind* characters) are furnished with canopy beds and handmade armoires.

🍴 EAT

$$ Cedar Grove Mansion Inn – 2200 Oak St., Vicksburg, MS. Closed Mon. 📞601-636-1000. www.cedargroveinn.com. **Southern.** Rustic brick walls, white linens and floor-to-ceiling windows create an ideal romantic setting. The chef's special blend of Creole seasonings jazzes up his New Orleans-style dishes.

$$ The Carriage House – 401 High St., Natchez, MS. 📞601-445-5151. www.stantonhall.com. **Southern.** Down-home Southern food is presented with formal trappings (fine linen and silver) at Stanton Hall's lovely dining room housed in a charming dependency of the main mansion. Chef Bingo Starr helms the kitchen, turning out the restaurant's signature miniature biscuits (try them with a dollop of jelly), and juicy, shatteringly crisp fried chicken. Top it all off with sweet peach cobbler.

Longwood, Natchez

Natchez★★

The architectural splendor of the antebellum plantation is lovingly preserved in Natchez, which avoided destruction during the Civil War by promptly surrendering to invading Union troops. Many of Natchez's wealthiest citizens had friends and family in the North and, in general, opposed secession.

▶ **Population:** 15,590.

🔢 **Info:** 𝓟601-446-6345; www.visitnatchez.com.

🚫 **Don't Miss:** The Oriental architecture of Longwood.

🕐 **Timing:** Plan your trip in the spring or fall so you can enjoy the Natchez Pilgrimage tours.

A BIT OF HISTORY

The oldest city on the Mississippi River, Natchez takes its name from its first known settlement, the **Grand Village of the Natchez Indians** (400 Jefferson Davis Blvd. 𝓟601-446-6502; www.natchezgrandvillage.com), where ceremonial plazas and mounds date back to the mid-16C. In 1716 the French explorer and governor of Louisiana, Jean-Baptiste Le Moyne de Bienville, established Fort Rosalie on a bluff over the river. The first steamboat docked in Natchez in 1811, opening new possibilities for trade and lavish lifestyles. A burgeoning plantation aristocracy, supported by far-flung cotton fields and slave labor, built elaborate "town estates" in and around Natchez, where they lived dur-

Mississippi Pilgrimages

A pilgrimage in Mississippi is not a religious experience; rather, it is a journey back in time. In the spring of 1932, Natchez society leader Katherine Miller, president of the Pilgrimage Garden Club, organized the first "pilgrimage," or tour, through some of the city's stately antebellum homes to fund the club's program to restore historic houses. Complemented by a pageant (a hoop-skirted musical extravaganza) presided over by the pilgrimage queen, the event attracted tourists as well as interior designers seeking a uniquely American style. Since then, many more home owners have opened their doors to visitors and pilgrimage weeks have been added in October and December.

During Natchez's month-long spring pilgrimage season (mid Mar–mid Apr), visitors are strongly advised to make advance reservations for lodging and home tours. Between pilgrimages, however, at least a dozen historic homes (most in public or institutional hands) are open for daily tours anytime (fees average $12 per house). For information on antebellum house tours, schedules and tickets, contact **Natchez Pilgrimage Tours** (𝓟601-446-6631; www.natchezpilgrimage.com).

For a glimpse of how the interior-design and home-furnishings professions have adapted "the Natchez style" to contemporary American tastes, visit the decorator's showroom of the **Historic Natchez Collection** (204 State St.), where you'll see high-end, licensed reproductions of Natchez-inspired antique furniture and decorative arts.

Additional Natchez mansions open for tours include the following. The designation (B&B) indicates properties that operate as bed-and-breakfast inns.
The Burn (c.1834) – 712 N. Union St., 𝓟601-442-1344 (B&B);
Dunleith (c.1856) – 84 Homochitto St., 𝓟601-446-8500 (B&B);
Linden (c.1800) – 1 Linden Pl., 𝓟601-445-5472 (B&B);
Monmouth Plantation (c.1818) – 36 Melrose Avenue, 𝓟601-442-5852 (B&B).

Natchez Trace Parkway

A 444mi National Park Service parkway (no traffic lights, no commercial traffic) running diagonally from Natchez, Mississippi, to Nashville, Tennessee, the Natchez Trace follows an ancient path first traced by buffalo and prehistoric hunters more than 8,000 years ago. At **Bynum Mounds** (milepost 232.4, about 25mi south of Tupelo), archaeologists discovered flint tools and clay cooking pots dating from 100 BC. The most impressive evidence of early cultures along the Trace can be found at **Emerald Mound** (milepost 10.3, 10mi north of Natchez), an eight-acre earthen mound crowned with a broad ceremonial plaza, probably constructed around AD 1200.

Until the steamboat brought speedy two-way traffic to the Mississippi River in the mid-19C, the trail carried some 10,000 travelers a year. Most were "Kaintucks"—hardy adventurers from Kentucky and points north—who floated goods downriver to New Orleans, sold their barges for lumber, then trekked home along the Trace. Plagued by bad weather, wild animals, hostile Indians and rough terrain, they often sought overnight shelter at roadside "stands" like **Mount Locust** (milepost 15.5) or **French Camp** (milepost 180.7), named after French trader Louis LeFleur. At **Grinder House** (milepost 385.9), a traveler named **Meriwether Lewis**—the famed commander of the Lewis and Clark Expedition—died of a gunshot wound one night in 1809. Whether his death was murder or suicide remains a mystery. Lewis is memorialized here by a marker in the form of a tall, broken column.

Contemporary travelers will find no operating inns or other commercial establishments on the Natchez Trace, but plenty of wildlife, cyclists, hikers and horse trailers heading for park-maintained riding trails. The **Natchez Trace Parkway Visitor Center** (℘662-680-4025; www.nps.gov/natr), located at milepost 266.0, just north of Tupelo, offers a film, interpretive exhibits and a bookstore.

ing the winter months between trips to Europe or New York. Emulating the great estates of Europe, they named their houses, landscaped their "parks," and filled their rooms with decorative arts: oil portraits and imported silver; fine French and Chinese porcelain; gold-leaf mirrors to rival Versailles; unique wall coverings; hand-carved pediments; cornice boards with Grecian motifs; and custom-made furniture of the finest walnut, mahogany and rosewood.

In present-day Natchez, many of these vast estates have been rescued and restored by civic and public organizations . Others operate as bed-and-breakfast inns hosting tours, overnight guests and special events. Many of these homes can be toured during the semi-annual **Natchez Pilgrimage** (see sidebar on previous page) in the spring and fall.

For a less genteel view of Natchez, visitors have long turned to the riverfront enclave of saloons and bawdy houses known as **Natchez-under-the-Hill** (Silver St. at Broadway). Today Silver Street is lined with shops, restaurants and bars catering to tourists from town and from two riverboats that offer cruises on the Mississippi.

SIGHTS
Longwood★★★

140 Lower Woodville Rd. ♿🅿 ℘601-446-6631. www.stantonhall.com/longwood.htm.

From a distance, this octagonal "Oriental villa," as its architect Samuel Sloan described it, is an elegant shell. The house was constructed for a wealthy planter but only the nine-room lower floor was ever finished; work on the upper floors was halted in 1861 when the Yankee workmen fled after the Confederates fired on Fort Sumter.

Longwood's architecture is elaborate and rare. The house boasts 120 Corinthian columns on verandahs on the first and second floors, 26 fireplaces and a stunning circular fourth-floor observatory with openings for 16 floor-to-ceiling windows offering panoramas of Natchez and the Mississippi River. Atop the observatory is a reproduction of the original Byzantine-style onion dome, topped by an ornate spire.

The tour takes visitors through the below-ground rooms, where many of the original furnishings remain, and then up into the unfinished floors. In the cavernous rooms, 150-year-old woodworking tools and half-carved timbers lie abandoned in the corners.

Melrose Plantation/Natchez National Historical Park★★★

1 Melrose-Montebello Pkwy. ℘601-446-5790. www.nps.gov/natc.

Now owned by the National Park Service, Melrose is an authentic antebellum town estate (c.1845) complete with slave quarters and other "dependencies," including a kitchen, stables and privies. A guided tour of the house and grounds informs visitors about the lives of slave owners and the enslaved alike, including the slaves' individualized bell-summoning system and the tragedies linked to a then-innovative lead-lined cistern system.

In 1910 an heir of the former owners moved to Melrose with his bride, who restored the house and opened it for the first pilgrimage tour in 1932. Original furnishings include a set of carved Rococo Revival chairs in the drawing room, from whose rose pattern the Gorham sterling-silver flat-ware pattern "Melrose" was derived.

Rosalie★★

100 Orleans St. ⤢🅿℘601-446-5676. www.rosaliemansion.com.

From the second-story portico of Rosalie (c.1820), visitors get a marvelous view of the broad Mississippi—a feature that also appealed to invading Union general Walter Gresham when he arrived and commandeered the house as his personal residence for three years beginning in 1863. With Gresham's consent, the Wilson family, Rosalie's owners, protected their belongings during the Union occupation by locking everything, including the 20-piece John Henry Belter rosewood parlor set, safely away in the attic and storing two huge gilt mirrors (swathed heavily in cotton) in a nearby cave. Amazingly, the mirrors reflect Rosalie's glory as clearly today as they did in 1863.

Stanton Hall★★

401 High St. ✂⤢🅿℘601-442-6282. www.stantonhall.com.

Master builder Thomas Rose completed this grand, white-stucco mansion in 1857. Built for Irish-immigrant cotton broker and planter Frederick Stanton, the house boasts Corinthian columns, 17ft-high ceilings and 50ft-long double parlors. Stanton called his home "Belfast," and planted 19 live oak trees (17 survive) on his property, which encompasses an entire block in the heart of downtown. Unfortunately, Stanton died only nine months after moving in. Over the next 80 years, the house went through a succession of owners before being bought by the Pilgrimage Garden Club in 1938. Intricate gas-lit chandeliers (called gasoliers) in the dining room depict scenes from Natchez history, and the original Sheffield silver doorknobs miraculously remain.

Magnolia Hall★

215 N. Pearl St. ✂⤢🅿℘601-443-9065. www.natchezgardenclub.com.

Distinguished by ornately carved magnolia-motif ceiling medallions, Magnolia Hall was built in 1858, and was one of the few Natchez mansions to suffer shelling damage (from a gunboat) during the Civil War. Now owned by the Natchez Garden Club, the house includes a small costume museum, with hoop skirts, corsets, and mannequins in antebellum garb worn by Natchez belles at the Spring Pilgrimage pageants the past 20 years.

Vicksburg★

Sitting proudly on a 200ft bluff at a sharp bend of the mighty Mississippi River, Vicksburg was so strategically positioned that it took Union commanders Ulysses S. Grant and William T. Sherman more than a year of planning, canal-digging and fierce fighting before they were able to besiege the city and capture it in July 1863. Called "the Gibraltar of the Confederacy," Vicksburg was a key commercial, cultural and transportation center whose fall spelled a turning point in the American Civil War.

A BIT OF HISTORY

First settled by the Spanish in 1790, Vicksburg got its name from a Methodist minister, Newit Vick, who bought 1,120 acres and laid out a town just before his death from yellow fever in 1819. The new town soon became a booming river port and railroad center, hosting 4,500 residents at the beginning of the Civil War.

As the crow flies, the heart of downtown is well within artillery range from

▶ **Population:** 23,450.
🛈 **Info:** ✆601-636-9421; www.vicksburgcvb.com.
👁 **Don't Miss:** The lovely view from the double balconies at Cedar Grove Mansion. Confederate trenches at Vicksburg National Military Park.

the famous Civil War battlefield. The **Old Courthouse** (1860), high on a hill above downtown, suffered a major hit; it now houses a museum with historical mementos and artifacts (1008 Cherry St.; ✆601-636-0741; http://old-courthouse.org).

Of the many fine houses built during antebellum prosperity, only a handful have survived, primarily by heroic eleventh-hour conversions into bed-and-breakfast inns in the face of unrelenting neighborhood decline. These properties include **Anchuca** (1010 First East St.; ✆601-661-0111; www.anchuca.com), where Jefferson Davis is said to have addressed a crowd from the balcony; the **Duff Green Mansion** (1114 First East

Vicksburg National Military Parkt

© Brian Swartz/iStockphoto.com

Mississippi Writers

For Southerners, "The past is never dead. It's not even past," observes a troubled resident of Yoknapatawpha County, the fictitious Mississippi setting of some 20 novels (*The Sound and the Fury* (1929); *As I Lay Dying* (1930); *Absalom, Absalom!* (1936)) and short-story collections by **William Faulkner** (1897-1962). Faulkner, who won the 1949 Nobel Prize for Literature, is perhaps the best known among a pantheon of Deep South writers. Born in New Albany, Mississippi, Faulkner lived in an 1840s plantation house, **Rowan Oak** (Old Taylor Rd., in Oxford, MS; 662-234-3284; www.rowanaok.com), from 1930 until his death.

Serious readers the world over carry an image of the struggling 20C South — faded aristocracy, deluded hopes and lost fortunes, bitter but resilient descendants of African slaves—based on the fictional works of an extraordinary generation of Mississippi writers such as Faulkner, Jackson's **Eudora Welty** (1909-2001), Columbus' **Tennessee (Thomas Lanier) Williams** (1911-83) and Natchez native **Richard Wright** (1908-60). Contemporary movie and crime-novel fans, meanwhile, stay up late to read thrillers by former Oxford resident **John Grisham** (*The Firm* 1993). Still others seek out lesser-known writers such as Oxford resident Barry Hannah (1942-2010), Civil War historian Shelby Foote (1916-2005), the father (1907-1972)-and-son (b. 1935) Hodding Carters and Walker Percy (1916-1990), the latter four all Greenville, Mississippi residents; or the newest issue of the prize-winning general-interest quarterly *The Oxford American* (revived in Oxford with Grisham's support, but now published by the University of Central Arkansas).

St.; 601-636-6968; www.duffgreenmansion.com), used as a Civil War hospital while its owners lived in a nearby cave; and the **Cedar Grove Mansion** (2200 Oak St.; 601-636-1000; www.cedargroveinn.com), with river views and four acres of antebellum gardens. The **Martha Vick House** (1300 Grove St.; 601-831-7007) was built for a daughter of Vicksburg's founder and is open for tours.

VICKSBURG NATIONAL MILITARY PARK★★

3201 Clay St, .25mi west of I-20. 601-636-0583. www.nps.gov/vick. Ranging over the meadows, hills and forests of this 1,800-acre site, Confederate and Union armies clashed in a decisive 1863 Civil War battle for Vicksburg, a critical Confederate port. After a 47-day siege and incessant cannon fire, Vicksburg surrendered on July 4, 1863, thus giving the North control of the "Father of Waters" and slicing the Confederacy in two from north to south. More than 10,000 Union troops died and some 9,000 Confederate soldiers lost their lives.

At the park **visitor center**, realistic displays show tents, trenches and furnished caves where Vicksburg residents waited out the shelling. A fiber-optic display map illustrates the effect of the Vicksburg campaign on the surrounding area, and the excellent film *Here Brothers Fought* gives a blow-by-blow account of the battle.

Be sure to take 16mi self-guided **driving tour** (audio, GPS and cellphone tours available), which leads past more than 1,324 memorials marking the positions of various state regiments. The park is vast and the memorials and statuary are numerous. Highlights include the **Illinois Memorial**, whose dome is modeled after Rome's Pantheon; the **Wisconsin Memorial** with "Old Abe," the war eagle; and a statue of General Grant on his horse.

At the northern edge of the park, a small museum presents artifacts and the raised hulk of the **USS Cairo**, an ironclad gunboat sunk by Confederates in 1862.

New Orleans Area

The Gulf Coast regions of Louisiana, Mississippi and Alabama comprise a varying landscape of beach-rimmed shorelines along the Mississippi Sound and bayou-laced swamps of the Mississippi delta. Punctuated by the charming and diverse southern cities of New Orleans, Biloxi and Mobile, each area affords myriad recreational opportunities. Seekers of sun and sand gravitate to Mississippi's waterside resorts. History buffs delight in touring Mobile's stately homes or the plantations that line the Mississippi River between New Orleans and Baton Rouge. Despite the devastation from Hurricane Katrina, the moniker, "The Big Easy" still applies to New Orleans. It lives up to its reputation as a haven for pleasure-seekers; its restaurants serve up finely crafted traditional Cajun and Creole dishes redolent of seafood and spices. And the genial peculiarities of the Cajun Country around Lafayette, Louisiana, can make a visit here feel like a trip to a foreign land.

Highlights

1 Soaking up the atmosphere of the **French Quarter** (p405)

2 A bowl of gumbo, a plate of jambalaya or a dish of étouffée (p409)

3 Remembering and honoring at the **National World War II Museum** (p410)

4 Going back in time at the **Rosedown Plantation** (p418)

LA — New Orleans

A Tropical Frontier

Sections of this region have changed hands numerous times since European explorers laid their claims in the 17C. France, Spain and England all grappled for control throughout the 18C, and all left their marks on regional culture before the US acquired the territories by treaty and by purchase in the early 19C. During the heyday of the slave trade, ships bearing human cargo for sale arrived here from Africa and the West Indies. On the backs of these slaves were built the massive cotton, indigo, rice and sugarcane plantations that fueled the region's economic prosperity in the 18C-19C.

Life along the coast during this period was difficult at best; epidemics of mosquito-borne yellow fever and malaria regularly swept through the cities, and hurricanes threatened each summer and fall. Transportation was limited to steamboats that plied the gulf waters between the population centers of Mobile, Biloxi and New Orleans. Today Interstate 10 links these cities.

A profusion of exotic plants flourishes in this subtropical climate, including moss-draped **live oak trees** (which maintain their green foliage year-round), fragrant magnolias, azaleas, hibiscus and bougainvillea.

High temperatures and inland humidity quell tourism in the summer, except at the breeze-cooled beachfront areas. The months from November to April are generally mild and comfortable. Pre-Lenten Mardi Gras celebrations in Lafayette, Mobile and New Orleans pack hotels and restaurants with thousands of visitors from all over the country and beyond.

At the end of August 2005, vast areas of New Orleans were flooded due to catastrophic levee breaches after Hurricane Katrina, bringing devastation to many of the city's poorer neighborhoods. Like most parts of town developed before the late 19C, the historic French Quarter escaped relatively unscathed, with most businesses able to reopen within two months. Other residential areas of the city, particularly New Orleans East, the Lower Ninth Ward, and St. Bernard Parish continue to recover, with rebuilding programs ongoing.

ADDRESSES

🛏 STAY

$$$$ Madewood Plantation House – 4250 Hwy. 308, Napoleonville, LA. 🅿 🖂 📞985-369-7151 or 800-375-7151. www.madewood.com. 8 rooms. This 1846 Greek Revival mansion sits in the middle of an active sugarcane plantation 75mi from New Orleans. Period antiques, including scrolled canopy, fourposter and half-tester beds, add authenticity. Breakfast, evening wine and cheese in the library, and candlelit dinners around the dining room's huge oak table are part of the deal. Private dining in the Music Room can be reserved in advance.

$$$$ Windsor Court Hotel – 300 Gravier St., New Orleans, LA. ✕♿🅿🖂 📞504-523-6000 or 800-928-7898. www.windsorcourthotel.com. 316 rooms. Frequented by European royalty and celebrities, this opulent hotel on the outskirts of the French Quarter received a complete interior renovation in 2012. Guest rooms and suites are outfitted with fine linens (note the custom toile depicting New Orleans landmarks), flat-screen TVs and elegant furnishings. High tea is served Thursday through Sunday in the lobby's Le Salon lounge.

$$$ Dauphine Orleans – 415 Dauphine St. New Orleans, LA. ♿🅿🖂 📞504-586-1800. www.dauphineorleans.com. 111 rooms. This lovely, well-run hotel sits in a prime French Quarter location just steps from historic attractions. Choose a room in the main hotel or in the historic Hermann House; the latter boast jacuzzis and upgraded amenities. Continental breakfast is included along with afternoon snacks, and the courtyard pool is the perfect place to cool off after a day of sightseeing.

$$$ Soniat House – 1133 Chartres St., New Orleans, LA. ♿🅿 📞504-522-0570. www.soniathouse.com. 30 rooms. A short walk from Cafe du Monde, this classic Creole-style town house in the French Quarter hasn't changed much since its beginnings in 1930. Spiral staircases lead to rooms decorated with European and Louisiana antiques and hand-carved canopy beds, leading out to flower-filled balconies. Comfortable guest rooms feature luxurious amenities like bathrobes, Molton Brown products, Egyptian cotton bed linens and goosedown pillows..

$$ T'Frere's House – 1905 Verot School Rd., Lafayette, LA. 🅿 🖂 📞337-984-9347 or 800-984-9347. www.tfreres.com. 8 rooms. You'll be immersed in Acadiana at this Colonial house on the edge of town. Antiques from the 18C and 19C take you back to 1880, when it was built. Guests particularly enjoy the ritual daily "Twilight Time" gatherings complete with juleps and crab canapés. The huge Cajun breakfast is the highlight: eggs, spicy smoked sausage, and crepes topped with sugar-cane syrup.

🍽 EAT

$$$ Arnaud's – 813 Bienville St., New Orleans, LA. 📞504-523-5433. www.arnaudsrestaurant.com. **Creole.** One of New Orleawns' cherished old-line culinary favorites, Arnaud's serves mouthwatering dishes that embody the pinnacle of fine Creole cuisine. Try mouthwatering duck breast with blueberry sauce, Oysters Bienville (simmered with shrimp, green onions and mushrooms) or tender pompano, perfectly seasoned. Try a Café Brulot (flavored with spices and flamed) with your desserts.

$$$ Cafe Vermilionville – 1304 W. Pinhook, Lafayette, LA. 📞337-237-0100. www.cafev.com. **Louisiana French.** Site of Vermilionville's first inn back in the early 1800s, this cafe in Lafayette's Oil Center now houses one of Lafayette's finest restaurants. The unvarnished wooden beams, hanging plants and candlelight blend romance with country elegance (jackets required). Raveworthy specialties include jumbo shrimp in a spicy herb sauce, crawfish beignets and pan-seared amberjack.

$$$ Emeril's Delmonico Restaurant and Bar -- 1300 St. Charles Ave., New Orleans, LA. ☏504-525-4937. www.emerilsrestaurants.com. **Creole.** When celebrity chef Emeril Lagasse restored the former Delmonico restaurant, he framed the 18ft windows in ultra suede and velvet panels, covered the walls with neutral shades of grass cloth, linen and cotton and updated the menus with modern twists on traditional Creole cuisine. Located on the edge of the Garden District, Delmonico features such updated classics as crabcakes with mango butter and cucumber kimchi; Louisiana drumfish Meuniere and jerk-spiced lamb sirloin with rum-glazed yams.

$$$ Mr. B's Bistro – 201 Royal St., New Orleans, LA. ☏504-523-2078. www.mrbsbistro.com. **Creole.** A French Quarter supper club known for its contemporary spin on local favorites. Mr.B's BBQ shrimp in a fiery pepper sauce and Gumbo Ya Ya (a soupy version of hearty chicken-and-andouille sausage stew) keep fans coming back. Bread pudding is the signature dessert.

$$$ The Grill Room – 300 Gravier St. in the Windsor Court Hotel, New Orleans, LA. ☏504-522-1994 . www.windsor court hotel.com. **American.** Regularly heading lists of New Orleans' finest restaurants, The Grill Room offers seasonal menus featuring locally sourced ingredients such as Gulf snapper, ribeyes with black truffle butter and pecan-crusted quail. It's all served up in one of New Orleans' most elegant dining rooms by well-trained staff.

$$ Jolie's Louisiana Bistro – 507 W. Pinhook Rd., Lafayette, LA. ☏337-504-2382. www.jolieslouisianabistro.com. **Creole.** This unfussy bistro melds traditional Creole cooking with an updated farm-to-table philosophy, serving up delicious steaks and local seafood creations such as the Zapp's Crawtator-Crusted Louisiana drumfish. The charcuterie and cheese boards are both winners.

$$ Dick & Jenny's – 4501 Tchoupitoulas St., New Orleans, LA. ☏504-894-9880. www.dickandjennys.com. **American.** You feel you've stepped in for a home-cooked meal at your best friend's house in this relaxed Uptown cottage. Best bets on the eclectic menu: the shrimp and tasso cheesecake, Louisiana flounder with sweet potato grits; and any of the gumbos du jour.

$$ Jacques-Imo's – 8324 OakSt., New Orleans, LA. ☏504-861-0886. http://jacques-imos.com. **Creole and Cajun.** With wild paint covering every inch of surface, an effusive and welcoming owner and a dedicated crowd of regulars, this Uptown spot wins points for its funky ambiance and delicious local fare, such as expertly cooked fish or steak dishes.

$$ La Crepe Nanou – 1410 Robert St., New Orleans, LA. Dinner only; closed Sun. ☏504-899-2670. www.lacrepenanou.com. **French.** Behind the velvet maroon curtains of this uptown bistro's doorway is a casual, French-flairdining room with vivid original paintings of Garden District street scenes. On the menu: typical bistro fare with a New Orleans twist, along with authentic classic *moules frites*.

Jackson Square, New Orleans

New Orleans★★★

In its topography, architecture, people and music, New Orleans resembles no other American city. Straddling the Mississippi River in southeastern Louisiana, the metropolis lies an average of 5ft below sea level. Its naturally swampy lands—laced with secondary tributaries called bayous—are made livable by an extensive system of levees, pumping stations and drainage canals. The city's long succession of inhabitants—encompassing the Native American indigenous population, French Creole and Spanish colonists, West Indian and African slaves, and settlers from Europe and the eastern US—has created a rich mix of peoples and cultures. The city's distinctive architecture is the result of European ideas adapted to the subtropical climate.

▶ **Population:** 368,250.
⊙ **Michelin Map:** p382.
🖹 **Info:** ℘504-566-5011 or 800-672-6124; www.neworleanscvb.com.
⊛ **Don't Miss:** The antebellum mansions of the Garden District.
🕒 **Timing:** Eating is a sport here; leave time to sample plenty of Cajun cooking.
🙎 **Kids:** The Audubon Zoo, the Audubon Insectarium, and the Aquarium of the Americas.

NEW ORLEANS TODAY

Its colorful cultural ambience, excellent restaurants and nowhere-else-but-here traditions make New Orleans one of the most popular tourist destinations in the US. Creativity, romance, drama and fun are always encouraged here. The American music form of jazz was born in Sunday-afternoon slave assemblages at Congo Square, and refined in the ballrooms, brothels and riverboats of the early20C city; today the annual New Orleans Jazz & Heritage Festival (**Jazzfest**) attracts hundreds of thousands of music fans.

Recovery continues from the effects of **Hurricane Katrina**, which struck the Gulf Coast in 2005 and caused the levee system around New Orleans to fail, inundating nearly 80 percent of the city and displacing tens of thousands of residents. Tourist attractions are fully restored to their pre-Katrina state,

Street musicians in the French Quarter

© Leslie Forsberg/Michelin

NEW ORLEANS

0   1/4 mi
0   300 m

AUDUBON PARK   NATIONAL WWII MUSEUM, GARDEN DISTRICT, OGDEN MUSEUM OF SOUTHERN ART, AUDUBON ZOO

and recovery is marching through the affected residential areas as well. New Orleans received a huge boost when its beloved **New Orleans Saints** football team won the 2009 Super Bowl, and the annual **Mardi Gras** celebration in February remains a world-renowned event. The storied **Superdome** covered sports arena, less than 3mi west of downtown, has hosted half a dozen NFL championship Super Bowl football games.

A BIT OF HISTORY

New Orleans was founded in 1718 by French explorer **Jean-Baptiste Le Moyne**, sieur de Bienville, in an effort to solidify French claims in the New World. The site he chose, atop a naturally raised embankment along the Mississippi, was militarily and economically important as the gateway to the Louisiana Territory, but proved inauspicious for settlement. French engineers laid out a town plan in 1721, and early colonists (forerunners of the city's non-indigenous Creole population) battled hurricanes, floods and epidemics as they maintained the trappings of French society in the muddy outpost. In 1769 the city came under Spanish rule, but was returned to France in 1803. A month later Napoleon sold the entire Louisiana Territory including New Orleans to the US for approximately $15 million.

The decades following the **Louisiana Purchase** saw an explosion in the city's population as settlers flooded west to occupy the new American territory. New Orleans grew to be the fourth-largest city in the US by 1840, its prosperity buoyed by the river trade. Shunned by the Creoles, Anglo-American newcomers settled in suburbs upriver from the French Quarter. Staunchly Confederate on the eve of the Civil War, New Orleans capitulated to a Union takeover in 1862 and was spared destruction.

The 20C saw numerous improvements to public-works systems, most importantly the development of flood-control measures that diverted river swells into shallow **Lake Pontchartrain** north of the city. The discovery of oil beneath the waters of the Gulf of Mexico brought new economic prosperity, along with continued port activities and increasingly, tourism.

Stroll through the **Garden District★★★**, the rectangle formed by St. Charles Avenue, Jackson Avenue, Magazine Street and Louisiana Avenue, to see an unmatched assortment of **antebellum mansions** (Greek Revival and Italianate styles predominate) erected mostly for Anglo-Saxon newcomers to New Orleans in the mid-19C. Built in the center of large plots of land, the houses allow space for front "gardens" where exotics such as banana, bougainvillea, magnolia, crape myrtle and oleander still flourish.

To explore **St. Charles Avenue★★**, a wide thoroughfare overhung with enormous live-oak trees, hop aboard the **St. Charles Streetcar★★ ▲▲** line that traces the 5mi from Carondelet and Canal Streets to Carrollton Avenue. Gracious antebellum and Victorian mansions edge either side of the avenue.

FRENCH QUARTER★★★

Historically known as the Vieux Carré, the fabled rectangle that for many embodies the essence of New Orleans, the French Quarter occupies roughly 100 blocks bounded by Canal Street, Rampart Street, Esplanade Avenue and the great curve of the Mississippi River. The grid pattern laid out in 1721 survives today, but devastating fires in 1788 and 1794 wiped out most early French colonial constructions. The distinctive archi-tectural flavor of the French Quarter—with its stucco surfaces in bright pastel tints, intricately patterned cast-iron galleries and secluded interior courtyards—developed during the city's Spanish and early American periods. New Orleans' French Creole population remained firmly entrenched here from the city's earliest days through the Civil War and Reconstruction, but by the late 19C an influx of immigrants had moved in and the genteel quarter became a rowdy commercial and nightlife district. Today most Quarter residents live quietly behind the closed shutters of Creole cottages and town houses lining the streets on the lake side of Bourbon Street and downriver of Dumaine. But on Bourbon, Royal and Decatur Streets, on the broad pedestrian malls surrounding Jackson Square, and on the plazas near the French Market, the vibrant public life of the Quarter plays out daily like an urban musical comedy.

Jackson Square★★

Bounded by Chartres, St. Philip, Decatur & St. Ann Sts.

Laid out as a military parade ground known as Place d'Armes, the fenced and landscaped square at the foot of Orleans Street was renamed in 1851 to honor **Andrew Jackson** (1767-1845), hero of the Battle of New Orleans and seventh US president.

The monumental statue of Jackson astride a rearing horse was dedicated in 1856. Surrounded by elegant St. Louis Cathedrala (1794), government buildings and the 1840s **Pontalba Buildings★** (E on map), the square served as the focal point of the old city; today street performers, artists and vendors set up shop on the square's flagstone perimeter. Across Decatur Street downriver from the square, **Café du Monde** (B on map) serves up café au lait and beignets (square donuts dredged in powdered sugar). Opposite looms handsome **Jax Brewery**, erected in 1891 and now renovated as a mall. A stairway between the two leads to the **Moonwalk**, a boarded promenade where visitors can watch ships navigating the bend in the Mississippi that gave rise to New Orleans' nickname "the Crescent City."

For a view of the city from the Mississippi River, take one of the paddlewheeler **cruises** that depart from the waterfront upriver from Jackson Square.

Cabildo★★

701 Chartres St. & ℰ504-568-6968. www.crt.state.la.us.

To the left of the cathedral stands the Cabildo (A on map), erected by the Spanish government in 1799; the papers completing the territory transfers of the Louisiana Purchase were signed here in 1803. Today the handsome building and the adjacent Arsenal contain excellent displays of Louisiana history; on view here is one of the four original bronze death masks made of Napoleon in 1821. Complementing the Cabildo to the right of the cathedral, the 1813 **Presbytère★★** (F on map) was built to house the bishops of Louisiana; today it showcases Katrina & Beyond, a sobering exhibit leading visitors through New Orleans residents' experience of the natural disaster that will forever mark the city. The upper level houses exhibits about the colorful history of Mardi Gras in New Orleans.

French Market★

1008 N. Peters St. ℰ504-522-2621. www.frenchmarket.org.

Extending downriver from Jackson Square, this bustling marketplace (1813) served the daily needs of New Orleans' Creole population. Stores (mostly gift shops) and restaurants occupy the structures today; the building remains open to the air, as it was in the 19C, and populated by vendors selling tables of crafts and flea-market wares.

Step across Decatur Street to the old **Central Grocery** (923 Decatur St.) and pick up a muffuletta, the pungent New Orleans sandwich made of Italian deli meats and cheeses layered on round bread and spiked with chopped-olive salad. But be sure to have plenty of napkins on hand.

Royal Street★★

Elegant Royal Street is best-known for the many shops and galleries occupying the street-level facades of its early-19C town houses. It is a street for meandering, with pauses to poke through galleries and to gaze upward at intricately whorled galleries of wrought and cast iron. The massive white marble and granite **Louisiana Supreme Court Building** (no. 400), was completed in 1910. Selections from the holdings at the **Historic New Orleans Collection★** (ℰ504-523-4662; www. hnoc.org) furnish changing exhibits presented in the ground-floor gallery of the 1792 **Merieult House** (D on map) at no. 533. Departing from the Forever New Orleans shop (no. 624; ℰ504-568-1801; www.mondecreole.com), Le Monde Creole conducts excellent guided **walking tours★** that access several romantic interior courtyards while illustrating the intricacies of the city's French and West African Creole society. You can tour the **Gallier House★** (nos. 1118-1132; ℰ504-525-5661; www.hgghh.org), a fine example of Creole and American style elements; the same organization offers tours of the beautifully restored Federal-style **Hermann-Grima House** (820 St. Louis St.).

Bourbon Street★

Year-round, but especially at Mardi Gras time, Bourbon Street teems with cocktail-toting revelers who come to celebrate, to drown their sorrows or simply to indulge in the pleasures of this unabashedly hedonistic city. Lights flash, music booms and hawkers stand in doorways touting the dubious wanton pleasures within.

Some of the finest traditional jazz is performed nightly just off Bourbon at **Preservation Hall★** (726 St. Peter St.; ℰ504-522-2841; www.preservationhall. com), one of the city's best-known and historic jazz venues.

MARDI GRAS★★★

New Orleans' **Mardi Gras** celebration is world-renowned as an unabashed invitation and tribute to escapism, ribaldry and decadence, a final hurrah before the spartan, sober season of Lent. The day before Ash Wednesday, Mardi Gras crowns the Carnival season, which officially begins on Twelfth Night (6 January). This season of parties, private masked balls and parades organized by exclusive social clubs known as "krewes" reaches its crescendo during the week and a half before Mardi Gras, during which time some 60 parades roll along established routes through various parts of the

Mardi Gras masks

© SuperStock / age fotostock

city. Costumed riders aboard elaborately designed floats, toss strings of beads, aluminum doubloons, plastic cups, toys and other trinkets to the crowds who line the streets begging for handouts. On Fat Tuesday itself, businesses and services shut down as residents and visitors alike take to the streets for a day-long citywide binge. Families dressed in costumes or in the Mardi Gras colors of purple, green and gold congregate along the St. Charles Avenue parade route to try for the prized coconuts handed out by the members of the Zulu Social Aid and Pleasure Club; or to toast Rex, King of Carnival, as he passes by with the Krewe of Rex. Die-hard revelers don costumes and head for the French Quarter to pack themselves like sardines into the throngs of people on Bourbon Street. Here they gape at the outrageous creations of costume-contest participants, drink and dance, and indulge in New Orleans' quintessential celebration of escape from life's worries to focus on the pleasures of today.

© Charles Bowman / age fotostock

MUSEUMS OF THE QUARTER

Many of the historic French Quarter's buildings were built on land 5ft above sea level in the late 19C, and therefore remained substantially dry after Hurricane Katrina struck. You'll find several interesting museums residing in the Quarter. **Musée Conti Wax Museum**★ (917 Conti St.; & ℘504-525-2605; www.neworleanswaxmuseum.com) offers a surprisingly informative walk through New Orleans history via a series of tableaux depicting key events and personages as waxen figures in the city's development.

During the late 1940s, beloved American author **Frances Parkinson Keyes** (1885-1970) restored her gracious home, **Beauregard-Keyes House**★ (1113 Chartres St.; ℘504-523-7257; www.bkhouse.org), where she lived until the 1970s. The house had been the residence of Con-federate general P.G.T. Beauregard for 18 months following the Civil War. It now contains a collection of fans, folk costumes and more than 200 antique dolls. Nearby, the **New Orleans Historic Voodoo Museum** (724 Dumaine St.; ℘504-680-0128; www.voodoomuseum.com) provides, through mysterious artifacts and artwork,glimpses into the world of voodoo, the occult religion that arrived in New Orleans with the slave trade, and continues to flourish today.

Like its sister Audubon institutions (the Aquarium and the Zoo), the **Audubon Insectarium**★ (423 Canal St.; ✕& ℘504-581-4629; www.auduboninstitute.org), which occupies the lower floor of the historic U.S. Custom House, makes learning about the natural world fun. Bugs—their habits, their biology, and (in some cases) their flavor—are the focus of kid-oriented exhibits. Enticing interactive displays and lots of live specimens highlight the adaptability of nature's supreme survivors. Exhibit areas include the **Louisiana Swamp**, the **Metamorphoses Gallery** (where butterflies emerge regularly from racks of chrysalises) and the **Termite Gallery**. Stop in at the Bug Appetit cafe to sample snacks made of edible insects. The visit ends with a walk through the **Butterflies in Flight Gallery**, where 400 of the beautiful creatures flit, flutter and perch (sometimes on visitors!).

Innovative exhibits highlighting marine specimens from North, Central and South America delight visitors to the **Aquarium of the Americas**★★ (1 Canal St.; ✕&🄿 ℘504-861-2537; www.auduboninstitute.org). This fine aquarium is distinguished by its slanted blue-green cylinder rising at the foot of Canal Street. Moray eels, silvery tarpon and other colorful creatures glide overhead as visitors navigate the walk-through tunnel of the **Caribbean Reef**. The aquarium's playful sea otters cavort in their see-through tank, while fearsome piranhas glide in the **Amazon Rain Forest**. The **Mississippi River** exhibit reveals a wealth of catfish, bass, crappies and a rare white alligator. Other features include Adventure Island, an interactive play zone for kids with a touch pool filled with bullnose and cownose rays; a colony of playful penguins; **Parakeet Pointe**, home to hundreds of colorful parakeets flitting in their free-flight exhibit; and an IMAX theater.

WAREHOUSE DISTRICT★

In the once-bland industrial sector extending upriver from Poydras Street thrives the center of visual arts in New Orleans. Warehouses that sprang up behind riverfront docks in the early 19C are now reborn as studios and museums, while street-level storefronts along **Julia Street** house a variety of contemporary art galleries. Occupying a handsome former factory and warehouse, the **Contemporary Arts Center** (900 Camp St.; ✕&🄿 ℘504-528-3800; www.cacno.org) mounts live performances and edgy temporary exhibits of modern visual art in its sleekly renovated gallery spaces. **Riverwalk Marketplace** (℘504-522-1555), a festival shopping mall, stretches along the area where riverfront loading docks once fringed the Mississippi (Poydras, Canal & Julia Sts.). At the upriver end of the Riverwalk,

NEW ORLEANS CUISINE

Rooted in traditions more than two centuries old, New Orleans cuisine reveals the divergent influences of the varied cultures who populated the city. The origins of Cajun cooking lie in the simple foodways of agrarian France, brought to Louisiana by Acadian farmers and adapted with local ingredients. Considered more complex, Creole cuisine began in New Orleans and was influenced by the culinary traditions of the city's Spanish, African, West Indian and Native American populations.

Dependent as they are on the use of fresh local ingredients, many Cajun and Creole specialties are difficult to duplicate outside the region, making eating out, for some visitors, the raison d'être of a visit to the "Big Easy." Fish and seafood drawn from Louisiana rivers, lakes, brackish coastal wetlands and the Gulf of Mexico headline many a menu, accompanied by mellow Creole tomatoes, sweet satsuma oranges and other fruits and vegetables unique to the region's soil and climate.

Complex combinations of herbs and spices spike many dishes. **Roux**, a mixture of flour and fat cooked until dark brown, forms the base of sauces and soups. These include **gumbo**, a rich stew typically made with okra, **andouille** (a spicy smoked pork sausage) and chicken or seafood, and thickened with **filé** (powdered sassafrass, first used by the region's Choctaw Indians). Shrimp, oysters and crawfish (a freshwater shellfish resembling a miniature lobster) appear in countless forms: **étouffée**, or "smothered," in rich, vegetable-laced sauce; simmered with rice, tomato, meats and spices in **jambalaya**; chilled and dressed with piquant **rémoulade** sauce; or dusted with cornmeal, then fried and heaped on French bread in a **po' boy** sandwich. Amberjack, redfish, pompano and trout are all fished locally and served up sautéed with almonds, napped with meunière sauce, or broiled and topped with sweet lump crabmeat. For dessert, try **bananas Foster**, a decadent preparation of bananas sautéed in butter and brown sugar then flamed with rum at table and served over ice cream.

Spicy Cajun crawfish étouffée

© GWMullis/iStockphoto.com

be sure to explore the **Southern Food and Beverage Museum**★ (℘504-569-0405; http://southernfood.org), celebrating the multilayered culinary culture of the southern US with emphasis on New Orleans. A separate gallery devoted to cocktails tells the colorful history of liquor in the US.

The fine **Louisiana Children's Museum** (420 Julia St.; ℘504-523-1357; www.lcm.org) wows creative kids with its fun activities and displays like a pint-sized grocery store, a miniature art studio, a playground of simple machines and a giant bubble play area.

National World War II Museum★★

945 Magazine St. (entrance on Andrew Higgins Dr.) ✕&🅿 ℘504-528-1944. www.nationalww2museum.org.

This sobering but ultimately inspirational museum occupying a complex of state-of-the-art facilities in the Warehouse District presents the American experience of the most wide-ranging and transformative armed conflict in modern history. Displays about the enormously complicated amphibious landing operations that turned the tide of the war are the focus of the museum's earliest section. Expansions in recent years employ artifacts, fiber-optic maps, letters, personal articles, uniforms, and in particular photographs and videos, to detail the entire scope of the conflict from the expansionist policies of Germany, Italy and Japan in the 1930s through the US entry into the war in 1941 to the August 1945 dropping of the atomic bomb on Hiroshima.

Enter the grand Louisiana Memorial Pavilion where you'll see large artifacts, including a restored C-47 troop carrier aircraft and a **Higgins boat**, one of the shallow-draft 36-passenger transports—designed and built in New Orleans—credited by General Dwight D. Eisenhower with winning the war by enabling amphibious landings. Throughout the main building, video stations continuously screen short films highlighting personal histories and major conflicts such as the bat-

tles of Midway, the Philippines and the Leyte Gulf.

Across the street, the museum's theater screens an emotion-packed 4-D presentation **Beyond all Boundaries**★★, featuring immersive special effects that plunge the viewer into the story of this war. In the **Restoration Pavilion**, visitors can see pieces from the museum's ever-expanding collection of large artifacts (boats, vehicles, weapons) undergoing restoration. Exhibits in the **Freedom Pavilion** detail soldiers' lives as well as life on the homefront.

Confederate Memorial Hall

929 Camp St. ℘504-523-4522. www.confederatemuseum.com.

This handsome, Romanesque-style building (1891) houses a fine collection of paintings, photographs, uniforms, battle memorabilia and other artifacts of the Civil War, including personal belongings of Robert E. Lee, Stonewall Jackson and Jefferson Davis.

Adjacent, the **Ogden Museum of Southern Art** (925 Camp St.; ℘504-539-9650; www.ogdenmuseum.org) showcases selections from its permanent collection of paintings, crafts and works in mixed-media. Watercolorist Walter Inglis Anderson, visionary artist Howard Finster and sculptor Ida Kohlmeyer are represented here along with studio glass from the Penland School.

ADDITIONAL SIGHTS
Magazine Street

This colorful commercial and residential thoroughfare winds its way from the Warehouse District to Audubon Park. The blocks are jammed with restaurants and coffeehouses, designer boutiques and second-hand stores, upscale furniture and import showrooms, and gift shops of every stripe.

Audubon Zoo★★

6500 Magazine St. ✕&🅿 ℘504-581-4629. www.auduboninstitute.org.

With its lush landscaping and exhibits featuring exotic animals from around the globe, this well-designed zoo is a treat. The **Louisiana Swamp** exhibit mimics life on the bayou and features fish, nutria, and a large group of alligators (including a rare white alligator). The Reptile House boasts a rare Komodo dragon, and Monkey Hill offers kids the chance to run and climb. Don't miss the daily giraffe and elephant feedings. On sweltering days, the Cool Zoo splash park offers welcome relief.

Across Magazine Street from the zoo lies **Audubon Park★★** (bounded by St. Charles, Walnut & Calhoun Sts.). Formerly the site of a 400-acre sugar plantation, this space served as a Union encampment during the Civil War and as the site of the 1884 World's Cotton Centennial, which sparked residential development of uptown New Orleans.An oak-lined path curves along the park perimeter around a golf course.

City Park★

Entrance at Espplanade Ave. & Wisner Blvd. 🅿 𝒫504-482-4888. www.neworleanscitypark.com.
Northwest of Jackson Square, this expansive urban park encompasses 1,300 acres at the head of gracious **Esplanade Avenue★**, which traces an old Choctaw path from the river to the Bayou St. John. Attractions include the **New Orleans Botanical Garden**, the just-for-kiddies Storyland and **Carousel Gardens** amusement parks.

New Orleans Museum of Art★

1 Collins Dibboll Circle. 𝒫504-658-4100. www.noma.org.
Housed in a handsome Beaux-Arts-style building (1911) within City Park, this collection of more than 40,000 pieces encompasses major European and American schools of painting, but focuses on French works (Dégas, Monet, Renoir, Pisarro and Gaugin are represented), Louisiana and African-American artists. You'll also find Japanese Edo-period paintings, a significant collection of pre-Colombian art, and several exquisite eggs by Russian jeweler Peter Carl Fabergé.

Adjacent to the museum lies a **Sculpture Garden**, with more than 60 works by well known masters (Rodin, Oldenburg, Noguchi, Kohlmeyer and Moore, among others) artfully placed amid winding landscaped paths.

EXCURSIONS

Chalmette Battlefield★

▶ 5mi southeast of New Orleans in Chalmette. Go east on Rte. 46 to park entrance at 8606 W. St. Bernard Hwy. 𝒫504-281-0510 or 504-589-2133. www.nps.gov/jela.
At this riverside battlefield on January 8, 1815, Gen. Andrew Jackson and a force of about 5,000 soldiers successfully defended New Orleans against British invasion in the final major confrontation of the War of 1812, thus securing US ownership of the Louisiana Territory. In the visitor center, displays and interactive exhibits recount the battle. Afterward, you can drive or walk the 1.5mi road leading past key battle sites, and visit the peaceful National Cemetery.

Barataria Preserve

▶ 6588 Barataria Blvd. in Marrero, 17mi south of New Orleans near Crown Point. Take US-90 West over the Mississippi River; exit at Barataria Blvd. and go south on Rte. 45 to park. 𝒫504-589-3690 or 504-589-2133. www.nps.gov/jela.
This 20,000-acre wetland wilderness characterizes the constantly shifting terrain of the Mississippi delta region. Ranger-led hikes and guided canoe trips unlock the mysteries of this unique environment, as do exhibits in the preserve's visitor center.
An adventurous way to see the Bayou Barataria up close is to take one of several privately operated **swamp tours** (𝒫504-566-5011 or 800-672-6124).

Cajun Country★

A broad landscape of sugarcane and rice fields, boggy swamps and sinuous bayous, Cajun Country offers visitors an excellent opportunity to sample the rich cultural heritage of one of the nation's best-known ethnic groups. Comprising 22 parishes (the Louisiana term for counties), the region extends north of the ragged Gulf Coast and west of the Mississippi River, encompassing the boggy Atchafalaya Basin and relatively high prairies ranging west of Lafayette to the Texas border.

- ⚅ **Michelin Map:** 584 M 13.
- 🚹 **Info:** ☎225-342-8119; www.louisianatravel.com.
- 😋 **Don't Miss:** The beauty and authenticity of Shadows-on-the-Teche.
- 👫 **Kids:** Little ones love to imagine the past at Vermilionville, a restored farmstead.

A BIT OF HISTORY

Formally nicknamed "Acadiana," the Cajun Country is principally inhabited by descendants of French colonists who were deported from Acadia (now Nova Scotia, Canada) in 1755 for refusing to swear allegiance to the British Crown. After suffering terrible hardships, Acadian refugees began arriving in southern Louisiana in the late 18C, infusing the region with the distinctive culture that flourishes today. Tourist attractions are sparse outside the regional capital of Lafayette, but the charm of a visit to this area lies in its people and their lifestyle.

Explore the small towns of **St. Martinville**, **Breaux Bridge** or **Opelousas**, where fun-loving, hardworking and fervently Catholic Cajuns (the word is derived from "Acadian") welcome visitors to join their enthusiastic pursuit of a good time. Fiddles and accordions set feet flying in rural dance halls; headily spiced gumbos, seafood stews and *boudin* (rice and pork sausage) appear on local tables; and Cajun French is as prevalent as English on the sidewalks.

SIGHTS

Lafayette★

135mi west of New Orleans via I-10. Visitor center at 1400 N.W. Evangeline Thruway. ☎800-346-1958. www.lafayettetravel.com.

Founded in 1836 as Vermilionville and renamed in 1884, Louisiana's fourth-largest city is known as the "Hub City of Acadiana." Several Acadian-related

Jean Lafitte National Historical Park and Preserve

© National Parl Service

sights lie within its boundaries, and its many hotels and restaurants make it a natural headquarters for explorations of the surrounding region.

Acadian Cultural Center★★

501 Fisher Rd. ♿ 🅿 ℘ 337-232-0789. www.nps.gov/jela.

This well-conceived visitor center operated by the **Jean Lafitte National Historical Park and Preserve** is an ideal place to begin forays into the Cajun Country. Displays focus on various aspects of Cajun life in Louisiana, highlighting the ways in which Acadian traditions and methods—farming and building techniques, clothing, language, crafts, music—were adapted to conditions in the new land. A 40min video dramatizes the Acadian expulsion from Nova Scotia.

In spring and fall, the center operates guided **boat tours** on languid Bayou Vermilion, former home to trappers, farmers and fishermen; it's a great way to get a feel for the traditional Cajun lifestyle of yesteryear.

👥 Vermilionville★

300 Fisher Rd. ✕ 🅿 ℘ 337-233-4077. www.vermilionville.org.

Eighteen colorfully re-created and restored buildings, including a 1790 farmstead, range along tranquil Bayou Vermilion at this living-history museum and folklife park devoted to commemorating the Acadian way of life c.1765-1890. Costumed artisans demonstrate traditional crafts such as weaving, boatbuilding and blacksmithing, while Cajun bands perform regularly in a large performance hall. Don't miss a browse through the gift shop for locally-produced handcrafted items.

Acadian Village★

200 Greenleaf Dr. 🅿 ℘ 337-981-2364. www.acadianvillage.org.

Set around a placid "bayou," this rustic re-created village offers a glimpse of life in Acadiana around the mid-19C. Most of the structures are originals, moved here from other locations in the region; others were constructed on-site

Acadian Village

© Michelle Broussard Photography

with period materials. Helpful plaques provide insights into architectural practices of the time, while displays in each building focus on Acadian culture and traditions.

Shadows-on-the-Teche★★

317 E. Main St., New Iberia. 🚌 Visit by guided tour only. ℘ 337-369-6446. www.shadowsontheteche.org.

Moss-draped live oak trees create a play of light and shadow over this elegant brick Greek Revival mansion, built by sugarcane planter David Weeks in 1834. Distinguished by its dignified columned facade, the house remained in the Weeks family for four generations before being left to the National Trust for Historic Preservation.

You'll feel you've traveled back in time on a visit here, as nearly every item in the house is original, including fine Federal and Empire-style furniture from New York and Philadelphia, Staffordshire china and family portraits.

Family members lie interred in a tranquil corner of the formally landscaped grounds fringing the slow-moving Bayou Teche.

Guided tours are offered daily, as well as a lively schedule of activities, from Halloween events in the gardens to arts and crafts fairs.

Gulf Coast★

Long a popular resort haven, the coastline fringing the Gulf of Mexico from Mobile, Alabama, to New Orleans, Louisiana, boasts a wide variety of attractions for gamblers, sportsmen and history buffs, as well as those seeking the pleasures of sun and sand.

A BIT OF HISTORY

Beginnings

Claimed by the French government in the late 17C, this area came under British rule in 1763 following French defeat in the French and Indian War, and was ceded to Spain following the American Revolution. The American flag was first raised over the territory in 1811, and resort communities sprang up. Staunchly Confederate through the Civil War, the Gulf Coast fell to Union forces in 1864.

Modern-day Disasters

In the years following Reconstruction, tourism again boomed in the area. Hurricane Katrina devastated much of this area in 2005; recovery efforts were ongoing in April 2010 when an explosion occurred at the Deepwater Horizon oil drilling platform offshore, sending the entire rig to the bottom and leaving the oil well at the seafloor uncapped. Before the well was sealed, an estimated 4.9 million barrels of oil gushed into the Gulf, slicking waterways, beaches and wetlands all along the Louisiana, Mississippi and Alabama shores with raw crude.

The environmental and economic damage of the disaster are still being calculated. Tourism at the resort communities of **Gulf Shores, Pascagoula, Biloxi, Ocean Springs** and **Gulfport** slowed in the aftermath of the disaster but today, after successful cleanup efforts, these cities are again attracting visitors to their white-sand beaches, warm gulf waters and moderate year-round temperatures, although some historic structures were lost.

- ◔ **Michelin Map:** 584 O 13.
- 🛈 **Info:** ℘225-342-8119; www. louisianatravel.com; ℘228-896-6699, www.gulfcoast.org (Biloxi); ℘251-208-2000, www.mobile.org (Mobile).
- 🅿 **Parking:** Long distances between resort towns make driving essential here. During the winter, parking lots will be full of cars with license plates from northern states.
- 😋 **Don't Miss:** Mardi Gras in Mobile.
- 👪 **Kids:** Curious kids may like exploring the gun turret of the USS Alabama, World War II battleship.

BILOXI

This bustling coastal Mississippi city teems with activity from its resorts, fishing port, seafood canneries and boatyards, all blessings of its water-bound location on a peninsula between Biloxi Bay and the Mississippi Sound. Founded in 1699, Biloxi was accessible only by steamboat during the antebellum period; it nevertheless became one of the most popular resorts on the Gulf Coast.

Biloxi was hard hit by Hurricane Katrina in 2005; the massive storm came ashore just west of the city and flooded the entire shorefront area, bringing water into beachfront hotels and washing barge-based casinos inland.

Today both new and rebuilt casinos dot the miles of beach along Biloxi's shorefront. Katrina's winds and tidal surge wiped away the charming homes that used to line the residential stretches of Beach Boulevard. Continuing to rebuild from that devastating event, the city welcomes thousands each May to the popular Biloxi Shrimp Festival.

Ocean Springs★

1mi east of Biloxi via US-90.

This waterside artists' colony in Mississippi invites strolls along pleasant sidewalks lined with antique shops, potteries, art galleries and cafes.

Also in town is the **William M. Colmer Visitor Center** (3500 Park Rd., off US-90; 228-875-0821; www.npslgov/guis) of the **Gulf Islands National Seashore**, a national park that preserves the Gulf Coast barrier islands.

MOBILE★

Third-largest city in Alabama, this gracious port combines the genteel atmosphere of the antebellum era with the bustle and verve of a contemporary southern metropolis. Mobile (pronounced mow-BEEL) served as the capital of French Louisiana from 1711 to 1719. Its prime location at the head of Mobile Bay made the city a major Confederate port during the Civil War, one of the last to fall to Union control. Today the Port of Mobile and shipbuilding activities at the Alabama Shipyards fuel Mobile's economy.

The city prides itself on its French heritage; the Mardi Gras celebration here predates the better-known festivities in New Orleans and signals the start of the dazzling annual **Azalea Trail Festival**. Local maps and information are available at the visitor center downtown in **Fort Condé** ♣♣ (150 S. Royal St.; 251-208-7569; www.museumofmobile), a reconstructed version of the early-18C French outpost. Mobile's population exploded in the last decade as people moved from New Orleans in the wake of Hurricane Katrina.

♣♣ USS Alabama Battleship Memorial Park★★

2703 Battleship Pkwy., off US-90 1mi east of downtown. ✕♿🅿 251-433-2703. www.ussalabama.com.

Launched in 1942, this massive ship served in both the Atlantic and Pacific theaters of World War II, and earned nine battle stars shooting down 22 enemy planes and participating in six land bombardments.

The self-guided tour offers a rare opportunity to enter a massive barbette supporting one of the ship's 16-inch gun turrets. Other attractions in the park include the World War II submarine USS Drum, and 27 historic aircraft.

Museum of Mobile★

111 S. Royal St. ♿ 251-208-7569. www.museumofmobile.com.

An extensive and varied collection of documents, portraits, Civil War artifacts, and Mardi Gras memorabilia housed in Mobile's historic market building tells the story of Mobile from colonization to the present. Exhibits change frequently; there's also a fun hands-on Discovery Room for kids.

♣♣ Gulf Coast Exploreum Museum of Science★

65 Government St. at Water St. 251-208-6873. www.exploreum.com.

Sleek and sparkling, the Exploreum features interactive exhibits that encourage kids to get excited about physics. In Hands-On Hall, more than 50 interactive physics displays entertain and educate visitors. Visitors can conduct a variety of biologically oriented experiments in BioLab, in-vestigate the workings of the human body in BodyWorks, and explore the world of chemistry in ChemLab.

EXCURSION

Bellingrath Home and Gardens★★

▶ 20mi south of Mobile via I-10 to US-90. 12401 Bellingrath Rd., Theodore, AL. ✕♿🅿 251-973-2217. www.bellingrath.org/gardens.

Begun in 1927, some 65 acres of beautifully landscaped gardens surround this Mediterranean-style villa (1935) of antique brick and ironwork. Mobile soft-drink magnate Walter Bellingrath and his wife created this exquisite haven on the bank of the Fowl River as a personal retreat, decorating the house with Mrs. Bellingrath's extensive collection of European antique furniture, china and porcelain. The rose garden ranks among the finest in the country; you can also stroll a Bayou Boardwalk.

River Road★★

One of the finest collections of antebellum plantation houses in the South lies along the historic River Road between New Orleans and Baton Rouge, Louisiana. Lined with more than 2,000 plantations in its early-19C heyday, these banks of the Mississippi have since been marred by a glut of 20C oil and chemical plants.

> **Michelin Map:** 584 N 13.
> **Info:** 225-342-8119; www.louisianatravel.com.
> **Location:** The River Road traces both banks of the Mississippi for approximately 120mi between New Orleans and Baton Rouge.

A BIT OF HISTORY

Beginning in the early 18C, Louisiana's French colonial government encouraged agricultural development of this area by granting plots of land to individuals who established plantations. Cotton, indigo, rice and especially sugarcane all thrived in the rich soil of the Mississippi River flood-plain, providing planters with the means to live extravagantly.

Large homes built by slave labor formed the heart of most plantations; the principal entryway faced the river. After 1803, Greek Revival became the popular style, and many Creole-style homes were updated with Classical ornamentation.

Madewood★ (1846), designed by noted Louisiana architect Henry Howard, is considered among the finest examples of Greek Revival architecture in the area (4250 Hwy. 308, 2mi south of Napo-leonville; ✗ 🅿 985-369-7151; www.madewood.com).

The term "River Road" designates roadways on both sides of the river and incorporates sections of several state highways (notably Highway 18 on the west bank, and Highway 44 on the east bank). Route numbers change along the way; it's best to keep to the levees. The Hale Boggs Bridge (I-310), the Veterans Memorial Bridge (Hwy. 641) and the Sunshine Bridge (Hwy. 70) allow access between the east and west banks.

EAST BANK

◗ The following sights are organized from south to north.

Destrehan★★

13034 River Rd., Destrehan. &🅿 985-764-9315. www.destrehan plantation.org.

Completed in 1790 as the heart of a 6,000-acre indigo (later sugarcane) plantation, this raised Creole-style manor is considered the oldest documented plantation house in the Mississippi Valley.

Destrehan Plantation

© Richard Sexton

In 1793, it was purchased by Jean Noel Destrehan who, with his brother-in-law Etienne de Boré, perfected the process of granulating sugar. The house was expanded in 1810, and Greek Revival ornamental details were added in 1839 to conform to antebellum tastes. Historic **craft demonstrations** (indigo-dyeing, candlemaking) take place daily.

San Francisco★

2646 Hwy. 44, Garyville. 🅿 ✆985-535-2341. www.sanfranciscoplantation.org.
The eye-catching exterior style of this ebulliently decorated plantation house (1856), with its latticework, scrolled cornices and balustraded captain's walk, was dubbed "Steamboat Gothic" style for its fancied resemblance to riverboats passing on the Mississippi. The interior is restored to c.1860.

Houmas House★

40136 Hwy. 942, Burnside. ✆225-473-9380. www.houmashouse.com.
This stately plantation home gained its name from the land it was built upon, which was originally owned by the Houmas Indians.

Houmas pairs a modest four-room c.1790 house with an 1840 Greek Revival mansion built for John Smith Preston, a son-in-law of Revolution-ary War hero Wade Hampton. The stunning gardens nurture native Louisiana and exotic tropical plants.

WEST BANK

❿ The following sights are organized from north to south.

Nottoway★

31025 Hwy. 1, White Castle. ✖🅿 ✆225-545-2730. www.nottoway.com.
Largest plantation home in the South, this ornate white mansion (1859) on the Mississippi displays a fanciful mix of Greek Revival and Italianate styles. Designed by Henry Howard for Virginia sugarcane planter John Hampden Randolph and his family, the 53,000sq ft house boasts 64 rooms sporting elegant appointments.

Oak Alley★

3645 Hwy. 18, Vacherie. ✖&🅿 ✆225-265-2151. www.oakalleyplantation.com.
Named for the gracious quarter-mile-long **allée★** of 28 live oak trees that approaches it on the river side, this stately Greek Revival mansion was completed in 1839 as the heart of a flourishing sugarcane plantation. (The trees predate the house by more than a century.) A total of 28 massive columns support the two-story gallery surrounding the house. The interior is furnished with fine period antiques.

Laura★★

2247 Hwy. 18, Vacherie. 🅿 ✆225-265-7690. www.lauraplantation.com.
The Creole culture of New Orleans and the lower Mississippi Valley are the focus of excellent guided tours of this colorfully painted raised Creole cottage (1805). Also on the site are 12 historic outbuildings, including original **slave cabins** where, in the 1870s, the African folktales of Br'er Rabbit (👁 see ATLANTA) were first recorded.

BATON ROUGE★

Incorporated in 1817, this busy port and and university city on the banks of the Mississippi has been Louisiana's state capital since 1849.

Its colorful name comes from the "red stick" placed by local Indians to mark a hunting boundary. Louisiana's **State Capitol★★** building (State Capitol Dr. at N. 4th St.; ✆225-342-7317; www.crt.state.la.us/tourism/capitol/), a striking 34-story Art Deco skyscraper (1932), is the tallest state capitol in the US, and dominates the surrounding landscape, as was the intention of its creator, the controversial and redoubtable governor Huey P. Long. (Long was buried in the Capitol's garden after being assassinated in 1935.) Views from the spire's 27th-floor **observation gallery** encompass the river and the **Pentagon barracks**, established in 1819 to house a US army garrison serving the southwestern US. The **Old Arsenal** (1838) situated amid pretty gardens to the east of the spire, contains a small military museum.

Music on the Bayou

In Cajun Country, the fun begins when the day's work is done, and for many Cajuns fun means heading to local stages or dance halls to step, swing and stomp to the pulse-quickening sounds of **Cajun** and **zydeco** music. Typical Cajun bands incorporate accordions, fiddles and guitars along with bass and percussion (including washboards and tambourines), all accompanying a lead singer warbling in French about ill-fated love, family relationships and the joys of eating, drinking, dancing and living life to the fullest. In the course of its evolution from its roots in Acadian folk music, Cajun music has been much influenced by African, country and bluegrass musical traditions. Today it is enjoying a resurgence thanks to star performers such as Michael Doucet and his band BeauSoleil. Also accordion-based, zydeco music developed in the mid-20C on the prairies of southeastern Louisiana at the hands of such pioneers as Clifton Chenier and Boozoo Chavis, who applied rhythm-and-blues elements to traditional Creole music forms. Soul, disco and reggae music continue to exert an influence on zydeco, and a profusion of zydeco dance halls attests to its growing popularity.

♣♣ Louisiana State Museum★

660 N. 4th St. ♿ ✆225-342-5428.
www.crt.state.la.us/museum/
properties/LSMbr.aspx.

The sleek new building across from the capitol contains colorful, fun exhibits about the state's history, economy and culture. Look for the Civil War-era submarine, or try your feet at dancing to zydeco or Cajun music.

Old State Capitol★

100 North Blvd. ♿ ✆225-342-0500.
www.louisianaoldstatecapitol.org.

At this castle-like, Gothic Revival-style structure (1850), representatives in 1861 voted to withdraw from the Union and form a separate nation (it existed for four weeks). Today the building has displays on Louisiana's colorful political history.

A concrete promenade along the east bank of the river near the Old State Capitol makes for a pleasant stroll past riverboat casinos and the **USS Kidd** ♣♣, a decommissioned World War II destroyer (305 S. River Rd.; ✆225-342-1942).

♣♣ Louisiana Art & Science Museum

100 River Rd. ♿ ✆225-344-5272.
www.lasm.org.

This riverfront structure mounts good temporary exhibits on artistic and cultural themes. A permanent Egypt gallery intrigues with its full-size mummy. In the planetarium you can explore space exhibits and take in a show in the domed theater.

Magnolia Mound Plantation★

2161 Nicholson Dr. ✆225-343-4955.
www.friendsofmagnoliamound.org.

Visitors may view an open-hearth cooking demonstration in the working detached kitchen before touring the gracious house (c.1791), considered one of the finest examples of Creole-style architecture in the area.

EXCURSION

Rosedown Plantation State Historic Site★★

▶ 12501 Hwy. 10, 26mi north of Baton Rouge off US-61, St. Francisville. ✆225-635-3332. www.crt.state.us/parks/rosedown.aspx.

Don't miss this faithfully restored Greek Revival-style home (1835) and its 28-acre historic formal **garden★** where owner Daniel Turnbull's wife, Martha, experimented with exotic plant species, successfully introducing azaleas and camellias to the southeastern US.

Southeast

Sunrise, Harbour Town, Hilton Head Island
©Leslee Alexander/Michelin

Atlanta Area

Framed by the foothills of the Blue Ridge Mountains, and blessed with a temperate climate, Atlanta is Georgia's capital and largest city. The Atlanta metropolitan area today encompasses a sprawling 6,126sq mi in 20 surrounding counties, and harbors more than four million people. Within an hour-and-a-half drive south of the city, near Macon, you'll find historic memorials to those who shaped Georgia's past, from its prehistoric mound-builders to its Civil War prisoners. Stretching along Georgia's 105mi section of Atlantic coastline, the gracious city of Savannah and the nearby Golden Isles offer a respite from Atlanta's frenetic pace.

Highlights

1 **Civil War** sites, a boon for history buffs (p428)

2 The noble profiles at **Stone Mountain Park** (p429)

3 Gracious Savannah's genteel **Historic District** (p431)

4 Beach living on Georgia's **Golden Isles** (p433)

The Peach State

The state now known as Georgia began as a vast tract of land between the 31st and the 36th parallels that England's King Charles II granted in 1663 as the Carolina colony to eight Lords Proprietor. In 1732 King George II gave the land between the Savannah and Altamaha rivers to 21 trustees, including English soldier and philanthropist **James Edward Oglethorpe**. European settlers established plantations in this new land, and an agrarian economy grew up around the cultivation of rice and indigo. The invention of the cotton gin by Eli Whitney, in 1793, made cotton cultivation highly profitable; it efficiently accomplished the arduous task of separating the fiber from the seed (previously done by hand). Textile mills and railroads were soon established, and Atlanta was founded in 1836 as a rail center.

At the dawn of the 21C, Atlanta ranked as the country's twelfth-largest metropolitan area (eleventh-largest today): transportation, along with finance and retail, contributed the lion's share of the city's revenue. Atlanta Hartsfield International Airport has surpassed Chicago's O'Hare as the country's busiest, and now ranks number-one in the world in passenger traffic.

Lenox Square and **Phipps Plaza** malls create consumer heaven in Buckhead, while the 2.2-million-sq ft **Mall of Georgia** (north of Altanta off I-85) is the largest in the state. Atlanta has a symphony orchestra, a ballet company and myriad museums, as well as 20 colleges and universities. Emory University's **Michael C. Carlos Museum★★** (𝄞404-727-4282; www.carlos.emory.edu) maintains one of the finest collections of Ancient Art in the Southeast; holdings range from Greek, Roman and ancient Egyptian pieces to Asian and African works. Inviting restaurants round out Atlanta's menu of offerings, serving up everything from simple Southern dishes to sophisticated continental cuisine.

To say nothing of sports would be a serious omission. Atlanta fields three major league teams: the Atlanta Braves MLB team holds its games at Turner Field; the Atlanta Falcons NFL team plays in the Georgia Dome; the home court for MBA's Atlanta Hawks is Philips Arena.

ADDRESSES

🏠 STAY

$$$ The Eliza Thompson House – 5 W. Jones St., Savannah, GA. ⌨. ☎912-236-3620. www.elizathompson house.com. 25 rooms. Named after the society widow who built the stately historic-district house in 1847, this B&B has antique furnishings and a pretty courtyard with a fountain. Room rate includes a free downtown parking pass.

$$$ The Gastonian – 220 E. Gaston St., Savannah, GA. ⌨☎912-232-2869. www. gastonian.com. 17 rooms. Two adjoining Regency-style mansions (1868) house this luxurious historic-district inn near Forsyth Park. All guest quarters have working fireplaces and are individually decorated with antique four-poster beds and Oriental rugs. Some come with whirpools. Relax with hors d'œuvres and wine in the evening. You'll find the attentive service here is the epitome of Southern hospitality.

$$$ The Jekyll Island Club Hotel – 371 Riverview Dr., Jekyll Island, GA. ☎912-635-2600. www.jekyllclub.com. 157 rooms. Victorian architecture and period reproductions give the restored historic landmark resort a palatial feel. With three 18-hole golf courses, 13 tennis courts, horseback riding and a nearby beach club, you may never want to leave the family-friendly complex.

$$$ The Ritz-Carlton, Buckhead – 3434 Peachtree Rd., Atlanta, GA. ☎404-237-2700. www.ritzcarlton.com. 517 rooms. Buckhead seems a logical setting for one of the city's most opulent hotels. The mahogany-paneled lobby is brimming with 18C and 19C English antiques and artwork. Guest rooms are comparatively spacious and **The Café** ($$$) receives constant praise. There's an on-site spa as well.

🍴 EAT

$$$ Elizabeth on 37th – 105 E. 37th St., Savannah, GA. ☎912-236-5547. www. elizabethon37th.net. **New Southern.** Traditional 18C and 19C dishes with a nod to health-conscious fare headline menus in this Greek Revival-style mansion. Seasonal selections might include black-eyed-pea patty with tomato relish and sesame-almond-crusted grouper. Reservations required.

$$$ Restaurant Eugene – 2277 Peachtree Rd. N.E. Atlanta, GA. ☎404-355-0321. www.restauranteugene.com. **New Southern.** There's a reason Chef Linton Hopknis won the James Beard Award for Best Chef Southeast in 2012. At Restaurant Eugene, the likes of guinea hen with spoonbrread purée and foie gras with kumquat marmalade, white cornbread and sorghum, win diners over too.

$$ Canoe – 4199 Paces Ferry Rd. N.W., Atlanta, GA. ☎770-432-5440. www.canoe atl.com. **New American.** A rustic dining room that looks like the interior of a spruced-up cabin (soaring cherry-wood ceilings, shiny limestone walls) is the setting for this beloved restaurant in the Vinings area. Dishes such as slow-roasted Carolina rabbit with Swiss chard, and Enchanted Springs Rainbow trout with spring pea sauté get raves. The landscaped patio overlooks the Chattahoochee River.

$$ South City Kitchen – 1144 Crescent Ave., Atlanta, GA. ☎404-873-7358. www. southcitykitchen.com. **New Southern.** Determined to dispel the image that Southern cuisine is heavy, the chef at this high-energy Midtown bungalow fuses regional ingredients with a light touch. Stellar results include shrimp and Red Mule grits and smoked pork chops with local butterbeans.

$$ The Crab Shack – 40 Estill Hammock, Tybee Island, GA. ☎912-786-9857. www. thecrabshack.com **Seafood.** This bare-bones eatery, 17mi east of Savannah, offers the freshest shellfish around. Huge portions of boiled or steamed crabs, shrimp and oysters come with corn on the cob and potatoes, and are served on wooden tables.

$ Gladys Knight and Ron Winans' Chicken & Waffles – 529 Peachtree St N.E., Atlanta, GA. ☎404-874-9393. www. gladysandron.net. **Southern.** A classic southern experience, this late-night eatery serves soul food to groups, couples, families and those leaving the clubs after a night of dancing. Don't miss the peach cobbler or the grits.

Atlanta★★

As the commercial center of the Southeast, Atlanta pulses with activity, while retaining its signature Southern hospitality. The city sprawls atop a high granite ridge against a leafy backdrop of wooded hills. From its gleaming downtown skyscrapers to the pricey boutiques of Buckhead, contemporary Atlanta offers visitors a smorgasbord of cultural, entertainment, shopping and dining opportunities.

▶ **Population:** 432,427.

🛈 **Info:** Atlanta Convention & Visitors Bureau, 233 Peachtree St., NE. ☎404-521-6688; www.atlanta.net.

🅿 **Parking:** If you decide to drive, ask those at your destination if they validate parking. Validation rates are often substantially discounted.

⊛ **Don't Miss:** The insider look at broadcast news at the CNN Studio.

👥 **Kids:** A tour of the New World of Coca-Cola.

A BIT OF HISTORY

Incorporated in 1845, Atlanta became an important Confederate transportation hub. As such it was the prime target of Union General William T. Sherman during the Civil War. On Kennesaw Mountain north of Atlanta on 2 July 1864, Sherman drove Gen. Joseph E. Johnston and his 65,000 men from the Kennesaw line. Today **Kennesaw Mountain National Battlefield Park** (off I-75 near Marietta at Old Hwy. 41 & Stilesboro Rd.; ☎770-427-4686; www.nps.gov/kemo) preserves more than 2,800 acres, including 11mi of original earthworks from the battle. Sherman pushed on, his advance culminating in the bloody **Battle of Atlanta** on July 22. In September 1864 Sherman occupied the city; two months later he burned Atlanta to the ground.

Like its symbol, the phoenix, Atlanta rose from the ashes of the Civil War and re-established itself as the South's transportation and distribution center. In the early 20C, the practice of racial segregation blocked Atlanta's efforts to become a major US city, but the civil rights movement (👈 see INTRODUCTION) in the early 1960s, led by Dr. Martin Luther King, Jr., ultimately resulted in the end of legal segregation.

The city gained international status in 1996 as host of the Centennial Olympic Games. Two lasting legacies from that event are the 21-acre **Centennial Olympic Park** (Marietta St. & International Blvd., ☎404-223-4412; www.centennialpark.com) and **Turner Field** (755 Hank Aaron Dr.; ☎404-522-7630; www.atlantabraves.mlb.com). The park, with its centerpiece Olympic Rings fountain, hosts special events downtown; Turner Field is now home to the Atlanta Braves baseball team. In spring of 2014, the new 42,000sq ft **National Center for Civil and Human Rights**, currently under construction, is slated to open at Pemberton Place, on land donated by its neighbor the Coca-Cola Company; content will focus on human rights around the world.

Atlanta Skyline

Georgia Department of Economic Development

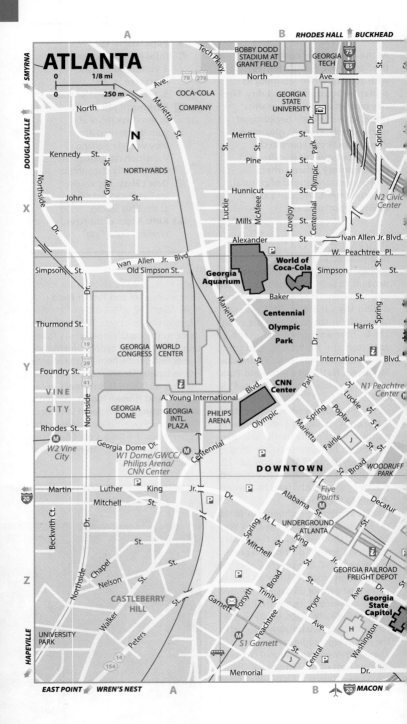

ATLANTA

SMYRNA

DOUGLASVILLE

HAPEVILLE

0   1/8 mi
0   250 m

N

RHODES HALL   BUCKHEAD

Tech Pkwy.

78   278

North

BOBBY DODD
STADIUM AT
GRANT FIELD

GEORGIA
TECH

75
85

St.

Ave.

COCA-COLA
COMPANY

GEORGIA
STATE
UNIVERSITY

North

Marietta St.

Ave.

St.

NORTHYARDS

Kennedy   St.

John   St.

Gray   St.

North

Northside   Dr.

X

Merritt   St.

Pine   St.

Hunnicut   St.

Mills   St.

Alexander   St.

St.

St.

Luckie   St.

McAfeee

Lovejoy

Centennial

Olympic

Park   Dr.

Spring

N2 Civic
Center

Ivan Allen Jr. Blvd.

W. Peachtree Pl.

Simpson   St.

Ivan   Allen   Jr.   Blvd.
Old Simpson St.

Georgia
Aquarium

World of
Coca-Cola

Simpson   St.

Spring

Thurmond St.

Baker   St.

Harris   St.

Foundry St.

19
29
41

GEORGIA
CONGRESS

WORLD
CENTER

Marietta

Centennial

Olympic

Park

International   Blvd.

Dr.

Y

VINE

CITY

Rhodes St.

Northside   Dr.

A. Young International

GEORGIA
DOME

GEORGIA
INTL.
PLAZA

PHILIPS
ARENA

St.

Blvd.

Olympic

CNN
Center

Park

Spring

Marietta

Poplar

Fairlie

Luckie   St.

N1 Peachtree
Center

St.

St.

St.

Broad

WOODRUFF
PARK

W2 Vine
City

Georgia   Dome   Dr.
W1 Dome/GWCC/
Philips Arena/
CNN Center

Centennial

DOWNTOWN

20

Martin   Luther   King

Mitchell   St.

Jr.   Dr.

Five
Points

Decatur

Alabama   St.

UNDERGROUND
ATLANTA

Beckwith Ct.

Northside   Dr.

Chapel   St.

Nelson   St.

St.

Spring

M. L.

Mitchell   St.

King

St.

Jr.   St.

GEORGIA RAILROAD
FREIGHT DEPOT

Z

CASTLEBERRY
HILL

UNIVERSITY
PARK

Walker   St.

Peters   St.

Garnett   St.

Forsyth   St.

Trinity

Broad   St.

Peachtree   St.

Pryor   St.

Central   Ave.

Washington

GEORGIA
State
Capitol

H

14
154

S1 Garnett

Memorial   Dr.

EAST POINT   WREN'S NEST

MACON
20

A   B

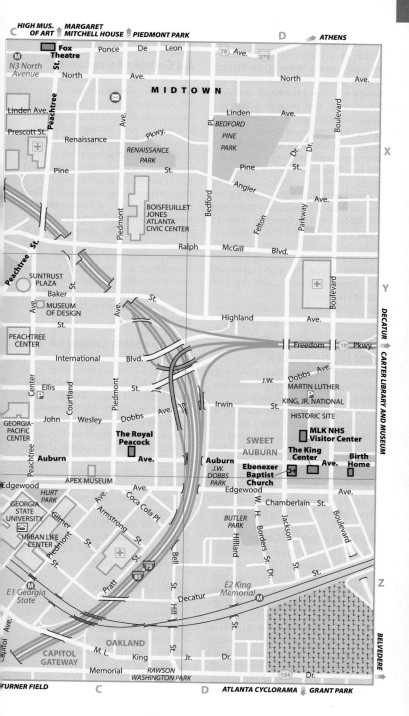

MIDTOWN AND DOWNTOWN

Atlanta's attractions range along its main artery, **Peachtree Street**, which runs north to south from **Buckhead★★**—site of the city's trendiest restaurants and shopping areas—through the arts district of **Midtown★★** to the office towers of **Downtown★★**. Midtown is the place to find the city's best-known performing-arts centers: the **Fox Theatre★** (660 Peachtree St.; ♿ ✆404-881-2100; www.foxtheatre.org), a grand restored 1920s movie palace that now stages live productions; and the **Woodruff Arts Center★** complex (Peachtree at 16th St.; ✕♿ ✆404-733-4200; www.woodruffcenter.org), which includes Atlanta Symphony Hall, the Alliance Theatre, the High Museum of Art, Young Audiences, and the 14th Street Playhouse.

◖ Sights below are organized from south to north, beginning with Downtown.

CNN Studio Tour★★

CNN Center, Techwood Dr. & Marietta St., Downtown. ✕♿ ✆404-827-2300 (ticket office). www.cnn.com/StudioTour.

In 1980 Atlanta entrepreneur Ted Turner launched the Cable News Network (CNN), the first 24-hour cable news station, which broadcasts from 14-story **CNN Center**. The 55min studio tour shows visitors the inner workings of the network and allows access to a glassed-in gallery where visitors can watch CNN reporters and newscasters at work.

♟♙ New World of Coca-Cola★★

121 Baker St., Downtown. ♿ ✆404-676-5151. www.worldofcoca-cola.com.

Located in a gleaming fairly new facility (2007) near the Georgia Aquarium, this enticing museum celebrates the world's best-selling soft drink, born in Atlanta in 1886. Displays here trace the Coca-Cola story from its humble beginnings at a downtown Atlanta drug store to its multinational pres-ence today. The visit features a 4D theater and fully-functional bottling line. At the exhibit's end, enjoy Coca-Cola products from around the globe in the tasting experience exhibits.

♟♙ Georgia Aquarium★

225 Baker St., Downtown ✕♿🅿 ✆404-581-4000. www.georgiaaquarium.org.

This fine aquarium in the heart of downtown boasts animal species rarely seen in captivity. Walk through the viewing tunnel in the massive **Ocean Voyager★** exhibit tank to see **whale sharks** gliding overhead; they're some of the largest fish in the world. Another highlight is the gallery and multimedia show **Dolphin Tales**, which stars the aquarium's newest residents. Other exhibit areas include **Cold Water Quest** (featuring denizens of cold ocean waters); **River Scout** (highlighting freshwater species from Africa, Asia and South America) and **Tropical Diver** (with its lovely coral reef). The 4D Theater presents undersea films with the latest in high-tech special effects.

Georgia State Capitol★★

Washington & Courtland Sts., Downtown. ✆404-656-2846. www.sos.state.ga.us.

Situated on five acres of one of Downtown's highest ridges, Georgia's Classical Renaissance 1889 limestone capitol, with its four-story portico, is a scaled-down version of the US Capitol in Washington, DC. Its gold-leaf dome, topped with a statue of Freedom, is a recognizable landmark amid the Downtown skyline.

Inside the central **rotunda**, an impressive three-story atrium rises just over 237ft to the dome. Housed on the fourth floor, the **Capitol Museum** recounts the building's history. Here, you can sign up for tours of the Capitol.

Piedmont Park★

Piedmont Ave. & 12th St., Midtown. ✆404-875-7275. www.piedmontpark.org.

Developed for the 1895 Cotton States Exposition, Piedmont Park's 185 acres encompass the **Atlanta Botanical Garden★** (✆404-876-5859; www.atlantabotanicalgarden.org). Both the park and garden have been expanded and renovated.

A Street Named Peachtree

One of Atlanta's most puzzling paradoxes is represented by the city's main artery, Peachtree Street. More than 37 streets in Atlanta bear the name Peachtree, yet, surprisingly, you would be hard-pressed to find a single peach tree in the city. Although the name dates back to 1825, no one truly knows its origin. Some believe that it derives from a Cherokee word for pine tree.

Rhodes Hall★

1516 Peachtree St. N.W., Midtown. **P**
✆404-885-7800. www.rhodeshall.org.
This 1904 castle-like structure of Stone Mountain granite serves as headquarters of the Georgia Trust for Historic Preservation. It is also open as a house museum, noteworthy for its grand mahogany **staircase**, flanked by nine **stained-glass panels** depicting the rise and fall of the Confederacy.

Margaret Mitchell House and Museum★★

990 Peachtree St. NE at 10th St., Midtown. ♿**P** ✆404-249-7015.
www.margaretmitchellhouse.org.
Nicknamed "the dump" by the sprightly Atlanta writer who penned the Pulitzer Prize-winning novel *Gone with the Wind* (1936), this restored house is the city's only surviving building with a connection to Margaret Mitchell (1900-49) and her epic novel of the Civil War. Visitors can view the tiny, ground-floor apartment where the author lived (1925-32) and the living-room nook where she wrote the renowned classic, which has sold more copies worldwide than any other book except the Bible. An exhibit on the novel and blockbuster movie features memorabilia, props and footage from the 1939 film.

High Museum of Art★

1280 Peachtree St. N.E., Midtown.
✗♿✆404-733-4444. www.high.org.
The jewel in the Woodruff Arts Center's crown is this striking contemporary **structure**★ (1983, Richard Meier) covered with white porcelain-enameled steel panels. Rodin's sculpture The Shade, a gift from the French government, presides over the front lawn.

Highlights from the permanent collection—some 12,000 works—include American decorative arts, 19C American landscapes (the Hudson River school is a particular strength), African art, folk art, photography and contemporary American art.

♟ Atlanta History Center★★

130 W. Paces Ferry Rd., Buckhead.
✗♿**P**✆404-814-4000.
www.altantahistorycenter.com.
This complex comprises the Atlanta History Museum, the Centennial Olympic Games Museum, a research library and archives, two historic houses, a series of gardens and a restaurant. Excellent permanent exhibits in the **Atlanta History Museum**★★ bring the city's defining experiences to life, highlighting the Civil War, the Centennial Olympic Games, and the city's transformation from agrarian crossroads to metropolitan capital.
Visit the elegant 1928 **Swan House**★ (✐visit by guided tour only), designed by Philip Shutze. In contrast, the simple frame buildings of **Smith Family Farm** (1845) provide a glimpse into the lifestyle of an early Georgia farm family.

Georgia Governor's Mansion★★

391 W. Paces Ferry Rd. N.E., Buckhead.
✆404-261-1776.
http://mansion.georgia.gov.
Its Doric-columned facade facing one of Buckhead's main thoroughfares, the 24,000sq ft Greek Revival-style brick structure contains a museum-quality collection of **Federal antiques**. Upstairs rooms are reserved for the use of the current governor and his family.

ADDITIONAL SIGHTS
Grant Park
Entrance at intersection of Boulevard & Cherokee Ave. S.E.; www.grantpark.org.
Grant Park is the name given to both the city's oldest park and the adjacent neighborhood. Its rolling terrain, created in 1903 by the Olmsted brothers (sons of Frederick Law Olmsted) is home to two popular attractions: the Cyclorama and the 40-acre **Zoo Atlanta** (800 Cherokee Ave.; 👥✕♿🅿 𝒸404-624-5600; www.zooatlanta.org), one of four zoos in the US featuring giant pandas.

Atlanta Cyclorama★★
800 Cherokee Ave. S.E. ♿🅿 𝒸404-658-7625. www.atlantacyclorama.org.
One of three existing cycloramas in the country (the others are in Gettysburg, PA (👁see GETTYSBURG); and at New York City's Metropolitan Museum of Art), this 42ft-tall painting-in-the-round weighs more than 9,000 pounds and measures 358ft in circumference. Its scenes—which took a group of German, Austrian and Polish artists 22 months to complete—depict the Battle of Atlanta, the Civil War standoff that broke the back of the Confederacy. Visitors sit on a viewing platform surrounded by the painting and watch the events of July 22, 1864 unfold as the stage revolves.

Jimmy Carter Library and Museum★★
441 Freedom Pkwy. ✕♿🅿 𝒸404-865-7100. www.jimmycarterlibrary.org.
The official library and museum of **Jimmy Carter**, the 39th president of the US (1977-81), was built in 1986 and renovated in 2009. Its **Carter Library Museum★** features a pictorial biography of Carter's rise from a Georgia peanut farmer to president, exhibits describing his major political accomplishments, and a replica of the Oval Office.
Next door, the nonprofit Carter Center was established by the former president to promote worldwide democracy and to fight disease and poverty.

Sweet Auburn
Known as "Sweet Auburn," Atlanta's **Auburn Avenue** saw its heyday as the commercial and social hub of Atlanta's black community from 1890 to the 1960s. The street blended a rich mixture of African-American businesses, retail outlets, nightclubs and churches. In the 1960s, it became a gathering spot for leaders of the burgeoning Civil Rights Movement. Auburn Avenue also claims the birthplace and pulpit of the movement's leading voice, **Dr. Martin Luther King, Jr.** (1929-68), who won the Nobel Peace Prize in 1964 and was assassinated four years later in Memphis, Tennessee.

During the 1980s, a revitalization of the historic street began when the blocks where Dr. King had lived and worked were designated a National Historic District. Begin a tour at the **Martin Luther King, Jr. National Historic Site★★** (450 Auburn Ave NE.; t404-331-5190; www.nps.gov/malu), which tells the history of black America, including the civil rights movement and the pivotal role played by Dr. King. Across the street is the **The King Center★** (449 Auburn Ave.; 𝒸404-526-8900), where a number of King's pastoral accoutrements are displayed. King is buried outside in a simple marble tomb.

Other King-related sights on Auburn Avenue include the Queen Anne-style **Birth Home★** (no. 501), and **Ebenezar Baptist Church** (no. 407). Dr. King, his father and maternal grandfather all served as pastors of this 1922 brick church.

Several blocks west stands **The Royal Peacock** nightclub (186 Auburn Ave; now closed). Founded during the 1930s as a performance venue for black entertainers, The Peacock hosted the likes of Ray Charles, James Brown and Aretha Franklin.

Wren's Nest

1050 Ralph David Abernathy Blvd.
📞404-753-7735. www.wrensnest.org.
The sprawling c.1867 Wren's Nest is the Victorian home of **Joel Chandler Harris** (1848-1908), journalist and author of the Uncle Remus tales for children. The man who brought to life Brer Fox and Brer Rabbit wrote the tales in the dialect of coastal Georgia slaves. Especially popular here are the lively storytelling sessions 👥.

EXCURSIONS

👥 Stone Mountain Park★★

◐16mi east of Atlanta via US-78.
Take Ponce de Leon Ave. to Stone Mountain Freeway; follow signs to park.
△✕⌖ 770-498-5690.
www.stonemountainpark.com.
Recreational opportunities abound in this 3,200-acre park, built around 825ft-high **Stone Mountain**, the world's largest granite outcropping. The park's focal point is the giant **Confederate Memorial** relief carving of Jefferson Davis and generals Robert E. Lee and Stonewall Jackson on the face of the mountain. Covering 3 acres of the mountain face, it's the largest relief carving in the world. Stone sculptor Gutzon Borglum, known for the presidential profiles on Mt. Rushmore, began work here in 1923; the carving was completed in 1972. In the **Discovering Stone Mountain** Museum, you'll learn how the on-again, off-again project was finally realized. Bring the family and take a cable car ride to the top, or enjoy a scenic train ride around the mountain. More adventurous types can take a **SkyHike** through the treetops and navigate rope bridges and tunnels through **Geyser Towers**.

Georgia Sports Hall of Fame

◐84mi south of Atlanta in Macon.
301 Cherry St. 📞478-752-1585.
www.gshf.org.
Honoring more than 300 of Georgia's most accomplished athletes, including MLB slugger Hank Aaron (b. 1934) and golf great Bobby Jones (1902-1971), the Hall is the largest state sports museum in the US. In its 43,000sq ft of space,

you'll discover the history of Georgia sports in exhibits that celebrate both the coaches and players of high school, college, amateur and professional teams.

Ocmulgee National Monument★

◐90mi south of Atlanta in Macon.
Take I-75 South to Macon and go east on I-16 to Exit 4; go east on US-80 and follow signs to Ocmulgee at 1207 Emery Hwy. ⌖📞478-752-8257.
www.nps.gov/ocmu.
Humans have inhabited this fertile Ocmulgee River bottomland for more than 12,000 years, but it wasn't until 1934 that archaeological digs unearthed artifacts here dating to the last Ice Age. Several mounds remain on the property as relics of the advanced Mississippian culture, a farming people who inhabited the site between 900 and 1100 AD.
Start your visit by viewing the short introductory film, then set out to explore the site on foot. The best-preserved structure is the **earthlodge**, thought to have been used as a council chamber; the highest earthen mound is the 55ft-high **Great Temple Mound**.

Andersonville National Historic Site★

◐160mi south of Atlanta in Andersonville. Take I-75 South to Exit 41. Take Rte. 26 West to Montezuma; pick up Rte. 49 and follow it south 7mi. 760 Pow Rd. ⌖📞229-924-0343.
www.nps.gov/ande.
This peaceful meadow once contained one of the most horrific Civil War prison camps. More than 45,000 Union soldiers were held at this site over the 14 months of the camp's existence; thousands were interred here, having died after succumbing to the effects of disease, poor sanitation and malnutrition. Today the 26.5-acre prison site encompasses the National Prisoner of War Museum, replicas of portions of the stockade that once enclosed the grounds, and memorials erected by Union survivors.
Adjacent to the prison is Andersonville National Cemetery, burial site for Union soldiers and other US war veterans.

Savannah and the Golden Isles★

Set on a bluff between the Savannah and Altamaha rivers, Savannah survives as a testimony to visionary 18C city planning and modern historic preservation. The city, with its stately mansions, landscaped plazas, Spanish moss-draped live oaks and friendly populace, is a quintessentially Southern city. An hour's drive south of Savannah via Interstate 95 brings you to St. Simons and Jekyll islands, and to the wild shores of Cumberland Island, all beads on a string of Atlantic Coast resorts known as the Golden Isles. Despite its humid summers, the coast of Georgia entices visitors with its beautiful beaches, abundant seafood and rich history.

▶ **Population:** 139,491 (Savannah).

Michelin Map: 584 R 12

Info: ℰ877-728-2662; www.savannahvisit.com.

Don't Miss: The remarkable historic district and one of the country's oldest synagogues, as well as one of the oldest black churches.

Kids: Girl Scouts will want to see Andrew Low House, while older kids get to hear ghost stories about the haunted city.

SAVANNAH★★

The city of Savannah was born in 1733 when English army officer and philanthropist **James Oglethorpe** and a group of more than 100 settlers landed at Yamacraw Bluff above the Savannah River. One of 21 trustees to whom King George II had granted the tract of land between the Savannah and Altamaha rivers, Oglethorpe envisioned the colony of Georgia as an environment where the British working poor and "societal misfits" could carve out a living cultivating agricultural products desired by the Crown.

In its early years, the region's agrarian economy, based on rice and tobacco and later cotton, fueled Savannah's growth as a port and a center for commodities trading. By 1817 Savannah's City Exchange, which occupied the site now taken by City Hall, was setting the market price for the world's cotton. All that, however, ended with the Civil War. When General Sherman finally reached Savannah in December 1864, city leaders surrendered without a fight. Sherman, acknowledging the city's beauty, chose not to level Savannah as he had

Historic Houses in Savannah

Georgia Department of Economic Development

St. Patrick's Day in Savannah

Since 1813 when the local Irish Hibernian Society marked its favorite feast day with a parade, Savannah has prided itself on its rambunctious celebration of St. Paddy's Day. The party starts when the water in the downtown fountains is dyed green, and culminates in a 2-hour parade through the Historic District. The bacchanalia draws partygoers from all over the US.

Atlanta; instead he presented the city to President Lincoln as a Christmas gift. Revitalization efforts begun in the 1940s have led to a growing economy based on industry, manufacturing, port commerce and tourism. Today, Savannah's landmark historic district attracts more than 12 million visitors a year, and its year-round host of festivities culminates in Savannah's famed **St. Patrick's Day** celebration, when the riverfront becomes one big festival ground.

HiSTORIC DISTRICT★★

Oglethorpe's revered original city plan incorporates a series of 21 grassy squares connected by broad thoroughfares and edged with stately examples of 19C Greek Revival, Federal, Regency and Georgian architecture. Today these plazas are preserved in downtown's 2.5mi historic district (bounded by Gaston St., E. Broad St., Martin Luther King Jr. Blvd. and the river). With its graceful fountain, 20-acre **Forsyth Park★**

anchors the south end of Bull Street. Begin at the **Savannah Visitor Center** (301 Martin Luther King Jr. Blvd.; ℘912-944-0455; www.savannahvisit.com), where you can catch a trolley tour. Adjoining the center is the **Savannah History Museum** (℘912-651-6825; www.chsgeorgia.org). Take a break at the outdoor cafes and myriad shops of **City Market** (Jefferson St. at West St. Julian St.; ℘912-232-4903; www.savannahcitymarket.com).

Scarbrough House★

41 Martin Luther King Jr. Blvd. 🅿 ℘912-232-1511. www.shipsofthesea.org
A block west of City Market, a charming garden invites visitors into this 1819 Regency villa designed by English architect William Jay. Today the villa houses the **Ships of the Sea Maritime Museum★**, which presents nautical history and seafaring culture through a fine selection of paintings, model ships and maritime antiques.

Midnight in the Garden of Good and Evil

A stately Italianate manor overlooking Savannah's Monterey Square, the c.1860s **Mercer House**—designed by New York architect John Norris—became famous as a crime scene. It was in this house in 1981 that resident antiques dealer Jim Williams was accused of fatally shooting 21-year-old Danny Hansford.

Jim Williams' murder trial set staid Savannah on its ear, and was later immortalized in John Berendt's best-selling 1994 book, Midnight in the Garden of Good and Evil. Both the book and the movie that followed in 1997 painted a vivid picture of Savannah's eccentric populace, from Jim Williams—the alleged shooter, whose favorite game, Psycho Dice, was his own invention—to Lady Chablis, an oversexed transvestite. The most recognized icon from both the book and the movie is perhaps the Bird Girl statue (1938), which appears on the book's cover. The work of artists Sylvia Shaw Judson, the statue once stood in Savannah's **Bonaventure Cemetery**.

♿Visitors can now find *Bird Girl* in the Telfair Academy in the Historic District.

First African Baptist Church★

23 Montgomery St. ℘912-233-6597, www.firstafricanbc.com.

Established in 1773 by freed slave George Leile, this church is considered the oldest black Baptist church in North America. By 1826, church members had established the first African-American Sunday School in the US. The current structure was built in 1859 by members of the congregation.

Congregation Mickve Israel

20 Gordon St. ℘912-233-1547. www.mickveisrael.org

The only Gothic-style synagogue building in the country, Congregation Mickve Israel is also of interest for being the third-oldest Jewish congregation in America. The synagogue faces Monterey Square and is open for architectural tours as well as worship.

Factors Walk★★

Shops and restaurants now occupy the riverfront warehouses along Bay Street (between Bay & Rivers Sts.), surrounding Factors Walk, a 19C center of cotton commerce. Here cotton traders would buy and sell from the bridgeways that connect the offices on the upper portion of the bluff with the warehouses below. The 1887 **Old Cotton Exchange** (100 E. Bay St., at Drayton St.; now a Masonic Lodge) was the center of Savannah's post-Civil War cotton trade. Separating East and West Factors Walk, 1905 **City Hall** (corner of Bay & Bull Sts.), with its golden dome, reigns as a vibrant local landmark.

Telfair Academy★

121 Barnard St. ℘912-790-8800. www.telfair.org.

Designed by architect William Jay, the Regency-style mansion was initially built in 1818 as the home of Alexander Telfair. The structure now forms part of the **Telfair Museums**, which encompass a fine art collection of 4,000 pieces by American and European artists. Note especially the group of works by members of the Ash Can school—Robert Henri, George Luks and George Bellows—as well as American portraiture, and collections of early-19C furniture and silver.

Contemporary works and traveling exhibits are mounted in the nearby **Jepson Center** (207 W. York St.), a sleek facility designed by Moshe Safdie (2006).

Owens-Thomas House★★

124 Abercorn St. ℘912-790-8800. www.telfair.org.

Belle of Oglethorpe Square, the Owens-Thomas House is considered one of William Jay's finest works—and the only unaltered example of his surviving designs. Now administered by the Telfair Museums, this house was completed in 1819 when the architect was only 25 years old. The stately structure typifies Jay's English Regency style; its tabby and coadestone exterior as well as the elegant interior detailing have been carefully restored. Also on the grounds, the mansion's carriage house includes one of the earliest intact urban slave quarters in the South.

Davenport House★

324 E. State St. ℘912-236-8097. www.davenporthousemuseum.org.

When threatened by demolition, this fine two-story Federal structure became a rallying point for citizens interested in preserving Savannah's stately homes. The community effort resulted in saving the home and establishing the **Historic Savannah Foundation**, a grassroots organization that has played a key role in the rejuvenation of the historic district.

Cathedral of St. John the Baptist★

222 E. Harris St. ℘912-233-4709. www.savannahcathedral.org.

The white, twin spires of this dignified French Gothic cathedral (1876) loom over the historic district. The parish was founded by French and Haitian immigrants in the late 1700s; today it's the seat of the Diocese of Savannah. Step inside to see the results of the four-year restoration (completed in 2000) that returned the cathedral's Austrian

Little St. Simon's

Although it's separated from the mainland by the narrow Hampton River, Little St. Simon's Island feels worlds away from the resort bustle of the other Golden Isles. Privately owned by the same family since 1908, the island offers deluxe accommodations to just 30 guests at a time (transportation is by boat), in a 1930s bungalow or a three-bedroom house. You won't find golf courses, beach shops or hordes here. Instead it's 10,000 acres of unspoiled wilderness, native wildlife, peace and tranquility. Naturalists conduct in-terpretive programs if you choose (the island is paradise for birdwatchers); otherwise you're free to canoe the winding tidal creeks, bike the 15 miles of trails or stroll the 7 miles of gloriously deserted beach (☎912-638-7472; www.littlestsimonsisland.com).

stained-glass windows and Italian marble altar to their former glory.

Andrew Low House★

329 Abercorn St. ☎912-233-6854. www.andrewlowhouse.com.
In 1848 wealthy cotton merchant Andrew Low commissioned John Norris to create this Classical house with its elaborate cast-iron balconies. Low's daughter-in-law, Savannah-born **Juliette Gordon Low** (1860-1927), founded the Girl Scouts USA—the world's largest volunteer organization for girls— here on March 12, 1912, holding troop meetings in the carriage house on the property.

THE GOLDEN ISLES★

Forming part of Georgia's Atlantic Coast barrier islands, the Golden Isles of St. Simons, Little St. Simons (ⓒsee infobox above), Sea and Jekyll islands are located 70mi south of Savannah. These popular tourist destinations boast wide, sandy beaches, award-winning golf courses, wildlife refuges and historic resorts. One such hotel, **The Cloister** on **Sea Island** (entrance off Sea Island Dr.; ☎912-638-3611; www.seaisland.com) was designed by renowned Florida architect Addison Mizner. Just south of Jekyll Island as the crow flies, Cumberland Island claims a pristine national seashore.
By 1586 the Spanish had established missions along the coast and maintained a stronghold here until 1742, when James Oglethorpe defeated the Spanish on St. Simons Island during the

Battle of Bloody Marsh (a monument on Demere Rd. preserves the site). By the time he sailed for England in 1743, Oglethorpe had left behind the seeds of civilization that would blossom into playgrounds for the wealthy.
To access the Georgia coast, travel south on I-95 from Savannah to US-17. A detour to **Sapelo Island** (accessible by ferry from Meridian Ferry Dock, Rte. 99, Meridian, GA; ☎912-437-3224) will take you to one of the existing Gullah communities.

St. Simons Island★

77mi south of Savannah. From I-95, take Exit 9 and follow US-17 South to St. Simons Causeway.
Known for its beautiful beaches, St. Simon's heralds its past in the 1872 working **lighthouse** and the adjacent **Museum of Coastal History** (101 Twelfth St.; ☎912-638-4666; www.saintsimonslighthouse.org), and in the ruins of **Fort Frederica National Monument★** (at the end of Frederica Rd.; ☎912-638-3639; www.nps.gov/fofr) built by James Oglethorpe in 1736.

Jekyll Island★★

From I-95, take Exit 6 and follow US-17 South to Jekyll Island Welcome Center on Jekyll Island Causeway. ⚠✕&🅿☎912-635-3636. www.jekyllisland.com.
Purchased for $125,000 in 1886 by a consortium of East Coast millionaires—with names like Gould, Goodyear, Pulitzer and Rockefeller—Jekyll Island was a winter playground for the

Jekyll Island beach

Georgia Department of Economic Development

nation's captains of industry until World War II. In 1887, consortium members—calling themselves the Jekyll Island Club—hired architect Charles Alexander to build a 60-room clubhouse, then moved into their own "cottages" up to 8,000sq ft in size.

Today the **Jekyll Island Club Historic District**★★ preserves several of the structures and is in the process of restoring others. The Victorian clubhouse now operates as the **Jekyll Island Club Hotel** (371 Riverview Dr.; 912-635-2600; www.jekyllclub.com).

A guided tram tour of the historic district begins at the **Jekyll Island Museum** in the old club stables (100 Stable Rd.; P 912-635-4036; www. jekyllisland.com).

Cumberland Island National Seashore★★

Take Exit 2 off I-95 South; turn left on Rte. 40 and follow it 9mi east to St. Marys, GA. Accessible by ferry only from downtown St. Marys; reservations required. 912-882-4336. www.nps.gov/cuis.

Saltwater marshes, maritime forests and 18mi of lonely beaches compose the complex ecosystem that is Cumberland Island. The largest of Georgia's Golden Isles, the island lies across Cumberland Sound from the town of St. Marys, Georgia. Stately 1898 **Plum Orchard** (visit

by guided tour only; 912-882-4336) and the 1884 **Dungeness**—of which only eerie ruins remain—were both once occupied by members of Pittsburgh's monied Carnegie family.

Another former Carnegie mansion now operates as the upscale **Greyfield Inn**. Begin your visit on the mainland at **Cumberland Island National Seashore Visitor Center** (113 St. Marys St.; 912-882-4336).

Okefenokee Swamp Park★★

64mi southwest of Brunswick, GA. Take US-82 West to Hwy. 177; take Hwy. 177 11mi south to park. 912-283-0583. www.okeswamp.com.

Serving as the northern entrance to **Okefenokee National Wildlife Refuge**, the nonprofit park provides an excellent introduction to the swamp's 700sq mi of canals, moss-draped cypress trees and lily-pad prairies.

The Seminoles named this area, formed by the headwaters of the Suwannee and St. Mary's rivers, Okefenokee—"Land of Trembling Earth."

This is the only entrance to the swamp where you can take a guided boat tour. Park admission fee includes a ride on the 1.5mi railroad.

To penetrate the swamp's deeper reaches, rent a canoe and paddle through the tea-colored waters along the refuge's 120mi of canoe trails.

Blue Ridge Parkway

One of America's great roads, the Blue Ridge Parkway skirts several of the tallest peaks east of the Mississippi River, offering breathtaking vistas as it cuts through Virginia and heads southwest to North Carolina and Tennessee. The 469mi-long highway dips into the fragrant woodlands that encompass six national forests, anchored on the north by Virginia's Shenandoah National Park and on the south by Great Smoky Mountains National Park in North Carolina.

Blue Ridge Parkway
VA
NC

Highlights

1. Fall foliage along the **Linn Cove Viaduct** (p444)

2. Spying **Grandfather Mountain**'s noble profile through the clouds (p444)

3. Lunch at historic Michie Tavern (p447)

4. Wine-tasting in Virginia's **wine region** (p447)

America's Backbone

Stretching from Pennsylvania to Georgia, the Blue Ridge gets its name from a filmy haze (a combination of water vapor and organic compounds) that bathes its slopes in shades of velvety blue. The range is part of the Appalachian Mountain chain, a 2,000mi-long spine that runs from Newfoundland, Canada, south to Alabama.

For 10,000 years, Cherokee Indians and their ancestors occupied this area; but they were displaced in the 18C by European settlers who tried to impose their idea of civilization on the Native Americans. By the mid-19C, the new US government under President Andrew Jackson had forcibly relocated nearly all the Indians to grim reservations in the Midwest, in a series of marches known as the "Trail of Tears." A handful of Cherokees remained hidden in the mountains, where their descendants still live today. Opening Shenandoah and Great Smoky Mountains national parks and the Blue Ridge Parkway in the early 20C saved the land from mining interests. Experience the grandeur of this region by driving the parkway, hiking its wooded trails and rafting down its many waterways.

Great Smoky Mountains National Park

© Comstock, Inc

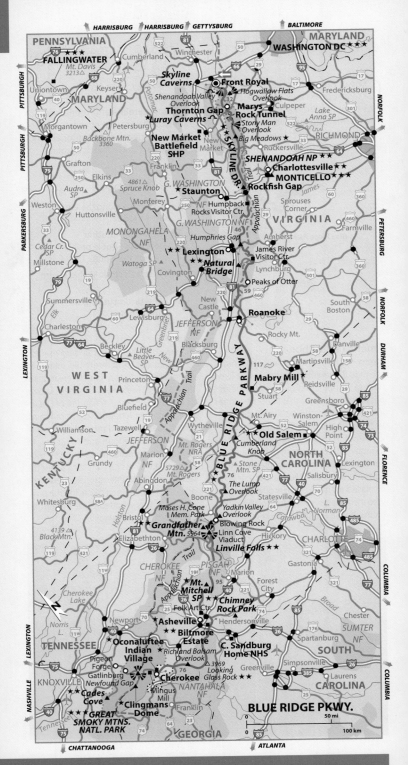

ADDRESSES

🏠 STAY

$$$$$ The Inn at Little Washington – Corner of Middle & Main Sts., Little Washington, VA. ☎540-675-3800. www.theinnatlittlewashington.com. 18 rooms. Described as "sumptuous and extraordinary," this plush inn and restaurant, 67mi west of the nation's capital, has become a destination in itself. Theatrical guest rooms are designed with reproduction William Morris wallcoverings and period antiques. Food lovers book up to a year in advance to savor chef Patrick O'Connell's artful prix-fixe meals (**$$$$**).

$$$$ The Grove Park Inn Resort – 290 Macon Ave., Asheville, NC. ☎828-252-2711. www.groveparkinn.com. 514 rooms. Set on 140 acres in the Blue Ridge Mountains, the historic hotel has been a haven for celebrities—including F. Scott Fitzgerald and Franklin D. Roosevelt—since its 1913 opening. Views from the front-facing rooms are exquisite. Rooms in the original wing are small request one of the newer rooms if space is an issue. An 18-hole golf course, an Incredible spa, well-equipped fitness center and several tennis courts are also on site. Save time for farm-to-table cuisine at Horizons restaurant.

$$$ Boar's Head Inn – 200 Ednam Dr., Charlottesville, VA. ☎434-296-2181. www.boarsheadinn.com. 175 rooms. Three miles from town, the main building resembles an English manor house in the Blue Ridge foothills. 17C antiques create an informal, pub-like feel in the common areas, and renovated guest rooms are done in neutral tones with antique furnishings and plush towels In the bath. Two restaurants, plus golf, tennis and spa facilities are also available at this 573-acre estate.

🍴 EAT

$$$ C and O – 515 E. Water St., Charlottesville, VA. Dinner only ☎434-971-7044. www.candorestaurant.com. **Contemporary.** Locals in search of a special-occasion meal head straight for this cozy, yet quietly upscale restaurant near Downtown. Chefs Nate and Rachel Kambic treat fresh local ingredients star in innovative preparations like warm artichoke pâté and Steak Chinoise with ginger, tamari and scallion pan sauce,.

$$$ Cúrate – 11 Biltmore Ave., Asheville, NC. ☎828-239-2946. www.curatetapasbar.com. **Tapas.** Chef Katie Buttons worked at the famous El Bulli in Spain, so it's no wonder that the array of tapas in her laid-back, downtown Asheville restaurant is so good. It's worth the splurge to sample the jamón ibérico de bellota, a ham made from free-range pigs fattened on acorns. House-made sangria makes a perfect accompaniment.

$$ L'Étoile – 817 W. Main St., Charlottesville, VA. CLosed Mon. ☎434-979-7957. www.letoilerestaurant.com. **American.** French techniques transform local produce into delicious dishes at this casual, unpretentious spot. il's a favorite Sunday brunch destination for regulars in the know.

$$ The Market Place – 20 Wall St., Asheville, NC. Closed Sun. ☎828-252-4162. www.marketplace-restaurant.com. **Contemporary.** Organic produce and local ingredients are staples . at this downtown restaurant. Inventive dishes—crispy potato cake with goat cheese; spinach, caper and polenta-stuffed trout; white chocolate mousse—are served in the contemporary dining room. In good weather, eat on the patio, which opens onto brick-paved Wall Street.

$ Salsas – 6 Patton Ave., Asheville, NC. Closed Sun. ☎828-252-9805. **Mexican/Caribbean.** Locals don't mind waiting for tables at the hottest place downtown, which fuses Latin and island flavors, such as roasted banana stuffed with spinach and goat cheese rolled in a flour tortilla.

$ Woodlands Barbecue – 8304 Valley Blvd. (Hwy. 321), Blowing Rock, NC. ☎828-295-3651. www.woodlandsbbq.com. **Barbecue.** The rustic atmosphere and live country and bluegrass music make a perfect foil for slow-smoked chicken, ribs and pulled pork dressed with your choice of signature sauces. Plates come loaded with your choice of sides (hushpuppies and slaw are good bets). Wash it all down with some sweet tea.

Shenandoah National Park★★

The best-known feature within the more than 196,030 acres of Shenandoah National Park, Skyline Drive follows former Indian trails along the backbone of the Blue Ridge as it runs through western Virginia from Front Royal to Rockfish Gap. Meticulously landscaped and punctuated by 75 overlooks girdled with low stone walls, the 105mi drive offers one dazzling view after another. To the east, the Piedmont's gentle, rounded hills slope down into the coastal plain. The western peaks give way to the Shenandoah Valley, named for the river that winds lazily past fields, woods and picturesque farms. More than 500mi of trails thread the Shenandoah, including 101mi of the 2,175mi-long Appalachian Trail, which runs from Maine to Georgia.

- ♿ **Michelin Map:** p412.
- **Info:** ☏540-999-3500; www.nps.gov/shen.
- ▶ **Location:** The park is in the Blue Ridge Mountains, just 75mi from the nation's capital. Four highways bisect the park.
- ☺ **Don't Miss:** Reflections of stalactites in Mirror Lake.
- ◷ **Timing:** Allow two days (Skyline Drive - 105mi).

A BIT OF HISTORY

Between 1928 and 1935, the state of Virginia purchased almost 280sq mi of private mountain land in more than 3,000 separate parcels, which it in turn ceded to the federal government. President Franklin D. Roosevelt dedicated Shenandoah National Park in 1936. To compensate for years of lumbering and grazing, the newly created Civilian Conservation Corps descended on the region in 1933 to plant trees, clear trails, grade the hillsides along Skyline Drive and control erosion. Weathered log cabins and rambling stone walls are all that remains of the mountaineers' world, as nature slowly reclaims its own.

SKYLINE DRIVE★★

Allow 2 days (105 mi).
The sights below are organized from north to south.

Skyline Drive through Shenandoah National Park

© National Park Service

VISITOR INFORMATION

Two park **visitor centers**, Dickey Ridge (mile 4.7) and Harry F. Byrd (mile 51) are open Apr–Nov. The Loft Mountain Wayside (mile 79.5) is open May–Oct weekends only. Maps, free backcountry permits, and information on accommodations, facilities and recreational activities are available at visitor centers and at **Park Headquarters** (3655 US-211 East, Luray, VA 22835-9036; ⚠✖♿🅿✆540-999-3500).The park is open year-round, though portions of Skyline Drive may be temporarily closed in winter due to weather conditions. Many facilities are closed during the winter (late Nov–Mar). Entrance to the park (valid for 7 consecutive days) is $15/vehicle and $8/ pedestrian or cyclist Mar–Nov; $10/ vehicle and $5/pedestrian or cyclist Dec–Feb. Mountain temperatures range from the mid-70s in summer to the teens in winter. Temperatures vary with elevation, so it's best to wear layers of clothing.

DRIVING IN THE PARK

The speed limit in the park is 35mph. Expect roads to be crowded during peak foliage season (Oct). Concrete mile markers located on the west side of the road are numbered in increasing order from north to south. Along the way, watch carefully for deer, bear, wild turkeys and other animals who may cross the drive without warning. Stay in your vehicle to view wildlife, and never feed animals in the park.

Skyline Caverns

10334 Stonewall Jackson Hwy., 1mi south of park entrance on US-340, Front Royal, VA . 🅿✆540-635-4545. www.skylinecaverns.com. Highlights in this 60-million-year-old limestone cave include a rare, calcite formation known as anthodites, or "cave flowers" because they resemble a profusion of spiky blooms. The glassy surface of **Fairyland Lake★** shimmers in the glow of multicolored lights. The massive, columnar space of **Capitol Dome** formed 12,000 years ago when a stalagmite on the cave floor fused with a stalactite on the ceiling.

Hiking the "A.T."

The Appalachian National Scenic Trail, the longest continuous marked footpath in the US, stretches from Springer Mountain in north Georgia, traversing 14 states, 2 national parks, and 8 national forests in a high, well-maintained but often rugged path of more than 2,000mi to the rocky summit of Mt. Katahdin in Maine. The popular hiking trail is open all year except during serious blizzards, and attracts thousands of day hikers, campers and backpackers from around the world, as well as a dedicated core of "through-hikers" who—after rigorous training—begin in Georgia in early spring and walk northward for three to four months, hoping to reach Maine before winter sets in.

A favorite of hikers for generations, the Appalachian Trail officially became a part of the National Park System in 1968.

The Official Appalachian Trail Guides are published by the Appalachian Trail Conference (ATC) and are available through retail bookstores worldwide (a catalog of ATC publications is available from their national office; Tsee National and State Lands, Hiking Trails). The Ultimate Appalachian Trail Store (✆304-535-6331 or 888-287-8673; www.atctrailstore.org) sells other Appalachian Trail-related items.

Front Royal to Thornton Gap

31.5mi.

Skyline Drive begins at US-340 at the south edge of Front Royal and climbs to **Shenandoah Valley Overlook** (mile 2.8), where the sweeping **view★★** west takes in Massanutten Mountain. Skyline Drive then ascends to 2,085ft at **Signal Knob Overlook** (mile 5.7), named for the point at the right end of Massanutten that served as a Confederate signal station. **Hogwallow Flats Overlook** (mile 13.8) looks east over lumpy peaks called monadnocks, lone remnants of a range that predates the Blue Ridge.

Luray Caverns★

970 US-211 West, 9mi west of Thornton Gap Entrance on US-211, Luray, VA. ✖🅿⌖540-743-6551. www.luraycaverns.com.

Lying 160ft underground, popular Luray Caverns is a wonderland of shimmering stalactites and flowstone that drips from the ceiling like wet fabric. Razor-sharp subterranean mounds rising up from the depths of **Mirror Lake** are only reflections of stalactites hanging above (the water is only 18 inches deep). In the Cathedral Room, you can hear the haunting notes made by the cave's unique **Stalacpipe Organ**.

After admiring the caverns, get a feel for local history at the **Luray Valley Museum**, featuring authentic structures relocated to this site to represent a 19C farming village.

New Market Battlefield State Historical Park

1mi west of Thornton Gap entrance on US-211, New Market, VA. ♿🅿⌖540-740-3101. www2.vmi.edu/museum/nm/index.html.

On these bucolic pastures west of the Blue Ridge, 257 cadets from the Virginia Military Institute in Lexington prevailed over Union forces in May 1864. Today the military institute oversees the historical park, which comprises the 287-acre battlefield; the **Hall of Valor**; and 19C **Bushong Farm**, which served as a hospital during the battle.

Marys Rock Tunnel to Rockfish Entrance Station★★

73mi.

The short length of **Marys Rock Tunnel** (mile 32.4) belies its arduous creation: For three months, workers drilled through more than 600ft of rock before cars be-gan driving through in 1932. From **Stony Man Overlook** (mile 38.6) you can see Old Rag Mountain, crowned in one-billion-year-old granite—the oldest rock in the park.

At mile 42, **Skyland** resort dates from the late 1880s. At **Big Meadows★** (mile 51), flat fields differ dramatically from other parts of the park. West of Big Meadows, **Byrd Visitor Center** houses changing exhibits.

Skyline Drive ends at **Rockfish Gap** (mile 105.4), where two major east-west highways, US-250 and I-64, cross the mountains.

Staunton★

13mi west of Rockfish Gap Entrance via US-250, I-64 West and I-81 North.

In this small hilly city (pronounced STAN-ton), the **Woodrow Wilson Presidential Library** (20 N. Coalter St.; ♿🅿⌖540-885-0897; www.woodrow-wilson.org) encompasses a museum and the birthplace of the nation's 28th president; and an attractive downtown of shops, bistros and restored homes. Maps of historic downtown are available at the **Staunton Visitor Center** (35 South New St.; ⌖540-332-3971; www.vis-itstaunton.com).

The **Frontier Culture Museum★★** (1290 Richmond Rd., 0.5mi west of I-81 Exit 222 off US-250 West; ♿🅿⌖540-332-7850; www.frontiermuseum.org) synthesizes the region's European heritage through a series of farm buildings that were dismantled and moved to this site. Costumed interpreters demonstrate farming techniques blacksmithing and sheep shearing.

Blue Ridge Parkway★★

Picking up where Skyline Drive leaves off, the magnificent Blue Ridge Parkway winds southwest from Rockfish Gap, Virginia, to North Carolina's border with Tennessee. At Ridge Junction (mile 355.3), the road leaves the crest of the stately Blue Ridge and enters the southern fringe of the Black Mountains, dominated by the tallest peak in the east, Mt. Mitchell (6,684ft). From there, it courses through the Great Craggy Range, the French Broad River Valley and the Balsam Mountains before meeting the Great Smokies.

- **Michelin Map:** p412.
- **Info:** America's Byway: The Blue Ridge Parkway; ☏540-767-2490; www.blueridgeparkway.org.
- **Location:** Sights on the Scenic Drive listed below are organized from north to south.
- **Don't Miss:** The majestic Biltmore Estate in Asheville.
- **Timing:** The Parkway is designed for leisurely driving: plan to take it slowly. We suggest 5 days (469mi).
- **Kids:** Watching the hawk migration from Humphries Gap is a once-in-a-lifetime experience.

A BIT OF HISTORY

When the idea of building a road between Great Smoky Mountains and Shenandoah national parks came to the attention of President Franklin D. Roosevelt in the 1930s, North Carolina and Tennessee had different ideas about where it would go. Construction began just south of the Virginia border at **Cumberland Knob** (mile 217.3) in 1935. The parkway, built in noncontiguous sections, opened in 1939. The entire road took more than 50 years to finish. Some 26 car tunnels had to be cut through solid rock; they were mostly dug by hand by the Civilian Conservation Corps.

SCENIC DRIVE
Rockfish Gap to Humphries Gap★
45.6mi.

Views along this stretch of the parkway, beginning at its northern terminus at Rockfish Gap, are broad and beautiful. At the **Mountain Farm Museum** on the grounds of **Humpback Rocks Visitor**

Linn Cove Viaduct along Blue Ridge Parkway and Grandfather Mountain, North Carolina

© Dave Allen/iStockphoto.com

VISITOR INFORMATION

The park's 15 **visitor centers** are open May–Oct (The Folk Art Center is open year-round). Maps and information on area activities and accommodations are available at visitor centers or from **Parkway Headquarters** at mile 384 (199 Hemphill Knob Rd., Asheville, NC, 28802; ⚠✕🚻♿🅿️✎828-298-0398). The parkway is open year-round, though sections may be closed by snow and ice during the winter months. The speed limit on the parkway is 45mph (35mph in developed areas). Expect roads to be crowded during peak foliage season (Oct). Concrete mile markers along the road are numbered in increasing order north-to-south starting at mile 0 (the north entrance to the parkway at Rockfish Gap, VA) and ending at mile 469 (the south entrance to the parkway off US-441 in Cherokee, NC). Temperatures on the parkway range from mid-70s in summer to the teens in winter, and vary with elevation. We recommend dressing in layers.

LODGING IN THE PARK

The nine campgrounds are open May–Oct. Most lodges and facilities along the parkway are closed during the winter. Reservations are recommended during the peak tourist season in fall.

Center (mile 5.8), you'll get a close-up look at five examples of 19C highland structures. From **Humphries Gap** (mile 45.6) you can watch hawks migrate in mid- to late September.

Lexington★★

11mi west of Humphries Gap on US-60. Information available at the Lexington Visitor Center, 106 E. Washington St. ✎540-463-3777. www.lexingtonvirginia.com.

The presence of two renowned Confederate generals, **Robert E. Lee** (1807-70) and **Stonewall Jackson** (1824-63) pervades this charming college town, home to Virginia Military Institute (1839) and Washington and Lee University (1749). Lee, asked by both the North and South to serve during the Civil War, was the president of the university that now bears his name.

Today he is honored at a small museum in the 1868 brick **Lee Chapel★** (Washington and Lee campus, park at 100 N. Jefferson St.; ♿🅿️✎540-458-8768), where he is interred.

General Thomas J. Jackson's last home was at 8 E. Washington Street (t540-463-2552). He is buried at the **Stonewall Jackson Memorial Cemetery** (S. Main & McDowell Sts.).

Natural Bridge★★

16mi west of Terrapin Hill Overlook (mile 61.4) on Rte. 130, Natural Bridge, VA. ✕🅿️✎540-291-2121. www.naturalbridgeva.com.

Called one of "the most sublime of Nature's works" by Thomas Jefferson, Natural Bridge soars 215ft above Cedar Creek. Designated a National Historic Landmark in 1998, this limestone span began forming about 100 million years ago. Geologists believe the water level was once much higher. As the level dropped over time, the arch grew taller and wider, worn away by the rushing waters.

Beyond the bridge, a moderate hike (1mi) leads to lovely **Lace Falls**.

Terrapin Hill Overlook to Roanoke★

58.6mi.

The parkway drops to its lowest point—649ft—at a verdant spot near Virginia's James River. A short trail from the **James River Visitor Center** (mile 63.6) leads to a restored lock from the Kanawha Canal (1851), which once linked tidewater Virginia to the frontier. South of the visitor center, you'll find a lodge and restaurant at the **Peaks of Otter** (mile 85.6), which is closed in winter.

At **Roanoke**, the landscape flattens to rolling hills as the parkway crosses the Roanoke River.

Mabry Mill★

Mile 176.2.

One of the most charming spots on the parkway, this rustic mill was built in 1910 by Ed and Lizzie Mabry. The massive wheel of the wooden gristmill still churns through a small pond.

Cumberland Knob to Moses H. Cone Memorial Park

76mi.

You'll cross the border from Virginia into North Carolina at **Cumberland Knob** (mile 217.5), the location of another visitor center. Continuing south, you will pass through **The Lump Overlook**

(mile 264.4) and eventually **Yadkin Valley Overlook** (mile 289.8), which surveys the valley where famed explorer **Daniel Boone** (see WESTERN KENTUCKY) honed his hunting skills.

The Blowing Rock★

3.8mi east of Moses H. Cone Memorial Park (mile 293.5) on US-321, Blowing Rock, NC. ✕&🅿 ☎828-295-7111. www.theblowingrock.com.

Jutting out over the Johns River Gorge, this 4,000ft-high cliff is named for a phenomenon caused by the walls of the gorge 3,000ft below. The gorge walls form a flume through which winds often gust upward with enough force to return light objects tossed off the cliff. The rock lent its name to the charming village of **Blowing Rock**, now

Old Salem

In the mid 18C, the area around present-day Winston-Salem, North Carolina was owned by Earl Granville, heir to one of the eight Lords Proprietor charged with governing England's holdings in the colony of Carolina. Hoping to populate his domain with law-abiding citizens, Granville approached members of the Moravian sect, a Protestant group who had escaped religious persecution in their native Germany. The Moravians purchased 100,000 acres from Granville, and in 1753 they established the settlement of **Bethabara** (Hebrew for "house of passage"). Nineteen years later, the group moved 6mi southeast to the permanent site of Salem.

Saved from demolition after World War II, **Old Salem★★** (70mi east of the Parkway, via US-421 East through Wilkesboro to Winston-Salem. Exit on Business 40, take Main St. Exit and go south 1mi; ✕🅿☎336-721-7300; www.oldsalem.org) is a charming mixture of 18C and 19C houses, shops and taverns set along brick streets (centered on Main St. between Race & Cemetery Sts.).

Begin your visit at the **Old Salem Visitor Center** (**900 Old Salem Rd.**), where you can purchase tickets and obtain self-guided-tour maps to the 10 buildings open to the public. Costumed docents inside these structures provide information about life in the early Moravian community. Cross the bridge from the Visitor Center and stop in the **Museum of Southern Decorative Arts**, where a stellar collection of Southern furniture and interiors spans the centuries from 1670 to 1895 (☎336-721-7360; www.mesda.org). Across from Salem Square, the **Single Brothers House★★** provided living space for unmarried men from the age of 14 until they either married or died. The original part of this three-story structure, with its half-timbered facade, dates to 1769. Salem Square is bordered on the east by **Home Moravian Church** (1800). A short distance up Church Street, the imposing 1802 **Vierling House★** (at Bank St.) overlooks the Moravian cemetery, **God's Acre**. Rows of identical white headstones here illustrate the sect's belief that all are equal in death as well as in life. Stop in the 1818 **Winkler Bakery** (Main St. between Academy & Bank Sts.), to sample traditional goodies such as Moravian sugar cake and thin, crisp ginger cookies.

a year-round resort center for skiing and upscale shopping.

Grandfather Mountain★★

1mi south of milepost 305 on US-22, 2mi north of Linville, NC. ✖🅿️ 🖉828-733-4337. www.grandfather.com.

The world's only privately owned international biosphere reserve, Grandfather Mountain (5,964ft) lies within a 4,000-acre park. The mountain is named for the elderly profile visible as you approach Linville from US-105. In the park, you'll find the **Mile High Swinging Bridge**, strung between two peaks; a nature museum; and a network of beautiful, but rigorous, hiking trails.

Be sure to traverse Grandfather's perimeter via the elevated roadway of **Linn Cove Viaduct** (mile 304), from which you'll enjoy panoramic views of the valleys below. Building the viaduct in 1987 marked the completion of the Blue Ridge Parkway, more than 50 years after it was begun.

Linville Falls★★

0.5mi off the parkway from milepost 316.4, Linville, NC. 🅿️.

The Linville River once flowed over the top of the 2,000ft-deep gorge here, until a flood in 1916 cracked the rock, creating the falls that exist today. You can hike to the foamy chutes via two different trails (ranging from .6mi to 1mi) hacked though rhododendron thickets.

Mount Mitchell State Park★

4.8mi northwest of parkway via Rte. 128 from milepost 355, Burnsville, NC. △✖&🅿️ 🖉828-675-4611. www.ncparks.gov.

Driving to the top of the tallest mountain east of the Mississippi is an ear-popping ride around hairpin turns with amazing views of the landscape below. From atop the 6,684ft peak unfolds a haunting scene of wind-stunted trees ravaged by air pollution, acid rain and an insect called the Balsam Woolly Adelgid.

Just north of Asheville at the **Folk Art Center** (mile 382; &🅿️ 🖉828-298-7928; www.southernhighlandguild.org), there's

an assortment of pottery, quilts and other handmade items from members of the Southern Highland Craft Guild.

Biltmore Estate★★

Take US-25 North Exit off the parkway and continue 4mi north on US-25 to Biltmore entrance. ✖&🅿️ 🖉828-225-1333. www.biltmore.com.

Asheville's most popular tourist attraction, George Vanderbilt's 250-room mansion (1895) embodies architect Richard Morris Hunt's interpretation of a Loire Valley château. Allow at least a half-day to see the estate, including **Antler Hill Village and Winery** and Frederick Law Olmsted's 75 acres of formal **gardens★★**.

Commissioned by George Vanderbilt (grandson of New York railroad tycoon Cornelius Vanderbilt), this extravagant castle was a technological marvel in its day, boasting central heating, electricity and two elevators. Highlights include the vast **Banquet Hall**, hung with richly hued 16C Flemish tapestries; the **Salon**, which displays chess pieces used by Napoleon Bonaparte; and the two-story **Library**, lined with some 10,000 leather-bound volumes. Upstairs you'll see family and guest bedrooms; downstairs are the kitchens, pool, bowling alley and servants' quarters.

Across from Biltmore's entrance, **Biltmore Village** was laid out in 1889 by Frederick Law Olmsted. Now the village houses boutiques, restaurants and galleries. Look out for high-quality crafts at **New Morning Gallery** (7 Boston Way).

Asheville★

From the parkway, drive 3mi west on US-74; take I-240 West to downtown exits. 🖉828-258-6101. www.exploreasheville.com.

This artsy town boasts an impressive collection of Art Deco buildings downtown, where art galleries, antique shops, bookstores and an eclectic group of restaurants line Haywood Street and Patton and Lexington Avenues.

Nearby, at 48 Spruce Street, you can tour the **Wolfe Memorial**, the Queen Anne-style home on which author **Thomas**

Wolfe (1900-38) based the boarding house in his most famous work, *Look Homeward, Angel* (1929).

Adjacent to the house, the **Wolfe Memorial Visitor Center** (52 N. Market St.; 828-253-8304; www.wolfememorial.com) maintains an exhibit detailing Wolfe's life and work.

Chimney Rock at Chimney Rock State Park★★

25mi south of Asheville on US-74; entrance on right in the village of Chimney Rock. 828-625-9611. www.chimneyrockpark.com.

Ascending the summit of this 2,280ft-high granite monolith can be a rigorous hike or a short elevator trip up the equivalent of 26 stories.

At the top, sweeping **views★★** overlook the terrain that provided the backdrop for the film The Last of the Mohicans (1992). Millions of years ago, rock and mountain were one. Over the eons, water filled fractures within the mountain, eventually isolating Chimney Rock.

Carl Sandburg Home National Historic Site

24mi south of Asheville in Flat Rock, NC. Take I-26 to Exit 22 (US-25) and follow signs to 81 Carl Sandburg Ln. 828-693-4178. www.nps.gov/carl.

Named Connemara by a previous owner, this secluded farmhouse (c.1838) reflects the unpretentious comfort favored by American poet **Carl Sandburg** (1878-1967). The writer, who won a Pulitzer Prize for history (1940) for his six-volume biography of Abraham Lincoln, spent the last 22 years of his life here.

French Broad River to Cherokee

75.6mi.

Some of the parkway's most dramatic scenery adorns its southernmost leg. Beginning at the French Broad River (mile 393.5), this rugged stretch passes through 17 tunnels as it courses through Pisgah and Nantahala national forests. At mile 417, the smooth granite face of 3,969ft **Looking Glass Rock★★** is

breathtaking. The road then curves west and climbs to its highest point (6,053ft) at **Richland Balsam Overlook★** (mile 431.4). From here, the parkway continues to its southern terminus at US-441 just north of Cherokee.

Cherokee

Cherokee Welcome Center, 498 Tsali Blvd. 800-483-1601. www.visitcherokeenc.com.

Gateway to Great Smoky Mountains National Park (see GREAT SMOKY MOUNTAINS), this small burg lies within the 82,600-acre Qualla Boundary Indian Reservation, home to some 9,000 members of the Eastern Band of Cherokees, who have occupied these mountains for centuries. Amid the souvenir shops, motels and the popular Harrah's Cherokee Casino, the town maintains sights that detail the history of the Cherokee tribe.

Museum of the Cherokee Indian★

From US-441 North, turn left on Drama Rd. 828-497-3481. www.cherokeemuseum.org.

This well-interpreted museum walks visitors chronologically through Cherokee history from the Paleo-Indian period to the present. The journey begins with a 5min film introducing the Cherokee version of creation. Afterward, visitors are free to walk through the exhibits, which include a fine collection of Indian artifacts enhanced by lively dioramas and poignant recorded narratives. Don't miss the Cherokee language **Bible**, translated in the mid-19C by Cherokee intellect Sequoyah (see EAST TENNESSEE).

Oconaluftee Indian Village★

.5mi off US-441 North at the end of Drama Rd. 800-483-1601. www.visitcherokeenc.com.

A living re-creation of the Cherokee's past, the village contains structures ranging from a 16C thatched-roof cottage to an 18C sweathouse, similar to those that were used by Cherokee ancestors.

Charlottesville★★

Set amid the eastern foothills of the Blue Ridge Mountains and surrounded by the lush horse farms of Albemarle County, this university town takes pride in its natural beauty, rich history and cultural attractions.

A BIT OF HISTORY

Founded as the county seat in 1762, Charlottesville became the heart of a network of tobacco plantations, and farms raising wheat and corn. Well removed from Vir-ginia's established aristocracy, the area fostered a tough self-reliance that would produce many leaders, including three of the country's first five presidents—**Thomas Jefferson** (1743-1826), **James Madison** (1751-1836) and **James Monroe** (1758-1831).

In addition to Jefferson's Monticello, **Ash Lawn-Highland★** (Rte. 53 east of Rte. 20; ℘434-293-8000; www.ashlawn-highland.org) preserves the remains of Monroe's tobacco plantation; and **Montpelier★★** (24mi northeast of Char-lottesville via Rte. 20; ℘540-672-2728; www.montpelier.org), where the pains-takingly restored mansion affords visi-tors a look at Madison's former estate as it appeared during the period following his presidency.

In recent years Charlottesville has been consistently ranked high for quality of living, a recognition that has fueled its growth without diminishing its

▶ **Population:** 43,475.

Info: Charlottesville Albemarie Convention and Visitors Bureau; ℘434-293-6789; www.visitcharlottesville.org.

◗ **Location:** Charlottesville is located 25mi east of the Blue Ridge Parkway from the Rockfish Gap Entrance via I-64.

Parking: A free trolley will take you from downtown to campus and back, no car necessary.

⊛ **Don't Miss:** Two of the country's most significant architectural sights.

appeal. One of the town's most popu-lar locales for strolling, the seven-block pedestrians-only **downtown mall** (Main St. between 2nd St. N.W. & 6th St. N.E.) is graced by fountains, plantings and benches, as well as boutiques, restau-rants and bars that occupy brick com-mercial buildings from the early 20C. Charlottesvillelies in the heart of Vir-ginia's wine-growing region.

Winery tours in the surrounding area are popular year-round, but especially during the fall harvest season when foli-age reaches its peak of color. The city also claims an active indie music scene.

Monticello

Virginia's Wine Country

Thomas Jefferson may have been one of the earliest to spot the potential for growing wine grapes in Virginia. With its gently rolling terrain and weather conditions very like those in Europe's wine regions, the area proved perfect for the cultivation of European-style varietals like Cabernet Franc, Cabernet Sauvignon and Merlot. Horticultural diseases stunted Jefferson's winemaking efforts and Prohibition proved another stumbling block, but the Virginia wine industry has experienced remarkable growth since the mid 1970s and today Virginia wines are routinely recognized both here and abroad. Some 228 wineries, mostly small, family-owned operations, thrive in the state and welcome visitors for tours and tastings. Arm yourself with a map of Virginia's 9 Wine Regions and a calendar of wine events; then relax and enjoy some time among the vines. ☑ Virginia Wine ℘804-344-8200; www.virginiawine.org.

SIGHTS

Monticello★★★

On Rte. 53, east of Rte. 20, following signs. ♿🅿 Open daily 8:30am–6pm. ⬥$24. ℘434-984-9800. www.monticello.org.

Included on the UNESCO World Heritage List of international treasures, Thomas Jefferson's remarkable "essay in architecture" stands as an enduring monument to the guiding spirit of the birth of America. Best known as the author of the Declaration of Independence, Thomas Jefferson held positions including governor of Virginia, minister to France, secretary of State, vice president and third US President (1801-09). An accomplished statesman, musician, draftsman and naturalist, Jefferson began building his home in 1768 on the little mountain ("Monticello") that commands views of the countryside.

A **visitor center** at the base of the mountain (Rte. 20, just south of I-64, Exit 121; ℘434-977-1783) offers exhibits and a film.

Tours of the house begin in the **entrance hall**, which Jefferson used as a museum. Thoughtful innovations are evident at every turn, from heat-conserving double doors to skylights and a dumbwaiter. On the way up the mountain, stop at **Historic Michie Tavern★** (683 Thomas Jefferson Pkwy.; ✗♿🅿℘434-977-1234). Established in 1784, this rambling white structure is popular today for its set midday fare of fried chicken, stewed tomatoes, black-eyed peas and cornbread.

University of Virginia★★

US-29 & US-250 Business (Emmet St. & University Ave.). Campus maps available at University Police Department (US-29 & Ivy Rd.). ℘434-924-0311. www.virginia.edu.

One of only four works of architecture in the country to rate inclusion on the UNESCO World Heritage List, the university began in 1817 as Thomas Jefferson's retirement project, a carefully planned "academical village" that embodies the limitless freedom of the human mind. Today the university enrolls some 21,000 students and ranks as one of the top universities in the East.

The heart of Jefferson's village, the graceful **Rotunda★★** (University Ave. & Rugby Rd.), completed in 1826, was patterned on the Pantheon in Rome, its shape more or less a perfect sphere seated within a cube. Although the Rotunda is undergoing an extensive multi-stage renovation, from the south Rotunda steps you can still take in a sweeping view of the **Lawn**, flanked by colonnades that link student rooms with 10 pavilions, each modeled after a different Greek or Roman temple.

Great Smoky Mountains National Park★★★

Straddling the North Carolina-Tennessee border, the lofty mountains that form the nation's most visited park are named for the ever-present shroud of blue-gray mist that inspired Cherokee Indians to call them *Shaconage*, or "place of blue smoke." Water and hydrocarbons released by the leafy woods and by more than 1,600 kinds of blooming plants that grow on the slopes, produce the vaporous "smoke"' (pollution has added to the mix, cutting visibility by about 60 percent since 1940 and damaging the red spruces). Today Great Smoky is a UNESCO World Heritage Site and an International Biosphere Reserve; it preserves the best examples of eastern deciduous forest and provides habitat for more than 60 species of mammals, including black bears (some 1,500 live in the park), white-tailed deer, elk and more than 200 types of birds.

- **Info:** National Park Service; ✆865-436-1200; www.nps.gov/grsm.
- **Don't Miss:** Great views and sunsets at Clingmans Dome.
- **Timing:** Allow a day. Park sights listed below are organized beginning at the south entrance in North Carolina.
- **Kids:** Find plenty of amusement-park fun at Dollywood.

A BIT OF HISTORY

In 1920, 75 percent of the 521,621 acres that would become Great Smoky Mountains National Park was owned by lumber companies. These lands were saved from being clear-cut through the support of national auto clubs anxious to provide their members with scenic drives, and the combined efforts of the legislatures of North Carolina and Tennessee. To defray the costs of acquiring thousands of parcels of property, oil magnate John D. Rockefeller pitched in $5 million in 1928; the park opened in 1934.

Near the park's northern entrance lie the regional commercial centers of **Gatlinburg** and **Pigeon Forge**, Tennessee. As US-441 enters Gatlinburg, it becomes a vast strip of hotels, fast-food restaurants and outlet malls that make for a jarring contrast to the peaceful parkland. Seven miles farther west on US-441, Pigeon Forge attracts visitors to its 118-acre theme park, **Dollywood** (✆865-428-9488; www.dollywood.com), owned by country music diva Dolly Parton, who grew up nearby.

SIGHTS
Oconaluftee Visitor Center

At the park's south entrance on US-441 in Cherokee, NC. ✆828-497-1900. After driving south down the Blue Ridge Parkway, begin here, at the southern entrance to the Great Smokies, where wall panels chronicle area logging in the 19C. Rangers are on hand to answer questions and sell books about and guides to the park. **Mountain Farm Museum** showcases a restored early-19C mountain homestead, including an apple house and a working blacksmith.

Newfound Gap Road★

Leading northwest from Oconaluftee Visitor Center, this scenic route (closed to commercial vehicles) winds up the crest of the Great Smokies and provides numerous pullouts from which to enjoy breathtaking vistas. Just up the road (.5mi north of visitor center) is **Mingus Mill**, with an 1886 water-powered gristmill. Stop for **views★★** from the crest of **Newfound Gap** (15.5mi north

ADMISSION

The park is open year-round, though roads may close due to severe winter weather. Entrance to the park is free. Facilities and roads within the park may be closed due to severe weather during the winter (Nov–Mar). Expect roads to be crowded in summer (Jul–Aug) and during the peak foliage season (Oct).

VISITOR CENTERS

The park's visitor centers, **Oconaluftee** (2mi north of Cherokee, NC on US-441; ✆865-436-1200), **Sugarlands** (2mi south of Gatlinburg, TN on US-441; ✆865-436-1200), and **Cades Cove** (on Cades Cover Loop Rd.; access via Little River Rd. off the northern end of US-441; ✆865-436-1200) are open year-round. Newfound Gap Road (33mi) connects the park's north and south entrances (at Oconaluftee and Sugarlands visitor centers). Maps and information, including accommodations, weather conditions and recreational activities, may be obtained at visitor centers or from **Park Headquarters** (107 Park Headquarters Rd., Gatlinburg, TN 37738; ✆865-436-1200).

ACCOMMODATIONS

The park maintains more than 800mi of trails, 10 developed campgrounds ($14-$23/night; reservation information ✆877-444-6777 or www.recreation.gov) and 5 horse camps. Permits (free; available at visitor centers or ranger stations) are required for all backcountry camping (Backcountry reservations ✆865-436-1297). The only lodging in the park is LeConte Lodge, accessible only by hiking trail (advance reservations required; ✆865-429-5704).

SAFETY

Mountain temperatures range from mid-70s in summer to the teens in winter. Never undertake a hike without first consulting local weather forecasts. Temperatures vary with elevation, so be sure to wear layers of clothing. Decent hiking footwear is advised, whatever the weather.

---

of visitor center), **where the Appalachian Trail crosses the road.**

Clingmans Dome★

From Newfound Gap, pick up the winding 7mi spur to the park's tallest mountain (6,643ft). Take the steep, paved .5mi trail from the parking lot to the **observation tower** for a dizzying panorama that extends across the Carolinas, Georgia and Tennessee, and for sunset views.

Cades Cove★★

From the north end of US-441 at Sugarlands Visitor Center, take Little River Rd. 24mi west.

Nestled in a secluded valley surrounded by the forested peaks of the Great Smoky Mountains, Cades Cove was settled in the early 19C by pioneers from Virginia, North Carolina and East Tennessee who came here in search of affordable farmland. At the beginning of the 11mi one-way loop road is an orientation shelter, where you can purchase a booklet that details the cabins, mills and churches you'll discover along the way—vestiges of a community that thrived until the park's creation in the 1920s. Of special note is the Gregg-Cable House, built in 1879.

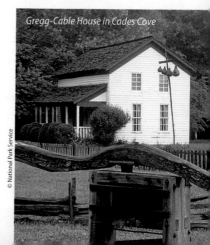

Gregg-Cable House in Cades Cove

© National Park Service

Coastal Carolinas

Countless barrier islands, sounds, inlets and bays define the jagged Atlantic edge of the Carolinas' coastal plain. The area ranges from the high, windswept dunes of the Outer Banks of North Carolina to the golf courses of Hilton Head, South Carolina. National seashores, wildlife refuges and state parks offer ample outdoor activity for naturalists, while well-developed resorts such as Nags Head, North Carolina, and Myrtle Beach and Isle of Palms, South Carolina, pack in sunseekers who desire the more urban pursuits of golf, tennis and family amusement parks.

A Bit of History

European settlement began in the late 16C with Sir Walter Raleigh's ill-fated colony on Roanoke Island and Huguenot Jean Ribault's short-lived settlement on Parris Island in Port Royal Sound. In 1633 King Charles II deeded the land south of Virginia between the 31st and 36th parallels to eight Lords Proprietor to show his gratitude for their political support. The new colony, named

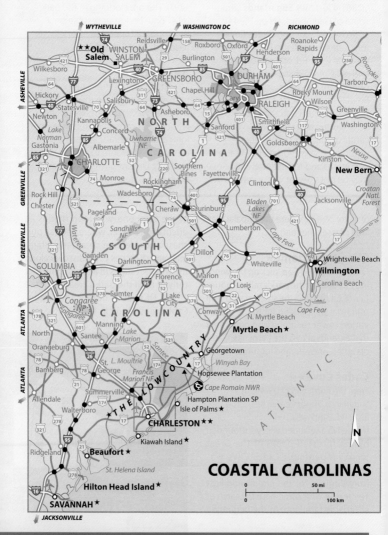

COASTAL CAROLINAS

Highlights

1 Reliving the Wright's triumph at **Kill Devil Hills** (p454)

2 Peeking into courtyards in Charleston's **Historic District** (p456)

3 Browsing sweetgrass baskets at the **Old Market** (p458)

4 Watching sunsets on **Kiawah Island** (p463)

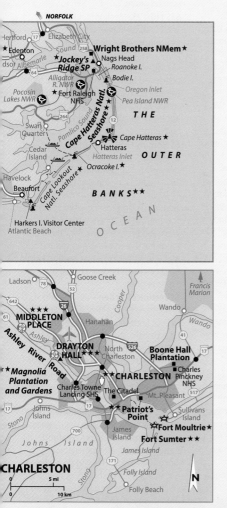

Carolina, was split into North and South in 1712 and reflected an economic schism. Charleston was a thriving South Carolina port, while North Carolina claimed only three small towns: Bath, Edenton and New Bern.

In the ensuing years, this region witnessed great moments in the country's history, such as the victory over the British at Fort Moultrie (after the battle, the palmetto tree was adopted as the South Carolina state symbol), the opening volleys of the Civil War fired at Fort Sumter in Charleston Harbor, and the first airplane flight by the Wright brothers at Big Kill Devil Hill on North Carolina's Outer Banks.

Today vacationers flock to the wide, sandy beaches that line the coast, while Charleston, the area's largest city, extends its mannerly charms to some 4 million visitors a year. The surrounding Lowcountry has its own cuisine and folkways, and descendants of early Creole slaves still speak their distinctive Gullah dialect in isolated pockets here. Farther north, North Carolina's chief port of Wilmington (169mi north of Charleston on US-17), on the Cape Fear River, celebrates its history in a number of colonial and Civil War sites.

ADDRESSES

🛏 STAY

$$$$$ Charleston Place Hotel – 205 Meeting St., Charleston, SC. ☎843-722-4900. www.charlestonplace.com. 440 rooms. A curving central staircase graces the lobby of this recently renovated Charleston institution, now operated by Orient Express Hotels, Inc. Guest rooms are elegantly appointed with 19C period furnishings. Don't miss the fine service and award-winning Southern cuisine at the hotel's Charleston Grill.

$$$$ Harbour View Inn – 2 Vendue Range, Charleston, SC. ☎☎843-853-8439. www.harbourviewcharleston.com. 52 rooms. This historic district property overlooks Charleston Harbor. Lowcountry-style guest rooms feature four-poster beds, wicker chests and seagrass rugs. Rates include a host of extras like afternoon wine and cheese and milk and cookies before bedtime.

$$$$ John Rutledge House Inn – 116 Broad St., Charleston, SC. ☎☎843-723-7999. www.johnrutledgehouseinn.com. 19 rooms. A rough draft of the Constitution was written in this 1763 house, and John Rutledge was one of the 55 men who signed it. Inlaid parquet floors, canopied rice beds and carved plaster moldings mark the National Historic Landmark's restoration to its mid-18C appearance.

$$$$ Planters Inn – 112 N. Market St., Charleston, SC. ☎843-722-2345. www.plantersinn.com. 64 rooms. Most accommodations in the original 1844 building of this historic-district Relais & Châteaux property are elegantly designed in subtle colors with four-poster canopy beds. Lowcountry cuisine at the inn's Peninsula Grill gets raves.

$$$ The Beaufort Inn – 809 Port Republic St., Beaufort, SC. ☎☎843-379-4667. www.beaufortinn.com. 25 rooms. An 1897 mansion in historic downtown where Lowcountry hospitality shines. Each guest room is uniquely decorated: you could stay in a different one every night and never get bored. Styles range from rich Victorian to cotton-candy pastels with hand-painted furniture.

$$$$ The White Doe Inn – 319 Sir Walter Raleigh St., Manteo, NC. ☎☎252-473-9851. www.whitedoeinn.com. 8 rooms. The aromas of early-morning coffee and French toast will make you feel right at home here. All of the guest rooms have bedside fireplaces and 19C antiques befitting the Queen Anne-style house.

🍽 EAT

$$$ Husk – 76 Queen St., Charleston, SC. ☎843-577-2500. www.huskrestaurant.com. **Southern.** Only ingredients—most of them local—sourced below the Mason-Dixon Line go into Chef Sean Brock's bill of fare at Husk. Be sure to order a skillet of Benton's bacon cornbread to pair with entrées such as cornmeal-dusted North Carolina catfish with Appalachian tomato gravy.

$$$ FIG – 252 Meeting St., Charleston, SC. ☎843-805-5900. www.eatatfig.com. **Contemporary.** Chef Mike Lata's restaurant, FIG (it stands for Food Is Good), wows foodies with brilliantly conceived dishes and a dedicated farm-to-table culinary bent. Try the pancetta-wrapped tilefish; the Wagyu beef tartare appetizer, or chicken with wild nettles and farro.

$$ Hominy Grill – 207 Rutledge Ave., Charleston, SC. ☎843-937-0930. www.hominygrill.com. **Southern.** Set in an 1897 Charleston single house, about 12 blocks outside the historic district, Hominy Grill represents Chef Robert Stehling's vision of a Southern diner. Weekend brunch is wildly popular here for dishes like a fried green tomato BLT and the Big Nasty Biscuit, stuffed with fried chicken, cheddar cheese and sausage gravy.

$$ Jestine's Kitchen – 251 Meeting St., Charleston, SC. ☎843-722-7224. **Southern.** Expect Southern soul food at this Charleston institution, named for founder Jestine Matthews. You can't go wrong with fried chicken, meatloaf or pecan-crusted whiting here, paired, of course, with "Jestine's table wine"—aka Southern sweet tea.

$$ Lee's Inlet Kitchen – 4460 Bus. Hwy. 17, Murrell's Inlet, SC. ☎843-651-2881. www.leesinletkitchen.com. **Seafood.** This casual seafood joint, family-owned since 1948, knows how to do seafood. Succulent piles of shrimp, oysters and scallops arrive grilled, broiled or fried with plenty of extras.

The Outer Banks★★

One of the major beach destinations in the southeastern US, the Outer Banks comprise a 125mi-long system of narrow Atlantic barrier islands wedged between inland sounds and ocean. These fragile dunes and marshlands, constantly pounded by wind and surf, are notorious for their offshore shoals where more than 600 shipwrecks have occurred, earning the coastline the dubious sobriquet, "Graveyard of the Atlantic." Once occupied by the Secotan Indians, this area was the site of the first English colony in the Americas in 1585.

A BIT OF HISTORY

A popular resort spot for more than a century now, the northern end of the

Info: ☎ 252-473-2138; www.outerbanks.org.

Location: The Banks extend from North Carolina's northern border south to its midsection.

Don't Miss: History in flight at the Wright Brothers National Memorial.

Outer Banks is packed with vacation homes, hotels, shops and restaurants. But south of the town of **Nags Head**, commercialism subsides, as Route 12, the only road threading the length of the contiguous northern Banks, passes occasional villages and the Pea Island National Wildlife Refuge on its way to **Cape Hatteras**.

The **Graveyard of the Atlantic Museum** (59200 Museum Drive, Hatteras, NC, 27943; ☎ 252-986-2995; www.graveyardofthe

The Lost Colony

In 1585 **Sir Walter Raleigh** sent forth seven English ships bearing 108 colonists with instructions to establish a settlement in the "most fertile and pleasant ground" of Virginia. Landing on the shores of **Roanoke Island** (southeast of Nags Head via US-158 South & US-64 West) in Roanoke Sound, the colonists built a fort and made a tentative peace with the local Indians, but by the spring of 1586, the group feared for their survival and returned to England.

In the spring of 1587, Raleigh sent another group forth, and by August the colony could boast the first English child born in the New World—**Virginia Dare**, granddaughter of the settlers' leader, John White. Soon after her birth, White sailed for England to re-supply the colony, but his return to the colony was delayed by several years. When at last he sailed up to the fort, he found it deserted, with no clue to the colonists' fate save the Indian word "CROATAN" carved into a post. Were the colonists killed by Indians? Did they move to another location? To this day, no one knows for certain—the fate of these colonists remains one of American history's most compelling mysteries.

The colonists' Elizabethan-style encampment and a replica of the Elizabeth II— one of seven vessels that brought the 16C English settlers to Roanoke Island —are re-created at **Roanoke Island Festival Park★** (Dare St. near downtown Manteo; ☎ 252-475-1500; www.roanokeisland.com); the **American Indian Town** exhibit here replicates Coastal Algonquin life and culture before European contact. The actual location of the first colony is preserved at **Fort Raleigh National Historic Site★** (off US-64 in north Manteo; ☎ 252-473-5772; www.nps. gov/fora) on Roanoke Sound. Outdoor productions of the stage play, **The Lost Colony★**, have been staged at the Waterside Theater here each summer since 1937 (for information, call ☎ 252-473-2127; www.thelostcolony.org).

atlantic.com) offers an introduction to the Outer Banks' maritime heritage.

Just beyond the town of Hatteras, where the road ends, state ferries (𝒫877-368-4968; www.ncdot.org/ferry) carry passengers and cars across Hatteras Inlet to **Ocracoke Island★**. Here wide beaches and tiny Ocracoke Village attract travelers looking for a quiet vacation (ᗙsee www.oracokevillage.com for accommodations and dining information). At the southern tip of the Outer Banks, **Cape Lookout National Seashore★** preserves a 55mi-long paradise of uninhabited sand beaches (accessible via ferry from Harkers Island, Davis, Atlantic, Beaufort & Morehead City; for ferry schedules and general information, contact the national seashore's **Harkers Island Visitor Center**, off Rte. 70 on Harkers Island Rd.; 𝒫252-728-2250; www.nps.gov/calo).

Just west of the Outer Banks, lining the sounds and rivers that chisel the mainland, lie some of North Carolina's earliest settlements. Established in 1712, the colonial seaport of **Edenton★** (northwest of Nags Head on Rte. 32) graces the banks of Albemarle Sound. On the Neuse River, **New Bern**—settled in 1710 by Germans and Swiss who named it after Bern, Switzerland—became the seat of the colonial government from 1766 to 1776 and the state capital from 1776 to 1794. And west of Cape Lookout, the fishing village of **Beaufort** (pronounced BOW-furt) on US-70 preserves its early-18C heritage in the restored buildings at **Beaufort Historic Site★** (130 Turner St.; 𝒫252-728-5225; www.beauforthistoricsite.org), and at the **North Carolina Maritime Museum** (315 Front St.; 𝒫252-728-7317; www.ncmaritimemuseums.com).

SIGHTS
Cape Hatteras National Seashore★★

Information about the seashore is available at the Bodie Island Visitor Center, near the Bodie Island Lighthouse on Rte. 12. 🅿 𝒫252-473-2111. www.nps.gov/caha.

Protecting several noncontiguous units of beaches, dunes and marshlands on the sound, the seashore encompasses 45sq mi of land. Shelling, birdwatching, windsurfing and sunbathing are favorite pastimes along the park's windswept shore.

Aside from its natural attractions, the seashore is famous for its historic lighthouses. Tallest lighthouse in the US, the 208ft (equal to 12 stories) **Cape Hatteras Lighthouse★** (off Rte. 12 near

Cape Hatteras Lighthouse

© National Park Service

Buxton) was built in 1870, but moved inland 2,900ft to the southwest in the summer of 1999 to protect it from the advancing ocean. During the summer visitors can climb the 248 steps to its tower (painted with distinctive diagonal spirals of black and white) for panoramic **views★★** of the sweeping arc of the Outer Banks. The 1823 **Ocracoke Island Lighthouse★** (on the southern end of the island in Ocracoke Village), measuring just 75ft tall, is the oldest in the state. The **Bodie Island Lighthouse** (southern tip of Bodie Island), painted in horizontal stripes, is the third to occupy the site and still functions as a navigational aid.

Wright Brothers National Memorial★

Milepost 8 off US-158, in Kill Devil Hills, NC. ♿ P ℰ252-473-2111. www.nps.gov/wrbr.

On this site on December 17, 1903, brothers **Wilbur and Orville Wright**, owners of a bicycle shop in Dayton, Ohio, made the first successful controlled, powered airplane flights. The current 431-acre memorial houses a **visitor center** with exhibits on the brothers' life and achievements and reproductions of their 1902 glider and 1903 *Flyer*.

Daily lectures explain the Wrights' struggles to solve the problem of powered flight, and their final victory here on the high dune of Big Kill Devil Hill, where soft sands and consistent winds allowed them to experiment with aerodynamic principles.

In December 1903, after several seasons of failed experimentation, they made four successful powered flights, the longest measuring 852ft and lasting 59 seconds. On the grounds of the memorial stand reconstructions of the Wrights' simple 1903 **camp buildings**, and the **Wright Brothers Monument**, a 60ft-high pylon of gray granite topping Big Kill Devil Hill.

Jockey's Ridge State Park★

Milepost 12 on US-158 bypass. ♿ P ℰ252-441-7132. www.jockeysridge statepark.com.

The 420-acre park protects the highest natural sand dune on the East Coast, 80-100ft (its height varies due to shifts in the sand) Jockey's Ridge. Its soft, forgiving sides and the winds that sweep off its top also make it one of the East's most popular hang-gliding sites.

Stop in the **visitor center** to learn about dune formation, then head out along the boardwalk for views of the ridge, or climb to the top of the dune (bring a kite). You can also take the 1.5mi interpretive **Tracks in the Sand Trail** that leads to Roanoke Sound.

ADDITIONAL SIGHT
Tryon Palace Historic Sites and Gardens★★

On US-17 in New Bern, NC. 529 S. Front St. ♿ P ℰ252-639-3500. www.tryonpalace.org.

Set amid the shaded residential streets of **New Bern**, the multi-building complex features restored and re-created buildings from the 18C and early 19C. Centerpiece of the complex, stately Georgian **Tryon Palace★★** is a reconstruction of the structure built in the late 1760s as the official colonial assembly meeting place and residence of Royal Governor William Tryon. After the American Revolution, the building served as the North Carolina capitol until 1798, when it burned to the ground.

Inside, 18C furnishings and ornate paneling depict the opulence of a royal governor's life. Attached to the palace by curved colonnades are two brick dependencies: the Kitchen Office (east side), where costumed interpreters demonstrate 18C cooking; and the **Stable Office** (west side), the only original palace building to survive into the 21C. Surrounding the palace, flower-and-boxwood parterred **gardens★** are reminiscent of colonial landscaping.

Charleston★★

Set on a narrow peninsula of land at the confluence of the Ashley and Cooper rivers on the South Carolina coast, the city of Charleston fancies itself a grand Southern dame, venerable in her history, elegant in her architecture, and genteel in her manner. On this 5.2sq mi peninsula, you will discover some of the city's most legendary sights and its loveliest structures, along with a multitude of boutiques, antique shops and restaurants that cater to a wide range of tastes and wallets. The area boasts some of the prettiest and most-challenging golf courses in the country; if you're a fan of the links, don't forget to pack your clubs. Beaches line the coast north and south of the city, and the Ashley River plantations and Civil War-era sights beckon history buffs.

- ▶ **Population:** 124,632.
- **Info:** ℘843-853-8000; www.explorecharleston.com.
- **Don't Miss:** The regional pleasures of the Magnolia Plantation and Gardens.
- **Timing:** Plan time to stroll at a leisurely pace through the Historic District.
- **Kids:** Kids won't get bored at the Charleston Museum thanks to hands-on history exhibits.

A BIT OF HISTORY

In 1670 a group of English colonists landed on the western bank of the Ashley River, just south of a Kiawah Indian village. The archaeological ruins of the settlement they named Charles Towne, after King Charles II, remain at the living-history park at **Charles Towne Landing State Historic Site** (northwest of Charleston on Rte. 171; ℘843-852-4200; www.charlestowne.org). Plagued by disease and mosquitoes on their swampy site, the colonists relocated their town to the peninsula across the river in 1680. Charles Towne grew to be the fifth-largest city in colonial America by 1690, with a wealthy merchant class supporting its bustling port. Rice, indigo and cotton thrived in the Lowcountry's temperate, humid climate, and soon hundreds of plantations—largely dependent on slave labor for their prosperity—were established.

Charles Towne witnessed the first great victory of the Revolutionary War in 1776, when the colonists trounced the British in the **Battle of Fort Moultrie**. After the war, Charleston was incorporated as South Carolina's first city in 1783.

The Civil War, which began in Charleston Harbor in the early morning hours of April 12, 1861, changed the city forever. By war's end, the once-thriving port had been shelled and burned into a virtual ghost town. With the abolition of slavery, the region's plantation economy gradually disintegrated.

Plagued by natural disasters over the years, plucky Charleston has rebuilt itself after repeated fires, hurricanes

The Single House

The city's distinctive contribution to American architecture is based on a typical West Indian design (many of Charleston's early settlers were planters from Barbados). One room wide and two rooms deep, the classic Single House includes a long piazza—or porch—lying behind a "false" front door on the narrow side of the house that opens onto the street (the real entrance to the house is off the piazza). A variation on this theme, the Double House is a near square with a room in each corner, divided by a central hall.

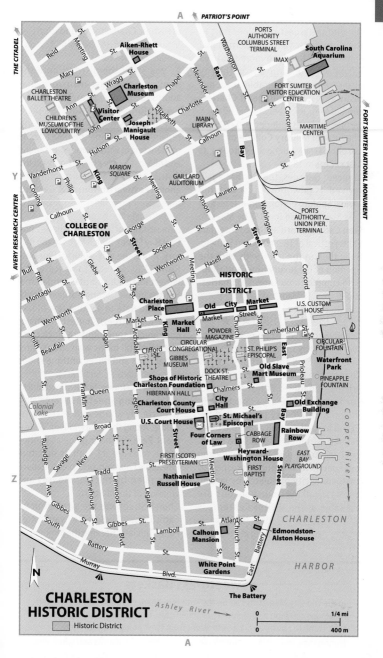

CHARLESTON
HISTORIC DISTRICT

Historic District

and earthquakes (the city sits on the second most active fault in the US). In order to protect its historic structures, Charleston became the first American city to enact a historic zoning ordinance in 1931, thus becoming a model for the preservation movement in other US cities. Today Charleston's stunning **18C and 19C architecture★★★** alone merits a visit.

One of the Carolina coast's top tourist destinations, Charleston boasts the eighth-largest container port in the US in dollar value of international shipments—handling more than $63 billion worth of cargo a year. The city also claims two venerable academic institutions: the **College of Charleston** (66 George St. between St. Philip & Coming Sts.) was founded in 1770; and **The Citadel Military College of South Carolina** (171 Moultrie St.) enrolled its first cadets in 1842.

In recent decades, the city has again revived its downtown, first with the annual **Spoleto** performing-arts festival (late May), started in 1977 by Maestro Gian Carlo Menotti as the counterpart to his Festival of Two Worlds in Spoleto, Italy; then in the late 1980s with the opening of the luxury hotel and shopping complex now known as **Charleston Place** (130 Market St.).

HISTORIC DISTRICT★★★

Occupying the lower tip of the peninsula formed by the Ashley and Cooper rivers—named for Anthony Ashley Cooper, one of the English Lords Proprietor—Charleston's historic district encompasses the area specified in the original 17C city plan, called the **Grand Modell**. A stroll along the brick, palmetto-fringed streets here hearkens back to the days when Charleston was London in miniature: a prosperous aristocratic city populated by landed gentry. Walking-tour booklets are available at the **Visitor Center** (375 Meeting St.; ☏843-853-8000; www. explorecharleston.com) and at the **Shops of Historic Charleston Foundation** (108 Meeting St.; ☏843-724-8484; www. historiccharleston.org).

As you stroll the district, note the wrought- and cast-**ironwork** that adorns the garden gates. This decorative art form evolved from 19C plantation blacksmiths who made and repaired tools. Inside the gates nestle gardens bright with oleander, jessamine and hibiscus. Many private homes in the district are open for tours during the annual **Festival of Houses & Gardens** (mid-Mar–Apr; ☏843-723-1623; www. historiccharleston.org).

Fine restaurants and art galleries line **East Bay Street**, which leads to the Battery. Along the way, colorful **Rainbow Row** (79-107 E. Bay St.) showcases the largest intact cluster of Georgian row houses in the US; the earliest dwellings here date to 1680. A few blocks away, **King Street**, Charleston's major commercial thoroughfare since colonial days, still brims with shops, inns, restaurants and pricey **antique shops** (between Market & Broad Sts.).

Recently, the formerly run-down blocks of **Upper King Street** have come alive with trendy shops and restaurants galore. Along the Cooper River, **Waterfront Park** (main entrance at Vendue Range, off E. Bay St.), with its signature Pineapple Fountain, occupies the space once filled by the warehouses and wharves of the old port.

Church Street was the inspiration for Catfish Row in DuBose Heyward's story *Porgy*. This later became the jumping off

---

Sweetgrass Baskets

In the Old City Market and along the streets in Charleston, you will see women making and selling a wide variety of coiled grass baskets. The coiled basketry craft came to South Carolina with slaves from West Africa 300 years ago.

During the pre-Civil War plantation era, slaves stored foodstuffs and winnowed rice in baskets made by coiling marsh grass with strips of palmetto leaves. In the early 20C women began producing and selling "show baskets" made of sweetgrass, a now-scarce dune grass found along the South Carolina coast. Today, this art form, passed down from generation to generation, is prized as a dying folk art. Labor-intensive sweetgrass baskets take anywhere from 12 hours to 3 months to make.

Edmondston-Alston House

©Janette Siler/Michelin

point for Gershwin's opera *Porgy and Bess*, which was based on real Charleston residents.

The Battery★★

Bordered by East & South Battery at the point of the peninsula.

The high seawall that lines the Cooper River side of Charleston Harbor replaced the masonry wall built in 1700 to fortify the city. Strengthened over the years to ward off hurricanes, this wall became known as the High Battery for the gun emplacement stationed here during the War of 1812. Today this popular promenade attracts strollers, joggers and bikers, who enjoy views★ of the river and of the graceful homes that line East and South Battery. These elegant pastel structures, positioned so that their airy piazzas catch the prevailing breezes, provide stellar examples of Charleston's noted antebellum residential architecture★★★. At the tip of the point, White Point Gardens★— named for the mounds of oyster shells that once accumulated here—were laid out by John Charles Olmsted in 1906.

Edmondston-Alston House★★

21 East Battery. ☎843-722-7171.
www.edmonstonalston.com.
Scotsman and cotton trader Charles Edmondston built this home in 1825. When the cotton market turned sour 13 years later, Edmondston sold the house to monied Charleston rice planter Charles Alston, who added the third-floor piazza and other Greek Revival details. A tour of the manse, with its triple-storied piazza supported by Doric and Corinthian columns, depicts the life of Charleston's 19C elite. The second-floor library contains more than 1,000 rare volumes.

Calhoun Mansion★★

16 Meeting St. ☎843-722-8205.
www.calhounmansion.net.
With 24,000sq ft of living space, Calhoun Mansion ranks as Charleston's largest single residence. Built in 1876 for wealthy banker George Williams, the home passed to William's daughter Sally and her husband, Patrick Calhoun (grandson of statesman John C. Calhoun). The mansion encompasses 35 rooms, fitted with lavish Victorian-era furnishings. The airy second-floor music room rises 45ft high to a glass skylight.

Nathaniel Russell House★★★

51 Meeting St. ☎843-724-8481.
www.historiccharleston.org.
Called an "urban plantation" when it was completed in 1808, Nathaniel Russell's Federal-style residence is still flanked by a formal English garden. Inside, the reception room opens onto a hall containing a "flying" staircase★★★—a freestanding spiral that circles up to the third floor. Restored to its 1808 glory, the home exemplifies the Adamesque style in the ornate carved woodwork and moldings that adorn the rooms.

Spanish Moss

You see it everywhere in the Lowcountry, hanging like fringe over the branches of live oak and cypress trees. A symbol of the South, Spanish moss is quite the misnomer: it's neither Spanish, nor moss. It is, in fact, an epiphyte, or air plant, which wraps its long silvery-green stems around a host tree and drapes from the tree's branches. The plant's narrow leaves are covered with scales that trap moisture and nutrients from the air. In the 18C, Spanish moss was used in many Southern households to stuff mattresses. The insects that were often trapped in this natural filler became known as bed bugs, as in "don't let the bed bugs bite."

Heyward-Washington House★★

87 Church St. ✆843-722-2996. www.charlestonmuseum.org.
Lawyer and patriot Thomas Heyward was the original owner of this red-brick double house. The site on which the home stands is within the boundaries of the old walled city. Inside, the rooms are decorated with a remarkable collection of 18C Charleston-made **furniture★**, including pieces attributed to **Thomas Elfe**, one of the early city's most prominent cabinetmakers.

Four Corners of Law

Originally intended to be a grand public square, the intersection of Broad and Meeting Streets is now graced with public buildings that represent state, federal and municipal law: the 1788 Charleston **County Court House** (northwest corner); the 1896 Renaissance Revival **U.S. Court House and Post Office** (at the southwest corner and the oldest continually used post office in the Carolinas); and the 1801 Palladian-style **City Hall** (northeast corner). Georgian-style **St. Michael's Episcopal Church★** (southeast corner) represents God's law.

Old Exchange Building★

122 E. Bay St. ♿ ✆843-727-2165. www.oldexchange.org.
Built by the British in 1771 as an Exchange and Customs House, this Palladian-style building was the site where South Carolina Patriots ratified the US Constitution in 1788. Some of the very men who signed the document had been imprisoned downstairs in the gloomy **Provost Dungeon** (👁visit by guided tour only) during the British occupation of the city. Visitors to the dungeon today can see part of the original wall built in 1690 to fortify the city.

Old City Market★★

Stretching from Meeting St. to the harbor along Market St.
Consisting of a three-block row of vendors' sheds, the market is fronted by 1840 Greek Revival **Market Hall** (Market St. at Meeting St.), designed by Edward Brickell White to resemble the Temple of Fortuna Virilis in Rome. Today the long sheds offer a virtual flea market of foodstuffs, T-shirts, jewelry and sweetgrass baskets.

Charleston Museum★

360 Meeting St. ✆843-722-2996. www.charlestonmuseum.org.
Across the street from the visitor center, America's first museum was founded in 1773. Now housed in a contemporary structure, the collections cover Charleston and the Lowcountry's social and natural history from pre-settlement days to the present. A fine exhibit of **Charleston silver** reflects the changing tastes of Charleston society (the christening cup of George Washington is one of the treasures here). **👥 Kidstory** features hands-on natural history and interactive displays designed to spark kids' interest in Charleston's rich cultural history as well.

Miami Area

Called the Gold Coast in part because of its proliferation of valuable real estate, Florida's most heavily developed strip extends 70mi along the Atlantic from Miami to Palm Beach, and encompasses one-third of the state's population. In sharp contrast, just to the west lie the nearly unpopulated expanses of the Everglades, linked to Miami by the Tamiami Trail (US-41).

Miami

Highlights

1 Dolphin shows at **Miami Seaquarium** (p473)

2 Chilled claws and key lime pie at **Joe's Stone Crab** (p474)

3 People-watching on **Ocean Drive** in Miami Beach (p475)

4 Sunset at Key West's **Mallory Square Dock** (p479)

A Bit of History

Before the arrival of the first European explorers, such as Spaniards Pedro Menéndez de Avilés and Ponce de León, Tequesta and Calusa Indians inhabited South Florida. With the exception of the swampy Everglades, the interior of the region—still predominantly agrarian—was conducive to the hunting and gathering methods of these early inhabitants, who supplemented their diet with fish and mollusks.

Synonymous with warm sunshine and fresh oranges, the Miami area became an established tourist mecca in the 1890s after the Florida East Coast Railway, bankrolled by railroad tycoon Henry Flagler,

South Beach nightlife

© VISIT FLORIDA

GETTING THERE

Miami International Airport (MIA): ☎305-876-7000 or www.miami-airport.com; 7mi northwest of downtown. Multilingual Information Service in Concourses B, D, G & E. Transportation to downtown via SuperShuttle ($15; ☎305-871-2000; www.supershuttle.com), taxi ($15-$25), Metrobus and hotel courtesy shuttles. Rental car offices are located near the airport, accessible by rental company shuttle buses at the terminal.

Amtrak train station: 8303 N.W. 37th Ave., ☎800-872-7245, www.amtrak.com. **Greyhound/Trailways bus** stations: Miami International Airport; 4111 N.W. 27th St, Miami Beach.; 16000 NW 7th Ave., North Miami Beach; ☎800-231-2222, www.greyhound.com.

GETTING AROUND

Miami-Dade Transit Agency connects Greater Miami and the beaches via Metrorail, Metromover, and Metrobus. **Metrorail** trains connect downtown Miami to surrounding areas ($2, EASY Card or exact change required). The **Metromover** elevated rail system links the Brickell Ave. and Omni areas, and loops around downtown (free). **Metrobus** operates county-wide ($2, EASY Card or exact change required).

Reloadable EASY Card farecards available at all Metrorail stations, at retail outlets and online at www.miamidade.gov/transit. Schedules and route information: ☎305-770-3131. Disabled visitors: ☎305-499-8971. **Tri-Rail** commuter rail service runs between West Palm Beach and greater Miami, and connection to Metrorail (fares are based on zones traveled but range from $2.50 to $6.90 one way). Schedules and route information: ☎800-874-7245, www.tri-rail.com. **Taxi:** Metro Taxi (☎305-888-8888); Yellow Cab (☎305-444-4444). **Water Taxi** shuttle (☎954-467-6677, www.watertaxi.com) operates all week throughout Ft. Lauderdale ($20 adults, $13 children, all day pass).

VISITOR INFORMATION

For a free visit planner, maps and information on accommodations, shopping, entertainment, festivals and recreational activities, contact the **Greater Miami Convention and Visitors Bureau**, 701 Brickell Ave., Suite 2700, Miami FL 33131, ☎305-539-3000, www.miamiandbeaches.com; or **Miami Beach Visitor Center**, 1920 Meridian Ave., Miami Beach FL 33139, ☎305-674-1300, www.miamibeachchamber.com.

---

finally reached Palm Beach and Miami. The Royal Palm Hotel opened in Miami the very next year, and between 1945 and 1954, more new hotels were established in the Greater Miami area than in all other US states combined. Real-estate development quickly followed, with the establishment of Miami Beach, Coral Gables, Hialeah and Miami Springs. Today southeast Florida still attracts hordes of visitors to its year-round warm weather, clear blue waters and white-sand beaches.

Greater Miami embraces all of Miami-Dade County plus several islands, including Miami Beach, a long barrier island 2.5mi off the mainland between Biscayne Bay and the Atlantic Ocean. Seven causeways line the mainland to Miami Beach.

The Miami area has a diverse mix of Latinos, Caucasians and African Americans. While distinct ethnic communities exist (such as Little Havana, Little Haiti and Brownsville), the broad area is a cultural melting pot of peoples, foods, festivals and languages. The Miami area offers a diverse range of entertainment; snorkeling on off-shore coral reefs; dancing to Latino rhythms in Miami nightclubs; admiring the Art Deco architecture of Miami Beach; and alligator-watching in the grassy expanses of the Everglades.

ADDRESSES

🛏 STAY

Hotel reservation services: Greater Miami & the Beaches Hotel Association, ☎305-531-3553; Central Reservation Service, ☎407-740-6442, www.reservation-services.com. **Bed & Breakfast reservations**: Florida Bed and Breakfast Inns, ☎561-223-9550, www.florida-inns.com. **Hostels**: Hostelling International: Miami Beach, ☎305-534-2988, www.ClayHotel.com; and Key West, ☎305-296-5719; www.keywesthostel.com.

$$$$$ Delano South Beach – 1685 Collins Ave., Miami Beach, FL. ☎305-672-2000. www.delano-hotel.com. 238 rooms. South Beach's minimalist trend started with Philippe Starcke's redo of this 1947 beachside oasis. Contemporary white-on-white guest quarters boast top amenities.

$$$$$ The Biltmore Hotel – 1200 Anastasia Ave., Coral Gables, FL. ☎305-445-1926. www.biltmorehotel.com. 275 rooms. Coral Gables' National Historic Landmark looks like a misplaced Spanish palace. Vaulted hand-painted ceilings, palm-filled courtyards and balustraded balconies are just some of the features that have attracted royalty and movie stars here since 1926. Then there's the 1.25-million-gallon pool and personalized service.

$$$$ The Marquesa Hotel – 600 Fleming St., Key West, FL. ☎305-292-1919. www.marquesa.com. 27 rooms. Four 1884 Conch houses—a cross between Federal and Bahamian—make up the historic-district favorite. A palm-filled garden with trellised orchids surrounds two pools nestled behind the houses. Breezy guest rooms mix soft tropical colors with Chippendale pieces and West Indies wicker. The hotel's **Cafe Marquesa** specializes in Caribbean-inspired dishes with Asian and Central American influences.

$$$ The Hotel – 801 Collins Ave., Miami Beach, FL. ☎305-531-2222. www.thehotelofsouthbeach.com. 73 rooms. Todd Oldham designed nearly everything in this renovated Art Deco gem (1939) off Ocean Drive. A huge tile mosaic and velveteen couches, in rose, green and gold, pick up colors from the lobby's original terrazzo floor. The colors of the sand, sea and sky brighten up bedrooms.

$$ Hotel St. Michel – 162 Alcazar Ave., Coral Gables, FL. 🛏 ☎305-444-1666. www.hotelstmichel.com. 28 rooms. This comfortable European-style bed-and-breakfast inn enjoys a great location in walker-friendly downtown Coral Gables. The parquet floor in the reception area and subdued, Old World-style decor in the guest rooms are reminiscent of homey European inns. Amenities include fresh fruit on arrival, French chocolates at turndown, and morning newspaper.

🍴 EAT

$$$ Joe's Stone Crab – 11 Washington Ave., Miami Beach, FL. Closed Aug–mid-Oct. ☎305-673-0365. www.joesstonecrab.com. **Seafood.** Located at the southern end of Miami Beach, this high-energy eatery has been a local institution since 1913. Stone-crab claws are conveniently cracked open and served chilled with the house mustard sauce. Sides—coleslaw and creamed spinach—are big enough for two, and don't forget to save room for the famous key lime pie. To avoid long lines, order from the take-away counter and have a surfside picnic.

$$ Versailles Restaurant – 3555 S.W. 8th St., Miami, FL. ☎305-445-7614. www.versaillesrestaurant.com. **Cuban.** Local transplants get their fix of home cooking at this Little Havana mainstay. Most rib-sticking dishes, such as roast pork and grilled palomilla steak with garlic and onions, come with generous portions of black beans and white rice. Finish your meal with a shot of potent, ultra-sweet café cubano.

$ News Cafe – 800 Ocean Dr., Miami Beach, FL. ☎305-538-6397. www.newscafe.com. **American.** People-watching is a 24-hour activity at this sidewalk cafe that opened in the 1988 to give production crews and models a casual place for a quick bite. Everything from French toast to salads is listed on the extensive menu.

Miami★★★

One of the most popular resort destinations in the US, Miami draws upwards of 9 million visitors from around the world yearly with promises of golf, water sports, deep-sea fishing, lively nightlife and a seemingly inexhaustible supply of sunshine. With a population of more than 2.5 million, Miami-Dade County is ethnically diverse; close to 50 percent of the county's inhabitants are Latino. The proximity of Miami to Cuba (180mi) and its similar climate have made this American city a logical destination for Cuban exiles.

▶ **Population:** 413, 892.

🛈 **Info:** Greater Miami Convention and Visitors Bureau. ℰ305-539-3000; www.miamiandbeaches.com.

🕓 **Timing:** Leave time to eat at one of the city's many excellent Cuban eateries.

👥 **Kids:** Today's kids may not remember Flipper, the TV show that was filmed at Miami Seaquarium, but they will still enjoy a stop here.

A BIT OF HISTORY

Since the first permanent settlement founded by Spaniard **Pedro Menéndez de Avilés** in 1567, early inhabitants found life in the Miami area to be challenging; peace had to be negotiated with local Indian tribes, and pirates scavenged the coast.

By the mid-1830s only a handful of pioneers had settled in the area. **Julia Tuttle**—who came to be known as the "Mother of Miami"—was largely responsible for putting Miami on the map. Tuttle convinced railroad magnate **Henry Flagler** to bring his **Florida East Coast Railway** (FEC) south, trading half of her land for Flagler's work as city developer and planner. The first train rolled into Miami in 1896; the fledgling city was incorporated three months later. While Miami's growth corresponded directly to the development of the railroad and the federal highway system, a handful of visionaries, including Miami Beach developer **Carl Fisher** and Coral Gables planner **George Merrick**, earned the real credit for creating the pastel boomtowns that turned Miami into a winter resort for wealthy Northerners, the "Sunshine of America."

The tide, however, started turning in the mid-1920s. In 1925 a cargo embargo laid the city low. Then a one-two punch—delivered by a deadly hurricane that damaged nearly every building downtown in 1926, and the stock market crash of 1929—knocked the city to its knees. After such a beating, Miami recovered slowly, bolstered by liquor supplied by rumrunners during Prohibition and the legalization of pari-mutuel betting in 1931.

Today's metropolis benefits from an amalgamation of ethnic groups and enterprises. Its international population is evident in the distinct ethnic communities of Little Havana and Little Haiti. Downtown Miami sports architecturally innovative office towers. Miami-Dade County hosts some 1,000 multinational corporations.

The **Port of Miami**, the world's busiest cruise harbor, serves a total of eight cruise lines and boasts an annual passenger count nearing 4 million. Despite the income generated by the port and other commerce, tourism still reigns as king of industry in Miami.

DOWNTOWN

Defined by the Miami River on the south and by **Bayfront Park** on Biscayne Bay, the vibrant 1.5sq mi quarter known as Miami's downtown exudes the bustling atmosphere of a Latin city. In recent years a large cluster of contemporary high-rise hotels and office buildings, including the tiered **Miami Tower** (100 S.E. 2nds St.) and Southeast **Financial Center** (200 S. Biscayne Blvd.) have created a dramatic skyline—illuminated at night in neon outlines. The spread of downtown south of the Miami River along **Brickell Avenue** has resulted in the emergence of that area—once lined with the homes of Miami's richest citizens—as an international financial district. Downtown Miami is in the midst of a development boom. Currently, a $1.05 billion construction project called **Brickell CityCentre** will transform 9.1 acres along South Miami Avenue between 6th and 8th Streets, bringing 5.4 million sq ft of commercial, residential, entertainment, retail and hotel space to the area. In addition, a new 40-acre **Museum Park** on the waterfront along Biscayne Blvd. will serve as the new home of the **Pérez Art Museum Miami**, formerly the Miami Art Museum, in December 2013 (305-375-3000, www.pamm.org) and a new science museum for the city (2014).

Miami-Dade Cultural Center★

101 W. Flagler St. 305-375-1896. A complex of three Mediterranean Revival buildings—including HistoryMiami and the Miami-Dade Public Library—the center rests atop a tiled plaza, illustrating architect Philip Johnson's design for a cultural oasis above the busy downtown streets.

HistoryMiami★★

305-375-1492. www.historymiami.org. Housed on the museum's second floor, the permanent exhibit **Tropical Dreams: A People's History of South Florida** recounts the area's colorful past via a wealth of artifacts and mixed-media presentations, including an early Tequesta Indian settlement and treasures from sunken Spanish galleons. HistoryMiami also offers walking, bike, boat and coach tours of the city led by historians, eco-historians and tour guides.

Bayside Marketplace★

401 Biscayne Blvd. 305-577-3344. www.baysidemarketplace.com. Composed of buildings, plazas and open-air walkways, Bayside and its profusion of boutiques, chain stores and eateries overlooks Biscayne Bay.

ADDITIONAL SIGHTS
Museum of Contemporary Art★

Joan Lehman Building, 770 N.E. 125th St., in North Miami. 305-893-6211. www.mocanomi.org.

Designed by architect Charles Gwathmey, the simple but elegant building on palm-studded grounds within the North Miami civic complex features a permanent collection of works by notables such as Roy Lichtenstein, Dennis Oppenheim, Julian Schnabel, John Baldessari and José Bedia. Mixed-media works are a particular focus of changing exhibits featuring work by, for example, video artist Corey Arcangel and American pop artist Keith Haring.

Ancient Spanish Monastery★★

16711 W. Dixie Hwy., in North Miami. 305-945-1461. www.spanishmonastery.com.

A superb example of early Gothic architecture, the Cloister of St. Bernard of Clairvaux was completed in 1141 in Segovia, Spain. Wealthy newspaperman **William Randolph Hearst** purchased the monastery in 1925, intending to reconstruct it on the grounds of his California estate, San Simeon. But Hearst never finished his estate, and after his death in 1951 the cloister was sold to two South Florida developers who planned to open it as a tourist attraction. Reconstructing the cloister, however, was tantamount to a giant jigsaw puzzle; the shipping boxes had been dismantled and re-crated years earlier in New York due to a quarantine. The resulting 10,751 jumbled packages that arrived in Florida took 19 months to assemble.

Inside the 200-pound wrought-iron entrance gate lies a lush subtropical garden. On the garden's southern perimeter stands the entrance to a long cloister. Once serving as the monks' refectory, the **Chapel of St. Bernard of Clairvaux** occupies the first corridor.

FLORIDA'S TURNPIKE · FORT LAUDERDALE

CAROL CITY · Palmetto · Expwy. · NORTH MIAMI · Ancient Spanish Monastery

BEACH

Opa-locka · BISCAYNE GARDENS

OPA-LOCKA · NORTH MIAMI

OLETA RIVER SP · HAULOVER BEACH PARK

AMELIA EARHART PARK · Pkwy. · Museum of Contemporary Art · BAL HARBOUR · SURFSIDE

HIALEAH · HIALEAH PARK RACETRACK · MIAMI SHORES · BISCAYNE PARK · GREATER MIAMI NORTH

W. 21st St. · E. 25th St. · E. 21st St. · NORTH BAY VILLAGE · LITTLE HAITI

Airport · Expwy. · Fontainebleau Miami Beach

N.W. 36th St. · MIAMI JAI ALAI · MIAMI · J. Tuttle Causeway · Pérez Art Museum Miami · VENETIAN IS.

Miami International · Dolphin · Expwy. · MIAMI BEACH · Collins · South Beach

W. Flagler St. · Bayside Marketplace · Jungle Island · STAR I. · Port of Miami · Brickell CityCentre · FISHER I.

LITTLE HAVANA · Calle Ocho

S.W. 8th St. · CORAL GABLES · Coral Way · VIZCAYA · Miami Seaquarium · VIRGINIA KEY

Biltmore Hotel · Venetian Pool · COCONUT GROVE · UNIV. OF MIAMI MARINE LAB · CRANDON

Univ. of Miami · The Barnacle Historic State Park · KEY BISCAYNE · ATLANTIC OCEAN

SOUTH MIAMI · Sunset Dr. · Kendall

MATHESON HAMMOCK COUNTY PARK · BILL BAGGS CAPE FLORIDA SP · GREATER MIAMI

Fairchild Tropical Botanic Garden · CAPE FLORIDA · N

ZOO MIAMI, EVERGLADES NATL. PARK, BISCAYNE NATL. PARK

0 — 3 mi
0 — 5 km

Two circular stained-glass **telescopic windows**★ (named for the three rings of receding frames that encase them) are as old as the monastery.

CORAL GABLES★★

The grandest and most successful of South Florida's boomtown developments, Coral Gables covers a 12.5sq mi area just southwest of downtown Miami, encompassing the **University of Miami** campus. The area's fine **Mediterranean Revival architecture**, featuring clay roof tiles, breezy courtyards and loggias, as well as mature tropical landscaping, helps make Coral Gables one of the most desirable residential enclaves in Greater Miami.

"Miami's Master Suburb" was the brainchild of developer **George Merrick** (1886-1942), who began laying out Coral Gables in 1925. He incorporated

Little Havana

Immediately west of downtown, Little Havana is one of the city's most lively and exotic neighborhoods. **Calle Ocho**, or Eighth Street—the heart of activity in Little Havana—vibrates with a spirited street life where pungent tobacco and heady *café Cubano* scent the air, and English is rarely spoken. Each year on the second Sunday in March, over 1 million revelers flock to this thoroughfare for the gala street party **Calle Ocho Open House**, a culmination of the week-long Lenten festival known as Carnaval Miami. Stretching along Calle Ocho (between S.W. 17th & S.W. 12th Aves.), the **Latin Quarter** invites tourists to walk its brick sidewalks set with stars bearing the names of an international array of prominent Hispanic entertainers, including Julio Iglesias and Gloria Estefan.

Since the influx of Cubans escaping the Cuban Revolution in 1959, Little Havana has remained a magnet for refugees from a variety of Spanish-speaking nations as well as the political nerve center of the influential Cuban exile colony. Cuban history is remembered in places such as **José Martí Park** (362 S.W. 4th St.), named after the apostle of Cuban independence who was killed in Cuba in 1895. Commemorating the chief of the Cuban Liberating Army, **Máximo Gómez Park** (southeast corner of S.W. 15th Ave.)—also known as Domino Park—is where locals assemble daily for games of dominoes, chess and checkers. Before you leave, be sure to sample Little Havana's profusion of authentic Cuban restaurants.

broad boulevards—like the main east-west artery **Coral Way**—and park-like landscaping associated with European cities. Designed to set Coral Gables apart, grand drive-through portals like the **Douglas Entrance** (Tamiami Trail & Douglas Rd.) border the eastern and northern perimeters.

The Biltmore Hotel★★

1200 Anastasia Ave. ✕⚫🅿 ☎305-445-1926. www.biltmorehotel.com.
Inaugurated in 1926 as South Florida's premier winter resort, this 275-room Mediterranean Revival "wedding cake" incorporates a 300ft-high tower with triple cupola that is visible from miles around.
In its heyday, the Biltmore attracted Hollywood stars such as Bing Crosby, Judy Garland and Ginger Rogers. Now restored to its former glory, the hotel boasts an ornate **lobby★**, an elegant **ballroom** with a vaulted ceiling, and a 1.25-million-gallon **pool**.

Venetian Pool★★

2701 de Soto Blvd. ✕⚫🅿 ☎305-460-5306. www.coralgablesvenetianpool.com.
A limestone quarry that supplied building materials for the area's early homes forms the base of this whimsical municipal pool. Footbridges and striped light poles reminiscent of those lining Venice's Grand Canal adorn the free-form swimming area. Today the renovated pool, ornamented with waterfalls and pocked with rock caves, provides a unique recreational venue.

Fairchild Tropical Botanic Garden★★

10901 Old Cutler Rd. ✕⚫🅿 ☎305-667-1651. www.fairchildgarden.org.
Named after plant explorer David Fairchild, the largest botanical garden in

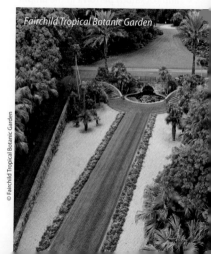
Fairchild Tropical Botanic Garden

© Fairchild Tropical Botanic Garden

Venetian Pool

the continental US is set on 83 well-tended acres studded with a series of 12 man-made lakes. The garden boasts more than 2,500 species of plants and trees from around the world, arranged in spaces that vary dramatically from narrow allées to open beds; the collection of palms and cycads is nationally recognized. A tram tour (45min) takes visitors past a sampling of the garden's flora.

👥 Jungle Island★

1111 Parrot Jungle Trail. 🍴♿🅿✆305-400-7000. www.jungleisland.com.

A rainbow of vivid-colored macaws perched inside the entrance greets visitors who come to view exotic birds, including cockatoos, emus, cranes and pink flamingos. Winding through lush tropical gardens, a pathway leads to a walk-through aviary; trained macaws and cockatoos perform in the amphitheater. Among the park's newer exhibits are the only colony of African penguins in South Florida and two leopards, one black and one spotted.

COCONUT GROVE★★

Stretching 4mi south of Rickenbacker Causeway along Biscayne Bay, Miami's oldest community owes its name to Horace Porter, a Connecticut doctor who dreamed of starting a post office here in 1873. By the early 20C, bayfront estates here were a prime winter address for affluent industrialists such as James Deering. The Grove's intellectual and artistic community flourished in the 1920s and 30s, drawing notables such as poet Robert Frost.

Annexed by the city of Miami in 1925, this area has managed to retain a strong sense of history in its quiet residential neighborhoods. Catering to the under-40 crowd, **Coconut Grove Village★** (Grand Ave. & Main Hwy.) is a haven of sidewalk cafes and tony boutiques, including the **Mayfair** (2911 Grand Ave.; www.mayfairinthegrove.com) and **CocoWalk** (3015 Grand Ave.), an ensemble of bars, chain stores and movie theaters. Inaugurated in 1963, the annual, three-day **Coconut Grove Arts Festival** (www.cgaf.com) in late winter celebrates the Grove's long-standing interest in the arts.

Vizcaya★★★

3251 S. Miami Ave. 🍴♿🅿✆305-250-9133. www.vizcaya.org.

Overlooking the calm blue waters of Biscayne Bay, this ornate Italian Renaissance-style villa and its formal gardens embody the fantasy winter retreat of their builder, Illinois entrepreneur **James Deering** (whose family developed the International Harvester Company).

Under the supervision of decorator Paul Chalfin, New York architect **F. Burrall Hoffman, Jr.**, designed a villa to hold all of Deering's European treasures. Vizcaya (named after the Spanish merchant Vizcaino) took 1,000 workers more than two years to complete.

The 34 rooms that are open to the public incorporate elements of four major styles: Renaissance, Baroque, Rococo and Neoclassical. Two floors of rooms surround a central courtyard (now roofed to protect the priceless art within). Looking out over the gardens, the **Tea Room** is actually an enclosed loggia with a stained-glass wall displaying Vizcaya's emblematic sea horse and caravel. The **East Loggia**, with its striking colored-marble floor, opens out onto the terrace that fronts Biscayne Bay. Just off the terrace sits the **Stone Barge**, an ornamental Venetian-style breakwater.

More than 10 acres of formal **gardens** flank the mansion's south side. The fan-shaped Italian hill garden, with its curvilinear parterres, centers on a two-room Baroque **Casino**, or garden house, set on an artificial hill.

The Barnacle Historic State Park★★

3485 Main Hwy. ✆305-442-6866. www.floridastateparks.org/thebarnacle.

This five-acre bayfront site preserves one of the last patches of tropical hardwood hammock in Coconut Grove, along with the 1891 home of yacht designer **Ralph Middleton Munroe**. Munroe first came to the Grove in 1877. In 1886 he purchased a 40-acre tract of property and, using lumber salvaged from a shipwreck, built a five-room home. The Bahamian-style, hip-roofed structure was nicknamed "The Barnacle" for its octagonal roof that tapers to a small open-air vent. In 1908 Munroe enlarged the single-story house by adding a new ground floor in concrete. Virtually unchanged since Munroe's day, the house remained in the family until the 1970s and still contains the original furnishings.

👪 Miami Seaquarium★

4400 Rickenbacker Causeway, just east of Coconut Grove on Key Biscayne. 🍴🅿✆305-361-5705. www.miamiseaquarium.com.

In the 1960s, this 38-acre marine park served as the set for the TV series *Flipper* and as home to its star. Today numerous live shows feature dolphins, sea lions and orcas, focusing on entertainment with an educational subtext, and demonstrate these denizens' amazing abilities. Seals, manatees and stingrays, tropical fish and birds are all housed in specially designed habitats that allow viewing to best effect.

EXCURSIONS

👪 Zoo Miami★★

➲1 Zoo Blvd., 18mi southwest of Miami. Take the Florida Turnpike south to Exit 16. Go west on S.W. 152nd St. and follow signs to zoo at 12400 S.W. 152nd St. 🍴♿🅿✆305-251-0400. www.miamimetrozoo.com.

The best way to see the more than 2,000 reptiles, birds and mammals in this popular cageless zoo is to wander along the 3mi loop trail that winds through the 300-acre park; an elevated monorail also makes regular runs around the grounds, offering its riders a bird's-eye view of the animal habitats. Among the highlights are an affectionate band of **lowland gorillas** (a walk-in viewing cave permits a close-up look) and a group of **Bengal tigers**.

Biscayne National Park★

➲38mi south of Miami in Homestead. Take the Florida Turnpike south to N. Canal Dr. Convoy Point Visitor Center is at the end of S.W. 328th St. ⛺♿🅿 ✆305-230-7275. www.nps.gov/bisc.

Located in the Atlantic Ocean and Biscayne Bay, the largest marine park in the US was established in 1980 to help protect a 270sq mi area of coastal wetlands, mangrove shorelines, coral reefs and a string of barrier islands.

The **reefs★★★** are located about 10mi offshore, where warm Gulf Stream currents nurture some 50 species of living coral. For those wishing to explore the reefs, the park sponsors glass-bottom boat tours (reservations: ✆305-230-1100) and rents scuba and snorkeling gear.

Miami Beach★★★

Touted as one of the country's great tropical paradises, Miami Beach is justifiably famed for its fabulous palm-studded shoreline, eccentric architecture and colorful locals. The city of Miami Beach was built on the dreams and speculation of northern developers and entrepreneurs such as Pennsylvania nurseryman Henry Lum, New Jersey horticulturalist John C. Collins and Indiana automobile magnate Carl Fisher.

▶ **Population:** 89,840.
🛈 **Info:** ✆305 539-3000; www.miamiandbeaches.com.
🅿 **Parking:** You'll need a car to cruise down the legendary Ocean Drive.
👁 **Don't Miss:** The Art Deco architecture on Collins Avenue.

A BIT OF HISTORY

The city occupies a narrow barrier island (7mi long and 1.5mi wide) located 2.5mi off the mainland. After World War I, Collins and Fisher pooled their resources, promoting Miami Beach to monied northerners. By 1921 the former mangrove swamp was alive with sprawling Mediterranean Revival estates, luxury hotels, polo grounds and tennis courts. Today, the famous South Beach area (below 23rd St.) and rejuvenated Art Deco Historic District, with its fashionable clubs and boutiques, are reached directly by the MacArthur Causeway. People-watching is a prime pastime in

SoBe (local slang for South Beach), now a magnet for fashion models, designers and assorted glitterati. The real stars, however, are the buildings themselves.

ART DECO HISTORIC DISTRICT★★★

Listed on the National Register of Historic Places in 1979, this enclave of small-scale Art Deco hotels and apartment houses dating from the late 1920s to the early 40s amounts to the largest concentration of architecture of its kind in the world. (Interestingly, Miami Beach's North Shore Historic District was added to the National Register of Historic Places in 2009, for its post-war Miami Modernism, or MiMo, architecture.) Derived from the European minimalist **International Style**, Art Deco used decorative stylized elements to embellish simple massive forms. Miami Deco went a step further, outlining structures in neon lights at night, and incorporating flamingos, palm trees and other tropical motifs into exuberant door grills, bas-relief plaques, murals and etched windows.

The district measures about 1sq mi and is roughly bounded by the Atlantic Ocean on the east, Alton Road on the west, Sixth Street on the south and Dade Boulevard to the north. A commercial thoroughfare encompassing chic restaurants, hip dance clubs and Cuban coffee shops, **Washington Avenue** is enlivened by the colorful Mediterranean Revival architecture of **Española Way★** (between Washington &

Stone Crabs

Harvested off Florida's Gulf Coast between October and May, stone crabs are sought after for their succulent claw meat, which rivals lobster for sweetness. The rust-colored crustaceans possess the ability to generate new claws within 12 to 18 months (fishermen take only the claws, since they contain the crab's only edible meat). Miami Beach's legendary restaurant **Joe's Stone Crab** (11 Washington Ave.; closed Sept-mid-Oct; ✆305-673-0365) serves its namesake delicacy to droves of diners who are willing to brave the long lines (*Joe's doesn't take reservations*).

Drexel Aves.). Along the oldest commercial street on the island, **Lincoln Road Mall** is a pedestrians-only enclave with shops, galleries, restaurants and a central mall. Cultural offerings here range from New World Symphony concerts at the Frank Gehry-designed **New World Center** (no. 500; www.newworldcenter.com) to working artisans' studios at **Artcenter South Florida** (no. 924; www.artcentersf.org).

The **Miami Design Preservation League (MDPL)** offers Art Deco district tours guided by historians, architects and other trained guides (walking tours depart from Art Deco Welcome Center in Oceanfront Auditorium, 1001 Ocean Dr.; 305-672-2014; www.mdpl.org; bike and Segway tours depart from Bike and Roll, 210 10th St.; 305-604-0001; http://segwaymiami.com).

Ocean Drive★★

Along this lively north-south boulevard bordering the Atlantic Ocean beats the heart of the SoBe scene. Locals and tourists lunch at shaded sidewalk cafes, while scantily clad youths streak by on in-line skates; nightfall brings revelers to some of Miami's hottest bars and dance clubs. Across the street lies lovely **Ocean Beach★★**, which offers a great **view★** of Ocean Drive and its pastel parade of Art Deco hotels: the seven-story blue-tinted **Park Central** (no. 640); the neon-lit **Colony** (no. 736); and the 11-story **The King & Grove Tides** (no. 1220). Located in **Lummus Park**, fronting the beach, is the Oceanfront Auditorium, which houses the **Art Deco Welcome Center** (305-672-2014; www.mdpl.org).

The Wolfsonian-FIU★★

1001 Washington Ave.
305-531-1001. www.wolfsonian.org.
The former Washington Storage Company building (1927, Robertson and Patterson) is distinguished by an elaborate gold-colored Moorish relief facade of cast concrete. Owned and operated by Florida International University, the building now houses a museum and research center that oversees more than 150,000 works of American and

European art and design dating from 1851 to 1945. The museum devotes its fifth floor to a permanent collection of some 300 works that illustrate how design has been used to help people adjust to the modern world.

Seven blocks north at 111 Lincoln Road stands a striking new (2010) multi-story car park designed by Swiss-based firm Herzog & de Meuron.

Bass Museum of Art★

2121 Park Ave. 305-673-7530.
www.bassmuseum.org.
This landmark 1930 Art Deco structure was named after New York entrepreneur John Bass, who donated his art collection to the city of Miami Beach. The permanent collection includes European paintings from the 15C to 20C, with an emphasis on the **Dutch and Flemish Masters**; an outstanding display of 16C-19C **textiles**; as well as decorative arts. A new wing completed in 2002 by Japanese architect Arata Isozaki more than doubled the museum's size.

Collins Avenue★

One of the main traffic arteries in Miami Beach, Collins Avenue boasts such lauded 1940s Art Deco hotels as the **National** (no. 1677), the **Delano** (no. 1685) and the **Ritz Plaza** (no. 1701), with their squared, stepped-back facades and quirky central towers. Just beyond 44th Street rises the iconic **Fontainebleau** Miami Beach, a massive, 1,500-room hotel overlooking an exclusive stretch of waterfront homes known as Millionaire's Row.

ADDITIONAL SIGHT
The Fillmore Miami Beach at the Jackie Gleason Theater★

1700 Washington Ave. 305-673-7300. www.fillmoremb.com.
This concrete and glass block theater (1951) hosted comedian Jackie Gleason's popular TV series from 1964 to 1970; today it hosts music festivals and live shows from jazz musicians and flamenco dancers to the divas of soul. Look for Roy Lichtenstein's red-and-white-striped **Mermaid** on the south lawn.

Everglades National Park★★★

Renowned throughout the world, the vast "river of grass" known as the Everglades covers the southern end of the Florida peninsula. Everglades National Park is one of only a few American parks that enjoy status as a UNESCO World Heritage Site and as an International Biosphere Reserve. This immense subtropical wetland nurtures such diverse ecosystems as hardwood hammocks and mangrove swamps that harbormammals, reptiles and many bird species.

- **Michelin Map:** 584 S 15
- **Info:** 305-242-7700; www.nps.gov/ever.
- **Location:** The Everglades at the southern tip of mainland Florida.
- **Don't Miss:** The different ecosystems of this landscape.
- **Kids:** Will love nature in action, as seen from a tour of Shark Valley.

A BIT OF HISTORY

The Everglades is actually a slow-moving river—formed during the last Ice Age—which starts at Lake Okeechobee in south-central Florida and slopes south, where it drains into the Gulf of Mexico. Although this sheet of moving water is 50mi wide, it averages only 6in in depth. The fragile ecosystem of the Everglades was seriously compromised in the early 20C when Florida governor Napoleon Broward implemented a plan to divert water from the Glades to irrigate farmland and provide suburban drinking water.

In 1916 the tide of development was stemmed as the first Everglades preserve, **Royal Palm State Park**, was set aside. When 107,600 acres were added to its boundaries with the 1989 **East Everglades Expansion Act**, the 1.5-million-acre park became the third-largest national park in the continental US.

VISITOR INFORMATION

Everglades National Park is open daily year-round. Admission is $10/car for a seven-day pass. The southern (main) entrance, park headquarters and the **Ernest Coe Visitor Center** (40001 State Rd. 9336; 305-242-7700; www.nps.gov/ever) are 11mi southwest of Homestead, FL, some 45mi south of Miami International Airport via Rte. 821. The northern entrance and **Shark Valley Visitor Center** (36000 SW 8th St., Miami; 305-221-8776) is 30mi west of Miami via US-41.

Winter is the best time to visit; daytime temperatures range from 60° to 80°F, mosquitoes are tolerable, and wildlife is easier to spot. During the **summer**, the rainy season (May–Oct), temperatures often soar to 95°F, and high humidity attracts clouds of biting insects (*bring insect repellent*). Parts of the park may close in summer due to flooding.

For maps, information facilities and recreational activities, contact **Park Headquarters**, 40001 State Road 9336, Homestead, FL 305-242-7700.

ACCOMMODATIONS

If you're planning a visit in the winter high season, make lodging and tour reservations several months in advance. **Campsites** are located at Long Pine Key and Flamingo. Permits are required (available at visitor centers) for **backcountry camping**. The **$ Hotel Redland** (5 S. Flagler Ave., Homestead, FL; 305-246-1904; www.hotelredland.com) has 13 rooms all bursting with character and reproduction Victorian furnishings. It's an historic property close to shops and restaurants.

Everglades Wildlife

One of the major wetlands left on this continent, the Everglades supports some 600 species of animals—including 350 types of birds, 60 species of mosquitoes and 26 kinds of snakes. The southern Everglades is the only place in the world to find both crocodiles and alligators. Only a few hundred **American crocodiles** inhabit the Glades' brackish mangrove inlets. Once a species with a poor prognosis for survival, the **alligator** has made a strong comeback in the park. These sluggish-looking reptiles can sprint at speeds nearing 15mph for distances of 50 yards. Birds provide the greatest spectacle in the park, with herons, egrets, ibis, cranes and **anhingas** almost always within sight. Bald eagles, ospreys and the small, endangered **snail kite** also make their home here. Florida's designated state animal, rare **Florida panthers** roam the Everglades' wetlands, the only habitat left for them in the eastern US. These big tawny cats avoid humans, and their nocturnal hunting habits make them difficult to spot.

Preserving the Everglades' ecosystem and managing its water flow has long been a critical issue, as human needs continue to encroach on conservation efforts. Championed by activists such as Florida journalist **Marjory Stoneman Douglas** (1890-1998), the Everglades have benefited from legislation that attempts to re-establish water flow and exterminate human-introduced natural enemies such as the water-consuming Australian Melaleuca tree) that threaten the Everglades' native vegetation.

SOUTHERN EVERGLADES

While you can see the park highlights in a day, the best way to experience the Everglades and its wildlife is to spend some time hiking its trails and boating on its waters. The southern entrance (on Rte. 9336) leads past designated stops along its 38mi course to Flamingo, the southern terminus of the park.

Pahayokee Overlook★★

This elevated platform provides a sweeping **view★★** of a seemingly end-less prairie of sawgrass, the Everglades' most dominant flora.

Flamingo

This small outpost overlooking Florida Bay has a park visitor center and pro-vides the only place to get food in the southern part of the park. Here nature lovers can take **wilderness cruises★★** that tour the backcountry canals and

the open waters of Florida Bay (depart from park visitor center; ☏239-695-2945).

NORTHERN EVERGLADES

Cutting across the Everglades, the Tami-ami Trail (US-41) links Miami with Naples on the west coast. The main entrance into the national park along this route is at Shark Valley. Coursing through the Everglades' western coastal region, the navigable **Wilderness Waterway** winds for 99mi from Flamingo to Everglades City. The park offers cruises of the **Ten Thousand Islands★★** (☏239-695-2591), affording visitors a look at the marine world of Chokoloskee Bay. Also within the scope of the northern Everglades are **Big Cypress National Preserve** (52mi west of Miami; accessible from US-41 & I-75), habitat of the endangered Florida panther, and **Fakahatchee Strand State Preserve★** (north of Everglades City; accessible from US-41 and Rte. 29).

Shark Valley★★

30mi west of Miami, entrance on south side of US-41. ☏305-221-8776.
Actually a basin lying a few feet lower than the rest of the Everglades, Shark Valley is named for the shallow, slow-flowing slough that empties into the brackish—and shark-infested—Shark River. The park's naturalist-led **tram tours★** (☏305-221-8455; www.sharkval-leytramtours.com) provide the best glimpse of the expansive landscape.

The Florida Keys★★

Curving southwest 220mi from Biscayne Bay to the Dry Tortugas, these thousand-plus islands scribe a narrow archipelago that separates the Atlantic from the Gulf of Mexico. Just 50mi south of Miami, the Keys are known for their laid-back atmosphere, enhanced by the diverse characteristics of the individual islands. Along the Overseas Highway (US-1), green mile-marker posts signal the locations of sights, giving distances from Key West.

- **Michelin Map:** 584 R, S 16
- **Info:** ℘305-451-4747 (Key Largo); ℘305-664-4503 (Middle Keys); ℘305-872-2411 (Lower Keys); www.fla-keys.com.
- **Location:** 50mi southwest of Miami, the Keys extend 220mi to the Dry Tortugas as an archipelago among the waters of the Atlantic, Florida Bay and the Gulf of Mexico.

A BIT OF HISTORY

In 1904 railroad magnate Henry Flagler launched plans to extend his Florida East Coast Railway from Miami to Key West. Known as the Overseas Railroad, the train first pulled into Key West in 1912. Though destroyed in 1935 by a hurricane that killed 400 people, the railroad literally paved the way for the Overseas Highway, completed in 1938 along the former railroad bed.

The **Upper and Middle Keys** serve as jumping-off points for anglers, divers, snorkelers and wildlife enthusiasts interested in the wealth of marine life that thrives on the offshore **Florida Reef Tract★★★**, the largest living coral-reef system in North American waters. Stretching 26mi in length, but only 1mi at its widest point, **Key Largo★** (MM 110) is the largest and northernmost in this chain of coral-rock isles. Below Key Largo (MM 85-MM 45), the **Middle Keys**—notably **Islamorada**—offer anglers such deep-sea trophies as sailfish, tarpon and marlin.

Spanning the distance from **Marathon** to the **Lower Keys, Seven-Mile Bridge★★** (MM 47-40), with its 288 135ft sections, ranks as the world's longest segmental bridge. Driving its length affords expansive **views★★** of blue-green waters.

Hemingway in Key West

One of Key West's legendary figures, novelist **Ernest Hemingway** (1899-1961) spent his most productive years on the island. Hemingway and his second wife, Pauline, wintered here in the late 1920s, and in 1931 they purchased a home in the town Hemingway dubbed "the St. Tropez of the poor." Here in Key West, the author cultivated his macho "Papa" image, spending his days writing, fishing and drinking with a coterie of locals. Hemingway's legacy continues to infuse the island, and is the impetus behind the annual **Hemingway Days** festival, held in conjunction with the writer's birthday (July 21).

Fans can visit the **Ernest Hemingway Home & Museum★★** (907 Whitehead St.; ℘305-294-1575; www.hemingwayhome.com), the gracious yellow stucco house where "Papa" wrote such classics as *Death in the Afternoon* (1932) and *For Whom the Bell Tolls* (1940) in his **studio★** above the carriage house. Other Hemingway landmarks include "Papa's" favorite hangout, **Sloppy Joe's Bar** (201 Duval St.), and **Blue Heaven** (729 Thomas St.), a former brothel (now a cafe) where Hemingway attended boxing matches.

A Key to Wildlife

The Keys provide visitors an opportunity to see and interact with a variety of wildlife. For a close-up view of the dazzling kaleidoscope of vivid coral and sea creatures—parrot fish, sea fans, sponges—on the offshore reef, rent gear at one of the many dive shops on Key Largo and try snorkeling or diving at **John Pennekamp Coral Reef State Park★★** (MM 102.5, Key Largo; △✖&🄿 ℘305-451-1202; www.pennekamppark.com). The park also offers glass-bottom boat tours of the reef (Coral Reef Park Co.; ℘305-451-6300). Another good place for underwater exploration is **Bahia Honda State Park** (MM 36.8, Bahia Honda Key; △✖🄿 ℘305-872-3210), which boasts one of the chain's largest stretches of sand **beach★★**—rarely found in the Keys.

Visitors can learn about dolphin behavior, socialization and physiology, and then interact with these playful mammals in a special program offered at the **Dolphin Research Center★** ♟♙ (MM 59, Grassy Key; &🄿 ℘305-289-1121; www.dolphins.org). And you can spot the smallest species of North American deer, the petite **Key Deer** (*Odocoileus virginianus clavium*), at the **National Key Deer Refuge★** (MM 30.5, Big Pine Key; ℘305-872-2239; www.fws.gov/nationalkeydeer).

KEY WEST★★★

Tourist information is available at the Key West Chamber of Commerce, 510 Greene St, ℘305-294-2587.

Pirates, wreckers, writers, US presidents and Cuban freedom fighters have at one time all found a haven on this small island at the southernmost tip of the continent. Closer to Havana, Cuba, than to Miami, Key West cultivates an atmosphere of sublime laissez-faire that appeals to artists, the gay community and droves of tourists who flock to the eateries, boutiques and bars on 14-block-long **Duval Street**, hub of the 200-square-block historic area known as Old Town.

Named *Cayo Hueso* ("Island of Bones") by Spanish explorer Ponce de León in 1513, Key West became the 19C headquarters for the lucrative enterprises of wrecking (finding sunken treasure from shipwrecks) and later, cigar-making. When Henry Flagler's Overseas Railroad reached its terminus at Key West in 1912, the town began its incarnation as a tourist resort. Writers Ernest Hemingway, Tennessee Williams and John Dos Passos, Cuban liberator José Martí, and President Harry Truman number among the notables drawn to Key West over the years.

Old Town★★

One of the largest National Historic Districts on the National Register, Old Town boasts diverse architecture, from simple wood-frame vernacular Conch houses and gingerbread-trimmed Victorians to imported Bahamian houses and gracious Classical Revival mansions built by transplanted New England seafarers in the 19C. One indigenous feature is the "**eyebrow**": this West Indian element designed to block the tropical sun consists of eaves that partly overhang second-story windows, resembling a brow over squinting eyes.

Though Old Town is easily navigated on foot, the narrated **Old Town Trolley tours** (℘305-296-6688) provide a good introduction to the area. At dusk, locals and visitors gather at **Mallory Square Dock** (behind Mallory Sq.) for the Key West ritual of watching the island's spectacular **sunsets★★**.

Key West Shipwreck Museum★

1 Whitehead St. in Mallory Square. ✖℘305-292-8990. www. keywestshipwreck.com.

The feel of a 19C dockside warehouse is evoked here as actors recount the thrills and hazards of the shipwreck salvage and recovery business. Exhibits fill two floors with items salvaged from the

Overseas Highway, Florida Keys

©PhotoDisc

wreck of the merchant ship *Isaac Allerton*, caught in a hurricane in 1856.

Facing the Shipwreck Museum, the **Key West Aquarium** 👥 (Whitehead St.; ♿ 🅿 ☎305-296-2051; www.keywestaquarium.com) allows visitors a look at some of the sea life found in the waters off the Keys. Don't miss the shark tank, or the opportunity to see rays and barracudas gliding about the outdoor pool.

Mel Fisher Maritime Museum★

200 Greene St. ♿ 🅿 ☎305-294-2633. www.melfisher.org.

Exhibits here chronicle the story of treasure-hunter Mel Fisher's 16-year search for the 1622 wreck of the Spanish galleon *Nuestra Señora de Atocha*. A video details the 1985 discovery of the *Atocha* and its mother lode—valued at more than $400 million—while displays on the first floor highlight the fabulous gold, silver, gems and other artifacts recovered from the dive site.

Harry S. Truman Little White House Museum★★

111 Front St., in Truman Annex. Entrance on right just past the corner of Front St. ♿ ☎305-294-9911. www.trumanlittlewhitehouse.com.

This large, unpretentious white clapboard home (1890) gives a rare glimpse into the private life of America's 33rd president, **Harry S Truman** (1884-1972). Prior to Truman, Thomas Edison had

lived here while working on his depth charge for the US Navy during World War I. Beginning with a sojourn to Key West in 1946, Truman spent his "working vacations" over the next seven years of his term in office at this former naval station duplex, which he called his "Little White House." While here, he ran the country from the **desk** that still sits in a corner of the living room.

San Carlos Institute

516 Duval St. ♿ ☎305-294-3887. www.institutosancarlos.org.

The roots of this 1924 Spanish Colonial structure date back to 1871, when it served as the hub of social and revolutionary activity for Cubans in Key West. Ground-floor displays focus on **José Martí** (1853-95), organizer of the second effort for Cuban independence.

EXCURSION
Dry Tortugas National Park★

⬭ 69mi west of Key West. Accessible only by boat or seaplane (☎305-296-5666, www.sunnydayskeywest.com; or ☎305-293-9300, www.keywestseaplanecharters.com). ⚠☎305-242-7700, www.nps.gov/drto.

Encompassing 100sq mi in the Gulf of Mexico, the park protects the cluster of reef islands known as the Dry Tortugas. One of these, Garden Key, is the site of **Fort Jefferson**, the largest coastal stronghold built by the US in the 19C.

Palm Beach★★

Occupying the northern part of a 16mi-long subtropical barrier island, this strip of real estate harbors one of the highest concentrations of multimillion-dollar mansions in the world. The picture-perfect island of palm-lined thoroughfares attracts streams of tourists—particularly in winter—who come to sample fine restaurants, stay in world-class hotels and shop along chic Worth Avenue.

> ▶ **Population:** 8,532.
> ⓖ **Michelin Map:** 584 S 15
> ▣ **Info:** ℰ561-233-3000; www.palmbeachfl.com.
> ⊛ **Don't Miss:** The luxurious Breakers Hotel.
> ⓞ **Timing:** Leave plenty of time (and money) for shopping. Worth Avenue rivals Chicago's Michigan Avenue and New York's Fifth Avenue.

A BIT OF HISTORY

Railroad magnate Henry Flagler proclaimed Palm Beach "a veritable paradise" in the late 19C when he was scouting a site for a new South Florida resort. Flagler's Royal Poinciana Hotel (now gone) opened in 1894, the same year his railroad made the town accessible from points north. Today, Flagler's indelible mark on the city is most apparent in The Breakers hotel and in Whitehall, his former home.

The growth of Palm Beach in the early 20C owes much to architect **Addison Mizner** (1872-1933), who gave the city its elegant look. Taking inspiration from Spanish Colonial manor houses and Italian Renaissance villas, Mizner designed estates with pink stucco walls, red-tile roofs and breezy loggias. His Mediterranean Revival style is exemplified in many of the two-story villas along swanky **Worth Avenue★★** (between Ocean Blvd. & Cocoanut Row), lined with pricey shops and delightful alleyways that thread off the avenue into courtyards graced by tilework fountains and tropical flowers. Among these, **Via Mizner★** stands out for its labyrinthine passages and pastel walls.

SIGHTS

The Breakers★★

1 S. County Rd. ✕ & ℰ561-655-6611. www.thebreakers.com.
The third incarnation of Henry Flagler's famous hotel (the first two, constructed of wood, were destroyed by fire) cost $6 million and took 75 Italian artisans and more than 1,200 craftsmen close to a year to build. The present grand hotel features belvedere towers with open arches, and a colonnaded porte cochere. The lobby runs the entire 200ft length of the center section with an 18ft-high vaulted ceiling. Behind the lobby, the **Florentine Dining Room** is adorned with a domed ceiling painted with frescoes and Italian pastoral scenes.

Flagler Museum★★

1 Whitehall Way, off Cocoanut Row.
✕ & ▣ ℰ561-655-2833.
www.flaglermuseum.us.
Built by **Henry Morrison Flagler** (1830-1913) as a wedding gift for his third wife, Mary Lily Kenan, **Whitehall** (1902, Carrère and Hastings) served as the Whitehall Hotel from 1925 to 1959.

Now a museum, the mansion is fronted by a landscaped walkway leading to a two-story verandah that spans the facade. Inside the mansion, now restored to its Flagler-era appearance with many of its original furnishings, **Marble Hall**, an imitation of a Roman villa's atrium, dazzles the eye with its masterful ceiling mural by Italian artist Benvenuti. Hung with Baccarat-crystal chandeliers, the **Louis XIV Music Room** was Kenan's favorite; the ornate **Ballroom** was used to entertain society's elite.

The second floor contains the Rococo-style **Master Suite** (dressed in yellow watered-silk damask) and 14 guest suites.

Norton Museum of Art★★

1451 S. Olive Ave., West Palm Beach.
✗&🅿 ℘561-832-5196.www.norton.org.
Founded in 1941 by steel tycoon Ralph
H. Norton (1875-1953), who wintered in
West Palm Beach, this museum boasts
a wonderful spectrum of some 7,000
works in its collections. Permanent
holdings place special emphasis on
19C-20C American (O'Keeffe, Homer,
Marin, Warhol, Pollock) and European
artists (Monet, Renoir, Matisse, Picasso,
Klee). A renowned **Chinese collection★**
encompasses tomb jades, ceramics and
ritual bronzes dating from as far back
as 1500 BC.

The serene **Ann Norton Sculpture Gardens** (253 Barcelona Rd.; ℘561-832-5328;
www.ansg.org) display the works of Norton's second wife.

Southern Gulf Coast★

Florida's southern Gulf Coast
stretches south from Sanibel and
Captiva Islands to the Ten Thousand
Islands that border Everglades
National Park. Life runs at a calmer
pace here, with smaller cities and
waters lapping gently on the shore.

A BIT OF HISTORY

Though Ponce de León and other 16C
Spanish explorers sailed along this
coast, they concentrated their attentions for the most part on Tampa Bay
and left the south-west coast to the
Calusa Indians. White settlement began
in the mid-19C and proceeded in fits
and starts until the turn of that century.
The railroad finally reached Naples in
1927, opening the way for sun seekers
to revel in the gulf's lovely beaches and
breathtaking sunsets.

NAPLES★

Basking on the gulf shore just north of
the Everglades, Naples has grown from
a fishing hamlet to a high-end city of
culture and fashion. Opportunities
abound here for fine dining, upscale
shopping and golfing.

Naples' historic downtown, **Old
Naples★** (5th Ave. S. & 3rd St. S.), offers
chic shops and restaurants on palm-
lined streets, as well as shaded courtyards perfect for sipping tea or taking
a respite from shopping. Numerous art
galleries line **Third Street South**; other

> 🅸 **Info:** ℘239-262-6141
> www.napleschamber.org
> (Naples); ℘239-472-1080,
> www.sanibel-captiva.
> org (Sanibel & Captiva).
> 😊 **Don't Miss:** Alligators at
> the J.N. "Ding" Darling
> National Wildlife Refuge.
> 🕓 **Timing:** This area can
> get hit during hurricane
> season (Jun–Nov).
> 👪 **Kids:** Nothing entertains kids
> like building a sand castle on
> the beach. Try Lowdermilk
> Park, a perfect public beach.

upscale shops can be found along **Fifth
Avenue South**. To see some of the city's
most luxurious beachfront homes, take
the **scenic drive★** along **Gulf Shore
Boulevard** south to Gordon Pass. Along
the way you'll pass popular **Lowdermilk
Park★** with its pristine public beach,
volleyball court and picnic area.

Located just west of Big Cypress
National Reserve, Naples makes a good
base for excursions to the Everglades
or to the **Ten Thousand Islands**, an
archipelago of islets that are covered
collectively with one of the largest mangrove forests in the world (cruises depart
from Everglades National Park Gulf Coast
Visitor Center on Rte. 29 in Everglades
City; ℘239-695-2591). At this chain's
northern end lies the popular resort of
Marco Island (from Naples take US-41
South to Rte. 951 West; www.marcoisland
chamber.org).

Shelling: A Popular Island Pastime

Combing Sanibel and Captiva beaches for the islands' bountiful cache of shells is a popular pastime. The islands' unusual east-west orientation acts as a natural catchment for the more than 200 species of mollusks that inhabit the Gulf of Mexico's shallow continental shelf. Arrive an hour before low tide, or after a northwesterly wind for the best finds. And keep an eye out for common varieties such as calico scallops, kitten's paws, fighting conchs and tiny coquina clams (taking live specimens is prohibited by state law). Lovely **Bowman's Beach** (3mi north of Ding Darling Refuge) and **Turner Beach** (at Blind Pass) are popular with beginning shellers. For those wishing to venture farther afield, a number of **shelling excursions** are also available (for information, contact the Sanibel-Captiva Islands Chamber of Commerce, 1159 Causeway Rd., Sanibel; 239-472-1080; www.sanibel-captiva.org).

SANIBEL AND CAPTIVA ISLANDS★★

Spanish explorers first discovered these lovely barrier islands, which arc 20mi into the Gulf of Mexico. Now a shell collector's paradise and winter resort in close proximity to Fort Myers, Sanibel and Captiva were slow to develop until the building of a causeway in 1963 linked them to the mainland. By the 1990s, the islands had become so popular that conservationists rallied to protect the land from unchecked development. One noteworthy result of their efforts, the "Ding" Darling National Wildlife Refuge, preserves more than one-third of Sanibel's total acreage and provides a haven for native species.

J.N. "Ding" Darling National Wildlife Refuge★★

1 Wildlife Dr., off Sanibel-Captiva Rd. & P 239-472-1100. www.fws.gov/dingdarling.

This pristine parcel of unspoiled land was narrowly preserved from real-estate development in the 1940s, thanks to the efforts of cartoonist and ardent conservationist "Ding" Darling. Today it's a showcase of barrier-island wildlife in canals, bogs, inlets, mangrove swamps and upland forests. Begin at the **visitor center**, where displays and videos offer insight into the natural history of the 6,300-acre refuge. For a glimpse of alligators and a host of water birds, including roseate spoonbills, egrets and great blue herons, take

the unpaved 5mi **Wildlife Drive**. Be sure to leave your car and meander along the 4mi of interpretive hiking trails, or paddle the 6mi of marked canoe courses. *Visitors can rent canoes and bicycles in the refuge. Guided canoe excursions, pontoon boat and tram tours are also available* (call Tarpon Bay Explorers; 239-472-8900; www.tarponbayexplorers.com).

EXCURSION
Edison and Ford Winter Estates★★

17mi northeast of Sanibel Island in Fort Myers. Take Rte. 867 (McGregor Blvd.) to no.2350. & P 239-334-7419. www.edisonfordwinterestates..org.

This riverside complex holds the winter homes and tropical gardens of inventor **Thomas Alva Edison** (1847-1931) and auto manufacturer **Henry Ford** (1863-1947). Edison built his spacious "Seminole Lodge" with its wide verandahs in Fort Myers in 1885. The house tour includes Edison's **laboratory** and the adjacent **Edison Museum**, chockablock with his inventions and displays about Ford and his life as well.

The grounds contain more than a thousand varieties of plants from around the world. After meeting at a conference in 1896, Edison and Ford forged a life-long friendship. In 1916 Ford bought a modest cottage on a piece of land adjacent to Edison's Florida home. The "Mangoes," as the two-story frame house was called, is furnished with reproductions in the Ford fashion.

Orlando Area

One of the most popular tourist destinations in the US, the Orlando area in central Florida attracts more than 50 million visitors annually. Best known as the home of Walt Disney World, the region also boasts the elaborate theme parks of Universal Studios, SeaWorld and a number of major corporate headquarters. Orlando itself, the state's largest inland city, serves as the region's hub.

Highlights

1 Sitting in the splash zone at **SeaWorld** marine shows (p488)

2 Closing the day with a **light show** at a theme park (p490)

3 Space Shuttle Atlantis at **Kennedy Space Center** (p495)

4 Lolling on the **beach**: Sarasota (p502) **and St. Pete** (p501)

Orlando

A Bit of History

Central Florida experienced its first influx of settlers—largely north Florida cattlemen who were attracted to the area's lush grasslands—after the end of the Second Seminole War in 1842. Forty years later, towns mushroomed along the line of Henry Plant's **South Florida Railway**. Railroad access encouraged tourism and other economic ventures, including lumbering and the naval stores industry.

After a killing frost in the 1890s, citrus farmers from northern Florida migrated south to this area, and the citrus industry burgeoned. The growth of tourism increased exponentially in the early 1970s with the opening of Walt Disney World, 20mi southwest of Orlando. The corridor stretching between the two, and south to **Kissimmee** (pronounced kiss-SIM-ee) quickly sprouted a host of commercial attractions hoping to ride on Disney's coattails. Orlando's central location provides easy access to the historic riches of St. Augustine (to the northeast), the Kennedy Space Center (east), culturally diverse Tampa Bay (southwest) and the arts scene of Sarasota on the Gulf Coast.

ADDRESSES

🛏 STAY

$$$$$ Disney's Grand Floridian Resort & Spa – 4401 Floridian Way, Lake Buena Vista, FL. ☏407-824-3000. www.disneyworld.com. 867 rooms. Disney's most luxurious property is a Victorian-era waterside resort set on 40 acres along the Magic Kingdom's monorail. The five-story lobby—with an aviary, carved moldings, and an open-cage elevator—is topped by illuminated stained-glass domes and metal scrollwork. Elegant guest rooms feature late-19C-style woodwork and old-fashioned sink fittings.

$$$$ Loews Don CeSar Hotel– 3400 Gulf Blvd., St. Petersburg Beach, FL. ☏727-360-1881. www.loewshotels.com. 277 rooms. A massive flamingo-pink sand castle towering off the St. Petersburg coast, the Don, built in 1928, recalls its jazz-age heyday—when F. Scott Fitzgerald was a regular—with crystal chandeliers and tropical gardens. Guest rooms are designed in Florida pastels and light woods. The hotel spa includes a rooftop garden.

$$$$ The Peabody Orlando – 9801 International Dr., Orlando, FL. ☏407-352-4000. www.peabodyorlando.com. 1,641 rooms. The modern outpost of

Memphis' original Peabody is situated in the Plaza International district and is linked to the convention center. Its palm-studded atrium lobby features a two-story waterfall. In keeping with tradition, the red carpet is rolled out twice a day for the resident ducks to march to the marble fountain.

$$$ Casa Monica Hotel – 95 Cordova St., St. Augustine, FL. ☎904-827-1888. www.casamonica.com. 138 rooms. Downtown's resurrected Medieval-style fort was built in 1888 as a winter getaway for America's top-tier families. Its regal features—gilded iron tables and chairs, columns and arches—will make you think you're in Moorish Spain. Designed with plush velvets and tapestry fabrics, accommodations exceed the expectations of yesteryear's monarchs. .

$$$ Longboat Key Beachfront Resort – 4711 Gulf of Mexico Dr., Longboat Key, FL. ☎941-383-2451. www.longboatkeyhilton.com. 102 rooms. Located offshore on a barrier island 12 miles west of Sarasota, this Hilton property sits on a white-sand beach offering views of gorgeous sunsets. The relative lack of close proximity to cultural attractions makes for a quieter, more relaxing getaway. Guests can enjoy the hotel pool as well as kayaking and other watersports close at hand.

$$$ Vinoy Rennaissance Resort – 501 Fifth Ave. N.E., St. Petersburg, FL. ☎727-894-1000. www.renaissancehotels.com. 361 rooms. Babe Ruth was among the elite group who wintered at downtown's opulent 1925 landmark. A 2002 renovation brought the salmon color back to its exterior, and restored the lobby's quarry-tile floors and stenciled cypress beams. Bedrooms are done in contemporary furnishings.

$$ The Courtyard at Lake Lucerne – 211 Lucerne Circle N.E., Orlando, FL. ☎407-648-5188. www.orlandohistoricinn.com. 30 rooms. Four historic residences (1893-1940) center on a tropical courtyard overlooking downtown Orlando's Lake Lucerne. Each one reflects the period of its heyday, from Victorian fabrics and sleigh beds to Art Deco suites. Breakfast is served on the verandah of the antebellum house.

⧎/ EAT

$$$$ Bern's Steak House – 1208 S. Howard Ave., Tampa, FL. ☎813-251-2421. www.bernssteakhouse.com. **American.** Hyde Park's 40-year-old landmark offers meat connoisseurs six cuts of aged US prime beef, from chateaubriand to T-bone, served with garlic butter and baked potatoes. The encyclopedic wine list boasts more than 6,800 entries. Gilded plaster columns, red wallpaper and vineyard murals set the mood.

$$ White Wolf Cafe – 1829 N. Orange Ave., Orlando, FL. Closed Sun dinner. ☎407-895-9911.www.whitewolfcafe.com. **American.** A breezy, Bohemian atmosphere, packed with antiques, welcomes hungry visitors to choose from an incredibly varied menu encompassing tasty breakfasts (lobster omelet, fluffy French toast), hearty lunches and excellent fresh seafood and pizza.

Shrek 4-D, Universal Studios Florida

Orlando★★★

Once a sleepy agrarian area filled with citus groves, the sprawling metropolitan Orlando region ranked among the nation's fastest-growing cities through the last half of the 20C. It's also a tourist mecca, of course. While the southwestern corridor is filled with malls, hotels, restaurants and entertainment parks, the older downtown area retains the charm of early 20C Florida in its historic architecture.

▶ **Population:** 9,562.
⚲ **Michelin Map:** p472
▯ **Info:** ☏407-363-5872; www.visitorlando.com.
◉ **Don't Miss:** The non-Disney attractions in this city known for Mickey Mouse.
👥 **Kids:** Wizarding World of Harry Potter is a delight for the whole family.

A BIT OF HISTORY

In 1824 swampy Mosquito County stretched southward from St. Augustine and westward to Alachua County, encompassing the 2,558sq mi of land that today defines the Orlando metropolitan area. Some 700 settlers inhabited Mosquito County when the Second Seminole War broke out near Ocala in 1835. To protect the area's pioneers, the US government established several forts in the county, including **Fort Gatlin**, built in 1838. After hostilities ended in 1842, the Fort Gatlin settlement formed the nucleus of the future city of Orlando.

In the early 19C, cattle and cotton reigned as the major moneymakers in central Florida. Citrus was introduced as a major crop in the 1870s when the new South Florida Railway provided access to wider markets. Despite the financial havoc wreaked by two disastrous freezes in 1894–95, Orlando rebounded into a thriving agricultural town by the early 20C. Its economy remained rooted in agriculture until 1965, when **Walt Disney**—animated-film wizard and creator of California's Disneyland—announced his plans to build a new theme park here.

Overnight, land values in the area skyrocketed. During the remainder of the 1960s, development engulfed the southwestern part of the city. Walt Disney World opened to great fanfare in 1971. SeaWorld followed two years later, and Universal Studios joined the local theme-park ranks in 1990. Since Walt Disney World's inauguration, metropolitan Orlando has tripled in population. The area currently ranks as one of the world's top commercial tourist destinations and boasts the second-largest concentration of hotel rooms in the US.

DOWNTOWN AREA

Since Orlando's incorporation in 1875, Downtown has been the city's administrative hub. Revitalized in the late 20C, an eight-square-block core, designated the **Orlando Downtown Historic District** centers on **Orange Avenue★**. North of Downtown, Lock Haven Park encompasses several cultural institutions.

Orlando Museum of Art★

2416 N. Mills Ave., in Loch Haven Park. ♿▯ ☏407-896-4231. www.omart.org. The permanent collection is rotated in four large contemporary galleries. More than 600 works of 19C and 20C **American art** include paintings by John Singer Sargent, George Inness, Maurice Prendergast, and Gene Davis. The African collection features Yoruba beadwork, Asante statuary and Benin metalwork.

👥 Orlando Science Center★

777 E. Princeton St., in Loch Haven Park. ✕♿▯ ☏407-514-2000. www.osc.org. This cylindrical building with its four-story central atrium has five interactive display areas on four levels, covering subjects from Florida ecosystems to computer technology. KidsTown and the Science Park Gallery are chockablock with hands-on exhibits. The **Crosby**

Observatory houses one of Florida's largest refractor telescopes.

UNIVERSAL ORLANDO★★★

👤👤 6000 Universal Blvd. Take I-4 to Exit 75A (from the east or from Orlando International Airport) or 74B (from the west); follow signs to Universal Orlando's main parking garage or the park's three hotels. ✕🚹🅿 ✆407-363-8000. www.universalorlando.com.

Formerly a single theme park and working movie studio, Universal Studios expanded its focus (and its name) in 1999 with an impressive new theme park, **Universal Studios Islands of Adventure**, home to some of the wildest roller coasters in Orlando. "Islands" is linked to **Universal Studios Florida** (the original park), by way of **Universal Studios CityWalk**, a dining, entertainment and shopping complex. CityWalk is designed as a two-tiered, 30-acre promenade of individually themed entertainment venues wrapped around a four-acre harbor.

Highlights include jazz, rock and reggae nightclubs (Jimmy Buffett's Margaritaville is a perennial favorite); live-performance venues (the Blue Man Group has set up shop here); and a variety of restaurants, including Emeril's Restaurant Orlando and the world's largest Hard Rock Cafe. Three resort hotels, including the first-ever Hard Rock Hotel, and more studio production space have nearly tripled the size of the park.

Universal Studios Florida★★★

The original 444-acre theme park and working studio (with nine soundstages), Universal Studios Florida ranks as the largest motion-picture and television facility outside Hollywood. Created as a park where visitors can "ride the movies," it bases its attractions on popular films and television shows.

Taking in all the shows and rides requires an entire day (plan to arrive 30 min to 1hr prior to opening time). Head for thrill rides first and see shows during midday, when ride lines are longest. The Express Plus Pass and the VIP Studio Tour (reservations required) give visitors

priority entrance to leading attractions (✆407-363-8295). Over 20 rides, shows and attractions here will keep you amused for the entire day. From activities for kids of all ages (**A Day in the Park with Barney** and **Fievel's Playland**) to live shows and action movies enhanced by multisensory special effects (**Twister! Ride It Out** and **Shrek 4-D**) to thrill rides and coasters bumped up with cinematic special effects (**Hollywood Rip Ride Rockit** and **Revenge of the Mummy**) the park guarantees fun and excitement for children and adults alike. Newly opened in 2013 are the immersive rides **Despicable Me Minion Mayhem** and **TRANSFORMERS: The Ride 3-D**.

Universal Studios Islands of Adventure★

Cutting-edge rides and attractions in this thrill-packed park are organized on five themed islands around a lagoon. Characterized by a unique and eclectic architecture representing a variety of international cultures, **Port of Entry** is principally a shopping and dining area. **Seuss Landing** features the whimsical characters of the late children's writer Theodor "Dr. Seuss" Geisel in rides like the **Cat in the Hat**, plus an interactive playland, **If I Ran the Zoo**. **Toon Lagoon** brings cartoon characters like Popeye, Rocky and Bullwinkle to life; prepare for a drenching as you help Dudley save Nell on the thrilling flume ride **Dudley Do-Right's Ripsaw Falls**. Realistic dinosaurs stalk visitors at **Jurassic Park** (the **River Adventure** is a favorite here), while high-tech thrill rides are the main attractions of **The Lost Continent** and **Marvel Super Hero Island**; the latter is home to some of the park's most popular attractions, including the 3-D **Amazing Adventures of Spider-Man** and **The Incredible Hulk Coaster**.

Rides, shows and shops in the recently opened **Wizarding World of Harry Potter** transport visitors to the village of Hogsmeade and Hogwarts Castle, where wizards-in-training get to join our hero on **Harry Potter and the Forbidden Journey**. An expansion scheduled for 2014 will introduce Diagon

Alley, with new rides, restaurants and shops.

🧑‍🤝‍🧑 SEAWORLD ORLANDO★★★

7007 Sea World Dr. Main entrance on Central Florida Pkwy.; take I-4 to Exit 71 (from the west) or exit 72 (from the north) and follow signs to park entrance. ✕♿ 🅿 𝒫407-351-3600. www.seaworld.com. This 200-acre marine adventure park mixes entertainment and education in its numerous animal shows, touch pools and aquariums. Opened in 1973, the park is one of three SeaWorlds nationwide, which together support one of the world's largest collections of marine life. From the park entrance, an elliptical maze of walkways is dotted with pools, aquarium tanks and other habitats displaying tropical fish, sharks, stingrays, turtles, penguins and manatees.

Marine Mammal Shows

The main attractions at SeaWorld are its ever-popular shows featuring trained sea creatures and staged in specially constructed theaters and stadiums. (*Check schedules when you arrive and plan your visit around show times.*)
One Ocean, SeaWorld's all-new Shamu show, stars the five-ton orca Shamu and his protégés, who leap and twirl to music in a wholesome water ballet staged in a three-story set. **Blue Horizons** combines the talents of trained dolphins, whales, birds and stunt actors in a spectacular cutting-edge theatrical presentation. In 2013, the park opened the doors to the largest attraction in its history: **Antarctica: Empire of the Penguin**, a combination of family rides and exploration of a penguin colony.

Thrill Rides

On **Journey to Atlantis**, a high-speed water coaster carries passengers through dark passageways, and down a nearly vertical 60ft waterfall. The flying coaster **Manta** seamlessly blends thrills with face-first animal encounters. **Wild Arctic** takes passengers on a virtual-reality helicopter ride over a northern landscape featuring above- and below-water

views of beluga whales, polar bears, walruses and harbor seals. And the **Kraken**, a floorless monster coaster, is one of the fastest rides of its kind in Orlando.

🧑‍🤝‍🧑 Aquatica★

5800 Water Play Way, across the street from SeaWorld. ✕♿🅿 𝒫888-800-5447. http://aquaticabyseaworld.com. SeaWorld's water park is a collection of water slides, pools and animal encounters. The crowd favorite is the Dolphin Plunge, which sends visitors down an enclosed tube slide through an underwater realm populated by a pod of black-and-white Commerson's dolphins.

🧑‍🤝‍🧑 DISCOVERY COVE★★

6000 Discovery Cove Way (International Dr.) adjacent to SeaWorld. ✕♿🅿 𝒫877-434-7268. www.discoverycove.com. Up close and personal animal encounters are the focus of this 30-acre marine park, where visitors can swim and snorkel around a coral reef; walk through a net aviary to pet hundreds of colorful birds; float along a lazy river on an inner tube; or lollygag on the beach. For most visitors, the highlight is the 45min trainer-guided interaction with a bottlenose dolphin at Dolphin Lagoon, including a supervised and safe dolphin ride.

EXCURSION
🧑‍🤝‍🧑 LEGOLAND Florida

▶ 47mi south of Orlando in Winter Haven at 1 LEGOLAND Way. 𝒫877-350-5346. www.legoland.com. Check website for hours and prices. Built on the former site of the **Cypress Gardens** botanical garden and theme park, this 150-acre tribute to the famous building blocks is especially entertaining for the 10 years-and-under set. The park is divided into 11 sections and includes more than 50 rides, shows, and attractions. Fortunately, the gardens were preserved and remain a key draw. Other highlights include: **The Factory Tour**, where kids can see the colorful pieces being made from beginning to end; **Miniland USA**, comprised of miniature Lego replicas of American cities; and **LegoLand Water Park**.

Walt Disney World®★★★

Located 20mi southwest of Orlando, this immense 47sq mi complex encompasses four extensive theme parks; Magic Kingdom, Epcot, Disney's Animal Kingdom and Disney's Hollywood Studios. The four combine the romantic nostalgia of Disney's mid-20C vision with today's technology. In addition, 25 separate resort hotels—with nightclubs, water parks, five 18-hole golf courses and a 255-acre sports complex—enhance the world's most visited theme park.

Info: ℰ407-824-4321 https://disneyworld.disney,go,com.

Parking: Shuttle buses and trains will take you from one park to another: no need to drive.

Don't Miss: The movie-themed rides at Disney's Hollywood Studios.

Timing: Days at the theme parks are tiring. Plan enough days to get everything in and have time for afternoon naps.

Kids: Disney character meet-and-greets: the thrill of a lifetime.

A BIT OF HISTORY

Born in Chicago, **Walter Elias Disney** (1901-66) showed early signs of a keen imagination and an aptitude for drawing—talents that would be key to his career. Disney was operating an animation studio in Kansas City, when, at the age of 22, Walt and his brother Roy left to establish the Disney Brothers Studios in Hollywood, California. Their studio scored its first hit in 1928 with *Steamboat Willie*, starring a character named Mickey Mouse. In 1937, *Snow White*, Disney's first feature-length animated film, was met with instant success.

More than a decade later, disillusioned with the tawdriness of existing amusement parks, Disney began planning his own in Anaheim, California. Inaugurated in 1955, Disneyland changed the face of global amusement. Disney launched plans in 1965 to open a second park on nearly 30,000 acres of land in central Florida.

Disney envisioned this property as an **Experimental Prototype Community of Tomorrow** (Epcot), a place that would function as a model for future communities and highlight the creativity behind American industry. However, as construction began, the renowned cartoonist died in 1966. In deference to his brother, Roy Disney named the Florida complex Walt Disney World,

preserving Walt's concept for the park. In 1971 Magic Kingdom opened, followed by Epcot in 1982, and seven years later by Disney-MGM Studios (now Disney's Hollywood Studios)—a combination working film studio and theme park. Animal Kingdom was added in 1998. The immensely popular Disney concept has also been exported abroad. In 1983 Tokyo Disneyland was launched, followed in 1992 by Disneyland Paris and Disneyland Hong Kong in 2005.

▲▲ MAGIC KINGDOM★★★

The 107-acre Magic Kingdom includes six areas—Main Street, U.S.A., Tomorrowland, Fantasyland (which is currently undergoing the largest expansion in park history), Liberty Square, Frontierland and Adventureland—radiating out from the Central Plaza in front of Cinderella Castle. Shops, eateries, attractions and costumed "cast members" (ride attendants, shopkeepers and other staff) in each area echo the dominant theme of their "land."

Magic Kingdom is the most popular of the four parks and the most time-consuming to access. Thrill rides—Space Mountain, Splash Mountain and Big Thunder Mountain Railroad—along with the ever-popular Pirates of the Caribbean, attract the greatest crowds; head for them first. Tidy Vic-

GETTING THERE

BY AIR - Orlando International Airport (MCO): ☏407-825-2001; www.orlandoairports.net. 28mi northeast of Walt Disney World. Airport information booths located in main lobby of airport and in third-level atrium. Mears Motor Shuttle provides shuttle service to Walt Disney World (departs from baggage claim area; $21/one-way; ☏407-839-1570; www.mearstransportation.com). Limo and taxi service is also available. Rental car agencies are located at the airport. If you are driving from Orlando airport, take the Beeline Expressway/Rte. 528 West (toll), then continue on I-4 West and follow signs to individual parks.

BY BUS AND TRAIN - Amtrak train station: 1400 Sligh St., Orlando (24mi from park), ☏800-872-7245, www.amtrak.com. **Greyhound/Trailways bus** stations: 555 N. McGruder Blvd., Orlando (26mi from park), and 103 E. Dakin Ave., Kissimmee (16mi from park); ☏800-231-2222; www.greyhound.com.

BY CAR - Walt Disney World is located 20mi southwest of downtown Orlando. Take I-4 West to Exit 67 for best access to Epcot, Typhoon Lagoon, Downtown Disney, River Country and Discovery Island. To reach Disney's Animal Kingdom, Wide World of Sports, take Exit 65 (Rte. 192) West, and follow signs. For Disney's Hollywood Studios and Magic Kingdom, take Exit 64. Trams shuttle visitors to the main gates from pick-up areas throughout the parking lots.

GETTING AROUND

Monorail trains, buses, ferries and water taxis (all free) link all attractions, including hotels and resorts, throughout the complex. Buses operate approximately every 20min, from one hour prior to the park opening until closing. Bus routes painted in red are direct after 4pm, with the exception of service to Magic Kingdom, Epcot and Disney's Hollywood Studios from Disney's Old Key West Resort and the Disney Institute, which operates on scheduled pick-up times between noon and 6pm.

VISITOR INFORMATION

Disney parks are open year-round daily 9am-9pm, with some parks staying open until 11pm during peak season; Animal Kingdom is open dawn to dusk. Hours vary seasonally; call for information ☏407-824-4321. △✗♿🅿 For general information and to request a free Vacation Guide, contact Walt Disney World Guest Information, P.O. Box 10000, Lake Buena Vista FL 32830-0040, ☏407-939-6244, www.disneyworld.com. For visitor services (foreign-language maps, information for guests with disabilities, baby facilities, storage lockers, banking facilities, camera centers and information about Disney character greetings), see Guest Relations at individual parks: City Hall, Main Street, USA at Magic Kingdom; near Gift Stop at Epcot; Hollywood Boulevard at Disney's Hollywood Studios; and next to Creature Comfort at Animal Kingdom.

torian storefronts holding commercial shops re-create the milieu of an early 19C town on **Main Street, U.S.A.** During the summer and Christmas holidays, the nighttime parade of lights fills the street each evening.

Disney's "fantasy future city" of **Tomorrowland** is the location of the favorite thrill ride **Space Mountain**, a roller coaster that hurtles passengers through near-darkness. **Fantasyland** is the most popular area in all Walt Disney World. With its rides based on Disney's animated feature films, Fantasyland centers on the 189ft-high **Cinderella Castle**—a Gothic extravaganza ornamented with turrets, towers and gold spires. The expansion of this area ush-

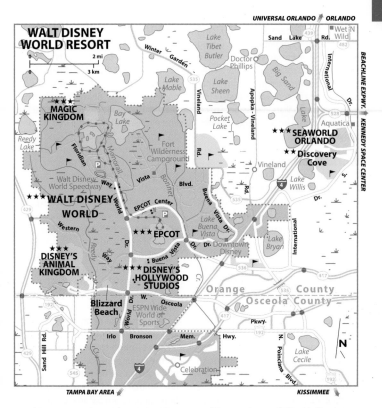

ered in two new themed areas in 2013: the Enchanted Forest, inspired by The Little Mermaid and Beauty and the Beast, and Storybook Circus, inspired by *Dumbo*. The Old West lives on in the wooden walkways, country stores and saloon of **Frontierland**. Inside the ever-popular **Splash Mountain**, riders board dugouts and careen down the mountain to a soaking splash. The **Big Thunder Mountain Railroad** rollercoaster negotiates a terrain of hoodoos, caves and canyons. **Adventureland** features one of the most beloved amusement park rides ever created, **Pirates of the Caribbean**. Here visitors board boats for a cruise through a darkened swamp to a Caribbean village, where they drift past sets peopled with lifelike buccaneers, pigs, parrots and more.

EPCOT★★★

The 300-acre Epcot is divided into two distinct areas: Future World, housing pavilions devoted to technology and ingenuity, and World Showcase, where the culture and architecture of 11 nations are represented. The Future World complex celebrates American industry and serves as a "showcase for new ideas," as Disney intended. The Living with the Land Epcot Seas pavilions function as working research centers as well as attractions.

Future World

Encircling the 180ft-high, faceted geo-sphere that symbolizes Epcot, nine large pavilions house rides, interactive display areas and films, all saluting humankind's ingenious technological achievements.

Spiral up 18 stories in a time machine vehicle inside Epcot's giant landmark sphere, **Spaceship Earth**, where you'll ride past animated scenes depicting the history of human communication from prehistoric tribes to present-day technology. Then go on to explore **The Seas with Nemo and Friends**, a

5.7-million-gallon aquarium, and **Living With the Land**, an enormous working greenhouse. In Future World you'll also soar over California in a simulated hang glider in **Soarin'**, design and drive your own virtual concept car at **Test Track**, train for a trip to Mars in **Mission: Space**, and journey into **ImageWorks**, an interactive funhouse.

World Showcase

The 1.3mi promenade at World Show-case circles a 40-acre lagoon and passes the pavilions of 11 different countries (including Mexico, Norway, China, Germany and Morocco). Each pavilion—staffed by natives of the country it represents—reflects the architecture, foods, crafts, costumes and traditions of that culture. The Norway pavilion includes **Maelstrom**, which plunges riders through treacherous northern seas; other pavilions screen films in a CircleVision 360 Theater or feature multi-media presentations.

Located in front of the American Adventure pavilion, the **America Gardens Theatre** hosts a variety of live outdoor stage shows. In the evenings, World Show-case lagoon and pavilions become the setting for an extravaganza of laser lights, music, fountains and fireworks.

👥 DISNEY'S ANIMAL KINGDOM★★★

Disneyworld's latest park is devoted to the natural world: animals living and extinct. The largest animal theme park in the world, Animal Kingdom has placed 1,700 animals (of 250 species) and 4 million plants (of 3,000 species) on more than 500 acres of land. Here, visitors can move from colorful parades to a re-created African savanna, from sophisticated rides and exhibits to primitive native villages. Moreover, visitors can meet with animal-behavior experts, monitor animal-care facilities and learn about the depletion of world rain forests and grasslands.

Animal Kingdom extends in four directions from its hub **Discovery Island**, a tropical artists' colony occupying a man-made riverine island around the 145ft **Tree of Life**.

A delightful cast of animated insects and arachnids inhabits the 3-D experience **It's Tough to Be a Bug** (look out for the termite sneeze).

In the **Africa** section of the park you'll find Animal Kingdom's leading attraction, **Kilimanjaro Safaris**. On this ride, open-sided all-terrain trucks carry passengers down a twisting dirt road, across river fords to the grasslands of the Serengeti Plain. Here, travelers can

Big Thunder Mountain Railroad® attraction

© Disney

observe rhinoceroses, elephants, lions, cheetahs, zebras, and other residents of the savanna.

The **Asia** area centers on a rural Asian village set amid rainforest vegetation. Departing from here, the **Maharajah Jungle Trek** winds past decaying temple ruins and allows passengers a glimpse of Bengal tigers and Komodo dragons roaming without apparent barriers. **Kali River Rapids** combines a white-water thrill ride with an environmental theme. And **Expedition Everest** takes you on a careening train ride through the Himalayas.

Constructed to resemble a paleontological research camp, **DinoLand U.S.A.** appeals mostly to the elementary-school set. In the popular ride **Dinosaur**, visitors journey back to late Cretaceous times along a twisting and bumpy route, where riders dodge nine different species of Audio-Animatronics® dinosaurs and narrowly escape meteoric disaster.

Interactive demos and high-tech exhibits of animal behavior are the focus in **Rafiki's Planet Watch**, where a petting zoo and animal surveillance cameras express the conservation message.

👥 DISNEY'S HOLLYWOOD STUDIOS★★★

This 154-acre theme park/studio celebrates the magic of filmmaking, from animation and stuntsmanship to adventure and romance. The attractions include rides, film performances and live shows that explain behind-the-scenes moviemaking. As a working studio, Disney's Hollywood Studios produces scores of television shows and Disney animated films.

The least crowded of the four parks, this one also has a more compact design for an easier visit. Like elsewhere, thrill rides and newest attractions tend to have the longest lines. Head for Tower of Terror, Star Tours, and the **Rock 'n' Roller Coaster Starring Aerosmith** first. Lined with palm trees and sleek Art Deco buildings filled with commercial shops, **Hollywood Boulevard** opens onto a central plaza next to a replica of the former Grauman's Chinese Theatre in Los Angeles.

Visitors can take a trip through the celluloid classics on **The Great Movie Ride**, explore the wonders of the animation process at **The Magic of Disney Animation**, or take the pirate's oath and embark on a sea adventure with **The Legend of Captain Jack Sparrow**. The inner workings of filmmaking are revealed on the **Backlot Tour**, and the mysteries of movie stunts are unraveled in **Indiana Jones Epic Stunt Spectacular.** Visitors can audition to take the stage at the **American Idol Experience,** or serve as a judge in deciding who among the hopefuls stays and who goes.

At the end of Sunset Boulevard looms the Hollywood Tower Hotel, where guests travel back in time in **The Twilight Zone Tower of Terror** ride. Based on an episode from the popular 1960s television series The Twilight Zone, the ride culminates in a 13-story plunge in the old service elevator. The futuristic thrill ride **Star Tours** takes travelers on a simulated high-speed voyage to the Moon of Endor.

ADDRESSES

🏨 STAY

Walt Disney World complex offers more than 27,000 rooms at 25 properties including resort hotels, villas, condominiums, cabins and campgrounds. Rates vary by season and property. For all reservations, call ☎407-934-7639.

OUTSIDE THE DISNEY COMPLEX
Numerous lodgings, ranging from luxury to budget, lie within a 5-10min drive of the main entrances. Many offer free shuttle service to Disney attractions. Make reservations 3 to 5 months in advance, especially for summer and holidays.

For further Information, contact the **Orlando/Orange County Convention and Visitors Bureau**, 6700 Forum Dr., Suite 100, Orlando FL 32821, ☎407-363-5872, www.visitorlando.com.

Kennedy Space Center★★★

Protruding from Florida's Atlantic coast, Merritt Island is home to the nation's space program. Every US rocket, from the one that carried the Explorer I satellite in 1958 to modern space shuttles, has blasted off from here or from adjoining Cape Canaveral. Opened to the public in 1966, the Kennedy Space Center Visitor Complex, Florida's fourth-largest tourist attraction, receives more than 1.5 million visitors a year.

- ♿ **Michelin Map:** 584 S 14
- 🚹 **Info:** ℰ321-449-4444; www.kennedyspacecenter.com.
- 🅿 **Parking:** Leave the car in the parking lot and take one of the bus tours.
- 👁 **Don't Miss:** The Merritt Island National Wildlife Refuge.
- 👪 **Kids:** Touch a piece of genuine moon rock at the Apollo/Saturn V Center.

A BIT OF HISTORY

The National Aeronautics and Space Administration (NASA) was founded in 1958 and charged with the mission of space exploration. In May 1961, President John F. Kennedy challenged the nation "to achieve the goal, before the decade is out, of landing a man on the moon and returning him safely to Earth." Based on Kennedy's speech, the press soon declared a "space race" between the two Cold War superpowers, and NASA began buying land on Merritt Island for its main launch facility. In 1963 the US Fish and Wildlife Service gained management of the 95 percent of land not needed by NASA and created the **Merritt Island National Wildlife Refuge★★** (4mi east of Titusville on Rte. 402; ℰ407-861-0667; www.fws.gov/merrittisland) as a haven for migratory waterfowl.

Between 1961 and 1966, the Mercury and Gemini programs captured the world's attention. In 1961 Alan Shepard became the first American in space. The following year, John Glenn was the first US astronaut to orbit the earth. In 1965 Edward White walked in space, another first. Kennedy's goal was accomplished on 20 July 1969, when Neil Armstrong and Buzz Aldrin became the first humans to walk on the moon.

NASA's answer to a reduction in funding in the late 1970s was a fleet of reusable space shuttles, which formed the centerpiece of the space program from the maiden voyage of *Columbia* in 1981 to the final mission in 2011. NASA continues its participation in the **International Space Station** research facility,

Apollo/Saturn V Center

©VISIT FLORIDA

Watching a Rocket Launch

To obtain a launch schedule, consult www.spacecoastlaunches.com or www.kennedyspacecenter.com for up-to-the-second information and current and projected launch status. Tickets for launch viewing go on sale approximately four to six weeks prior to the launch date and may be purchased at the Kennedy Space Center website or in person at the Kennedy Space Center Visitor Complex Ticket Pavilion. For updated information, call ✆866-737-5235.

a combined effort with Russia, Canada, Japan and the 14 member nations of the European Space Agency. NASA's long-range plans call for a permanent lunar base and a manned mission to Mars.

VISIT

♿Hwy. 405 between Range Rd. and East Ave. SW, Orsino, FL.

Exhibits

Admission to the Visitor Complex includes all exhibits, IMAX films, bus tours and the **Astronaut Hall of Fame**. You'll also find an art gallery, playground, and the **Rocket Garden**, where eight rockets and other equipment are displayed.

You can speak with an astronaut at the **Astronaut Encounter**, and board a virtual space shuttle to experience the sensation of blasting into space in the simulated **Shuttle Launch Experience**. Across from the simulator, get up close to an awe-inspiring full-size replica of the space shuttle *Explorer*. In the two IMAX theaters, screens looming more than five stories high project compelling large-format **films★**, many in 3-D and featuring footage shot from space. Behind the IMAX theaters, the **Astronauts Memorial** is a moving tribute to astronauts who have made the ultimate sacrifice.

The newest attraction is the **Space Shuttle Atlantis**, a 90,000sq-ft exhibit in which the actual shuttle is breathtakingly displayed as if in mid-orbit and replete with scorch marks and space dust from its last mission.

Visitors can also experience more than 60 multimedia and simulator exhibits detailing the achievements of NASA's more than 30-year Space Shuttle program. Be sure not to miss the International Space Station Gallery or the Astronaut Training Simulators.

Bus Tours

Bus tours depart year-round daily every 15min. Special operations may alter tour itineraries.

The best way to visit the facility is the **Kennedy Space Center Tour★★** (2-4hrs). Buses first pass the 525ft-high **Vehicle Assembly Building** (VAB) where the shuttle is assembled.

At **Launch Complex 39**, visitors can climb an observation gantry. Here, a short video provides an overview of the beginnings of the space-flight era, and a second film replays the launching of *Apollo 8*, the first manned spaceship to orbit the moon.

Next, a stirring multimedia review of the Apollo series and an excellent movie about the *Apollo 11* mission culminate at the **Apollo/Saturn V Center** with a close-up inspection of a 363ft *Saturn V* moon rocket, one of three such rockets in the world.

In the **International Space Station Center**, visitors learn about the venture that is driving the space industry in the 21C.

Focusing on space-flight history, the **Cape Canaveral: Then and Now** tour takes in shuttle facilities and the ships that salvage rocket boosters. The tour includes a visit to complexes where the first manned space flights were launched.

Launch site of the first US satellite, the **Air Force Space and Missile Museum**, a 30min stop, offers an impressive array of rockets and historical artifacts.

St. Augustine★★★

The oldest continuously occupied European settlement in the US lies on Florida's east coast. Historic St. Augustine mingles one-story 18C structures with 19C architectural showpieces and 20C tourist attractions. Today "America's Oldest City" attracts more than 2 million visitors annually.

▶ **Population:** 13,407.
◉ **Michelin Map:** 584 R 13
▤ **Info:** ℘904-829-1711; www.floridashistoriccoast.com.
◈ **Don't Miss:** Castillo de San Marcos National Monument, the oldest masonry fort in the US.
▲ **Kids:** What kid could resist the St. Augustine Alligator Farm?

A BIT OF HISTORY

In 1565 Spanish explorer **Pedro Menéndez de Avilés** made landfall near present-day St. Augustine, charged by Philip II of Spain with obtaining a Spanish foot-hold in Florida. A 208ft stainless-steel cross today marks the spot where Menéndez and his men came ashore. Menéndez's chaplain celebrated the event by saying Mass, thus establishing the **Mission de Nombre de Dios★** (27 Ocean Ave.; ℘904-824-2809; www.missionandshrine.org), the first Catholic mission in the US. St. Augustine, the colony Menéndez built between the Matanzas and San Sebastián rivers, became the capital of Spanish Florida in 1587.

In the first half of the 17C, new French and English settlements along the coast to the north challenged Spain's tenuous foothold in Florida. To defend their city, the Spanish began construction on a massive coquina (stone formed from the sedimentation of seashells) fort, Castillo de San Marcos, which fended off Spain's enemies until 1763 when Spain relinquished possession of Florida to England in exchange for Cuba.

The British ruled St. Augustine for the next 20 years; in 1783 the terms of the Treaty of Paris gave Florida back to Spain. Unable to maintain economic independence, Spain ceded Florida to the US in 1819.

But it was tourism—ushered in by New York industrialist **Henry Morrison Flagler** (1830-1913)—that finally put St. Augustine on the map. By 1889 Flagler had linked the city to the rest of the East Coast via his Florida East Coast Railway and built a triumvirate of hotels. They attracted throngs of visitors. Today the city still relies on tourism as its eco-

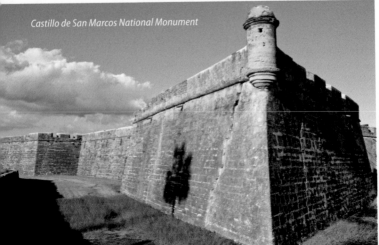

Castillo de San Marcos National Monument

© Terry J Alcorn/iStockphoto.com

nomic mainstay, capitalizing on its history and miles of beachfront.

SIGHTS

The **Visitor Center** (10 S. Castillo Dr., near San Marco Ave.; ☎904-825-1000) sells tickets for the **sightseeing trains** that tour the city daily. Some three dozen structures from the Spanish-Colonial period are preserved today, and bear witness to this historic city's long past.

Castillo de San Marcos National Monument★★★

1 S. Castillo Dr. ☎904-829-6506. www.nps.gov/casa.

Defender of St. Augustine since the beginning of the 18C, the oldest masonry fort in the US stolidly overlooks Matanzas Bay at the northern boundary of the old city. The increasing threat from English and French forces, coupled with a pirate raid in 1668 that left St. Augustine a smoldering ruin, convinced Spanish officials in Madrid that the city needed a permanent stone fortification. By 1695 the four-sided coquina rock fortress was largely complete: pointed triangular bastions formed each corner of the structure's 12ft-thick outer walls. The Castillo withstood every enemy attack that beset it, including an attack by English general James Moore in 1702. In 1924 the fort was designated a national monument, and today ranks among the best-preserved examples of Spanish colonial fortifications in the New World.

Ranger talks and audiovisual presentations provide an introduction to the Castillo's long history. Afterward, you can explore the fort and climb the staircase to the **gundeck**, outfitted with some of the Castillo's original cannons and mortars. The panoramic **view** of the Matanzas River from here demonstrates the ease with which sentries could monitor an intruder's approach.

After visiting the fortress, stroll down **St. George Street**. This city backbone retains its historic flavor despite a host of gift shops, craft boutiques and restaurants. The **St. Photios National Greek Orthodox Shrine★** (no. 41;

☎904-829-8205; www.stphotios.com) resides in the former Avero House. At number 143, the **Peña-Peck House★** (☎904-829-5064; www.penapeckhouse.com) was erected in the 1740s but was many times renovated and expanded; it operates today as a house museum.

Colonial Spanish Quarter★★

33 St. George St. ☎904-342-2857. www.colonialquarter.com.

Behind a low wall, the heart of colonial St. Augustine beats on in a living-history museum dedicated to re-creating the 18C city. Based on historical and archaeological research, eight structures have been rebuilt here, including the dwellings of a foot soldier, an artilleryman and a calvalryman.

Upon entering through Florencia House, visitors can explore St. Augustine's grassy "streets." Costumed guides demonstrate spinning, carpentry, basketry and other daily activities of 18C life. Don't miss the **De Mesa-Sanchez House★**, one of the city's fine restored historic residences.

Cathedral-Basilica of St. Augustine★★

North side of Plaza de la Constitución. ☎904-824-2806. www.thefirstparish.org.

The scalloped facade and tower gracing the north side of the Plaza de la Constitución mark the home of the parish of St. Augustine. Founded in 1565 at the first Mass said upon Pedro Menéndez's landing, this cathedral ranks as the nation's oldest Catholic parish. After an 1887 fire destroyed all but the walls and facade of this church (originally constructed in 1793), noted architect James Renwick aided in the reconstruction, enlarging the structure and adding a transept and a bell tower.

Government House Museum★

48 King St. ☎904-825-5034. www.staugustine.ufl.edu.

Throughout 400 years of existence, this stately, two-story masonry edifice has retained its official purpose. Now

Florida's resident reptile

restored to its 1764 appearance, Government House holds colorful displays that document the city's development.

Lightner Museum★★

75 King St. ✕ ⛟ 🅿 ✆904-824-2874.
www.lightnermuseum.org
Across from Flagler College rises the former Hotel Alcazar, a poured-concrete structure completed in 1888 for Flagler. After closing its doors as a hotel in 1937, the building was purchased in 1946 by Chicago publisher Otto C. Lightner to house his assemblage of decorative arts that today form an intriguing look at the aesthetics of the Gilded Age.

Of note on the first level is a steam engine created entirely of blown glass. The second level holds Lightner's extensive collection of **art glass★★**, grouped according to type, style and manufacturer. Lightner's collection of decorative arts graces the third level.

Ximenez-Fatio House★★

20 Aviles St. ✆904-829-3575.
www.ximenezfatiohouse.org.
This two-story coquina residence was built in 1798 by Spanish merchant Andrés Ximenez as his residence and general store. It exemplifies the way early St. Augustine buildings were expanded and adapted for various uses—including incarnations as a boarding house and an inn. Today the house, which is beautifully restored, reflects the period from 1830 to 1850.

González-Alvarez House★★

14 St. Francis St. 🅿 ✆904-824-2872.
www.staugustinehistoricalsociety.org.
This National Historic Landmark is thought to be St. Augustine's oldest extant residential structure. It offers a fascinating look at the progress of St. Augustine from Spanish colony to British outpost to American city. The house was built in the early 18C for Tomás González y Hernández, a settler from the Canary Islands. The second story and balcony were added during the British period.

In 1918 the St. Augustine Historical Society purchased the property and restored it to its 18C appearance.

EXCURSIONS

👥 St. Augustine Alligator Farm★★

◗ On A1A, 1mi south of St. Augustine on Anastasia Island. ⛟ 🅿 ✆904-824-3337.
www.alligatorfarm.com.
Founded in 1893, the alligator farm houses some 2,500 crocodilians in landscaped habitats. A special indoor exhibit, **Gomek Forever★**, pays homage to a 1,700-pound saltwater crocodile from New Guinea who was the park's star resident until his death in 1997.

Don't miss the **Land of Crocodiles★**, a rare collection of all 23 species of crocodilians that hail from every tropical area of the world.

Fort Matanzas National Monument★★

◗ 15mi south of St. Augustine via A1A.
🅿 ✆904-471-0116. www.nps.gov/foma.
This 300-acre park preserves the site where Pedro Menéndez's forces slaughtered some 250 French Huguenots in 1565. After the 1740 siege of Castillo de San Marcos, the Spanish realized the threat of British invasion and built an armed coquina fortification at this site. In the visitor center, a short film describes the turbulent history and restoration of Fort Matanzas. From a nearby landing, you can board a ferry to cross the Matanzas River to the fort itself, which includes a coquina watchtower erected in 1742 to defend Matanzas Inlet.

Tampa Bay Area★★

Blessed with perennially fine weather, Florida's second-largest metropolitan area is known as the state's west-coast capital. Tampa Bay, the state's largest open-water estuary, opens onto the Gulf of Mexico. Its two densely populated centers—Tampa on the east side of the bay and St. Petersburg on the west—are linked by three causeway bridges. Just north, Tarpon Springs★ (on the Gulf Coast 35mi north of St. Petersburg) adds international flair, supporting a community of Greek sponge divers with a host of authentic Greek restaurants. On the Gulf Coast, just south of Bradenton, Sarasota attracts visitors to its fine museums and white-sand beaches.

- ⓒ **Michelin Map:** 584 R 14
- ⓘ **Info:** ☏813-226-0293, www.visittampabay.com (Tampa); ☏727-464-7200, www.viststpeteclearwater.com (St. Petersburg); ☏941-957-1877, www.sarasotafl.org (Sarasota).
- ⊘ **Don't Miss:** The weird world exposed at the Salvador Dalí museum.
- 👪 **Kids:** The entertainment and rides at Busch Garden Tampa Bay are made for kids.

TAMPA★★

Set on the blue waters of Tampa Bay, Florida's third-largest city is both port and resort. Its subtropical climate makes Tampa a year-round recreational paradise with a host of attractions ranging from the Latin accents of Ybor City to the thrill rides of Busch Gardens.

On Good Friday, 1528, Spanish explorer Pánfilo de Narváez landed near what is now Clearwater, Florida, and marched north with his men to the site of modern Tallahassee. More than two and a half centuries later, Cuban and Spanish fishermen established the village of Spanishtown Creek west of present-day downtown.

In the 1880s railroad tycoon **Henry Bradley Plant** (1819-99) chose Tampa as the port for a new railroad that would connect Florida with the rest of the East Coast. Plant built a multimillion-dollar transportation empire that eventually included 14 railway companies and several steamship lines. Railroad transportation and a bustling port assured Tampa's growth by attracting new businesses. One such venture, the cigar industry, flourished here in the late 19C and early 20C, particularly in the Ybor City district. After recovering from a 1921 hurricane, Tampa hit its peak during the Roaring Twenties' real-estate boom. Unfortunately, the land boom did not last, and Tampa's economy failed even before the Great Depression. Its economy eventually revived, however, and today the city holds its own among Florida's tourist destinations.

Bayshore Boulevard★

From the Hillsborough River to Mac-Dill Air Force Base, this scenic drive provides some of the finest **views**★ of Hillsborough Bay and the downtown skyline. The boulevard rims the historic **Hyde Park** neighborhood (centered on Swann Ave.) and continues south to Ballast Point.

Henry B. Plant Museum★

401 W. Kennedy Blvd., on the University of Tampa campus. ✕ & 🅿 ☏813-254-1891. www.plantmuseum.com.

Facing the Hillsborough River and a clutch of downtown skyscrapers, the silver minarets atop the former **Tampa Bay Hotel**★★ have been synonymous with Tampa since the hotel's lavish opening in 1891.

Built by Henry Plant to fortify his transportation empire, the red-brick, Moorish Revival-style structure with its distinctive white wood **fretwork** today

The minarets of the Tampa Bay Hotel
(Henry B. Plant Museum)

preserves rooms from the original hotel; note the domed Fletcher Lounge, which served as the hotel's main dining room and the Grand Salon, where guests socialized. Much of the rest of the building houses University of Tampa offices.

🏛 Florida Aquarium★

701 Channelside Dr. at Garrison Seaport Center. ✕ 🚻 🅿 ☎813-273-4000. www.flaquarium.org.

Beneath a signature green glass dome, Tampa's aquatic-life facility harbors more than 1 million gallons of fresh- and saltwater and provides a home for some 10,000 aquatic plants and animals both from Florida and across the globe. Opened in 1995, the 200,000sq ft aquarium is unique in that it focuses solely on Florida ecosystems (except, of course, for the penguins). Viewing galleries are laid out in a self-guided tour of four aquatic habitats: **Wetlands** (cypress swamps, mangrove forests and sawgrass marshes), **Bays and Beaches** (bay bottoms), the **Coral Reefs** (stag-horn coral, dark grottoes) and **Sea Hunt** (deep sea). Marine-life videos are shown in a main-floor theater.

🏛 Busch Gardens Tampa Bay★★

10165 N McKinley Dr. ✕ 🚻 🅿 ☎813-987-5082. www.buschgardens.com.

In 1959 August A. Busch, Jr., then president and chairman of Anheuser-Busch, Inc., opened a bird sanctuary and garden on the grounds of the Busch brewery. Now it's an animal-oriented theme park complete with live animal shows and thrill rides in addition to the animal attractions. More than 2,000 animals roam 300 acres of tropical gardens while rides, trams, trains and shows add to the entertainment.

The park is divided into 10 sections that correspond to African countries (Morocco, The Congo, etc.). Arrive early to avoid long lines, and note that thrill rides (roller coasters, including SheiKra, Cheetah Hunt, Montu and Kumba; and water rides Tanganyika Tidal Wave, Stanley Falls and Congo River Rapids) are the most popular attractions.

🏛 Museum of Science and Industry (MOSI)★★

4801 E. Fowler Ave. ✕ 🚻 🅿 ☎813-987-6000. www.mosi.org.

One of the largest science centers in the Southeast, this quintessential hands-on science museum houses some 450 permanent exhibits that address subjects from butterflies to nuclear fusion. Tops among the permanent exhibits are **Gulf Coast Hurricane**, where you'll get to experience the feel of high-speed winds; and the 25-acre **Back Woods**, featuring nature trails, habitats and several acres of wetlands. These are complemented by annual special exhibits. The museum also features large-format films in its five-story **IMAX Dome theater**, space shows in the **Saunders Planetarium** and a delightful **butterfly garden**.

ST. PETERSBURG★★

Lying on the west side of Tampa Bay, sunny St. Petersburg is Tampa on holiday. A thriving mix of young professionals, retirees and sun-seeking vacationers enjoy St. Pete's relaxed lifestyle, first-rate museums and sparkling gulf beaches.

Pánfilo de Narváez and Hernando de Soto landed on the Pinellas Peninsula in the early 16C in search of gold but abandoned the area after encountering hostile natives. In 1888 the peninsula caught the attention of Russian speculator **Peter Demens**, who brought his Orange Belt Railroad to the estate of **John Williams**, a retired Union general. By beating Williams in a lottery, Demens earned the right to name St. Petersburg after his hometown.

Around the early 20C, the city began attracting a large number of tourists. By the beginning of World War I, another railroad connected St. Pete to Tampa and development of the beaches began. The 1920s land boom elevated St. Pete to resort status.

Today St. Petersburg ranks as Florida's fourth most populous city, with tourism as its leading industry. Downtown, handsomely landscaped waterfront parks attract visitors to the bayside, where you can stroll **The Pier★** with its distinctive upside-down pyramid, and take in the art museums. A 30-minute drive west, **Gulf Boulevard** stretches from **St. Petersburg Beach** up to **Clearwater**, the most popular strand of sand on Florida's Gulf Coast.

Museum of Fine Arts★★

255 Beach Dr. N.E. ♿🅿 ℘727-896-2667. www.fine-arts.org.

Housed in an attractive Palladian-style building and a sympathetic two-story addition, this museum presents an impressive range of masterpieces from around the globe ranging from antiquities and world masterpieces to contemporary works. Starting from the marble-floored Great Hall, the museum features **Impressionist** treasures, a remarkable trove of early **Asian sculpture**, as well as modern American paintings. You'll also find pre-Columbian art and fine pieces from ancient Greece and Rome, the Renaissance and 18C Europe.

Don't miss the lovely interior sculpture garden, or the luminous collection of **Steuben glass★**.

The Dalí Museum★★★

1 Dali Blvd. ♿🅿 ℘727-823-3767. www.salvadordalimuseum.org.

The world's most comprehensive collection of works by the flamboyant Spanish surrealist **Salvador Dalí** (1904–89) resides in this museum. First opened in 1982, the museum moved in 2011 to a new, purpose-built structure befitting the artist, replete with a massive geodesic bubble known as the "enigma". The collection contains 2,140 pieces, including 96 oil paintings and more than 100 watercolors and drawings. Early paintings and various self-portraits demonstrate young Dalí's talent and the strong influence of painters from the 17C Flemish masters to the Impressionists and Cubists. Between 1929 and 1940, Dalí experimented with Surrealism, often attenuating figures to emphasize his obsession with time, death and sex. The third-floor galleries in the James Wing contain a permanent retrospective of oil paintings arranged in chronological order, beginning with Dalí's childhood works (1914) and ending with his monumental **masterworks★★**. Painted between 1948 and 1970, each of the masterworks took more than a year to complete.

SARASOTA★★

Lying on Florida's Gulf Coast, Sarasota offers numerous and diverse attractions. Here you'll find the official art museum of Florida, a host of cultural and sports activities, upscale shopping districts, a variety of restaurants and a 35mi stretch of pristine white-sand beach.

The bulk of the area's pioneers began arriving in the late 1860s. In 1902 the town elected its first mayor, John Hamilton Gillespie, who built one of the country's first golf courses in Sarasota, thus introducing a sport that is now played on more than 40 area courses. Another influential city father, **John Ringling** (1866-1936), of the Ringling Bros. and Barnum & Bailey Circus, bought a house in Sarasota in 1912. Five years later he founded a local real-estate development company in the city and for a decade thereafter poured much of his time, money and energy into the area. In 1927 Ringling moved the circus' winter headquarters to Sarasota, providing a boost to the local economy in the wake of the Florida land bust. That same year, Ringling and his wife began the construction of a grand Italian Renaissance residence and museum to house their growing art collection.

Today the Ringling complex, the adjacent Florida State University Center for the Performing Arts, and the Van Wezel Performing Arts Hall present the best in art, music, dance and theater. Along Palm Avenue and Main Street lies the hub of Sarasota's **Downtown Art District★**, full of galleries, theaters and restaurants.

John and Mable Ringling Museum of Art★★

5401 Bayshore Rd. ✗🚻🅿🖉941-359-5700. www.ringling.org.

Spreading over 66 landscaped acres, the museum complex comprises the art gallery, Ringling's mansion and the circus

---

Ybor City

1.6mi northeast of downtown Tampa. The visitor center is located at 1600 E. 8th Ave. 🖉813-241-8838; www.ybor.org. Center of Tampa's 19C cigar-making industry, **Ybor City★** retains its historic heritage even as it evolves into one of the city's hippest nightspots. Off-beat galleries, chic retail shops, nightclubs and ethnic restaurants line **Seventh Avenue★**, Ybor City's main thoroughfare. On weekend evenings, the district takes on a carnival atmosphere as crowds spill onto Seventh Avenue from dozens of bars and nightclubs.

The district is named after cigar manufacturer **Vicente Martínez Ybor**, who chose Tampa as the new site for his operations when labor-union pressures in Key West forced him to relocate here in the late 19C. Ybor's cigar factory opened in 1886 and soon became the largest in the world. By the 20C, cigars fired Tampa's main industry with some 150 factories and Ybor City teemed with a lively mix of young laborers—Cubans, Spaniards, Italians and Germans. The advent of machine-rolled cigars, the popularity of cigarettes, and the Depression caused Ybor City's cigar industry—and the community itself—to decline.

The 1990s ushered in a resurgence of interest in Ybor City, resulting in the restoration of many historic landmarks. The **Ybor City Museum** (1818 9th Ave.; ♿🖉813-247-6323; www.ybormuseum.org) sells self-guided walking tours through the historic district. Housed in the 1923 yellow brick Ferlita Bakery, the museum outlines the development of Ybor City. Guided tours take in adjacent **La Casita** (1895), an early-20C cigar-maker's cottage. Ybor City's oldest and largest hand-rolled-cigar factory, the Martínez Ybor Cigar Factory, was once housed in a three-story 1886 building in **Ybor Square**.

For a taste of traditional Spanish cuisine and culture, head to the **Columbia Restaurant** (2117 E. Seventh Ave.; 🖉813-248-4961; www.columbiarestaurant.com), Florida's oldest operating restaurant (1905). The Columbia specializes in authentically prepared paella, snapper Alicante and pompano en papillote; its wine list is extensive. Colorfully attired dancers take the stage nightly (except Sunday) to present well performed classical flamenco.

museum. A visitor complex, the Historic Asolo Theater and Mrs. Ringling's rose garden are also included on the site.

A treasury of European culture, the museum of art stands as the artistic triumph of southwest Florida, and was designated as the official state art museum in 1946. Complemented by magnificent architecture, the Ringling boasts more than 10,000 objects, the majority of which were acquired after Ringling's death. Inside and out, the building displays an abundance of architectural flourishes including friezes, mosaics, medallions, cartouches and other ornamentation that Ringling found in his travels. The collection concentrates on paintings of the late Renaissance and Baroque periods (1550-1750), and features an extensive private collection of works by Baroque master **Peter Paul Rubens** (1577-1640). The museum's **Baroque Collection** is considered one of the finest in the US.

©VISIT FLORIDA

John and Mable Ringling Museum of Art

Art Galleries

A wing of 11 rooms, the **North Galleries** offer a broad survey of late Medieval through early Baroque art of Italy and northern Europe, with an emphasis on 16C and 17C Italian works. The **Rubens Gallery** consists of four huge paintings, part of a series called *The Triumph of the Eucharist*, executed around 1625. Continuing through this wing, you'll find many other Baroque masterpieces, as well as fine examples from the Middle Ages and Renaissance. The **South Galleries** present a survey of 17C-19C European art, and 18C-19C American art, as well as Dutch Garden Painting and Art of France. The Ulla R. and Arthur F. Searing wing opened in 2007 to showcase special exhibis.

Cà d'Zan

A pathway leads from the museum to Ringling's extravagant Venetian-style palace (1926) overlooking Sarasota Bay. The Cà d'Zan (Venetian dialect meaning "House of John") incorporates Italian and French Renaissance, Venetian Gothic, Baroque and modern architectural elements. Inside, note the 30ft-high **court room** with painted cypress beams and the stained glass in the **tap room**. The **marble terrace** offers a sweeping **view** of the bay. Ceiling panels in the **ballroom**, depicting dance costumes from various nations, were painted by Willy Pogany, set designer for the New York Ziegfeld Follies.

Circus Museum

The recently renovated museum boasts the largest miniature circus in the world, created over a period of more than 50 years. The model depicts the Ringling Bros. and Barnum & Bailey Circus from 1919-1938. You'll also find circus memorabilia, posters, wagons, calliopes and other objects from the old days of the big top.

Barrier Islands

Flung out north and south along Sarasota's Gulf Coast lie several idyllic barrier islands, connected to the mainland by causeways. To the northwest, **Longboat Key** offers vacation condos and a wide variety of beachside hotel accommodations. **St. Armands Key**, across the John Ringling Causeway from downtown Sarasota, boasts the area's upscale shopping district, **St. Armands Circle★**. Just west of St. Armands Key lies **Lido Key★**, home of **Mote Marine Aquarium** (1600 Ken Thompson Pkwy.; ℘941-388-4441; www.mote.org) as well as several popular beaches.

INDEX

INDEX

INDEX

INDEX

🏨 STAY

🍽 EAT

INDEX

Thematic Maps

Maps and Plans

Companion Publications

Map 583 Northeastern USA/ Eastern Canada, Map 584 Southeastern USA
Large-format map providing detailedn road systems; includes driving distances, interstate rest stops, border crossings and interchanges.
◆ Comprehensive city and town index
◆ Scale 1 : 2,400,000 (1 inch = approx. 38 miles)

Map 761 USA Road Map
Covers principal US road networks while also presenting shaded relief detail of overall physiography of the land.
◆ State flags with statistical data and state tourism office telephone numbers
◆ Scale: 1 : 3,450,000 (1 inch = approx. 55 miles)

North America Road Atlas
A geographically organized atlas with extensive detailed coverage of the US, Canada and Mexico. Includes 246 city maps, a distance chart, state and provincial driving requirements, and a climate chart.
◆ Comprehensive city and town index
◆ Easy to follow "Go-to" pointers

★★★ **Worth the trip**
★★ **Worth a detour**
★ **Interesting**

Sight Symbols

━━━ ◉ ━━━━━━━━━ Recommended itineraries with departure point

🏛 🕎	Church, chapel – Synagogue	▢ Building described
O	Town described	▢ Other building
AZ B	Map co-ordinates locating sights	▪ Small building, statue
▪ ▲	Other points of interest	⊚ ♣ Fountain – Ruins
⚒ ⌒	Mine – Cave	🛈 Visitor information
🌾 ⌁	Windmill – Lighthouse	⊂ ⟋ Ship – Shipwreck
☆ ⛪	Fort – Mission	☀ ⋁ Panorama – View

Other Symbols

🛡 Interstate highway (USA)	🛡 US highway	⬭ Other route
🍁 Trans-Canada highway	🛡 Canadian highway	🛡 Mexican federal highway
═══ Highway, bridge		Major city thoroughfare
═●═ Toll highway, interchange		City street with median
═══ Divided highway		◄ One-way street
─── Major, minor route		Pedestrian Street
15 (21) Distance in miles (kilometers)		⊁⊰⊱ Tunnel
2149/655 Pass, elevation *(feet/meters)*		▸▪▪▪▪ Steps – Gate
△6288(1917) Mtn. peak, elevation *(feet/meters)*		△ 🛡 Drawbridge - Water tower
✈ ✛ Airport – Airfield		🅿 ✉ Parking – Main post office
⛴ Ferry: Cars and passengers		🖼 ✚ University – Hospital
⛴ Ferry: Passengers only		🚂 🚌 Train station – Bus station
≺≺⊃ Waterfall – Lock – Dam		● Ⓐ Subway station
—··—··— International boundary		➊ ⛬ Digressions – Observatory
- - - - - State boundary		▦ ⛱ Cemetery – Swamp

Recreation

▪○○○○○▪ Gondola, chairlift	⟨⟩ ►	Stadium – Golf course
🚂 Tourist or steam railway	✳ ▦	Park, garden – Wooded area
⛴ ♨ Harbor, lake cruise – Marina	🌍	Wildlife reserve
⚓ ☑ Surfing – Windsurfing	🌍 ✡	Wildlife/Safari park, zoo
▨ ⚓ Diving – Kayaking	- - - - -	Walking path, trail
⚓ ⚓ Ski area – Cross-country skiing	🚶	Hiking trail

Sight of special interest for children

Abbreviations and special symbols

NP	National Park	NMem	National Memorial	SP	State Park
NM	National Monument	NHS	National Historic Site	SF	State Forest
NWR	National Wildlife Refuge	NHP	National Historical Park	SR	State Reserve
NF	National Forest	NVM	National Volcanic Monument	SAP	State Archeological Park

🛡 National Park 🛡 State Park 🛡 National Forest 🛡 State Forest

All maps are oriented north, unless otherwise indicated by a directional arrow.

The Michelin Adventure

It all started with rubber balls! This was the product made by a small company based in Clermont-Ferrand that André and Edouard Michelin inherited, back in 1880. The brothers quickly saw the potential for a new means of transport and their first success was the invention of detachable pneumatic tires for bicycles. However, the automobile was to provide the greatest scope for their creative talents. Throughout the 20th century, Michelin never ceased developing and creating ever more reliable and high-performance tires, not only for vehicles ranging from trucks to F1 but also for underground transit systems and airplanes.

From early on, Michelin provided its customers with tools and services to facilitate mobility and make traveling a more pleasurable and more frequent experience. As early as 1900, the Michelin Guide supplied motorists with a host of useful information related to vehicle maintenance, accommodation and restaurants, and was to become a benchmark for good food. At the same time, the Travel Information Bureau offered travelers personalised tips and itineraries.

The publication of the first collection of roadmaps, in 1910, was an instant hit! In 1926, the first regional guide to France was published, devoted to the principal sites of Brittany, and before long each region of France had its own Green Guide. The collection was later extended to more far-flung destinations, including New York in 1968 and Taiwan in 2011.

In the 21st century, with the growth of digital technology, the challenge for Michelin maps and guides is to continue to develop alongside the company's tire activities. Now, as before, Michelin is committed to improving the mobility of travelers.

MICHELIN TODAY

WORLD NUMBER ONE TIRE MANUFACTURER
- 70 production sites in 18 countries
- 111,000 employees from all cultures and on every continent
- 6,000 people employed in research and development

Moving
for a world

Moving forward means developing tires with better road grip and shorter braking distances, whatever the state of the road.

CORRECT TIRE PRESSURE

RIGHT PRESSURE

- Safety
- Longevity
- Optimum fuel consumption

-0,5 bar

- Durability reduced by 20% (- 8,000 km)

-1 bar

- Risk of blowouts
- Increased fuel consumption
- Longer braking distances on wet surfaces

forward together
where mobility is safer

It also involves helping motorists take care of their safety and their tires. To do so, Michelin organises "Fill Up With Air" campaigns all over the world to remind us that correct tire pressure is vital.

WEAR

DETECTING TIRE WEAR

The legal minimum depth of tire tread is 1.6mm.
Tire manufacturers equip their tires with tread wear indicators, which are small blocks of rubber moulded into the base of the main grooves at a depth of 1.6mm.

Tires are the only point of contact between the vehicle and road.

The photo below shows the actual contact zone.

If the tread depth is less than 1.6mm, tires are considered to be worn and dangerous on wet surfaces.

NEW TIRE

WORN TIRE
(1,6 mm tread)

Moving forward
means sustainable mobility

INNOVATION AND THE ENVIRONMENT

By 2050, Michelin aims to cut the quantity of raw materials used in its tire manufacturing process by half and to have developed renewable energy in its facilities. The design of MICHELIN tires has already saved billions of litres of fuel and, by extension, billions of tons of CO2.

Similarly, Michelin prints its maps and guides on paper produced from sustainably managed forests and is diversifying its publishing media by offering digital solutions to make traveling easier, more fuel efficient and more enjoyable!

The group's whole-hearted commitment to eco-design on a daily basis is demonstrated by ISO 14001 certification.

Like you, Michelin is committed to preserving our planet.

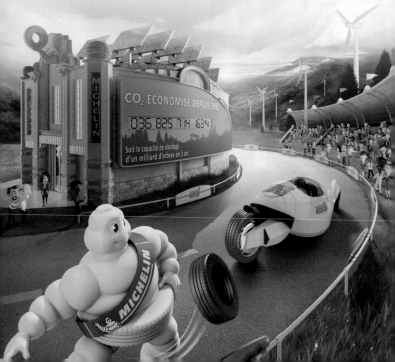

Chat with Bibendum

Go to
www.michelin.com/corporate/en
Find out more about
Michelin's history and the
latest news.

QUIZ

Michelin develops tires for all types of vehicles.
See if you can match the right tire with the right vehicle…

Solution : A-6 / B-4 / C-2 / D-1 / E-3 / F-7 / G-5

THEGREENGUIDE **USA EAST**

Editorial Director	Cynthia Clayton Ochterbeck
Editorial Manager	Gwen Cannon
Contributing Writers	Zain Deane, M. Linda Lee, Claiborne Linvill, Connor Morrison, Anne-Marie Scott
Production Manager	Natasha G. George
Cartography	Peter Wrenn
Photo Editor	Nicole D. Jordan
Photo Researcher	Nicole D. Jordan, Charles Anton Attebury
Interior Design	Chris Bell, Natasha G. George, Jonathan P. Gilbert
Cover Design	Chris Bell, Christelle Le Déan
Layout	Nicole D. Jordan, Natasha G. George
Cover Layout	Michelin Travel Partner, Natasha G. George

Contact Us

Michelin Travel and Lifestyle North America
One Parkway South
Greenville, SC 29615
USA
travel.lifestyle@us.michelin.com
www.michelintravel.com

Michelin Travel Partner
Hannay House
39 Clarendon Road
Watford, Herts WD17 1JA
UK
✆01923 205240
travelpubsales@uk.michelin.com
www.ViaMichelin.com

Special Sales

For information regarding bulk sales, customized editions and premium sales, please contact us at:
travel.lifestyle@us.michelin.com
www.michelintravel.com

Michelin Travel Partner

Société par actions simplifiées au capital de 11 288 880 EUR
27 cours de l'Ile Seguin - 92100 Boulogne Billancourt (France)
R.C.S. Nanterre 433 677 721

© Michelin Travel Partner
ISBN 978-2-067188-70-9
Printed: November 2013
Printed and bound in France - N° 201311.0162